Foundations of Risk Management and Insurance

Foundations of Risk Management and Insurance

Charles M. Nyce, PhD, CPCU, ARM
Senior Director of Knowledge Resources
American Institute for CPCU/Insurance Institute of America

Second Edition • Fifth Printing

American Institute for Chartered Property Casualty
Underwriters/Insurance Institute of America
720 Providence Road, Suite 100
Malvern, Pennsylvania 19355-3433

Second Edition • Fifth Printing • April 2009

Library of Congress Control Number: 2006928976

ISBN 978-0-89463-284-6

Foreword

The American Institute for Chartered Property Casualty Underwriters and the Insurance Institute of America (the Institutes) are not-for-profit organizations committed to meeting the evolving educational needs of the risk management and insurance community. The Institutes strive to provide current, relevant educational programs in formats that meet the needs of risk management and insurance professionals and the organizations that employ them.

The American Institute for CPCU (AICPCU) was founded in 1942 through a collaborative effort between industry professionals and academics, led by faculty members at The Wharton School of the University of Pennsylvania. In 1953, AICPCU coordinated operations with the Insurance Institute of America (IIA), which was founded in 1909 and remains the oldest continuously functioning national organization offering educational programs for the property-casualty insurance sector.

The Insurance Research Council (IRC), founded in 1977, is a division of AICPCU supported by industry members. This not-for-profit research organization examines public policy issues of interest to property-casualty insurers, insurance customers, and the general public. IRC research reports are distributed widely to insurance-related organizations, public policy authorities, and the media.

The Institutes' new customer- and solution-focused business model allows us to better serve the risk management and insurance communities. Customer-centricity defines our business philosophy and shapes our priorities. The Institutes' innovation arises from our commitment to finding solutions that meet customer needs and deliver results. Our business process is shaped by our commitment to efficiency, strategy, and responsible asset management.

The Institutes believe that professionalism is grounded in education, experience, and ethical behavior. The Chartered Property Casualty Underwriter (CPCU) professional designation offered by the Institutes is designed to provide a broad understanding of the property-casualty insurance industry. Depending on professional needs, CPCU students may select either a commercial or a personal risk management and insurance focus. The CPCU designation is conferred annually by the AICPCU Board of Trustees.

In addition, the Institutes offer designations and certificate programs in a variety of disciplines, including the following:

- Claims
- Commercial underwriting
- Fidelity and surety bonding
- General insurance
- Insurance accounting and finance
- Insurance information technology
- Insurance production and agency management
- Insurance regulation and compliance
- Management
- Marine insurance
- Personal insurance
- Premium auditing
- Quality insurance services
- Reinsurance
- Risk management
- Surplus lines

You can complete a program leading to a designation, take a single course to fill a knowledge gap, or take multiple courses and programs throughout your career. The practical and technical knowledge gained from Institute courses enhances your qualifications and contributes to your professional growth. Most Institute courses carry college credit recommendations from the American Council on Education. A variety of courses qualify for credits toward certain associate, bachelor's, and master's degrees at several prestigious colleges and universities.

Our Knowledge Resources Department, in conjunction with industry experts and members of the academic community, develops our trusted course and program content, including Institute study materials. These materials provide practical career and performance-enhancing knowledge and skills.

We welcome comments from our students and course leaders. Your feedback helps us continue to improve the quality of our study materials.

Peter L. Miller, CPCU
President and CEO
American Institute for CPCU
Insurance Institute of America

Preface

This text was written for use, along with the *Code of Professional Ethics* and the CPCU 510 *Course Guide*, as required study material for the gateway course in the education program leading to the Chartered Property Casualty Underwriter (CPCU®) professional designation. The CPCU 510 course, Foundations of Risk Management, Insurance, and Professionalism, is probably the course that most CPCU candidates will take first. This text is designed to help students understand the foundations on which the insurance industry is built and to prepare them for the remainder of the courses in the CPCU curriculum.

The CPCU program is designed to provide an advanced education for risk management and insurance professionals. The goals of this text are the following:

- To enable CPCU candidates to understand and apply the fundamental principles on which the practice of insurance is based.

- To provide CPCU candidates with an understanding of insurance within the context of enterprise risk management principles and practices. Enterprise risk management takes a broader view of risk and risk management techniques than traditional risk management, which tends to focus on hazard risks and insurance as the primary risk financing technique.

- To equip CPCU candidates to apply a formal approach in analyzing any property-liability insurance policy, using up-to-date examples and insurance policy extracts.

This edition of *Foundations of Risk Management and Insurance* is a substantial revision of the previous textbook. It contains additional chapters and expanded information about risk management, risk assessment, risk control, and the functioning of insurance markets. It also provides detailed instruction in analyzing insurance policies. The text begins with a broad discussion of risk, then narrows the focus to risk management and, further, to one risk financing measure—insurance. It ends with a focus on the insurance policy.

The fifteen chapters in *Foundations of Risk Management and Insurance* can be summarized as follows: Chapters 1 and 2 set the basis for understanding risk by providing an overview of risk and risk management. Chapters 3 through 5 continue the study of risk management by examining risk assessment, risk control, and risk financing, respectively. The focus narrows to insurance in

Chapters 6 through 8, with discussions of insurance markets and competition and an examination of the insurance mechanism from a variety of viewpoints, including functional, economic, financial, and social. The focus narrows again in Chapters 9 and 10, which examine the legal foundation of the insurance policy. Chapters 11 through 13 provide detailed instruction on policy analysis. The final two chapters examine how to determine the amounts payable under insurance policies—Chapter 14 covering property insurance policies, and Chapter 15 covering liability insurance policies.

The Institutes are grateful to the following individuals, who reviewed one or more chapters of the manuscript:

Max Abrams, CPCU, AIM, ARM

Charles A. Lankau III, JD

Joanna Mahoney, CPCU, CPIW, ARM

David W. Sommer, PhD

Their thoughtful review of the material has contributed to making this text accurate and relevant to current industry conditions. The Institutes remain equally thankful to individuals who contributed to the development of earlier texts for this course. Although they are too numerous to name here, the current updated and revised text still reflects the valuable insight of these insurance professionals.

For more information about the Institutes' programs, please call our Customer Service Department at (800) 644-2101, e-mail us at customerservice@cpcuiia.org, or visit our Web site at www.aicpcu.org.

Charles M. Nyce

Contributing Authors

The American Institute for CPCU, the Insurance Institute of America, and the author of this text acknowledge, with deep appreciation, the work of the following contributing authors:

M. Martin Boyer, PhD
Professor, Department of Finance
HEC Montréal, University of Montréal

Michael W. Elliott, MBA, CPCU
Assistant Vice President
AICPCU/IIA

Contents

Chapter 1

Direct **Direct Your Learning**

Risk

After learning the content of this chapter and completing the corresponding course guide assignment, you should be able to:

- Describe each of the following in the context of risk:
  - Uncertainty
  - Possibility
  - Possibility compared with probability
- Explain the following elements for property, liability, personnel, and net income loss exposures:
  - Assets exposed to loss
  - Causes of loss, including associated hazards
  - Financial consequences of loss
- Classify a given risk within the following categories:
  - Pure or speculative
  - Subjective or objective
  - Diversifiable or nondiversifiable
- Describe the three financial consequences of risk.
- Define or describe each of the Key Words and Phrases for this chapter.

Develop Your Perspective

What are the main topics covered in the chapter?

Risk is the uncertainty about outcomes, some of which can be negative. Risk is explored by examining loss exposures, categories of risk, and financial consequences of risk.

Identify potential sources of risk.

- What assets can be exposed to loss?
- What are the associated financial consequences of loss?
- What differentiates pure and speculative losses?

Why is it important to learn about these topics?

Risk is present in all activities and affects both individuals and organizations. Identifying risk and its implications, associated loss exposures, and financial consequences will help in managing risk.

Consider why people and organizations are willing to take certain risks.

- Why are some loss exposures considered more risky than others?

How can you use what you will learn?

Examine the risks facing a family or an organization.

- What types of loss exposures associated with those risks are present?
- How would you classify these risks?
- What are the associated financial consequences?

Chapter 1
Risk

Although risk may intuitively seem undesirable, it can yield both positive and negative outcomes. Risk, in terms of the possibility of negative outcomes, is a byproduct of opportunity and reward. For example, an organization might commit some of its capital to a major marketing campaign (risk) for the opportunity to significantly improve its market share (reward). Opportunities cannot be pursued, and reward cannot be obtained, without incurring some risk. Because of this risk/reward relationship, individuals and organizations seek to maximize reward while minimizing the associated risk. Risk management helps individuals and organizations to avoid, prevent, reduce, or pay for the negative outcomes of risk so that opportunities for reward can be pursued.

The study of risk management and insurance in this text begins with understanding risk and how it is quantified. Based on this understanding, the risks faced by an individual or an organization can be identified, analyzed, controlled, and financed through the risk management process. A wide variety of risk management techniques are available, one of the most significant of which is the risk financing technique of transfer of risk via an insurance policy. Insurance can be viewed as an industry and as an economic, financial, and social mechanism, as well as a risk transfer measure. However, from the perspective of a risk management or insurance professional, the insurance policy is the central mechanism for delivering the promise of risk transfer and coverage to the customer.

The foundation for learning about risk management and insurance rests on the fundamentals of risk. Consequently, this chapter addresses understanding and quantifying risk, types and elements of loss exposures and associated hazards, the classifications of risk, and the financial consequences of risk. Understanding these topics is essential to finding ways to address the possible negative outcomes faced by individuals and organizations. In short, risk must be understood before it can be effectively managed.

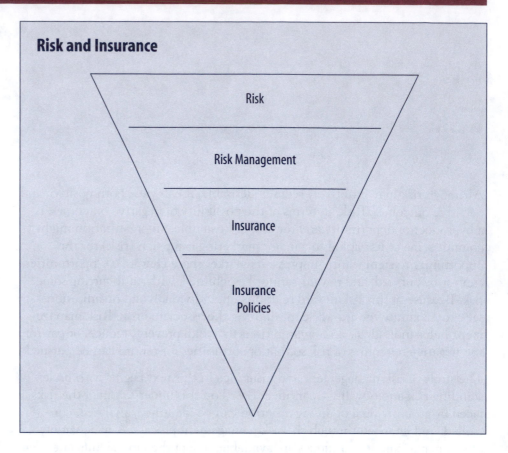

Risk and Insurance

- Risk
- Risk Management
- Insurance
- Insurance Policies

UNDERSTANDING AND QUANTIFYING RISK

Risk is a term regularly used by individuals in both their personal and professional lives and is generally understood in context. However, properly defining risk is often difficult because it can have many different meanings. In this text, **risk** is defined as the uncertainty about outcomes, some of which can be negative. A negative outcome is a loss or reduction in value. For example, owning property exposes an individual or organization to risk because that property can suffer a reduction in value. Property values can be reduced by specific damage to the property, such as by a fire or flood, or simply by the property's age or condition. Owning property can also expose the owner to the risk of loss resulting from liability. For example, a homeowner faces the risk that an individual who suffers an injury while on the property may demand compensation for his or her injuries. Although this type of loss does not reduce the value of the property, it is a reduction in value to the homeowner in that the homeowner may have to compensate the individual.

The two elements within the definition of risk used in this text are as follows:

1. Uncertainty of outcome
2. Possibility of a negative outcome

Risk
The uncertainty about outcomes, some of which can be negative.

> ## Industry Language—Risk
>
> ### What is risk?
>
> Risk can be used in many contexts in risk management and insurance and can have any of the following meanings:
>
> - The subject matter of an insurance policy, such as a structure, an auto fleet, or the possibility of a liability claim arising from an insured's activities
> - The insurance applicant (the insured)
> - The possibility of bodily injury or property damage
> - A cause of loss (or peril), such as fire, lightning, or explosion
> - The variability associated with a future outcome

First, risk involves uncertainty about the type of outcome (what will actually occur), the timing of the outcome (when the outcome will occur), or both the type and timing of the outcome. Consider an individual who buys a share of stock in a publicly traded corporation. This individual may experience a positive outcome if the value of the stock increases or a negative outcome if the value of the stock decreases. The timing of either outcome is uncertain because the individual does not know if or when the stock price is going to change or what the new stock price will be. Whether uncertainty involves *what* will actually happen, *when* something will happen, or both, it results from the inability to accurately predict the future.

Second, risk involves the possibility of a negative outcome. Possibility means that an outcome or event may or may not occur. The fact that something *may* occur does not mean that it *will* occur. For example, it is possible that an individual may be injured while driving to or from work, loading a truck at work, moving some furniture at home, or falling in an icy parking lot at the mall. However, the possibility that these events may occur does not mean that they will occur. Nonetheless, because of the possibility of a negative outcome (injury), risk exists.

The possibility that something may occur does not indicate its likelihood of occurring. Possibility does not quantify risk; it only verifies that risk is present. To quantify risk, one needs to know the probability of the outcome or event occurring. **Probability** is the likelihood that an outcome or event will occur. Unlike possibility, probability is measurable and has a value between zero and one. If an event is not possible, it has a probability of zero, whereas if an event is certain, it has a probability of one. If an event is possible, but not certain, its probability is some value between zero and one. Probabilities can be stated as a decimal figure (.4), a percentage (40 percent), or a fraction (four-tenths or two-fifths).

Probability
The likelihood that an outcome or event will occur.

To help understand the difference between possibility and probability, consider the possibility that an individual will be injured in an auto accident while driving to or from work tomorrow. That person will not necessarily be injured in an auto accident tomorrow, and the fact that it is possible does not give any indication of its likelihood. The risk exists and has simply been identified. Contrast this with there being a 5 percent probability that the same individual will be injured in an auto accident while driving to or from work tomorrow. This statement not only indicates that it is possible the individual will be injured tomorrow, it gives the likelihood. The risk has now not only been identified but also quantified.

Understanding the probability of various outcomes helps focus risk management attention on those risks that can be appropriately managed. Probability can also be used to help decide which activities (and associated risks) to undertake and which risk management techniques to use. In the previous example, if the probability of injury while driving to or from work was 5 percent, and the probability of injury if the individual took the train to work was 1 percent, the individual may decide to take the train. However, if the risk of auto injury was reduced to 1 percent by driving a car with airbags and antilock brakes, and if it was more convenient and quicker to drive, then the individual may decide (cost permitting) to buy a new car with airbags and antilock brakes and then drive to work. The use of probability in decision making is discussed in more detail in subsequent chapters.

Risk is present in many of the activities that individuals and organizations undertake on a day-to-day basis. However, the definition of risk does not identify what can be lost when a negative outcome does occur. In managing the risks that an individual or organization faces, those areas in which a loss could occur must first be identified.

LOSS EXPOSURES

Loss exposure
Any condition that presents a possibility of loss, whether or not an actual loss occurs.

Individuals and organizations incur losses when assets they own decrease in value. Situations or conditions that expose assets to loss are called loss exposures. More specifically, a **loss exposure** is any condition that presents a possibility of loss, whether or not an actual loss occurs. In order to effectively manage risk, individuals and organizations must identify all the loss exposures they face.

Elements of Loss Exposures

Every loss exposure has the following three elements:

1. An asset exposed to loss
2. Cause of loss (also called a peril)
3. Financial consequences of that loss

These three elements are necessary to completely describe a loss exposure. For example, identifying a building (an asset exposed to loss) is not sufficient for describing that building as a loss exposure. It is also necessary to identify the causes of loss associated with that building (such as fire, flood, or hurricane) and the financial consequences of that loss (such as a decline in the market value of the building or in the income produced by the use of the building).

Asset Exposed to Loss

The first element of a loss exposure is an asset exposed to loss. This asset can be anything of value an individual or organization has that is exposed to loss. Assets owned by organizations can include property (such as buildings, automobiles, and office furniture), investments, money that is owed to them, and cash. In addition to these are assets that are often overlooked, including intangible assets (such as patents, copyrights, and trademarks) and human resources. Individuals may have many of the same assets as organizations (property, money, investments, and so on). In addition, individuals may have intangible assets such as professional qualifications, a unique skill set, or valuable experience.

Cause of Loss

The second element of a loss exposure is cause of loss. Fire, windstorm, explosion, and theft are examples of causes of loss that present a possibility of loss to property. Exhibit 1-1 shows causes of loss that have resulted in homeowners making claims on their insurance policies and the frequency with which these claims are made. Although this list is far from exhaustive, it does indicate the range of potential causes of loss.

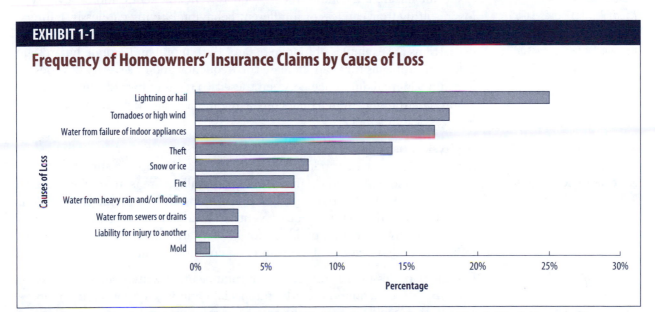

EXHIBIT 1-1

Frequency of Homeowners' Insurance Claims by Cause of Loss

Source: Insurance Research Council, *Public Attitude Monitor 2003: Protecting Homes From Natural Disasters and Household Perils, Homeowners Insurance Discounts and Claims* (Malvern, Pa.: Insurance Research Council, 2003), p. 17.

Hazard
A condition that increases the frequency and/or severity of loss.

Loss exposures and causes of loss that affect them can be influenced by hazards. A **hazard** is a condition that increases the frequency and/or severity of loss. For example, a fire hazard, such as storing oily rags next to a furnace, increases the frequency and/or severity of loss caused by fire. Insurers typically define hazards according to the following four classifications:

1. Moral hazard
2. Morale hazard
3. Physical hazard
4. Legal hazard

Moral hazard
A condition that increases the frequency and/or severity of loss resulting from a person acting dishonestly.

A **moral hazard** is a condition that increases the frequency and/or severity of loss resulting from a person acting dishonestly. Examples of acting dishonestly include intentionally causing, fabricating, or exaggerating a loss. For example, one moral hazard incentive is financial difficulty. Someone who is facing overwhelming debt might be tempted to intentionally cause a loss in an attempt to profit from the situation and thereby reduce or eliminate the debt. Purchasing an insurance policy is another moral hazard incentive—some people might be inclined to behave differently once they enter into a contract that shifts the financial consequences of risk to another party. In insurance, this behavior can include filing false claims, inflating a claim on a loss that did occur, or intentionally causing a loss.

Insurance underwriters try to recognize signs of moral hazard, such as property that is grossly over-insured. Also, underwriters may look for situations that could lead to moral hazard, such as labor unrest that might increase the frequency of questionable workers' compensation claims.

Morale hazard
A condition that increases the frequency and/or severity of loss resulting from careless or indifferent behavior.

A **morale hazard** is a condition that increases the frequency and/or severity of loss resulting from careless or indifferent behavior. Driving carelessly, failing to lock an unattended building, or failing to clear an icy sidewalk to protect pedestrians are examples of morale hazard. Both moral and morale hazards are behavior problems that can increase the frequency and/or severity of losses. The fundamental difference between these two types of hazard is intent. A moral hazard results from a deliberate act; a morale hazard results from carelessness or indifference.

Physical hazard
A condition of property, persons, or operations that increases the frequency and/or severity of loss.

A **physical hazard** is a condition of property, persons, or operations that increases the frequency and/or severity of loss. For example, a slip-and-fall accident is more likely to occur on an icy sidewalk, a fire is more likely to start in a building with defective wiring, and an explosion is more likely to occur in a painting area that has inadequate ventilation. Inadequate ventilation may also create environmental problems for workers and therefore increase the frequency and/or severity of workers' compensation claims.

Fire safety professionals and property insurance underwriters subdivide physical hazards into common hazards and special hazards. Common hazards are hazards that could potentially be present at most properties, such as unsafe heating systems. Special hazards are those considered unique to an individual property, such as drying ovens in a metalworking plant.

Moral and Morale Hazards—An Example

James purchased a new vacation home located on a wooded lot in a remote area. In his first year of ownership, James did not have homeowners insurance coverage and was extremely careful about keeping the property clear of debris that could burn in a wildfire, maintaining all of the utilities in the house to prevent water or gas leaks and electrical fires, and locking the doors and windows to prevent unwanted intruders. After one year of owning the property, James purchased a homeowners policy with a low deductible. He no longer kept the property clear of debris, failed to maintain the utility systems, and was careless about locking the doors and windows. In his fifth year of owning the property, James began having financial troubles and decided selling the vacation home would help alleviate them. Unfortunately, it was not easy to sell, and James started a fire in the home in the hope of collecting the insurance proceeds.

The differences between moral and morale hazards in this case can best be understood by considering three time frames: year one, years two through four, and year five.

James's actions in year one are typical of the actions taken by individuals and organizations faced with risk—he was attempting to minimize the likelihood of having a loss at the property. Neither moral nor morale hazards are present.

Once James purchased insurance in year two, his circumstances and behavior changed. His carelessness and indifference to safety and theft during years two through four constitute a morale hazard.

In year five, James's financial difficulties led him to intentionally start a fire in the hope of collecting the insurance proceeds. Both the insurance policy and the financial difficulties provided the incentive for the dishonest behavior that constituted a moral hazard. There is no morale hazard, because James's behavior was deliberate, not careless or reckless.

A **legal hazard** is a condition of the legal environment that increases the frequency and/or severity of loss. For example, courts in some geographic areas are much more likely to find in favor of the plaintiff or to grant large damages awards in liability cases than are courts in other areas. Various trends can also be legal hazards. For example, an increasing number of decisions against tobacco manufacturers would present a legal hazard for companies participating in the tobacco industry.

The geographical variance in court judgments in the United States is the focus of an annual ranking of state liability systems by the Institute for Legal Reform (ILR).[1] This ranking is based on a survey of attorneys in public corporations that explores how U.S. corporations perceive the fairness and efficiency of the tort liability system. The higher its position in the ranking, the more "business friendly" a state's liability system is perceived to be. That is, courts in these states are more likely to find in favor of the defense or limit the size of damages awards. Exhibit 1-2 shows the top and bottom ten states from the 2005 Ranking of State Liability Systems and the reported effect the litigation environment has on business decisions (such as where to locate a business).

Legal hazard
A condition of the legal environment that increases the frequency and/or severity of loss.

EXHIBIT 1-2

2005 State Liability Systems Ranking Study

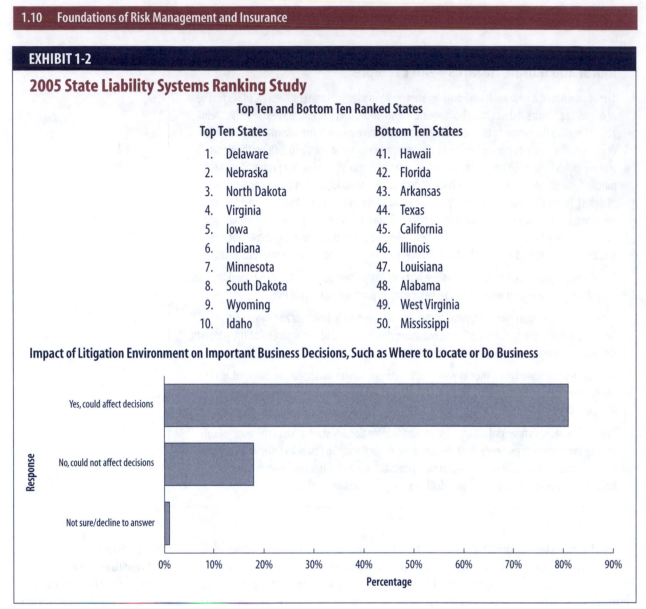

Top Ten and Bottom Ten Ranked States

Top Ten States		Bottom Ten States	
1.	Delaware	41.	Hawaii
2.	Nebraska	42.	Florida
3.	North Dakota	43.	Arkansas
4.	Virginia	44.	Texas
5.	Iowa	45.	California
6.	Indiana	46.	Illinois
7.	Minnesota	47.	Louisiana
8.	South Dakota	48.	Alabama
9.	Wyoming	49.	West Virginia
10.	Idaho	50.	Mississippi

Impact of Litigation Environment on Important Business Decisions, Such as Where to Locate or Do Business

Source: 2005 State Liability Systems Ranking Study, www.instituteforlegalreform.com/harris/pdf/HarrisPoll2005-FullReport.pdf, p. 13 (accessed September 27, 2005).

Regardless of whether they are moral, morale, physical, or legal, hazards can have a compounding effect. For example, the loss frequency associated with a safe driver in a safe car is increased by either the physical hazard of an unsafe car or the moral hazard of an unsafe driver. The frequency is further increased by the compound effect of an unsafe driver in an unsafe car. Therefore, risk management and insurance professionals need to carefully monitor any situation that may involve multiple hazards.

Financial Consequences of Loss

The third element of loss exposures is the financial consequences of the loss. The financial consequences of a loss depend on the type of loss exposure, the cause of loss, and the loss frequency and severity. Some financial consequences can be established with a high degree of certainty; for example, the value of a building that has been damaged by fire. Other financial consequences may be more difficult to determine, such as the value of business lost while the building damaged by fire is being restored. In addition, although some financial consequences are known as soon as a loss occurs, such as the value of property lost in a robbery, others may take months or years to determine, such as the ultimate value of liability claims regarding a defective product.

Types of Loss Exposures

For insurance and risk management purposes, loss exposures are typically divided into the following four types:

1. Property loss exposures
2. Liability loss exposures
3. Personnel loss exposures
4. Net income loss exposures

The three elements of loss exposures apply to each of these four types. However, each type is distinguished in relation to how it affects the first element of a loss exposure, that is, the asset exposed to loss.

Property Loss Exposures

A **property loss exposure** is a condition that presents the possibility that a person or an organization will sustain a loss resulting from damage (including destruction, taking, or loss of use) to property in which that person or organization has a financial interest. Property can be categorized as either tangible property or intangible property. **Tangible property** is property that has a physical form, such as a piece of equipment. **Intangible property** is property that has no physical form, such as a patent or copyright. Tangible property can be further subdivided into real property and personal property. **Real property** is tangible property consisting of land, all structures permanently attached to the land, and whatever is growing on the land. **Personal property** is all tangible property other than real property.

Damage to property can cause a reduction in that property's value, sometimes to zero. For example, when property is stolen, the owner suffers a total loss of that property because the owner no longer has use of it. In addition to these losses, property damage can result in a loss of income (net income loss exposure) because the property cannot be used to generate income or because extra expenses are incurred to continue operations.

Exhibit 1-3 reviews the three elements of a loss exposure as they apply to property loss exposures.

Property loss exposure
A condition that presents the possibility that a person or an organization will sustain a loss resulting from damage (including destruction, taking, or loss of use) to property in which that person or organization has a financial interest.

Tangible property
Property that has a physical form.

Intangible property
Property that has no physical form.

Real property
Tangible property consisting of land, all structures permanently attached to the land, and whatever is growing on the land.

Personal property
All tangible property other than real property.

EXHIBIT 1-3

Elements of Property Loss Exposures

1. **Asset Exposed to Loss**

   - Tangible property

     - Real property, such as offices and warehouses

     - Personal property, such as office furniture and office equipment

   - Intangible property, such as patents, copyrights, trademarks, trade secrets, and customer goodwill

2. **Cause of Loss**

   Some of the more frequent causes of loss, as shown in Exhibit 1-1, include the following:

   - Lightning or hail

   - Tornadoes or high wind

   - Water from failure of indoor appliances; heavy rain or flooding; or sewers or drains

   - Theft

   - Snow or ice

   - Fire

   - Mold

3. **Financial Consequences of Loss**

   The maximum financial consequence of a property loss is limited by the value of the property. However, a property loss may also have an effect on the financial consequences of liability, personnel, or net income losses.

Liability Loss Exposures

Liability loss exposure
A condition that presents the possibility that a person or organization will sustain a loss resulting from a claim alleging that the person or organization is legally responsible for injury and/or damage.

A **liability loss exposure** is a condition that presents the possibility that a person or organization will sustain a loss resulting from a claim alleging that the person or organization is legally responsible for injury and/or damage. The loss exposure results from the claim itself, not necessarily the payment of damages. Even if a claim is successfully defended, and therefore does not result in payment of damages, the party against whom the claim was made nonetheless incurs defense costs, other claim-related expenses, and potentially adverse publicity, all of which produce a financial loss. Exhibit 1-4 reviews the three elements of a loss exposure as they relate to liability loss exposures.

EXHIBIT 1-4

Elements of Liability Loss Exposures

1. **Asset Exposed to Loss**

    The asset exposed to loss for a liability loss exposure is money. Payments that may be required include the following:

    - Damages to the plaintiff if the claim is not successfully defended
    - Settlement costs if the claim settles out of court
    - Legal fees
    - Court costs

2. **Cause of Loss**

    Circumstances in which a liability loss exposure can arise include the following:

    - Breach of a legal duty, such as manufacturing a defective product, if that breach causes harm to another
    - Breach of contract, such as failure to pay on the agreed date
    - Failure to adhere to requirements set out in statutes, regulations, or local ordinances, such as a failure to provide a safe working environment

3. **Financial Consequences of Loss**

    In theory, the financial consequences of a liability loss exposure are limitless. In practice, financial consequences are limited to the total wealth of the person or organization. Although some jurisdictions limit the amounts that can be taken in a claim, liability claims can result in the loss of most or all of a person's or an organization's assets, as well as in a claim on future income.

Industry Language—Property and Liability Loss Exposures

Property

A property loss occurs when a person or an organization sustains a loss as the result of damage (including destruction, taking, or loss of use) to property in which that person or organization has a financial interest. The possibility that such a situation could occur is a property loss exposure.

Insurance professionals often use the term "loss" to mean the event itself. In addition, they often refer to the loss in terms of the applicable property, the cause of loss, the consequences, or the applicable policy.

- When focusing on the type of property, they often refer to a "building loss" or a "personal property loss," regardless of the peril involved.
- When focusing on causes of loss, they often refer to a "fire loss," a "smoke loss," or a "theft loss."

- When focusing on consequences, they often refer to a "business income loss," an "extra expense loss," or an "additional living expense loss," regardless of the type of property or causes of loss involved.

- When focusing on applicable policy, they often use the policy name or type, such as a "homeowners loss," "auto loss," or "business interruption loss."

Similar language is used for loss exposures. Insurance practitioners often refer to a building loss exposure, a fire loss exposure, a homeowners loss exposure, or a business interruption loss exposure.

Liability

Insurance and risk management professionals often refer to specific types of liability losses in terms of the applicable coverage or the activity leading to the loss. For example, a claim for damages arising out of a product defect might be referred to as a "products liability loss" and the possibility of such a claim might be referred to as a "products liability loss exposure." Similarly, owning, operating, maintaining, or using an automobile might be referred to as "auto liability" or "auto liability loss exposures."

Property Damage and Liability Damages

Risk management and insurance professionals use the term "damage" to refer to the harm done to property. The term "damages" refers to the monetary award that may be granted by a court in a liability case.

Personnel Loss Exposures

Personnel loss exposure

A condition that presents the possibility of loss caused by a key person's death, disability, retirement, or resignation that deprives an organization of that person's special skill or knowledge that the organization cannot readily replace.

A **personnel loss exposure** is a condition that presents the possibility of loss caused by a key person's death, disability, retirement, or resignation that deprives an organization of that person's special skill or knowledge that the organization cannot readily replace. A key person can be an individual employee, an owner, an officer or manager of the organization, or a group of employees who possess special skills or knowledge that is valuable to the organization. For example, the possibility that the CEO of an organization can resign to take a position in a more prestigious organization is a personnel loss exposure. Exhibit 1-5 reviews the three elements of a personnel loss exposure.

Personal loss exposure

A condition that presents the possibility of an individual's or a family's loss caused by a family member's illness, death, disability, or unemployment.

If the key person is viewed in terms of his or her family, the loss exposure associated with the loss of that key person is often called a personal or human loss exposure. Although the terminology is slightly different, the definition is almost the same. A **personal loss exposure** is a condition that presents the possibility of an individual's or a family's loss caused by a family member's illness, death, disability, or unemployment. For example, a family would face a personal loss exposure with the possibility of the primary wage earner dying.

EXHIBIT 1-5

Elements of Personnel Loss Exposures

1. **Asset Exposed to Loss**

   The asset exposed to loss for a personnel loss exposure is the value that the key person adds to the organization.

2. **Cause of Loss**

   Circumstances that can lead to a personnel loss exposure include the following:

   • Death

   • Disability

   • Retirement

   • Voluntary separation, such as resignation

   • Involuntary separation, such as layoff or firing

3. **Financial Consequences of Loss**

   The financial consequences of a personnel loss vary based on the cause of loss and can be partial or total as well as temporary or permanent. For example, the death of a key employee is a total, permanent loss. If the personnel loss is caused by a disability, the loss of value to the organization may only a partial loss if the employee is able to continue to add some value to the organization. It may also only be temporary, if a full recovery from the disability is expected.

Net Income Loss Exposures

A **net income loss exposure** is a condition that presents the possibility of loss caused by a reduction in net income. Net income equals revenues minus expenses and income taxes in a given time period. If you consider income taxes to be part of an organization's expenses, a net income loss is a reduction in revenue, an increase in expenses, or a combination of the two. Both individuals and organizations have net income loss exposures. For example, a potential fire at an organization's production facilities could not only destroy the facilities (a property loss exposure) but also force the organization to stop operations for a few weeks, resulting in a loss of sales revenue (a net income loss exposure). Similarly, if a tornado damages the retail store of a self-employed business owner, the inability to earn income while the store is being repaired represents a net income loss exposure. Exhibit 1-6 reviews the three elements of a net income loss exposure.

Net income losses are often the result of a property, liability, or personnel loss (all of which are direct losses). Therefore, net income losses are considered to be indirect losses.

Net income loss exposure
A condition that presents the possibility of loss caused by a reduction in net income.

EXHIBIT 1-6

Elements of Net Income Loss Exposures

1. **Asset Exposed to Loss**

    The asset exposed to loss for a net income loss exposure is the future stream of net income cash flows of the individual or organization.

2. **Cause of Loss**

    Circumstances that can lead to a net income loss exposure include the following:

    *   Property loss
    *   Liability loss
    *   Personnel loss
    *   Losses stemming from business risks; for example, losses resulting from poor strategic planning

3. **Financial Consequences of Loss**

    The financial consequences of a net income loss vary based on the cause of loss. A reduction in revenues, an increase in expenses, or a combination of the two can have financial consequences. The worst case scenario for a net income loss is a decrease in revenues to zero and a significant increase in expenses for a prolonged period.

Direct and Indirect Losses

Property, liability, and personnel loss exposures present the possibility of direct losses to an individual or organization, whereas net income loss exposures present the possibility of indirect losses.

A direct loss is a loss that occurs immediately as the result of a particular cause of loss, such as the reduction in the value of a building that has been damaged by fire. An indirect loss is a loss that results from, but is not directly caused by, a particular cause of loss. For example, the reduction in revenue an organization suffers as a result of fire damage to one of its buildings is an indirect loss.

Estimating indirect losses is often challenging because of the difficulty in projecting the effects that a direct loss will have on revenues or expenses. For example, a risk management professional working at a restaurant chain may be able to project the amount needed to settle a lawsuit brought by a customer accusing the restaurant of food poisoning (direct liability loss) with some certainty. However, projecting the effect that any negative publicity relating to the lawsuit would have on future restaurant sales (indirect loss) would be more difficult.

In the insurance industry, the term "net income losses" is usually associated with property losses, and some insurance policies provide coverage for net income losses related to property losses. However, there are many other causes of net income losses. Some net income losses are associated with the liability or personnel loss exposures that have traditionally been the focus of risk management. Other net income losses are associated with organizational activities that have not traditionally been the focus of risk management, such as strategic marketing or branding decisions. Besides these, other potential net income losses that may affect individuals or organizations include the following:

- *Loss of goodwill.* Organizations are concerned with maintaining goodwill among customers and other stakeholders. Goodwill can be lost in many ways, including providing poor service, offering obsolete products, or mismanaging operations. For a not-for-profit organization, goodwill is equivalent to reputation. Goodwill has broader implications than just reputation in for-profit organizations, because goodwill may have a monetary value. To maintain goodwill, many organizations choose to pay for certain accidents for which they are not legally responsible. For example, if a guest sustains an injury on an organization's premises, and the organization did not cause or contribute to the injury, that organization might still choose to pay any medical bills in order to maintain goodwill and avoid adverse publicity.

- *Failure to perform.* Net income losses may occur as a result of some type of failure to perform, including a product's failure to perform as promised, a contractor's failure to complete a construction project as scheduled, or a debtor's failure to make scheduled payments.

- *Missed opportunities.* An organization may suffer a net income loss as a result of a missed opportunity for profit. For example, an organization that delays a decision to modify its product in response to changes in market demand might lose market share and profit that it could have made on that updated product.

Once an individual or organization has identified the areas in which a loss could occur, that is, those loss exposures subject to risk, the individual or organization can determine the classifications of risk affecting those loss exposures.

CLASSIFICATIONS OF RISK

Risk forms part of the daily activities of individuals and organizations. Classifying the various different types of risk can help in assessing, controlling, and financing risk as part of the risk management process. Classification can help with assessing risks, because many risks in the same classification have similar attributes. It also can help with controlling and financing risk, because many risks in the same classification can be controlled or financed with similar techniques. Finally, classification helps with the administrative function of risk management by helping to ensure that risks in the same classifications are less likely to be overlooked.

The following classifications of risk are some of the most commonly used:

- Pure and speculative risk
- Subjective and objective risk
- Diversifiable and nondiversifiable risk

As shown in Exhibit 1-7, these classifications are not mutually exclusive, and all classification pairs can be applied to any given risk.

EXHIBIT 1-7

Classifications of Risk

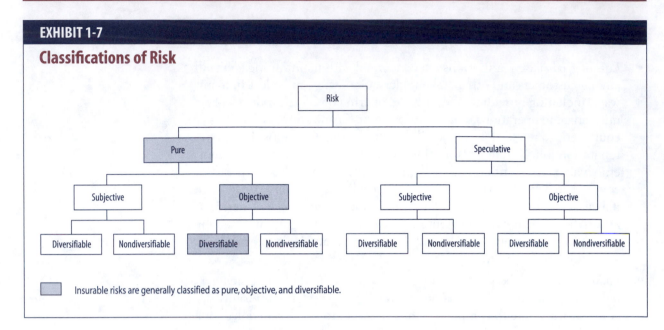

Insurable risks are generally classified as pure, objective, and diversifiable.

Pure and Speculative Risk

Pure risk

A chance of loss or no loss, but no chance of gain.

A **pure risk** is a chance of loss or no loss, but no chance of gain. For example, the owner of a house faces the risk associated with a possible fire loss. The house will either burn or not burn. If the house burns, the owner will suffer a financial loss. If the house does not burn, the owner's financial condition is unchanged. Neither of the possible outcomes would produce a gain. Because there is no opportunity for financial gain, pure risks are always undesirable.

Speculative risk

A chance of loss, no loss, or gain.

A **speculative risk** is a chance of loss, no loss, or gain. An example of speculative risk is gambling. Because speculative risk involves a chance of gain, it can be desirable, as evidenced by the fact that every business venture involves speculative risks. For example, an investor who purchases an apartment building to rent to tenants expects to profit from this investment, and so it is a desirable speculative risk. However, the venture could be unprofitable if, for example, the investor cannot attract sufficient tenants or if government-imposed rental price controls limit the amount of rent that can be charged.

Financial investments, such as the purchase of shares of stock, involve a distinct set of speculative risks, described in Exhibit 1-8. Other business activities can also involve speculative risks, such as the following:

- Price risk, that is, the uncertainty over the size of cash flows resulting from possible changes in the cost of raw materials and other inputs (such as lumber, gas, or electricity), as well as changes in the market for completed products and other outputs.

- Credit risk, that is, the risk that customers and other creditors will fail to make promised payments. Although a credit risk is particularly significant for banks and other financial institutions, it can be relevant to any organization with accounts receivable.

EXHIBIT 1-8

Speculative Risks in Investments

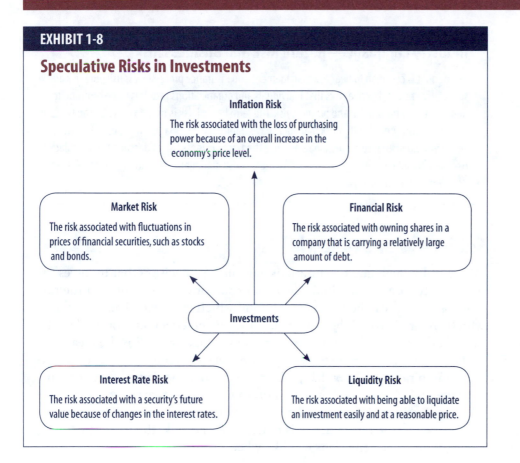

Inflation Risk

The risk associated with the loss of purchasing power because of an overall increase in the economy's price level.

Market Risk

The risk associated with fluctuations in prices of financial securities, such as stocks and bonds.

Financial Risk

The risk associated with owning shares in a company that is carrying a relatively large amount of debt.

Investments

Interest Rate Risk

The risk associated with a security's future value because of changes in the interest rates.

Liquidity Risk

The risk associated with being able to liquidate an investment easily and at a reasonable price.

Insurance deals primarily with risks of loss, not risks of gain; that is, with pure risks rather than speculative risks. However, the distinction between these two classifications of risk is not always precise—many risks have both pure and speculative aspects. For example, although a homeowner faces a pure risk from causes of loss such as fire, he or she also faces the speculative risk that the market value of the house will increase or decrease during any one year. Similarly, although an investor who purchases an apartment building to rent to tenants faces a speculative risk because rental income may produce a profit or loss, the investor also faces a pure risk from causes of loss such as fire. To properly manage these investments, the homeowner and the apartment owner must consider both the speculative and the pure risks. For example, they may choose to manage the pure risk by buying insurance or taking other measures to address property loss exposures. The speculative risk might be managed by obtaining a favorable mortgage and maintaining the property to enhance its resale value.

Distinguishing between pure and speculative risks is important because those risks must often be managed differently. For example, although insurers are developing new products designed to handle some speculative risks (discussed in subsequent chapters), most insurance policies are designed to handle pure risks.

> ### Industry Language—Hazard Risk and Business Risk
>
> Although it is common to hear risk management and insurance professionals use pure risk and speculative risk to describe risks that individuals and organizations face, it is more common to hear the terms hazard risk and business risk. The term hazard risk is used to describe the types of risk (typically pure risks) that risk managers have traditionally managed in the past. Risk management and insurance professionals also use the term business risk to describe the speculative risks associated with an organization's activities. As risk management continues to develop, so does industry terminology.

Subjective and Objective Risk

Subjective risk

The perceived amount of risk based on an individual's or organization's opinion.

Objective risk

The measurable variation in uncertain outcomes based on facts and data.

When individuals and organizations must make a decision that involves risk, it is usually based on the individual's or organization's assessment of the risk. The assessment can be based on opinions, which are subjective, or facts, which are objective. **Subjective risk** is the perceived amount of risk based on an individual's or organization's opinion. **Objective risk** is the measurable variation in uncertain outcomes based on facts and data. Because it is based on opinion rather than on fact, subjective risk may be quite different than the true underlying risk that is present. In fact, subjective risk can exist even where objective risk does not. The closer that an individual's or organization's subjective interpretation of risk is to the objective risk, the more effective their risk management plans will likely be.

The differences between objective risk and subjective risk in individuals are illustrated by a study that examined people's perceptions of the number of deaths caused by certain events or medical conditions.[2] Researchers asked participants to estimate how many people died in one year from different causes of death. These estimates were compared with the real number of deaths for each cause. Exhibit 1-9 illustrates the results of the study. If an estimate were exactly correct, then the point plotted on the graph would be on the diagonal line. For any point above the line, the number of deaths per year was overestimated. For any point below the line, the number of deaths per year was underestimated.

The study revealed that the number of deaths from dramatic events such as tornadoes and floods was overestimated. One reason for this phenomenon may be that these events receive more media attention than others. The number of deaths from causes that receive less media attention—including many medical conditions such as diabetes, heart disease, and stroke—was underestimated.

For causes that are on the same horizontal level in Exhibit 1-9, respondents estimated the same number of deaths, but the actual number of deaths was quite different. For example, people estimated that pregnancy and diabetes had the same death rate, but, in fact, diabetes accounted for about eighty times as many deaths as did pregnancy.

EXHIBIT 1-9

Subjective Versus Objective Risk

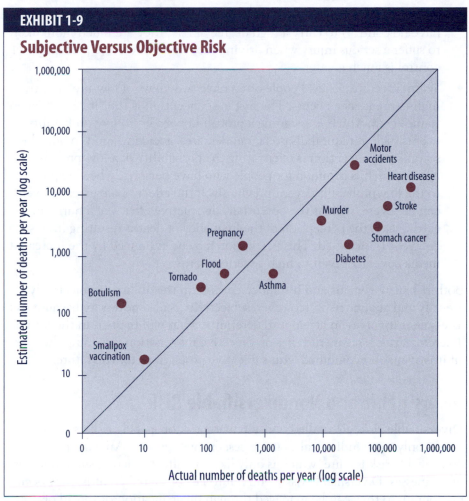

Estimated number of deaths per year (log scale)

Actual number of deaths per year (log scale)

Source: Lichtenstein, Slovic, Fischoff, Layman, and Combs, "Judged Frequency of Lethal Events," *Journal of Experimental Psychology: Human Learning and Memory*, vol. 4, no. 6, 1978, American Psychological Association, pp. 551–578, adapted with permission.

Causes of death on the same vertical line indicate that the respondents estimated quite different numbers of people dying from those causes, whereas the actual numbers of deaths were approximately the same. For example, roughly the same number of people died from motor accidents as from diabetes, yet the estimates were far different.

The reasons why subjective and objective risk can differ substantially include the following:

- *Familiarity and control.* People's perception of a particular risk is influenced by their level of familiarity with that risk and the control they may be able to exert over it. If the familiarity comes from facing the risk on a regular basis, then the greater the familiarity, the greater the likelihood that the person will understate the actual level of risk. Similarly, people generally understate the level of risk when they feel they are in control.

For example, although many people consider air travel (over which they have no control) to carry a high degree of risk, they are much more likely to suffer a serious injury when driving their cars, where the perception of control is much greater.

- *Severity over frequency.* People often have two views of low-probability, high-consequence events. The first misconception is the "it can't happen to me" view, which is assigning a probability of zero to low-probability events such as natural disasters, murder, fires, accidents, and so on. The second misconception is overstating the probability of a low-probability event, which is common for people who have personally been exposed to the low-probability event previously. If the effect of a particular event can be severe, such as the potentially destructive effects of a hurricane or earthquake, the perception of the frequency of deaths resulting from such an event is increased. This perception may be enhanced by the increased media coverage given to high-severity events.

Both risk management and insurance depend on the ability to objectively identify and analyze risks. However, subjectivity is also necessary because risk assessment involves an attempt to determine what will happen in the future. Therefore, risk assessment relies on objective information regarding the past (if it is available) combined with subjective projections for the future.

Diversifiable and Nondiversifiable Risk

Diversifiable risk

A risk that affects only some individuals, businesses, or small groups.

Diversifiable risk, also called nonsystematic risk or specific risk, is a risk that affects only some individuals, businesses, or small groups. An example of a diversifiable risk is a fire, which is only likely to affect one or a small number of businesses. Diversifiable risks tend not to be correlated (that is, they occur randomly), so they can be managed through diversification or spread of risk. For instance, an insurer can diversify the risks associated with fire insurance by insuring many buildings in several different locations. Similarly, business investors often diversify their holdings, as opposed to investing in only one business, hoping those that succeed will more than offset those that fail.

Nondiversifiable risk

A risk that affects a large segment of society at the same time.

Nondiversifiable risk, also called systematic risk or fundamental risk, is a risk that affects a large segment of society at the same time. Examples of nondiversifiable risks include inflation, unemployment, and natural disasters such as hurricanes. Nondiversifiable risks are correlated, that is, their gains or losses tend to occur simultaneously rather than randomly. For example, under certain monetary conditions, interest rates increase for all firms at the same time. If an insurer were to insure firms against interest rate increases, it would not be able to diversify its portfolio of interest rate risks by underwriting a large number of insureds, because all of them would suffer losses at the same time.

The distinction between diversifiable and nondiversifiable risks is not always clear, and some risks can fall under both classifications, depending on the circumstances. For example, a person's unemployment might be a consequence of poor work performance (diversifiable), disability resulting from injury (diversifiable), or the result of an economic downturn (nondiversifiable). A successful products liability claim against a particular tobacco company (diversifiable) might lead to similar claims against all manufacturers in that industry (nondiversifiable).

Although private insurance tends to concentrate on diversifiable risks, and government insurance is often suitable for nondiversifiable risks, a clear line of demarcation does not exist. Various social insurance programs and government-mandated private insurance plans do address diversifiable risks. Examples include workers' compensation plans and compulsory auto insurance programs. Also, private insurers have managed to deal with some nondiversifiable risks, such as earthquakes and hurricanes, either through diversification or by pooling their resources.

Having identified loss exposures and the classifications of risk affecting those loss exposures, an assessment of the financial consequences of those risks will assist in developing a full understanding of the extent to which an individual or organization is exposed to risk. This, in turn, will help to determine where risk management efforts should be focused.

FINANCIAL CONSEQUENCES OF RISK

The cost of risk represents the extent to which an individual's or organization's value has been affected by its risks and indicates how much value might be generated if those risks were reduced or eliminated. In theory, determining the cost of risk is fairly straightforward—calculate the individual's or organization's value if no risk were present and then subtract the individual's or organization's value calculated with risk present. The result is the true cost of risk.

In practice, however, calculating these values is difficult or impossible because it is often not possible to determine the value of the organization without risk present. Furthermore, not all risks reduce an individual's or organization's value. Speculative risks offer the possibility of gain as well as the possibility of loss or no loss. Such risks may actually increase an individual's or organization's value.

Therefore, it is more appropriate to concentrate not on the true cost of risk, but on its financial consequences. The financial consequences of risk faced by individuals or organizations can be broken into the following three components:

1. Expected cost of losses or gains
2. Expenditures on risk management
3. Cost of residual uncertainty

Expected Cost of Losses or Gains

The first financial consequence of risk is the expected cost of losses or gains. In his seminal work on calculating the expected cost of losses or gains, Herbert W. Heinrich discussed the cost of one specific risk, the cost of risk associated with industrial accidents (pure risk).[3] Industrial accidents can demonstrate the various costs that need to be accounted for when determining expected costs of losses. Heinrich observed that not only do industrial accidents include the cost of the compensation paid to the injured employee, but they also include other hidden costs, including the following:

- Time lost by the injured employee
- Time lost by other employees who stop work
- Time lost by foremen, supervisors, or other executives
- Time spent on the case by first-aid attendants and hospital department staff (when not paid for by the insurer)
- Damage to the machine, tools, or other property or the spoilage of material
- Interference with production, failure to fill orders on time, loss of bonuses, payment of forfeits, and other similar causes of loss
- Continuation of the injured employee's wages in full after the employee's return to work—even though the employee's services may temporarily be worth less than normal value
- Loss of profit on the injured employee's productivity and on the idle machines
- Lost productivity because of employee excitement or weakened morale resulting from the accident
- Overhead per injured employee, that is, the expense of light, heat, rent, and other items that continue while the injured employee is not productive

Many of these hidden costs are indirect costs and are more difficult to measure than direct accident costs. Consequently, the overall effect of losses is much greater than the direct losses themselves. Therefore, it is important to identify and try to assign a value to hidden costs in order to get a reasonably accurate view of expected costs.

Calculating the expected cost of losses or gains for speculative risks is more complex than calculating pure risk. For example, suppose a manufacturer was considering adding a second plant to its production facilities. The manufacturer would have to consider all of the expected costs associated with all the pure risks of the new plant, including industrial accidents, as well as the costs or gains associated with the speculative risks. Those costs or gains may include the cost of raw materials, the financing costs for the capital to build the plant, the market price at which the manufacturer can sell its goods, or the expected demand for its products. All of these expected costs and/or gains need to be considered with speculative risks. Actually determining the expected cost of losses or gains is discussed in greater detail in a subsequent chapter.

Expenditures on Risk Management

The second component of the financial consequences of risk is the individual's or organization's expenditures on risk management. The most widely known risk management technique used by individuals is risk financing by purchasing insurance. Homeowners insurance, auto insurance, health insurance, and life insurance are all risk financing measures used by individuals to manage some of the risks they face. Organizations tend to use a wider variety of risk control and risk financing techniques than do individuals. The expenditures on these activities are a financial consequence of risk and are discussed in further detail in a subsequent chapter.

Cost of Residual Uncertainty

The third component of the financial consequences of risk is the cost of residual uncertainty (cost of worry). Residual uncertainty is the level of risk that remains after individuals or organizations implement their risk management plans. This residual uncertainty is also influenced by an individual's or organization's subjective view of the risks to which they are exposed. For example, if an individual is unduly concerned about a particular risk, he or she may overestimate the frequency or severity of it, resulting in a subjective interpretation of the true objective risk. Residual uncertainty can be minimized, but doing so is costly because more has to be spent on attempts to control or finance the risks involved.

The cost of residual uncertainty may be difficult to measure and is largely ignored in cost of risk studies. However, it may still have a significant effect on the ultimate financial consequences of risk for an individual or organization. For example, because it may be more costly to an employer to hire an employee who is perceived as presenting a high risk (for example, because he or she changes jobs frequently), the employer may not be willing to hire or will not be willing to pay a high salary for such an individual. This lost salary opportunity is the cost of residual uncertainty for the individual. For organizations, the cost of residual uncertainty includes the effect that uncertainty has on consumers, investors, and suppliers. Consumers may not be willing to pay as much for products from organizations with a poor safety reputation, investors will require a larger rate of return on their investment from riskier organizations, and suppliers will be less willing to sell their supplies on credit to financially unstable organizations.

Individuals and organizations vary greatly as to how much residual uncertainty they are willing to accept. However, differences in willingness to accept uncertainty (risk) are beneficial to society and economic development. It allows different individuals and organizations to pursue a variety of risky activities that may offer substantial rewards, not just for the investors, but also for society as a whole.

Although it may be difficult to precisely calculate the financial consequences of risk, by considering all of its components and at least estimating its financial consequences, an individual or organization is better able to determine where to focus risk management efforts.

SUMMARY

The word risk can have many different meanings. In this text, risk is defined as the uncertainty about outcomes, some of which can be negative. The two elements within this definition of risk are uncertainty of outcome (uncertainty about what will actually occur, when the outcome will occur, or a combination of the two) and the possibility of a negative outcome. Possibility means that an outcome or event may or may not occur. This is not the same as probability, which is the likelihood that an outcome or event will occur. Unlike possibility, probability is measurable and has a value between zero and one. Understanding the probability of various outcomes helps focus risk management attention on those risks that can be appropriately managed and can help in making decisions as to which risks to undertake and which risk management techniques to use.

In managing the risks that an individual or organization faces, those areas in which a loss could occur must first be identified. Individuals and organizations incur losses when assets they own decrease in value. Situations or conditions that expose assets to loss are called loss exposures. More specifically, a loss exposure is any condition that presents a possibility of loss, whether or not an actual loss occurs.

Every loss exposure has the following three elements: (1) an asset exposed to loss, (2) a cause of loss (also called a peril), and (3) financial consequences of that loss. The asset exposed to loss can be anything of value an individual or organization has that is exposed to loss. Examples of causes of loss include fire, windstorm, explosion, and theft. These causes of loss can be influenced by hazards, which are conditions that increase the frequency and/or severity of a loss. Insurers often typically define hazards according to four classifications: moral hazard, morale hazard, physical hazard, and legal hazard. The financial consequences of a loss depend on the type of loss exposure, the cause of loss, and the loss severity. Some financial consequences can be established with a high degree of certainty; other financial consequences may be more difficult to determine.

For insurance and risk management purposes, loss exposures are typically divided into four types: property loss exposures, liability loss exposures, personnel loss exposures, and net income loss exposures. The three elements of loss exposures apply to each of these four types. However, each type is distinguished in relation to how it affects the asset exposed to loss.

Classifying the various types of risk can help in assessing, controlling, and financing risk as part of the risk management process. Some of the most commonly used classifications are pure and speculative risk, subjective and objective risk, and diversifiable and nondiversifiable risk. A pure risk is a chance of loss or no loss, but no chance of gain, whereas a speculative risk has the chance of loss, no loss, or gain. A subjective risk is the perceived amount of risk based on an individual's or organization's opinion, whereas an objective risk is measurable and is based on facts and data. A diversifiable risk is a risk that affects only some individuals, businesses, or small groups, whereas a nondiversifiable risk affects a large segment of society at the same time.

When managing risk, it is more appropriate to concentrate on the financial consequences of risk than on the actual cost of risk, which can be difficult to quantify. The financial consequences of risk faced by individuals or organizations can be broken into three components: (1) expected cost of losses or gains, (2) expenditures on risk management, and (3) the cost of residual uncertainty. In order to get a reasonably accurate view of the expected cost of losses or gains, it is important to identify and try to assign a value to hidden costs, such as lost productivity. Expenditures on risk management include risk financing measures such as the purchase of insurance policies. Residual uncertainty is the level of risk that remains after individuals or organizations implement their risk management plans. The cost of residual uncertainty may be difficult to measure and is largely ignored in cost of risk studies. However, it may still have a significant effect on the ultimate financial consequences of risk for an individual or organization.

Managing risk is part of every individual's or organization's activities. The degree of formality with which risk is managed varies. For example, an individual is unlikely to follow a formal risk management program. However, many organizations conduct their risk management according to a formal program that can be implemented using the risk management process. Understanding risk management is important in reducing the adverse effects of risk.

CHAPTER NOTES

1. "2005 State Liability Systems Ranking Study," www.instituteforlegalreform.com/harris/pdf/HarrisPoll2005-FullReport.pdf (accessed September 27, 2005).

2. Sarah Lichtenstein, Paul Slovic, Baruch Fischoff, Mark Layman, and Barbara Combs, 1978 "Judged Frequency of Lethal Events," *Journal of Experimental Psychology: Human Learning and Memory,* 4:6, pp. 551–578.

3. Herbert W. Heinrich, *Industrial Accident Prevention,* 4th ed. (New York: McGraw-Hill Book Co., 1959), pp. 51–52. In 1980, a fifth edition of *Industrial Accident Prevention* was published, containing revisions by Dan Peterson and Nester Roos.

Chapter 2

Direct Your Learning

Understanding Risk Management

After learning the content of this chapter and completing the corresponding course guide assignment, you should be able to:

- Contrast traditional and enterprise risk management.

- Describe the benefits of risk management and how it reduces the financial consequences of risk for individuals, organizations, and society.

- Summarize pre-loss and post-loss risk management program goals and the conflicts that can arise as they are implemented.

- Describe each of the steps in the risk management process.

- Define or describe each of the Key Words and Phrases for this chapter.

Develop Your Perspective

What are the main topics covered in the chapter?

Both traditional and enterprise risk management can benefit individuals, organizations, and society. Larger organizations typically conduct risk management through a formalized risk management program that has both pre-loss and post-loss goals designed to advance the organization's overall goals and that can be implemented using the risk management process.

Identify the benefits an organization can expect by applying risk management.

- How does risk management reduce the cost of risk?
- How are an organization's goals integrated with its risk management program?

Why is it important to learn about these topics?

Understanding how to manage risks can help an individual or organization reduce the adverse effects of losses or missed opportunities.

Consider the loss exposures your organization manages.

- Why is your organization willing to assume those risks?
- Who performs risk management functions within your organization?

How can you use what you will learn?

Evaluate the loss exposures facing your organization.

- What might the pre-loss and post-loss goals of your organization include?
- What information would you need to identify your organization's risks?
- What are the associated financial consequences?

Chapter 2
Understanding Risk Management

Risk management involves the efforts of individuals or organizations to efficiently and effectively assess, control, and finance risk in order to minimize the adverse effects of losses or missed opportunities. Individuals practice risk management to protect their limited assets from losses and to help meet personal goals. For an organization, sound risk management adds value and helps to ensure that losses or missed opportunities do not prevent it from meeting its goals.

Traditional risk management concerns managing hazard risk. Enterprise risk management (ERM) expands an organization's risk management professional's role to include management of business risk, such as strategic and financial risks. Whichever form of risk management is followed, its benefits affect individuals, organizations, and society.

Larger organizations typically conduct risk management through a formalized risk management program that has both pre-loss and post-loss goals that are designed to advance the organization's overall goals and that can be implemented using the risk management process. The risk management process consists of a series of six steps that enable an organization to identify, analyze, and, ultimately, manage its risk.

RISK MANAGEMENT

In its simplest form, risk management includes any effort to economically deal with uncertainty of outcomes (risk). For individuals, risk management is usually an informal series of efforts, not a formalized process. Individual or personal risk management may be viewed as part of the financial planning process that encompasses broader matters such as capital accumulation, retirement planning, and estate planning. Individuals and families often practice risk management informally without explicitly following a risk management process. For example, individuals purchase insurance policies to cover accidental or unexpected losses or they contribute to savings plans so that they have money available to cover unforeseen events. In smaller organizations, risk management is not usually a dedicated function, but one of many tasks carried out by the owner or senior manager. In many larger organizations, the risk management function is conducted as part of a formalized risk management program. A **risk management program** is a system for planning, organizing, leading, and controlling the resources and activities that an organization needs to protect itself from the adverse effects of accidental losses.

Risk management program
A system for planning, organizing, leading, and controlling the resources and activities that an organization needs to protect itself from the adverse effects of accidental losses.

Risk management process
The method of making, implementing, and monitoring decisions that minimize the adverse effects of risk on an organization.

Most risk management programs are built around the risk management process. The **risk management process** is the method of making, implementing, and monitoring decisions that minimize the adverse effects of risk on an organization. Although the exact steps in an organization's risk management process may differ from the process discussed in this text, all risk management processes are designed to assess, control, and finance risk.

Evolving Industry Language: Risk Classification and Risk Categories

Risk management and insurance professionals often use the terms pure risk and hazard risk interchangeably. They also often use the terms speculative risk and business risk interchangeably. When risk is described as either pure or speculative risk, the description is about the classification of risk. The classification is based on an attribute of the risk—whether there is the potential for gain or not. When risk is described as either hazard or business risk, the description is about a category of risk. The categories are based on terminology that has developed in the risk management industry. Hazard risk has traditionally been managed by risk management professionals, whereas business risk has traditionally been managed outside the risk management department. The pure or speculative risk classification is important in identifying insurable risks (discussed in a subsequent chapter). The hazard or business risk categories are important in understanding the evolution from traditional risk management to enterprise risk management.

Most hazard risks are pure risks, but not all pure risks are hazard risks, as shown subsequently. Similarly, most speculative risks are business risks, but not all business risks are speculative risks. As this chapter focuses on risk management, it will use the hazard and business risk categories.

Traditional Risk Management

Traditionally, the risk management professional's role has been associated with loss exposures related to hazard risk. This view excludes from the scope of risk management all loss exposures that arise from business risk. Therefore, organizational risk management has focused on managing safety, purchasing insurance, and controlling financial recovery from losses generated by hazard risk. Risk management professionals have dealt with activities such as monitoring safety programs or processing workers' compensation claims, rather than helping achieve organizational gains from exposure to business risk. This has often led traditional risk management departments to be viewed by other departments as cost centers, not as revenue centers—that is, they believe risk management only costs the organization money. This leads to the misconception that risk management does not add value to the organization.

Making sound decisions about individual hazard risks requires a basic understanding of an organization's overall financial condition and its capacity to withstand loss, both of which are influenced by its overall exposure to business risk as well as hazard risk. For example, how much cash an organization can access to pay for unanticipated property losses is directly affected by how well its products are selling and how well its investments are performing. As a result, the traditional role of risk management and of the risk management professional is expanding to include management of a broader array of risks.

Enterprise Risk Management by Organizations

Enterprise risk management (ERM) is the term commonly used to describe the broader view of risk management that encompasses both hazard and business risk. ERM is an approach to managing all of an organization's key risks and opportunities with the intent of maximizing the organization's value. An ERM approach allows an organization to integrate all of its risk management activities so that the risk management process occurs at the enterprise level, rather than at the departmental or business unit level. How ERM is implemented in practice varies significantly among organizations, depending on their size, nature, and complexity.

Enterprise Risk Management in Practice

If ERM is considered a part of a corporate culture in which all risk management decisions are made under the guidance of an individual executive, then it has been practiced by small organizations for years. In a small organization, one individual or a small group of individuals often assesses all risks the organization faces and determines how to allocate limited resources to best manage the risks that have the greatest effect on the organization.

However, ERM is now being implemented by large organizations as well. The risk management professional no longer needs to sell the importance of risk management to senior executives because risk management is no longer viewed as a cost center, but as a way to add value to the organization. In ERM, a risk management executive exhibits top-down control.

One of the barriers to successfully implementing ERM in large organizations involves the balance of control between the various departments. Some departmental managers may be reluctant to relinquish control of risk-related decisions previously made within their departments. For example, the finance department may be reluctant to surrender ultimate control of foreign exchange rate risk. In addition, the internal audit and risk management departments may disagree about who should be in charge of the ERM program.

Mid-sized organizations have been slower to adopt ERM, often because they are large enough to need a dedicated risk management function yet do not have the resources to implement a full ERM corporate structure.

Traditionally, risk management is departmentalized. That is, hazard risks are managed in the risk management department, financial risks in the finance department, and so on. Using this approach, an organization rarely makes relative comparisons among its risks to determine how they interact with one another or to evaluate their cumulative effect on the organization. ERM, by coordinating all risk management activities under a single executive, is designed to facilitate these comparisons and evaluations.

For ERM to be effective, an organization must have the culture and infrastructure to manage the risks that most affect its value. Therefore, ERM can be a challenge in organizations that have previously followed a traditional risk management approach.

Risk Maps

ERM is a holistic approach to risk management in that it addresses all risks faced by an organization. Although some aspects of risk are qualitative, individual risks can be best compared via a quantitative rating system that incorporates the loss exposures' loss frequency (likelihood of occurrence) and loss severity (significance of loss). One such system of comparison used in ERM programs is a risk map of the type shown in Exhibit 2-1. Risk maps can come in many forms, including geographical maps as well as two-dimensional and three-dimensional charts. Risk maps can also be tailored to show how often the frequency and severity of losses could interfere with achieving specific key business goals. The risk map in Exhibit 2-1 is a two-dimensional chart created by plotting the organization's risks on a grid relative to one another based on loss frequency (shown on the horizontal axis) and loss severity (shown on the vertical axis). Both frequency and severity are divided into two categories (high and low), yielding four quadrants. The more categories of frequency and severity included in a risk map, the more sectors the map depicts.

EXHIBIT 2-1

Risk Map

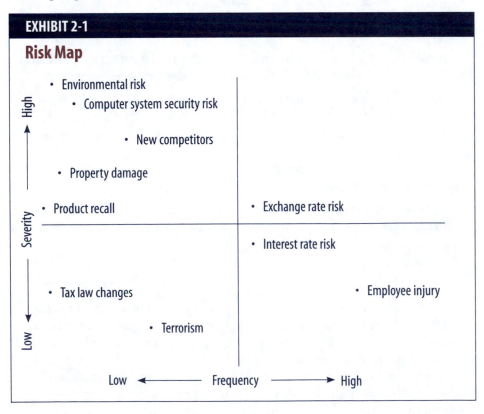

A risk map serves three functions in an ERM program. First, it helps to break down the departmentalization of risk under a traditional risk management program through a central diagram that depicts risks from all sources. Such a depiction enables the comparison of all risks, regardless of the department or area of the organization to which they are assigned. Second, a risk map is an efficient communication tool to help senior management better understand the risks inherent to the organization and can help determine which risks require the most attention and the greatest amount of risk management resources. Finally, risk maps, if tailored to key business goals, rank risks based on their relative effect on those goals. That is, the frequency and severity of the risks are assessed based on how often each would interfere with achieving a specific business goal.

In order to accommodate the volume and variety of risks organizations face, computerized risk management information systems are frequently used in measuring and rating risks to create risk maps. Because each organization has a different risk profile (risks faced) and risk appetite (risks willing to assume), one organization's risk map will not necessarily apply to another. Therefore, the risks an organization identifies and prioritizes in an ERM program will also vary.

Quadrants of Risk in an Organization

Although no consensus exists about how an organization should categorize its risks, one ERM approach involves dividing them into four risk quadrants: hazard, operational, financial, and strategic. As discussed previously, hazard risks are traditionally managed by risk management professionals. Operational risks are pure risks that fall outside of the traditional hazard risk category and could jeopardize service-related or manufacturing-related business functions. Financial risks directly affect an organization's financial position via changes in revenue, expenses, business valuation, or the cost or availability of capital. Strategic risks are fundamental to an organization's existence and business plan because they have a current or future effect on earnings or capital arising from adverse business decisions, improper implementation of decisions, or lack of responsiveness to changes in the industry or changes in demand.

The focus of the four risk quadrants is different from the risk classifications previously discussed; that is, pure and speculative, subjective and objective, and diversifiable and nondiversifiable. Whereas the classifications of risk focus on some aspect of the risk itself, the four quadrants of risk focus on the source of risk and who has traditionally managed it. Just as a particular loss exposure can fall into more than one classification, a loss exposure can also fall into multiple ERM risk quadrants. For example, intellectual property could be categorized as a strategic risk because protection of intellectual property has often fallen outside of the traditional risk management function. However, because intellectual property is a type of property, it can also be considered a hazard risk.

Exhibit 2-2 contains a list of common risks, categorized according to the four ERM risk quadrants. Each of the risks is also classified as either pure or speculative and diversifiable or nondiversifiable. They are not classified as subjective or objective, which is dependent on the organization, not on the risk.

Traditional Risk Management Contrasted With ERM

Enterprise risk management is an extension of traditional risk management. However, the following significant differences exist between the two:

- *Strategic application.* ERM is integrated into an organization's strategic business decisions. Organizations that practice ERM typically place an executive in charge of risk management, sometimes called a chief risk officer (CRO), to ensure that risk is effectively managed across the organization. Because ERM is applied enterprise-wide, it supersedes

---

EXHIBIT 2-2

Causes of Loss Categorized According to the Four Quadrants of Risk

Hazard Risks

Many of these risks are transferred by property-liability insurance policies. Insurance for some of these risks, such as workers' compensation, may be mandated by law.

Examples include:
- Property damage (pure, diversifiable)
- Third-party liability (pure, diversifiable)
- Directors and officers (D&O) liability (pure, diversifiable)
- Health and safety (pure, diversifiable)
- Natural hazards, such as flood or earthquake (pure, nondiversifiable)
- Asbestos (pure, diversifiable)
- Terrorism (pure, diversifiable)

Operational Risks

Although many operational risks are pure risks, traditional risk management deals less frequently with operational risks.

Examples include:
- Product recall (pure, diversifiable)
- Discrimination (pure, diversifiable)
- Embezzlement (pure, diversifiable)
- Workplace violence (pure, diversifiable)
- Kidnap (pure, diversifiable)
- Turnover (pure, diversifiable)
- Service provider failures, such as phone or utility service (pure, diversifiable)
- Supplier business interruption (pure, diversifiable)

Financial Risks

Financial risks are traditionally handled by the treasury or chief financial officer (CFO) function. These risks are normally speculative and can sometimes be managed with financial tools such as options or futures.

Examples include:
- Debt rating (speculative, diversifiable)
- Liquidity/cash (speculative, diversifiable)
- Asset valuation (speculative, diversifiable)
- Legislative changes (speculative, nondiversifiable)
- Commodity prices, such as fuel prices (speculative, nondiversifiable)
- Interest rates (speculative, nondiversifiable)
- Currency/foreign exchange rates (speculative, nondiversifiable)
- Economic growth/recession (speculative, nondiversifiable)

Strategic Risks

Many strategic risks are directly linked to management decisions.

Examples include:
- Intellectual property (speculative, diversifiable)
- Ethics (speculative, diversifiable)
- Planning (speculative, diversifiable)
- Technology (speculative, diversifiable)
- Union relations (speculative, diversifiable)
- New competitors (speculative, diversifiable)
- Media coverage (speculative, diversifiable)
- Industry consolidation (speculative, diversifiable)
- Product design (speculative, diversifiable)

departmental or functional autonomy that could impede risk management efforts. In contrast, traditional risk management focuses only on hazard risk without examining risk in other functional areas. For example, if an organization practices traditional risk management, then a decision about purchasing property insurance on a production facility would be made by its risk management professional, whereas a decision to hedge exchange rate risk would be made by the financial manager. The risk management professional and the financial manager would have very little, if any, interaction about these two decisions. If the same organization practiced ERM, then both of these decisions would be included in the risk management function.

- *Risks considered.* ERM involves managing all risks affecting an organization's ability to meet its goals, regardless of whether the risks are hazard or business. As shown in Exhibit 2-3, traditional risk management normally considers only hazard risks that involve fortuitous losses, that is, losses over which the organization has no control. ERM considers all risks that an organization faces, regardless of their source or potential outcomes. For example, traditional risk management would have focused on property loss exposures related to the fire cause of loss, whereas ERM would focus on those as well as the likelihood of the failure of new products.

- *Performance metrics.* ERM emphasizes results-based performance measurement. Results indicate whether a risk management technique helped achieve an underlying business goal, such as total sales or return on investment. In traditional risk management, success can be measured on both an activity and results basis. That is, in addition to measuring the success of risk management efforts based on results such as fewer property losses, traditional risk management also evaluates based on activity, such as the number of safety drills held in a year.

All forms of risk management are intended to help minimize the adverse effects of losses and missed opportunities. Understanding the specific benefits that risk management offers can help an individual or organization determine which risk management activities to undertake.

RISK MANAGEMENT BENEFITS

Properly managing risk reduces its negative financial consequences and thereby benefits individuals, organizations, and society. As discussed previously, the three components of the financial consequences of risk are (1) expected losses or gains, (2) the cost of risk management, and (3) the cost of residual uncertainty. A tradeoff exists between the second component, the cost of risk management, and the value generated by the corresponding reduction in risk. An organization that spends a relatively large amount on risk management (assessing, controlling, and financing risks) should see smaller expected losses (less frequent or less severe) and experience less residual uncertainty than an organization that spends less on risk management. For example, an organization that spends more on risk control by installing a state-of-the-art security system

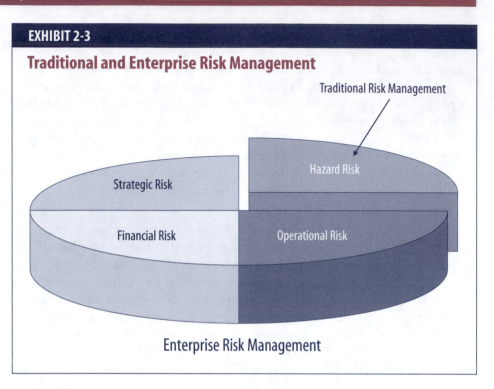

EXHIBIT 2-3

Traditional and Enterprise Risk Management

Traditional Risk Management

Strategic Risk

Hazard Risk

Financial Risk

Operational Risk

Enterprise Risk Management

would expect to have fewer thefts (and therefore lower expected losses) and a better sense of security (less residual uncertainty).

Whether for an individual, an organization, or society, the cost of risk management is the cost of resources expended to reduce either the expected losses or residual uncertainty associated with risk. A reduction in either of those two components represents the benefit of risk management. Exhibit 2-4 summarizes the benefits of risk management for individuals, organizations, and society in terms of its reduction of expected losses and residual uncertainty. An efficient risk management program helps to minimize the total of all three components of risk's costs.

EXHIBIT 2-4

Risk Management Benefits

	Component	
	Lower Expected Losses	**Less Residual Uncertainty**
Individuals	Preserves financial resources	Reduces anxiety
Organizations	Preserves financial resources Makes an organization more attractive as an investment opportunity	Reduces deterrence effect
Society	Preserves financial resources	Improves allocation of productive resources

Reducing the Financial Consequences of Risk

The overall financial consequence of risk for a given asset or activity is the sum of the following three costs: (1) the cost of the value lost because of actual events that cause a loss, (2) the cost of the resources devoted to risk management for that asset or activity, and (3) the cost of residual uncertainty. However, because it is difficult to assign a specific value to the cost of residual uncertainty, it is also difficult to establish a benchmark against which the performance of the risk management program can be assessed. As a result, organizations typically evaluate a subset of costs that form part of the financial consequences of risk and refer to this subset of costs as the cost of risk. For a particular asset or activity, the cost of risk can be broken down as follows:

- Cost of losses not reimbursed by insurance or other external sources
- Cost of insurance premiums
- Cost of external sources of funds, for example, the interest payments to lenders or the transaction costs associated with noninsurance indemnity
- Cost of measures to prevent or reduce the size of potential losses
- Cost of implementing and administering risk management

Each year, the Risk and Insurance Management Society (RIMS), a global organization of risk management professionals, conducts a survey to determine the cost of risk for industry categories in the United States and Canada. The survey reveals trends in different industries and is used as a benchmarking tool to compare cost of risks between organizations in the same industry. The survey also provides benchmarking measures in areas such as risk management staffing, insurance coverages, and insurance broker compensation. Exhibit 2-5 shows the cost of risk per $1,000 of revenue for all U.S. and Canadian organizations that answered the survey. The exhibit shows a pattern of declining cost of risk throughout the 1990s with a sharp upturn beginning in 2001. Although a portion of the falling cost of risk during the 1990s can be attributed to advancements in risk management, much of the decline is attributable to changes in the insurance market. As insurance rates fell during the mid-to-late 1990s, the cost of risk decreased. As insurance rates began to climb in 2000 and then rise sharply following the terrorist attacks of September 11, 2001, the cost of risk increased. One of the major components of the cost of risk has historically been workers' compensation costs, which make up approximately one-third of the total cost of risk in most years of the survey.

By reducing the long-term, overall cost of risk and devoting a minimum of resources to the actual process of managing risk without interfering with normal activities, risk management helps an individual or an organization to be more productive, promotes safety, and enhances profitability.

EXHIBIT 2-5

The Cost of Risk per $1,000 in Revenue

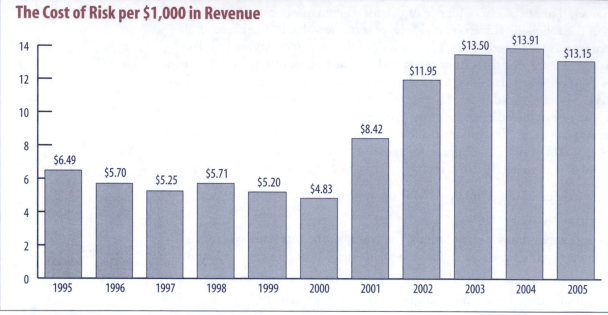

Source: 2005 RIMS Benchmark Survey.

Benefits to Individuals

Risk management can preserve an individual's financial resources by reducing his or her expected losses. Most individuals have limited financial resources and are therefore not able—or willing—to bear the financial consequences of substantial risks. For example, most people can not afford to pay thousands (or millions) of dollars in damages if they seriously injure or kill someone in an auto accident. For some, avoiding loss is a viable alternative, and they choose not to drive. However, for most individuals, driving is a necessity. Purchasing auto liability insurance enables them to transfer this liability risk to the insurer. Although auto liability insurance is required in most states, many individuals purchase liability coverage well above the minimum required limits.

The second benefit of risk management for individuals is that it reduces the residual uncertainty associated with risk. Most individuals are at least somewhat risk averse. Risk aversion means that, all else being equal, individuals prefer certainty to uncertainty, or less risk to more risk. For example, if given a choice between the 100 percent certainty of paying $100 or a 20 percent chance of paying $500 (and, therefore, an 80 percent chance of paying nothing), a risk-averse individual would choose the 100 percent certainty of paying $100. Risk management allows an individual to invest time and money into managing risks in order to reduce uncertainty and its associated anxiety.

Benefits to Organizations

Organizations tend to have more resources than individuals and therefore are better equipped to bear risk. Consequently, organizations do not exhibit the same degree of risk aversion as individuals. Nonetheless, organizations usually choose to manage their risks, because they, too, benefit from preserving their financial resources. Preservation of financial resources adds value to the organization and makes it a safer and more attractive investment, because shareholders or other investors want to know that their equity is safe and will generate future income and creditors seek assurance that the money they have loaned the organization will be repaid on time with interest. Risk management can protect the financial resources necessary to satisfy these parties and other stakeholders.

The protection that risk management affords an organization's financial resources can, in turn, provide confidence that capital is protected against future costs such as property loss, interruption of future income, liability judgments, or loss of key personnel. This sense of confidence is attractive both to suppliers and customers. As a result, suppliers may be more willing to allow the organization to buy on credit and customers may purchase more products or services the organization offers.

Risk management also can reduce the deterrence effect of risk; that is, it can improve an organization's capacity to engage in business activities by minimizing the adverse effects of risk. Consequently, the organization can plan for its future with less uncertainty about potential outcomes. The fear of possible future losses tends to make senior management reluctant to undertake activities or investments it considers too risky, thereby depriving the organization of their associated benefits. By making losses less frequent, less severe, or more predictable, risk management can alleviate management's fears about potential losses. This increases the feasibility of activities such as research and development, joint ventures, or investment in other organizations, that previously appeared too risky.

Benefits to Society

Society also faces a cost of risk, as well as uncertainty about future losses. Its cost of risk is slightly different from that of an individual or organization. Nonetheless, risk management benefits society in the same ways that it does individuals and organizations, by lowering expected losses and reducing residual uncertainty.

A nation's economy has limited resources with which to produce goods and services. When, for example, a fire or an earthquake demolishes a factory or destroys a highway, that economy's overall productive resources are reduced. Beyond the resources directly consumed in a loss, a significant portion of a nation's productive resources is devoted to preventing, repairing, or compensating for the results of losses.

When losses are possible, some portion of the economy's resources must be devoted to risk management for the benefit of society as a whole. Minimizing the resources consumed in running an economy's risk management program is analogous to an organization minimizing the administrative costs of its risk management department.

By reducing residual uncertainty, risk management also improves the allocation of productive resources. Risk management makes those who own or run an organization more willing to undertake risky activities, because they are better protected against losses that those activities might have produced. This makes executives, workers, and suppliers of financial capital more able to pursue activities that maximize profits, returns on investments, and, ultimately, wages. Such shifts increase productivity within an economy and improve the overall standard of living.

To make best use of the benefits that risk management can provide, a risk management professional first needs to establish the goals of the risk management program. Once these goals have been established, activities can be pursued that will maximize the potential to achieve those goals.

RISK MANAGEMENT PROGRAM GOALS

Senior management support is essential to an effective and efficient risk management program. To gain that support, a risk management program should promote the organization's overall goal. In most for-profit organizations, the overall goal is to maximize the organization's value. Public entity and not-for-profit organizations might emphasize other goals, such as service to members, subscribers, or benefactors. With a clear understanding of the organization's overall goals, a risk management program's goals can be tailored to support the organization's goals. Risk management program goals are typically divided into two categories: pre-loss goals and post-loss goals.

Pre-loss goals
Risk management program goals that should be in place even if no significant losses occur.

Pre-loss goals are risk management program goals that should be in place even if no significant losses occur. Pre-loss goals describe an organization's need to meet responsibilities as an ongoing operation. Possible pre-loss goals include economy of operations, tolerable uncertainty, legality, and social responsibility. A risk management program should incorporate these goals, regardless of the organization's actual loss experience.

Post-loss goals
Risk management program goals that should be in place in the event of a significant loss.

Post-loss goals are risk management program goals that should be in place in the event of a significant loss. Post-loss goals broadly describe the degree of recovery that an organization will strive to reach following a loss. Possible post-loss goals include survival, continuity of operations, profitability, earnings stability, social responsibility, and growth. These goals describe operating and financial conditions that the organization's senior management would consider acceptable after the most significant foreseeable loss.

Pre-Loss Goals

Regardless of loss experience, every organization has operational goals that are vital to its success that the risk management program should support. Four such operational goals are as follows:

1. Economy of operations
2. Tolerable uncertainty

3.   Legality

4.   Social responsibility

Although these are not the only possible operational goals, they are typical of the types of operational goals that pre-loss risk management activities are designed to support.

Economy of Operations

A risk management program should operate economically and efficiently; that is, the organization generally should not incur substantial costs in exchange for slight benefits. One way to measure the economy of a risk management program is through benchmarking, in which an organization's risk management costs are compared with those of similar organizations. The RIMS cost of risk benchmarking study shown previously in Exhibit 2-5 provides one way to measure the economy of an organization's risk management program.

Tolerable Uncertainty

Tolerable uncertainty involves keeping managers' uncertainty about losses at tolerable levels. Managers should be able to make and implement decisions effectively without being unduly affected by uncertainty. Therefore, risk management professionals typically seek to implement a risk management program that assures managers that whatever might happen will be within the bounds of what was anticipated and will be effectively treated by the risk management program. Although a risk management program should make all personnel aware of potential loss exposures, the program should also provide assurances through both risk control and risk financing that loss exposures are being managed well.

Legality

The risk management program should help to ensure that the organization's legal obligations are satisfied. These legal obligations will typically be based on the following:

- Standard of care that is owed to others
- Contracts entered into by the organization
- Federal, state, and local laws and regulations

A risk management professional has an essential role in helping the organization avoid liability by meeting the standard of care that it owes to others. The risk management professional and the organization's legal counsel manage lawsuits brought by others that arise from the organization's wrongful or negligent acts or omissions. Some public and charitable entities are immune from negligence claims because of long-standing constitutional and other judicial doctrines that exempt them. However, such immunities have eroded over time, and many entities that might be eligible for such immunity choose to purchase liability insurance rather than invoke it.

The risk management professional should be aware of the organization's contractual obligations as well as the contractual obligations that others owe to it. If the organization does not fulfill its obligations under a contract, the other party may bring a lawsuit against the organization for breach of contract. If the other party does not fulfill its obligation and the organization does not pursue the matter, the other party may be relieved of its obligations under the contract.

Risk management professionals also need to be aware of the federal, state, and local laws and regulations that apply to their organizations and should work with other employees to ensure compliance. Examples of laws and regulations of particular concern to the risk management function are occupational health and safety regulations, labeling requirements for consumer products, regulations about hazardous waste disposal, and statutes establishing mandatory insurance requirements.

Social Responsibility

Social responsibility, which is both a pre-loss and a post-loss goal for many organizations, includes acting ethically and fulfilling obligations to the community and society as a whole. Beyond the altruistic interests of the organization's owners, many organizations justify pursuing this goal because of its potential to enhance the organization's reputation.

For public entities and not-for-profit organizations, social responsibility might be the overriding pre-loss goal, even surpassing the need for economy of operations. Public entities exist to fulfill the needs of their constituents, so their purpose is to promote social goals. Similarly, not-for-profit organizations are chartered to meet the needs of members, subscribers, or students, and this often requires a social responsibility focus.

Post-Loss Goals

Post-loss goals are based on the operating and financial conditions that the organization's senior management would consider acceptable after a significant foreseeable loss. Six possible post-loss goals are as follows:

1. Survival
2. Continuity of operations
3. Profitability
4. Earnings stability
5. Social responsibility
6. Growth

After a severe loss, the most basic goal is survival, while the most ambitious goal is uninterrupted growth. The more ambitious a particular post-loss goal, the more difficult and costly it is to achieve.

Survival

Survival is a fundamental post-loss goal. For individuals, survival means staying alive. For organizations, survival means resuming operations to some extent after an adverse event. Survival does not necessarily mean returning to the condition that existed before loss. Within that context, an organization survives a loss whenever that loss does not permanently halt its production and the incomes of those who work for or own it.

Examples of losses that could prevent an organization's survival include the following:

- Its only office or plant is destroyed.
- A legal liability judgment or an out-of-court settlement drains its cash and credit resources.
- The death or disability of a key employee (such as an executive or technician) deprives it of essential leadership or of some vital expertise.

Continuity of Operations

Continuity of operations is an important post-loss goal for many private organizations and an essential goal for all public entities. Although the survival goal requires that no loss (no matter how severe) permanently shut down an organization, the goal of continuity of operations is more demanding. With continuity as a goal, no loss can be allowed to interrupt the organization's operations for any appreciable time. Within this context, "appreciable" is a relative term and depends on the goods or services produced. One organization may be unable to tolerate even a few days' shutdown, whereas another organization's output might be continuous even when some of its activities halt for a month or more. When an organization's senior management sets continuity of operations as a goal, its risk management professional must have a clear, detailed understanding of the specific operations whose continuity is essential and the maximum tolerable interruption interval for each operation.

Any organization for which continuous operation is essential must take steps, and probably incur additional expenses, to forestall an intolerable shutdown. These steps include the following:

- Identify activities whose interruptions cannot be tolerated
- Identify the types of events that could interrupt such activities
- Determine the standby resources that must be immediately available to counter the effects of those losses
- Ensure the availability of the standby resources at even the most unlikely and difficult times

The last step, ensuring the availability of standby resources, is likely to add to an organization's expenses, and, accordingly, achieving the continuity of operations goal tends to be more costly than the more basic goal of survival.

However, for organizations that give high priority to continuity of operations, this added cost is preferable to the alternative of business interruption.

For public entities—particularly cities, counties, and other governing bodies, as well as schools and public utilities—maintaining public services without interruption is perhaps the most important risk management goal. Any sustained interruption in police or fire protection, supplies of clean water, removal of trash or sewage, or public education can be catastrophic. The essential purpose of most public entities is to provide some service, and therefore they are willing to commit significant resources to comprehensive contingency plans.

Profitability

As well as considering the physical effects a loss might have on an organization's operations, senior management may also be concerned with how such a loss would affect the organization's profitability. In a for-profit organization, the goal is to generate net income. In a not-for-profit organization, the goal is to operate within the budget. An organization's senior management might have established a minimum amount of profit (or surplus in not-for-profit organizations) that no loss can be allowed to reduce. To achieve that minimum amount, the risk management program is likely to emphasize insurance and other means of transferring the financial consequences of loss so that actual financial results fall within an acceptable range. An organization that requires a minimum profit tends to spend more on risk management, particularly risk financing, than does an organization that is prepared to tolerate an occasional unprofitable financial result.

Earnings Stability

Rather than strive for the highest possible level of profit (or surplus) in a given period, some organizations emphasize earnings stability over time. Striving for earnings stability requires precision in forecasting risk management costs, as well as lower retention levels and a willingness on the part of the organization to spend more on risk transfer mechanisms. A risk management professional focusing on earnings stability would seek ways of creating consistent results over time, rather than choose actions that might produce fluctuating results.

Social Responsibility

As discussed previously, losses affect an organization's ability to fulfill its real or perceived obligations to the community and to society as a whole. Organizational disruptions have implications for relationships with customers, suppliers, employees, taxpayers, and other members of the public. These relationships, even though they may not involve legal obligations, are often the focus of the organization's overall mission. Many not-for-profit organizations and public entities are unable to distinguish between the post-loss goals of survival and social responsibility because of their focus on community service. However, the post-loss goal of social responsibility does not apply only to not-for-profit and public entities. For example, consider an organization with strong ties to the local community that relies heavily on the support of the customers and suppliers in its neighborhood. If such an organization makes a social commitment, such as sponsoring a local charity event, then the failure to honor that commitment could seriously damage its reputation and correspondingly affect its future business operations. Such an organization would want to ensure that its risk management program provided sufficient protection against losses so that the organization's ability to meet its social responsibilities would not be seriously diminished in the event of a loss.

Growth

Emphasizing the post-loss goal of growth—for example, increasing market share, the size and scope of activities or products, or assets—might have two distinctly opposing effects on an organization's risk management program. Those effects depend on the managers' and owners' tolerance for uncertainty. If striving to expand makes managers and owners more willing to accept greater uncertainty in exchange for minimizing risk management costs, the organization's explicit costs for risk management could be fairly low. Such an organization's risk management professional might find it difficult to obtain a budget adequate to protect against expanding loss exposures. Moreover, if such an organization suffers a severe loss for which it was not adequately prepared, its real cost of risk management—more accurately, its real cost of not effectively managing loss exposures—might be significant and involve sacrificing much of the growth it has attained.

In contrast, the goal of risk management in a growing organization might be to protect its expanding resources so that its path of expansion is not blocked or reversed by a substantial loss. Risk management costs in this scenario are likely to be high because such an organization might seek increased earnings (growth) rather than survival or earnings stability. Consequently, the organization lowers its tolerance for unanticipated loss and requires greater emphasis on risk control and risk financing.

Conflict Between Goals

Pre-loss and post-loss goals are interrelated and sometimes conflict with each other. Although conflicts may arise between post-loss goals, it is more common for post-loss goals to conflict with pre-loss goals, or for pre-loss goals to compete with each other. Therefore, an organization might discover that fully achieving all risk management program goals simultaneously is impossible.

Achieving any post-loss goal involves expending risk management resources, which may conflict with the pre-loss goal of economy of operations. The more ambitious and costly the post-loss goal, the greater the conflict with the economy of operations goal. The economy of operations goal may also conflict with the tolerable uncertainty goal. To provide management with the desired level of assurance, the risk management professional must be confident that certain organizational post-loss goals will be achieved. Gaining that confidence requires allocating some of the organization's limited resources, including money, to risk management efforts such as purchasing insurance, installing guards on machinery to prevent industrial accidents, or maintaining duplicate copies of records in case originals are destroyed.

The legality and social responsibility goals may also conflict with the economy of operations goal. Some externally imposed obligations, such as safety standards dictated by building codes, may be nonnegotiable. Therefore, the costs imposed by legal obligations must be accepted as unavoidable, regardless of the economy of operations goal. Obligations imposed by social responsibility, such as employee benefits subject to collective bargaining agreements, may be negotiable. However, although meeting social responsibility might raise costs in the short term, it can have worthwhile long-term benefits that make the costs acceptable.

Both pre-loss and post-loss goals should be integrated into an organization's overall risk management program. One way to achieve the pre-loss and post-loss risk management program goals is through the risk management process.

RISK MANAGEMENT PROCESS

To fulfill the goals of a risk management program, the risk management professional uses the risk management process, illustrated in Exhibit 2-6. The risk management process is a series of six steps that can be applied to any set of loss exposures. Anyone undertaking the risk management process should have a sound grasp of the organization's goals and be able to recognize which risks pose the most severe financial threat. Although the risk management process has six distinct steps, experienced risk management professionals may deal with several steps simultaneously.

The risk management process can be initiated by events such as the following:

- A pending insurance renewal that may prompt a thorough risk analysis
- A serious claim that stimulates a review of the organization's risk management activities
- A merger or acquisition proposal that creates a new organization whose risks require reevaluation
- A new law or regulation that affects the organization

However, the risk management process need not be initiated by events such as these, because it is continuous. The last step in the process, monitoring results and revising the existing risk management program, may lead to the identification of new or additional loss exposures.

EXHIBIT 2-6

The Risk Management Process

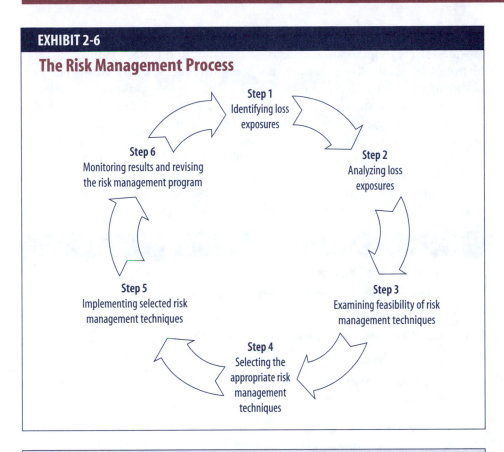

Step 1
Identifying loss exposures

Step 2
Analyzing loss exposures

Step 3
Examining feasibility of risk management techniques

Step 4
Selecting the appropriate risk management techniques

Step 5
Implementing selected risk management techniques

Step 6
Monitoring results and revising the risk management program

Saving Time and Money: Dealing With Steps in the Risk Management Process Simultaneously

Mary, an experienced risk management professional, is identifying and analyzing the property loss exposures of a newly acquired $5 million building financed with a bank loan. Based on experience, Mary realizes that the most practical way to finance these exposures is to purchase special-form open-perils ("all-risks") property insurance with an appropriate limit and deductible. Mary could spend much time and effort identifying all the various perils—such as fire, lightning, windstorm, and vandalism—that could cause building damage, but most of these perils would be covered by the special-form open-perils insurance. Therefore, Mary can combine the identification, analysis, and choice of the appropriate risk management technique into one step. Mary realizes that by combining steps, she is freeing up valuable time that can be spent on matters that require special treatment such as evaluating loss exposures subject to pollution, contamination, or flood damage. Even though insurance will be purchased on the building, Mary does not completely disregard loss exposure identification and analysis, because she realizes that property risk control measures should also be considered.

Step 1: Identifying Loss Exposures

A wide variety of methods, such as those listed in Exhibit 2-7, can be used to identify the specific loss exposures that could interfere with the achievement of the organization's goals. These methods offer a systematic approach to identifying loss exposures. They also can enable risk management professionals to identify missed opportunities. Although loss exposure identification methods are applied individually, they can overlap in their use and function. Despite this overlap, using different methods helps the risk management professional avoid overlooking important loss exposures. For example, loss history documents may not reveal the possibility of loss exposures related to flood, but studying a flood insurance rate map or a cause of loss checklist would.

EXHIBIT 2-7

Identifying Loss Exposures

No single method exists for identifying loss exposures. Risk management professionals may use some or all of the following:

- Document analysis (including any or all of the following):
    - Risk assessment questionnaires and checklists
    - Financial statements and underlying accounting records
    - Contracts
    - Insurance policies
    - Organizational policies and procedures
    - Flowcharts and organizational charts
    - Loss histories
- Compliance reviews
- Inspections
- Expertise within and beyond the organization

Step 2: Analyzing Loss Exposures

Analyzing loss exposures is completed by estimating the likely significance of possible losses identified in step one. Together, these two steps constitute the process of assessing loss exposures and are therefore probably the most important steps in the risk management process, because only a properly assessed loss exposure can be appropriately managed. Once a loss exposure has been assessed, the best ways to manage it often become immediately apparent. The remaining steps of the risk management process flow from this assessment.

Loss exposures are analyzed along the following four dimensions:

1. Loss frequency—the number of losses (such as fires, auto accidents, or liability claims) within a specific time period

2. Loss severity—the amount, in dollars, of a loss for a specific occurrence

3. Total dollar losses—the total dollar amount of losses for all occurrences during a specific time period

4. Timing—when losses occur and when loss payments are made

Reviewing these dimensions enables a risk management professional to develop loss projections and prioritize loss exposures so that resources can be properly allocated. Analyzing loss exposures is, in itself, expensive. The cost of risk includes the cost of acquiring risk-related information used in loss forecasts, estimates of future cash flows, and other planning activities. In some cases, this information can actually reduce losses. For example, recent advances in satellite technology and meteorology, although expensive, provide advance warning that enables people in a hurricane's path to board up windows, evacuate, and implement other loss reduction measures. Such detailed information improves forecast accuracy and can lead to better risk management decisions.

Step 3: Examining the Feasibility of Risk Management Techniques

Loss exposures arise from activities and circumstances that are essential to individuals and to organizations. These loss exposures can be addressed through the risk control techniques and risk financing techniques shown in Exhibit 2-8. Broadly speaking, risk control techniques are those risk management techniques that minimize the frequency or severity of losses or make losses more predictable. Risk financing techniques are those risk management

EXHIBIT 2-8

Risk Management Techniques

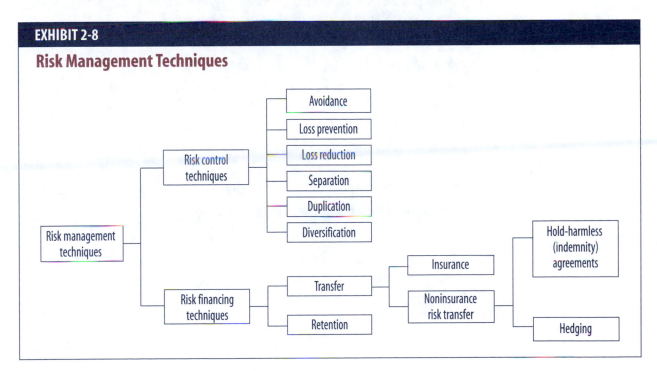

techniques that generate funds to finance losses that risk control techniques cannot entirely prevent or reduce.

Risk management techniques are not usually used in isolation. Unless the loss exposure is avoided, organizations typically apply at least one risk control technique and one risk financing technique to each of their significant loss exposures. The risk control technique alters the estimated frequency and severity of loss, and the financing technique pays for losses that occur despite the controls. Most risk control and risk financing techniques can be used with any other control or financing technique. Risk control techniques and risk financing techniques are discussed in detail in subsequent chapters.

Step 4: Selecting the Appropriate Risk Management Techniques

Once loss exposures have been identified and analyzed and possible risk management techniques considered, risk management professionals can select those techniques that best prevent or reduce losses and that will adequately finance losses that occur despite prevention and reduction efforts. Selecting the most appropriate mix of risk management techniques is usually based on quantitative financial considerations as well as qualitative, nonfinancial considerations.

Summary of Risk Control Techniques

Avoidance eliminates any possibility of loss. The probability of loss from an avoided loss exposure is zero because an entity decides not to assume a loss exposure in the first place (proactive avoidance) or to eliminate one that already exists (abandonment).

Loss prevention involves reducing the frequency of a particular loss.

Loss reduction involves reducing the severity of a particular loss.

Separation involves dispersing a particular activity or asset over several locations. Separation involves the routine, daily reliance on each of the separated assets or activities, all of which regularly form a portion of the organization's working resources.

Duplication involves relying on backups, that is, spares or duplicates, used only if primary assets or activities suffer loss.

Diversification involves providing a range of products and services used by a variety of customers.

Summary of Risk Financing Techniques

Retention involves generating funds from within the organization to pay for losses.

Transfer involves generating funds from outside the organization to pay for losses and includes insurance and noninsurance transfer.

Financial Considerations

Most private, for-profit organizations choose risk management techniques by using financial criteria, that is, they choose those techniques with the greatest positive (or least negative) effect on the organization's value. The risk management techniques selected should be effective and economical. A technique is effective if it enables an organization to achieve its desired goals, such as to maximize organizational value. A technique is economical if it is the least expensive of the possible effective options.

For all organizations, the potential costs if loss exposures are left completely untreated must be compared with the costs of possible risk management techniques when considering whether a technique is economical. A financial analysis of a risk management technique may be based on the following:

- A forecast of the dimensions of expected losses (frequency, severity, timing of payment, and total dollar losses).

- A forecast, for each feasible combination of risk management techniques, of the effect on the frequency, severity, and timing of these expected losses.

- A forecast of the after-tax costs involved in applying the various risk management techniques. These costs include, for example, the cost of insurance premiums or the expenses associated with installing and maintaining various risk control devices.

Based on those considerations, an organization can perform a cost/benefit analysis that identifies the risk management technique, or combination of techniques, that will maximize the organization's value while allowing it to stay within budgetary constraints.

Nonfinancial Considerations

Although an organization's goal should be to determine a level of risk management that will maximize its financial value, an organization's value may also stem from ethical and other nonfinancial considerations. Data based on objective risk factors usually are not the only criteria considered in determining appropriate risk management techniques. An organization might also place a great deal of value on maintaining operations or on peace of mind.

An organization's nonfinancial goals can constrain its financial goals, leading to the selection of risk management techniques that, although best for that organization, might be inconsistent with its value maximization goal. For example, a private, family-owned organization might emphasize stability of earnings over time, rather than maximum earnings in any one period. Consequently, the organization might over-invest in loss-prevention devices or safety practices rather than absorb the minor losses that these devices or practices are designed to prevent. For similar reasons, a private, family-owned organization would be likely to insure against losses that, from a value maximization standpoint, might be better to retain.

Step 5: Implementing the Selected Risk Management Techniques

After an organization decides which risk management technique(s) to use, the next step is to implement them, which requires cooperation among its departments. Implementing risk management techniques may involve any of the following measures:

- Purchasing loss reduction devices
- Contracting for loss prevention services
- Funding retention programs
- Implementing and continually reinforcing loss control programs
- Selecting agents or brokers, insurers, third-party administrators, and other providers for insurance programs
- Requesting insurance policies and paying premiums

Implementing risk management techniques does not necessarily end with the initial implementation of the selected technique. For example, if an organization purchases a building, it almost certainly will also decide to purchase property insurance. However, additional details, such as the exact placement of fire extinguishers, the terms and cost of insurance and noninsurance contract revisions, which insurer to use, the timing of insurance premium payments, or the actual deposit of funds for a retention program or to cover deductibles, must be addressed as the program is implemented.

Step 6: Monitoring Results and Revising the Risk Management Program

Once implemented, a risk management program must be monitored and periodically revised as necessary in order to ensure that it is achieving expected results and to adjust it to accommodate changes in loss exposures and the availability or cost-effectiveness of alternative risk management techniques. Monitoring and revising the risk management program requires the following four steps: (1) establishing standards of acceptable performance, (2) comparing actual results with these standards, (3) correcting substandard performance or revising standards that prove to be unrealistic, and (4) evaluating standards that have been substantially exceeded.

Establishing Standards of Acceptable Performance

Because of year-to-year variations and the random nature of fortuitous events, the best way to monitor a risk management program may be to combine standards that consider both results and activities. A results standard focuses on actual achievement of goals, regardless of the effort required to achieve them. For example, a risk management professional might judge a risk management program's performance in terms of a decline in the frequency or severity of employee injuries. However, those results depend largely on fortuitous events, which, by definition, are unpredictable. In contrast, an activity standard focuses on efforts made to achieve a goal regardless of actual results. These independent standards focus mainly on the quality and quantity of the risk management department's activities, such as the installation of new safety equipment designed to protect employees from injury, rather than the actual outcomes.

Risk management professionals often contend that their contribution is as great in years in which there are many losses as in years in which there are few losses, because the losses themselves are beyond their control. In fact, risk management professionals may be even more valuable to their organizations when losses are severe because of the assistance that they can give to the organization in dealing with those losses. Therefore, risk management professionals have sought performance standards that are not solely dependent on the organization's somewhat uncontrollable loss record. Although results standards are important, activities standards are necessary to obtain a complete picture of the success or failure of a risk management program.

Comparing Actual Results With Standards

A proper standard for evaluating risk management performance includes specifications for how results or performance will be measured. A good standard includes target activity levels or results, or at least desired directions of change. For example, if an organization had a risk management goal of preventing accidents involving its employees, a results standard could be formulated as a maximum number of accidents per employee hour worked, or at least as a decrease in the number of accidents from one year to the next. A comparison of the actual number of accidents that occur with the number established in the results standard will indicate whether risk management activities are achieving the desired results.

Alternatively, an activity standard relating to the same employee accidents could specify, and provide a schedule for, when an organization's employees should receive safety training updates. The comparison of results against this activity standard would not consider the number of employee accidents, but instead determine if all employees received the level of training established by the standard.

Correcting Substandard Performance

The risk management professional should also develop a plan for addressing substandard performance. For example, if the number of safety inspections is below that required by the standard, the risk management professional should include a plan to increase their frequency. If retained losses are growing faster than expected, then the risk management professional should determine how retention levels and, perhaps, risk control techniques should be reevaluated.

Substandard performance does not necessarily indicate that the performance itself is the problem. The standard may, in fact, be inappropriate. A risk management program should change when loss exposures change. Similarly, the standards by which that program is evaluated must be reexamined and possibly altered if the environment within which the risk management program operates also changes. For example, increases in inflation, changes in the volume or nature of an organization's activities, and cyclical or long-term movements in insurance markets or money markets may require adjustments in standards by which acceptable risk management performance is evaluated.

Although changes in risk management standards should not be arbitrary, the continuing need for change should be recognized. Therefore, when monitoring a risk management program, the standards for evaluating that program should also be evaluated, and, when appropriate, revised to accommodate new situations.

Evaluating Standards That Have Been Substantially Exceeded

Performance should ideally meet or exceed a standard. However, if performance substantially exceeds a standard, then the risk management professional should determine why. One reason may be the superior skills of the employee or employees involved in implementing the standard. Another alternative is that the standard is not sufficiently demanding. The risk management professional should, if appropriate, revise the standard so that it more accurately reflects the performance potential of the employees and the organization.

Although monitoring results and revising the risk management program is listed as the final step of the risk management process, it is often the first step for a risk management professional who is taking control of an organization's risk management program. Unless the organization is a start-up, it probably has some (either formal or informal) risk management program in place. Once the risk management program has been properly evaluated, the risk management professional begins the risk management process again. The steps of the risk management process are applied under the revised risk management program, which may now have different program goals or face a new set of organizational risks.

SUMMARY

In its simplest form, risk management includes any efforts to economically deal with the uncertainty of outcomes (risk). A risk management program is a system for planning, organizing, leading, and controlling the resources and activities that an organization needs to protect itself from the adverse effects of risk. Traditionally, risk management has been concerned only with hazard risk. The inclusion of business risk is part of the more recent field of enterprise risk management (ERM). ERM is an approach to managing all of an organization's key risks and opportunities with the intent of maximizing the organization's value.

Although no consensus exists about how an organization should categorize its risks, one ERM approach involves dividing them into four risk quadrants: hazard, operational, financial, and strategic. The focus of the four risk quadrants is different from the risk classifications previously discussed; that is, pure and speculative, subjective and objective, and diversifiable and nondiversifiable. Whereas the classifications of risk focus on some aspect of the risk itself, the four quadrants of risk focus on the source of risk and who has traditionally managed this risk. In the same way that a particular loss exposure can fall under more than one classification, a loss exposure can also fall into more than one of the four ERM risk quadrants.

Enterprise risk management is an extension of traditional risk management. However, the following significant differences exist between ERM and traditional risk management:

- Strategic application—Traditional risk management is conducted at the departmental level, whereas ERM is enterprise-wide and supersedes departmental or functional autonomy.

- Risks considered—Traditional risk management focuses on hazard risk, whereas ERM focuses on both hazard and business risk.

- Performance metrics—Traditional risk management emphasizes activity standards, whereas ERM emphasizes results standards.

For an individual, an organization, and for society, the cost of risk management is the cost of resources expended to reduce either the expected losses or residual uncertainty associated with risk. Therefore, the ultimate benefit of risk management is a reduction in either or both of these components. For an individual, the specific benefits are a preservation of financial resources and reduced anxiety. For an organization, the benefits are preservation of financial resources, increased attractiveness to investors, and a reduced deterrent effect. For society as a whole, the benefits are preservation of financial resources and an improved allocation of productive resources.

Risk management program goals are typically divided into two categories: pre-loss goals and post-loss goals. Pre-loss goals are risk management goals that should be in place even if no significant losses occur. Such goals include economy of operations, tolerable uncertainty, legality, and social responsibility. Post-loss goals are risk management goals that should be in place in the event of a significant loss. Such goals include survival, continuity of operations, profitability, earnings stability, social responsibility, and growth.

One way to implement a risk management program is through the risk management process, which is a method of making, implementing, and monitoring decisions that minimize the adverse effects of risk on an organization. The risk management process consists of the following six steps that can be applied to any set of loss exposures:

1. Identifying loss exposures
2. Analyzing loss exposures
3. Examining the feasibility of risk management techniques
4. Selecting the appropriate risk management techniques

5. Implementing the selected risk management techniques

6. Monitoring results and revising the risk management program

Effectively managing risk is vital to the success of organizations. Applying the risk management process helps to ensure risk is being properly managed. The first two steps of the risk management process comprise risk assessment. Once methods of identification have been used to identify the range of risks facing individuals and organizations, a variety of tools are available to help individuals and risk management professionals accurately evaluate those risks.

Chapter 3

Direct Your Learning

Risk Assessment

After learning the content of this chapter and completing the corresponding course guide assignment, you should be able to:

- Describe the following methods of loss exposure identification:
  - Document analysis
  - Compliance review
  - Personal inspections
  - Expertise within and beyond the organization
- Explain why data used in risk management decisions need to be relevant, complete, consistent, and organized.
- Describe the nature of probability with respect to the law of large numbers and theoretical and empirical probability.
- Interpret the information provided in a simple probability distribution and explain how that information can be used in making basic risk management decisions.
- Explain how various measures of central tendency and measures of dispersion can be used in analyzing the probabilities associated with risk.
- Explain how an insurance or a risk management professional can apply normal distributions to analyze loss exposures and project future losses more accurately.
- Explain how to analyze loss exposures considering the four dimensions of loss and data credibility.
- Define or describe each of the Key Words and Phrases for this chapter.

Develop Your Perspective

What are the main topics covered in the chapter?

Risk assessment combines identifying and analyzing loss exposures, the first two steps in the risk management process. This chapter outlines the documents and methods that can be used to identify loss exposures, describes the statistical tools for measuring the probability of potential losses, and considers the dimensions involved in analyzing a loss exposure.

Describe the methods of identifying loss exposures.

- What information is readily available, and from what source(s)?
- What information requires special expertise from either within or beyond the organization?

Why is it important to learn about these topics?

By understanding the available sources of data regarding loss exposures and examining the statistical tools used to analyze those loss exposures, you can learn how to develop loss projections and how these projections can help in making underwriting decisions and prioritizing the allocation of risk management resources.

Consider how an insurance or risk management professional can analyze the data gathered through the loss exposure identification step to discover prior patterns and project future patterns.

- How do measures of central tendency help to determine expected results?
- How do measures of dispersion help to determine the degree of variation that can be expected in losses?

How can you use what you will learn?

Consider the size of your organization and the types of losses to which your organization is exposed.

- What methods could you use to identify those loss exposures?
- For which loss exposures could you gather enough information to analyze loss frequency and loss severity?
- How could you use this information to project potential future losses?

Chapter 3
Risk Assessment

Risk assessment involves the first two steps of the risk management process: identifying and analyzing loss exposures. Individuals usually rely on the expertise of insurance professionals who have a variety of tools at their disposal to help assess their risks. Organizations also have access to insurance professionals as well as in-house risk management or insurance professionals to help assess their risks.

While individuals may rely on insurance professionals as the only method or source of information to identify loss exposures, organizations cannot. A risk management or insurance professional working for an organization must consider all available documents and information-gathering methods to determine which are most applicable to the organization.

Loss exposure analysis is based on probability and the statistical analysis of data. Reliable data are essential to providing meaningful estimates. An insurance or a risk management professional can then use that data to develop probability distributions, which assign probability estimates to each possible outcome. These probability distributions, in turn, enable the insurance or risk management professional to use statistical analysis when analyzing loss exposures.

The analysis step of the risk management process involves considering loss exposures from the perspective of four dimensions. Loss frequency concerns the number of losses that occur. Loss severity and total dollar losses consider the financial costs incurred as a result of those losses. Timing entails when losses occur and when loss payments are made—payments are not necessarily made at the time of loss or even shortly thereafter. In addition to the four dimensions, data credibility must be considered to determine how much confidence can be placed in the ability of both the available data and their analysis to accurately indicate future losses. Analyzing these four dimensions helps in developing the loss projections that are used by insurance professionals who make underwriting decisions and risk management professionals who make risk management decisions.

IDENTIFYING LOSS EXPOSURES

The first step in the risk management process is identifying all possible loss exposures. For individuals, common property and liability exposures can be identified by a property-casualty insurance producer as part of an assessment of insurance needs. Similarly, individuals' net income loss exposures can be identified by life insurance producers as part of a needs assessment for life and health insurance products. However, for organizations, loss exposure identification is typically more complex. Therefore, a variety of methods and sources of information are used, including the following:

- Document analysis, including any or all of the following:
  - Risk assessment questionnaires and checklists
  - Financial statements and underlying accounting records
  - Contracts
  - Insurance policies
  - Organizational policies and records
  - Flowcharts and organizational charts
  - Loss histories
- Compliance review
- Inspections
- Expertise within and beyond the organization

These methods and sources of information enable an organization to take a systematic approach to identifying loss exposures. Although it may not be possible or practical for an organization to use all methods and sources, a comprehensive identification of loss exposures requires using more than one.

Document Analysis

The variety of documents used and produced by an organization can be a key source of information regarding loss exposures. Some of these documents are standardized and originate from outside the organization, such as questionnaires, checklists, and surveys. These standardized documents broadly categorize the loss exposures that most organizations typically face and are completed with information that is exclusive to the organization. Other documents are organization-specific, such as financial statements and accounting records, contracts, insurance policies, policy and procedure manuals, flowcharts and organizational charts, and loss histories. Although the use and function of the various documents may overlap, causing possible duplication in loss exposure identification, reviewing multiple documents is necessary to avoid failing to identify important loss exposures.

In addition to the documents discussed in this section, virtually any document connected to an organization's operations also reveals something about its loss exposures. For example, Web sites, news releases, or reports from external organizations such as A.M. Best or D&B may indicate something about an organization's loss exposures. Although it is not feasible to review every document that refers to an organization, some of these additional sources may be useful.

Risk Assessment Questionnaires and Checklists

Standardized documents published outside of an organization, such as insurance coverage checklists and risk assessment questionnaires, broadly categorize the loss exposures that most organizations typically face. A variety of checklists and questionnaires have been published by insurers, the American Management Association (AMA), the International Risk Management Institute (IRMI), the Risk and Insurance Management Society (RIMS), and others. Although some organizations or trade associations have developed specialized checklists or questionnaires for their members, most are created by insurers and concentrate on identifying insurable hazard risks. Some focus on listing the organization's assets, whereas others focus on identifying potential causes of loss that could affect the organization.

Checklists typically capture less information than questionnaires. Although checklists can help an organization identify its loss exposures, they do not show how those loss exposures support or affect specific organizational goals. Linking loss exposures with the goals they support can be useful in analyzing the potential financial consequences of loss. Therefore, checklists are of limited benefit in the analysis step of the risk management process.

A questionnaire captures more descriptive information than a checklist. For example, as well as identifying a loss exposure, a questionnaire may capture information about the amounts or values exposed to loss. The questionnaire can be designed to include questions that address key property, liability, net income, and at least some personnel loss exposures. Questionnaire responses can enable an insurance or a risk management professional to identify and analyze an organization's loss exposures regarding real property, equipment, products, key customers, neighboring properties, operations, and so on. Additionally, the logical sequencing of questions helps in developing a more detailed examination of the loss exposures an organization faces.

Both checklists and questionnaires may be produced by insurers (such questionnaires are known as insurance surveys). Most of the questions on these surveys relate to loss exposures for which commercial insurance is generally available. Risk management or risk assessment questionnaires have a broader focus and address both insurable and uninsurable loss exposures. However, a disadvantage of risk assessment questionnaires is that they typically can only be completed with considerable expense, time, and effort, and still may not identify all possible loss exposures.

Standardizing a survey or questionnaire has both advantages and disadvantages. Standardized questions are relevant for most organizations and can be answered by persons who have little risk management expertise. However, no standardized questionnaire can be expected to uncover all the loss exposures particularly characteristic of a given industry, let alone those unique to a given organization. Additionally, the questionnaire's structure might not stimulate the respondent to do anything more than answer the questions asked; that is, it will only elicit the information that is specifically requested. Consequently, it may not reveal key information. Therefore, questionnaires should ideally be used in conjunction with other identification and analysis methods. Appendix A reproduces the table of contents and contents schedule of the standardized survey/questionnaire originally published by the American Management Association and subsequently revised by the Risk and Insurance Management Society. Additionally, Appendix B contains a more general survey/questionnaire in the form of a risk profile.

Because even a thoroughly completed checklist or questionnaire does not ensure that all loss exposures have been recognized, experienced insurance and risk management professionals often follow up with additional questions that are not on the standardized document. The following text box illustrates such a follow-up.

Follow-Up to Questionnaire: Shipton's Auto Body Shop

Insurance producer Amy Chung used a questionnaire when interviewing Damon Shipton for his property insurance application. The questionnaire was specially developed by the insurer for use with organizations in the auto business and asked whether the body shop had a spray-painting booth. The answer was "no," which was unusual for a modern body shop. Amy asked a few more questions and learned that this shop was using a newly developed air filtration system that was better than the standard spray-painting booth. When Amy submitted the insurance application, not only was this account not rejected because of the "no spray-painting booth" response on the questionnaire, but the answer prompted the property underwriter, James Day, to also visit the shop. James then granted a preferential insurance rate based on additional information his visit uncovered as well as Amy's information about the new air filtration system.

Financial Statements and Underlying Accounting Records

Risk management professionals with accounting or finance expertise sometimes begin the loss exposure identification process by reviewing an organization's financial statements, including the balance sheet, income statement, statement of cash flows, and supporting statements. As well as identifying current loss exposures, financial statements and accounting records can be used to identify any future plans that could lead to new loss exposures.

Balance sheet
The financial statement that reports the assets, liabilities, and owners' equity of an organization as of a specific date.

An organization's **balance sheet** is the financial statement that reports the assets, liabilities, and owners' equity of the organization as of a specific date. Owners' equity, or net worth, is the amount by which assets exceed liabilities. Asset entries indicate property values that could be reduced by loss. Liability entries show what the organization owes and enable the risk management professional to explore two types of loss exposures: (1) liabilities that could be increased or created by a loss and (2) obligations (such as mortgage payments) that the organization must fulfill, even if it were to close temporarily as a result of a business interruption. Exhibit 3-1 shows an example of a balance sheet for a hypothetical company, Lawton Manufacturing.

EXHIBIT 3-1

Lawton Manufacturing, Inc., Balance Sheet as of July 31, 2006 (in Thousands)

Assets

Cash and cash equivalents	$ 62
Marketable securities	—
Receivables (net)	469
Merchandise inventories	4,293
Other current assets	109
Property, plant, and equipment (net)	8,160
Notes receivable	26
Intangibles	268
Other assets	78
Total assets	$13,465

Inventory values can be used to identify property at risk as well as to determine the severity of potential losses at storage facilities.

Assets valued here can be used to identify property exposures and values at risk.

Liabilities and Owners' Equity

Accounts payable	$ 1,586
Other current liabilities	1,271
Long-term debt	1,566
Deferred income taxes	85
Other long-term liabilities	217
Total liabilities	$ 4,725
Common capital stock	74
Additional paid-in capital	2,854
Retained earnings	5,876
Accumulated comprehensive income adjustment	(61)
Less shares for compensation plans	(3)
Owners' equity	$ 8,740
Total liabilities and owners' equity	$13,465

Indication of funds available to pay for retained losses.

The **income statement** is the financial statement that reports an organization's profit or loss for a specific period by comparing the revenues generated with the expenses incurred to produce those revenues. This statement is particularly useful in identifying net income loss exposures; that is, those loss exposures that reduce revenue or increase expenses. Exhibit 3-2 shows an example of an income statement for Lawton Manufacturing.

Income statement
The financial statement that reports an organization's profit or loss for a specific period by comparing the revenues generated with the expenses incurred to produce those revenues.

EXHIBIT 3-2

Lawton Manufacturing, Inc., Income Statement for the Year Ended July 31, 2006 (in Thousands)

Net sales	$1,150,000	Property, liability, or personnel losses that decrease revenues, such as net sales, generate net income loss exposures.
Cost of goods sold	(850,000)	
Gross profit	300,000	
Selling, general, and administrative expenses	(271,000)	
Earnings from operations	29,000	Property, liability, or personnel losses that increase expenses, such as cost of goods sold, generate net income loss exposures.
Interest expense	(4,000)	
Earnings before income taxes	25,000	
Income taxes	(10,000)	
Net income	$ 15,000	Changes to this value are net income losses.

Statement of cash flows

The financial statement that summarizes the cash effects of an organization's operating, investing, and financing activities during a specific period.

The **statement of cash flows** (also called the statement of sources and uses of funds) is the financial statement that summarizes the cash effects of an organization's operating, investing, and financing activities during a specific period. Funds-flow analysis on the statement of cash flows can identify the amounts of cash either subject to loss or available to meet continuing obligations. For example, the statement of cash flows would indicate the amount of cash that is typically on hand to pay for any losses resulting from loss exposures that have been retained by the organization. Exhibit 3-3 shows an example of a statement of cash flows for Lawton Manufacturing.

Financial statements can reveal that an organization is subject to significant financial risks, such as fluctuations in the value of investments, interest rate volatility, foreign exchange rate changes, or commodity price swings. However, the primary advantage of financial statements from a risk management professional's perspective is that they help to identify major categories of loss exposures. For example, property loss exposures can be seen in the asset section of the balance sheet. Some liability loss exposures, especially contractual obligations such as loans or mortgages, can be seen in the liabilities section of the balance sheet. The potential effects of net income loss exposures can be seen by comparing revenues with expenses on the income statement.

The major disadvantage of using financial statements for identifying loss exposures is that although they identify most of the major categories of loss exposures (property, liability and net income are identified but personnel loss exposures are not), they do not identify or quantify the individual loss exposures. For example, the balance sheet may show that there is $5 million in property exposed to loss, but it does not specify how many properties make up that $5 million, where those properties are located, or how much each individual property is worth.

EXHIBIT 3-3

Lawton Manufacturing, Inc., Statement of Cash Flows for the Year Ended July 31, 2006 (in Thousands)

Cash flows from operating activities:

Net income	$ 15,000
Add (deduct) items not affecting cash:	
Depreciation expense	5,000
Increase in accounts receivable	(75,000)
Increase in raw materials inventory	(175,000)
Increase in current liabilities	55,000
Net cash used by operating activities	($175,000)

Cash flows from investing activities:

Cash paid for equipment	($ 45,000)
Net cash provided by investing activities	($ 45,000)

← Can be used to identify items of new equipment that are property loss exposures.

Cash flows from financing activities:

Cash received from issue of short-term debt	$ 15,000
Cash received from issue of long-term debt	50,000
Cash received from sale of common stock	200,000
Payment of cash dividend on common stock	(5,000)
Net cash provided by financing activities	$ 260,000
Net increase in cash for the year	40,000
Cash at beginning of year	0
Cash at end of year	$ 40,000

← Identifies a continuing expense when analyzing net income exposures.

← Identifies cash subject to loss as well as amount of cash available to pay losses.

Another disadvantage is that financial statements depict past activities—for example, revenue that has already been earned, expenses that have already been incurred, prior valuations of assets and liabilities, and business operations that have already taken place. They are of limited help in identifying projected values or future events. Therefore, even after using financial statements for loss exposure identification, insurance and risk management professionals still need to project what events might occur in the future, determine how these future events could change loss exposures, and analyze and quantify potential losses accordingly.

Contracts

A contract is an agreement entered into by two or more parties that specifies the parties' responsibilities to one another. Analyzing an organization's contracts may help identify its property and liability loss exposures and help determine who has assumed responsibility for which loss exposures. It is often necessary to consult with legal experts when interpreting contracts.

Entering into contracts can either increase or reduce an organization's property and liability loss exposures. For example, a contract to purchase property or equipment will increase the organization's property loss exposures, whereas a contract to sell property or equipment will reduce property loss exposures.

A contract can generate liability loss exposures in two ways. First, the organization can accept the loss exposures of another party through a contract, such as a hold-harmless agreement (sometimes referred to as an indemnity contract). A **hold-harmless agreement** is a contractual provision obligating one party to assume another party's legal liability in the event of a specified loss. For example, an organization may enter into a hold-harmless agreement with its distributor under which the organization agrees to indemnify the distributor (pay the losses for which the distributor is liable) if the distributor is found liable for a products liability claim. **Indemnification** is the process of restoring an individual or organization to a pre-loss financial condition.

Hold-harmless agreement
A contractual provision obligating one party to assume another party's legal liability in the event of a specified loss.

Indemnification
The process of restoring an individual or organization to a pre-loss financial condition.

The second way a contract may generate a liability loss exposure is if the organization fails to fulfill a valid contract. For example, if an organization agrees to deliver manufactured goods to a distributor and then fails to deliver those goods, the distributor is entitled to bring a legal claim against the organization. The distributor's claim presents a liability loss exposure for the organization.

Alternatively, an organization can reduce or eliminate liability loss exposures by entering into a contract that transfers its liability to another organization. For example, an organization can enter into a hold-harmless agreement under which the second party agrees to indemnify the organization in the event of a liability claim.

Contract analysis can both identify the loss exposures generated or reduced by an organization's contracts and ensure that the organization is not assuming liability that is disproportionate to its stake in the contract. Ongoing contract analysis is part of monitoring and maintaining a risk management program.

Insurance Policies

Although insurance is a means of risk financing, reviewing insurance policies can also be helpful in risk assessment. Insurance policies are a type of hold-harmless agreement. The insurer, in exchange for the premium, agrees to pay some portion of the insured organization's losses that are generated by the loss exposures covered by the insurance policy. Analyzing insurance policies reveals many of the insurable loss exposures that an organization faces. However, this analysis may either indicate the organization is insured for more loss exposures than it really has, or, alternatively, may not show all the loss exposures the organization faces. As insurance policies typically are standardized forms, an organization does not necessarily face every loss exposure covered by its policies. Furthermore, the organization may face many other loss exposures that either cannot be covered by insurance policies or are covered by policies the organization has chosen not to purchase. To identify insurance coverage that an organization has not purchased, and therefore potentially identify insurable loss exposures that have not been insured, a risk management professional can compare his or her organization's coverage against an industry checklist of insurance policies currently in effect.

Organizational Policies and Records

Loss exposures can also be identified using organizational policies and records, such as corporate by-laws, board minutes, employee manuals, procedure manuals, mission statements, and risk management policies. For example, policy and procedure manuals may identify some of the organization's property loss exposures by referencing equipment, or pinpoint liability loss exposures by referencing hazardous materials with which employees come into contact. As well as identifying existing loss exposures, some documents may indicate impending changes in loss exposures. For example, board minutes may indicate management's plans to sell or purchase property, thereby either reducing or increasing its property loss exposures.

Internal Documents as Loss Exposures

Internal documents, in addition to identifying loss exposures, need to be analyzed to determine their appropriateness and consistency with external publications. An organization's internal documents are not typically written in anticipation that they will be viewed outside the organization. However, many internal documents are used during legal proceedings and therefore may present a potential liability loss exposure to the organization. This illustrates the need for internal documents to be consistent with external information the organization releases.

One drawback to using policies and records to identify loss exposures is the sheer volume of documents that some organizations generate internally. It may be virtually impossible to have one employee or a group of employees examine every internal document. In these instances, insurance and risk management professionals would need to examine a representative sample of documents. This makes the task manageable, but increases the likelihood that not all loss exposures will be identified.

Flowcharts and Organizational Charts

A flowchart is a diagram that depicts the sequence of activities performed by a particular organization or process. An organization can use flowcharts to show the nature and use of the resources involved in its operations as well as the sequence of and relationships between those operations.

A manufacturer's flowchart might start with raw material acquisition and end with the finished product's delivery to the ultimate consumer. Individual entries on the flowchart, including the processes involved and the means by which products move from one process to the next, can help identify loss exposures—particularly critical loss exposures. For example, the flowchart might illustrate that every item produced must be spray-painted during the production process. This activity presents a critical property loss exposure, because an explosion at the spray-painting location might disable the entire production line.

The simplified flowchart in Exhibit 3-4 reveals that difficulties with getting the furniture through customs at the Los Angeles Port could disrupt the entire furniture supply chain.

EXHIBIT 3-4

Furniture Manufacturer Flowchart

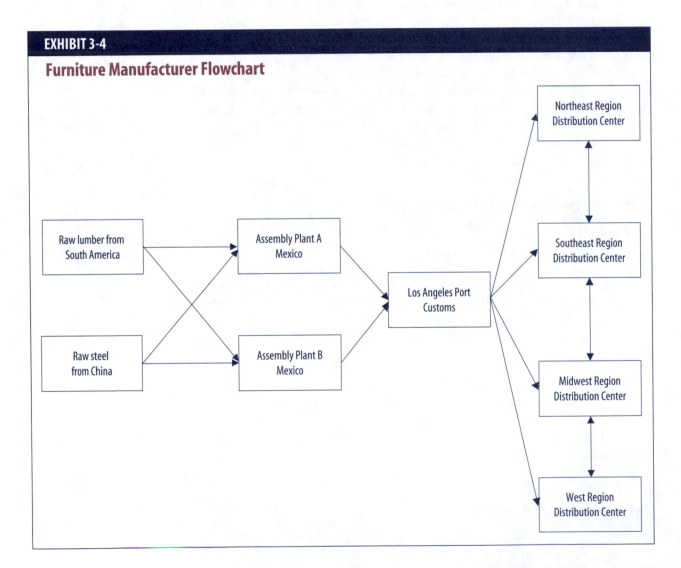

Information can also be obtained from organizational charts. An organizational chart depicts the hierarchy of an organization's personnel and can help to identify key personnel for whom the organization may have a personnel loss exposure. This chart can also help track the flow of information through an organization and identify any bottlenecks that may exist. Although organizational charts can be fundamental in properly identifying personnel loss exposures, an individual's place on an organizational chart does not guarantee that he or she is a key employee. The organizational chart does not necessarily reflect the importance of the individual to the continued operation or profitability of the organization.

Loss Histories

Loss history analysis, that is, reviewing an organization's own losses or those suffered by comparable organizations, can help a risk management or an insurance professional to both identify and analyze loss exposures. Loss histories of comparable organizations are particularly helpful if the organization is too small or too new to have a sizeable record of its own past losses, or if the organization's own historical loss records are incomplete.

Any past loss can recur unless the organization has had a fundamental change in operations or property owned. Accordingly, loss histories are often an important indicator of an organization's current or future loss exposures. However, loss histories will not identify any loss exposures that have not resulted in past losses. Therefore, use of loss histories alone is inadequate.

Compliance Review

In addition to document analysis, insurance and risk management professionals may also conduct compliance reviews to identify loss exposures. A compliance review determines an organization's compliance with local, state, and federal statutes and regulations. The organization can conduct most of the compliance review itself if it has adequate in-house legal and accounting resources. Otherwise, it may have to use outside expertise.

The benefit of compliance reviews is that they can help an organization minimize or avoid liability loss exposures. However, a drawback of compliance reviews is that they are expensive and time consuming. Furthermore, because regulations are often changing, remaining in compliance requires ongoing monitoring. As a result, conducting a compliance review simply to identify loss exposures is often impractical. However, because noncompliance is a liability loss exposure, loss exposure identification can be part of the justification of the cost of a compliance review and is an ancillary benefit once a review has been completed.

Personal Inspections

Some loss exposures are best identified by personal inspections, that is, information-gathering visits to critical sites both within and outside an organization. Such visits often reveal loss exposures that would not appear in written descriptions of the organization's operations and therefore should lead to a more complete list of loss exposures. Personal inspections should ideally be conducted by individuals whose background and skills equip them to identify unexpected, but possible, loss exposures. Additionally, the person conducting the inspection should take the opportunity to discuss the particular operations with front-line personnel, who are often best placed to identify nonobvious loss exposures. Therefore, a personal inspection can overlap with consulting expertise within and beyond the organization.

Expertise Within and Beyond the Organization

Thorough loss exposure identification should include soliciting expertise both inside and outside the organization. Doing so renders a more complete and objective picture of the organization's loss exposures.

Interviews with employees can be conducted to gather information about their jobs and departments. Whereas an inspection can only reveal what is happening during the inspection, interviews can elicit information about what occurred before the inspection, what might be planned for the future, or what could go or has gone wrong that has not been properly addressed. Interviews should include a range of employees from every level of the organization. Questionnaires can be designed for use in conjunction with these interviews to ensure that they are comprehensive and are eliciting as much information as possible.

To obtain an external perspective, practitioners in fields such as law, finance, statistics, accounting, auditing, and the technology of the organization's industry can be consulted. The special knowledge of experts in identifying particular loss exposures is an invaluable resource.

Hazard analysis

A method of analysis that identifies conditions that increase the frequency or severity of loss.

One area of specialization that often requires such expert services is hazard analysis. **Hazard analysis** is a method of analysis that identifies conditions that increase the frequency or severity of loss. For example, a business consultant might identify conditions that cause the organization to overlook opportunities for growth. Alternatively, concerns about environmental hazards might require a specialist to take air or water samples and a specialized laboratory to analyze them. Although hazard analysis is focused on loss exposures that have already been identified, the results of the analysis often identify previously overlooked loss exposures.

Because identifying loss exposures is the beginning of the risk management process, it should be done thoroughly and systematically. The efficacy of the subsequent steps of the process depends on the accuracy of the initial identification of loss exposures. If these loss exposures are not identified, their financial consequences might be inadvertently retained by an organization, which could result in disastrous consequences. Risk management professionals should be prepared to actively address each potential loss exposure. The various methods and sources of information available can help to identify the loss exposures that will direct these risk management activities.

Once loss exposures are identified, they need to be analyzed in order to determine which have the potential to most undermine organizational goals. Furthermore, analyzing loss exposures enables risk management and insurance professionals to prioritize the loss exposures that require the most attention during the remainder of the risk management process. Loss exposure analysis is based on probability and statistical data analysis. Therefore, it is important to understand the requirements of data on past losses, as well the nature and measures of probability that can be employed.

DATA, PROBABILITY, AND STATISTICAL ANALYSIS

The statistical analysis of loss exposures starts with gathering sufficient data in a suitable form. Once these data have been collected, they can be subjected to a variety of probability and statistical techniques that are frequently used by insurance and risk management professionals.

Data on Past Losses

The most common basis of an analysis of current or future loss exposures is information about past losses arising from similar loss exposures. For example, if an insurance or a risk management professional was trying to analyze the frequency and severity of workplace injuries, then a history of past workers' compensation claims would be a sound basis for analysis. However, gathering information from past losses is not always an ideal way to determine future loss exposures. To begin with, there may not be sufficient data on which to make a meaningful forecast. For example, if the organization was recently formed, information on past losses may be either unavailable or inadequate. In addition to insufficient data, the quality of the data may not be sufficient to produce a reliable analysis. To accurately analyze loss exposures using data on past losses, the data should meet four criteria. They should be relevant, complete, consistent, and organized.

Relevant Data

To analyze current loss exposures based on historical data, the past loss data for the loss exposures in question must be relevant to the current or future loss exposures the insurance or risk management professional is trying to assess. For example, if an organization was trying to assess its auto physical damage loss exposures for the next twelve months, it may examine its auto physical damage losses for the last four or five years and then take into account any changes in the makeup of its auto fleet and the rate of increase for repairs to determine potential losses for the next twelve months. Although the organization may have auto physical damage records for the last twenty or thirty years, much of that data may no longer be relevant because of advances in auto engineering. Modern cars use different designs and materials that provide more for passenger safety at the expense of increased physical damage to the auto in the event of an accident. Therefore, data from ten years ago may not be relevant to today's auto physical damage loss exposures.

Similarly, relevant data for property losses include the property's repair or replacement cost at the time it is to be restored, not the property's historical or book value. For liability losses, the data should relate to past claims that are substantially the same as the potential future claims being assessed. Even relatively minor differences in the factual and legal bases of claims can produce substantially different outcomes and costs. Data to analyze personnel loss exposures must relate to personnel with similar experience and expertise as those being considered as future loss exposures. The appropriate data for considering net income loss exposures would depend on the type of loss exposure being analyzed. Those data should involve similar reductions in revenue and similar additional expenses as would those loss exposures under consideration.

Complete Data

Obtaining complete data about past losses for particular loss exposures often requires relying on others, both inside and outside of the organization. What constitutes complete data depends largely on the nature of the loss exposure being considered. For example, considering loss exposures related to employee injuries would require historical loss data to include information regarding loss amounts, the employee's experience and training, the time of day of the loss, the task being performed, and the supervisor on duty at the time. Similarly, complete data on a property loss to a piece of machinery would include the cost of repairing or replacing any damaged or inoperative machinery, the resulting loss of revenue, any extra expenses, or any overtime wages paid to maintain production. Having complete information helps to isolate the causes of each loss. Furthermore, having complete data enables the risk management professional to make reasonably reliable estimates of the dollar amounts of the future losses.

Consistent Data

To reflect past patterns, loss data must also be consistent in at least two respects. First, the loss data must be collected on a consistent basis for all recorded losses. Second, data must be expressed in constant dollars, to adjust for differences in price levels. If data are inconsistent in either respect, the future loss exposures could be significantly underestimated or overestimated.

Loss data are often collected from a variety of sources, each of which may use different accounting methods. Consequently, these data are likely to be inconsistent in their presentation. For example, one common source of inconsistency results when some of the loss amounts being analyzed are reported as estimates and others are reported as actual paid amounts. Similarly, data will be inconsistent if some amounts are reported at their original cost and others are reported at their current replacement cost.

Differences in price levels will also lead to inconsistency. Two physically identical losses occurring in different years will probably have different values. Inflation distorts the later loss, making it appear more severe because it is measured in less valuable dollars. To prevent this distortion, historical losses should be adjusted (indexed) so that loss data is expressed in constant dollars. To express data in constant dollars means that the amounts reported are comparable in terms of the value of goods and services that could be purchased in a particular benchmark year. Price indices are used to adjust data so that they are in constant dollars.

When Is a Dollar Not Worth a Dollar?

When referring to historical values, a variety of terms are used, such as nominal dollars, current dollars, and real or constant dollars.

Nominal dollars—dollar values at the time of the loss. For example, if a fire destroyed a building in 1995 and it cost $100,000 to repair the building in 1995, then the loss in nominal dollars is $100,000.

Current dollars—dollar values today. This value involves inflating all historical dollar values to today's value by using some measure of inflation (such as the Consumer Price Index). For example, the $100,000 loss in 1995 is actually a $125,000 loss in today's (current) dollars.

Real or constant dollars—dollar values in some base year. This value enables comparison of losses that have occurred in different time periods. The choice of base year does not matter. For convenience, the most recent year is often chosen. For example, suppose losses were reported over the four-year window 2002–2005. To determine real or constant dollars, multiply 2002 values by 1.08 (to account for the 8 percent increase in prices from 2002 to 2005) to convert the 2002 values into 2005 values for comparison. Similarly, 2003 losses would have to be multiplied by 1.06 and 2004 losses by 1.03.

Organized Data

Even if data are relevant, complete, and consistent, if they are not appropriately organized they will be difficult for the insurance or risk management professional to use to identify patterns and trends that will help to reveal and quantify potential future loss exposures. Data can be organized in a variety of different ways, depending on which is most useful for the analysis being performed. For example, listing losses for particular loss exposures by calendar dates may be useful for detecting seasonal patterns, but may not disclose patterns that could be revealed by listing such losses by size. An array of losses—amounts of losses listed in increasing or decreasing value—could reveal clusters of losses by severity and could also focus attention on large losses, which are often most important for insurance and risk management decisions. Organizing losses by size is also the foundation for developing loss severity distributions or loss trends over time.

Once data have been collected, insurance and risk management professionals can apply probability and other statistical analyses to those data in order to better understand and project the future potential loss exposures faced by their organizations.

Nature of Probability

The probability of an event is the relative frequency with which the event can be expected to occur in the long run in a stable environment. For example, given many tosses, a coin can be expected to come up heads as often as it comes up tails. Given many rolls of one die from a pair of dice, a four can be expected to come up one-sixth of the time. According to one standard mortality table, slightly more than 1.2 percent of males aged sixty-two can be expected to die before reaching age sixty-three.[1] Statistics in 2001 indicated that of the many automobiles on the road, 1 out of every 194 could be expected to be stolen within the year.[2] Finally, statistical analysis of automobile collisions would show that there are approximately 220 to 230 crashes per 100 million vehicle-miles driven.[3]

Any probability can be expressed as a fraction, percentage, or decimal. For example, the probability of a head on a coin toss can be expressed as ½, 50 percent, or .50. The probability of an event that is totally impossible is 0 and the probability of an absolutely certain event is 1.0. Therefore, the probabilities of all events that are neither totally impossible nor absolutely certain are greater than 0 but less than 1.0.

Theoretical probability
Probability that is based on theoretical principles rather than on actual experience.

Probabilities can be developed either from theoretical considerations or from historical data. **Theoretical probability** is probability that is based on theoretical principles rather than on actual experience. In contrast, **empirical probability** is probability that is based on actual experience. Probabilities associated with events such as coin tosses or dice throws can be developed from theoretical considerations and are unchanging. For example, from a description of a fair coin or die, a person who has never seen either a coin or a die can calculate the probability of flipping a head or rolling a four. In contrast, the probability that a sixty-two-year-old male will die in a particular year cannot be theoretically determined, but must be estimated by studying the loss experience of a sample of men aged sixty-two.

Empirical probability
Probability that is based on actual experience.

The empirical probabilities deduced solely from historical data may change as new data are discovered or as the environment that produces those events changes. Therefore, empirical probabilities are only estimates whose accuracy depends on the size and representative nature of the samples being studied. In contrast, theoretical probabilities are constant as long as the physical conditions that generate them remain unchanged. Although it may be preferable to use theoretical probabilities because of their unchanging nature, they are not applicable or available in most of the situations that insurance and risk management professionals are likely to analyze, such as automobile accidents or workers' compensation claims. As a result, empirical probabilities must be used.

Probability analysis
A technique for forecasting events on the assumption that they are governed by an unchanging probability distribution.

Probability analysis is a technique for forecasting events on the assumption that they are governed by an unchanging probability distribution. Probability analysis is particularly effective for projecting losses in organizations that have (1) a substantial volume of data on past losses and (2) fairly stable operations so that (except for price level changes) patterns of past losses presumably will continue in the future. In organizations with this type of unchanging environment, past losses can be viewed as a sample of all possible losses that the organization might suffer. The larger the number of past losses an organization has experienced, the larger the sample of losses that can be used in the analysis. Consequently, the forecasts of future losses are more reliable (consistent over time) because the forecast is based on a larger sample of the environment that produced the losses. This is an application of the **law of large numbers**, which is a mathematical principle stating that the actual (empirical) relative frequency of each of the possible outcomes more nearly approaches the true (theoretical) probability of that outcome as the number of independent events increases.

Law of large numbers
A mathematical principle stating that the actual (empirical) relative frequency of each of the possible outcomes more nearly approaches the true (theoretical) probability of that outcome as the number of independent events increases.

As an example, suppose an urn holds four marbles. One of the marbles is red and three are black. Assume that the number of red or black marbles is not known. The task is to estimate the theoretical probability of choosing a red marble on one draw (sample) from the urn by repeatedly sampling the marbles and replacing each in the urn after the sampling. After 20 samples a red marble has been chosen 8 times, which yields an empirical frequency of 40 percent ($\frac{8}{20}$). However, this estimate is inaccurate because the theoretical probability is 25 percent ($\frac{1}{4}$), given that only one of the four marbles is red. According to the law of large numbers, the relative inaccuracy between the empirical frequency (40 percent in this case) and the theoretical probability (25 percent) will decline, on average, as the sample size increases. That is, as the number of samples increases from 20 to 200 or 2,000, the empirical frequency of choosing a red marble gets closer and closer to 25 percent.

The law of large numbers has some limitations. It can be used to more accurately forecast future events only when the events being forecast meet all three of the following criteria:

1. The events have occurred in the past under substantially identical conditions and have resulted from unchanging, basic causal forces.

2. The events can be expected to occur in the future under the same, unchanging conditions.

3. The events have been, and will continue to be, both independent of one another and sufficiently numerous.

Probability Distributions

Once empirical probabilities are determined, probability distributions can be constructed to assist with the statistical analysis. A **probability distribution** is a presentation (table, chart, or graph) of probability estimates of a particular set of circumstances and of the probability of each possible outcome. Because probability distributions include the probability of every possible outcome (making it certain that one of these outcomes and only one will occur), the sum of the probabilities in a probability distribution must be 1.0 (100 percent).

Probability distribution
A presentation (table, chart, or graph) of probability estimates of a particular set of circumstances and of the probability of each possible outcome.

Both theoretical probabilities (such as those involving tossing coins or rolling dice) and empirical probabilities (such as those involving the number or size of losses) have outcomes that are mutually exclusive and collectively exhaustive. For example, on a particular flip of a coin, only one outcome is possible: heads or tails. Therefore, these outcomes are mutually exclusive. Similarly, these two outcomes are the only possible outcomes and, therefore, are collectively exhaustive. A properly constructed probability distribution always contains outcomes that are both mutually exclusive and collectively exhaustive. For example, Exhibit 3-5 shows the hypothetical probability distribution of the number of hurricanes making landfall in Florida during any given hurricane season. Each outcome (hurricane) is mutually exclusive and the sum of the outcomes is 1.0, so they are collectively exhaustive. Exhibit 3-6 shows the distribution as a pie chart.

EXHIBIT 3-5

Number of Hurricanes Making Landfall in Florida During One Hurricane Season

Number of Hurricanes Making Landfall	Probability
0	.300
1	.350
2	.200
3	.147
4	.002
5+	.001
Total Probability	1.000

EXHIBIT 3-6

Probability of Hurricanes Making Landfall in Florida During One Hurricane Season

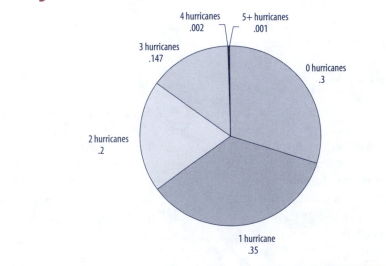

Theoretical Probability Distributions

Consider the probability distribution of the total number of points on one throw of two dice, one red and one green. There are thirty-six equally likely outcomes (green 1, red 1; green 1, red 2; … green 6, red 6). Exhibit 3-7 shows three alternate presentations of this probability distribution—a table, a chart and a graph. All possible outcomes are accounted for (they are collectively exhaustive) and the occurrence of any possible outcome (such as green 1, red 1) excludes any other outcome. Eleven point values are possible (ranging from a total of two points to a total of twelve points) and the probability of each of these eleven possible point values is proportional to the number of times each point value appears in the table of outcomes.

As the chart in Exhibit 3-7 indicates, the probability of a total of two points is $\frac{1}{36}$ because only one of the thirty-six possible outcomes (green 1, red 1) produces a total of two points. Similarly, $\frac{1}{36}$ is the probability of a total of twelve points. The most likely total point value, seven points, has a probability of $\frac{6}{36}$, represented in the table of outcomes by the diagonal southwest-northeast row of sevens. When the outcomes are presented as a graph, the height of the vertical line above each outcome indicates the probability of that outcome.

Although insurance and risk management professionals work with theoretical distributions on occasion, relatively few of the loss exposures they analyze involve theoretical probabilities. Therefore, most of the work they do involves empirical probability distributions.

Empirical Probability Distributions

Empirical probability distributions (estimated from historical data) are constructed in the same way as theoretical probability distributions. Exhibit 3-8 shows a hypothetical empirical probability distribution for auto physical damage losses. Because the first requirement of a probability distribution is that it provide a mutually exclusive, collectively exhaustive list of outcomes, loss categories (bins) must be designed so that all losses can be included. One method is to divide the bins into equal sizes, similar to Exhibit 3-8, with each bin size being a standard size (in this case, $5,000).

The second requirement of a probability distribution is that it define the set of probabilities associated with each of the possible outcomes. Exhibit 3-8 shows empirical probabilities for each size category in Column 3. To determine the empirical probabilities in Column 3, the number of losses for each category (Column 2) is divided by the total number of losses. The sum of the resulting empirical probabilities is 100 percent (that is, the outcomes are collectively exhaustive) and any given loss falls into only one category (the outcomes are mutually exclusive). Therefore, the empirical probability distribution for losses is described by Columns 1 and 3 and satisfies all the requirements of a probability distribution.

EXHIBIT 3-7

Probability Distribution of Total Points on One Roll of Two Dice

A. Table of Outcomes

		Red Die					
		1	2	3	4	5	6
Green Die	1	2	3	4	5	6	7
	2	3	4	5	6	7	8
	3	4	5	6	7	8	9
	4	5	6	7	8	9	10
	5	6	7	8	9	10	11
	6	7	8	9	10	11	12

B. Chart Format

Total Points Both Dice	Probability				
2	1/36	or	.028	or	2.8%
3	2/36	or	.056	or	5.6
4	3/36	or	.083	or	8.3
5	4/36	or	.111	or	11.1
6	5/36	or	.139	or	13.9
7	6/36	or	.167	or	16.7
8	5/36	or	.139	or	13.9
9	4/36	or	.111	or	11.1
10	3/36	or	.083	or	8.3
11	2/36	or	.056	or	5.6
12	1/36	or	.028	or	2.8
Total	36/36	or	1.000	or	100.0%

Note: Total may not sum to 1 or 100% because of rounding.

C. Graph Format

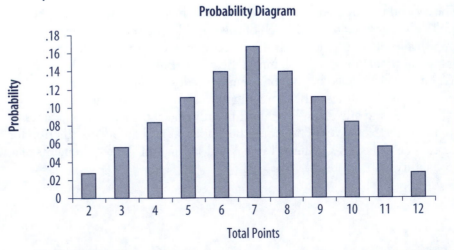

EXHIBIT 3-8

Estimated Probability Distribution of Auto Physical Damage Losses

(1) Size Category of Losses (bins)	(2) Number of Losses	(3) Percentage of Number of Losses	(4) Dollar Amount of Losses	(5) Percentage of Dollar Amount
$0–$5,000	7	36.84%	$ 18,007	10.64%
$5,001–$10,000	7	36.84	51,448	30.39
$10,001–$15,000	2	10.53	27,298	16.13
$15,001–$20,000	1	5.26	15,589	9.21
$20,001–$25,000	1	5.26	21,425	12.66
$25,001+	1	5.26	35,508	20.98
Total	19	100.00%	$169,275	100.00%

Mean dollar amount = $8,909

The empirical probability distribution for auto physical damage losses presented in Exhibit 3-8 differs in two ways from the theoretical probability distributions of the dice rolls shown in Exhibit 3-7. First, the outcomes shown in Column 1 of Exhibit 3-8 (size categories of losses) are arbitrarily defined boundaries, whereas the outcomes of a roll of dice are specific and observable. Second, whereas the maximum possible dice total is twelve, the largest size of machinery losses ($25,000+) has no evident upper limit.

Discrete and Continuous Probability Distributions

Probability distributions come in two forms: discrete probability distributions and continuous probability distributions. Discrete probability distributions have a finite number of possible outcomes, whereas continuous probability distributions have an infinite number of possible outcomes.

Discrete probability distributions are usually displayed in a table that lists all possible outcomes and the probability of each outcome. These distributions are typically used to analyze how often something will occur; that is, they are shown as frequency distributions. The number of hurricanes making landfall in Florida (Exhibit 3-5) is an example of a frequency distribution. Discrete probability distributions have a countable number of outcomes. For example, it is impossible to have 2.5 outcomes. In contrast, continuous probability distributions have an infinite number of possible outcome values and are generally represented in one of two ways: either as a graph or by dividing the distribution into a countable number of bins (as shown in Exhibit 3-8).

Exhibit 3-9 illustrates two representations of continuous probability distributions. The possible outcomes are presented on the horizontal axes and the likelihood of those outcomes is shown in the vertical axes. The height of the line or curve above the outcomes indicates the likelihood of that outcome. The outcomes in a continuous probability distribution are called probability density functions. Continuous probability distributions are typically used for severity distributions—they depict the value of the loss rather than the number of outcomes. Figure (a) in Exhibit 3-9, which has a flat line above the interval $0 to $1,000, illustrates that all of the outcomes between $0 and $1,000 are equally likely. Figure (b), which has a curve that starts at $0 and increases until it reaches a peak at $500 and then declines to $0 again at $1,000, illustrates that the very low (close to $0) and very high (close to $1,000) outcomes are unlikely and that the outcomes around $500 are much more likely.

As shown previously, the other way of presenting a continuous probability distribution is to divide the distribution into a countable number of bins. Exhibit 3-8 displays auto physical damage losses in a continuous probability distribution that has been divided into six bins described by various ranges of losses. Although the auto physical damage distribution is a continuous probability distribution, the dividing of the losses into bins makes the continuous distribution resemble a discrete probability distribution with several outcomes.

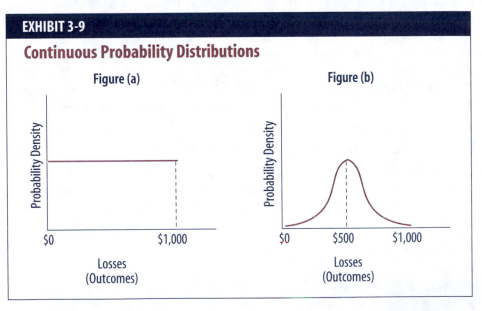

EXHIBIT 3-9

Continuous Probability Distributions

When working with continuous probability distributions used as severity distributions, the value lost can take any value between $0 and some upper limit (such as $1,000,000). By definition, continuous probability distributions have an infinite number of possible outcomes (otherwise they are discrete distributions). Therefore, the probability of any given outcome is zero, as there are an uncountable number of other outcomes. As a result, an insurance or risk management professional has to divide the continuous distribution into a finite number of bins. When divided into bins, a probability of an outcome falling within a certain range can be calculated. For example, in a discrete frequency distribution, the probability of a high-rise office building not having a fire (zero fires) may be .50, of having one fire—.35, and of having two fires—.15. If a fire occurs, the damage may be anywhere between $0 and $1,000,000,000, which is a continuous severity distribution. It is almost impossible for an insurance or risk management professional to assign a probability to the likelihood of having a loss amount of $35,456.32. However, if the severity distribution is divided into a finite number of bins, $0–$1,000,000, $1,000,001–$2,000,000, and so on, it is possible to assign a probability to each bin. For example, the probability of the damage being between $0 and $1,000,000 is .25 and the probability of the damage being between $1,000,001 and $2,000,000 is .30. By dividing a continuous distribution into bins, the insurance or risk management professional simplifies the analysis necessary to develop a forecast of future losses using frequency and severity distributions.

Central Tendency

Having determined empirical probabilities and constructed probability distributions, the insurance or risk management professional can use central tendency and dispersion to compare the characteristics of those probability distributions. The **central tendency** is the single outcome that is the most representative of all possible outcomes included within a probability distribution. Many probability distributions cluster around a particular value, which may or may not be in the exact center of the distribution's range of values. The three most widely accepted measures of central tendency are the expected value or mean, the median, and the mode.

Central tendency
The single outcome that is the most representative of all possible outcomes included within a probability distribution.

In analyzing a probability distribution, the measures of central tendency represent the best guess as to what the outcome will be. For example, if a manager asked an underwriter what the expected losses from fire would be on a store that the underwriter had insured, the underwriter's best guess would be one of the measures of central tendency of the frequency distribution multiplied by one of the measures of central tendency of the severity distribution. So, if the expected number of fires was two, and each fire had an expected severity of $5,000, the underwriter would expect $10,000 in losses.

Expected Value

The **expected value** is the weighted average of all of the possible outcomes of a theoretical probability distribution. The weights are the probabilities of the outcomes.

Expected value
The weighted average of all of the possible outcomes of a theoretical probability distribution.

The outcomes of a probability distribution are symbolized as $x_1, x_2, x_3, \ldots x_n$ (x_n represents the last outcome in the series), having respective probabilities of $p_1, p_2, p_3, \ldots p_n$. The distribution's expected value is the sum of $(p_1 \times x_1) + (p_2 \times x_2) + (p_3 \times x_3) + \ldots (p_n \times x_n)$. In the dice example, the distribution's expected value is shown in Exhibit 3-10 as the sum of the values in Column 3. The procedure for calculating the expected value applies to all theoretical discrete probability distributions, regardless of their shape or dispersion. For continuous distributions, the expected value is also a weighted average of the possible outcomes. However, calculating the expected value for a continuous distribution is much more complex and therefore is not discussed in this text.

EXHIBIT 3-10

Calculating the Expected Value of a Probability Distribution— The Two Dice Example

(1) Total Points– Both Dice (x)	(2) Probability (p)	(3) $p \times x$	(4) Cumulative Probability (sum of p's)
2	1/36	2/36	1/36
3	2/36	6/36	3/36
4	3/36	12/36	6/36
5	4/36	20/36	10/36
6	5/36	30/36	15/36
7	6/36	42/36	21/36
8	5/36	40/36	26/36
9	4/36	36/36	30/36
10	3/36	30/36	33/36
11	2/36	22/36	35/36
12	1/36	12/36	36/36 or 100%
Total	36/36 = 1	252/36 = 7.0	

Expected Value = 252/36 = 7.0.
Median = 7. (There is an equal number of outcomes (15) above and below 7.)
Mode = 7. (The most frequent outcome.)

Mean

Probabilities are needed to calculate a theoretical distribution's expected value. However, when considering an empirical distribution constructed from historical data, the measure of central tendency is not called the expected value, it is called the mean. The distribution's **mean** is the sum of the values in a data set divided by the number of values. In other words, the mean is the numeric average. Just as the expected value is calculated by weighting each possible outcome by its probability, the mean is calculated by weighting each observed outcome by the relative frequency with which it occurs. For example, if the observed outcome values are 2, 3, 4, 4, 5, 5, 5, 6, 6, and 8, then the mean equals 4.8, which is the sum of the values, 48, divided by the number of values, 10.

The mean is only a good estimate of the expected outcome if the underlying conditions determining those outcomes remain constant over time. Unlike the expected value, which is derived from theory, the mean is derived from

Mean

The sum of the values in a data set divided by the number of values.

experience. If the conditions that generated that experience have changed, the mean that was calculated may no longer be an accurate estimate of central tendency. Nonetheless, an insurance or a risk management professional will often use the mean, or expected value, as the single best guess as to forecasting future events. For example, the best guess as to the number of workers' compensation claims that an organization will suffer in the next year is often the mean of the frequency distribution of workers' compensation claims from previous years.

Median and Cumulative Probabilities

Another measure of central tendency is the median. The **median** is the value at the midpoint of a sequential data set with an odd number of values, or the mean of the two middle values of a sequential data set with an even number of values. In order to determine a data set's median, its values must be arranged by size, from highest to lowest or lowest to highest. In the array of nineteen auto physical damage losses in Exhibit 3-11, the median loss has an adjusted value of $6,782. This tenth loss is the median because nine losses are greater than $6,782 and nine losses are less than $6,782.

Median
The value at the midpoint of a sequential data set with an odd number of values, or the mean of the two middle values of a sequential data set with an even number of values.

EXHIBIT 3-11

Array of Historical and Adjusted Auto Physical Damage Losses

(1) Date	(2) Historical Loss Amount	(3) Adjusted Loss Amount*	(4) Rank
09/29/03	$ 155	$ 200	19
04/21/03	1,008	1,300	18
03/18/04	1,271	1,500	17
12/04/03	1,783	2,300	16
07/27/05	3,774	4,000	15
06/14/06	4,224	4,224	14
04/22/06	4,483	4,483	13
02/08/05**	5,189	5,500	12
05/03/03	4,651	5,999	11
01/02/06**	6,782	6,782	10
07/12/04	6,271	7,402	9
05/17/05**	7,834	8,303	8
08/15/04	7,119	8,403	7
06/10/06	9,059	9,059	6
12/19/05	12,830	13,599	5
08/04/05	12,925	13,699	4
11/01/04	13,208	15,589	3
01/09/06	21,425	21,425	2
10/23/06	35,508	35,508	1

* Adjusted amount column is the historical loss amount adjusted to current year (2006) dollars using a price index.

** Loss for which adjustment of historical amount to 2006 constant dollars changes ranking in array

A probability distribution's median has a cumulative probability of 50 percent. For example, seven is the median of the probability distribution of points in rolling two dice because seven is the only number of points for which the probability of higher outcomes ($^{15}\!/_{36}$) is equal to the probability of lower outcomes ($^{15}\!/_{36}$). That is, there are fifteen equally probable ways of obtaining an outcome higher than seven and fifteen equally probable ways of obtaining an outcome lower than seven.

The median can also be determined by summing the probabilities of outcomes equal to or less than a given number of points in rolling two dice, as in Exhibit 3-10. The cumulative 50 percent probability ($^{18}\!/_{36}$) is reached in the seven-points category (actually, in the middle of the seven-point class of results). Therefore, seven is the median of this distribution.

The cumulative probabilities in Column 4 of Exhibit 3-10 indicate the probability of a die roll yielding a certain number of points or less. For example, the cumulative probability of rolling a three or less is $^{3}\!/_{36}$ (or the sum of $^{1}\!/_{36}$ for rolling a two and $^{2}\!/_{36}$ for rolling a three). Similarly, the cumulative probability of rolling a ten or less is $^{33}\!/_{36}$, calculated by summing the individual Column 2 probabilities of outcomes of ten points or less. With probability distributions of losses, calculating probabilities of losses equal to or less than a given number of losses or dollar amounts of losses, individually and cumulatively, can be helpful in selecting retention levels. Similarly, calculating individual and cumulative probabilities of losses equal to or greater than a given number of losses or dollar amounts can help in selecting upper limits of insurance coverage.

Exhibit 3-12 shows how to derive a cumulative probability distribution of loss sizes from the individual probabilities of loss size in Exhibit 3-8. Column 3 of Exhibit 3-12 indicates that, on the basis of the available data, 36.84 percent of all losses are less than or equal to $5,000 and that another 36.84 percent are greater than $5,000 but less than or equal to $10,000. Therefore, the probability of a loss being $10,000 or less is calculated as the sum of these two probabilities, or 73.68 percent, as shown in Column 4 of Exhibit 3-12. Similarly, as shown in Column 7, individual losses of $10,000 or less can be expected to account for 41.03 percent of the total dollar amount of all losses.

Understanding the cumulative probability distribution will enable an insurance or risk management professional to evaluate the effect of various deductibles and policy limits on insured loss exposures. For example, if an insurance policy has a $5,000 policy limit, the insurance or risk management professional would know that 36.84% of losses covered by that policy would be below the deductible level and therefore would not be paid by the insurer.

The summed probabilities in Column 4 of Exhibit 3-12 indicate that the median individual loss is between $5,001 and $10,000, the category in which the 50 percent cumulative probability is reached. This result is consistent with the $6,782 median loss found by examining Exhibit 3-11.

EXHIBIT 3-12

Cumulative Probabilities That Auto Physical Damage Losses Will Not Exceed Specified Amounts

(1) Loss Size Category	(2) Number of Losses	(3) Percentage of Number of Losses	(4) Cumulative Percentage of Number of Losses Not Exceeding Category	(5) Dollar Amount of Losses	(6) Percentage of Dollar Amount	(7) Cumulative Percentage of Dollar Amount of Losses Not Exceeding Category
$0–$5,000	7	36.84%	36.84%	$18,007	10.64%	10.64%
$5,001–$10,000	7	36.84	73.68	51,448	30.39	41.03
$10,001–$15,000	2	10.53	84.21	27,298	16.13	57.16
$15,001–$20,000	1	5.26	89.47	15,589	9.21	66.37
$20,001–$25,000	1	5.26	94.74	21,425	12.66	79.02
$25,001+	1	5.26	100.00	35,508	20.98	100.00
Total		100.00%			100.00%	

Mode

In addition to mean and median, a further measure of central tendency is the **mode**, which is the most frequently occurring value in a distribution. For a continuous distribution, the mode is the value of the outcome directly beneath the peak of the probability density function. In the distribution of total points of two dice throws, the mode is seven points. In the empirical distribution of auto physical damage losses shown in Exhibit 3-12, the mode is the $0–$5,000 range or the $5,001–$10,000 range, because those ranges have the highest frequency of losses (seven). Knowing the mode of a distribution allows an insurance or risk management professional to focus on the outcomes that are the most common. For example, knowing that the most common auto physical damage losses are in the $0–$10,000 range may influence the risk financing decisions regarding deductible levels for potential insurance coverages.

The relationships among the mean (average), median, and mode for any data set are illustrated by the distribution's shape. The shape of a particular relative frequency or severity probability distribution can be seen by graphing a curve of the data as shown in Exhibit 3-13. In a symmetrical distribution, one side of the curve is a mirror image of the other. Distribution (a) is the standard (normal) distribution commonly called a bell-shaped curve, but both distributions are symmetrical. In a symmetrical distribution, the mean and median have the same value. In a standard bell-shaped distribution, the mode also has the same value as that of the mean and the median.

If a distribution is asymmetrical, it is skewed. Two skewed distributions are shown in Exhibit 3-13. Many loss distributions are skewed because the probability of small losses is large whereas the probability of large losses is small. Asymmetrical distributions are common for severity distributions where most losses are small losses but there is a small probability of a large loss occurring. If the distribution is skewed, the mean and median values will differ and the median value of the distribution is often a better guess as to what is most likely to occur than the mean. For example, if the distribution of workers' compensation claims was skewed by two years in which an organization experienced an unusually high level of claims, the mean would be higher than the median. In that situation, the median is more likely a better estimate of next year's claims than the mean.

Dispersion

As well as using central tendency to compare the characteristics of probability distributions, the insurance or risk management professional can use **dispersion**, which is the variation among values in a distribution. Dispersion describes the extent to which the distribution is spread out rather than concentrated around the expected value. The less dispersion around the distribution's expected value, the greater the likelihood that actual results will fall within a given range of that expected value. Therefore, less

EXHIBIT 3-13

Typical Shapes of Symmetrical and Skewed Distributions Showing Relative Locations of Mean, Median, and Mode

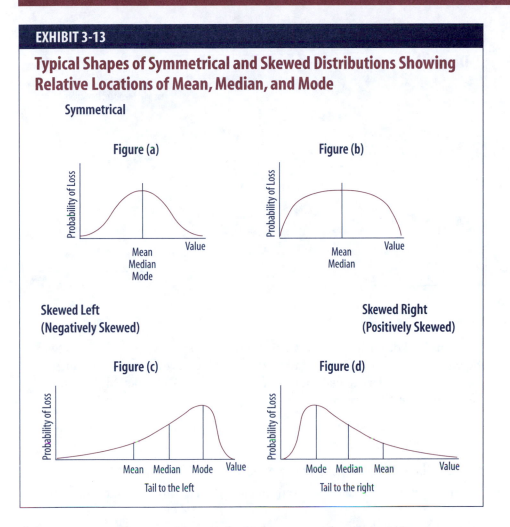

dispersion means less uncertainty about the expected outcomes. Insurance professionals may be able to use measures of dispersion around estimated losses to determine whether to offer insurance coverage to a possible insured. Dispersion also affects the shape of a distribution. The more dispersed a distribution (larger standard deviation), the flatter the distribution. A less dispersed distribution forms a more peaked distribution. Two symmetrical distributions with the same mean but different standard deviations are shown in Exhibit 3-14.

For example, if an underwriter is choosing between two accounts, both with the same expected loss, but one account has more variation in the possible losses then the other, the underwriter will likely choose to insure the account with less variation (lower dispersion). In general, the less dispersion around the central tendency, the less risk is involved in the loss exposure.

Two widely used statistical measures of dispersion are standard deviation and the coefficient of variation.

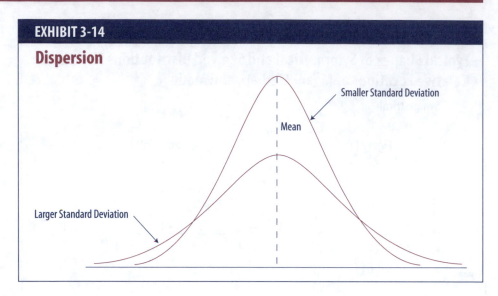

EXHIBIT 3-14

Dispersion

Standard Deviation

Standard deviation

The average of the differences (deviations) between the values in a distribution and the expected value (or mean) of that distribution.

The **standard deviation** is the average of the differences (deviations) between the values in a distribution and the expected value (or mean) of that distribution. The standard deviation therefore indicates how widely dispersed the values in a distribution are.

To calculate the standard deviation of a probability distribution, one must perform the following steps:

1. Calculate the distribution's expected value.
2. Subtract this expected value from each distribution value to find the differences.
3. Square each of the resulting differences.
4. Multiply each square by the probability associated with the value.
5. Sum the resulting products.
6. Find the square root of the sum.

Exhibit 3-15 illustrates how to calculate a standard deviation for the distribution of values in rolling two dice. This distribution's expected value was calculated as seven in Exhibit 3-10.

The standard deviation of auto physical damage losses can be estimated using the individual loss data reported in Exhibit 3-11. Calculating a standard deviation using a sample of actual outcomes is done in much the same way as for a probability distribution. To calculate the standard deviation using the actual sample of outcomes, it is not necessary to know the probability of each outcome, just how often each outcome occurred.

EXHIBIT 3-15

Calculation of Standard Deviation of the Probability Distribution of Two Dice

(1) Points (x_i)	(2) Probability (p)	(3) Step 1 EV	(4) Step 2 $x_i - EV$	(5) Step 3 $(x_i - EV)^2$	(6) Step 4 $(x_i - EV)^2 \times p$
2	1/36	7	−5	25	25/36
3	2/36	7	−4	16	32/36
4	3/36	7	−3	9	27/36
5	4/36	7	−2	4	16/36
6	5/36	7	−1	1	5/36
7	6/36	7	0	0	0
8	5/36	7	1	1	5/36
9	4/36	7	2	4	16/36
10	3/36	7	3	9	27/36
11	2/36	7	4	16	32/36
12	1/36	7	5	25	25/36
		Step 5		Total	210/36
		Step 6		$\sqrt{(210/36)} =$	2.42*

* Rounded

The steps for calculating the standard deviation of a set of individual outcomes not involving probabilities are as follows:

1. Calculate the mean of the outcomes (the sum of the outcomes divided by the number of outcomes).
2. Subtract the mean from each of the outcomes.
3. Square each of the resulting differences.
4. Sum these squares.
5. Divide this sum by the number of outcomes minus one (this value is called the variance).
6. Calculate the square root of the variance.

Exhibit 3-16 illustrates how to calculate a standard deviation using actual loss data (from Exhibit 3-11) rather than a theoretical probability distribution. An insurance or risk management professional needs to have a good understanding of how to measure the dispersion of the distributions of potential outcomes to gain a better understanding of the loss exposures being analyzed. For example, knowing the expected number of workers' compensation claims in a given year is important, but it is only one element of the information that can be gleaned from a distribution. The standard deviation can be calculated to provide a measure of how sure an insurance or risk management professional can be in his or her estimate of number of workers' compensation claims.

EXHIBIT 3-16

Calculation of Standard Deviation of Individual Outcomes

(1) Adjusted Loss Amount (ALA)	(2) Step 1 Mean Loss (ML)	(3) Step 2 ALA − ML	(4) Step 3 (ALA − ML)²
$ 200	$8,909	$−8,709	$ 75,846,681
1,300	8,909	−7,609	57,896,881
1,500	8,909	−7,409	54,893,281
2,300	8,909	−6,609	43,678,881
4,000	8,909	−4,909	24,098,281
4,224	8,909	−4,685	21,949,225
4,483	8,909	−4,426	19,589,476
5,500	8,909	−3,409	11,621,281
5,999	8,909	−2,910	8,468,100
6,782	8,909	−2,127	4,524,129
7,402	8,909	−1,507	2,271,049
8,303	8,909	−606	367,236
8,403	8,909	−506	256,036
9,059	8,909	150	22,500
13,599	8,909	4,690	21,996,100
13,699	8,909	4,790	22,944,100
15,589	8,909	6,680	44,622,400
21,425	8,909	12,516	156,650,256
35,508	8,909	26,599	707,506,801

Step 4	Sum	$1,279,202,694
Step 5	Variance [sum ÷ (n − 1)]	71,066,816
Step 6	Standard deviation (sqrt variance)	$8,430

Coefficient of Variation

Coefficient of variation

A distribution's standard deviation divided by its mean or expected value.

The coefficient of variation is a further measure of the dispersion of a distribution. The **coefficient of variation** is a distribution's standard deviation divided by its mean or expected value. For example, the coefficient of variation for the distribution of total points in rolling two dice equals 2.4 points divided by 7.0 points, or 0.34. Similarly the coefficient of variation of the sample of outcomes in Exhibit 3-16 is $8,430 divided by $8,909, or approximately 0.95.

In comparing two distributions, if both distributions have the same mean (or expected value), then the distribution with the larger standard deviation has the greater variability. If the two distributions have different means (or expected values), the coefficient of variation is often used to compare the two distributions to determine which has the greater variability relative to its mean (or expected value). For insurance and risk management professionals, comparing two distinct distributions with different means and standard deviations is difficult. Staying with the example of an underwriter trying to determine on which account to offer coverage, if the means are the same, all else being equal, the underwriter should choose the account with the lowest standard deviation. If the accounts have different means and standard deviations, the underwriter could compare the two accounts using the coefficient of variation and choose the account with the lowest coefficient of variation.

An insurance or a risk management professional can use the coefficient of variation to determine whether a particular loss control measure has made losses more or less predictable (that is, whether the distribution is more or less variable). For example, an insurance or a risk management professional may calculate that theft losses have a severity distribution with a mean of $3,590 and a standard deviation of $3,432 for a coefficient of variation of 0.96. If the organization installs a new security system, the theft losses may have a severity distribution with a mean of $2,150 and a standard deviation of $2,950 for a coefficient of variation of 1.37. Although the security system has reduced the mean severity, it has actually made the losses less predictable because the new severity distribution is relatively more variable than the old distribution without the security system.

The coefficient of variation is useful in comparing the variability of distributions that have different shapes, means, or standard deviations. The distribution with the largest coefficient of variation has the greatest relative variability. The higher the variability within a distribution, the more difficult it is to accurately forecast an individual outcome.

Normal Distribution

The **normal distribution** is a probability distribution that, when graphed, generates a bell-shaped curve. This particular probability distribution can help to accurately forecast the variability around some central, average, or expected value and has therefore proven useful in accurately forecasting the variability of many physical phenomena.

Exhibit 3-17 illustrates the typical bell-shaped curve of a normal distribution. Note that the normal curve never touches the horizontal line at the base of the diagram. In theory, the normal distribution assigns some probability greater than zero for every outcome, regardless of its distance from the mean. Exhibit 3-17 also shows the percentage of outcomes that fall within a given number of standard deviations above or below the mean of a distribution. For example, for all normal distributions, 34.13 percent of all outcomes are within one standard deviation above the mean and, because every normal

Normal distribution
A probability distribution that, when graphed, generates a bell-shaped curve.

distribution is symmetrical, another 34.13 percent of all outcomes fall within one standard deviation below the mean. By addition, 68.26 percent of all outcomes are within one standard deviation above or below the mean. The portion of a normal distribution that is between one and two standard deviations above the mean contains 13.59 percent of all outcomes, as does the portion between one and two standard deviations below the mean. Hence, the area between the mean and two standard deviations above the mean contains 47.72 percent (34.13 percent + 13.59 percent) of the outcomes, and another 47.72 percent are two standard deviations or less below the mean. Consequently, 95.44 percent of all outcomes are within two standard deviations above or below the mean and fewer than 5 percent of outcomes are outside two standard deviations above or below the mean.

EXHIBIT 3-17

The Normal Distribution—Percentages of Outcomes Within Specified Standard Deviations of the Mean

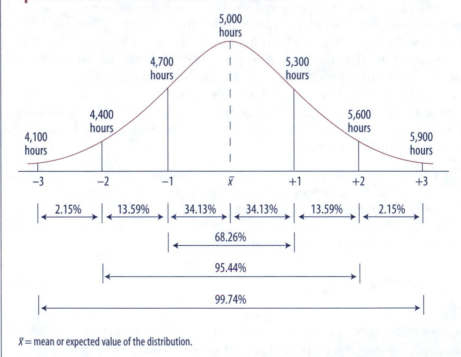

$\bar{X}$ = mean or expected value of the distribution.

Taking this a step further, 2.15 percent of all outcomes are between two and three standard deviations above the mean, and another 2.15 percent are between two and three standard deviations below the mean. Therefore, 49.87 percent (34.13 percent + 13.59 percent + 2.15 percent) of all outcomes are three standard deviations or less above the mean, and an equal percentage are three standard deviations or less below the mean. Consequently, the portion of the distribution between three standard deviations above the mean and three standard deviations below it contains 99.74 percent (49.87 percent × 2) of all outcomes. Therefore, only 0.26 percent (100 percent − 99.74 percent) of all outcomes lie beyond three standard deviations from the mean.

The relationship between the expected value and the standard deviation of a normal distribution can have useful practical application. For example, suppose that a plant uses 600 electrical elements to heat rubber. The useful life of each element is limited, and an element that is used for too long poses a substantial danger of exploding and starting an electrical fire. An insurance professional underwriting the plant's fire insurance would look for evidence that proper maintenance is performed and the heating elements are replaced to ensure proper fire safety. The issue is determining when to replace the heating elements. Replacing them too soon can be costly, whereas replacing them too late increases the chance of fire. The characteristics of the normal probability distribution provide a way of scheduling maintenance so that the likelihood of an element becoming very dangerous before it is replaced can be kept below a particular margin of safety that is specified by the organization based on its willingness to assume risk.

Assume that the expected safe life of each element conforms to a normal distribution having a mean of 5,000 hours and a standard deviation of 300 hours. Even if the maintenance schedule requires replacing each element after it has been in service only 5,000 hours (the mean, or expected, safe life), a 50 percent chance exists that it will become unsafe before being changed, because 50 percent of the normal distribution is below this 5,000-hour mean. If each element is changed after having been used only 4,700 hours [one standard deviation below the mean (5,000 – 300)], a 15.87 percent (50 percent – 34.13 percent) chance still exists that an element will become unsafe before being changed. If this probability of high hazard is still too high, changing each element after 4,400 hours [two standard deviations below the mean (5,000 – (2 × 300))] reduces the probability of high hazard to only 2.28 percent, the portion of a normal distribution that is more than two standard deviations below the mean. A still more cautious practice would be to change elements routinely after only 4,100 hours [three standard deviations below the mean (5,000 – (3 × 300))], so that the probability of an element becoming highly hazardous before replacement would be only 0.13 percent, slightly more than one chance in 1,000.

Using this analysis, management can select an acceptable probability that a heating element will become unsafe before being replaced and can schedule maintenance accordingly. Suppose, for example, that management accepts one chance in ten that an element would become dangerous before being replaced. That is, 90 percent of the elements should be replaced before they became dangerous. In terms of Exhibit 3-17, achieving this goal requires finding the point along the bottom of the diagram where 10 percent of the entire distribution (the portion of heating elements whose hazard could be tolerated) is below (to the left of) the time of replacement and the remaining 90 percent is above this point. This point is between one and two standard deviations below the mean—that is, between 15.87 percent of the total distribution and 2.28 percent. Statisticians have shown that a value of 1.65 standard deviations below the mean cuts off the lowest 10 percent of any normal distribution. Therefore, scheduling replacement of each element after 4,505 hours of use [calculated as 5,000 – (1.65 × 300)] would ensure that only 10 percent of the elements became hazardous before replacement. For still greater assurance, say, 95 percent (instead of 90 percent), one must move 1.96 standard deviations below the mean or replace each element after 4,412 hours of use [5,000 – (1.96 × 300)].

These statistical methods can help insurance and risk management professionals to perform the second step in the risk management process, that is, to analyze the loss exposures identified during the first step.

ANALYZING LOSS EXPOSURES

The analysis step of the risk management process involves considering the following four dimensions of a loss exposure:

1. Loss frequency—the number of losses (such as fires, auto accidents, or liability claims) that occur within a specific period.
2. Loss severity—the dollar amount of loss for a specific occurrence.
3. Total dollar losses—the total dollar amount of losses for all occurrences during a specific period.
4. Timing—when losses occur and when loss payments are made. (The time interval between loss occurrence and loss payment can be lengthy.)

Analyzing loss frequency, loss severity, total dollar losses, and timing helps insurance and risk management professionals develop loss projections, and, therefore, also helps them prioritize loss exposures so that risk management resources can be concentrated where they are needed most. The cost of analyzing loss exposures, which can be an expensive endeavor, is included in the cost of risk discussed in a previous chapter. The cost of risk includes the cost of acquiring risk-related information used in loss forecasts, estimates of future cash flows, and other analysis activities. Analyzing this information may ultimately lead to risk management decisions that result in fewer future losses, thereby helping to make the analysis of loss exposures more cost-effective.

If any of the four dimensions of loss exposure analysis involve empirical distributions developed from past losses, the credibility of the data being used needs to be determined. Data credibility is the level of confidence that available data are capable of being used as accurate indicators of future losses.

Loss Frequency

Loss frequency is the number of losses—such as fires, thefts, or floods—that occur within a specified period. The relative frequency is the number of losses that occur within a given period relative to the number of exposure units, such as the number of buildings or cars. If there is only one exposure unit, such as one building, the loss frequency and the relative frequency are the same. For example, an organization may experience, on average, five theft losses per year. That is, five is the mean of an empirical frequency distribution. If the organization has only one building, then both the loss frequency and the relative frequency of losses from theft is five per year. However, if the organization has five buildings, then the organization still has a loss frequency of five theft losses per year, but the relative frequency would be one loss per year per building. Two of the most common applications of relative frequency measures in risk management are injuries per man per hour in workers' compensation and auto accidents per mile driven.

Frequency distributions are usually discrete probability distributions that are based on past data regarding how often similar events have happened. For example, Exhibit 3-18 contains the frequency distribution of the number of hurricanes that make landfall in Florida during a single hurricane season. One way of describing the frequency of hurricanes is to report a mean frequency of occurrence, such as approximately 1.2 hurricanes making landfall per year. However, this ignores some of the other information that is available by looking at the entire frequency distribution. For example, the most likely outcome may be one hurricane per year (35.0 percent of the time). However, having zero hurricanes per year is also reasonably likely (30.0 percent of the time), but having five or more hurricanes make landfall in Florida is reasonably unlikely (0.1 percent of the time). Therefore, an insurance or risk management professional should also utilize other information from the frequency distribution, such as the standard deviation (~1.04) and skewness measures, to supplement the mean of 1.2.

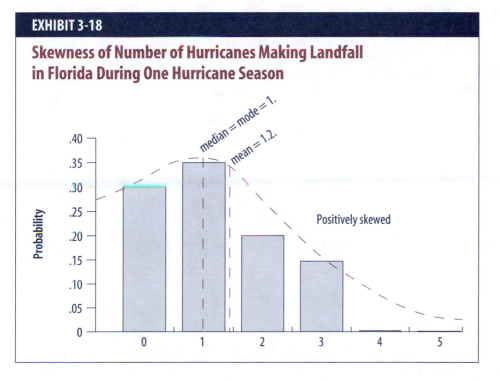

EXHIBIT 3-18

Skewness of Number of Hurricanes Making Landfall in Florida During One Hurricane Season

The accuracy of loss frequency data is influenced by the law of large numbers, which means that loss frequency can be projected with a fairly high degree of confidence for some loss exposures in large organizations. For example, a mail-order house that ships thousands of parcels each day probably can more accurately project the number of transit losses it will sustain in a year, based on past experience and adjusted for any expected changes in future conditions, than can a mail-order house that only ships hundreds of parcels each month.

Most organizations do not have enough exposure units to accurately project low-frequency, high-severity events (such as employee deaths). However, an estimate with a margin for error is better than no estimate at all, as long as its limitations are recognized.

Loss Severity

The purpose of analyzing loss severity is to determine how serious a loss might be. For example, how much of a building could be damaged in a single fire? Alternatively, how long could it be before operations can resume after a fire? Loss severity information is available from severity distributions such as the one shown in Exhibit 3-19, which contains the severity distribution for auto physical damage claims first introduced in Exhibit 3-8. This data can help determine both the probable maximum loss and the maximum possible loss.

EXHIBIT 3-19

PML and MPL of Loss Severity Distribution of Auto Physical Damage Losses

(1) Size Category of Losses (Bins)	(2) Number of Losses	(3) Percentage of Number of Losses	(4) Dollar Amount of Losses	(5) Percentage of Dollar Amount	
$0–$5,000	7	36.84%	$ 18,007	10.64%	
$5001–$10,000	7	36.84	51,448	30.39	A good estimate of MPL
$10,001–$15,000	2	10.53	27,298	16.13	
$15,001–$20,000	1	5.26	15,589	9.21	
$20,001–$25,000	1	5.26	21,425	12.66	
$25,001+	1	5.26	35,508	20.98	A good estimate of PML
Total	19	100.00%	$169,275	100.00%	

Mean = $169,275 ÷ 19 = $8,909.

Probable Maximum Loss

Probable maximum loss (PML)

An estimate of the largest loss that is likely to occur.

Probable maximum loss (PML) is an estimate of the largest loss that is likely to occur. From Exhibit 3-19, the mean of the distribution is approximately $8,909. That is, the average loss, given that a loss has occurred, is $8,909.

The PML is typically estimated to be near the mean for any given severity distribution. Provided that the probable maximum loss lies within one standard deviation of the mean, this is usually a reasonable estimation.

Maximum Possible Loss

Effectively managing risk requires identifying the worst possible outcome. The **maximum possible loss (MPL)** is the total value exposed to loss at any one location or from any one event. For example, in the case of fire damage to a building and its contents, the maximum possible loss is typically the value of the building plus the total value of the building's contents. From Exhibit 3-19, a good estimate of the MPL of auto physical damage losses would be approximately $36,000, close to the largest loss suffered.

To determine MPL for multiple exposure units, such as a fleet of cars, an insurance or risk management professional may want to consider things such as whether multiple vehicles travel together (so that one event, such as a collision, may affect several vehicles at once) or whether several vehicles are stored in the same location (so that one event, such as a fire, flood, or theft, may affect several vehicles). This will help determine the maximum number of vehicles that could be involved in any one loss and therefore the maximum possible loss from that event.

Although maximum possible property losses can be estimated based on the values exposed to loss, this estimation is not necessarily appropriate or possible for assessing maximum possible liability losses. In theory, liability losses are only limited by the defendant's total wealth. Therefore, some practical assumptions must be made about the MPL in liability cases to properly assess that loss exposure. In liability cases, instead of focusing on the defendant's total wealth, a common assumption is that the maximum amount that would be exposed to loss 95 percent (or 98 percent) of the time in similar cases is the MPL.

Focusing only on the PML or MPL estimates from a severity distribution is equivalent to only focusing on the mean of the frequency distribution. Such a focus ignores other information in the severity distribution that is relevant to properly managing risk. For example, focusing on the PML and MPL numbers does not take into account how different risk control or risk financing techniques may affect the severity distribution. The severity distribution in Exhibit 3-19 shows that nearly 74 percent of all losses are less than $10,000. If the organization in that example was interested in insuring its auto physical damage loss exposures, neither the PML nor MPL would indicate the best choice of deductible. Similarly, the PML and MPL would not identify whether the premium savings generated by choosing a higher deductible would be worth the additional risk in retained loss exposures. In order to fully analyze the significance of a particular loss exposure, it is important to consider both severity and frequency distributions and how they interact.

Maximum possible loss (MPL)
The total value exposed to loss at any one location or from any one event.

Frequency and Severity Considered Jointly

One method of jointly considering both loss frequency and loss severity is the Prouty Approach, which identifies four broad categories of loss frequency and three broad categories of loss severity. Another method is more statistically based and involves combining the frequency and severity distributions to create a single total claims distribution.

As shown in Exhibit 3-20, the four categories of loss frequency in the Prouty Approach are as follows:

1. Almost nil—extremely unlikely to happen; virtually no possibility
2. Slight—could happen but has not happened
3. Moderate—happens occasionally
4. Definite—happens regularly

The three categories of loss severity are as follows:

1. Slight—organization can readily retain each loss exposure
2. Significant—organization cannot retain the loss exposure, some part of which must be financed
3. Severe—organization must finance virtually all of the loss exposure or endanger its survival

EXHIBIT 3-20

The Prouty Approach

		Loss Frequency			
		Almost Nil	**Slight**	**Moderate**	**Definite**
Loss Severity	**Severe**	Reduce or prevent / Transfer	Reduce or prevent / Transfer	Reduce or prevent / Retain	Avoid
	Significant	Reduce or prevent / Transfer	Reduce / Transfer	Reduce or prevent / Retain	Avoid
	Slight	Reduce or prevent / Retain	Reduce / Retain	Reduce or prevent / Retain	Prevent / Retain

These broad categories of loss frequency and loss severity are somewhat subjective. One organization may view losses that occur once a month as moderate while another would consider that to be definite. Similarly, one organization may view a $1 million loss as slight while another might view it as severe. However, these categories can help insurance and risk management professionals justify the priority that should be placed on certain loss exposures.

Loss frequency and loss severity tend to be inversely related for any given loss exposure. In other words, the more severe a loss tends to be, the less frequently it tends to occur. Conversely, the more frequent a loss to a given exposure, the less severe the loss tends to be. Loss exposures that generate slight but definite losses are typically retained and incorporated in an organization's budget. At the other extreme, loss exposures that generate intolerably high losses are typically avoided. So, most risk management decisions, like the risk control and risk financing techniques shown in Exhibit 3-20, concern loss exposures for which individual losses, although tolerable, tend to be either significant or severe and have a moderate, slight, or almost nil chance of occurring.

A given loss exposure might generate financially serious losses because of either high individual loss severity or high-frequency, low-severity losses that aggregate to a substantial total. There may be a temptation to focus on high-profile "shock events," such as a major fire, a violent explosion, or a huge liability claim. However, smaller losses, which happen so frequently that they become routine, can eventually produce much larger total losses than the single dramatic event. For example, many retail firms suffer greater total losses from shoplifting, which happens every day, than they do from large fires that might happen once every twenty years. Minor, cumulatively significant losses usually deserve as much risk management attention as do large individual losses.

Another way of jointly considering frequency and severity is to combine both frequency and severity distributions into a total claims distribution. This new distribution can provide additional information to use in the remaining steps of the risk management process about the potential losses that may occur in a given period. Combining distributions can be difficult because as the number of possible outcomes increases, the number of possible combinations of frequency and severity grows exponentially.

Exhibit 3-21 presents a simple example of three possible frequencies (0, 1, and 2) and three possible severities ($100, $250, and $500) that represent shoplifting losses from a hardware store. The frequency and severity distributions for a given year are shown in Exhibit 3-21, along with the total claims distribution created by considering all the possible combinations of the frequency and severity distributions. For example, a 33 percent chance exists of a loss not occurring during the year (frequency = 0). Therefore, in the total claim distribution, a 33 percent chance exists of the total losses being $0. There is only one possible way for there to be a $100 loss. That is, with a frequency of 1 and a severity of $100. Therefore that probability is .11 [.33 (frequency 1) × .33 (severity $100) = .11]. There are two ways that the total claims for the year could equal $500. Either the organization could have one loss of $500, or it could have two losses of $250. Therefore, the probability of a $500 loss is the probability of one $500 loss plus the probability of two $250 losses.

Once an insurance or a risk management professional has created this distribution, he or she can calculate the measures of central tendency and dispersion and evaluate the effect that various risk control and risk financing techniques will have on this loss exposure.

EXHIBIT 3-21

Total Claims Distribution for Hardware Store Shoplifting Losses

Frequency

	Number of Losses	Probability
F0	0	.33
F1	1	.33
F2	2	.34

Severity

	Dollar Loss	Probability
S1	$100	.33
S2	$250	.33
S3	$500	.34

Total Claims Distribution

Dollar Loss	Probability*	Probability Calculation
$ 0	.33	$p(F0)$
100	.11	$p(F1) \times p(S1)$
200	.04	$p(F2) \times p(S1) \times p(S1)$
250	.11	$p(F1) \times p(S2)$
350	.07	$p(F2) \times p(S1) \times p(S2)$
500	.15	$[p(F2) \times p(S2) \times p(S2)] +$ $[p(F1) \times p(S3)]$
600	.08	$p(F2) \times p(S1) \times p(S3)$
750	.08	$p(F2) \times p(S2) \times p(S3)$
1,000	.04	$p(F2) \times p(S3) \times p(S3)$

There is only one possible way to have $0 losses: the frequency = 0. That happens 33% of the time.

There are two possible ways to have $500 in losses in a given year: two $250 losses or one $500 loss.

There is only one possible way to have $1,000 in losses: two $500 losses.

*   Rounded

Total Dollar Losses

The third dimension to consider in analyzing loss exposures is total dollar losses, which are calculated by multiplying loss frequency by loss severity. Total dollar losses represent a simplified version of combining frequency and severity distributions and can be used when analyzing frequency and severity distributions that have more than a few possible outcomes. Expected total dollar losses can be projected by multiplying expected loss frequency by expected loss severity, and worst-case scenarios can be calculated by assuming both high frequency and the worst possible severity. For example, Exhibit 3-22 includes the frequency and severity distributions that were shown in Exhibit 3-21 if they were expanded to include more possible outcomes. Combining the frequency and severity distributions in Exhibit 3-22 would be difficult given the total number of possible combinations. An insurance or a risk management professional could make some simpler calculations to determine what the potential total dollar losses may be. From Exhibit 3-22, expected total dollar losses would be $1,878.33 and the worst-case scenario could be $7,950.00. These estimates could then be used to determine the appropriate risk management techniques for managing these loss exposures, such as evaluating whether to insure the loss exposures for the premium the insurer is charging.

EXHIBIT 3-22

Total Dollar Losses

Frequency

	Number of Losses	Probability
F0	0	.03
F1	1	.05
F2	2	.08
F3	3	.10
F4	4	.15
F5	5	.20
F6	6	.15
F7	7	.10
F8	8	.08
F9	9	.05
F10	10	.01

Severity

	Dollar Loss	Probability
S1	$100	.30
S2	$250	.25
S3	$500	.20
S4	$683	.15
S5	$883	.10

Expected value = $383.33.

Expected value = 4.9.

Expected total dollar losses = 4.9 × $383.33 = $1,878.33.

Worst case total dollar losses = 9 × $883.00 = $7,950.00.

Timing

The fourth dimension to consider in analyzing loss exposures is timing of losses. Risk assessment requires considering not only when losses are likely to occur, but also when payment for those losses will likely be made. The timing dimension is significant because money held in reserve to pay for a loss can earn interest until the actual payment is made. Whether a loss is counted when it is incurred or when it is paid is also significant for various accounting and tax reasons that are beyond the scope of this text.

Funds to pay for property losses are generally disbursed relatively soon after the event occurs. In contrast, liability losses often involve long delays between the time of the adverse event, the time when an occurrence is recognized, the period of possible litigation, and the time when payment is actually made. Disability claims, for example, might be paid over a long period. In some cases, especially those involving environmental loss exposures or health risks, the delay can span several decades. Although this delay increases the uncertainty associated with the loss amount, it does give greater time for reserves to earn interest or investment income.

Data Credibility

After analyzing the four dimensions of a loss exposure, an insurance or a risk management professional then evaluates the credibility of the projections of loss frequency, loss severity, total dollar losses, and timing. The term data credibility refers to the level of confidence that available data can accurately indicate future losses. There are two related issues regarding data credibility that may prevent data from being good indicators of future losses. The first issue is the age of the data and the second issue is whether the data represent actual losses or estimates of losses. Ideally, data used to forecast losses are generated in the same environment that will apply to the projected period. However, the environment for most loss exposures changes, even if those changes happen slowly. The changing environment renders more recent data a more credible predictor of future losses than older data. However, because of delays in reporting and paying of claims, more recent data are not always actual losses, but estimates of what the ultimate losses will be. This leaves insurance and risk management professionals with a dilemma. Use older data, which is accurate but may have been generated in an environment that is substantially different from the period for which they are trying to predict, or use more recent data and sacrifice some accuracy to maintain the integrity of the environment.

How Credible Are Your Data?

There are several factors, both internal and external, that may influence data credibility for an organization. Internally, changes in the way that an organization operates, such as alterations to manufacturing processes or changes in data collection methods, may significantly reduce the credibility of previously collected data. Externally, events such as natural catastrophes, large liability awards, or terrorist attacks not only alter the data that are collected in that time frame, but also may cause shifts in the operating environment that render previously collected data less credible.

Once the projections are made along the four dimensions of loss exposures, the analysis of the loss exposures will often dictate which type of risk control or risk financing measures should be implemented. For example, the pattern shown in Exhibit 3-23 illustrates the expected transportation losses for a large shipper who has been in business for ten years and who has a steadily increasing volume of transportation services. The average losses during the coming years might be projected to fall along the line labeled "projected" and the probable maximum loss might be projected to fall along the line labeled "maximum." Probable minimum loss levels might also be projected, as shown by the "minimum" line. If such projections can be made with a high degree of confidence in the data used for the projections, actual losses would be expected to follow a pattern like the "actual" line on the graph, deviating from the average from one year to the next but in no case exceeding the maximum or falling below the minimum. Because the shipper can reasonably anticipate the degree of uncertainty, it may choose to retain these losses instead of insuring them.

EXHIBIT 3-23

Projected Losses Versus Actual Losses Within Minimum and Maximum Bounds

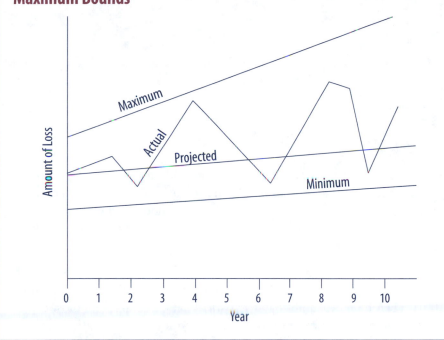

Similarly, Exhibit 3-24 represents products liability losses experienced by a large manufacturer. A few losses usually occur each year. However, in Year 4, almost no losses occurred, whereas, in Year 8, at least one major loss occurred. (The losses in Year 8 are so high that total losses exceeded even maximum projections.) It may have been possible to project these losses to a certain extent at lower levels, but possibilities existed for substantial losses above the expected and maximum levels. It might be disastrous to attempt to finance such losses solely out of the organization's operating budget.

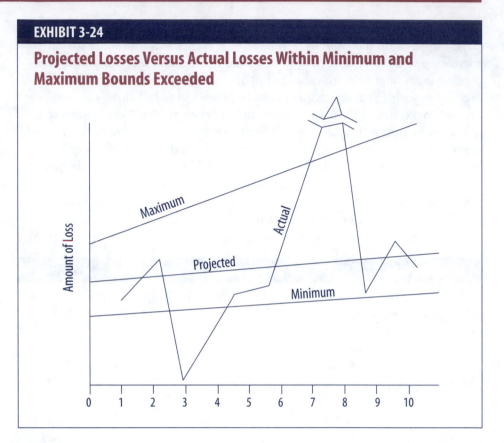

EXHIBIT 3-24

Projected Losses Versus Actual Losses Within Minimum and Maximum Bounds Exceeded

SUMMARY

The first step in the risk management process is identifying all possible loss exposures. Methods and sources of information available to help an organization systematically identify loss exposures include document analysis, compliance reviews, personal inspections, and using expertise within and beyond the organization.

Once loss exposures are identified, they need to be analyzed to determine their probable frequency, severity, total dollar amount, and timing. Loss exposure analysis is based on probability and statistical data analysis. The most common basis of an analysis of current or future loss exposures is information about past losses arising from similar loss exposures. To accurately analyze loss exposures using data on past losses, the data should be relevant, complete, consistent, and organized. Whether data are relevant and complete depends on the loss exposures being analyzed. However, unless sufficient data exist based on similar loss exposures, accurately projecting future losses is not possible. To reflect past patterns and avoid underestimation or overestimation of future losses, loss data must also be consistent in at least two respects: data must be collected on a consistent basis for all recorded losses and data must be expressed in constant dollars to adjust for differences in price levels. Finally, if data are not appropriately organized, identifying patterns and trends that will help to reveal and quantify future loss exposures will be difficult.

Once data have been collected, probability and other statistical analyses can be applied to those data. Probabilities can be developed either from theoretical considerations or from historical data. Theoretical probability is probability that is based on theoretical principles rather than on actual experience. In contrast, empirical probability is probability that is based on actual experience. Although it may be preferable to use theoretical probabilities because of their unchanging nature, theoretical probabilities are not applicable or available in most situations that insurance and risk management professionals are likely to analyze. Consequently, empirical probabilities must be used, even though these probabilities are only estimates.

Probabilities can be used to perform probability analysis, which is a technique for forecasting events based on the assumption that they are governed by an unchanging probability distribution. Probability analysis is particularly effective for projecting losses in organizations that have (1) a substantial volume of data on past losses and (2) fairly stable operations so that (except for price level changes) patterns of past losses presumably will continue in the future. The larger the number of past losses an organization has experienced, the more reliable the forecasts of future losses will be. This is an application of the law of large numbers, which is a mathematical principle stating that as the number of independent events increases, the actual (empirical) frequency (percentage) of each of the possible outcomes more nearly approaches the true (theoretical) probability of that outcome.

Once empirical probabilities are determined, a probability distribution can be constructed. A probability distribution is a presentation (table, chart, or graph) of probability estimates of a particular set of circumstances and of the probability of each possible outcome. A properly constructed probability distribution always contains outcomes that are both mutually exclusive and collectively exhaustive. There are two forms of probability distributions: discrete probability distributions and continuous probability distributions. Discrete probability distributions have a finite number of possible outcomes and are typically used as frequency distributions. Continuous probability distributions have an infinite number of possible outcomes and are typically used as severity distributions.

The insurance or risk management professional can use central tendency and dispersion to compare the characteristics of probability distributions. The central tendency is the single outcome that is the most representative of all possible outcomes included within a probability distribution. The three most widely accepted measures of central tendency are expected value or mean, median, and mode. The expected value is the weighted average of all of the possible outcomes of a probability distribution. The mean is the sum of the values in a data set divided by the number of values. The median is the value at the midpoint of a sequential data set with an odd number of values, or the mean of the two middle values of a sequential data set with an even number of values. The mode is the most frequently occurring outcome in a distribution.

Dispersion, which is the variation between values in a distribution, can be used as well as central tendency to compare the characteristics of probability distributions. The less dispersion around a distribution's expected value, the greater the likelihood that actual results will fall within a given range of that expected value. Two widely used statistical measures of dispersion are standard deviation and the coefficient of variation. The standard deviation is the average of the differences (deviations) between the values in a distribution and the expected value (or mean) of that distribution. The coefficient of variation is a distribution's standard deviation divided by its mean. In comparing two distributions, if both distributions have the same mean (or expected value), then the distribution with the larger standard deviation has the greater variability. If the two distributions have different means (or expected values), the coefficient of variation is often used to compare the two distributions to determine which one has the greater variability relative to its mean (or expected value). The coefficient of variation is also useful in comparing the variability of distributions that have different shapes, means, or standard deviations. The higher the variability within a distribution, the more difficult it is to accurately forecast an individual outcome.

The normal distribution is a probability frequency distribution that, when graphed, generates a bell-shaped curve. This particular probability distribution can help to accurately forecast the variability around some central, average, or expected value and has therefore proven useful in accurately forecasting the variability of many physical phenomena.

The analysis step of the risk management process involves considering the following four dimensions of a loss exposure: loss frequency, loss severity, total dollar losses and timing. Loss frequency is the number of losses (such as fires, auto accidents, or liability claims) that occur within a specific period. Loss severity is the dollar amount of loss for a specific occurrence. To fully analyze a loss exposure, loss frequency and loss severity should be considered jointly. Total dollar losses are the total dollar amounts of losses for all occurrences during a specific period. Timing refers to when losses occur and when loss payments are made (the time interval between loss occurrence and loss payment can be lengthy). Data credibility concerns the level of confidence that available data are capable of being used as accurate indicators of future losses.

CHAPTER NOTES

1.   The CSO 2001 Ultimate Male Composite Mortality Table, available from American Academy of Actuaries. www.actuary.org (accessed March 10, 2006).

2.   Insurance Information Institute, *III Insurance Fact Book 2004* (New York: Insurance Information Institute, 2004), p. 106.

3.   Bureau of Transportation Statistics http://www.bts.gov/publications/national_transportation_statistics/2005/html/table_02_17.html (accessed January 12, 2006).

Appendix A
Standardized Survey/Questionnaire

CONTENTS

CONTENTS SCHEDULE

Schedule number:_____

Location number: _____

Building number: _____

1. Machinery, equipment, tools, and dies:
    a. Replacement cost new _____
    b. Actual cash value _____
    c. Basis for (b)—obtain appraisal if available _____

    _____

    d. Any chattel mortgage? _____
        Name _____
        Address _____

    _____

2. Furniture and fixtures, equipment, and supplies:
    a. Replacement cost new _____
    b. Actual cash value _____
    c. Basis for (b)—obtain appraisal if available _____

    _____

    d. Any chattel mortgage? _____
        Name _____
        Address _____

    _____

3. Improvements and betterments:
    a. Date installed _____
    b. Original cost _____
    c. Replacement cost _____
    d. Actual cash value _____
    e. Describe _____
    f. Obtain appraisal if available _____

4. Stock (raw, in process, and finished):
    a. Maximum—at cost _____   at selling price _____
    b. Minimum—at cost _____   at selling price _____
    c. Average—at cost _____   at selling price _____
    d. Present—at cost _____   at selling price _____
    e. How and when inventoried_____

    _____

    f. Any fluctuations between buildings?_____

5. Property of others for repair, processing, or other purpose (including goods held on consignment): _____

6. Is there any agreement covering your responsibilities for these values?

   _____

7. Property of concessionaires: _____ Consignors: _____

8. Employee's belongings: _____

9. Valuable papers or drawings: _____

   a. Value _____   Reproduction cost _____

   b. Where kept _____

   c. Description _____

10. Value of exhibits—sales office:

11. Describe type, size, and value of signs:

   a. On premises _____

   b. At other locations _____

12. Care, custody, or control problems:

   Property in bailment _____

   Any warehouseperson's legal liability? _____

   Innkeeper's legal liability? _____

13. Water damage and sprinkler leakage exposure, including flood exposure, distance from nearest mass of water and height above water, and percentage of contents value subject to loss:

   _____

14. Earthquake exposure and amount subject to loss: _____

   _____

15. Any unusual cameras, scientific equipment, or valuable instruments?

   _____

16. Any fine arts in office? _____ If so, secure appraisals.

17. Any data processing equipment? _____

   a. If owned, indicate value. _____

       If leased, secure copy of rental agreement. _____

   b. If leased, who is responsible for damage or destruction? _____

       _____

       _____

   c. Cost to replace data stored in destroyed units _____

       _____

   d. Are duplicate cards and tapes maintained? _____
       Where? _____

       _____

   e. Any potential business interruption exposure? _____

     f.   Any use by others? _____ If so, qualifications of senior personnel

          _____

          _____

          _____

     g.   Secure copy of contract form used and estimate liability exposure _____

18. Is stock subject to:

    a.   Consequential loss _____

    b.   Crime loss _____

    c.   Damage by heat or cold _____

19. Animals, if any: _____

20. Crops, if any: _____

Appendix B
Risk Profile

Yes   No

☐   ☐   1. Do you have a brochure or other written material that describes your business operations or products?

☐   ☐   2. Is your business confined to one industry?

☐   ☐   3. Is your business confined to one product?

☐   ☐   4. Do you own buildings?

☐   ☐   5. Do you lease buildings from others?

☐   ☐   6. Do you lease buildings to others?

☐   ☐   7. Do you plan any new construction?

☐   ☐   8. Are your fixed asset values established by certified property appraisers?

☐   ☐   9. Do you own any vacant land?

☐   ☐   10. Are any properties located in potential riot or civil disturbance areas?

☐   ☐   11. Are any properties located in potential flood or earthquake areas?

☐   ☐   12. Do your properties have security alarm systems? (Fire-sprinkler discharge, burglary, smoke detection, etc.)

☐   ☐   13. Are there any unusual fire or explosion hazards in your business operation? (Welding, painting, woodworking, boilers or pressure vessels, etc.)

☐   ☐   14. Do you take a physical count of inventory at least once a year?

☐   ☐   15. Do you lease machinery or equipment other than automotive?

☐   ☐   16. Do you stockpile inventory, either raw or finished?

☐   ☐   17. Could you conveniently report inventory values on a monthly basis?

☐   ☐   18. Do you buy, sell, or have custody of goods or equipment of extremely high value? (Radium, gold, etc.)

☐   ☐   19. Do you use any raw stock, inventory, or equipment that requires substantial lead time to reproduce?

☐   ☐   20. Do you export or import?

☐   ☐   21. Do you buy or sell on consignment?

❏ ❏ 22. Do you buy or sell goods that must be shipped via waterway?

❏ ❏ 23. Do you handle any material with a high damageability factor (i.e., subject to loss from temperature changes, dampness, prolonged shelf life, etc.)?

❏ ❏ 24. Do you handle any goods or merchandise in the form of pairs or sets?

❏ ❏ 25. Are most incoming shipments made via common carrier?

❏ ❏ 26. Are most outgoing shipments made via common carrier?

❏ ❏ 27. Are your purchase terms F.O.B. your location?

❏ ❏ 28. Are your selling terms F.O.B. the customer?

❏ ❏ 29. Do you consider your trade area to be local?

❏ ❏ 30. Do you have goods or equipment located on the premises of subcontractors, bailees, or others?

❏ ❏ 31. Is your business seasonal?

❏ ❏ 32. Does your business generate accounts receivable?

❏ ❏ 33. Do you work with drawings, manuscripts, plans, or other records that, if lost or destroyed, could cause serious loss?

❏ ❏ 34. Do you have or use electronic data processing (EDP) equipment or facilities?

❏ ❏ 35. Do you sell on a contract basis with long-term obligations to your customers?

❏ ❏ 36. Do you buy from any single source suppliers with only one production or warehousing location?

❏ ❏ 37. Does one firm account for more than 1 percent of your gross sales?

❏ ❏ 38. If you suffer a major property loss, would you take every available emergency measure to continue servicing your customers during the period of repair or restoration to avoid losing the market?

❏ ❏ 39. Is your business subject to regulation by federal, state, or local authority?

❏ ❏ 40. If more than one location, are they interdependent?

❏ ❏ 41. Do you have property of others in your custody?

❏ ❏ 42. Does your business regularly call for the execution of written contracts?

❏ ❏ 43. Do you conduct business outside the United States?

❏ ❏ 44. Do you operate a company infirmary or hospital?

❏ ❏ 45. Do you operate an employee restaurant?

❏ ❏ 46. Do you have occasion to use boats or aircraft, other than scheduled commercial?

❏ ❏ 47. Do any employees hold a pilot's license?

❒ ❒ 48. Do you hold meetings or conventions outside the United States?

❒ ❒ 49. Do you subcontract work to others?

❒ ❒ 50. Do you require subcontractors to furnish evidence of liability and workers compensation insurance?

❒ ❒ 51. Do you perform subcontract work for others?

❒ ❒ 52. Are your sales achieved by direct salespeople?

❒ ❒ 53. Do you install or test your products on the customer's premises?

❒ ❒ 54. Do you provide a written warranty as to the use or fitness of the products you sell?

❒ ❒ 55. Do you manufacture or sell finished products?

❒ ❒ 56. Does your operation involve any risks of pollution or contamination?

❒ ❒ 57. Do you sell or provide service directly to the customer?

❒ ❒ 58. Do you lease automotive equipment?

❒ ❒ 59. Do you provide autos for the use of officers or salespeople?

❒ ❒ 60. Do you regularly operate vehicles beyond a fifty-mile radius of their home garages?

❒ ❒ 61. Do you operate any vehicles that are subject to the jurisdiction of the Interstate Commerce Commission?

❒ ❒ 62. Do you normally mortgage new automotive equipment?

❒ ❒ 63. Is it usual to have persons other than employees riding in your vehicles?

❒ ❒ 64. Do you require some form of driver training or participation in safety activities?

❒ ❒ 65. Do you require pre-employment physical examinations?

❒ ❒ 66. Do you routinely check with previous employers to determine the work record of new job applicants?

❒ ❒ 67. Is there an active safety committee to prevent employee injuries?

❒ ❒ 68. Do employees have regular occasion to travel and work in other states?

❒ ❒ 69. Do employees have occasion to work or be aboard ship or on navigable waters?

❒ ❒ 70. Do groups of employees have frequent occasion to travel together?

❒ ❒ 71. Are any employees based outside the United States?

❒ ❒ 72. Has there been an OSHA inspection of your premises?

❒ ❒ 73. Have you established appropriate internal systems and procedures for compliance with OSHA?

❒ ❒ 74. Are there any outstanding citations from OSHA?

❒ ❒ 75. Has your company ever sustained an employee dishonesty loss?

☐   ☐   76. Can your company accumulate more than $1,000 cash at a single location?

☐   ☐   77. Is countersignature required on outgoing checks?

☐   ☐   78. Are incoming checks immediately recorded and stamped for deposit?

☐   ☐   79. Are bank deposits made daily?

☐   ☐   80. Do you use armored car service?

☐   ☐   81. Do you employ outside auditors?

☐   ☐   82. Is your company a public corporation subject to federal and/or state securities and exchange commission(s) (SEC) jurisdiction?

☐   ☐   83. Do you employ security personnel, including guards?

☐   ☐   84. Do you have a need for surety bonds?

☐   ☐   85. Do you advertise nationally?

☐   ☐   86. Do you provide a group medical program for employees?

☐   ☐   87. Do you provide a group life program for employees?

☐   ☐   88. Do you provide a disability income program for employees?

☐   ☐   89. Do you provide a qualified pension or profit-sharing plan for employees?

☐   ☐   90. Are most employees union members?

☐   ☐   91. Have you been doing business with the same insurance broker for more than five years?

☐   ☐   92. Do you have a formal or declared risk management program?

☐   ☐   93. Is each division or location a separate profit center?

☐   ☐   94. Is your company currently paying taxes at a surtax level?

☐   ☐   95. Are the company asset schedules heavily depreciated for book value purposes?

☐   ☐   96. Is your net quick ratio at least two to one?

☐   ☐   97. Is cash flow a problem?

☐   ☐   98. Would a $100,000 uninsured loss be ruinous?

☐   ☐   99. Does the company have substantial investment in research and development?

☐   ☐   100. Is management of a mind to retain risk or "self-insure" when circumstances are favorable?

☐   ☐   101. Is short-term credit available if needed?

☐   ☐   102. Has your company ever sustained any unusually large or unique losses, either insured or uninsured?

Chapter 4

Direct Your Learning

Risk Control

After learning the content of this chapter and completing the corresponding course guide assignment, you should be able to:

- Illustrate the six risk control techniques.

- Explain how an organization can use risk control techniques and measures to achieve the following risk control goals:

  - Implement effective and efficient risk control measures

  - Comply with legal requirements

  - Promote life safety

  - Ensure business continuity

- Explain how an insurance or risk management professional evaluates the effects of proposed risk control measures on loss frequency and loss severity.

- Explain how risk control techniques can be applied to property, liability, personnel, and net income loss exposures.

- Explain how business continuity management is designed to ensure an organization's survival and continued operations.

- Define or describe each of the Key Words and Phrases for this chapter.

Develop Your Perspective

What are the main topics covered in the chapter?

Risk control encompasses techniques and measures that reduce the frequency and/or severity of losses. Although each loss exposure must be evaluated to determine which risk control techniques will best help an organization achieve its goals, many loss exposures within a given category—property, liability, personnel, or net income—warrant application of the same risk control techniques. In addition to risk control, organizations often use business continuity plans to ensure uninterrupted operations following a loss that threatens the organization's survival.

Compare an organization's loss exposures with the risk control techniques that may be used to address them.

- Why is avoidance often an impractical technique?
- How might techniques be combined to address a single loss exposure?

Why is it important to learn about these topics?

By examining an organization's operations, an insurance or risk management professional should be able to recognize actual and potential causes of loss. Using that information, he or she can select effective and efficient risk control techniques and ultimately reduce the organization's cost of risk related to those causes of loss.

Examine the risk control techniques that can reduce loss frequency and loss severity in each loss exposure category.

- Which risk control techniques are most effective in reducing or preventing property loss exposures for each category?
- In what way are net income loss exposures addressed by steps taken to address loss exposures in the other categories?

How can you use what you will learn?

Analyze the losses that have occurred or will likely occur in your organization and the risk control techniques that could be used to control them.

- What changes would you make to the risk control techniques that are currently being used by your organization to prevent or reduce losses?
- How might a business continuity plan promote your organization's recovery following a significant loss?

Chapter 4
Risk Control

The third step in the risk management process is examining the feasibility of risk management alternatives. This step facilitates the subsequent steps of selecting and implementing the appropriate risk management techniques. To make these selection decisions, an insurance or risk management professional must determine which risk management techniques most effectively address an organization's loss exposures. All risk management techniques fall into one of two categories: risk control or risk financing. The focus of this chapter is on risk control.

An insurance or risk management professional uses risk control techniques to reduce loss frequency and/or loss severity or to make losses more predictable. The six risk control techniques are avoidance, loss prevention, loss reduction, separation, duplication, and diversification. Multiple risk control measures may be used to implement a given technique.

Risk control goals are designed to support the risk management program goals, which in turn support the individual's or organization's goals. To that end, risk control techniques must be effective and efficient, comply with legal requirements, assist in promoting life safety, and that ensure that a business can retain continuity during and immediately following a loss.

Not every risk control technique can successfully be applied to every type of loss exposure. Therefore, each loss exposure must be evaluated to determine which risk control techniques will best help an organization achieve its goals However, many loss exposures within a given category—property, liability, personnel, or net income—warrant application of the same risk control techniques.

RISK CONTROL TECHNIQUES

Risk control is a conscious act or decision not to act that reduces the frequency and/or severity of losses or makes losses more predictable. Risk control techniques can be classified into one of the following six broad categories:

1. Avoidance
2. Loss prevention
3. Loss reduction
4. Separation
5. Duplication
6. Diversification

Each of these six categories aims to reduce either loss frequency or severity, or make losses more predictable, as shown in Exhibit 4-1.

Risk control
A conscious act or decision not to act that reduces the frequency and/or severity of losses or makes losses more predictable.

EXHIBIT 4-1

Target of Risk Control Techniques

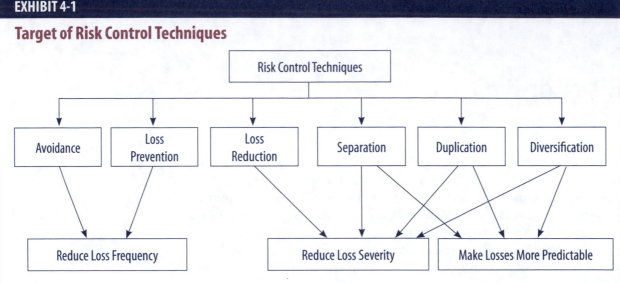

Avoidance

The most effective way of managing any loss exposure is to avoid the exposure completely. If a loss exposure has successfully been avoided, then the probability of loss from that loss exposure is zero. **Avoidance** is a risk control technique that involves ceasing or never undertaking an activity so that the possibility of a future loss occurring from that activity is eliminated. The aim of avoidance is not just to reduce loss frequency, but to eliminate any possibility of loss. Avoidance should be considered when the expected value of the losses from an activity outweighs the expected benefits of that activity. For example, a toy manufacturer might decide not to produce a particular toy because the potential cost of products liability claims would outweigh the expected revenue from sales, no matter how cautious the manufacturer might be in producing and marketing the toy.

Avoidance can either be proactive or reactive. Proactive avoidance seeks to avoid a loss exposure before it exists, such as when a medical student chooses not to become an obstetrician because he or she wants to avoid the large professional liability (malpractice) claims associated with that specialty. Reactive avoidance seeks to eliminate a loss exposure that already exists, such as when manufacturers of hand-held hair dryers stopped using asbestos insulation in their dryers once the cancer-causing properties of asbestos became known. Reactive avoidance, that is, discontinuing an existing activity, avoids loss exposures from future activities but does not eliminate loss exposures from past activities. For example, the hair dryer manufacturer may avoid claims from consumers who purchase the hair dryers produced after asbestos is no longer used, but would remain legally liable for associated harm suffered by prior consumers.

Because loss exposures do not exist in a vacuum, avoiding one loss exposure can create or enhance another. For example if an individual is concerned about dying in an airplane crash, he or she can choose not to travel by air. However, by avoiding air travel, the individual increases the loss exposure to injury or death from the other means of transport chosen in its place.

Complete avoidance is not the most common risk control technique and is typically neither feasible nor desirable. Loss exposures arise from activities that are essential to individuals and to organizations. Therefore, it is not possible to avoid these core activities. For instance, if a manufacturer's principle product is motorcycle safety helmets, it could not stop selling them in order to avoid liability loss exposures. Similarly, an organization cannot decline to occupy office space in order to avoid property loss exposures. Nonfinancial concerns also can render avoidance impossible. For example, a municipality cannot arbitrarily stop providing police protection or water to its inhabitants in order to avoid the associated liability loss exposures.

Loss Prevention

Loss prevention is a risk control technique that reduces the frequency of a particular loss. For instance, pressure relief valves on a boiler are intended to prevent explosions by keeping the pressure in the boiler from reaching an unsafe level. The valve is a type of loss prevention, not avoidance, because a boiler explosion is still possible, just not as likely.

Loss prevention
A risk control technique that reduces the frequency of a particular loss.

To illustrate a loss prevention measure, consider a hypothetical manufacturing company, Etchley Manufacturing (Etchley). Etchley has 500 employees working at a single plant. The workers' compensation loss history for this plant shows a significant number of back injuries. Etchley is considering hiring a back injury consultant to host a series of educational seminars for its employees. The consultant estimates that, based on the results of his past seminar series, Etchley will see a 20 percent reduction in the frequency of back injuries. The chart in Exhibit 4-2 shows the frequency distributions of back injuries both with and without the educational seminar in order to demonstrate the estimated effect of this loss prevention measure. The frequency distribution without the educational seminar has a mean of 30, a standard deviation of 5.48 and a coefficient of variation of 0.1827. The frequency distribution with the educational seminar has a lower mean of 24, a lower standard deviation of 4.20, and a lower coefficient of variation of 0.1750. Based on these figures, not only would the consultant's educational seminar reduce the expected frequency of back injuries, it would also reduce their variability from year to year, which would allow Etchley to budget more effectively for those injuries that do occur.

EXHIBIT 4-2

Example of a Loss Prevention Measure: Etchley Manufacturing

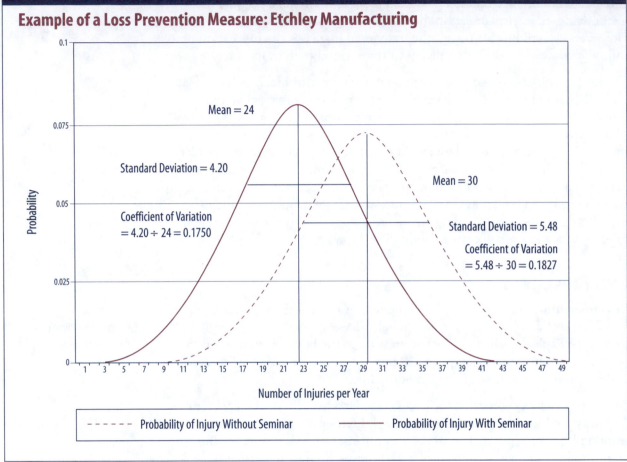

Loss prevention measures that reduce frequency may also affect the loss severity of the specified loss exposures. For example, as a result of the educational seminar, both the number of back injuries that occur and their severity may be reduced.

Generally, a loss prevention measure is implemented before a loss occurs in order to break the sequence of events that leads to the loss. Because of the close link between causes of loss and loss prevention, determining effective loss prevention measures usually requires carefully studying how particular losses are caused. For example, according to Heinrich's domino theory, as described in the following text box, most work-related injuries result from a chain of events that includes an unsafe act or an unsafe condition. Workplace safety efforts have therefore focused on trying to eliminate specific unsafe acts or unsafe conditions to break this chain of events and prevent injuries.

As is the case with avoidance, a loss prevention measure may reduce the frequency of losses from one loss exposure but increase the frequency or severity of losses from other loss exposures. For example, a jewelry store that installs security bars on its windows would likely reduce the frequency of theft. These same bars, however, might make it impossible for firefighters to enter the building through the windows or might trap employees inside the store if a fire occurs.

Heinrich's Domino Theory

In 1931, H. W. Heinrich published the first thorough analysis of work injuries caused by accidents.[1] He determined that work injuries were actually a result of a series of unsafe acts and/or mechanical or physical hazards (dominoes) that occurred in a specific order. Furthermore, he concluded that if any one of these dominoes could be removed from the chain, the work injury could be prevented. Heinrich's theory included the following five dominoes: (1) social environment and ancestry, (2) the fault of persons, (3) personal or mechanical hazards, (4) the accident, and (5) the injury. For example, if risk control measures could minimize mechanical hazards, the domino chain would be broken and fewer injuries would occur. Many of the principles that Heinrich outlined in his publication became the basis of modern risk control measures.

Loss Reduction

Loss reduction is a risk control technique that reduces the severity of a particular loss. Automatic sprinkler systems are a classic example of a loss reduction measure; sprinklers do not prevent fires from starting, but can limit or extinguish fires that have already started. Some loss reduction measures can prevent losses as well as reduce them. For example, using burglar alarms is generally considered a loss reduction measure because the alarm is activated only when a burglary occurs. However, because burglar alarms also act as a deterrent, they can prevent loss as well as reduce it.

Loss reduction
A risk control technique that reduces the severity of a particular loss.

As an example of a loss reduction measure, assume the consultant Etchley hired to conduct the educational seminars suggested that Etchley provide back braces for all of its employees because back braces help prevent back injuries and reduce the severity of back injuries that do occur. Exhibit 4-3 contains the original severity distribution for Etchley and the new severity distribution with all employees using back braces. As with most severity distributions, the severity distribution for back injuries is not symmetrical, but skewed. Most back injuries are grouped in the left-hand portion of the distribution (lower severity values), with some very serious injuries grouped as outliers to the right. This positively skewed distribution pulls the tail of the distribution to the right and increases the mean.

Note the difference between the means and modes with and without back braces. The use of back braces lowers the average severity (mean) by $13,792 ($29,800 − $14,008 = $13,792) as well as the severity of the injuries that would occur most often (mode) by $5,000 ($8,000 − $3,000 = $5,000).

The two broad categories of loss reduction measures are pre-loss measures, applied before the loss occurs, and post-loss measures, applied after the loss

EXHIBIT 4-3

Example of a Loss Reduction Measure: Etchley Manufacturing

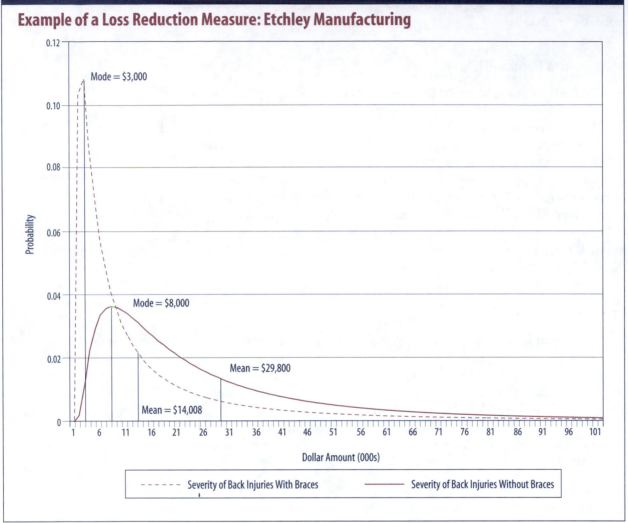

occurs. The aim of pre-loss measures is to reduce the amount or extent of property damaged and the number of people injured or the extent of injury incurred from a single event. For example, Etchley's use of back braces is a pre-loss measure erecting firewalls to limit the amount of damage and danger that can be caused by a single fire is also a pre-loss measure.

Post-loss measures typically focus on emergency procedures, salvage operations, rehabilitation activities, public relations, or legal defenses to halt the spread or to counter the effects of loss. An example of a post-loss loss reduction measure is to temporarily move an organization's operations to a new location following a fire so that operations can continue while the main premises is repaired, thus reducing loss severity.

Disaster recovery plan
A plan for backup procedures, emergency response, and post-disaster recovery to ensure that critical resources are available to facilitate the continuity of operations in an emergency situation.

Disaster recovery planning is a specialized aspect of loss reduction. A **disaster recovery plan**, also called catastrophe recovery plan or contingency plan, is a plan for backup procedures, emergency response, and post-disaster recovery to ensure that critical resources are available to facilitate the continuity of operations in an emergency situation. For many organizations, disaster recovery planning is especially important in addressing the risks associated with those systems without which the organization could not function. Disaster recovery plans typically focus on property loss exposures and natural hazards, not on the broader array of risks and associated loss exposures that may also threaten an organization's survival.

Separation

Separation is a risk control technique that disperses a particular asset or activity over several locations and regularly relies on that asset or activity as part of the organization's working resources. Separation is appropriate if an organization can operate with only a portion of these separate units left intact. If one unit suffers a total loss, the portion of the activity or assets at the other unit must be sufficient for operations to continue. Otherwise, separation has not achieved its risk control goal.

Separation
A risk control technique that disperses a particular asset or activity over several locations and regularly relies on that asset or activity as part of the organization's working resources.

Separation is rarely undertaken for its own sake, but is usually a byproduct of another management decision. For example, few organizations build a second warehouse simply to reduce the potential loss severity at the first warehouse. However, if an organization is considering constructing a second warehouse to expand production, the risk control benefits of a second warehouse could support the argument in favor of the expansion.

The intent of separation is to reduce the severity of an individual loss at a single location. However, by creating multiple locations, separation most likely increases loss frequency. For example, using two distantly separated warehouses instead of one reduces the maximum possible loss at each individual location, but increases loss frequency, because two units are exposed to loss. The insurance or risk management professional should be confident that the benefits of reduced loss severity from separation more than offset the increased loss frequency.

As an example of separation, consider a hypothetical organization, Ryedale Shipping Company (Ryedale), which has to decide between the following options for shipping its clients' products:

- Option A—use one central warehouse
- Option B—use two warehouses

Under Option A, the central warehouse would contain $500,000 worth of merchandise and have a 5 percent chance of experiencing a fire in any given year. For simplicity, assume that only one fire per year can occur and that if a fire occurs, all of the warehouse's merchandise is completely destroyed. Under Option B, the two warehouses would each have the same probability of a fire (5 percent), but would each house $250,000 worth of merchandise. For simplicity, assume that the two locations are independent of one another.

Exhibit 4-4 shows the severity distributions for these options and how the expected loss is calculated. Under Option A, the severity distribution is just the single outcome of a loss of $500,000. There are two possible outcomes in any one year: a fire at the central warehouse or no fire at the central warehouse. Given a probability of fire of .05 (5 percent), Ryedale would expect a $500,000 loss 5 percent of the time and a $0 loss 95 percent of the time. Therefore, the expected loss in any given year is $25,000 (.05 × $500,000 = $25,000).

EXHIBIT 4-4

Example of Separation: Ryedale Shipping Company

Option A

	Central Warehouse
Value of merchandise	$500,000
Probability of a fire	.05

Severity distribution (maximum loss in a fire)	**$500,000**
Probability of a fire in the central warehouse	.05
Expected loss (.05 × $500,000)	**$25,000**

Option B

	Warehouse 1 (W1)	Warehouse 2 (W2)
Value of merchandise	$250,000	$250,000
Probability of a fire	.05	.05

Severity distribution (maximum loss in a fire)	**$250,000**
Probability of fire at W1 and fire at W2 (.05 × .05)	.0025
Probability of fire in W1 but not W2 [.05 × (1 − .05)]	.0475
Probability of fire in W2 but not in W1 [(1 − .05) × .05]	.0475
Probability of one fire in either W1 or W2 (.0475 + .0475)	.095
Probability of zero fires (1 − .05) × (1 − .05)	.9025
Expected loss [(.0025 × $500,000) + (.095 × $250,000)]	**$25,000**

Under Option B, only $250,000 worth of merchandise is at risk in any one fire. Therefore, having two warehouses reduces Ryedale's severity distribution from $500,000 to $250,000. Increasing the number of warehouses increases the number of possible outcomes. Either there will be no fire at either location, there will be a fire at the first warehouse (W1) but not at the second warehouse (W2), there will be a fire at W2 but not at W1, or there will be a fire at both W1 and W2. The probability of each of these possible outcomes is shown in Exhibit 4-4. Given a probability of fire of .05, Ryedale would expect a $500,000 loss (fires at both W1 and W2) 0.25 percent of the time, a $250,000 loss at W1 4.75 percent of the time, a $250,000 loss at W2 4.75 percent of the time, and a $0 loss 90.25 percent of the time. The expected loss remains $25,000, but the likelihood of suffering a $500,000 loss has fallen from 5 percent to 0.25 percent, whereas the likelihood of suffering a $250,000 loss has increased from 0 percent to 9.5 percent. This results in a total claims distribution for Option B that has a lower standard deviation than the total claims distribution for Option A. The standard deviation of losses under Option A would be $108,973, and the standard deviation for Option B falls to $77,055.18, which makes losses under Option B more predictable than Option A.

Duplication

Duplication is a risk control technique that uses backups, spares, or copies of critical property, information, or capabilities and keeps them in reserve. Examples of duplication include maintaining a second set of records, spare parts for machinery, and copies of keys. Duplication differs from separation in that duplicates are not a part of an organization's daily working resources. For example, an organization may make arrangements with more than one supplier of a key raw material. That alternative supplier would be used only if a primary supplier could not provide needed materials because of, for example, a major fire at the primary supplier's plant. Duplication is only appropriate if an entire asset or activity is so important that the consequence of its loss justifies the expense and time of maintaining the duplicate.

Like separation, duplication can reduce an organization's dependence on a single asset, activity, or person, making individual losses smaller by reducing the severity of a loss that may occur. Duplication is not as likely as separation to increase loss frequency because the duplicated unit is kept in reserve and is not as exposed to loss as is the primary unit. For example, a duplicate vehicle that is ordinarily kept garaged is not as vulnerable to highway accidents as the primary vehicle. Duplication is likely to reduce the average expected annual loss from a given loss exposure because it reduces loss severity without increasing loss frequency. Similar to separation, duplication can also make losses more predictable by reducing the dispersion of potential losses.

There are several measures an organization can implement that are similar to duplication and that incorporate nonowned assets. One option is for an organization to contractually arrange for the acquisition of equipment or facilities in the event that a loss occurs. For example, a plant that manufactures aircraft can pay an annual fee for a contract in which a supplier agrees to deliver within thirty days the hydraulic tools and scaffolding required to continue operations in a rented hanger if the manufacturer's assembly plant incurs a loss. In this way, the aircraft manufacturer can continue operations with minimal business interruptions and avoid the expense associated with the ownership or storage of the duplicate equipment.

Diversification

Diversification is a risk control technique that spreads loss exposures over numerous projects, products, markets, or regions. Although diversification

Duplication
A risk control technique that uses backups, spares, or copies of critical property, information, or capabilities and keeps them in reserve.

Diversification
A risk control technique that spreads loss exposures over numerous projects, products, markets, or regions.

closely resembles the risk control techniques of duplication and separation, it is more commonly applied to managing business risks, rather than hazard risks.

Organizations engage in diversification of loss exposures when they provide a variety of products and services that are used by a range of customers. For example, an insurer might diversify its exposures by type of business and geographically by selling both personal and commercial insurance and both property-casualty and life insurance in multiple regions. Investors employ diversification when they allocate their assets among a mix of stocks and bonds from companies in different industry sectors. An investor might diversify investments by purchasing stock in a bank and stock in a pharmaceutical manufacturer. Because these are unrelated industries, the investor hopes that any losses from one stock might be more than offset by profits from another.

As with separation and duplication, diversification has the potential to increase loss frequency, because the organization has increased the number of loss exposures. However, by spreading risk, diversification reduces loss severity and can make losses more predictable.

Organizations implement risk control techniques and the measures that support them to address one or more specific loss exposures. Each measure should be tailored to the specific loss exposure under consideration. Furthermore, the application of risk control techniques should serve to support an organization's overall goals, pre-loss and post-loss risk management goals, and risk control goals.

RISK CONTROL GOALS

An insurance or risk management professional can use risk control techniques to prevent losses, reduce the severity of losses that do occur, and speed recovery following a loss. Through the implementation of specific risk control measures such as theft prevention devices or fire suppression systems, risk control preserves resources for individuals, organizations, and society. The persons and property protected through effective risk control either remain unharmed and productive or they are returned to productivity as quickly as possible.

Individuals and organizations have a variety of goals when implementing a risk management program. Just as the risk management program goals are designed to support the overall organizational goals, risk control goals are designed to support the risk management program goals, as outlined in Exhibit 4-5.

It is the risk management professional's responsibility to apply the risk control techniques through specific risk control measures that most effectively and efficiently support the risk management program and thereby help the organization achieve its goals. To this end, risk control techniques are used to support the following risk control goals: implement effective and efficient risk control measures, comply with legal requirements, promote life safety, and ensure business continuity.

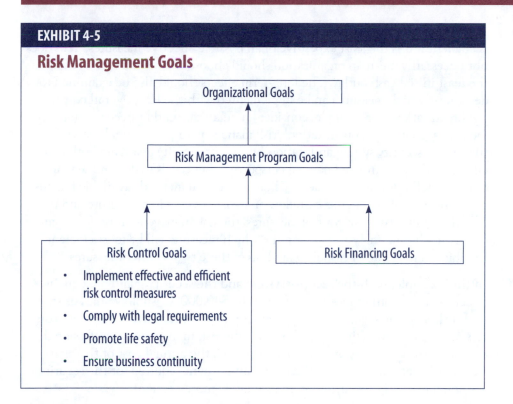

EXHIBIT 4-5

Risk Management Goals

Risk Control Goals
- Implement effective and efficient risk control measures
- Comply with legal requirements
- Promote life safety
- Ensure business continuity

Risk Financing Goals

Organizational Goals

Risk Management Program Goals

Implement Effective and Efficient Risk Control Measures

An individual or organization generally undertakes risk control measures that have a positive financial effect. Most risk control measures are implemented at a cost to the individual or organization. These costs are typically cash outlays, like the costs of the losses they aim to control, and are considered part of the cost of risk. However, so that risk control does not unduly increase the cost of risk, one of the goals of risk control is to employ measures that are effective and efficient.

A measure is effective if it enables an organization to achieve desired risk management goals, such as the pre-loss goals of economy of operations, tolerable uncertainty, legality, and social responsibility or the post-loss goals of survival, continuity of operations, profitability, earnings stability, growth, and social responsibility. Some risk control measures will be more effective than others. For example, both a sprinkler system and employees patrolling a warehouse with fire extinguishers may be effective risk control measures. However, a sophisticated sprinkler system with heat and flame sensors will likely be more effective than employee patrols. The effectiveness of various risk control measures is often based on both quantitative and qualitative standards. For example, determining whether measures to ensure worker safety are effective may rely not only on statistics regarding workers' compensation claims, but also on employee satisfaction with the measures taken.

As well as being effective, a risk control measure should be efficient. A measure is efficient if it is the least expensive of all possible effective measures. This does not necessarily mean an organization should choose the measure that entails the least initial cash outlay. The long-term effects should also be examined to determine which measure can be implemented with the least overall cost to the organization. For example, consider an organization that needs to improve security at night. The organization's risk management professional determines that a new security system and stationing a night security guard are both equally effective measures from a financial perspective, but needs to determine which of these methods is most efficient. There are several methods available for this comparison, one of which is cash flow analysis. Given a loss exposure and the effective alternative risk control measures, the risk management professional can use cash flow analysis to determine which measure will be most efficient. Exhibit 4-6 illustrates a cash flow analysis of these two security measures.

In this example, both the security system and the security guard are equally effective; they both reduce annual losses by $40,000. Cash flow analysis shows that although the security system requires a larger initial investment, it costs less to operate and maintain each year. If the risk management professional examines these choices over a ten-year period, the annual cost of the security guard eventually eclipses the initial investment required for the security system, making the security system ultimately more efficient.

The major advantage of using cash flow analysis for selecting risk control measures is that it provides the same basis of comparison for all value-maximizing decisions and thereby helps the organization achieve its value-maximization goal. It is also very useful for not-for-profit organizations that want to increase their efficiency by reducing unnecessary expenditures on risk control.

The disadvantages of cash flow analysis include the weaknesses of the assumptions that often must be made to conduct the analysis and the difficulty of accurately estimating future cash flows. Moreover, cash flow analysis works on the assumption that the organization's only goal is to maximize its economic value and does not consider any of the nonfinancial goals or selection criteria. For example, legality and social responsibility goals are not directly considered in cash flow analysis.

Comply With Legal Requirements

An organization may be required to implement certain risk control measures if a state or federal statute mandates specific safety measures, such as protecting employees from disability or safeguarding the environment against pollution. These risk control measures are a means of implementing the risk control techniques of avoidance, loss prevention, and loss reduction and they also support the risk management program pre-loss goal of legality. The cost of adhering to legal requirements becomes part of the cost of risk.

EXHIBIT 4-6

Using Cash Flow Analysis to Determine the More Efficient of Two Effective Risk Control Measures

Security System

NCF Calculations

Reduction in annual losses:		$40,000
Less: Differential cash expenses		
System annual monitoring fees	$ 4,200	
System annual maintenance expenses	$ 400	($ 4,600)
Before-tax NCF:		$35,400

> Annual savings by installing a security system

NCF Analysis

Factors:

Initial investment	$200,000
Life of system	10 years
Differential annual cash flow	$ 35,400
Minimum acceptable rate of return (annual)	10.00%

> The system's initial cost must be considered in cash flow analysis.

> To discount cash flows for ten years at 10 percent discount rate, the equivalent net present value factor is 6.145.

NPV Analysis

PV of differential annual cash flow	
($35,400 × 6.145)	$217,533
Less: PV of initial investment	($200,000)
Net present value:	$ 17,533

> Installing a security system would be effective, in that the cost of the risk control measure is less than the savings in prevented losses. In present value terms, the security system would save the organization over $17,000.

Security Guard

NCF Calculations

Reduction in annual losses:		$40,000
Less: Differential cash expenses		
Security guard salary and benefits	$ 38,000	($38,000)
Before-tax NCF:		$2,000

> Annual savings by hiring security guard.

NCF Analysis

Factors:

Initial investment	$0
Life of system	10 years
Differential annual cash flow	$ 2,000
Minimum acceptable rate of return (annual)	10.00%

> The security guard does not have upfront costs like the cost of the security system.

NPV Analysis

PV of differential annual cash flow	
($2,000 × 6.145)	$ 12,290
Less: PV of initial investment	($0)
Net present value:	$ 12,290

> Hiring a security guard would be effective, in that the cost of the risk control measure is less than the savings in prevented losses. However, it is not as efficient as the security system.

Many laws and regulations require organizations to implement specific risk control measures. For example, the fire safety code mandates certain fire safety procedures; environmental regulations govern the nonuse or use and disposal of toxic material; workers' compensation laws require employers to provide a safe working environment; and disability laws require organizations to make certain accommodations for people with disabilities. All of these examples would include risk control measures that support avoidance (ban of some toxic substances), loss prevention (safety procedures for machinery usage), and loss reduction (fire suppression systems). Some laws and regulations are amended fairly frequently, so it is important for the risk management professional to stay apprised of these amendments. For example, the privacy issues and enforcement regulations regarding the Health Insurance Portability and Accountability Act of 1996 (HIPAA) continue to evolve. Failure to comply with legal requirements exposes the individual or organization to additional fines, sanctions, or liability.

Promote Life Safety

Life safety

The portion of fire safety that focuses on the minimum building design, construction, operation, and maintenance requirements necessary to assure occupants of a safe exit from the burning portion of the building.

Safeguarding people from fire has grown in importance from a risk control perspective because of the emphasis legislative bodies have placed on health and safety issues and because of the increasing frequency and severity of liability claims. In the context of risk control, **life safety** is the portion of fire safety that focuses on the minimum building design, construction, operation, and maintenance requirements necessary to assure occupants of a safe exit from the burning portion of the building. Life safety must consider both the characteristics of the people who occupy buildings and the types of building occupancies (such as residences, office work, or manufacturing). Consideration of the general characteristics of both building occupants and occupancy has led to the development of specific fire safety standards for buildings. These standards are codified in the *Life Safety Code®* published by the National Fire Protection Association (NFPA), and cover the risk control techniques of avoidance, loss prevention, and loss control.[2]

Promoting life safety can be expanded beyond fire safety to incorporate any cause of loss that threatens the life of employees or customers. Therefore, organizations must be concerned about other causes of loss, such as product safety, building collapse, industrial accidents, environmental pollution, or exposure to hazardous activities that may create the possibility of injury or death. For example, a toy manufacturer should have an established product recall procedure in the event that a safety issue arises with one of its toys. Alternatively, a car manufacturer should install appropriate safety guards on machinery, equip employees with appropriate safety gear, and give employees sufficient training to enable them to carry out their jobs in reasonable safety.

Ensure Business Continuity

In addition to implementing effective and efficient measures, complying with legal requirements, and promoting safety, risk control should aim to ensure business continuity—that is, minimize or eliminate significant business interruptions, whatever their cause. Business continuity is designed to meet both the primary risk management program post-loss goal of survival and the post-loss goal of continuity of operations.

Loss exposures and their associated losses vary widely by industry, location, and organization. Some organizations are more susceptible to terrorism, some are more susceptible to information technology problems, and others are more susceptible to natural disasters. Because each organization is unique in its potential losses, each must also be unique in its application of risk control measures to promote business continuity. For example, there are many causes of loss, such as fire, theft or vandalism, that can be prevented through appropriate loss prevention measures. If left untreated, these causes of loss could easily result in a business interruption. However, there are other causes of loss (including natural disasters such as hurricanes or earthquakes) that an organization may not be able to avoid or prevent. Nonetheless, the organization may be able to minimize any business interruption that could occur during and after a natural disaster through appropriate loss reduction techniques.

In working to achieve these risk control goals, an insurance or risk management professional needs to assess how he or she can use risk control techniques (and the measures that support those techniques) to reduce loss frequency and losses severity.

LOSS FREQUENCY AND LOSS SEVERITY

To properly evaluate the effect of risk control measures on loss frequency and loss severity, the insurance or risk management professional should conduct an analysis of the effect that each control measure will have both on the specified loss exposure and on any other loss exposures. A particular risk control measure may reduce the loss frequency of the specified loss exposure but increase its loss severity. Conversely, a risk control measure could reduce loss severity but increase loss frequency. For example, an organization may be concerned that a fire or flood at its only warehouse would destroy its entire inventory. Accordingly, the organization may choose to acquire a second warehouse in a different location. Although this separation decreases the loss severity at each of the two warehouses, it doubles the loss exposure units, which may increase the frequency of loss occurrence for the organization. Exhibit 4-7 shows the inverse relationship between loss frequency and loss severity as the number of exposure units increases. In this exhibit, as the number of warehouses increases from one to four, the expected severity at each location declines, while the potential frequency increases.

EXHIBIT 4-7

Inverse Relationship Between Loss Frequency and Loss Severity

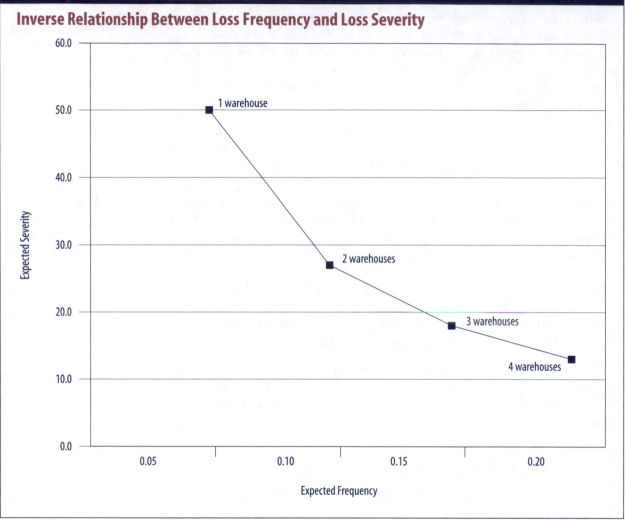

In addition to this inverse relationship between loss frequency and loss severity, a measure to control one kind of loss exposure may alter the frequency and severity of other loss exposures. When a risk control measure has implications outside of its intended purpose in this way, it is described as having externalities. Externalities can be either positive or negative. A positive externality exists when a risk control measure implemented for one particular loss exposure reduces the loss frequency or loss severity related to another loss exposure. For example, an organization may institute random drug testing to lower the frequency of employee injuries. The organization may also find a positive externality exists, such as that drug testing also reduces the incidences of employee theft. Conversely, if a risk control measure increases loss frequency or loss severity for another loss exposure, it is described as having a negative externality. For example, if an organization installs a sprinkler system, the sprinkler system can reduce losses resulting from fire, but it has a negative externality in that it might also increase losses caused by sprinkler leakage.

The existence of negative externalities does not necessarily rule out a risk control measure. For example, if the expected damage (losses) from sprinkler leakage were less than the expected damages resulting from fire, the danger of sprinkler leakage should not necessarily prevent the organization from installing a sprinkler system.

Insurance and risk management professionals need to examine all changes in loss frequency and loss severity of not only the targeted loss exposure, but also any loss exposure that may have its frequency or severity altered by the risk control measure under consideration, to ensure that the result of implementing a risk control measure is that the organization's overall expected losses are reduced.

The various risk control techniques that a risk management professional may examine can be divided into particular types, each of which can be implemented through a variety of risk control measures.

APPLICATION OF RISK CONTROL TECHNIQUES

Not all of the six risk control techniques are applicable to every loss exposure. However, many loss exposures within a given category of loss exposures—property, liability, personnel, and net income—warrant application of the same risk control techniques.

Property Loss Exposures

Property loss exposures are generally divided into two categories—tangible property loss exposures (covering real property, such as land and buildings, and tangible personal property) and intangible property loss exposures. The risk control techniques that are most applicable to property loss exposures vary based on the type of property as well as the cause of loss threatening the property. For example, risk control measures to prevent or reduce damage caused by fire are substantially different than those to prevent or reduce damage resulting from theft. Because of the broad array of property loss exposures and causes of loss, all of the categories of risk control techniques can be applied in some way to property loss exposures. Insurance producers and underwriters commonly examine commercial property loss exposures based on construction, occupancy, protection, and environment (known by their acronym—COPE). Each factor inherent in COPE can be addressed through the application of risk control techniques, as demonstrated in Exhibit 4-8.

Liability Loss Exposures

To implement effective risk control for liability losses, individuals and organizations need to understand the bases of legal liability. Legal actions can be brought under torts, contracts, or statutes. The liability loss exposures facing most individuals and organizations are presented in Exhibit 4-9. Three risk control techniques can be used to control liability losses: (1) avoid the activity that creates the liability loss exposure, (2) decrease the likelihood of the losses occurring (loss prevention), and (3) if a loss does occur, minimize its effect on the organization (loss reduction). The other risk control techniques of separation, duplication, and diversification are not as effective in treating liability loss exposures.

EXHIBIT 4-8

Application of Risk Control Techniques to COPE

COPE Factor	Description	Risk Control Technique
Construction	Construction materials and techniques range from simple frame construction (least resistive to fire) to fire-resistive construction (most fire resistive), with a wide variety of choices in between.	Loss prevention and loss reduction through construction techniques designed to minimize frequency and severity of losses.
Occupancy	There are nine different classifications of occupancy, ranging from residential to industrial, with each classification presenting its own unique risk to real property.	Loss reduction through safety training and emergency evacuation procedures.
Protection	There are two categories of protection, internal or external. Internal protection refers to what the organization does to protect its own real property. External protection refers to what fire departments and other public facilities do to safeguard the general public, including the organization, from fire and other causes of loss.	Two loss reduction measures used for internal fire protection are fire detection and suppression. External protection could involve security systems and security guard services.
External Environment	A building is exposed to many hazards from outside sources, such as neighboring buildings. COPE factors are used to evaluate neighboring buildings' fire risk and the risk of transfer to the organization's real property.	The loss prevention and reduction measures may include relocation away from external hazards and fire protection to the exterior of the property to prevent or reduce the likelihood of fire from another building to the organization's property.

Although avoidance is sometimes an effective risk control technique for liability losses, particularly proactive avoidance, it is often either not practicable or not possible to avoid undertaking the activity or activities that can lead to liability losses. Therefore, loss prevention and loss reduction measures are more typically used. The most common loss prevention measure is to control hazards (conditions that increase loss frequency or severity). Limiting the number or magnitude of hazards surrounding the loss exposures can prevent losses from occurring. For example, to limit liability claims arising from employee or customer injuries that occur in a parking lot, an organization could implement loss prevention measures such as clearing ice and snow, providing adequate signs, repairing potholes and cracks in walking surfaces, or conducting periodic inspections.

EXHIBIT 4-9

Typical Liability Loss Exposures

Liability Loss Exposure	Description
Premises liability	Created by having visitors to an organization's premises.
Operations liability	Created by conducting operations on an organization's premises.
Products liability	Created by manufacturing products.
Workers' compensation liability	Created by state statutes to cover employees for work-related injuries and illnesses.
Professional liability	Created by common law, which imposes a higher duty of care on professionals. A professional owes a duty of care to refrain from an action that carries an undue risk of causing harm to someone else.
Completed operations liability	Created because organization is responsible for bodily injury or property damage caused by completed work when the work is completed away from the organization's premises.
Automobile liability	Created because drivers and owners of autos owe a duty to others to use their autos in a reasonable, prudent manner and to exercise care for the safety of others.
Watercraft liability	Created because drivers and owners of watercraft owe a duty to others to use their watercraft in a reasonable, prudent manner and to exercise care for the safety of others.
Management liability	Created by the various duties that those in positions of trust owe to those they serve. Directors, officers, and managers hold such positions.

Once a liability loss has occurred, individuals and organizations can implement loss reduction measures to reduce the severity of the liability loss. These measures can include the following:

- Consulting with an attorney for guidance through the legal steps necessary to resolve liability claims.
- Properly responding to the liability claim and to the claimant in order to avoid feelings of ill-will that may increase the claimant's demands.

- Participating in alternative dispute resolution. Litigation is a long and costly process. Some forms of alternative dispute resolution, such as mediation or arbitration, often help to resolve liability claims more quickly and more economically than litigation.

Personnel Loss Exposures

Personnel loss exposures are unavoidable, because all organizations have key employees. These loss exposures can arise from events both inside and outside the workplace. Organizations generally incorporate three different risk control techniques when addressing personnel loss exposures: loss prevention, loss reduction, and separation.

The risk control measures that organizations find most cost-effective are those that can be instituted in the workplace. Therefore, most risk control measures regarding personnel loss exposures involve preventing and reducing workplace injury and illness. Loss prevention measures used to control work-related injury and illnesses typically involve education, training, and safety measures. Loss reduction measures include emergency response training and rehabilitation management. Although all organizations must comply with federally mandated safety measures issued by OSHA (the Occupational Safety and Health Administration), additional training and safety precautions are often cost-effective.

An organization may attempt to prevent personnel causes of loss that occur outside the workplace by controlling key employees' activities through employment contracts; for example, placing restrictions on hazardous activities such as sky diving, flying personal aircraft, riding motorcycles, and so on. Alternatively organizations may use a form of separation, such as restricting the number of key employees who can travel on the same aircraft.

Net Income Loss Exposures

Net income loss exposures can be associated with property, liability, or personnel loss exposures. Therefore, any of the risk control measures that control these three categories of loss exposures also indirectly control net income loss exposures. For example, to prevent a net income loss associated with a property loss exposure, an organization needs to prevent the property loss from occurring.

In addition to reducing the immediate effect of property, liability, or personnel losses on net income, risk control efforts must also control long-term effects, such as a loss of market share that can result from the net income loss. For example, if a manufacturer conducts a product recall, that manufacturer loses sales in the short term, causing a temporary loss of revenue. If the manufacturer's customers switch to purchasing products from other organizations, permanent market share could be lost, which is a long-term effect that translates into permanent revenue loss.

Two risk control measures that are directly aimed at reducing the severity of net income losses are separation and duplication. Separation and duplication enable an organization to reduce net income losses by maintaining operations or quickly resuming operations following a loss. Diversification is also a viable risk control technique for many because it helps to ensure that an organization's entire income is not dependent on one product or customer.

One of the goals of risk control is to ensure business continuity. Business continuity management is a particular process that focuses on those loss exposures that present a threat to the organization's continued operations.

BUSINESS CONTINUITY MANAGEMENT

Business continuity management is a process that identifies potential threats to an organization and provides a methodology for ensuring an organization's continued business operations. It is far broader in scope than risk control, but the two functions share many of the same goals. In some ways, business continuity management shares many of the same characteristics of enterprise risk management, but it has a narrower focus on risks that threaten the organization's existence. Business continuity management is designed to minimize or eliminate significant business interruptions, regardless of cause. That is, it is designed to meet the organizational post-loss goals of survival and continuity of operations.

Business continuity management, developed during the 1990s, typically focused on information technology (IT) concerns that could disrupt operations at organizations. A key IT issue during the 1990s was the year 2000 (Y2K) issue, which concerned the potential disruption that could be caused when software programs that were originally programmed with only two digits for the date (for example, 95 for 1995) had to switch to using four digits (going from 1999 to 2000).

Business continuity management has developed beyond the initial IT focus to encompass issues such as terrorism; corporate scandals; and economic developments that have led to more outsourcing, less duplication in production, greater reliance on just-in-time delivery, and more interdependence between organizations and key suppliers or buyers. Business continuity management plans have been expanded to help an organization handle interruptions from property losses, IT problems, human failures (such as fraud, sabotage, or terrorism), loss of utility services or infrastructure, reputation losses, human asset losses (personnel losses), and so on. These risks vary widely by industry, location, and organization. Some organizations are more susceptible to a particular loss exposure than others. Because each organization is unique in its loss exposures, it will also have to be unique in its application of business continuity management.

To help ensure the survival of the organization, business continuity management relies on the business continuity process and the business continuity

Business continuity management
A process that identifies potential threats to an organization and provides a methodology for ensuring an organization's continued business operations.

plan. The business continuity process assesses the threats to critical functions and develops a methodology for handling those threats. The business continuity plan is the planned response an organization will follow once a survival-threatening loss has occurred. By assessing threats to critical functions and pre-determining the organization's response to losses associated with those threats, business continuity management maximizes the probability of an organization's survival of a critical loss.

Steps in the Business Continuity Process

The business continuity process provides a systematic approach to developing and implementing a business continuity plan. The process involves the following six steps:

1. Identify the organization's critical functions
2. Identify the risks (threats) to the organization's critical functions
3. Evaluate the effect of the risks on those critical functions
4. Develop a business continuity strategy
5. Develop a business continuity plan
6. Monitor and revise the business continuity process

These steps are similar to the six steps of the risk management process and are designed to assess and control risks that are significant enough to warrant special attention because of the effect they can have on the organization's survival. The process involves identification of both the critical functions (processes) of the organization and the risks that could have a substantial effect on those functions. The duration of interruption necessary to produce a substantial effect depends on the function. For example, even a very brief loss of electricity to a hospital can seriously impede the staff's ability to provide basic medical care. Once the risks have been identified and evaluated, a business continuity strategy and plan are developed to establish how to maintain critical functions during a survival-threatening loss. Finally, similar to the risk management process, the entire process must be monitored and evaluated to ensure that it is functioning properly.

The business continuity process provides organizations with the framework to develop a systematic response to a variety of risks that could potentially threaten their future viability. Although following this process cannot ensure the survival of an organization, it can help to minimize the scope of threats that can cause its demise. The following text box discusses some practical issues that may arise during the business continuity process.

Business Continuity Management in Practice

Organizations that have implemented business continuity management face some common issues. One issue is deciding whether to outsource business continuity management to an organization that specializes in business continuity on a consulting or implementation basis. Another issue is determining the location of a backup site. Ideally, the backup site is close enough to the primary site so that employees can access the site quickly, but far enough away from the primary site so that the cause of the crisis cannot affect both locations simultaneously. The backup site would ideally have different telecommunications, power, and utilities from the primary site, in case the original cause of the crisis prevented those from functioning properly. A third issue is deciding the amount of detail that should be in a business continuity plan. The plan needs to be simple enough to follow in an emergency, but detailed enough to provide guidance in a wide variety of scenarios that may evolve. Finally, organizations need to be concerned about cost. How much time, energy, and money should be invested in business continuity is difficult to determine and is unique to each organization.

Business Continuity Plan

A business continuity plan details the activities the organization will take in response to an incident that interrupts its operations. An important part of the business continuity process is to develop such a plan before a significant loss occurs that disrupts business. The plan should be designed with the understanding that it is going to be used during a crisis; that is, it should be clear and able to be quickly read and understood. All relevant parties should have a copy of the plan and should receive appropriate training, including periodic rehearsals of crisis procedures.

Although business continuity plans vary widely by organization, some content is fairly general. Most business continuity plans contain the following:

- Strategy the organization is going to follow to manage the crisis
- Information about the roles and duties of various individuals in the organization
- Steps that can be taken to prevent any further loss or damage
- Emergency response plan to deal with life and safety issues
- Crisis management plan to deal with communication and any reputation issues (reputation management) that may arise
- Business recovery and restoration plan to deal with losses to property, processes, or products
- Access to stress management and counseling for affected parties

Exhibit 4-10 contains the emergency management considerations developed by a public-private partnership with the Federal Emergency Management Association (FEMA).

EXHIBIT 4-10

Suggested Emergency Management Considerations

Section 2: Emergency Management Considerations

- Direction and Control
  - Emergency Management Group (EMG)
  - Incident Command System (ICS)
  - Emergency Operations Center (EOC)
  - Planning Considerations
  - Security
  - Coordination of Outside Response
- Communications
  - Contingency Planning
  - Emergency Communications
  - Family Communications
  - Notification
  - Warning
- Life Safety
  - Evacuation Planning
  - Evacuation Routes and Exits
  - Assembly Areas and Accountability
  - Shelter
  - Training and Information
  - Family Preparedness
- Property Protection
  - Planning Considerations
  - Protection Systems
  - Mitigation
  - Facility Shutdown
  - Records Preservation
- Community Outreach
  - Involving the Community
  - Mutual Aid Agreements
  - Community Service
  - Public Information
  - Media Relations
- Recovery and Restoration
  - Planning Considerations
  - Continuity of Management
  - Insurance
  - Employee Support
  - Resuming Operations
- Administration and Logistics
  - Administrative Actions
  - Logistics

Source: Adapted from *Emergency Management Guide for Business and Industry*, www.fema.gov/library/bizindex.shtm (accessed November 7, 2005).

Ultimately, both business continuity management and risk control are aimed at enabling an individual or organization to not only deal with hazards and loss exposures, but to deal with them in the most efficient and cost-effective way in order to reduce the exposure to, and cost of, risk.

ETHICAL CONSIDERATIONS

One of the major issues confronting insurance and risk management professionals deciding to implement risk control techniques is deciding how much to spend on risk control. Risk control goals dictate that individuals and organizations implement risk control measures that are effective and efficient. One method of determining investment in risk control is performing a cost/benefit analysis. The cost/benefit decision criteria state that an individual or organization should continue to spend money on risk control until the next dollar spent (cost) returns less than one dollar in benefit. For example, if spending $1,000 on an alarm system saves $5,000 in theft losses, the alarm system should be installed. However, a $2,000 alarm system that is going to save $5,500 is not a worthwhile investment. Cost/benefit analysis would not advocate spending the extra $1,000 to save $500. One of the problems with cost/benefit analysis is that the insurance or risk management professional needs to take into account all the costs and all the benefits associated with the risk control measure. Many of these costs and benefits may be difficult to value.

The cost/benefit decision criteria lead to some ethical issues. For example, to what extent should an organization aim to reduce the risk to the average members of the population? To what extent should an organization aim to reduce the risk to the most vulnerable subgroup of the population? How much should an organization spend to save a human life? Also, is all human life worth the same amount?

Any risk control measure applied to risks involving the possibility of human fatality needs to determine the value of a human life. There are a variety of ways to do this. One method is to calculate the present value of an individual's future earnings. Another is to determine how much compensation would persuade someone to accept a career that involves possibility of death. The additional compensation divided by the increased probability of death is the implicit value of that human life. For example, consider a construction worker making $30,000 per year on a job that involves a 0 percent chance of death who accepts a new job at $32,000 per year that has a .05 percent chance of a fatal accident. The construction worker's additional compensation is $2,000 per year and the increase in the probability of death is .0005. By dividing $2,000 by .0005, the construction worker has implicitly valued his or her life at $4,000,000.

Another way to value human life is to examine the cost of the risk control measure being considered and the number of lives that the measure would save. By determining the cost per life saved, an implicit value of human life is determined. For example, the Department of Transportation spends between $390 million and $516 million per year on head impact protection that saves between 8,360 and 10,007 lives per year.[3] The cost per life saved is between $50,000 and $53,000. Similarly, the Occupational Safety and Health Administration (OSHA) spends $112 million per year on controlling methylene chloride, which and this saves 96 lives per year.[4] The cost per life saved is $1.16 million.

If the cost to save one life is less than $1,000, most people would agree that the risk control measure's benefits outweigh its costs. The question remains, however: At what level do its costs start to outweigh its benefits?

SUMMARY

Risk control is a conscious act or decision not to act that reduces the frequency and severity of losses or makes losses more predictable. Risk control techniques prevent losses, reduce the severity of losses, and speed recovery following a loss.

Risk control techniques can be categorized into one of six broad categories:

1. Avoidance
2. Loss prevention
3. Loss reduction
4. Separation
5. Duplication
6. Diversification

Avoidance involves ceasing or never undertaking an activity so that the possibility of a future loss occurring from that activity is eliminated. Loss prevention is a risk control technique that reduces the frequency of a particular loss. Loss reduction reduces the severity of a particular loss. Separation disperses a particular asset or activity over several locations and regularly relies on that asset or activity as part of the organization's working resources. Duplication uses backups, spares, or copies of critical property, information, or capabilities and keeps them in reserve. The difference between duplication and separation is that duplicates are not a part of an organization's daily working resources. Diversification spreads loss exposures over numerous projects, products, markets, or regions. Although diversification closely resembles duplication and separation, it is more commonly applied to managing business risks rather than hazard risks.

The goals of risk control are as follows:

- Implement effective and efficient risk control measures
- Comply with legal requirements
- Promote life safety
- Ensure business continuity

A measure is effective if it enables an organization to achieve desired risk management goals. A measure is efficient if it is the least expensive of all the possible effective measures. Some risk control measures are required by laws and regulations. For example, the fire safety code mandates certain fire safety procedures. In the context of risk control, life safety is that portion of fire safety that focuses on the minimum building design, construction, operation, and maintenance requirements necessary to assure occupants of a safe exit from the burning portion of the building. Promoting life safety can be expanded beyond fire safety to incorporate any cause of loss that threatens the life of employees or customers. Risk control measures should also aim to ensure business continuity—that is, minimize or eliminate significant business interruptions, whatever the cause. Business continuity management is designed to meet both the primary risk management program post-loss goal of survival and the post-loss goal of continuity of operations.

To properly evaluate the effect of risk control measures on loss frequency and loss severity, the insurance or risk management professional should conduct an analysis of the effect that each measure will have both on the specified loss exposure and on any other loss exposures.

Not all of the six risk control techniques are applicable to every loss exposure. Although each loss exposure must be evaluated to determine which risk control techniques will best help an organization achieve its goals, many loss exposures within a given category—property, liability, personnel, and net income—warrant application of the same risk control techniques. All of the categories of risk control techniques can be applied in some way to property loss exposures. Three risk control techniques can be used to control liability losses: (1) avoid the activity that creates the liability loss exposure, (2) decrease the likelihood of the losses occurring (loss prevention), and (3) if a loss does occur, minimize the effect of that loss on the organization (loss reduction). Organizations generally incorporate three different risk control techniques when addressing personnel loss exposures: loss prevention, loss reduction, and separation. Net income loss exposures can be associated with property, liability, or personnel loss exposures. Therefore, any of the risk control measures that control property, liability, or personnel loss exposures also indirectly control net income loss exposures. Risk control efforts for net income loss exposures consider both short-term and long-term effects. Two risk control measures that are directly aimed at reducing the severity of net income losses are separation and duplication.

Business continuity management is a process that identifies potential threats to an organization and provides a methodology for ensuring an organization's continued business operations. The business continuity process assesses the threats to critical functions and develops a methodology for handling those threats. It also provides organizations with the framework to develop a systematic response to a variety of risks that could potentially threaten the future viability of the organization.

The business continuity plan is the planned response an organization will follow once a survival-threatening loss has occurred. A business continuity plan details the activities the organization is going to take in response to an incident that interrupts its operations. By assessing threats to critical functions and pre-determining the organization's response to losses associated with those threats, business continuity management maximizes the probability of an organization's survival of a critical loss.

CHAPTER NOTES

1. H. W. Heinrich, *Industrial Accident Prevention*, 4th Edition (New York: McGraw-Hill, 1959).

2. Ron Coté, PE, and Gregory E. Harrington, PE, eds., *Life Safety Code® Handbook*, 9th ed. (Quincy, Mass.: National Fire Protection Association, 2003). Life Safety Code® is a registered trademark of the National Fire Protection Association, Quincy, Mass. 02169.

3. www.whitehouse.gov/omb/inforeg/spec24.pdf, table 24.1 (accessed January 20, 2006).

4. www.whitehouse.gov/omb/inforeg/spec24.pdf, table 24.1 (accessed January 20, 2006).

Chapter 5

Direct Your Learning

Risk Financing

After learning the content of this chapter and completing the corresponding course guide assignment, you should be able to:

- Explain how individuals or organizations can achieve their overall and risk management goals by fulfilling the following risk financing goals:
  - Pay for losses
  - Manage the cost of risk
  - Manage cash flow variability
  - Maintain an appropriate level of liquidity
  - Comply with legal requirements
- Describe the following aspects of retention and transfer:
  - Retention funding measures
  - Limitations on risk transfer measures
  - The advantages of both retention and transfer
- Explain how the following can affect the selection of the appropriate risk financing measure:
  - Ability of a risk financing measure to meet risk financing goals
  - Loss exposure characteristics
  - Characteristics specific to an individual or organization
- Explain how an organization meets its risk financing goals by using the following risk financing measures:
  - Guaranteed cost insurance
  - Self-insurance
  - Large deductible plans
  - Captives
  - Finite risk plans
  - Pools
  - Retrospective rating plans
  - Hold-harmless agreements
  - Capital market solutions
- Explain how risk financing measures are applied to the four types of loss exposures.
- Define or describe each of the Key Words and Phrases for this chapter.

Develop Your Perspective

What are the main topics covered in the chapter?

Risk financing generates the funds to pay for losses or offset variability in cash flows. Most risk financing options are a combination of retention and transfer, so the risk financing decision involves determining retention levels as well as choosing the most appropriate transfer measures.

Identify the problems in applying pure retention or pure transfer risk financing measures.

- Why are most applications of risk financing measures a combination of retention and transfer?

Why is it important to learn about these topics?

Application of risk financing measures requires a balance between the degree of risk that an organization will retain and the risk it must transfer. Determining this balance involves comparing an organization's risk management program goals with the advantages and disadvantages that the various risk financing measures offer in meeting those goals.

Consider how retention and transfer are applied in specific situations.

- What goals will an organization attempt to achieve through risk financing?
- What organization-specific characteristics affect desired retention levels?

How can you use what you will learn?

Evaluate your organization's overall mix of retained and transferred loss exposures.

- What are the advantages to your organization of retaining those loss exposures that have been retained?
- How would you compare the types of risk financing measures that your organization uses for property, liability, personnel, and net income loss exposures?

Chapter 5
Risk Financing

The third step in the risk management process—examining the feasibility of risk management alternatives—involves reviewing both risk control and risk financing options. This review enables an individual or organization to proceed to the subsequent steps of selecting and implementing the appropriate risk management techniques.

Examining the feasibility of risk financing alternatives requires understanding what risk financing measures are available and how they enable the individual or organization to achieve overall risk financing goals. Although risk financing has traditionally been divided into two types of techniques—retention and transfer—most risk financing measures available are actually combinations of retention and transfer. Therefore, a major part of the risk financing decision for every loss exposure involves determining the most appropriate retention levels. Once the level of retention has been decided, there are many transfer measures available, some of which are more suited to particular types of loss exposures than others. It is therefore important to understand what can be achieved through each of these measures in order to make the most appropriate risk financing decision.

OVERVIEW OF RISK FINANCING

Most loss exposures are managed through a combination of risk control and risk financing. Once an individual or organization has assessed all of the loss exposures it faces, the individual or risk management professional selects the appropriate risk control measures and decides how to finance them and the remaining variability in cash flows. Risk financing is a conscious act or decision not to act that generates the funds to pay for losses and risk control measures or to offset variability in cash flows. Traditionally, risk financing measures have been grouped under the following two techniques:

1. **Retention**—a risk financing technique by which losses and variability in cash flows are financed by generating funds within the organization.
2. **Transfer**—a risk financing technique by which the financial responsibility for losses and variability in cash flows is shifted to another party.

Risk financing
A conscious act or decision not to act that generates the funds to pay for losses and risk control measures or to offset variability in cash flows.

Retention
A risk financing technique by which losses and variability in cash flows are financed by generating funds within the organization.

Transfer
In the context of risk management, a risk financing technique by which the financial responsibility for losses and variability in cash flows is shifted to another party.

Insurance
A risk financing measure that transfers the potential financial consequences of certain specified loss exposures from the insured to the insurer.

Alternative risk transfer (ART)
Those risk financing measures that do not fall into the category of guaranteed cost insurance.

Transfer includes insurance and a variety of other risk financing measures that are often collectively called alternative risk transfer. **Insurance** is a risk financing measure that transfers the potential financial consequences of certain specified loss exposures from the insured to the insurer. **Alternative risk transfer (ART)** refers to those risk financing measures that do not fall into the category of insurance. The distinction between insurance and ART is often not clear. Several risk financing measures could be categorized either as insurance or as ART, such as a large deductible plan (an insurance policy with a large deductible) or a retrospective rating plan (an insurance policy with a premium that varies with current loss experience). Furthermore, as the insurance industry continues to evolve, the development of nontraditional insurance products such as finite risk plans (insurance policies with limited risk transfer) and insurance-linked securities (capital market products linked to insurable risks) further erodes the distinction between insurance and ART.

Unless avoidance is used, an organization or individual should apply at least one risk control measure *and* at least one risk financing measure to each significant loss exposure. Organizations and individuals with effective risk management programs follow a pattern in addressing loss exposures; they first control losses through cost-effective risk control, then apply risk financing techniques. The individual or organization should use risk control measures to control the frequency and severity of losses and apply risk financing measures to pay for both the risk control measures incorporated and any remaining losses or cash flow variability.

When choosing risk financing measures, it is important to understand the risk financing goals the individual or organization is trying to achieve, because each risk financing measure will help the individual or organization achieve the risk financing goals with varying degrees of effectiveness and efficiency. Once the individual or organization has developed risk financing goals, the proper balance of retention and transfer needs to be determined. This balance plays a major role not only in selecting the appropriate risk financing measures, but also in determining how those risk financing measures will be structured.

RISK FINANCING GOALS

Although individuals may have a variety of personal goals, every organization has an overall goal to maximize value. For example, the managers of publicly traded firms may attempt to maximize organizational value by maximizing the market value of their stock. This goal can be achieved by maximizing the present value of expected future cash flows.

Organizational Value and Future Cash Flows

Future cash flows are a projection of the amount of cash that will flow into an organization in a future period minus the amount of cash that will flow out of the organization during that same period. The present value of expected future cash flows is what the projected cash flows for that future period are worth today. This value is derived by a calculation (called discounting) that accounts for the time value of money. In theory, investors value a publicly traded organization by projecting the timing and size of its future cash flows. They then discount the expected cash flows back to the present to estimate the organization's current market value.

The degree of risk or uncertainty associated with future cash flows also influences a publicly traded organization's market value. The higher the degree of risk, the greater the discount rate that investors apply to an organization's projected future cash flows. The greater the discount rate, the lower the present value of the organization's cash flows, and the lower the organization's current market value. Therefore, increased variability (uncertainty) in an organization's future cash flows reduces the organization's market value.

Risk management program goals are designed to support an individual's or organization's overall goals. Because risk financing is an integral part of a risk management program, risk financing goals should support risk management program goals. Exhibit 5-1 illustrates this interrelationship and outlines common risk financing goals.

In order to support risk management program goals, most individuals and organizations adopt several risk financing goals, such as: pay for losses, manage the cost of risk, manage cash flow variability, maintain an appropriate level of liquidity, and comply with legal requirements, that are directly linked to the three financial consequences of risk: (1) expected cost of losses, (2) expenditures on risk management, and (3) residual uncertainty. Exhibit 5-2 relates each risk financing goal with the financial consequence of risk it attempts to manage.

Pay for Losses

Individuals and organizations need to ensure that funds are available to pay for losses when they occur. The availability of funds is particularly important in situations that disrupt normal activities, such as when an individual needs to replace an automobile used to commute to work or when an organization needs to replace damaged property necessary for continued operations. However, paying for losses is also important for other reasons, such as to promote public relations. For example, an organization does not want to damage its reputation by not paying liability losses resulting from legitimate third-party claims (claims filed against the insured by a party who is not a party to the insurance contract). Similarly, it may want to launch an advertising campaign to demonstrate its commitment to resolving a product liability issue.

EXHIBIT 5-1

Risk Management Goals

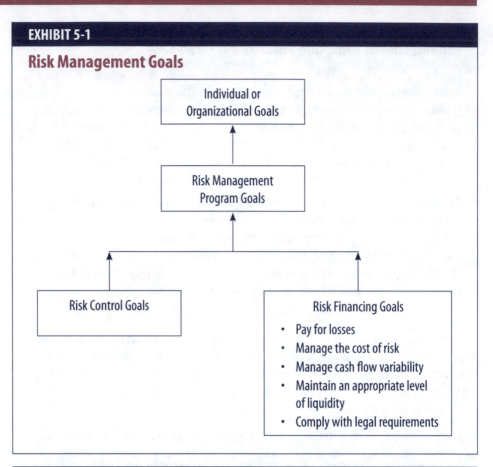

EXHIBIT 5-2

How Risk Financing Goals Address Financial Consequences of Risk

Consequences / Goals	Expected Costs of Losses	Expenditures on Risk Management	Residual Uncertainty
Pay for Losses	✓		
Manage the Cost of Risk		✓	
Manage Cash Flow Variability			✓
Maintain an Appropriate Level of Liquidity	✓		✓
Comply With Legal Requirements	✓		

For many individuals or organizations, paying for losses does not only entail paying for the actual losses or portions of losses retained, it also covers transfer costs, which are costs paid in order to transfer responsibility for losses to another party. For financial risks, transfer costs could be the price of buying options to hedge the costs associated with currency exchange rate risk. For hazard risks, transfer costs are often insurance premiums. In return for the premium, the insurer accepts the uncertainty of the cost of the insured's covered losses and agrees to reimburse the insured for covered losses or to pay covered losses on the insured's behalf. The premium would also need to cover expenses and profit margins for the insurer.

This text considers paying for losses and paying transaction costs separately. Paying for losses is one risk financing goal, whereas paying transaction costs is part of managing the cost of risk, a separate risk financing goal. For example, an insurance premium would cover both paying for losses and the transaction costs associated with the insurance policy. These two separate goals are parallel to being effective and efficient. Risk financing measures should be effective (pay for losses that do occur) as well as efficient (pay for losses in the most economical way).

Manage the Cost of Risk

Risk financing seeks to manage an individual's or organization's cost of risk. The following expenses form part of the cost of risk, regardless of whether losses are retained or transferred:

- Administrative expenses
- Risk control expenses
- Risk financing expenses

Administrative expenses include the cost of internal administration and the cost of purchased services, such as claim administration or risk management consulting. Although many of these expenses are unavoidable if a risk financing program is to be properly managed, an individual or organization may have an opportunity to save on some expenses by modifying procedures or eliminating unnecessary tasks. For example, an organization with a loss retention program might save expenses by outsourcing the claim administration function to a third party who can adjust the claims more cost effectively.

Risk control expenses are incurred to reduce frequency, reduce the severity of losses that do occur, or increase the predictability of future losses. An individual or organization can best analyze risk control expenses by conducting a cost-benefit analysis. Therefore, to ensure that risk control expenses promote an individual's or organization's long-term financial goals, resources should be devoted to risk control only if the benefit of a risk control measure exceeds its cost.

Risk financing expenses are incurred to manage the risk financing measures used to meet risk financing goals. Many of these risk financing measures involve transaction costs, including commissions paid to brokers, fees paid to banks or other investment institutions in order to establish accounts, and fees paid for trades on capital market transactions. Depending on the transaction's size, these costs can be substantial, sometimes millions of dollars. Transaction costs vary based not only on the risk financing measure chosen but also on varying market conditions. For example, the commissions paid to brokers are often a percentage of the total insurance premium that the broker places with an insurer. If insurance prices increase, the commission paid will be higher. If market conditions dictate lower insurance premiums, commissions will be lower as well.

Managing the administrative expenses, risk control expenses, and risk financing expenses does not necessarily mean minimizing those costs in an attempt to operate economically or increase profitability. In fact, many of those costs are necessary to manage an effective risk management program. Individuals and organizations should be aware of the value of the risk financing measures used to ensure that they are receiving adequate service for the price that is being paid for them. In other words, an individual or organization should be wary of sacrificing effectiveness for efficiency.

Manage Cash Flow Variability

The level of cash flow variability that an individual or organization is able or willing to accept depends on the individual's or organization's tolerance for risk. Determining that level of tolerance can be difficult. For an individual, risk tolerance often depends on financial strength, family obligations, and the individual's aversion to risk. For example, an individual with two young children may desire more stable income than an individual without children. Therefore, the individual with children may be more inclined to choose a career in which the majority of the compensation comes from salary rather than commissions.

For an organization, the maximum cash flow variability level depends on factors such as the organization's size, its financial strength, and management's own degree of risk tolerance. For example, if management is prepared to accept risk in order to gain a possible benefit, then the cash flow variability levels will be higher than if management prefers to avoid risk. An organization's maximum cash flow variability level also depends on the degree to which the organization's other stakeholders, such as shareholders, suppliers, or customers, are willing to accept risk. For example, suppliers may be less willing to sell supplies on credit to organizations with high variability in their cash flows because of concern about the organization's ability to make its repayments. Therefore, individuals or organizations can achieve their goals for managing cash flow variability by determining the maximum cash flow variability they are willing to tolerate and arranging their risk management programs within those parameters.

Maintain an Appropriate Level of Liquidity

A certain level of cash liquidity (liquid assets) is required to pay for retained losses. A liquid asset is one that can easily be converted into cash. For example, marketable securities are liquid because they can readily be sold in the stock or bond markets. Assets such as real property and machinery are typically not liquid because they are difficult to sell quickly at prices close to their market values.

As an individual or organization's retention level increases, so does the level of liquidity required. Therefore, to meet risk financing goals, individuals or organizations must determine the appropriate level of liquidity for retained losses and consider both internal and external sources of capital to meet those needs. Internally, individuals or organizations can look to the liquidity of their assets and the strength of their cash flows. Liquidity can be increased by selling assets or by retaining cash flow instead of using it to fund capital projects or to pay dividends. Externally, an organization can increase liquidity by borrowing, issuing a debt instrument (a bond), or issuing stock (for a publicly traded organization). For an individual, borrowing is typically the only external option.

One problem with maintaining high levels of liquidity is that liquid assets do not typically offer the same return on investments as other, longer-term, less liquid investments. Individuals and organizations must consider the balance between desire for long-term returns in less liquid investments and the liquidity needs of retained losses.

Comply With Legal Requirements

Individuals and organizations need to consider the legal environment when making risk financing decisions. Sometimes laws and regulations will require specific risk financing measures. For example, most states require drivers to purchase auto liability insurance policies. Similarly, state workers' compensation statutes require most employers to purchase workers' compensation insurance or to qualify as self-insurers. Alternatively, legal requirements will affect how risk financing measures are implemented. For example, an organization that intends to raise its liquidity by issuing bonds may be required by the bond purchasers to insure its property for a specific amount. Similarly, contractual obligations, such as leases on automobiles or aircraft, may also require insurance coverage on the leased property. Ultimately, the goal of complying with legal requirements is a fundamental requirement of all risk financing goals. How individuals and organizations comply with these requirements depends on the individual requirements imposed by the applicable statutory or contractual obligations.

The various risk financing measures that can be used to help an individual or organization achieve these risk financing goals have traditionally been grouped into two types: retention and transfer.

RETENTION AND TRANSFER

Because most risk financing measures involve elements of both retention and transfer, the distinction between the two is eroding. Therefore, it is more appropriate to view pure retention and pure transfer as the extreme points on a continuum of risk financing measures, with almost all risk financing measures, including insurance, falling somewhere between the two extremes. That is, most risk financing measures are risk-sharing mechanisms, part retention and part transfer. Whether any specific risk financing measure involves more retention or more transfer depends on the measure. For example, Exhibit 5-3 shows that an individual or organization that purchases an insurance policy (the insured) retains the deductible amount and any losses above the policy limit. The insured transfers to the insurer losses that are above the deductible but below the policy limit. In the example in Exhibit 5-3, the majority of the risk financing measure involves transfer.

Determining the best mix of retention and transfer requires understanding how both retention and transfer operate, the advantages of each, and how each enables an individual or organization to meet risk financing goals. This information can be combined with consideration of the specific loss exposure characteristics, plus any characteristics specific to the individual or organization, in order to determine the most appropriate levels of retention and transfer.

Retention

Retention can be the most economical form of risk financing. However, it also exposes the individual or organization to the most cash flow variability. Provided risks have been adequately identified and analyzed (assessed), retention is an intentional form of risk financing and is called planned retention. Unplanned retention occurs when either losses cannot be insured or otherwise transferred or an individual or organization fails to correctly identify or assess a loss exposure. In these two situations, retention becomes the risk financing method of last resort, which is why retention is often called the default risk financing technique. Unplanned retention can have a severe effect on risk financing goals and limits the choice of retention funding techniques. Conversely, planned retention allows the risk management professional to choose the most appropriate retention funding measure.

EXHIBIT 5-3

Insurance Risk Sharing

Cara has just purchased a homeowners policy from Radley Insurance with a $1,000 deductible and a $300,000 limit. It would cost Cara $350,000 to rebuild her home today using the same construction materials. Assuming a total loss of the home from fire, Cara would retain the first $1,000 in loss because of her deductible. Radley would then pay the next $300,000 (risk transfer) in losses. Cara would be responsible for the last $49,000 in losses, as she would retain any losses above the limit. With the maximum retained amount of the losses being $50,000 and the maximum transferred amount of the losses being $300,000, this example of risk financing is closer to pure transfer than pure retention.

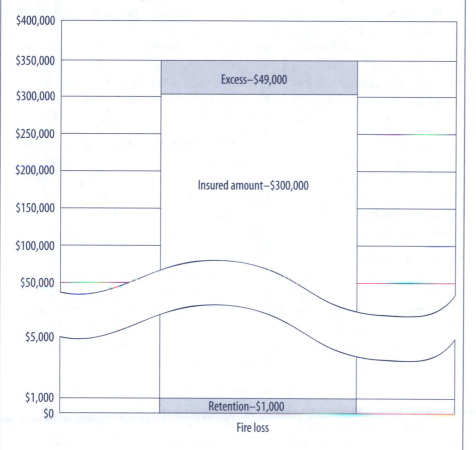

Cara can adjust the levels of retention and transfer in this example by adjusting her deductible and policy limit. Cara can decrease (increase) her retention by reducing (increasing) her deductible and raising (lowering) her policy limit.

Retention Funding Measures

Retention funding measures rely on funds that originate within the organization. In order of increasing administrative complexity, the four planned retention funding measures available to an organization are as follows:

1. Current expensing of losses
2. Using an unfunded reserve
3. Using a funded reserve
4. Borrowing funds

Current expensing of losses is the least formal funding measure (and therefore the least expensive to administer), but it also provides the least assurance that funds will be available, especially to pay for a major loss. Current expensing relies on current cash flows to cover the cost of losses. This may be feasible for losses with a low expected value, but becomes less advisable the larger the expected value of the loss. Generally, the larger the potential loss an organization wants to retain relative to its cash flows, the more formal and better funded the type of retention should be.

An unfunded loss reserve appears as an accounting entry denoting potential liability to pay for a loss. Although this reserve recognizes in advance that the organization may suffer a loss, the organization does not support that potential for loss with any specific assets. A typical example of an unfunded loss reserve is the reserve for uncollectible accounts. Organizations establish this reserve based on an estimation of the portion of accounts receivable that will not be paid.

In contrast to an unfunded loss reserve, a funded loss reserve is supported with cash, securities, or other liquid assets allocated to meet the obligations that the reserve represents. For example, a reserve for taxes payable at the end of the coming calendar quarter is usually supported by cash to pay them when they become due. Funded loss reserves can be fairly informal, such as identifying assets that would be sold in the event of a loss, or highly complex transactions such as forming a captive insurer, discussed in detail subsequently in this chapter.

Although borrowing funds does not appear to be a retention measure, when individuals or organizations use borrowed funds to pay losses, they suffer a resulting reduction in their line of credit or ability to borrow for other purposes. This reduction ultimately depletes their resources. Consequently, the individuals or organizations are indirectly using their own resources to pay for losses and, in time, use their own earnings to repay the loan. In the short term, the external source of capital is paying for the loss. In the long term, however, the individuals or organizations pay the entire loss.

Advantages of Retention

The advantages of using retention as a risk financing technique include the following:

- Cost savings
- Control of claims process
- Timing of cash flows
- Incentives for risk control

The primary advantage that retention offers an individual or organization is cost savings. Retention is typically the most economical risk financing alternative and can generate cost savings in several ways. For example, suppose that an organization is deciding whether to retain its commercial auto liability loss exposures or transfer them through a commercial auto insurance policy. If the organization chooses to retain the risk of auto liability, then it can save money by avoiding the following costs that are often included in insurance premiums:

- Administrative costs—underwriting, claims, and investment costs incurred by the insurer as well as the additional amounts added to these costs in order to generate the profit needed by the insurer.
- Premium taxes—taxes on insurance premiums imposed by many states.
- Moral hazard costs—costs that are often included in underwriting and claims to verify information submitted or claims filed (often included with administrative costs).
- Social loading costs—if the state funds a residual pool through which high-risk individuals or organizations are able to purchase insurance that was unavailable from insurers, the insurers who sell insurance in that state will pass the costs of the residual pool on to all insureds who have purchased policies.
- Adverse selection costs—cost of being pooled with high risk policyholders (this only applies to individuals and organizations that typically have losses below average losses).

In addition to cost savings, retention allows an organization to maintain control of the claims process. This control allows greater flexibility in investigating and negotiating claims settlements. For example, an organization that is very concerned with its reputation may want to litigate liability claims against it, whereas an insurer may be more willing to settle the claim to reduce the payout that may be required on its part.

Another advantage of retention is the timing of cash flows. Most transfer measures require the individual or organization to make an up-front payment (such as a premium for an insurance policy). At some point after the loss occurs, the individual or organization is reimbursed by the other party. Retention avoids the up-front payment and can shorten the delay between the time of the loss and the payment by the other party. It also allows the individual or organization to maintain any use of the funds that would have otherwise been paid. These funds can either be used in day-to-day operations or even invested to generate additional income.

Retention also has the advantage of being an incentive for risk control. When individuals or organizations directly pay for their own losses, they have a strong incentive to prevent and reduce those losses. This encourages risk control in order to maximize the reduction in loss frequency and loss severity. Although not without consequences in terms of the cost of risk control measures, these efforts should ultimately save costs.

Industry Language—Self-Insurance and Retention

The term "self-insurance" is sometimes used to describe a risk financing plan for which a person or an organization retains its own losses—or simply decides not to buy insurance. Used this way, the term "self-insurance" is interchangeable with the term "retention."

Some argue that self-insurance is an inaccurate term because insurance involves a transfer of risk, thereby making it impossible to insure one's self. Others assert that certain forms of self-insurance are not insurance at all and that the label "self-insurance" should be applied only to a formal program in which an organization keeps records of its losses and maintains a system to pay for them. This text uses "self-insurance" in this context, that is, when an organization uses a formal program to record and pay for losses.

Insurance professionals should be aware that some statutes, regulations, and contracts use "self-insurance" and "retention" interchangeably. In addition, "self-insurance" and "retention" are also used together: self-insured retention. Self-insured retentions are similar to deductibles. A self-insured retention (SIR) is defined as a risk financing measure in which the insured organization adjusts and pays its own losses up to the self-insured retention level.

Transfer

The opposite of pure retention is pure transfer. A pure transfer shifts the responsibility for the entire loss from one party (transferor) to another party (transferee). However, most, if not all, transfer arrangements contain limitations that prevent them from being regarded as pure transfers.

Limitations on Risk Transfer Measures

There are two main limitations on the risk transfer measures available to individuals and organizations. First, risk transfer measures (including insurance) are not typically pure transfers, but are some combination of retention and transfer. Most, if not all, risk transfer measures involve some type of limitation on the potential loss amounts that are being transferred. These limitations can be deductibles, limits, or other restrictions so that the individual or organization (transferor) pays at least some portion of the loss. Second, the ultimate responsibility for paying for the loss remains with the individual or organization. Risk financing does not eliminate the transferor's legal responsibility for the loss if the transferee fails to pay. For example, if an employee gets injured at work, the employer's workers' compensation insurer would pay for the medical bills of the injured employee. If the workers' compensation insurer cannot or will not pay the medical bills for some reason, the employer is still responsible for paying the bills. Therefore, the transferor is reliant on the good faith and financial strength of the transferee as well as on the judicial enforceability of the transfer agreement. The transferee might not pay because of lack of funds, a dispute about whether the loss falls within the transfer agreement's scope or financial limits, or as a result of a successful court challenge to the agreement's enforceability.

Risk Transfer and Counter-Party Credit Risk

By entering into a risk transfer agreement, one organization (Organization A) can transfer risk to another organization (Organization B). Ultimately, however, Organization A is responsible for its own losses. This creates another risk, the risk that the Organization B cannot or will not pay for any losses that are incurred. In options and futures markets, this risk is often called counter-party credit risk. Counter-party credit risk is not usually an issue with exchange-traded options and futures contracts because the exchange itself typically has a clearinghouse that guarantees payment on the exchange contracts. For example, the Chicago Board of Trade (CBOT) advertises that since 1925 no contract on the CBOT has failed to pay as per the contract. When the risk transfer contracts are insurance contracts, rating organizations such as A. M. Best or Moody's assign the insurers a claims paying ability rating to help insureds identify potential counter-party credit risk. When ART products are used for risk transfer that is not exchange-traded, the counter-party credit risk is generally considered more substantial.

Advantages of Transfer

Despite these limitations, there are significant advantages to using risk transfer measures as part of a risk financing program. These advantages include the following:

- Reducing exposure to large losses
- Reducing cash flow variability
- Providing ancillary services
- Avoiding adverse employee and public relations

The principal advantage of risk transfer measures is that they reduce an individual's or organization's exposure to large losses. Retaining large loss exposures increases the probability that the individual or organization will incur financial distress. Financial distress can have negative effects on relationships with suppliers and customers and may ultimately lead to bankruptcy. Retaining large loss exposures also increases the probability that the individual or organization will need to either raise funds from external sources, such as a stock or bond issue, or borrow funds, which can be costly. Risk transfer measures can help lessen the variability of the cash flows of an organization or activity by reducing the effect of losses associated with retaining large loss exposures. Many publicly traded organizations try to reduce variability of cash flows and earnings on those cash flows because this lack of variability appears to be valued by investors. Therefore, as well as achieving the risk financing goal of managing cash flow variability, risk transfers can increase an organization's attractiveness to investors and thereby potentially increase the overall value of the organization.

Risk transfer has the advantage that ancillary services can be included in the transfer arrangement; for example, insurers often offer risk assessment and control services as well as claims administration and litigation services. Being able to access these services can be a major factor in deciding to transfer some loss exposures. The level of efficiency and expertise that some organizations, such as insurers, have developed in these areas often makes the risk transfer agreement very appealing to organizations that cannot provide these services efficiently. Although it is possible to obtain these ancillary services outside of transfer arrangements through third-party providers, this can be expensive.

Finally, risk transfer can have the advantage of avoiding adverse employee and public relations because as well as transferring responsibility for the loss itself, the organization can transfer responsibility for the claims administration process. Therefore, any issues with claims administration are less likely to harm the reputation of the organization and consequently are less likely to generate adverse employee and public relations.

Because most risk financing measures involve elements of both retention and transfer, selecting a risk financing measure involves determining how much of a particular loss exposure the individual or organization is willing to retain.

SELECTING APPROPRIATE RISK FINANCING MEASURES

When selecting the appropriate risk financing measures to be used in a risk management program, an individual or organization needs to evaluate the relative advantages of all the available measures and consider the ability of each to meet the risk financing goals. How much risk transfer a risk financing measure provides is the primary determinant of whether it is appropriate for the individual or organization. In addition, the relative amount of retention and transfer that the measure provides helps determine whether it will successfully fulfill the individual's or organization's risk financing goals. Selecting the appropriate risk financing measures also involves consideration of the specific characteristics of both the loss exposure involved and the characteristics of the individual or organization.

Ability of Retention and Transfer to Meet Risk Financing Goals

One of the major factors influencing the ability of a risk financing measure to meet an individual's or organization's risk financing goals is how much of the loss exposure is retained and how much is transferred. An organization's risk financing program needs to balance retention and transfer in light of the specific risk financing goals that the organization is trying to accomplish. This balance can be achieved through the appropriate mix of risk financing measures. Some loss exposures may be fully retained, others mostly transferred, and the remainder addressed with risk financing measures that balance retention and transfer. Exhibit 5-4 summarizes how retention and transfer measures can meet each of the risk financing goals.

Because retention can be the most economical risk financing measure, it enables an organization to meet its risk financing goal of managing the cost of risk. However, depending on the magnitude of the actual losses sustained, retention programs may have difficulty paying for losses. The ability to pay for losses depends on the structure of the retention measure implemented and the relative strength of the individual's or organization's cash flows. For example, if a loss exposure suffers a substantial loss that was retained, the ability to pay for the loss depends on whether the retention measure was pre-funded (such as funded reserve) or post-funded (such as cash flows or borrowing), how large the loss is relative to what was expected when the retention decision was made, and how large the loss is relative to cash flows or assets of the individual or organization.

Retention also generates the highest level of cash flow variability and may threaten an organization's liquidity level. Often, how an organization structures and manages its retention determines how effective it is at achieving risk financing goals compared with transfer.

Risk transfer measures typically offer the greatest certainty regarding the ability to pay losses, offer the greatest cash flow certainty, and are useful in preventing liquidity problems, but they may be costly to arrange. Furthermore, some organizations are required by statute or contractual obligation to transfer some risk. For example, most mortgage lenders require that the property owner carry adequate limits of property insurance coverage. Similarly, many states require that motor vehicle owners, including organizations, have auto liability coverage. These requirements add to the overall cost of transfer and may therefore affect the benefit of transfer relative to retention.

EXHIBIT 5-4

Ability of Retention and Transfer to Meet Risk Financing Goals

Risk Financing Goal	Retention	Transfer
Pay for Losses	Depends on magnitude of losses and structure and management of retention measure, as well as the relative strength of cash flows	Primary benefit of transfer measures
Manage the Cost of Risk	Primary benefit of retention	Rarely the most cost effective option
Manage Cash Flow Variability	Typically exposes the individual or organization to more variability in cash flows	Important benefit of transfer measures
Maintain an Appropriate Level of Liquidity	Depends on magnitude of losses and structure and management of retention measure, as well as the relative strength of cash flows	Generally reduces the level of liquidity needed
Comply With Legal Requirements	Depends on structure and management of retention measure	Secondary benefit of transfer measures

Loss Exposure Characteristics Affecting the Selection of Appropriate Risk Financing Measures

The frequency and severity of losses associated with each loss exposure are vital to determining whether a loss exposure should be fully retained or whether some form of transfer is appropriate. Exhibit 5-5 shows a simple, four-quadrant table illustrating frequency and severity with two possible outcomes (high or low). The low-frequency, low-severity quadrant covers losses that occur infrequently and are not severe. Retaining these exposures is economical because they should have a minimal effect on liquidity or cash flow variability. These types of loss exposures often lend themselves to unfunded retention plans, in which small, infrequent losses are paid out of cash flow.

The high-frequency, low-severity quadrant covers losses that occur frequently but are not severe. The administrative expenses associated with filing small, frequent claims with an insurer or other transferee often outweigh the benefits gained from the transfer agreement. Therefore, these types of loss exposures are often retained, with the administration of the claims process done in-house or by a third party.

The low-frequency, high-severity quadrant covers losses that occur infrequently but are severe. These loss exposures are ideally suited for transfer to another party. Insurance products are often designed around these types of loss exposures.

The high-frequency, high-severity quadrant covers losses that occur frequently and are severe. These loss exposures should be avoided. Neither risk retention nor risk transfer is adequately designed to handle these types of loss exposures. If risk control measures can be applied to reduce the frequency or severity of the losses (or both), the loss exposure can be reclassified into the appropriate quadrant to be re-evaluated in terms of risk financing options.

EXHIBIT 5-5

The Effect of Frequency and Severity on the Retention or Transfer Decision

	Low Frequency	High Frequency
Low Severity	Retain	Retain
High Severity	Transfer	Avoid (if possible) Retain (last resort)

Exhibit 5-5 indicates that risk financing through retention is the appropriate technique for most loss exposures. It is only for loss exposures with low frequency, high severity losses that risk transfer measures are appropriate.

Individual- or Organization-Specific Characteristics Affecting the Selection of Appropriate Risk Financing Measures

The optimal balance between retention and transfer varies for each individual or organization, depending on specific characteristics. Therefore, individuals and organizations will make different decisions in selecting the appropriate risk financing measures. Even if two organizations have the same set of loss exposures, differences between the organizations may result in vastly different selections. The following individual- or organization-specific characteristics can affect the selection of appropriate risk financing measures:

- Risk tolerance
- Financial condition
- Core operations
- Ability to diversify

- Ability to control losses
- Ability to administer the retention plan

Individuals and organizations vary widely in their willingness to assume risk. A risk-averse organization may decide not to produce a certain type of product because of the high instance of associated product liability claims, whereas another organization's primary source of revenue could be that same product. The level of risk an organization is willing to assume directly affects its optimal balance between retention and transfer. All else being equal, the higher an individual's or organization's willingness to accept risk, the higher the likelihood that more risk will be retained.

The financial condition of the individual or organization has a significant effect on ability to retain risk. The more financially secure an individual or organization is, the more loss exposures can be retained without causing liquidity or cash flow variability problems. However, even financially secure individuals or organizations need to be careful. They may experience short-term liquidity problems if a significant loss has been retained and short-term cash flow or liquid assets are not sufficient to cover the loss.

An organization is often better able to retain the loss exposures directly related to its core operations because it has an information advantage regarding those operations. That is, the organization knows and understands its core operations and the loss exposures associated with them better than any outside party, including insurers. Because of this information advantage, an outside party would likely need higher compensation to enter into a transfer agreement. Therefore, it would be more economical to retain these loss exposures.

If an organization can diversify its loss exposures, similar to the way many individuals and organizations diversify their investment portfolios, it can gain the advantage of offsetting losses that occur to one loss exposure with the absence of losses associated with the other loss exposures. The organization is then better able to accurately forecast future losses. This increased level of loss accuracy would reduce uncertainty about losses and therefore allow the organization to retain more loss exposures.

Because risk control reduces loss frequency and/or loss severity, the more risk control an organization is able to undertake, the more loss exposures it is typically able to retain. All else being equal, the reductions in frequency and/or severity make it more likely that the organization will have the ability to fund the retention of that particular loss exposure.

Risk retention requires more administration than risk transfer. Such administration may include claim administration, risk management consulting, or retention fund accounting. Organizations that have a better ability to fulfill these administrative requirements are able to use retention more efficiently.

Determining the optimal balance between risk transfer and risk retention measures keeps the risk financing program aligned with the individual's or organization's overall risk management goals. For the portion of those loss exposures that an individual or organization decides to transfer, a variety of risk financing measures are available.

RISK FINANCING MEASURES

Once an individual or organization has made the decision to use risk transfer, there are several risk financing measures to consider. Each risk financing measure is unique in not only its operation but also in its ability to meet an individual's or organization's risk financing goals. The decision to use a specific risk financing measure depends on the specific characteristics of the targeted loss exposure, as well as the characteristics of that risk financing measure, including its implementation cost, loss sensitivity, and ease of administration. Loss sensitivity refers to how sensitive the risk financing measure is to actual losses. Some risk financing measures pay for losses actually incurred (such as guaranteed cost insurance), whereas others pay based on some general measure or index (such as hedging using option contracts). If the general measure or index does not provide a payout that is available when the loss occurs, the risk financing measure does not provide the needed protection. These types of risk financing measures can expose an individual or organization to a new risk—basis risk. In the context of risk management, basis risk is the risk that the payout on a risk financing measure is not perfectly aligned with the individual's or organization's actual losses. Basis risk is most relevant for the capital market solutions discussed subsequently in this chapter.

Individuals and organizations implementing a specific risk financing measure need to understand how the measure operates and whether it will enable them to meet their risk financing goals.

Guaranteed Cost Insurance

This text uses the term guaranteed cost insurance to refer to insurance policies in which the premium and limits are specified in advance. The premium is guaranteed in that it does not depend on the losses incurred during the period of coverage. Guaranteed cost insurance is different from the many newer insurance products, such as finite risk, multi-trigger, or retrospective rating insurance products that are discussed as separate risk financing measures in this chapter.

Guaranteed cost insurance policies are designed to cover property, liability, and net income loss exposures from various causes of loss and have been widely used in the property-casualty insurance industry for many years. Insurance is a funded risk transfer measure. The insurance buyer (insured) transfers the potential financial consequences of certain loss exposures to an insurer. The insured pays the insurer a relatively small, certain financial cost in the form of an insurance premium. In exchange, the insurer agrees to pay for all the organization's losses that are covered by the insurance policy, typically subject to a deductible and policy limit. The insurer also agrees to provide necessary services, such as claim handling and liability-claim defense.

Organizations that have large loss exposures often have difficulty finding a single insurer that is willing or able to supply adequate guaranteed cost insurance coverage. To solve this problem, many organizations purchase multiple guaranteed cost insurance policies as part of an overall insurance program. An insurance program is typically divided into two layers—a primary layer and an excess layer. The **primary layer** is the first level of insurance coverage above any deductible. It is also referred to as the working layer because it is the layer used most often to pay losses. An **excess layer** is a level of insurance coverage above the primary layer. Insureds who want more insurance coverage than that offered by the primary layer usually purchase one or more excess layers. The insurance policies issued to provide coverage in excess layers are often referred to as excess coverage. **Excess coverage** is insurance that covers losses above an attachment point, below which there is usually another insurance policy or a self-insured retention. Some insurers do not provide primary layers of coverages; they specialize in supplying excess layers.

In between primary and excess layers in an insurance program, an organization may use an umbrella policy. An **umbrella policy** is a policy that provides coverage above underlying policies and may also offer coverage not available in the underlying policies, subject to a self-insured retention. A buffer layer is used when the umbrella policy requires underlying coverage limits that are higher than those provided by the primary layer. A **buffer layer** is a level of excess insurance coverage between a primary layer and an umbrella policy.

As an example of using layers of coverage, consider a large hotel chain that uses a layered liability insurance program to insure its large liability loss exposures. The primary layer of the insurance program consists of three primary (underlying) policies covering general liability, commercial auto liability, and employers' liability. Coverage above the primary layer is provided by an umbrella policy, which provides coverage for all three areas of liability. For the auto liability coverage, the umbrella policy requires a buffer layer above the primary layer because the primary auto liability policy limits are below the umbrella policy's minimum requirements. Finally, the hotel chain has three layers of excess insurance above the umbrella policy, providing layers of coverage for loss exposures not covered by the umbrella policy. Exhibit 5-6 illustrates the hotel chain's multilayered liability insurance program.

The number of layers the insured purchases depends on both the limits the insured desires and the limits that are available from insurers. The premium per $100 of coverage (the rate) usually decreases for each layer of coverage (for example, in Exhibit 5-6, excess layer 3 would probably be cheaper than excess layer 2) because there is a corresponding decrease in the probability that losses will be large enough to use higher layers.

Before using guaranteed cost insurance for risk financing, an organization should assess the extent to which such insurance meets the organization's risk financing goals. Exhibit 5-7 describes how guaranteed cost insurance can meet these goals. An additional benefit offered by guaranteed cost insurance is that generally the individual or organization can deduct the insurance premium for tax purposes.

Primary layer
The first level of insurance coverage above any deductible.

Excess layer
A level of insurance coverage above the primary layer.

Excess coverage
Insurance that covers losses above an attachment point, below which there is usually another insurance policy or a self-insured retention.

Umbrella policy
A policy that provides coverage above underlying policies and may also offer coverage not available in the underlying policies, subject to a self-insured retention.

Buffer layer
A level of excess insurance coverage between a primary layer and an umbrella policy.

EXHIBIT 5-6

Multilayered Liability Insurance Program Including a Buffer Layer

Excess layer 3
Excess layer 2
Excess layer 1
Umbrella policy

General liability (primary layer)	Buffer layer	Employers' liability (primary layer)
	Auto liability (primary layer)	

EXHIBIT 5-7

Ability of Guaranteed Cost Insurance to Meet Risk Financing Goals

Risk Financing Goal	How Guaranteed Cost Insurance Meets the Goal
Pay for Losses	Insurance can meet this goal, provided the loss exposures are covered by the guaranteed cost insurance policies.
Manage the Cost of Risk	Insurance can meet this goal, but it is not ideal because insurance premiums are designed to cover not only expected losses, but also insurer administrative costs, adverse selection and moral hazard costs, premium taxes, and any social loadings.
Manage Cash Flow Variability	Insurance can meet this goal because much of the uncertainty about future losses is transferred to the insurer.
Maintain Appropriate Level of Liquidity	Insurance can meet this goal because the organization requires less liquidity with guaranteed cost insurance compared with retention or ART measures.
Comply With Legal Requirements	Insurance can meet this goal, especially regarding loss exposures that are required (by law or contractual obligation) to be transferred.

Self-Insurance

Self-insurance
A form of retention under which an organization records its losses and maintains a formal system to pay for them.

Self-insurance is a form of retention under which an organization records its losses and maintains a formal system to pay for them. Self-insurance can be contrasted with an informal retention plan, under which an organization simply pays for its losses with its cash flow or current (liquid) assets but has no formal payment procedures or method of recording losses. Self-insurance is particularly well-suited for financing losses that are paid out over a period of time, thereby providing a cash flow benefit (compared with guaranteed cost insurance) to the organization retaining its losses. Consequently, workers' compensation, general liability, and automobile liability loss exposures are often self-insured because they have claim payouts that extend over time. Self-insurance (retention) is usually combined with a risk financing measure (transfer), such as an excess coverage insurance policy that covers any infrequent, high-severity losses that may occur.

Self-insurance is usually used for high-frequency loss exposures because it is more efficient than filing many claims with an insurer. Because of the large volume of claim transactions, self-insurance requires claim administration services similar to those provided by an insurer. Such services include the following:

- *Recordkeeping.* A self-insured organization needs a recordkeeping system to track its self-insured claims.

- *Claim adjustment.* As with an insured plan, claims must be investigated, evaluated, negotiated, and paid.

- *Loss reserving.* A self-insured organization must determine reserve amounts needed for estimated future payments on self-insured losses that have occurred. The reserves for self-insured loss payments can be funded or unfunded.

- *Litigation management.* Litigation management involves controlling the cost of legal expenses for claims that are litigated. This includes evaluating and selecting defense lawyers, supervising them during litigation, and keeping records of their costs. It also involves specific techniques such as auditing legal bills and experimenting with alternative fee-billing strategies.

- *Regulatory requirements.* In most states, an organization must qualify as a self-insurer in order to self-insure workers' compensation or auto liability loss exposures. The qualification requirements specify items such as financial security requirements; filing fees, taxes, and assessments that must be paid; excess coverage insurance requirements; and periodic reports that the organization must submit to the regulatory body to qualify as a self-insurer.

- *Excess coverage insurance.* Many states require a self-insurer to purchase excess coverage insurance. Some states specify conditions for the purchase of this coverage. In other states, the state agency responsible for self-insurance reviews each applicant and decides whether to require excess coverage insurance.

Before adopting a self-insurance plan, an organization should evaluate the plan's ability to meet the organization's risk financing goals. Exhibit 5-8 explains how a self-insurance plan can meet these goals.

EXHIBIT 5-8

Ability of a Self-Insurance Plan to Meet Risk Financing Goals

Risk Financing Goal	How a Self-Insurance Plan Meets the Goal
Pay for Losses	Self-insurance can help meet this goal if an organization carefully chooses the loss retention level, purchases appropriate excess coverage, and has sufficient cash flow or liquid assets.
Manage the Cost of Risk	A self-insured organization must administer its own claims (either with its own staff or a third-party administrator) but can save insurer operating expenses, profits, and risk charges. These significant savings are the primary benefit of self-insurance.
Manage Cash Flow Variability	With self-insurance, retained loss outcomes are uncertain. The higher the retention, the higher the degree of uncertainty of retained loss outcomes.
Maintain Appropriate Level of Liquidity	Self-insurance can help meet this goal if an organization carefully chooses the loss retention level, purchases appropriate excess coverage, and accurately forecasts paid amounts for retained losses.
Comply With Legal Requirements	A self-insurer must meet certain legal requirements. In most states, an organization must qualify as a self-insurer for workers' compensation and auto liability.

Large Deductible Plans

A **large deductible plan** is an insurance policy with a per occurrence or per accident deductible of $100,000 or more. A large deductible plan is similar to a self-insurance plan combined with excess coverage insurance in that it exposes the organization to a relatively large amount of loss. In exchange for this exposure, the insurer provides a premium reduction relative to guaranteed cost insurance. A key difference between self-insurance and large deductible plans is that with self-insurance, the insured is responsible for adjusting and paying its own losses up to the attachment point of the excess coverage insurance. Under a large deductible plan, the insurer adjusts and pays all claims, even those below the deductible level. The insurer then seeks reimbursement from the insured for those claims that fall below the deductible. In effect, the insurer is guaranteeing the payment of all claims.

Large deductible plan
An insurance policy with a per occurrence or per accident deductible of $100,000 or more.

The insured usually must provide the insurer with a form of financial security (such as a letter of credit) to guarantee payment of covered losses up to the deductible. Both self-insurance and large deductible plans are common for workers' compensation, auto liability, and general liability policies.

Before adopting a large deductible plan, an organization should evaluate the plan's ability to meet the organization's risk financing goals. Exhibit 5-9 describes how a large deductible plan can meet these goals.

EXHIBIT 5-9

Ability of a Large Deductible Plan to Meet Risk Financing Goals

Risk Financing Goal	How a Large Deductible Plan Meets the Goal
Pay for Losses	The plan meets this goal because the insurer pays for losses as they become due, including losses less than the deductible for which the insured eventually reimburses the insurer.
Manage the Cost of Risk	The plan may meet this goal because the insurer administers the claims process, even for the small claims the insured has retained. The plan will meet this goal better than guaranteed cost insurance but not as well as retention plans.
Manage Cash Flow Variability	The plan meets this goal because the organization can effectively manage cash flow uncertainty if the deductible amount is chosen carefully. The plan will meet this goal better than self-insurance but not as well as guaranteed cost insurance.
Maintain Appropriate Level of Liquidity	The plan meets this goal because liquidity is maintained if the deductible level is carefully selected. The liquidity needed is lower with a large deductible plan than with retention, but higher than the liquidity needed with guaranteed cost insurance.
Comply With Legal Requirements	The plan meets this goal because it can meet legal requirements for purchasing insurance because an insurer issues a policy guaranteeing that all covered claims will be paid.

Captive Insurers

Captive insurer, or captive
A subsidiary formed to insure the loss exposures of its parent company and the parent's affiliates.

A **captive insurer**, or **captive**, is a subsidiary formed to insure the loss exposures of its parent company and the parent's affiliates. Captives can be owned by a single parent or by multiple parents. A captive owned by multiple parents is called a group captive. Single-parent captives, also called pure captives, typically operate as a formalized retention plan and only provide insurance coverage for their parent or sibling organizations, known as affiliated business.

Group captives typically operate as formalized pools in which several organizations group together to share the financial consequences associated with their collective loss exposures. Because of the sharing of loss exposures with other parents, group captives act more like transfer measures. If a significant portion of the captives' revenues are generated by underwriting loss exposures from unrelated, third-party organizations (unaffiliated business), captives operate much more as a transfer measure than as a retention measure. Captives also have the potential to transfer the financial consequences of some of the insured loss exposures to other insurers through a variety of arrangements, including reinsurance.

Operation of a Captive

A captive requires an investment of capital by its parent(s) in order to have the ability to pay losses and to manage its accounting, auditing, legal, and underwriting expenses. Just as any other insurer does, a captive collects premiums, issues policies, invest assets and pays covered losses. Nearly 5,000 captive insurers operate worldwide, with many large organizations using one or more captives to finance their loss exposures.

Deciding how a captive will operate includes the following considerations:

- What types of loss exposures the captive will insure
- Where the captive will be domiciled
- Whether the captive will accept unaffiliated business

Similar to self-insurance, captives are commonly used to cover loss exposures that substantially drain cash flow, such as workers' compensation, general liability, and automobile liability. An advantage to covering these types of losses through a captive is that the captive can earn investment income on the substantial loss reserves necessary for these exposures. Captives are also used to cover property loss exposures that are difficult to insure in the primary insurance market, as well as loss exposures that fall under specialized types of business, such as products liability and environmental liability. The decision on the types of loss exposures covered by the captive is often made prior to the captive's formation. In that case, the captive is specifically formed to handle particular loss exposures for the parent. Once in operation, many captives expand their operations to manage a wider variety of loss exposures.

Many jurisdictions, known as domiciles, encourage captives to locate within their territories by offering favorable regulations and low (or no) taxes. These domiciles see captive insurance as an industry that boosts their economies by providing employment and income such as annual registration fees. Examples of these domiciles include offshore locations such as Barbados, Bermuda, Dublin, Isle of Man, Guernsey, Singapore, and the Cayman Islands, as well as onshore locations such as Hawaii, Vermont, Colorado, and Tennessee. Although a captive insurer can be domiciled anywhere in the world, most organizations choose a domicile that is favorable toward the formation and operation of captives. Corporate governance concerns about the transparency of financial transactions have increased the appeal of onshore captive domiciles and offshore domiciles that offer reputable regulatory oversight. When selecting the domicile for a captive, the captive's parent should consider the following:

- Initial capital requirements, taxes, and annual fees
- Reputation and regulatory environment
- Premium and investment restrictions
- Support of infrastructure in terms of accountants, bankers, lawyers, captive managers, and other third-party service providers within the domicile

Some organizations operate a captive not only to underwrite their own loss exposures, but also to insure third-party business; that is, business that is not directly related to the captive's parent and affiliates. Some organizations use their captives in this way to enable them to operate in the insurance business. Others have found a benefit to writing third-party business over which they have some control, such as warranties on the products they sell.

There are several considerations to take into account when deciding whether to insure third-party business. For example, many domiciles have different capital and regulatory requirements for captives that are involved in third-party business. Such requirements are much more restrictive than the requirements for captives writing only affiliated business. For example, Bermuda only requires $120,000 of initial capital to form a pure captive that will provide coverage only for the parent organization's loss exposures. If the captive is going to provide coverage for unaffiliated organizations, Bermuda requires $1,000,000 of initial capital. Furthermore, writing third-party business may require additional actuarial, underwriting, and marketing expertise that the captive does not currently present. Finally, insuring third-party business adds additional risk to the captive resulting from the possibility of adverse results from that business.

Special Types of Group Captives

In addition to the single-parent and group captive structures discussed previously, there are several special types of group captives. The most common special types of group captives include the following:

- Risk retention group (RRG)
- Rent-a-captive
- Protected cell company (PCC)

Risk retention group
A group captive formed under the requirements of the Liability Risk Retention Act of 1986 to insure the parent organizations.

Rent-a-captive
An arrangement under which an organization rents capital from a captive to which it pays premiums and receives reimbursement for its losses.

A **risk retention group (RRG)** is a group captive formed under the requirements of the Liability Risk Retention Act of 1986 to insure the parent organizations. The Liability Risk Retention Act allows the formation of these groups to provide liability coverage, other than personal insurance, workers' compensation, and employers' liability. Risk retention groups were formed in direct response to the lack of liability insurance coverage available in insurance markets during the mid-1980s.

A **rent-a-captive** is an arrangement under which an organization rents capital from a captive to which it pays premiums and receives reimbursement for its losses. By using a rent-a-captive, an organization can benefit from using a captive without having to supply its own capital to establish such a company. Each insured keeps its own premium and loss account, so no risk transfer occurs among the members. However, there is no statutory separation of capital and assets in a rent-a-captive structure as there is in the protected cell company structure. Because of this, it is possible that the capital rented by the insured in a rent-a-captive structure could be diminished by losses of another insured in the structure.

A **protected cell company (PCC)** is a corporate entity separated into cells so that each participating company owns an entire cell but only a portion of the overall company. A PCC is similar in structure to a rent-a-captive. An organization pays premiums to the PCC and receives reimbursement for its losses while also receiving credit for underwriting profit and investment income. As with a rent-a-captive, each organization keeps its own premium and loss account in a separate cell from those of other members. Because the PCC is required by statute to be separated into cells, each member is assured that other members and third parties cannot access its assets in the event that any of those other members becomes insolvent. This protection is not necessarily provided by a rent-a-captive.

Protected cell company (PCC)
A corporate entity separated into cells so that each participating company owns an entire cell but only a portion of the overall company.

Ability of a Captive to Meet Risk Financing Goals

Before forming a captive, an organization should evaluate the captive insurer plan's ability to meet the organization's risk financing goals. Exhibit 5-10 explains how a captive plan can meet those goals.

EXHIBIT 5-10

Ability of a Captive Plan to Meet Risk Financing Goals

Risk Financing Goal	How a Captive Plan Meets the Goal
Pay for Losses	The captive can meet this goal if properly capitalized and managed.
Manage the Cost of Risk	The captive can reduce an organization's costs over time if properly funded and managed, despite large start-up costs.
Manage Cash Flow Variability	The captive can meet this goal by charging level premiums to the parent and affiliates and by retaining earnings in the years with lower losses to pay for higher losses in the other years.
Maintain Appropriate Level of Liquidity	The captive can meet this goal if it is properly capitalized.
Comply With Legal Requirements	The captive can be structured to meet all legal requirements, although captives are rarely licensed to operate as a primary insurer in the United States.

Finite Risk Insurance Plans

Finite risk insurance plan
A risk financing plan that transfers a limited amount of risk to an insurer.

A **finite risk insurance plan** is a risk financing plan that transfers a limited amount of risk to an insurer. Finite risk insurance differs from guaranteed cost insurance in that a large part of the insured's premium under a finite risk insurance agreement creates a fund (experience fund) for the insured's own losses. The remaining amount of the premium is used to transfer a limited portion of risk of loss to the insurer. The insurer under a finite risk insurance plan usually shares with the insured a large percentage of its profit from the plan.

A finite risk insurance plan is often used for especially hazardous loss exposures (such as those leading to environmental liability and earthquake damage) for which insurance capacity is limited or unavailable.

Unlike a guaranteed cost insurance policy, the premium for a finite risk insurance plan is a very high percentage of the policy limits. For example, an insurer might provide a limit of $10 million for a $7 million premium. The insurer's risk is limited because the most it would ever have to pay is $10 million, and it has the opportunity to earn investment income on the $7 million premium until losses are paid. By charging a substantial premium for the risk and applying a relatively low policy limit, the insurer has only a small chance that its losses and expenses will exceed its premium and earned investment income.

As with most ART measures, finite risk insurance combines many of the advantages of both risk retention and risk transfer. An insured that can control its losses receives profit sharing, including investment income, on the cash flow of the experience fund. In addition, the insured is protected by a limited amount of risk transfer in the event that losses are much higher than expected.

A finite risk plan often enables an insured to obtain higher limits than it could get using guaranteed cost insurance. Underwriters are willing to provide the higher limits because premiums and limits are combined over several years under a single plan. In addition, by using a finite risk plan, an insured can certify to third parties that it has insurance that might not otherwise be available.

Ethical Considerations: Accounting for Finite Risk Transactions

Insurers have often used finite risk insurance products as a risk financing measure to manage their own risks. When insurers purchase a finite risk insurance policy from a reinsurer, it is referred to as finite risk reinsurance. Because finite risk insurance products do not involve much risk transfer, ethical questions have been raised regarding how insurers and reinsurers should account for finite risk reinsurance arrangements in their financial statements.

Premiums paid for finite risk reinsurance can be accounted for as reinsurance premiums (reinsurance accounting) if there is sufficient risk transfer; otherwise the premiums are accounted for as a deposit (deposit accounting), similar to a deposit at a bank. Although the accounting standards (FAS #113 and SSAP #62) do not specify exactly how much risk transfer needs to occur, common interpretation of the standards is that they require at least a 10 percent chance of a loss of 10 percent or more of the coverage limits for the transaction to qualify for reinsurance accounting.

Investigations by the New York State Attorney General, the Securities and Exchange Commission, and state regulators have questioned whether the risk transfer requirements were met by certain insurers and reinsurers that accounted for some finite risk reinsurance arrangements as reinsurance transactions. These investigations are not questioning the finite risk financing measure itself. They are questioning the accounting involved in specific transactions to determine if some of these transactions have not been properly accounted for.

Before adopting a finite risk plan, an organization should evaluate the plan's ability to meet the organization's risk financing goals. Exhibit 5-11 explains how a finite risk insurance plan can meet those goals.

EXHIBIT 5-11

Ability of a Finite Risk Plan to Meet Risk Financing Goals

Risk Financing Goal	How a Finite Risk Plan Meets the Goal
Pay for Losses	The plan can meet this goal because the insurer pays for losses as they become due. However, because of the limited risk transfer, the insured ultimately pays for almost all of its own losses.
Manage the Cost of Risk	The plan can meet this goal because the profit-sharing feature encourages and rewards successful risk control efforts and thereby reduces an organization's cost of risk.
Manage Cash Flow Variability	The plan can meet this goal because cash flows are smoothed over multiple periods; however, large premiums may be due at outset.
Maintain Appropriate Level of Liquidity	The plan cannot meet this goal because premium payments are usually paid upfront.
Comply With Legal Requirements	The plan can meet this goal because the insurer issues a policy guaranteeing that all covered claims will be paid.

Pools

Pool
A group of organizations that insure each other's loss exposures.

A **pool** is a group of organizations that insure each other's loss exposures. Each insured member of the pool contributes premium based on its loss exposures and in exchange the pool pays for each insured's covered losses. In some pools, the members also contribute capital. Pools can be organized in a variety of ways, including as a stock insurer or as a not-for-profit unincorporated association governed by its members. However, the structure of most pools is less formal than the structure of a group captive.

A pool operates like an insurer by collecting premiums, paying losses, purchasing excess insurance or reinsurance, and providing other services such as risk control consulting. Pools can be formed to cover various types of loss exposures and are well-suited for organizations that are too small to use a captive insurer. For example, in the United States, workers' compensation pools are common and are permitted in most states. The individual states regulate the formation and operation of these pools. Public entities are commonly members of workers' compensation pools.

The pool achieves savings through economies of scale in administration, claim handling, and the purchase of excess insurance or reinsurance. Each pool member might realize a savings in premium compared with that for guaranteed cost insurance, yet still benefit from some risk transfer to the other pool members. A suitably designed pool can reduce an organization's cost of risk and keep the uncertainty of the cost associated with its retained losses at a tolerable level.

Before joining a pool, an organization should evaluate the pool's ability to meet the organization's risk financing goals. Exhibit 5-12 explains how pools can meet those goals.

Retrospective Rating Plans

Retrospective rating plan
A risk financing plan under which an organization buys insurance subject to a rating plan that adjusts the premium rate after the end of the policy period based on a portion of the insured's actual losses during the policy period.

A **retrospective rating plan** is a risk financing plan under which an organization buys insurance subject to a rating plan that adjusts the premium rate after the end of the policy period based on a portion of the insured's actual losses during the policy period. Retrospective rating plans are used to finance low-to-medium-severity losses and are usually combined with other risk financing plans (such as excess liability insurance) to cover high-severity losses. An organization must have a substantial insurance premium, usually amounting to several hundred thousand dollars per year, to benefit from a retrospective rating plan.

At its inception, a retrospective rating plan appears to operate in the same way as a guaranteed cost insurance plan. The insured pays a premium (the deposit premium) at the beginning of the policy period and the insurer issues an insurance policy and agrees to pay covered losses up to the policy limit. However, in a retrospective rating plan, the insured's losses during the policy period are considered in calculating a major portion of the premium. The

---

EXHIBIT 5-12

Ability of a Pool to Meet Risk Financing Goals

Risk Financing Goal	How a Pool Meets the Goal
Pay for Losses	A pool can meet this goal because there is some risk transfer to other members of the pool. However, ultimately, the pool must pay for its own losses.
Manage the Cost of Risk	A pool can meet this goal through economies of scale in administration.
Manage Cash Flow Variability	A pool can meet this goal through risk sharing with the other members. This risk sharing can be a major benefit of a pool if it has enough loss exposures to benefit from the law of large numbers.
Maintain Appropriate Level of Liquidity	A pool can meet this goal if adequately funded and managed, reducing an organization's necessary level of liquidity.
Comply With Legal Requirements	A pool can meet this goal if organized and managed within state regulations.

---

insurer (using a rating formula agreed on at policy inception) adjusts the premium after the end of the policy period to include a portion of the insured's covered losses that occurred during the policy period. If the premium due is more than the original deposit premium, the insurer will collect additional premium from the insured. If the premium due is less than the deposit premium, the insurer will issue a refund to the insured. Because the premium is adjusted upward or downward based directly on a portion of covered losses, the insured is, in effect, retaining a portion of its own losses.

Organizations commonly use retrospective rating plans for losses arising from their liability loss exposures that are covered by workers' compensation, auto liability, and general liability insurance policies. Organizations also use retrospective rating plans to finance auto physical damage and crime losses.

Comparison of Retrospective Rating and Experience Rating Plans

Retrospective rating is frequently confused with experience rating because both consider the insured's loss experience. Experience rating adjusts the premium for the current policy period to recognize the loss experience of the insured during *past* policy periods. In contrast, retrospective rating adjusts the premium for the current policy period to recognize the insured's loss experience during the *current* policy period.

Loss limit
The level at which a loss occurrence is limited for the purpose of calculating a retrospectively rated premium.

Retrospective premiums are calculated using a loss limit. A **loss limit** is the level at which a loss occurrence is limited for the purpose of calculating a retrospectively rated premium. The loss limit can vary and is negotiated by the insurer and the insured. For example, the loss limit under a retrospective rating plan might be $100,000 per occurrence. In this case, the first $100,000 of each covered loss occurrence is included in the retrospective premium, and the amount of each loss occurrence that exceeds $100,000 and is less than the policy limit is transferred to the insurer.

The adjusted premium under a retrospective rating plan is subject to a maximum and a minimum amount, called the maximum premium and the minimum premium, respectively. For example, a retrospective rating plan might have a minimum premium of $200,000 and a maximum premium of $1,000,000. If the insured experiences no losses during the policy period, the minimum premium of $200,000 still applies. If, during the policy period, the insured experiences a total of $1,400,000 in losses subject to the policy's loss limit, the premium is limited to the maximum premium of $1,000,000.

Because the premium for a retrospective rating plan includes a portion of the insured's covered losses during the policy period and is subject to maximum and minimum amounts, an insured retains a portion of its losses. If an insured incurs higher-than-average losses during a policy period, the final adjusted premium under a retrospective rating plan is higher than the premium that the insured would pay under a guaranteed cost insurance plan to cover the same losses. The opposite is true if losses are lower than average. The portion of losses not retained is transferred to the insurer, which is compensated through risk transfer premium charges that are built into the retrospective rating plan premium. The retrospective rating plan premium also includes charges for other components, such as residual market loadings, premium taxes, and insurer overhead and profit. Such charges are also found in guaranteed cost insurance policies.

Retrospective rating plans require only a moderate amount of administration by the insured. The insured's responsibility is limited to making premium payments and arranging for any required security, such as a letter of credit, to guarantee future payments. The insurer is responsible for many of the administrative tasks, such as adjusting claims, making necessary filings with the states, and paying applicable premium taxes and fees. Because a portion of the premium includes the insured's covered losses, the insured should periodically audit the insurer's claim handling, loss payment, and loss reserving practices. Often, a broker or a risk management consultant performs this audit on the insured's behalf.

An organization can save certain expenses by retaining a portion of losses under a retrospective rating plan instead of transferring all losses under a guaranteed cost insurance plan. One significant expense saved is insurer risk charges, which are extra charges that an insurer includes as part of its risk transfer premium to cover the chance that losses will be higher than expected.

Retrospective rating plans encourage risk control. With a retrospective rating plan, an organization that is able to prevent and/or reduce its losses quickly realizes a premium savings compared with what it would pay under a guaranteed cost insurance plan. This direct link between losses and premium is a major incentive for an insured to control its losses.

If designed correctly, a retrospective rating plan also provides financial stability. If the loss limit and the maximum premium are set so as to reduce the uncertainty of the insured's premium adjustments to a level that it can tolerate, then the insured benefits from the relative stability that the retrospective rating plan provides for its earnings, net worth, and cash flow. If a retrospective rating plan covers more than one type of loss exposure, then the insured also benefits from the stability provided through diversification by retaining losses from different types of loss exposures under a single plan.

A retrospective rating plan can help an organization meet its risk financing goals by providing an appropriate balance between risk retention and risk transfer. Before adopting a retrospective rating plan, an organization should evaluate the plan's ability to meet the organization's risk financing goals. Exhibit 5-13 describes how a retrospective rating plan can meet these goals.

EXHIBIT 5-13

Ability of a Retrospective Rating Plan to Meet Risk Financing Goals

Risk Financing Goal	How a Retrospective Rating Plan Meets the Goal
Pay for Losses	The plan can meet this goal because, as with any insurance plan, the insurer pays for losses as they become due.
Manage the Cost of Risk	The plan can meet this goal because it includes a significant amount of retention and can reduce an organization's cost of risk over the long run.
Manage Cash Flow Variability	The plan can meet this goal because it helps manage some cash flow uncertainty, but because of the retrospective nature of the premium, some cash flow uncertainty remains.
Maintain Appropriate Level of Liquidity	The plan can meet this goal if the loss limit and maximum premium are chosen carefully.
Comply With Legal Requirements	The plan can meet this goal because an insurer issues a policy guaranteeing that all covered claims will be paid.

Hold-Harmless Agreements

Hold-harmless agreements are a noninsurance risk transfer measure; that is, a risk financing measure that transfers all or part of the financial consequences of loss to another party, other than an insurer.

A hold-harmless agreement can be a stand-alone contract or a clause within a contract. An example of the latter would be the inclusion of the following hold-harmless agreement as part of a leasing arrangement:

> To the fullest extent permitted by law, the lessee shall indemnify, defend, and hold harmless the lessor, agents, and employees of the lessor from and against all claims arising out of or resulting from the leased premises.

Hold-harmless agreements are commonly used to assign the responsibility for losses arising out of a particular relationship or activity. For example, it is common for manufacturers to enter into hold-harmless agreements with distributors whereby the manufacturer agrees to assume the liability losses the distributor suffers as a result of distributing the manufacturer's products. This type of hold-harmless agreement is a risk financing measure that transfers the financial responsibility for liability losses from the distributor to the manufacturer.

Before using a hold-harmless agreement as a risk financing measure, an organization should evaluate its ability to meet the organization's risk financing goals. Exhibit 5-14 explains how a hold-harmless agreement can meet those goals.

EXHIBIT 5-14

Ability of a Hold-Harmless Agreement to Meet Risk Financing Goals

Risk Financing Goal	How a Hold-Harmless Agreement Meets the Goal
Pay for Losses	The agreement can meet this goal provided the loss exposures are covered by the agreement.
Manage the Cost of Risk	The agreement can meet this goal subject to any other contractual demands the other party requires before accepting the hold-harmless agreement.
Manage Cash Flow Variability	The agreement can meet this goal subject to the extent of the agreement.
Maintain Appropriate Level of Liquidity	The agreement can meet this goal because the organization requires less liquidity with a hold-harmless agreement compared with retention or other ART measures.
Comply With Legal Requirements	The agreement can meet this goal, especially regarding loss exposures that are required (by law or contractual obligation) to be transferred.

Capital Market Solutions

A **capital market** is a financial market in which long-term securities are traded. Bonds and other financial assets having a maturity of more than one year are bought and sold. Recent innovative approaches to risk financing have used capital market products such as securitization, derivatives, and contingent capital arrangements as additional ART measures.

Because these new capital market products involve significant time and expense to implement, only a few, large organizations (including insurers and reinsurers) have used them to finance risk. Nonetheless, these organizations have been able to use capital market products to finance a variety of organization- and industry-specific risks. For example, insurers have used capital market products mainly for catastrophe risks, such as the risk of large earthquake or hurricane losses. However, these products could also be used to finance any type of insurable risk, and some predict that the use of capital market products by insurers and reinsurers will expand rapidly.

Capital market
A financial market in which long-term securities are traded.

Securitization

Securitization is the process of creating a marketable investment security based on a financial transaction's expected cash flows. For example, a bank might securitize its mortgage receivables and sell them through an intermediary (called a special purpose vehicle or SPV) to investors. In this case, the bank (mortgagee) lends money to both individuals and organizations (mortgagors) to purchase real property. The mortgagors make a promise to repay the mortgage through periodic payments to the bank. These mortgage payments are mortgage receivables to the bank. The bank, through an SPV, may sell a mortgage-backed security to investors. The bank collects the money from the investors, and transfers the mortgage receivables to the investors. In this type of transaction, the bank is no longer exposed to any risk of nonpayment by the mortgagors. That risk has been transferred from the bank to the investors through the mortgage-backed securities. These securities appeal to investors when they offer a sufficiently attractive return for the perceived risk of non-payment by the mortgagor. The bank exchanges one asset for another. It sells its mortgage receivables, which are subject to the possibility of default and other risks, and it receives the investors' money in exchange. Through securitization, the risk inherent in the mortgage receivables is transferred from the bank to the investors.

Securitization
The process of creating a marketable investment security based on a financial transaction's expected cash flows.

Insurance securitization, a unique form of securitization, is the process of creating a marketable insurance-linked security (similar to a mortgage-backed security) based on the cash flows that arise from the transfer of insurable risks. These cash flows are similar to premium and loss payments under an insurance policy. The most common insurance securitizations are catastrophe bonds. Exhibit 5-15 contains graphs of catastrophe bond activity and the number of catastrophe bonds issued up to April 2005.

Insurance securitization
The process of creating a marketable insurance-linked security based on the cash flows that arise from the transfer of insurable risks.

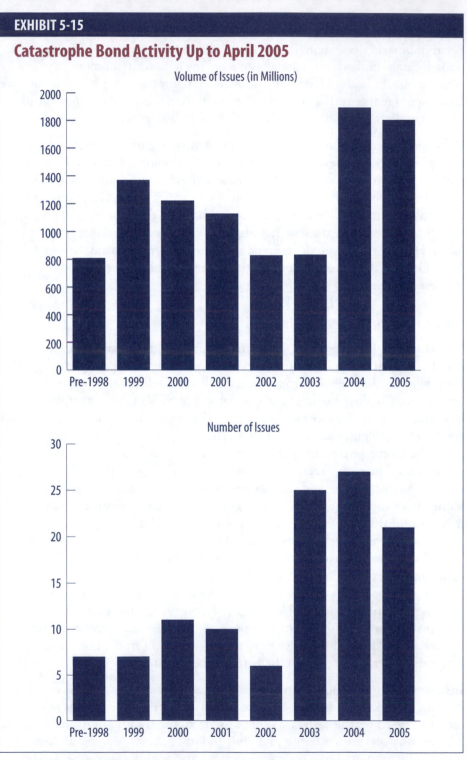

EXHIBIT 5-15

Catastrophe Bond Activity Up to April 2005

Source: Lane Financial LLC, *2005 Review of Trends in Insurance Securitization*, www.lanefinancialllc.com/pub/
sec1/20050430_Game_On_2005_Review_of_Trends_in_Insurance_Securitization4.pdf, p. 6 (accessed
December 15, 2005).

Insurers or reinsurers sell insurance policies that cover losses related to natural catastrophes. For example, the insurance policies may cover property damage caused by hurricanes or earthquakes. Because of the catastrophic nature of the coverage, insurers and reinsurers may have difficulty using pooling and the law of large numbers to adequately mitigate the catastrophic risk. One solution is to transfer that risk to the capital markets where investors holding diversified portfolios have a larger pool of assets to absorb catastrophic losses.

Similar to mortgage-backed securities, insurers and reinsurers can purchase insurance from an SPV, which will use the premiums to sell a catastrophe bond to investors. The investor pays the principal to the SPV. At the end of the bond term (typically one to three years), provided no covered catastrophe has occurred, the investor receives both the principal and interest payment from the SPV. If a catastrophe did occur, the investor receives less in return. Depending on the terms of the bond issue, the investor may only receive the principal with no interest income, or may only receive a portion of the principal. The premiums paid by the insurer are used by the SPV to offset the cost of bond issue and to cover any interest payments (payment to the investor) promised by the bond.

The payoff on catastrophe bonds is linked to the occurrences of major catastrophes during the bond's term. For example, suppose an investor purchases a bond from an SPV that provides a rate of return higher than a similarly rated corporate bond or a U.S. Treasury bond of comparable maturity. The investor assumes the risk that a hurricane might occur during the bond's term in exchange for a higher rate of return. If a hurricane does occur and causes losses that exceed a specified dollar threshold, the investor's return on the bond is reduced. If total property losses are high enough to trigger a reduced return on the bond, either the investor's interest income or the interest income and principal repayments on the bond may be lowered, depending on the terms of the bond and the extent of the losses. The SPV uses the savings in interest and principal repayments to pay cash to the issuing insurer or reinsurer, which uses the cash to offset its hurricane losses. Through the process of insurance securitization, the risk of loss caused by a hurricane has been securitized by linking it with the returns provided to investors in a marketable security.

Securitization passes some of the catastrophe risk that an insurer has accumulated through its insurance policies on to investors, thereby reducing the insurer's overall risk. From the investor's perspective, insurance-linked securities help diversify the investor's portfolio because the insurable risk embedded in insurance-linked securities is not closely correlated with the risks normally involved in other investments.

Hedging

Hedging is the purchase or sale of one asset to offset the risks associated with another asset. The asset held to offset the risk is often a contract, such as an option or futures contract. Hedging as a risk financing measure is well suited

Hedging
The purchase or sale of one asset to offset the risks associated with another asset.

to business risks created by price changes. For example, commodities (such as energy, metal, or agricultural), foreign exchange rates or currencies, and interest rates are all frequently hedged. The risk transferred is the exposure to loss from declines or increases in an asset's market price. The asset concerned is one that the hedging party holds for an extended period as a normal part of doing business. For example, suppose a manufacturer knows that it is going to require a substantial quantity of oil to support its manufacturing activities. If the manufacturer is concerned about the volatility in oil prices, it can hedge against changes in oil prices by entering a contract to buy the oil at a certain price and time at some point in the future. This type of hedging of speculative business risks allows an organization to protect itself against possible price-level losses by sacrificing possible price-level gains.

As another example, suppose that a soybean farmer is exposed to loss if the market price of soybean drops significantly between when he or she plants the crop and when he or she sells the harvest. Although the farmer is exposed to loss if the market price decreases, soybean consumers, such as a soy milk manufacturer, may profit from such a price decrease. If the market price were to rise, the farmer would profit but the manufacturer would be exposed to a loss. To manage this market price risk, the farmer could enter into a soybean hedge with the manufacturer during the soybean growing season, locking in a future sales price via a futures contract before bringing the soybeans to market. Changes in market prices—whether increases or decreases—would no longer affect the farmer's anticipated revenue on a per-unit basis, just as they would no longer affect the manufacturer, because the price has already been agreed upon. Both manufacturer and farmer are insulated from gains or losses associated with market price changes.

Any price or other financial value that is uncertain in the future and that can be objectively measured, such as a stock market index, common stock price, commodity price, or consumer or industrial price index, can be the basis for a hedge. Those prices or financial values are called underlying assets. The hedging contracts that are based on those underlying assets are called derivatives. A **derivative** is a financial contract that derives its value from the value of another asset.

Derivative
A financial contract that derives its value from the value of another asset.

For a derivative contract to be a successful hedging contract, two parties must be willing to hedge the underlying asset. For example, the soybean farmer (exposed to loss when prices decrease) would not be able to hedge the soybean prices for his or her harvest if there were no consumer (such as the soy milk manufacturer) who was exposed to loss when prices increase. There are several exchanges in which derivative contracts are traded that are easily accessible by organizations seeking to hedge.

One advantage of hedging is that hedging against possible net income losses from price changes can reduce an organization's business risk loss exposures. Consequently, an organization that uses hedging has a greater capacity to bear both business risks and hazard risks and at the same time reduces its dependence on traditional financial and insurance markets for its risk transfer needs.

A disadvantage of hedging is that it can destabilize not only an organization's general risk financing plans but also its entire financial structure. If an organization's retained earnings or capital are seriously jeopardized by unwise speculative investments in hedging instruments, the earnings or capital may no longer reliably pay for retained losses. Consequently, the financial security that they provide could be greatly impaired. The goal of reducing an organization's cost of risk for losses by generating high returns for loss reserves must be balanced against the goal of ensuring that funds will be available when needed to pay for losses.

Finally, the value of the derivative contract might not correspond exactly with organizations' losses. As hedging contracts are based on some general measure or index, if the general measure or index does not provide a payout that is highly correlated with an organization's losses, the risk financing measure does not provide the needed protection. As mentioned previously, these types of risk financing measures can expose an organization to basis risk.

Contingent Capital Arrangements

A **contingent capital arrangement** is an agreement, entered into before any losses occur, that enables an organization to raise cash by selling stock or issuing debt on prearranged terms after a loss occurs that exceeds a certain threshold. The organization pays a capital commitment fee to the party that agrees in advance to purchase the debt or equity after the loss.

With a contingent capital arrangement, the organization does not transfer its risk of loss to investors. Instead, it receives a capital injection in the form of debt or equity after a loss occurs to help it pay for the loss. Because the terms are agreed to in advance, the organization generally receives more favorable terms than it would receive if it were to try to raise capital after a large loss, when it is likely to be in a weakened capital condition. For example, a publicly traded pharmaceutical manufacturer may have a contingent capital arrangement with an investment bank that requires the investment bank to purchase a specified number of the manufacturer's shares at a pre-determined price if the manufacturer suffers a significant property loss at its main manufacturing plant for which it was unable to acquire property insurance. The manufacturer pays the investment bank a fee at the beginning of the agreement. If the loss occurs, the investment bank purchases the shares at the pre-determined price, providing the manufacturer with the capital necessary to rebuild the plant. If no loss occurs, the agreement expires without any stock sale occurring. Similar agreements for bond issues have also been structured.

Ability of Capital Market Solutions to Meet Risk Financing Goals

Before using capital market solutions as risk financing measures, an organization should evaluate their ability to meet the organization's risk financing goals. Exhibit 5-16 explains how capital market solutions can meet those goals.

Contingent capital arrangement
An agreement, entered into before any losses occur, that enables an organization to raise cash by selling stock or issuing debt at prearranged terms after a loss occurs that exceeds a certain threshold.

EXHIBIT 5-16

Ability of Capital Market Solutions to Meet Risk Financing Goals

Risk Financing Goal	How Capital Market Solutions Meet the Goal
Pay for Losses	They can meet this goal because some of the financial consequences of the losses are transferred to investors.
Manage the Cost of Risk	They cannot typically meet this goal. Capital market solutions are expensive relative to other risk financing measures.
Manage Cash Flow Variability	They can meet this goal because some of the financial consequences of the losses are transferred to investors.
Maintain Appropriate Level of Liquidity	They can meet this goal because capital market solutions can reduce the necessary level of liquidity that an organization needs to maintain.
Comply With Legal Requirements	They can meet this goal if correctly structured.

Combinations of Risk Financing Measures

Rather than using a single risk financing measure, individuals or organizations often combine two or more measures in order to meet their risk financing goals. Many combinations can be used, and frequently risk financing measures that transfer a substantial portion of risk are combined with retention and other risk financing measures that retain a significant portion of the risk. For example, an organization might self-insure its low-to-medium severity loss exposures and purchase guaranteed cost insurance for its high-severity loss exposures. Similarly, captives may be combined with guaranteed cost insurance or reinsurance or guaranteed cost insurance may be combined with contingent capital arrangements. Many possible combinations are available to meet an organization's risk financing goals. The combinations are limited only by the ingenuity of the organization, its broker, its risk management professional, and any participating transfer parties.

APPLICATION OF RISK FINANCING MEASURES

Not all risk financing measures are applicable to every loss exposure an organization faces. Some measures are more suitable than others, depending on which of the four categories of loss exposures (property, liability, personnel, or net income) that they are intended to address.

Property Loss Exposures

Property loss exposures can be divided into two categories: tangible property loss exposures and intangible property loss exposures. Tangible property consists of real property (land and buildings or other structures attached to the land) and tangible personal property. The risk financing measures that are most applicable to property loss exposures vary based on the type of property as well as the cause of loss threatening the property. However, the measures most applicable to property loss exposures are those that are closely related to guaranteed cost insurance.

For real property loss exposures, the most commonly used risk financing measures are guaranteed cost insurance, captives, pools, and large deductible plans. Real property losses tend to be low-frequency, high-severity losses that are typically transferred rather than retained. These types of loss exposures are well suited to the use of pooling and the law of large numbers to help reduce the volatility of losses. An exception is organizations that have a sufficient number of real properties that they can pool the loss exposures themselves or organizations that have such unique real property loss exposures that they would be unable to pool their loss exposures with those of other organizations. For these organizations, retention measures are often required.

Capital market solutions for real property loss exposures are typically tied to a particular cause of loss. For example, catastrophe bonds usually define the trigger as a windstorm or earthquake of a particular magnitude. Catastrophe bonds have been used almost exclusively by insurers or reinsurers who have insured a sizeable portfolio of real property loss exposures within a geographic region prone to natural disasters. Some notable exceptions include the Disney Corporation and the Taiwanese government. Disney, instead of purchasing a property insurance policy that provided coverage against the earthquake cause of loss on its Tokyo theme park, opted to go directly to the capital markets with a catastrophe bond issue to provide a source of capital if an earthquake caused substantial damage to the theme park. The Taiwanese government issued an earthquake catastrophe bond to reinsure the government's earthquake insurance pool.

Personal property loss exposures, because they tend to have more frequent and less severe losses than real property exposures, are often better managed with retention measures. For example, a rental car agency may only have one building (one real property loss exposure) but hundreds of automobiles to rent (hundreds of personal property loss exposures). The rental car agency is in a better position to retain the risk of loss to automobiles than to its building. The loss of one automobile is more likely than the loss of the building, but not as financially damaging to the agency.

In addition to retention, transfer measures such as guaranteed cost insurance can be used for personal property loss exposures. Hold-harmless agreements are also often used. In the rental car agency example, the agency can use a hold-harmless agreement to transfer the risk of auto physical damage and liability to the renter.

Although a number of insurers have developed policies to provide coverage for electronic data, risk financing measures are not typically used with intangible property loss exposures. Risk control measures are better suited to these loss exposures. Whereas it is possible to insure electronic data, it is often difficult to insure the theft of trade secrets or loss of brand reputation, because intangible property and its related causes of loss are not as well defined for insurance purposes as tangible property.

Liability Loss Exposures

An individual or organization can be held legally liable because of three causes of loss: torts, statutes, and contracts. Liability loss exposures can be managed with a combination of risk retention and risk transfer measures, such as large deductible plans, captives, finite risk plans, or pools. In addition, the guaranteed cost insurance market has several well-developed insurance products designed for liability loss exposures, such as products liability, professional liability, and environmental liability. The availability and affordability of risk transfer measures for liability loss exposures varies widely based on the specific loss exposure and on supply-side factors in the insurance industry.

Personnel Loss Exposures

Personnel loss exposures arise from events occurring both inside and outside the workplace and are unavoidable because all organizations have key employees. Very few risk transfer measures are available to organizations seeking to finance their personnel loss exposures. Therefore, these loss exposures are typically retained. An organization can purchase life insurance on key employees to help defer some of the losses it would incur in the event of the untimely death of a key employee. However, if a key employee were to retire, become disabled, or leave the organization for another career opportunity, the organization's losses would not be offset by a life insurance policy. Personnel loss exposures are better handled through risk control than through risk transfer measures.

Net Income Loss Exposures

Net income loss exposures are generally associated with property, liability, or personnel loss exposures. Therefore, any of the risk financing measures previously discussed in relation to those categories of loss exposures also indirectly finance net income loss exposures. In addition, guaranteed cost insurance policies such as business income insurance are specifically designed to provide coverage for net income losses that are generated by hazard risks. Capital market solutions (such as contingent debt or equity) can be used to offset net income losses caused by a specific trigger, such as property losses at a manufacturing facility or liability losses resulting from products liability. In addition, capital market solutions such as derivatives are ideally suited as risk financing measures for many net income losses generated by speculative risks, including rising commodity prices or rising interest rates.

Each of the risk financing measures discussed in this chapter can be implemented as part of the organization's risk financing program. For example, an organization that chooses to use guaranteed cost insurance to transfer the financial consequences of some of its property loss exposures must develop and implement an overall program that puts this risk financing measure to the best possible use for the organization. The program should address matters such as covered causes of loss, policy limits, deductible levels, and types and amounts of excess insurance, if any. An organization's risk financing program will likely use many risk financing measures simultaneously.

SUMMARY

Risk financing is a conscious act or decision not to act that generates the funds to pay for losses and risk control measures or offset variability in cash flows. Similar to risk control, individuals and organizations have risk financing goals that are designed to support the overall risk management goals. Risk financing goals include the following:

- Pay for losses—both paying for the actual losses or portions of losses that an organization retains and paying transfer costs, which are the costs paid in order to transfer responsibility for losses to another party

- Manage the cost of risk—including administrative, risk control, and risk financing costs

- Manage cash flow variability—requires determining the organization's maximum tolerance levels and arranging the risk management program within those parameters

- Maintain an appropriate level of liquidity—preserving a level of cash liquidity that is sufficient to pay for retained losses

- Comply with legal requirements—adhering to laws and regulations that either mandate risk financing measures or affect how risk financing measures are implemented

Traditionally, risk financing measures have been classified into two groups—retention and transfer. However, because most risk financing measures involve elements of both retention and transfer, the distinction between retention and transfer is eroding. Retention is a risk financing technique by which losses and variability in cash flows are financed by generating funds within the organization. The four planned retention funding techniques are current expensing of losses, using an unfunded reserve, using a funded reserve, and borrowing funds. The advantages of using retention as a risk financing technique include cost savings, control of claims process, timing of cash flows, and incentives for risk control.

Transfer is a risk financing technique by which the financial responsibility for losses and variability in cash flows is shifted to another party. Although a pure transfer would shift the responsibility for the entire loss to another party, most transfer measures involve some type of deductible, limit, or other restriction so that the organization pays (retains) at least some portion of the loss.

In addition, the ultimate responsibility for paying for the loss remains with the organization (transferor). The transferor is reliant on the good faith and financial strength of the transferee as well as on the judicial enforceability of the transfer agreement.

Despite the limitations, there are significant advantages to using risk transfer measures as part of a risk financing program, including reducing exposure to large losses, reducing cash flow variability, avoiding adverse employee and public relations, and providing ancillary services.

When making risk financing decisions, an individual or organization needs to evaluate the ability of the retention and transfer measures to meet the risk financing goals. Often, how effective retention is at achieving a risk financing goal compared with transfer depends on how an organization structures and manages its retention.

Making risk financing decisions should also involve consideration of the specific characteristics of both the loss exposure involved and the characteristics of the individual or organization. The frequency and severity of losses associated with each loss exposure are vital to determining whether a loss exposure should be fully retained or whether some form of transfer is appropriate. Even if two individuals or organizations have the same set of loss exposures, differences between individuals or organizations may result in vastly different optimal retention levels. Factors that affect individual retention levels include risk tolerance, financial condition, core operations, ability to diversify, ability to control losses, and ability to administer the retention plan.

A variety of risk financing measures are available that enable an individual or organization to meet risk financing goals, including the following:

- *Guaranteed cost insurance.* Guaranteed cost insurance policies are a form of funded risk transfer. In exchange for a premium, the insurer agrees to pay for all the organization's losses that are covered by the insurance policy, typically subject to a deductible and policy limit. The insurer also agrees to provide necessary services, such as claim handling and liability claim defense.

- *Self-insurance.* Self-insurance is a form of retention under which an organization records its losses and maintains a formal system to pay for them.

- *Large deductible plans.* A large deductible plan is an insurance policy with a per occurrence or per accident deductible of $100,000 or more. A large deductible plan is similar to a self-insurance plan in that it exposes the organization to a relatively large amount of loss. In exchange for this exposure, the large deductible plan insurer provides a premium reduction.

- *Captive insurers.* A captive insurer, or captive, is a subsidiary formed to insure the loss exposures of its parent company and the parent's affiliates. Captives can be owned by a single parent or by multiple parents. Special types of captives include risk retention groups (RRGs), rent-a-captives, and protected cell companies (PCCs).

- *Finite risk insurance plans.* A finite risk insurance plan is a risk financing plan that transfers a limited amount of risk to an insurer. A large part of the insured's premium under a finite risk insurance agreement creates a fund (experience fund) for the insured's own losses. The remaining amount of the premium is used to transfer a limited portion of risk of loss to the insurer. The insurer under a finite risk insurance plan usually shares with the insured a large percentage of its profit from the finite risk insurance plan.

- *Pools.* A pool is a group of organizations that insure each other's loss exposures. Each insured member of the pool contributes premium based on its loss exposures and in exchange the pool pays for each insured's covered losses. In some pools, the members also contribute capital.

- *Retrospective rating plans.* A retrospective rating plan is a risk financing plan under which an organization buys insurance subject to a rating plan that adjusts the premium rate after the end of the policy period based on a portion of the insured's actual losses during the policy period.

- *Hold-harmless agreements.* A hold-harmless agreement is a contractual provision requiring one party to assume another party's legal liability in the event of a specified loss. Hold-harmless agreements are a noninsurance risk transfer measure; that is, a risk financing measure that transfers all or part of the financial consequences of loss to another party, other than an insurer.

- *Capital market solutions.* Recent innovative approaches to risk financing have used capital market products such as securitization, derivatives, and contingent capital arrangements as additional ART measures.

Not all risk financing measures are applicable to every loss exposure an organization faces. For real property loss exposures, the most commonly used risk financing measures are guaranteed cost insurance, captives, pools, and large deductible plans. Real property losses tend to be low frequency, high severity losses that are typically transferred rather than retained.

Liability loss exposures can be managed with a combination of risk retention and risk transfer measures, such as large deductible plans, captives, finite risk plans, or pools. In addition, the guaranteed cost insurance market has products designed for liability loss exposures such as products liability, professional liability, and environmental liability.

Very few risk transfer measures are available to organizations seeking to finance their personnel loss exposures. An organization can purchase life insurance on a key employee, but if that employee were to retire, become disabled, or leave the organization for another career opportunity, the organization's losses would not be offset by a life insurance policy.

Any of the risk financing measures for property, liability, or personnel loss exposures also indirectly finance net income loss exposures. In addition, an organization can use guaranteed cost insurance policies, such as business income insurance, and capital market solutions, such as derivatives.

Chapter 6

Direct Your Learning

Financial Services and Insurance Markets

After learning the content of this chapter and completing the corresponding course guide assignment, you should be able to:

- Compare each type of consumer based on the following: insurance needs, knowledge of the market, market access methods, negotiating ability, and choice of risk financing alternatives.

- Explain how producers provide consumers with access to insurers.

- Describe the role of banks in the distribution of insurance products and services.

- Explain how admitted insurers, nonadmitted insurers, residual markets, and government programs meet the insurance needs of customers.

- Explain how insurers use reinsurance and financial markets as risk financing techniques.

- Explain the role in insurance markets of third-party administrators (TPAs), special investigative units (SIUs), inspectors, consultants, and regulators.

- Explain how each of the following influences competition in insurance markets: number and size of competing insurers, substitutes for insurance, knowledge of the market, and size and growth of overall market.

- Define or describe each of the Key Words and Phrases for this chapter.

Develop Your Perspective

What are the main topics covered in the chapter?

The insurance industry is a major component of the financial services sector and it provides insurance products and services to individuals and organizations both nationally and internationally. Insurance markets can be reviewed by examining the parties involved—consumers, producers, insurers, and various third parties—as well as the competitive environment in which insurance transactions occur.

Identify all of the parties involved in your insurance transactions.

- Are any of your risks insured in the excess and surplus lines market?
- Are any of your risks reinsured?

Why is it important to learn about these topics?

Several factors affect the functioning of insurance markets. By understanding the interaction of the factors and the parties involved, you can develop a deeper appreciation of the behaviors and reactions in response to events that change the market.

Consider how individuals and organizations are affected by competition in the insurance markets.

- What recent legislation has affected competition in the insurance market?
- How can mergers and acquisitions change the competitive environment for insurers and insureds?

How can you use what you will learn?

Examine the insurance market in your state.

- How many insurers are admitted in your state?
- What types of residual markets operate in your state?

Chapter 6
Financial Services and Insurance Markets

The financial services market, both in the United States and internationally, is an enormous market that is expanding every year. The insurance industry, which is a major component of that financial services market, employs millions of individuals and controls trillions of dollars of assets. The primary function of the insurance industry is to provide products and services used as risk financing mechanisms by individuals and organizations as part of their overall risk management plans. Property-casualty insurers in the U.S. alone collect over $400 billion in net premiums written annually.[1]

Insurance markets consist of the insurers, their marketing systems (producers), consumers, and a variety of third parties, all of whom are involved in developing, marketing, distributing, and purchasing insurance products and services. The transactions between these parties occur in an increasingly competitive market. This competition is an important aspect of the functioning of insurance markets. Understanding how insurance markets function will enable insurance professionals to better comprehend their role in the insurance market and how market changes will affect their professional responsibilities.

INSURANCE MARKETS OVERVIEW

Millions of insurance transactions occur in the U.S. each year. Insurance markets are the business environment in which buyers and sellers of insurance products and services come together to negotiate insurance transactions. As with any market, insurance markets can be described in a variety of ways, such as by the participants involved (buyers and sellers), the transactions that occur, or the competitive functioning of the market.

Buyers of insurance (consumers) can be divided into individuals and organizations. Individuals purchase personal lines insurance products, including homeowners, auto liability, auto physical damage, and umbrella liability coverages. Organizations purchase commercial lines insurance products, such as commercial property, general liability, products liability, workers' compensation, and umbrella and excess liability coverages. Sellers of insurance products and services include insurers, their marketing systems or producers (agents, brokers, banks, and excess and surplus lines intermediaries), and other third-party providers. Insurance transactions include purchasing insurance policies and purchasing any of the related products or services. These transactions are affected by market elements such as the number and size of insurers, availability of substitutes, the information available to consumers, and the size and growth of the overall market.

In the U.S., there are millions of consumers, tens of thousands of producers, and thousands of insurers and reinsurers. There are also thousands of third-party providers of products and services associated with insurance products. Exhibit 6-1 illustrates the transaction framework discussed in this chapter. The relationships discussed are general in nature and will not necessarily govern all transactions.

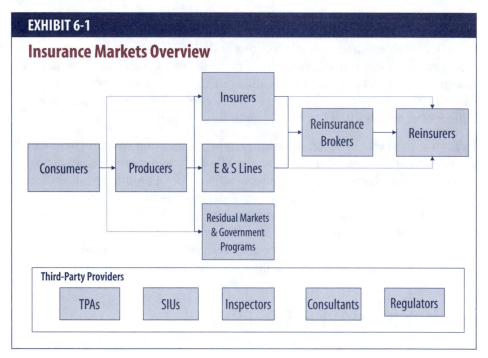

EXHIBIT 6-1

Insurance Markets Overview

Consumer Profile

Insurance markets are highly segmented—by products, by regions, and by the types of consumers they serve. One of the major segmentations of property-casualty insurance is the distinction between personal lines and commercial lines of insurance. Personal lines of insurance are insurance products targeted at and purchased by individuals. The most common personal lines of insurance are homeowners and private passenger auto. Commercial lines of insurance are insurance products targeted at and purchased by organizations. The most common commercial lines of insurance include commercial property, commercial general liability, and workers' compensation. Exhibit 6-2 contains a breakdown by line of net written premiums for 2004. This exhibit shows that the premium volume in the insurance industry is reasonably evenly split between personal lines and commercial lines, with the largest line being personal auto.

EXHIBIT 6-2

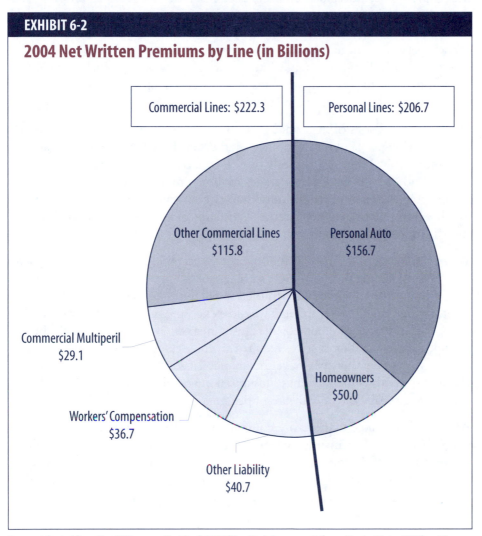

2004 Net Written Premiums by Line (in Billions)

Commercial Lines: $222.3

Personal Lines: $206.7

Other Commercial Lines $115.8

Personal Auto $156.7

Commercial Multiperil $29.1

Homeowners $50.0

Workers' Compensation $36.7

Other Liability $40.7

Source: Adapted from *The III Insurance Fact Book 2006* (New York: Insurance Information Institute, 2006), p. 33, using information from the NAIC Annual Statement Database.

In addition to the segmentation between personal customers and commercial customers, commercial lines customers are further segmented, based on the size of the organization, into small businesses, middle markets, and national accounts. Each type of insurance customer can be distinguished in terms of insurance needs, knowledge of the insurance markets, methods of accessing the insurance market, negotiating ability, and access to alternative risk financing measures. These five distinguishing characteristics are significant to consumers because they influence their demand for insurance products and services. They are equally important to insurers because they directly affect the products and services they are willing to supply to each type of customer.

Individuals

From an insurance perspective, individuals generally share the same needs. On the property side, individuals typically need insurance for personal property such as furniture, electronics, or automobiles, or for real property such as their homes. On the liability side, individuals typically need insurance for liability arising out of their personal actions and out of their ownership and use of property (such as automobiles). Because so many individuals have the same insurance needs, insurers are able to pool individual insureds' loss exposures based on relevant underwriting factors to determine the appropriate premiums for their policies.

Of all the categories of insurance consumers, individuals are typically the least knowledgeable about insurance markets and the insurance mechanism. Therefore, they often need to rely on the expertise of a producer to help them decide which types of coverages, policy limits, and deductible levels are most appropriate for their individual circumstances. Individuals may also use direct access to insurers through Web sites or call centers to purchase their insurance products.

When deciding how to manage their property-casualty loss exposures, individuals have few risk financing alternatives available besides retention and insurance. In addition, they are sometimes required to purchase insurance, regardless of whether they would prefer to retain the loss exposures concerned. For example, mortgage lenders require homeowners insurance on properties for which they provide funding, and most states require drivers to have auto liability insurance or to provide proof that they have the financial assets to pay for auto liability claims. Unless the individual has substantial financial assets, insurance purchases are typically the only means of risk financing for such loss exposures.

Although insurance markets are competitive, individuals do not have much negotiating power in insurance transactions. Most personal lines insurance contracts are offered on an as-written basis by the insurer. Therefore, very little negotiation occurs. If the individual consumer is not satisfied with the policy's terms or price, typically his or her only option is to look to other insurers for coverage.

Small Businesses

The distinction between personal lines and commercial lines of insurance is based on the whether the insured is an individual or organization. The distinction between small businesses, middle markets, and national accounts in the commercial lines markets is not as clear. No established definitions distinguish between these commercial accounts. Some insurers distinguish them based on the level of premium revenue the insured generates. Similarly, some brokers make the distinction based on the commissions the client generates. Other distinctions could be based on the number of employees or the organization's revenue or income. For example, one insurer may define small businesses as organizations with less than $500,000 in revenue, whereas another may define them as organizations with less than $1,000,000 in revenue.

In general, "small business" is a descriptor for organizations with few employees and limited revenue. Small businesses do not usually have any employees with full-time risk management responsibilities. Often it is the owner, or a designated partner or manager with a limited knowledge of insurance markets, who is responsible for making risk management decisions—including the risk financing decision to purchase insurance. This decision is often made with the help of a local insurance agent or a small local broker. Small businesses are not the typical target market for regional or national brokers because such businesses often do not generate sufficient commissions. Although the insurance needs of small businesses are typically more complicated than those of individuals, small business can still be covered by a limited number of commercial insurance policies, such as a businessowners policy, a workers' compensation policy, and commercial auto policies.

Small Businesses and the Businessowners Policy (BOP)

Insurers offer a combination of property and liability coverages in one policy, the businessowners policy (BOP), to meet the insurance needs of relatively uncomplicated small organizations. BOPs provide coverage for buildings and personal property, as well as for liability. Many BOPs also include business income coverage and have optional coverages for employee dishonesty, money and securities, and mechanical breakdown. BOPs are designed to meet the insurance needs of a wide range of small businesses, such as retail stores, offices, and apartment buildings. However, they are not designed to provide coverage for bars, financial institutions, or organizations in the automobile business.

Similar to individuals, small businesses have little negotiation power with insurers and a limited number of choices when it comes to risk financing alternatives. Some small businesses have been able to join with other similar organizations to form small risk retention groups or purchasing groups as alternatives to the standard commercial insurance market.

Middle Markets

Organizations that can be classified as middle markets may have substantially more complex insurance needs than individuals or small businesses. In addition to the property, liability, and workers' compensation exposures of small businesses, larger organizations' insurance needs vary considerably according to the products or services they provide. For example, a company that manufactures airplane components will have significant products liability insurance needs.

Middle market organizations will need higher policy limits and will often have unique insurance needs that require special attention during the underwriting process. For example, a college will have loss exposures associated with the well-being and fair treatment of the students that live on campus. This type of exposure, although common among colleges and universities, is not typical of most organizations.

Whereas most small businesses do not have sufficient loss exposures to be able to accurately project future losses, middle market organizations are often large enough that their loss histories provide credible statistics for use in projecting future losses. These organizations may be large enough to have a risk manager (or a small risk management department) with a reasonable level of knowledge of the insurance markets to assist with coverage decisions.

Middle market organizations typically use brokers to access the insurance markets and may be targeted by small (local), regional, or national brokers. They typically have some negotiating power with insurers because they have a more credible loss history, generate more premium income for the insurer, and have broker representation that can assist in their presentation to the insurers. Furthermore, the middle market organizations have increasing access to risk financing alternatives such as captives, protected-cell companies, risk retention groups, and contingent capital programs.

National Accounts

The national accounts segment contains the largest organizations seeking insurance coverage. These organizations, such as Fortune 500 companies, chemical and other manufacturing organizations, and large municipalities, have the most complex insurance needs, the most knowledge of the insurance market (with a large risk management department and regional or national broker representation), and the widest variety of risk financing alternatives. These factors, coupled with the fact that national accounts often generate millions of dollars in premiums annually, give national account organizations the most negotiating power with insurers. This power can be used to negotiate broader coverages, lower deductibles, higher limits, or premium reductions.

National account organizations are likely to have complex insurance programs that combine commercial insurance coverages with sophisticated retention plans and captive insurers. The use of captives by large organizations provides them with additional flexibility to bypass the standard commercial insurance market and access reinsurance markets directly.

Furthermore, unique loss exposures that require extremely high limits or highly specialized underwriting consideration are often insured by a consortium of insurers who work together to provide the necessary insurance program. For example, the property insurance program for the World Trade Center that was providing coverage during the terrorist attacks on September 11, 2001, had more than twenty insurers and reinsurers involved in the coverage.

Exhibit 6-3 summarizes the differences between the various types of consumers of insurance products. To meet the insurance demands of consumers, insurers have developed a variety of marketing systems, collectively referred to as producers, to supply insurance products and services.

EXHIBIT 6-3

Comparison of Insurance Consumers

	Individuals	Small Business	Middle Markets	National Accounts
Insurance Needs	Least complex	Somewhat complex	Complex	Highly complex
Knowledge of the Insurance Market	Least knowledgeable	Some knowledge	Risk manager on staff—more knowledgeable	Full-time risk management department—most knowledgeable
Access Method	Direct access/agents	Agents/small brokers	Brokers—small/regional/national	Brokers—regional/national
Negotiating Ability	Little, if any, negotiating ability	Little, if any, negotiating ability	Some negotiating ability	Most negotiating ability
Choice of Risk Financing Alternatives	Retention only alternative	Retention/few other alternatives	Some alternatives—rent-a-captives, risk retention groups	Wide variety of alternatives

Producers

Insurance producers are primarily agents and brokers but also include banks, excess and surplus lines intermediaries, stockbrokers, financial planners, retailers, and direct writing systems. This section focuses on agents, brokers, banks, and excess and surplus lines intermediaries because they are the most common means, outside of direct contact with the insurer, used by consumers to purchase insurance products.

Producers are involved in the primary insurance market, in which the insurance transaction occurs between the insured and the insurer. Exhibit 6-4 shows the various types of agents and brokers used by the different types of consumers. Individuals commonly use agents and brokers or direct contact (through direct writing systems, Internet, call center, or direct response) with an insurer to complete their insurance transactions. Organizations use both agents and brokers. Many agents and brokers are now owned by banks.

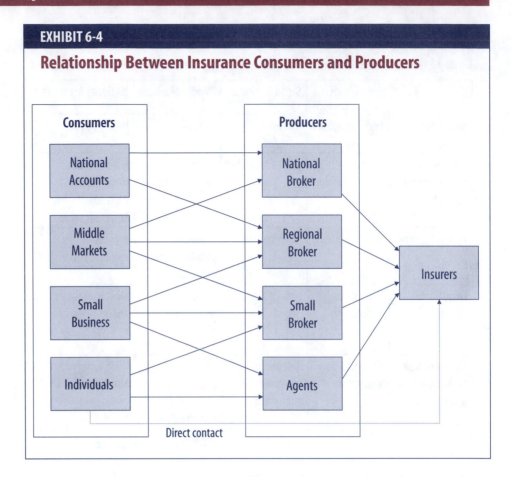

EXHIBIT 6-4

Relationship Between Insurance Consumers and Producers

Agents

In 2003, independent agents and brokers produced more than 50 percent of the property-casualty insurance sold.[2] Agents are contractors who are the authorized representatives of one or many insurers. As well as marketing personal lines insurance products to individuals, agents market commercial lines insurance products to small businesses and middle markets. A portion of the premium paid by the insured is used to compensate the agents, typically through a commission. Agents can be independent agents, representing multiple insurers, or exclusive agents, representing a single insurer. In addition to facilitating the insurance purchase, agents can offer other services such as risk management consulting, premium collection, and minor claim handling.

Brokers

Brokers are insureds' authorized representatives for the purposes of negotiating and obtaining insurance coverages. A broker may also serve as an insurer representative for certain purposes, such as issuing certificates of insurance or collecting premiums. Similar to agents, brokers have traditionally been compensated through commissions. In addition to offering insurance placement services, brokers also typically offer additional services such as risk assessment and control services, actuarial consulting services, and claim handling. They may be compensated on a fee basis for these services. Brokers typically fall into three categories depending on the scope of their operations: local, regional, or national.

Local brokers operate in a small geographic area targeting individuals, small businesses, and middle markets, and they often compete with agents for business from individuals and small commercial insurance customers. They also compete with regional brokers for smaller middle market accounts. Local brokers operate in a highly competitive environment.

Regional brokers typically operate in multi-state regions such as the southeast, mid-Atlantic, or western regions. Their target markets are the middle market and national account organizations, but they may also represent larger small business accounts. Although regional brokers are full service brokers, they do not have the same resources as national brokers and therefore often outsource some of the services offered. Regional brokers often compete with local brokers at the lower end of the middle markets and with national brokers on the remaining middle markets and national accounts.

National brokers operate nationally and cater to the risk management and insurance needs of middle market and national account organizations. They are typically full-service brokers, offering not only insurance placement but also other risk management services such as risk assessment, risk control, alternative risk financing options, and actuarial and claim administration services. Some national brokers also operate internationally in order to service those clients with global operations. The fifteen largest brokers in the U.S. all had revenues over $100 million in 2004, and eight of the ten largest brokers in the world are U.S. brokers. The level of competition at the national brokerage level has become more concentrated over the last decade as a result of mergers and acquisitions.

Is My Agent an Agent or a Broker?

Although this text distinguishes between agents and brokers, many independent agents act as both agents and brokers, depending on the specifics of the transaction being processed. Based on the Producer Licensing Model Act (PLMA) of 2000 issued by the National Association of Insurance Commissioners (NAIC), state licensing of producers no longer distinguishes between agents and brokers—states now license producers. Whether that producer is acting as an agent or a broker will depend on the specific activity in which the producer is engaged at that time.

Both agents and brokers serve insurers by delivering applications for underwriting. Although not all applications will be accepted, agents and brokers represent the flow of potential policyholders to an insurer.

Ethical Implications: Contingent Commissions

In May 2004, the New York State Attorney General, Elliot Spitzer, began an investigation into how insurance brokers are compensated. Specifically, Spitzer began investigating contingent commissions. Brokers are typically paid a commission based on a percentage of the premiums paid for the policies placed with an insurer. Contingent commissions are commissions paid by insurers to brokers based on additional factors, such as the profit the insurer realizes from the business provided by the broker or the volume of the business provided by the broker. The ethical question raised is whether a broker can act in the best interests of the consumer and still collect substantial income from insurers. The receipt of contingent commissions potentially makes it uncertain whether a broker is encouraging consumers to place their business with a particular insurer because that insurer provides the best policy at the best price, or because that insurer pays the best contingent commissions. This type of compensation structure may present a conflict of interest to brokers. A second ethical question raised by this practice is the level of transparency of broker compensation. The brokers' clients should be fully aware of the contingent commission arrangements that the broker has in place with insurers if they are to make a fully informed decision.

Banks

Many banks have become active in insurance markets as a result of the provisions of the Gramm-Leach-Bliley Act of 1999. The preferred mode of entry into the insurance industry has been by acquiring independent agents and brokers rather than becoming insurers. Banks appear to have more interest in distributing insurance products and services than in underwriting them. Although 60 percent of top-tier bank holding companies engaged in sales activities that produced insurance commissions and fees in the first half of 2005, less than 5 percent reported earning some insurance underwriting fee income.[3]

Banks have become involved in the distribution of insurance products and services for several reasons, including the following:

- Growing and diversifying the sources of revenues
- Increasing product offerings to current customers
- Cross-selling banking and insurance products and services

Banks seeking to grow and diversify revenues have started to distribute insurance products and services. The agent and broker revenues generated through the distribution of insurance products offer an additional revenue stream that is not directly tied to interest rates (as are most bank revenues). Another reason that banks have chosen to distribute insurance products rather than underwrite insurance is the rate of return on their investment. Although volatile, agent and broker revenues have been less volatile than insurer revenues and have yielded a greater return on equity over the ten-year period 1996 to 2005.[4]

Banks selling insurance products hope that offering the additional products will help to solidify the banking relationship with the customer. Cross-selling attempts to sell insurance products to current bank customers and banking products to current insurance customers. The advantage of cross-selling is that the customer already has a relationship with either the bank or the broker, which ideally makes the customer more receptive to affiliated offers. Cross-selling does not necessarily require the acquisition of an agent or broker; it can also be achieved through alliances and agreements with agents and brokers.

Excess and Surplus Lines Intermediaries

Excess and surplus lines intermediaries (surplus lines intermediaries) are producers who place business with nonadmitted insurers. A **nonadmitted insurer** is an insurer not licensed to do business in the insured's home state. Conversely, an **admitted insurer** is an insurer licensed by a state insurance department to do business in the insured's home state.

Nonadmitted insurer
An insurer not licensed to do business in the insured's home state.

Admitted insurer
An insurer licensed by a state insurance department to do business in the insured's home state.

Industry Terminology—Admitted, Nonadmitted, and Surplus Lines Insurers

Many industry practitioners use the terms nonadmitted insurers and surplus lines insurers (as well as nonadmitted market and surplus lines market) interchangeably. Although there is substantial overlap between these terms, there are differences. The following diagram shows that surplus lines insurers are a subset of the nonadmitted insurers that is deemed eligible by the state to insure risks exported by intermediaries to the surplus lines market. The remaining, nonadmitted insurers are not licensed in the state and are restricted to operating in the nonadmitted market only.

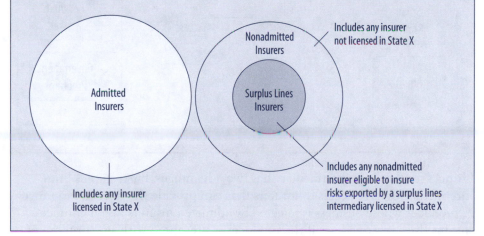

Most producers are usually limited to placing business with admitted insurers. The circumstances under which business can be placed with a nonadmitted insurer through a surplus lines intermediary vary by state. Usually, the loss exposures placed with nonadmitted insurers are unique loss exposures, such as amusement parks or day nurseries, or unusual or hard-to-place coverages, such as directors and officers (D&O), errors and omissions (E&O), or medical malpractice coverages. Normally, the producer must first make a reasonable effort to place the coverage with an admitted insurer (in the admitted market). For example, the producer, who must be licensed to place surplus lines business in that state, is required to conduct a diligent search and may be required to certify that a specified number (often two or three) of admitted insurers have refused to provide the coverage before attempting to access the nonadmitted market.

When producers need to access the nonadmitted market, as shown in Exhibit 6-5, they must usually go through surplus lines intermediaries rather than contacting the nonadmitted insurer directly. Occasionally, some nonadmitted insurers deal directly with the producer.

EXHIBIT 6-5

Relationship Between Producers and Insurers

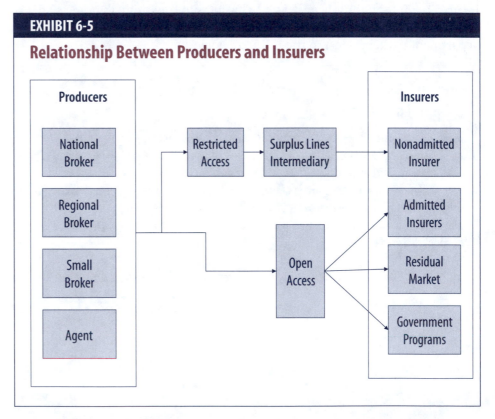

Using a surplus lines intermediary has two advantages. First, surplus lines intermediaries have access to insurers that can provide the needed insurance. A producer whose business is rejected by admitted insurers might contact a surplus lines intermediary if the producer is presented with one or more of the following:

- An unusual or a unique loss exposure
- A customer who requires high limits of insurance (high capacity)
- A distressed (significant recent losses) loss exposure that may present an underwriting problem in the admitted market

The second advantage is that the producer can use a surplus lines intermediary to place coverage on an unfavorable loss exposure (that is, one that has a poor claim history, difficult-to-treat exposures, and so on). Consequently, the producer preserves the relationships that his or her agency or brokerage has with its admitted insurers and prevents loss ratios from deteriorating should a significant loss occur.

Surplus lines intermediaries work with their producers to ensure that (1) coverage is placed only with eligible surplus lines insurers, (2) the customer's unique or unusual requirements can be met by a prospective nonadmitted insurer, and (3) the financial security of the nonadmitted insurer is correctly evaluated. Surplus lines intermediaries, like independent agents and brokers, can represent multiple insurers and are compensated by commissions generated by the business they place with eligible surplus lines insurers.

Insurers

Once the producer has established a relationship with the insurance consumer, it is the producer's responsibility to place the insurance business with an insurer who is willing to accept the risk transfer. The insurer may be an admitted insurer, a nonadmitted insurer, the state-run residual or assigned-risk market (discussed subsequently), or a government program such as the National Flood Insurance Program.

Admitted and Nonadmitted Insurers

In 2004, admitted insurers collected almost 93 percent of all premiums written, with the remainder written in the nonadmitted and residual markets.[5] If the consumer cannot obtain coverage in the admitted market, nonadmitted insurers offer a source of coverage for unique, high-capacity, or distressed loss exposures. Such coverages commonly include products liability, professional liability, employment practices liability, special events liability, and excess and umbrella liability.

Residual Markets

The inability to obtain coverage in the admitted market can be of particular concern to the insured if the insurance that the individual or organization is trying to purchase is either required by statute (such as auto insurance or workers' compensation insurance) or is necessary to protect a substantial investment (such as homeowners' insurance or property insurance in urban areas). In addition to the nonadmitted market, individuals and organizations that cannot obtain coverage in the admitted market can also obtain insurance through residual markets. **Residual market**, or assigned risk, is the term referring collectively to insurers and other organizations that make insurance available through a shared risk mechanism to those who cannot obtain coverage in the admitted market.

Residual market
The term referring collectively to insurers and other organizations that make insurance available through a shared risk mechanism to those who cannot obtain coverage in the admitted market.

Residual markets are shared risk mechanisms because the admitted insurers selling insurance coverage in the state share some risk in the residual market. Although states vary widely on how residual markets are designed and operated, a common method of sharing the risk of the residual market is based on the market shares of the admitted insurers in that state. The most common residual markets are for homeowners, commercial property, auto, and (in some states) workers' compensation exposures. Typically, an individual needs to demonstrate that he or she was unable to obtain coverage in the admitted market. Once that is established, a producer can obtain the insurance coverage in the residual market.

Premiums in the residual market are higher than the average premiums in the admitted market; however, the risks being placed are not average. The insureds who purchase insurance in the residual market tend to be high-risk individuals or organizations that often obtain coverage at a subsidized rate compared with what is an actuarially fair premium. Some states assign each policyholder in the residual market to a specific admitted insurer operating in the state; others have each admitted insurer pay a share of the combined losses of the residual market.

Windstorm insurance residual markets are common in hazard-prone areas such as the coastal southeastern U.S. and Texas. Fair Access to Insurance Requirements (FAIR) plans are residual market mechanisms designed to meet the need for property insurance on urban properties. These plans provide basic insurance coverage to property owners who might otherwise be unable to obtain insurance because of the property's location. Auto insurance residual markets exist in every state, and workers' compensation residual markets operate in a majority of the fifty states.

Residual markets may compete with the surplus lines market in some lines of business. For example, property owners (residential and commercial) in urban areas that have difficulty obtaining property insurance in the admitted market may either apply to a FAIR plan or obtain coverage through a surplus lines intermediary who places the business with an eligible surplus lines insurer. Although the rates may be higher in the surplus lines market, the insured will generally be able to obtain higher limits and broader coverage than in a residual market.

Government Programs

Government programs generally provide insurance coverage for risks where there has been a market failure in the private insurance market; that is, government programs provide insurance coverage that private insurers are unwilling or unable to provide. These programs can play various roles in insurance markets. Some programs, such as the National Flood Insurance Program, enable the government to act as the primary insurer, whereas others, such as the Terror Risk Insurance Program, enable the government to act as a reinsurer. For the primary insurance programs, producers are authorized to sell the government insurance coverage at specified premiums. The producers are paid a commission for the sale, and the remainder of the premium is paid to the government agency responsible for administering the program. If the government is acting as a reinsurer, the program operates similar to reinsurance.

The role of government programs in property-casualty insurance is discussed in detail in a subsequent chapter.

Reinsurance

Insurers are like other organizations in that they have several property and liability loss exposures. The major liability loss exposure for insurers is the losses suffered by their policyholders (underwriting risk). An insurer can finance some of this underwriting risk using reinsurance. **Reinsurance** is transfer of insurance risk from one insurer to another through a contractual agreement under which one insurer (the reinsurer) agrees, in return for a reinsurance premium, to indemnify another insurer (the primary insurer) for some or all of the financial consequences of certain loss exposures covered by the primary insurer's policies. The loss exposures transferred (ceded) could relate to a single subject of insurance (such as a building), a single policy, or a group of policies.

Depending on the type of reinsurance agreement, the reinsurer may pay a commission back to the primary insurer, called a ceding commission. A **ceding commission** is an amount paid by the reinsurer to the primary insurer to cover part or all of the primary insurer's policy acquisition expenses.

Reinsurers, like primary insurers, can transfer to other reinsurers some of the liability they have accepted in reinsurance agreements. A **retrocession** is a reinsurance agreement whereby one reinsurer (the retrocedent) transfers all or part of the reinsurance risk it has assumed or will assume to another reinsurer (the retrocessionaire).

Reinsurance Intermediaries

As shown in Exhibit 6-6, reinsurance can be placed with a reinsurer through a reinsurance intermediary, although some reinsurers will write business directly with an insurer. A reinsurance intermediary provides various services to both primary insurers and reinsurers, including coverage and premium negotiation, claim adjusting, accounting, and underwriting advice. As compensation for its services, a reinsurance intermediary receives a commission, called a brokerage fee, from the reinsurer. Reinsurance intermediaries are commonly involved in both the cession from the primary insurer to the reinsurer and also in any retrocessions that may occur.

Reinsurance
The transfer of insurance risk from one insurer to another through a contractual agreement under which one insurer (the reinsurer) agrees, in return for a reinsurance premium, to indemnify another insurer (the primary insurer) for some or all of the financial consequences of certain loss exposures covered by the primary insurer's policies.

Ceding commission
An amount paid by the reinsurer to the primary insurer to cover part or all of the primary insurer's policy acquisition expenses.

Retrocession
A reinsurance agreement whereby one reinsurer (the retrocedent) transfers all or part of the reinsurance risk it has assumed or will assume to another reinsurer (the retrocessionaire).

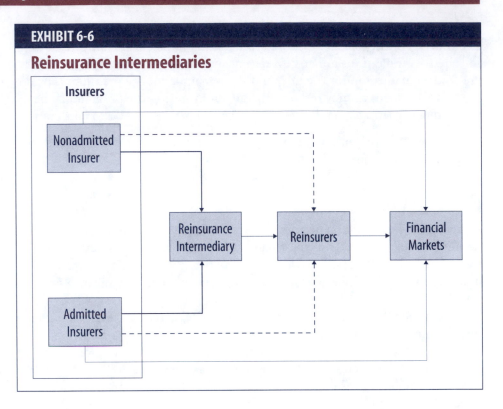

EXHIBIT 6-6

Reinsurance Intermediaries

Reinsurers

The reinsurance market is a global market. There are approximately 2,800 primary property-casualty insurers in the U.S. and approximately 4,000 reinsurers worldwide. Of those 4,000, more than 3,000 are involved in reinsuring U.S. insurers.[6] Similar to the primary insurance market, the reinsurance market is segmented, with some reinsurers specializing in property reinsurance, some specializing in liability insurance, and others involved in several lines of insurance. Some reinsurers (called direct writing reinsurers) use their own personnel to sell reinsurance and do not ordinarily accept loss exposures from reinsurance intermediaries.

Financial market
A mechanism used for trading securities.

Securities
Pieces of paper or electronic records that provide evidence of equity or debt instruments.

Money market
A financial market in which short-term securities are traded.

Financial Markets

Both insurers and reinsurers often access financial markets to share both risk and reward with third-party investors. A **financial market** is a mechanism used for trading securities. In financial markets, the items traded are financial assets or financial claims, collectively called securities. **Securities** are pieces of paper or electronic records that provide evidence of equity or debt instruments. Examples of securities include stocks, bonds, and Treasury bills. Different markets exist for different types of securities. Buyers and sellers may be individuals, corporations, or any other type of legal entity.

Financial markets are made up of money markets and capital markets. **Money markets** are financial markets in which short-term securities are traded.

"Short-term" means the securities will mature in one year or less. Capital markets are markets in which long-term securities are traded. "Long-term" means the securities will mature in more than one year.

Primary markets are mechanisms in which new securities are sold, with the proceeds going directly to the issuer. The primary markets enable corporations to raise additional cash by selling new shares of stock or by borrowing and issuing new bonds to investors. **Secondary markets** are mechanisms for investors to buy and sell previously issued securities. Although corporations are only directly involved in the primary markets, the secondary markets are critical to them because the liquidity of these markets means that buyers and sellers know they can resell their securities whenever desired. This makes the markets more attractive to buyers and sellers. Also, corporations can invest excess corporate funds using the secondary markets.

Primary market
A mechanism in which new securities are sold, with the proceeds going directly to the issuer.

Secondary market
A mechanism for investors to buy and sell previously issued securities.

Insurers and reinsurers are active in financial markets in two ways: as investors and as issuers. First, insurers manage billions of dollars in assets that need to be invested and are therefore some of the largest institutional investors active in financial markets. They provide capital for both short-term and long-term investments in bonds, stocks, and real estate. Second, insurers and reinsurers are active in financial markets as issuers. Some are publicly traded organizations that have issued stock on primary markets to investors to raise funds for operations. The stock issued is typically an equity investment, in that the purchaser of the stock becomes an owner of the insurer with an ownership claim on equity of the organization (the difference between assets and liabilities). Insurers and reinsurers have also issued debt instruments, typically bonds or surplus notes, on the primary markets. Individuals and organizations that purchase the insurers' debt instruments are creditors of the insurer, rather than owners. The one unique use of capital markets by insurers and reinsurers has been the securitization of natural hazard risk through catastrophe bonds, as discussed in a previous chapter.

The use of financial markets by insurers and reinsurers enables a further spreading of underwriting risk to a larger pool of investors than traditional insurance and reinsurance policies allow. This additional risk sharing provides insurers with additional capital to help keep premiums reasonable and to provide additional capacity to provide coverage.

ROLES OF THIRD PARTIES

In addition to the consumers, producers, underwriters, and reinsurers who are active in the insurance industry, a variety of third parties provide a range of vital products and services that allow the insurance markets to operate more effectively and efficiently. These individuals and organizations are called third parties because they are not directly involved in the insurance transaction between the consumer (first party) and the insurer (second party). Services that third-party providers supply include administrative services, investigative services, inspections, consulting services, and regulatory oversight.

Third-Party Administrators (TPAs)

Third-party administrator (TPA)
An organization that provides administrative services associated with risk financing and insurance.

Third-party administrators (TPAs) are organizations that provide administrative services associated with risk financing and insurance. Many organizations involved in self-insured plans, captives, risk retention groups, or other types of alternative risk financing find using TPAs an economical and efficient way to manage the administrative needs of their risk financing plans, rather than managing those services in-house. TPAs can provide almost all of the administrative services required for risk financing and insurance, including marketing, underwriting, loss control, claim handling, regulatory compliance, and legal assistance. TPAs can be independent organizations or they can be departments or subsidiaries of large insurers or brokers.

Special Investigative Units (SIUs)

Special investigative unit (SIU)
A division set up to investigate suspicious claims, premium fraud, or application fraud.

A **special investigative unit (SIU)** is a division set up to investigate suspicious claims, premium fraud, or application fraud. Some states require insurers to have SIUs. However, most medium to large insurers have voluntarily established these units. The SIUs generally consist of staff that have experience in claim handling, insurance investigation, and law enforcement, and have had some form of legal training. The most common activity of SIUs is investigating suspect claims. The units are also active in training insurer personnel to detect fraud, working with local attorneys and law enforcement to prosecute fraud, and promoting public awareness of fraud.

In addition to SIUs, insurers also have the support of state fraud bureaus and the National Insurance Crime Bureau (NICB) to prevent insurance fraud. The NICB is a not-for-profit organization that receives support from the property-casualty insurance industry and that assists insurers and law enforcement agencies in the identification, detection, and prosecution of insurance criminals. Many states have also established fraud bureaus, which are state law enforcement agencies that are designed to investigate and prosecute cases of insurance fraud. Fraud bureaus are typically established within the state's department of insurance.

Inspectors

Several types of inspectors are involved in the insurance industry. For example, inspectors are employed by the Occupational Safety and Health Administration (OSHA) to ensure that employers meet the minimum workplace safety standards that are vital to workers' compensation insurance. Many insurers employ safety inspectors as part of their risk control services to ensure that their insureds are meeting policy requirements. Also, a wide variety of independent inspectors related to all lines of property and liability insurance are available. For example, equipment breakdown policies are often issued only after the property being insured has been inspected by engineers to determine its condition and likelihood of suffering a loss. Similarly, both commercial and residential property is often inspected to determine its value and condition before issuing a property insurance policy.

Some states have also become involved in property inspection related to properties in hazard-prone areas. For example, the Texas Windstorm Insurance Association (TWIA), which is the insurer of last resort for windstorm and hail coverage in coastal Texas, requires that construction (including new structures, additions, and repairs) in hurricane-prone coastal communities be inspected to meet insurance requirements.

Consultants

Insurance consultants offer a wide variety of services including consulting on insurance policies and coverages, insurance placement or claims management, actuarial services, expert witness and litigation management, risk assessment, risk control, and risk financing. Often an insurance consultant will specialize in a specific area, such as workers' compensation, transportation, property, or life and health.

Some states require insurance consultants to be licensed, and requirements for a consultant's license vary by state. Separate examinations are usually required to be an insurance consultant in both life-health insurance and property-casualty insurance.

Regulators

Insurers are regulated mainly to protect consumers, to maintain insurer solvency, and to prevent destructive competition. Insurance is regulated primarily by state insurance departments. State regulators, in turn, are members of the National Association of Insurance Commissioners (NAIC), a not-for-profit corporation that has no regulatory authority of its own but that plays an important coordinating role. Only the state and federal governments have authority to regulate insurers.

Other organizations—which can be called unofficial regulators—also substantially affect insurer activities. The most well-known unofficial regulators are financial rating agencies, which provide summary information about insurer financial strength in the form of a financial rating. Corporate risk managers, independent insurance producers, consumers, and others consult these ratings when choosing an insurer. Many corporate and public entity risk managers purchase insurance only from insurers whose financial rating meets or exceeds a specific rating.

INSURANCE MARKETS AND COMPETITION

The insurance industry is segmented by products and by regions, as shown in Exhibit 6-7. Insurers can be classified as property-casualty insurers, life-health insurers, or multi-line insurers that sell both property-casualty and life-health insurance. Property-casualty insurance can then be further classified by line, that is, into personal or commercial lines. Commercial lines can focus on property or liability insurance. Commercial property lines include commercial property, commercial auto physical damage, commercial inland marine, and business income. Commercial liability lines include commercial general liability, commercial auto liability, and workers' compensation.

Property-casualty insurers can be either monoline insurers or multi-line insurers. Monoline insurers sell only one line of business. Multi-line insurers sell any or all lines of property and liability insurance, including both personal and commercial lines. Furthermore, property and liability lines of insurance are also segmented geographically. Therefore, individuals seeking to purchase homeowners insurance in Pennsylvania would likely have the choice of many insurers who are licensed to sell homeowners insurance in Pennsylvania. Such individuals can choose between a small local insurer that only sells homeowners insurance in Pennsylvania, a regional insurer that sells only personal lines insurance products in the mid-Atlantic region, or a large national insurer that sells most lines of business in most states.

EXHIBIT 6-7

Insurer Segmentation

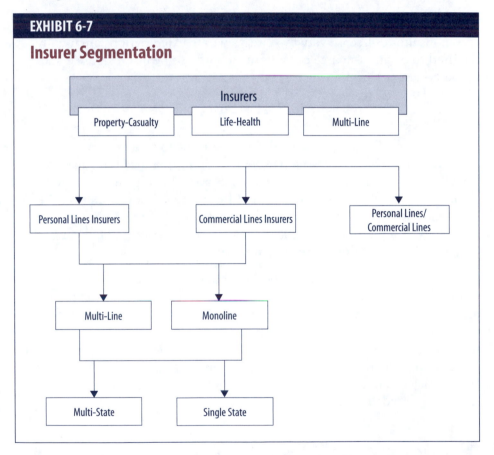

Competition between insurers is an important aspect in the functioning of insurance markets. Although the degree of competition varies by product line, insurance is typically perceived as highly competitive. The level of competition depends on the number and the size of competing insurers, the existence of insurance substitutes, the buyers' knowledge of the market, and the size and growth of the overall insurance market.

Competitive Markets and the Herfindahl Index

One measure used by economists to determine the competitive level of markets is known as the Herfindahl-Hirschman index, or more commonly just the Herfindahl index. The Herfindahl index is the sum of the squares of the percentage market shares of all organizations in the market. For example, if there are four insurers in a market and each insurer has 25 percent of the market share, the Herfindahl index value would be 0.25. The higher the Herfindahl index, the lower the level of competition.

Insurer	Market Share	Market Share Squared
A	0.25	0.0625
B	0.25	0.0625
C	0.25	0.0625
D	0.25	0.0625
Herfindahl index		0.2500

If the four insurers had different market shares, such as in the following example, the market would be less competitive (a higher Herfindahl index).

Insurer	Market Share	Market Share Squared
A	0.45	0.2025
B	0.35	0.1225
C	0.15	0.0225
D	0.05	0.0025
Herfindahl index		0.3500

The insurance industry's overall Herfindahl index score is fairly low, indicating that the insurance industry is competitive; however, some segments of the industry may not be particularly competitive. For example, the market for medical malpractice insurance in Pennsylvania may have a substantially higher Herfindahl index score (be less competitive) than the overall industry.

Number and Size of Competing Insurers

Competition in any industry is driven by the number of organizations in that industry, and it usually increases as the number of organizations increases. There is sometimes concern, from the public and government agencies, when there are not enough organizations to ensure a competitive market. For example, regulators and government agencies become concerned when mergers and acquisitions reduce the number of organizations in a particular market segment because this may limit competition and lead to increased prices for consumers. With several thousand property-casualty insurers writing business in the U.S., often through one of the many thousands of agents or brokers (producers), the U.S. property-casualty market has enough participants to form highly competitive markets.

One factor affecting the number of competitors is the ease with which competitors can enter the market. In recent years, entry into the insurance market has become easier. For example, in 1999, passage of the Gramm-Leach-Bliley Act, also called the Financial Services Modernization Act, removed some of the barriers that previously kept banks or other financial services organizations from competing with traditional insurers. Although only a small percentage of banks have entered the insurance market as insurers, entry is possible. Also, the Internet has made it easier for insurance organizations to develop a widespread presence without the cost of establishing a traditional marketing force.

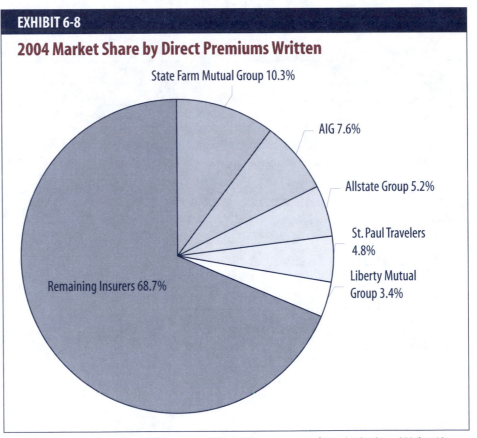

EXHIBIT 6-8

2004 Market Share by Direct Premiums Written

State Farm Mutual Group 10.3%

AIG 7.6%

Allstate Group 5.2%

St. Paul Travelers 4.8%

Liberty Mutual Group 3.4%

Remaining Insurers 68.7%

Source: Adapted from *The III Insurance Fact Book 2006* (New York: Insurance Information Institute, 2006), p. 10, using information from the NAIC Annual Statement Database.

Similar to the number of organizations, another important driver of competition is the size of the organizations in that industry. For a given number of organizations, the level of competition will usually be greater if all organizations are approximately the same size than if there are two or three large organizations and many small ones. Consider two markets for homeowners insurance, market A and market B. Each market has fifty insurers selling homeowners insurance. In market A, two insurers control 90 percent of the market share (approximately 45 percent each) and the remaining forty-eight competitors split the remaining 10 percent. In market B, the top twenty-five insurers each have roughly 3 percent of the market share, and the remaining twenty-five insurers share the remaining 25 percent. Market B is a more competitive market in which it is less likely that one or two insurers could exert undue influence on market conditions. Therefore, the number of competitors is not sufficient to establish that the market is highly competitive; the relative size of these competitors is also important. Exhibit 6-8 shows the market share of the top five property-casualty insurers in 2004, measured by direct premiums written.

As well as the number and the size of the competitors in the insurance market, geographic region is also important. Although the number of insurers that compete in the U.S. may be in the thousands, not all of them compete nationally. Many insurers are small organizations that only compete in one or a limited number of states. The level of competition also depends on the number and size of the insurance companies that have a presence in the county where their services are sought. For example, the level of competition in Malvern, Pennsylvania, is not affected by the number of insurers competing in Florida.

Substitutes for Insurance

For any product or service, the level of competition is also affected by the availability of close substitutes. For example, consider travel between two cities if only one airline provides service between them. Although the airline has a monopoly power over air travel between the two cities, substitute transportation may be available. For example, it may be possible to fly to or from a neighboring city. Alternatively, it may be possible to travel between the two cities by train, bus, rental car, private automobile, taxicab, or even by boat, private airplane, or helicopter. Moreover, if the airline keeps the air fares too high, competitors may decide to offer competing service between those two cities.

To some degree, insurance product sales are also affected by the risk financing alternatives available. Although most insurance consumers do not have the same variety of choices for risk financing as they do for transportation, there are alternatives to insurance that become increasingly appealing as the cost of insurance increases.

For example, a simple substitute may be the financial resources of the individual or organization. Some families find that their ability to retain losses increases over time as their wealth accumulates, and they become better able to absorb a moderate loss without going bankrupt or otherwise jeopardizing their financial stability. Likewise, a business that is in good financial condition might choose to retain certain losses rather than buy high-priced insurance. This is likely to reduce demand for insurance in two ways. First, individuals and organizations with the ability to retain more losses will be able to purchase insurance with larger deductibles, resulting in reduced premiums. Second, it will make individuals and organizations more price-sensitive to insurance products and more likely to use the other risk financing alternatives discussed previously.

Knowledge of the Market

Another aspect of competition is consumer knowledge of the market, which includes not only knowledge of prices, but also knowledge of the products and services offered. If a prospective insurance buyer knows that one insurer will charge $500 for a particular policy whereas another insurer will charge only $400, the customer will probably go to the insurer with the lower price, assuming that no substantial difference exists between the coverage or the service provided by either insurer. If substantial differences do exist, the consumer would need to weigh the benefits of the differential (additional) coverage or service against the differential cost.

Competition generally depends on knowledge of the market, and individuals do not generally have perfect knowledge of the market. For example, a customer who wants to buy a new washing machine may compare prices at some appliance stores in the region, but not every appliance store. This means that local competition is limited; an appliance store does not have to have a lower price than every other appliance store in the country to get this customer's business—just the appliance stores that this particular customer visited.

In the past, insurers benefited, to some extent, from the fact that it was not practical or convenient for a typical insurance purchaser to make a major investment in insurance shopping because of the cost in both time and effort to obtain information. Some personal lines insurance shoppers would contact a few insurers, whereas others would shop at one or more independent agents, each of whom represented several insurers. Several state insurance departments published rate surveys that listed many insurers' rates for a few typical situations, but prices varied depending on one's situation, and rates changed frequently. Similarly, commercial insurance buyers had more limited options for some types of insurance although they might obtain competing proposals from a few insurers.

The Internet has changed the amount of information available to insurance buyers and the speed with which that information can be obtained. The availability of this market information inevitably makes insurance marketing even more competitive. As consumers gain better access not only to pricing information but also to other information such as insurer financial ratings and consumer satisfaction surveys, the level of competition in the industry will continue to increase.

Size and Growth of the Overall Insurance Market

Drastic changes in the overall demand for insurance are unlikely, as are changes in the overall property-casualty insurance market in the U.S., because it is a mature market and presents limited growth potential. The existing base of loss exposures (houses, automobiles, commercial buildings, business receipts, and so on) is very large and growing at predictable rates.

Additions to the existing stock of insured loss exposures tend to closely follow the nominal growth of the overall economy. For the period from 1946 to 1990, the average annual growth rate of the insurance market was 9.4 percent. Since 1990, the growth rate has declined substantially. For example, the growth in property-casualty insurance premiums from 2001 to 2004 was 5.1 percent.[7] The following factors contributed to this decline:

- Saturation of the market demand for insurable products in both the property and casualty lines (such as automobile and homeowners insurance) and in the life insurance lines
- Decline in the average annual growth rate of the population
- The growth of alternative risk financing tools

Overall, insurance markets are considered competitive. Although segmented, most insurance markets have a sufficient number of similarly sized insurers competing in them to ensure competition. Some factors that may limit competition in certain insurance markets are the lack of substitutes and lack of knowledge of the market. In these instances, regulators may be needed to ensure competition remains. Finally, insurance markets in the U.S. are very large markets and are growing at predictable rates, which should preserve current levels of competition.

SUMMARY

Insurance markets are the business environment in which buyers and sellers of insurance products and services negotiate insurance transactions. Buyers can be segmented into individuals, small businesses, middle markets, and national accounts. Individuals typically need insurance for personal property, real property, and liability loss exposures. Of all the categories of insurance consumers, individuals are typically the least knowledgeable about insurance markets and often need to rely on the expertise of an agent or broker. Apart from insurance, retention is typically the only risk financing alternative available to individuals and they usually do not have much negotiating ability when buying insurance.

The insurance needs of small businesses can typically be covered by a limited number of commercial insurance policies. Similar to individuals, small businesses have little negotiation power with insurers and a limited number of choices when it comes to risk financing alternatives. Larger organizations' insurance needs vary considerably according to the products or services they provide. These middle market organizations typically use brokers to access the insurance markets and have increasing access to risk financing alternatives. The national account organizations have the most complex insurance needs, the most knowledge of the insurance market, and the widest variety of risk financing alternatives. Therefore, they also have the most negotiating power with insurers.

Agents are the authorized representatives of one or more insurers. As well as marketing personal lines insurance products to individuals, agents market commercial lines insurance products to small businesses and middle markets. Agents can be independent agents, representing multiple insurers, or exclusive agents, representing a single insurer. Brokers, whether local, regional, or national, are insureds' authorized representatives for the purposes of negotiating and obtaining insurance coverages. A broker may also serve as an insurer representative for certain purposes, such as collecting premiums. The preferred mode of entry into the insurance industry for banks has been by acquiring independent agents and brokers rather than becoming insurers. Excess and surplus lines intermediaries (surplus lines intermediaries) are producers who place business with nonadmitted insurers; that is, insurers that are not licensed to do business in the insured's home state.

The producer is responsible for placing the insurance business with an insurer who is willing to accept the risk transfer. The insurer may be an admitted insurer (licensed to do business in the insured's home state), a nonadmitted insurer, a state-run residual or assigned-risk market, or a government program. If the consumer cannot obtain coverage in the admitted market, nonadmitted insurers offer a source of coverage for unique, high-capacity, or distressed loss exposures. Alternatively, consumers may be able to obtain insurance through residual markets—insurers and other organizations that make insurance available through a shared risk mechanism to those who cannot obtain coverage in the admitted market. Government programs generally provide insurance coverage that private insurers are unwilling or unable to provide.

The major liability loss exposure for insurers is the losses suffered by their policyholders (underwriting risk). An insurer can finance some of this underwriting risk using reinsurance, which is the transfer of insurance risk from one insurer to another through a contractual agreement under which one insurer (the reinsurer) agrees, in return for a reinsurance premium, to indemnify another insurer (the primary insurer) for some or all of the financial consequences of certain loss exposures covered by the primary insurer's policies. Both insurers and reinsurers often access financial markets to share both risk and reward with third-party investors. Insurers and reinsurers are active in financial markets in two ways: as investors and as issuers. The use of financial markets by insurers and reinsurers enables a further spreading of underwriting risk to a larger pool of investors than traditional insurance and reinsurance policies allow.

A variety of third parties provide a range of products and services to the insurance markets, including administrative services, investigative services, inspections, consulting services, and regulatory oversight. Third-party administrators (TPAs) are organizations that handle claims on another organization's behalf. A special investigative unit (SIU) is a group set up to investigate suspicious claims, premium fraud, or application fraud. Several types of inspectors are involved in the insurance industry, such as safety inspectors, equipment breakdown inspectors, and property inspectors.

Insurance consultants offer a wide variety of services, including consulting on insurance policies and coverages, insurance placement or claims management, actuarial services, expert witness and litigation management, risk assessment, risk control, and risk financing. Regulators operate mainly to protect consumers, to maintain insurer solvency, and to prevent destructive competition.

The level of competition in the insurance market depends on the number and the size of competing insurers, the existence of insurance substitutes, the buyers' knowledge of the market, and the size and growth of the overall insurance market. Overall, insurance markets are considered competitive. Although segmented, most insurance markets have a sufficient number of similarly sized insurers competing in them to ensure competition. Some of the factors that may limit competition in certain insurance markets are the lack of substitutes and lack of knowledge of the market. In these instances, regulators may be needed to ensure competition remains. Finally, insurance markets in the U.S. are very large markets and growing at predictable rates, which should preserve current levels of competition.

CHAPTER NOTES

1. Insurance Information Institute, *III Insurance Fact Book 2006* (New York: Insurance Information Institute, 2006), p. 9.

2. A.M. Best, *Best's Review, The Guide to Understanding the Insurance Industry 2005* (Oldwick, N.J.: A.M. Best, 2005), p. 8.

3. Michael D. White, "Total Bank Insurance Revenue Up in First Half of 2005," (Michael White Associates (MWA), in conjunction with the American Bankers Association (ABIA)), October 31, 2005, www.bankinsurance.com/about/press-releases/2005-10-31-PR-MWA-ABIA%20Report.pdf (accessed March 22, 2006).

4. *III Insurance Fact Book 2006*, various pages; *Business Insurance*, Crain Communications, Inc., various issues.

5. Author's calculations based on *III Insurance Fact Book 2006*, various pages.

6. *III Insurance Fact Book 2006* and Reinsurance Association of America (www.reinsurance.org), various pages.

7. *III Insurance Fact Book 2006*, p. 20.

Direct Your Learning

Insurance Mechanism

After learning the content of this chapter and completing the corresponding course guide assignment, you should be able to:

- Explain how insurance benefits individuals, organizations, and society.

- Describe the core and supporting functions performed by insurers.

- Explain the dynamics of supply and demand in establishing product prices and the factors that affect the supply and demand for insurance.

- Describe the following economic issues related to insurance pricing:

  - Adverse selection

  - Moral and morale hazard

  - Actuarial compared with social equity

  - Timing

- Describe the main sources of revenues and expenses for insurers.

- Explain how the profitability of insurers is measured.

- Explain how pooling reduces risk in society.

- Compare pooling and insurance.

- Define or describe each of the Key Words and Phrases for this chapter.

Develop Your Perspective

What are the main topics covered in the chapter?

Gaining a complete picture of the insurance industry requires an examination of its functional, economic, financial, and social perspective. This examination reveals how the availability and pricing of insurance is affected by forces such as supply and demand, capacity requirements, and the risk transfer mechanism.

Identify the economic pressures facing your organization.

- How is your organization responding to those forces?
- How do other insurers respond differently within the same economic environment?

Why is it important to know these topics?

By examining the insurance industry's functional, economic, financial, and social views, you will begin to understand how and why insurers are able to assume risk and still meet their financial and nonfinancial goals.

Examine the different methods of determining the profitability of insurers.

- What do these ratios tell the insurer about its performance?
- What ratios are most effective in comparing one insurer's results to another's?

How can you use this information?

Consider the strategies an insurer might use to deal with inadequate organizational performance.

- Which functional areas within the insurer might implement the strategies?
- How are the other areas of the insurer affected?

Chapter 7
Insurance Mechanism

Building a complete perspective of the insurance mechanism requires multiple views. The functional view examines the functions performed by an insurer across the lifespan of the insured business, from marketing, through underwriting, to administration and claims. Insurers do not perform these functions in a vacuum. Each insurer exists and operates within the overall economic environment and is subject to the same issues concerning the laws of supply and demand as other types of organizations (the economic view). These economic factors have a bearing on the way an insurer can price its products. To operate successfully, an insurer must be financially successful. The financial view of insurance examines how an insurer generates revenues and expenses associated with the insurance products and services it offers, as well as how to determine the financial success of a particular organization. Finally, the social view examines how insurance applies pooling to benefit society by removing risk.

BENEFITS OF INSURANCE

When used as a risk financing measure within a risk management program, insurance can help an individual or organization achieve risk financing goals such as paying for losses, managing cash flow uncertainty, and complying with legal requirements. Insurance also provides benefits to individuals, organizations, and society as a whole by promoting insureds' loss control activities, enabling insureds to use resources efficiently, providing support for insureds' credit, providing insurers with a source of investment funds, and reducing social burdens.

Many of the benefits of insurance are consistent with an individual's or organization's risk financing goals. The primary role of insurance is to indemnify individuals and organizations for covered losses. This benefit is consistent with the risk financing goal of paying for losses. Provided that the loss is to a covered loss exposure and a covered cause of loss, insurance will indemnify the insured, subject to any applicable deductibles and policy limits.

Insurance also enables an individual or organization to meet the risk financing goal of managing cash flow uncertainty. Insurance provides the insured with some degree of financial security and stability. The insured can be confident that as long as a loss is covered, the financial effect on the insured's cash flow is reduced to any deductible payments and any loss amounts that exceed the policy limits. The remainder of the loss will be paid by the insurer, reducing the variation in the insured's cash flows.

The final risk financing goal that insurance meets is the goal of meeting legal requirements. Insurance is often used or required to satisfy both statutory requirements and contractual requirements that arise from business relationships. For example, all states have laws that require employers to pay for the job-related injuries or illnesses of their employees. Employers generally purchase workers' compensation insurance to meet this financial obligation. In addition, certain business relationships require proof of insurance. For example, building contractors are usually required to provide evidence of liability insurance before a construction contract is granted.

Individuals, organizations, and society also benefit from insurance beyond its ability to meet risk financing requirements. A major benefit of insurance is the promotion of risk control. Insurance often provides the insured with the incentive to undertake cost-effective risk control measures. Insurers provide this incentive through risk-sharing mechanisms such as deductibles, premium credit incentives, and contractual requirements. Because these incentives can lead to a reduction in losses paid by the insurer and therefore lower premiums, they benefit not only the individual insured but also all other insureds. Furthermore, risk control measures can save not only financial resources but also the lives of individuals or employees. Therefore, society as a whole benefits.

People and businesses that face an uncertain future often set aside funds to pay for future losses. However, insurance makes it unnecessary to set aside a large amount of money to pay for the financial consequences of loss exposures that can be insured. In exchange for a relatively small premium, individuals and organizations can free up additional funds. As a result, the money that would otherwise be set aside to pay for possible losses can be used to improve an individual's quality of life or to contribute to the growth of an organization.

Insurance can also provide support for an insured's credit. Before making a loan, a lender wants assurance that the money will be repaid. For example, when loaning money to a borrower to purchase property, the lender usually acquires a legal interest in that property. This legal interest enables the lender to take actions such as repossessing a car or foreclosing a home mortgage if the loan is not repaid. Without this ability to recover the loan amount, the lender would be less likely to make the loan. Insurance facilitates loans to individuals and organizations by guaranteeing that the lender will be paid if the collateral for the loan (such as a house or a commercial building) is destroyed or damaged by an insured event, thereby reducing the lender's uncertainty.

Insurance provides a source of investment funds for both insurer and insured. First, as discussed previously, insureds are not required to set aside large retention funds to pay for losses that are covered by insurance. Second, the premiums collected by insurers are invested until needed to pay claims. Such investments can provide money for projects such as new construction, research, and technology advancements. Insurers also invest in social projects, such as cultural events, education, and economic development projects. Investment funds promote economic growth and job creation that, in turn, benefit individuals, organizations, and society. Also, because investment brings additional funding to insurers in the form of interest, this additional income helps keep insurance premiums at a reasonable level.

Finally, insurance can help reduce social burdens. For example, the social costs of natural disasters, such as Hurricane Andrew in 1992, or Hurricanes Katrina and Rita in 2005, are increased by uninsured losses suffered by individuals and organizations that can amount to billions of dollars. Without other assistance, the victims of natural disasters would rely on the state or federal government. Insurance helps to reduce this burden by providing compensation to the affected parties. Compulsory auto insurance is another example, because it provides compensation to auto accident victims who might otherwise be unable to afford proper medical care or who might be unable to work because of the accident. Without insurance, victims of job-related or auto accidents might become a burden to society and need some form of state welfare.

Exhibit 7-1 summarizes the benefits of insurance to individuals, organizations, and society.

EXHIBIT 7-1

Benefits of Insurance

Benefit	Explanation
Pay for losses	The primary role of insurance is to indemnify (restore to pre-loss status) individuals and organizations for covered losses.
Manage cash flow uncertainty	Insurance provides financial compensation when covered losses occur. Therefore, insurance greatly reduces the uncertainty created by many loss exposures.
Comply with legal requirements	Insurance can be used both to meet the statutory and contractual requirements of insurance coverage and to provide evidence of financial resources.
Promote loss control activity	Insurance policies may provide insureds with incentives to undertake loss control activities as a result of policy requirements or premium savings incentives.
Efficient use of insured's resources	Insurance makes it unnecessary to set aside a large amount of money to pay for the financial consequences of loss exposures that can be insured. This allows that money to be used more efficiently.
Support for insured's credit	Insurance facilitates loans to individuals and organizations by guaranteeing that the lender will be paid if the collateral for the loan (such as a house or a commercial building) is destroyed or damaged by an insured event, thereby reducing the lender's uncertainty.
Source of investment funds	The timing of insurer's cash flows, premiums collected up front, and claims paid at a later date enable insurers to invest funds in a variety of investment vehicles.
Reduce social burden	Insurance helps to reduce the burden to society of uncompensated accident victims.

FUNCTIONAL VIEW OF INSURANCE

An insurer's core functions are marketing, underwriting, and claims. As shown in Exhibit 7-2, these core functions represent the lifespan of the business, from getting the business (marketing), to pricing the business (underwriting), and then to administering the business (claims). The remaining functions performed by insurers are designed to support these three core functions. An insurer performs these functions to facilitate risk transfer, to promote efficiency, and to meet its own financial and nonfinancial goals.

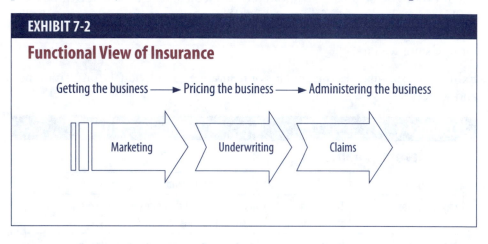

EXHIBIT 7-2

Functional View of Insurance

Getting the business ⟶ Pricing the business ⟶ Administering the business

Marketing   Underwriting   Claims

Marketing

An insurer's marketing department gets business by developing relationships with potential buyers of the insurer's products and services. These potential buyers must be adequately informed about the insurer's products, including its policies, rating plans, loss adjustment services, and loss control capabilities.

Marketing involves more than making sales calls. A successful marketing program is likely to include the following:

- Market research to determine potential buyers' needs
- Advertising and public relations programs to inform potential buyers about the insurer's products
- Training programs to equip the insurer's employees and producers to meet the public's needs
- Production goals and strategies tailored to the insurer's target audience
- Effective motivation and management of the producer network

The marketing department's goals must be balanced with other insurer goals. For example, the marketing department's goals should support the insurer's overall growth and customer retention goals. If the insurer has targeted specific regions or lines of business as targeted growth areas, the marketing department needs to align its efforts in those areas. An imbalance between the marketing department's goals and the goals of any other department within the organization may reduce the efficiency of the insurer.

Underwriting

Once the marketing department has developed a relationship with potential customers, it is the job of the underwriting department to determine if and under what conditions the insurer is willing to provide insurance products and services to these potential customers. **Underwriting** is the process of evaluating insurable loss exposures, accepting or rejecting them, classifying accepted risks, and determining the appropriate insurance premium. Underwriting serves both insurers and insurance buyers by helping the insurer avoid the information problem of adverse selection, discussed in detail subsequently in this chapter. Avoiding adverse selection helps the insurer stay profitable and keeps premiums reasonable for insureds.

The underwriting department counterbalances the marketing department because constraints on underwriting policy can reduce the number of applicants that are accepted. However, the underwriting and marketing departments must coordinate their efforts. Over time, an unduly restrictive underwriting policy combined with aggressive marketing will drive up the insurer's expenses. The cost of investigating and rejecting applicants increases an insurer's expenses, and the restricted premium volume reduces the revenue available to pay for those expenses.

The underwriting department assists the marketing department in developing marketable policy forms and rating plans and in trying to find ways to insure marginal risks by modifying the policy terms, the rating plan, or the risk.

Underwriting
The process of evaluating insurable loss exposures, accepting or rejecting them, classifying accepted risks, and determining the appropriate insurance premium.

Claims

An insurance policy is a promise to make a payment to, or on behalf of, the insured if an insured event occurs. The claim department's purpose is to fulfill the insurer's promise. To that end, the department is staffed by employees who are trained in the skills necessary to evaluate and settle claims and to negotiate or litigate the settlement of claims by or against insureds.

The claim handling process is designed to achieve a fair settlement in accordance with the applicable insurance policy provisions. Claim settlements that exceed the promised amount payable under the policy increase the cost of insurance for all policyholders. Settlements that are less than the promised amount deprive the insured of benefits to which he or she is entitled under the insurance policy. Insurers have developed expertise in claim adjusting in all categories of loss exposures that most individuals and organizations do not possess. Therefore, many insurance industry practitioners view the claim process as the primary service that insurers provide.

Supporting Functions

In order to support the core functions of marketing, underwriting, and claims, insurers provide a variety of other functions, including investments, loss control, premium auditing, reinsurance, actuarial activities, and information systems.

Although most insurers are able to provide these other functions in-house, many are available through third-party providers. The following functions are not only necessary to the efficient operation of insurers, but are also used by a variety of other risk financing organizations, such as captives, pools, risk retention groups, and self-insurers:

- Investments—An insurer's investment operations enable it to earn investment income on the funds generated by its underwriting activities. This investment income enables the insurer to reduce the premium that it must charge in exchange for the risks it assumes. The nature of the insurance risks that an insurer assumes is a factor in determining the types of investments it acquires. For example, liability losses are paid out over a longer period than property losses. Therefore, liability policies can support more long-term investments, such as corporate bonds with long maturity periods, whereas property policies need to be supported by more liquid and short-term investments. An insurer that assumes only moderate underwriting risks might be able to assume greater investment risks with potentially higher investment yield, whereas an insurer that assumes high underwriting risks might need to be more conservative in its investment strategy.

- Loss control—An insurer's loss control department provides information to the underwriting department to assist in selecting and rating risks. This department also works with commercial insureds to help prevent losses and to reduce the effects of those losses that cannot be prevented. Insurers may also market their loss control services as a stand-alone insurance product to third parties who have not purchased insurance policies from the insurer.

- Premium auditing—Although the premium for many types of insurance is known and guaranteed in advance, for some lines of insurance the premium is variable and cannot be precisely calculated until after the end of the policy period. For example, the premium for workers' compensation insurance policies is calculated using wages paid during the policy period. Other commercial insurance policies may use rating variables such as sales or revenue to calculate the premium. Premium auditors ensure equitable treatment of insureds by reviewing the insureds' records to obtain accurate information on rating variables.

- Reinsurance—When an insurer accepts a risk that is larger than it is willing or able to support, it can transfer all or part of that risk to other insurers through reinsurance transactions. Many insurers have a separate reinsurance department that arranges reinsurance and maintains reinsurance agreements.

- Actuarial—Functions carried out by the actuarial department include calculating insurance rates, developing rating plans, and estimating loss reserves. The actuarial department also conducts sensitivity analysis to determine the financial security of the insurer. Furthermore, the actuarial department coordinates with the accounting department in developing reports for regulators to ensure that the insurer is adhering to all regulatory requirements.

- Information systems—Insurers use information systems to conduct their daily operations, manage marketing efforts, underwrite policies, track investments, and pay claims. Information systems are especially important to insurers because of the vast amounts of data associated with insurance operations.

Insurers affect, and are affected by, the economic environment within which they operate. Therefore, they can be viewed from an economic perspective as well as a purely functional perspective.

ECONOMIC VIEW OF INSURANCE

There is supply and demand for insurance products just as there is supply and demand for other products, such as automobiles, tax preparation services, theater tickets, or video game consoles. Therefore, the fundamental supply-and-demand dynamics that apply to other products and services in the economy also apply to insurance policies. Although the remainder of this section describes supply and demand in terms of products, the dynamics affecting supply and demand of products apply equally to services.

The dynamics of supply and demand are such that the seller (supplier) will not offer a product at a price lower than the minimum possible price. Below this minimum possible price, the supplier prefers to keep the product rather than sell it. Similarly, the buyer will not pay more than the buyer's maximum possible price. Above this maximum possible price, the buyer would rather not have the product. If the seller's minimum possible price is lower than the buyer's maximum possible price, then a price exists between these two boundaries at which the transaction can occur such that both the seller and buyer are satisfied. The seller is paid an amount that is higher than the minimum the seller is willing to accept, and the buyer pays an amount lower than maximum the buyer is willing to pay, as illustrated in Exhibit 7-3.

EXHIBIT 7-3

Price Agreement Between Buyers and Sellers

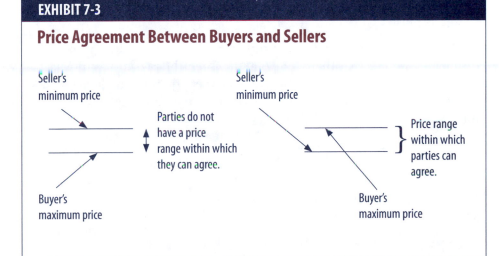

In insurance, the transaction can occur only when the premium charged by the insurer is higher than the minimum premium the insurer is willing to accept and lower than the maximum premium the insurance buyer is willing to pay. Provided the premium is higher than the minimum premium the insurer will accept, the insurer can make a profit.

Shopping for Insurance

Bridget is shopping for auto insurance. The most Bridget is willing to spend on auto insurance is $2,000 per year. She shops on XYZ Insurance Company's Web site, which states that XYZ is willing to sell her an auto insurance policy for $2,500 per year. The minimum price that XYZ is willing to accept, $2,500, is higher than the maximum premium that Bridget is willing to pay, $2,000. Therefore, Bridget and XYZ will not enter into an insurance contract.

Bridget then contacts her local insurance agent, who informs her that he has quotes from three different auto insurers with premiums that range from $1,500 to $1,800 per year. As all three premiums are below the maximum Bridget is willing to pay for auto insurance and above the minimum that the insurers are willing to accept, Bridget will be able to choose auto insurance from one of these three insurers based on not only the price, but also other factors that differentiate their products.

Examining how supply and demand interact in this manner in the insurance market provides useful insights about how insurers contribute to social well-being (buying insurance is financially advantageous to insureds), even when insurers are making profits.

For any product, demand is inversely proportional to its price: the higher the price, the smaller the quantity that consumers are willing to purchase. Alternatively, the smaller the quantity that can be purchased, the higher the price that consumers are willing to pay. The opposite is true for supply: the higher the price of a product, the greater the quantity that sellers are willing to offer, and vice versa. The effect of price and quantity on supply and demand is illustrated in Exhibit 7-4.

Combining the supply and demand curves on one graph, as shown in Exhibit 7-5, reveals that there is a point at which the two curves intersect. At this point, referred to in economics as market equilibrium, demand and supply are equal. Market equilibrium is reached at equilibrium price (P*) and equilibrium quantity (Q*).

Market equilibrium can be attained in a free market (a free market being one without constraints such as limits on price or quantity). In market equilibrium, all sales transactions occur at the equilibrium price (P*). Any price that is higher than the equilibrium price would generate a supply greater than demand

and would result in an over-abundance of the product. With an over-abundance of a product, the price declines back toward P*. Similarly, any price lower than the equilibrium price would generate a shortage, because demand would be greater than supply. With a shortage, the price rises back toward P*. Eventually, the price of the product will return to P*, and the amount supplied will return to Q*.

EXHIBIT 7-4

Supply and Demand Curves

Price

Demand
As the price declines,
the quantity demanded
increases.

Quantity

Price

Supply
As the price increases,
the quantity supplied
increases.

Quantity

EXHIBIT 7-5

Market Equilibrium

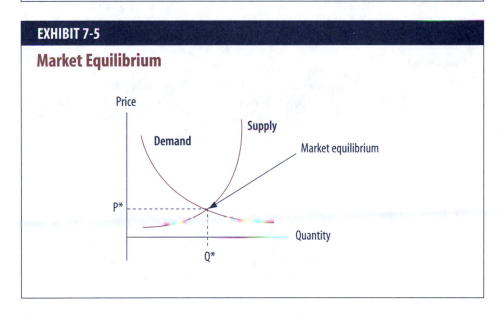

Price

Demand

Supply

Market equilibrium

P*

Quantity

Q*

Supply and Demand in the Video Game Console Market

Ellen wants to buy a new video game console and is considering a new Game Tower 500. Not many video game consoles of this model are available. Video Games, Inc. (Video), a nearby dealer, does have the Game Tower 500 in stock.

Supply

Video wants to maximize its profits. It wants to sell as many video game consoles as possible for as high a price as possible and to minimize the costs of keeping video game consoles in inventory. Conversely, video game console buyers want a low price; the lower the price, the more video game consoles will be purchased. Video seeks a price that maximizes sales revenue at its lowest cost for the number of units sold.

Demand

Ellen can only afford to spend a certain amount of money for a video game console. If she believes the price Video is charging is reasonable, Ellen may buy the video game console. If she thinks the price is too high, she will shop elsewhere, delay her purchase until the price is reduced, or consider a different brand of video game console. Each buyer determines what cost is within his or her price range.

Combining Supply and Demand

What price is appropriate for selling or buying a Game Tower 500? If Video's minimum price (for example, $500) is lower than Ellen's maximum price (for example, $600), the parties will probably be able to negotiate a price that is acceptable to both of them. If Video's price (for example, $550) is higher than Ellen is willing or can afford to pay (for example, $450), Ellen will delay her purchase or shop elsewhere.

Competition

Competition has a bearing on the supply and demand for a particular product or service. If a satisfactory substitute is available, a buyer can always decide to purchase the substitute. The presence of competition reduces the amount that buyers like Ellen are willing to pay for a Game Tower 500 (that is, it reduces the demand). As a result, sellers like Video are forced to lower their prices. Competition among suppliers tends to keep prices down.

The supply of, and the demand for, insurance is influenced by many factors that depend not only on consumers and insurers, but also on the economic and regulatory environment. Exhibit 7-6 presents a summary of the internal and external factors that determine the supply of, and the demand for, insurance products.

Insurance Supply

The supply of a manufactured product depends on many factors, such as the cost of the raw materials, administrative costs, manufacturing costs, and the total compensation of the workers. Similarly, for insurance products, the supply depends on factors such as how much the insurers must pay for rent, marketing services, and salaries. The premiums an insurer collects must cover these costs plus any losses that the insurer has to cover.

EXHIBIT 7-6

Insurance Supply and Demand Factors

Supply (Insurers)	Demand (Consumers)
• Capacity to assume new business	• Insurance mandates and regulation
• Investment opportunities	• Risk tolerance
• Production costs	• Financial status
• Regulatory environment	• Real services rendered
	• Tax incentives

One difference between an organization that sells insurance and a manufacturer or retailer is that an insurer sells a promise of a service that may be needed in the future, whereas a manufacturer or retailer sells a product that the consumer usually brings home (or consumes) immediately after the payment is made. At the time of sale, a manufacturer knows the exact production cost of each unit because these costs are incurred before the product is sold. The manufacturer can therefore price the product accordingly. The same is not true for an insurer. Some of the production costs of an insurance policy are known. For example, the insurer knows its marketing and underwriting costs. However, the major component of the production cost of an insurance policy, the losses and loss adjustment expenses, are not known at the time the premium is set. The fixed premium, combined with the unknown cost of the promise to pay losses, distinguishes insurance from most other products or services sold in the economy.

If the price an insurer could charge were unrestricted, it would seem that the supply of insurance could be virtually limitless. The more policies sold, the greater the premium income, which means more money to invest and thus greater investment income, as well as greater diversification of risk and better predictability of losses. However, insurers do not have an unlimited capacity to sell policies. Because an insurer sells a promise of a future payment in the event of a covered loss, an insurer could make too many promises and ultimately be unable to fulfill them. An insurer must eventually have enough resources to compensate all the policyholders who make a claim. Insurance regulators monitor insurers to help ensure that they have the financial resources to ultimately pay their claims.

The supply of insurance is therefore determined by the following important factors:

• Capacity to assume new business
• Investment opportunities
• Production costs
• Regulatory environment

Capacity to Assume New Business

An insurer's capacity to assume new business is limited by the risk that it will be unable to fulfill the payment promises that it has made. In other words, an insurer's capacity for new business is greatly affected by its **insolvency risk**, which is the risk of an insurer being unable to meet its financial obligations. Insolvency risk limits the supply of insurance provided by insurers. For most insurers, the probability of not being able to pay claims is low. For example, an insurer may want to keep its insolvency risk below 1 percent, meaning that there is only a 1 percent probability that the insurer will not have enough capital to pay all the claims that it must pay in the coming year. The two major variables that affect an insurer's claims-paying ability are (1) the number and the size of the policies sold (its liabilities) and (2) the funds available to pay for the promises made under those policies (its assets).

The first variable, liabilities, is usually measured by the insurer's total **written premiums**, that is, the total premium on all policies written (put into effect) during a particular period. A better measure would be the size of future claims that the insurer expects to pay, but accurately predicting those claims is difficult. Therefore, total written premiums is typically used as an approximation of the liability that the insurer is expected to face in the future. The second variable is measured by assets—such as stocks, bonds, real estate, and other investments—that can be liquidated to pay for claims. The difference between an insurer's assets and its liabilities is called the **policyholders' surplus**. Policyholders' surplus is a measure of how much capital the insurer has to pay claims that are greater than expected.

Insurance regulators closely monitor the relationship between an insurer's premiums and its policyholders' surplus. This relationship is measured by the **premium-to-surplus ratio** (also called the capacity ratio), which is a ratio that indicates an insurer's financial strength by relating net written premiums to policyholders' surplus. The premium-to-surplus ratio indicates the extent to which insurers can issue new policies, because it provides a rough measurement of how adequate available funds (measured by the policyholders' surplus) are to pay unexpected claims (measured by the total written premiums). Financial capacity constraints limit an insurer's ability to grow rapidly, because a rapid growth in new business increases an insurer's obligations faster than it increases policyholders' surplus. The premium-to-surplus ratio formula is calculated as follows:

Premium-to-surplus ratio = Written premiums ÷ Policyholders' surplus.

The policyholders' surplus represents the insurer's financial cushion for absorbing unexpected claims. If losses and expenses exceed written premiums, an insurer must draw on its policyholders' surplus to meet its obligations. Therefore, an insurer's new written premiums should not become too large relative to the policyholders' surplus.

Insolvency risk
The risk of an insurer being unable to meet its financial obligations.

Written premiums
The total premium on all policies written (put into effect) during a particular period.

Policyholders' surplus
The difference between an insurer's assets and its liabilities.

Premium-to-surplus ratio
A ratio that indicates an insurer's financial strength by relating net written premiums to policyholders' surplus.

Insurance regulators use the premium-to-surplus ratio as a benchmark to determine whether an insurer might be facing financial difficulty. A premium-to-surplus ratio above 3-to-1 is often considered a sign of financial weakness, and many consider a ratio above 2-to-1 to be too high. However, although this ratio is important, it is not the only measure of ability to absorb unexpected claims and is not the only indicator that should be used to evaluate an insurer's financial condition. More sophisticated measures recognize factors such as the lines of business written, the adequacy of the loss reserves, the quality of assets, and the amount of reinsurance. These measures are covered in other CPCU courses.

Insurer Capacity and Reinsurance

An insurer (primary insurer) can use a reinsurance arrangement to transfer some of its claim liability to another insurer in the reinsurance market. By using reinsurance, a primary insurer increases its capacity because it increases its ability to pay future claims by sharing the premium it collected and any future losses claimed with a reinsurer. This increase in the primary insurer's ability to indemnify losses is, however, not infinite. Just as the supply of primary insurance is limited, the supply of reinsurance is also limited. The factors that limit the supply of reinsurance are similar to those that limit the supply of primary insurance, such as investment opportunities, production cost, and financial capacity.

Investment Opportunities

When a consumer purchases an insurance policy, he or she purchases the right to claim an amount of money from the insurer at a future time, conditional on an event or a set of events occurring. Until the event occurs and the claim is made, the insurer has the opportunity to invest the premium it collected at the start of the policy.

The amount of investment income generated by the insurer reduces the premium the insurer has to collect to cover future losses. The premiums the insurer collects must be adequate to pay expenses plus the present value of future losses. The greater the income the insurer can earn on its investments, the lower its present value of future losses. An increase in the expected return on the insurer's investments increases the supply of insurance because although capacity may limit the total amount of premium an insurer can write, the insurer can charge a lower premium for coverage and therefore provide more coverage for the same total amount of premium written.

Production Costs

In addition to the actual losses that an insurer must pay, the production of insurance policies involves a variety of expenses that limit the supply of insurance policies that an insurer can provide. These expenses (discussed subsequently in more detail) can be associated with two of the insurer's primary assets: physical assets and human assets. Insurers, similar to manufacturers, need physical assets to produce insurance products and services. Although an insurer's office and equipment needs may not be as extensive as a manufacturer's, an insurer still has physical asset requirements. For example, an insurer needs an efficient information system to track information such as the premiums paid by the insureds, the payments made to claimants, investments, and regulatory filings. Information systems can also be used to assess applicants in order to determine the appropriate underwriting decisions. Other physical assets an insurer needs include office space and company vehicles for claim representatives who are adjusting claims in the field. The more expensive it is for the insurer to acquire and maintain its physical assets, the more costly it is for the insurer to produce insurance policies.

Human assets are also vital to the supply of insurance policies that an insurer can produce. The cost associated with the insurer's human assets influences the supply of insurance policies in the same way as the cost of the physical assets. The more the insurer expends on human assets, the fewer insurance policies it can supply. Employees who possess the appropriate knowledge and skills can help the insurer to accurately price policies, efficiently pay claims, and provide other services that are important to consumers, such as loss control. Salaries paid to claim representatives; producer commissions; and compensation paid to underwriters, actuaries, investment analysts, and other employees are the human asset costs for an insurer.

Regulatory Environment

Even if a particular loss exposure would be deemed acceptable by the underwriting department, an insurer may still be unable to sell an insurance policy for that loss exposure because of externally imposed regulatory constraints. The two main types of regulatory constraints on the supply of insurance are business practices regulation and price regulation.

Many business practices related to the supply of insurance policies, such as licensing, policy language, minimum financial requirements, and participation in residual markets, are regulated at the state level. State regulations also prescribe the minimum financial requirements (capital and policyholders' surplus requirements) that an insurer must have to transact business in that state. Some financial requirements may be high enough that an insurer decides not to sell that line of business in that state. State regulation on marketing practices and other insurer activities may also involve substantial administrative requirements, making it relatively unattractive for an insurer to offer certain insurance products and services. Because regulatory approval is often a slow process, it may constrain an insurer's ability to quickly provide new products and services.

The second regulatory constraint that insurers face is price regulation. State regulators have the power to limit prices by regulating insurance rate increases and the underwriting factors used in setting premiums for many lines of business. For example, insurers may be prohibited from using a driver's gender to determine auto insurance premiums. Regulators have used these powers primarily in automobile liability and in workers' compensation insurance lines, although other lines have also been affected on occasion, such as homeowners' insurance in areas susceptible to natural disasters (such as earthquakes and hurricanes) and title insurance.

Examples of Internal and External Obstacles to Supplying New Insurance Products

In addition to regulatory constraints on new product development, insurers often face other obstacles to the supply of new products. Some of these obstacles include the following:

- Personnel—The insurer may want to enter a certain line of business but concludes that its present staff is not capable of profitably writing and servicing this new line. Hiring additional personnel may not be feasible or might not generate sufficient volume to justify the cost.

- Reinsurance—The insurer's interest in writing a new line of business may depend on whether it can obtain reinsurance for large losses or catastrophes.

- Custom and tradition—Some insurers may hesitate to pioneer in areas that other insurers have not successfully tested.

- New business—A new line of insurance, in which losses are indeterminable, might lead to variable underwriting results, making it difficult to determine prices and leaving the insurer's assets exposed to catastrophic losses.

When regulation limits the price of insurance, some consumers pay less for coverage than before, but other consumers cannot find any coverage at any price. Insurers often limit the amount of insurance they are willing to sell if price regulation prevents them from charging a premium that is necessary to cover losses and expenses and to generate profits. If the coverage is mandatory, some consumers might have to purchase insurance through the state's residual markets, in which losses are often shared among all of the insurers selling insurance in the state.

Insurance Demand

Several factors affect the demand for insurance. These factors relate to both the market and the characteristics of the typical insureds. Factors affecting demand for insurance include the following:

- Insurance mandates and regulation
- Risk tolerance
- Financial status
- Real services rendered
- Tax incentives

Hurricane Andrew and the Supply of Property Insurance

After Hurricane Andrew struck in 1992, inflicting $15½ billion in insured damage, many Florida residents found it almost impossible to purchase property insurance. The supply of property insurance was dramatically reduced, even though demand increased as people became more aware of the extent of their loss exposure (subjective risk) to severe windstorms. These changes in supply and demand occurred despite the fact that the objective risk (the probability of windstorm damage to property) was essentially unchanged. Insurers and consumers, however, became much more aware of the risk of future windstorm damage.

The following three factors dramatically affected the supply of insurance:

- A change occurred in the assessment of the risk of bankruptcy to insurers. Although the probability of a hurricane did not change, the size of the losses and the correlation across the individual losses changed, so that insurers acquired more information about their exposure to catastrophic losses. In other words, insurers became better informed about the consequences of natural catastrophes. Many insurers that had been aggressively marketing property insurance in Florida decided they were no longer interested in expanding their market share, and most wanted to reduce their exposure in that market.

- Because most property insurers had to use their policyholders' surplus to pay the claims from Hurricane Andrew, the catastrophe reduced insurers' financial capacity to write new business because less capital was available after the storm.

- The supply of reinsurance decreased dramatically because reinsurers also suffered significant losses. A catastrophe like Hurricane Andrew has a major effect on insurers writing property reinsurance. Consequently, a decrease in reinsurance market capacity reduces the capacity of primary insurers.

Insurance Mandates and Regulation

Demand for insurance products and services does not necessarily have to be voluntary. There are insurance mandates in many common lines of insurance (including auto insurance and workers' compensation) that increase demand for those insurance products. For example, states impose financial responsibility requirements on auto owners or operators. These requirements are typically satisfied by purchasing auto liability insurance. In this case, the question is not whether to buy insurance, but from whom. Although self-insurance is usually permitted, it is not a common practice among most consumers. In self-insurance, a person or an organization with sufficient financial resources might post a bond, demonstrating to the state that adequate financial resources exist to pay for any losses resulting from an auto accident. Insurance mandates are often violated. For example, some motorists with limited financial resources weigh the risks of being caught and choose to go without insurance.

Most employers are required to provide the workers' compensation benefits prescribed by law. Although self-insurance alternatives are permitted for large employers, small employers with limited financial resources often have no choice about purchasing insurance.

In addition to regulatory mandates, some contracts that organizations and consumers enter into require insurance purchases. For example, most home purchases are financed by a mortgage, and the mortgage lender invariably requires insurance to protect its interest in the property and its ability to recover the loan amount. Creditors also require insurance on business property of many types when it is used as loan collateral. Similarly, many business contracts require one or more contractual parties to purchase liability insurance. All of these mandates and contractual requirements to purchase insurance increase the demand for insurance.

Risk Tolerance

The demand for insurance is strongly influenced by the insurance buyer's attitude toward risk. All else being equal, the greater the individual's risk tolerance, the less insurance that consumer will purchase. Although an insurance policy reduces the uncertainty of losses, this reduction comes at the expense of paying an insurance premium. The cost-benefit analysis (comparing the benefit of the reduced uncertainty with the premium cost of the insurance policy) determines who purchases insurance and who does not. A consumer who has a greater risk tolerance is less likely to purchase an insurance policy, because the cost of the premium outweighs the benefits of the reduced uncertainty.

A consumer's risk tolerance may change with age, with economic or social conditions, or with a significant loss event like a hurricane. For instance, an individual may feel more risk tolerant when younger. Alternatively, a change in economic conditions may increase the cost of retaining risk so that risk tolerance is reduced. For example, a wealthy individual who is suffering losses in an investment portfolio may no longer be willing to assume significant property loss exposures and therefore may choose to purchase a homeowners insurance policy. Ultimately, consumers' risk tolerance can increase or decrease the demand for insurance.

Financial Status

For individuals or organizations with severely limited financial resources, insurance purchases are often a luxury that cannot be afforded. Only individuals or organizations whose income exceeds a certain level are likely to purchase insurance. The higher an individual's (or an organization's) income, wealth, or asset level is, the more likely it is that an insurance policy will be purchased. However, as levels of income or wealth increase, the demand for some forms of insurance actually diminishes because individuals or organizations have the financial resources sufficient to retain losses as current expenses or to use various forms of retention, such as captive insurers.

Real Services Rendered

One of the factors that individuals and organizations consider when purchasing insurance is the services offered with the insurance policy. This can be the deciding factor for those that can afford to retain the risk but choose to insure it. Furthermore, insurers can achieve product differentiation by offering services that are valued by the consumers, such as fast claims service, loss control services, or a personable sales force. The real services an insurer chooses to offer often depend on the type of customer they are trying to attract and the lines of business that the insurer offers. For example, individuals often develop close business relationships with their insurance agent. Therefore, insurers operating in personal lines may want to ensure that they offer a personable sales force. Similarly, they may want to ensure fast claims service, which is another factor that individual consumers value. Alternatively, insurers that are active in commercial lines may focus on offering more extensive loss control services that are valuable to organizations.

Another way to increase demand, both for individual insurer's products and in the aggregate, is to introduce new insurance products, such as extended warranty products for automobiles, warranties for home buyers, and insurance against financial losses resulting from identity theft. An insurer who recognizes the consumer's need for a new insurance product (such as terrorism insurance) or for an old product in a new region, offers a valuable service for which consumers are willing to pay more. By distinguishing its insurance products and services from those of its competitors through new product development or additional services on existing products, an insurer can increase the demand for its insurance policies.

Tax Incentives

Tax incentives affect demand by encouraging people to purchase certain lines of insurance in which the premium is tax-deductible. For example, the cost of employer-provided group life and health insurance is not considered taxable income to an employee (subject to limitations), and it is a tax-deductible expense for the employer. A tax deduction has the same effect as a discount because it lowers the net cost of insurance to purchasers, thereby increasing demand. The difference between a tax deduction and a discount is that the deduction is provided by the government, not the insurance provider.

Tax considerations affecting the purchase of property or liability insurance policies are often more subtle. For example, an individual's or a family's casualty losses (as defined by the tax code) can be income-tax-deductible in some cases, but property-liability insurance premiums are not tax-deductible. The tax deduction helps subsidize the cost of uninsured losses. Recognizing this, wealthy individuals in a high tax bracket might decide to forgo the purchase of property insurance or to purchase insurance with a high deductible.

Alternatively, a business's casualty losses (as defined by the tax code) are tax-deductible at the time they are paid, not during the year when they are incurred. A long delay often exists between the date of an occurrence and the date the loss is paid. Some losses, such as those involving a serious disability, are paid over a period of many years. In contrast, insurance premiums are tax-deductible as a business expense when they are paid. In many cases, the annual cost of insurance is much more consistent from year to year than the amounts that would otherwise be paid as retained losses. This is a powerful argument for the purchase of insurance when earnings stability is a risk management program goal.

Economic Issues Related to Insurance Pricing

In a free market (one that is free of any external constraints), the structure of supply and demand dictates that an insurance transaction will occur at a price that is satisfactory to both the insurer and the consumer. Insurers supply insurance at a price that is greater than the expected value of the losses they cover (plus expenses and profits), and consumers purchase insurance when the premium is less than the cost to them of assuming the risk. For some individuals, the cost of retention can be substantially higher than the expected loss. Therefore, they will purchase insurance even if the premium is greater than the expected loss they face.

When selling insurance to a group of insurance buyers, an insurer's goal is to collect premiums that in the aggregate are adequate to generate an operating profit from the group. This goal is accomplished when the insurance premium for each policy reflects the loss exposures the policy covers, with an allowance for the insurer's expenses, profits, contingencies, and (perhaps) an adjustment for investment income. Insurers refer to this as a premium that is commensurate with the loss exposure. Actuaries develop insurance rating systems for many different types of coverage that match premiums with loss exposures, and underwriters ensure that the specific loss exposures being insured are properly classified within the rating system. Provided the actuaries have developed the proper rating system and the underwriters have accurately classified the individual loss exposures, the loss exposures should be adequately priced and the insurance markets should function properly.

Four key issues affect how insurance markets function with regard to pricing: adverse selection, moral hazard, actuarial compared with social equity, and timing. Any of these issues can affect the proper functioning of insurance markets and, in the extreme case, cause market failure. Market failure occurs when supply and demand do not intersect at a sustainable price and quantity. An example of a market failure was the general liability crisis in the mid-1980s, in which many organizations where unable to obtain liability insurance coverage at any price.

Adverse Selection

Appropriate insurance pricing requires that the insurer be able to gather sufficient information about the applicant to adequately assess and price a particular policy. This information gathering is typically handled by the underwriter and insurance producer. Although much information about an applicant is available from the application and other sources, it can be expensive for insurers to collect. After taking into account all of the information that can be collected cost-effectively, a portion of the information about the applicant remains unknown to the insurer. In economic terms, this is called information asymmetry and it occurs when one party has information that is relevant to the transaction that the other party does not have. Although this information is important to insurers, and would enable them to appropriately price their insurance products, the benefits to the insurer of appropriate pricing do not outweigh the costs of obtaining the additional information.

For example, Tamika lives in Savannah and wants to purchase auto insurance on her new minivan. For a relatively minor cost, the auto insurers that Tamika calls can obtain information from various statistical organizations on the number of auto accidents that occur in the Savannah area, the types of vehicles involved, the ages of the drivers, and the cost of claim settlements. In fact, if the insurers that Tamika calls sell a significant amount of auto insurance in the area, they will already have this information. Furthermore, those insurers can get a copy of Tamika's driving record to determine if she has been involved in any recent traffic violations or auto accidents. However, this information does not completely inform the insurers about what type of driver Tamika is. Assume that Tamika has not had any moving violations or been involved in any accidents. This could mean that Tamika is a very good driver (low risk) or it could mean that she is a very bad driver (high risk) who has just been lucky to avoid accidents and moving violations. The insurers could spend a considerable amount of money to attempt to verify which of the alternatives is correct. In theory, insurers could require a driving test, hire an investigator to follow Tamika and report on her driving habits, or, with Tamika's permission, install a tracking device in her minivan to track her movements to determine her driving habits. However, the additional information may not be worth the expense. Instead of obtaining this additional information, an insurer could charge Tamika an average rate (the same rate they would charge all drivers with the same characteristics as Tamika) and hope that she is a good driver (a low risk). If the insurer sells enough insurance policies to people with characteristics similar to Tamika, the insurer hopes that any poor drivers in the pool are more than offset by all of the good drivers in the pool so that the average rate is sufficient to cover losses and expenses of the group and also to generate profits.

When an insurer charges an average rate because it cannot differentiate between a high risk and a low risk, high-risk individuals have an incentive to buy the insurance policy because the premium is too low relative to their individual risk level. Conversely, low-risk individuals do not want to buy the insurance because the premium is too high. This results in adverse selection. Adverse selection is the process by which consumers with the greatest probability of loss are those most likely to purchase insurance. In the previous example, if the insurer were to offer the average rate to all the drivers, then the high-risk drivers in the group would buy the insurance and the low-risk drivers would not. Therefore, despite offering the average rate, the group of people the insurer has insured is not an average group—it is worse than average because of adverse selection. This group of insureds would tend to have more accidents and higher claims than the average group, because they are poor drivers.

There are significant ethical, social, and legal issues regarding the information insurers need to develop appropriate insurance prices. The continued advances in data collection and dissemination have given insurers the ability to access and analyze an increasing amount of information. However, this access to information has raised privacy concerns about what information is relevant to accurate pricing and how much information is too much.

Avoiding adverse selection is one of the main functions of underwriting and is the major information issue faced by insurers. Another key issue concerns moral and morale hazard.

Moral and Morale Hazard

Just as adverse selection can be thought of as an information problem, moral hazard and morale hazard can be thought of as behavior problems. As discussed in a previous chapter, moral hazard is a condition that increases the frequency and/or severity of a loss resulting from a person acting dishonestly. Morale hazard is a condition that increases the frequency and/or severity of loss resulting from careless or indifferent behavior. Both moral and morale hazard are behavior problems that often arise in risk transfer measures, especially insurance. Individuals and organizations do not behave in the same way when they are insured as when they are uninsured because they will not bear the entire cost of the loss as they would with retention. Some of the loss costs are assumed by the insurer and, therefore, the insureds are less careful.

Moral and morale hazard problems are common in automobile insurance and are also present in products liability and general liability insurance. Insurers need to be aware of the existence of moral and morale hazards, the two main behavior problems that affect insurance markets, when providing insurance to individuals and organizations. The most common method of reducing moral and morale hazard behavior issues is to ensure that the insured participates in the loss by including a risk-sharing mechanism (such as a deductible) in the insurance policy.

Examples of Moral and Morale Hazard

Vince has workers' compensation insurance and healthcare coverage through his employer. Doctors' visits covered by workers' compensation do not have a co-pay, although Vince's healthcare coverage does require him to pay a $25 co-pay per doctor's visit. Vince injures his knee skiing on a Sunday. To avoid having to pay the co-pay for a doctor's visit, he reports to his superior on the following Monday that the injury occurred at work early on Monday morning. Vince's situation is a moral hazard problem; he has intentionally caused a loss to the workers' compensation insurer who has to pay for the cost of treatment.

Abigail owns a two-and-a half-year-old car that she drives to work every day. The car is fully paid for and has a market value of $20,000. Abigail purchased a comprehensive automobile insurance policy that guarantees that if her car is stolen within the first three years of the policy, she receives a brand new car. This policy is a replacement-cost new insurance policy (similar clauses exist for homeowners insurance and commercial buildings). If Abigail purchased the same new car today, she would need $30,000. Because she has purchased the insurance policy, Abigail does not bear the cost of a new car if her car is stolen. Even if she does not want to have her car stolen, Abigail will not invest as much time, effort, and energy in preventing her car from being stolen as she would if she was uninsured. Abigail's situation is a morale hazard problem; she is indifferent to loss because she will not bear any of the cost if a loss occurs.

These are two classic cases of moral and morale hazard. The behaviors of Abigail and Vince are different when they are insured compared with when they were uninsured.

Actuarial Equity Compared With Social Equity

Ideally, the premiums charged to insureds should vary in direct proportion to the insureds' loss exposures and expected losses. Fair discrimination, which charges an equitable premium to each insured, is an essential element of insurance pricing. State insurance laws generally prohibit insurance rates that are unfairly discriminatory.

At issue is that equity has a different meaning for different people, and opinions often vary about whether insurance pricing should achieve actuarial equity or social equity. Insurers generally want to achieve actuarial equity, in which each insured pays a premium directly proportional to the loss exposures that are transferred to the insurer. The concept of actuarial equity is founded in cost-based pricing. The goal of cost-based pricing is to identify every variable that will signal the differences between otherwise identical loss exposures. Actuarial equity has been the traditional test applied by regulatory authorities to distinguish between fair and unfair discrimination, but there has been an increasing trend towards consideration of another test—social equity.

Neither the states nor the courts have specifically defined social equity, but it generally involves two concepts. The first of those concepts is that insurers should relate the amount each person should pay for insurance to his or her ability to pay rather than to the person's loss exposure or expense factor.

The second concept is that insurers should not increase an insured's insurance premium because of criteria that are beyond that individual's control. To help achieve social equity, legislators and the public have identified certain insurance rating variables that are socially unacceptable—including, in virtually every state, the use of race, religion, and national origin. Even if loss experience differs based on these variables, they cannot be reflected in rating plans. This can affect underwriters' decisions. For example, in some jurisdictions, sex has been eliminated as a rating factor for auto insurance—although insurers have gathered historical loss information that indicates that youthful male operators have more losses relative to youthful female operators. In those jurisdictions where sex has been eliminated as a rating factor, youthful males and youthful females with similar characteristics are required to pay the same rates.

When regulatory constraints distort actuarial equity, the effect is that some groups (such as youthful male operators) are undercharged for their insurance, whereas other groups (such as youthful female operators) are overcharged in order for the insurer to break even. Artificial restrictions on classification variables, such as the use of an operator's sex, create a situation in which the low risks subsidize the high risks. Whether this situation is commendable or even acceptable is not an insurance issue; it is a public policy issue.

When rules and regulation prevent insurers from using easily accessible information (such as age, sex, and race), they need to find costlier and less-efficient mechanisms to gather that information. In the case of age, for example, insurers may want to look at the type of automobile, income source, and any other variable that correlates with the age of an individual. If insurers can find variables that correlate to the characteristics they are forbidden to use, then insurers will often use these less-efficient characteristics in their risk classification schemes.

Timing

One final important issue in insurance pricing is timing. For some types of losses, especially large losses arising from liability exposures, a substantial delay can occur between the date of an occurrence, the date the loss is discovered, and the date the loss is paid. During this period, which can span several years, the insurer invests the premium paid for the coverage and generates investment income. The investment income partially offsets the cost of the insurer's expected losses. This partial offset is often reflected in the insurer's pricing. In other words, the insurer considers not the expected loss amount, but the present value of the expected loss amount, when determining the appropriate premiums. As the present value of the expected loss is lower than the expected loss amount, the effect is to reduce premiums.

As well as determining the timing of a loss, an insurer has to assess the value of future losses. In binary insurance policies (policies, such as life insurance policies, under which a lump sum of money is paid if a particular event occurs) this is not an issue because the insurer knows exactly what amount will be paid. The only thing the insurer needs to forecast is when the claim will be paid. However, for most property and liability insurance policies, the claim size is as much an unknown as is the time when the claim will be made. This means that insurers need to forecast the size of the payment that it will eventually disburse to the insured. The longer the time before the amount is paid, the harder it is for the insurer to forecast the size of payment. For example, it is more difficult for an insurer to predict the severity of claims ten years in the future than it is to predict the severity of claims six months in the future.

Because the level of uncertainty is much greater for certain liability lines of insurance (long-tail lines) than for other liability lines and for property lines of insurance (short-tail lines), the risk of mispricing the insurance policy is greater. Consequently, everything else being equal, insurers generally price long-tail line insurance policies higher than short-tail lines.

In order for insurers to operate effectively within the economy, they need to be financially successful. Therefore, as well as viewing insurers from a functional view and an economic view, it is important to assess the insurer from a financial perspective.

FINANCIAL VIEW OF INSURANCE

Insurers need to be financially successful in order to meet their organizational goals. As with any other organization, an insurer will be financially successful if, over time, its revenues exceed its expenses by a satisfactory margin. To understand how to measure the success of an insurer, an insurance professional needs to understand where to find the information related to insurer success. Most of this information is contained in the insurer's financial statements.

Insurer Financial Statements

The primary financial statements for any organization are the balance sheet and income statement. Exhibit 7-7 contains an example of an insurer's balance sheet in both Generally Accepted Accounting Principles (GAAP) and Statutory Accounting Principles (SAP) formats.

A balance sheet, sometimes called a statement of financial position, is a financial statement that reports the assets, liabilities, and owners' equity of an organization as of a specific date. The total assets must equal (balance with) the total liabilities and owner's equity. This results in the following accounting equation:

$$\text{Assets} = \text{Liabilities} + \text{Owners' equity.}$$

Loss reserve

A liability on an insurer's balance sheet that shows the estimated amount that will be required to settle claims that have occurred but have not yet been paid.

The assets typically accumulated by an insurer include money; stocks and bonds; tangible property, such as buildings, office furniture, and equipment; and accounts receivable from agents, brokers, and reinsurers.

An insurer's major liabilities are the loss reserve and the unearned premium reserve. The **loss reserve** is a liability on an insurer's balance sheet that shows the estimated amount that will be required to settle claims that have occurred

EXHIBIT 7-7

Insurer's Balance Sheet

Barnley Insurance Group, Balance Sheet as of December 31, 20X5

Assets/Admitted Assets	GAAP		SAP	
Cash & cash equivalents	$ 24.5	1.4%	$ 23.7	1.6%
Bonds	942.8	52.9	900.2	59.0
Stocks	408.5	22.9	461.1	30.2
Short-term investments	19.9	1.1	0.1	0.0
Accrued investment income	18.7	1.1	18.6	1.2
Agents' balances	63.8	3.6	28.8	1.9
Accrued retrospective premiums	52.8	3.0	48.7	3.2
Reinsurance recoverable	196.1	11.0	23.0	1.5
Other assets	53.5	3.0	20.4	1.3
Total assets/Admitted assets	$1,780.6	100.0%	$1,524.6	99.9%
Liabilities & Owners' Equity/Policyholders' Surplus				
Loss & LAE reserves	$ 895.9	50.3%	$ 723.3	47.4%
Unearned premium reserves	36.8	2.0	35.9	2.4
Provision for reinsurance	n.a.	n.a.	30.7	2.0
Accrued policyholder dividends	(2.5)	−0.1	1.7	0.1
Deferred income taxes	14.2	0.8	—	0.0
Other liabilities	81.8	4.6	75.6	5.0
Total liabilities	$1,026.2	57.6%	$ 867.2	56.9%
Common capital stock	2.4	0.1	4.5	0.3
Additional paid-in capital	102.9	5.8	59.0	3.9
Unassigned funds (surplus)	494.1	27.8	543.0	35.6
Unrealized capital gains	155.0	8.7	50.9	3.3
Owners' equity/Policyholders' surplus	$ 754.4	42.4%	$ 657.4	43.1%
Total liabilities & OE/Surplus	$1,780.6	100.0%	$1,524.6	100.0%

but have not yet been paid. The loss reserve is the insurer's best estimate of these final settlement amounts. The **uncarned premium reserve** represents the insurance premiums prepaid by insureds for insurance coverage that the insurer will provide in the future. Because it has yet to provide the coverage, the insurer has not earned the right to keep this portion of the premiums it has collected. If the insurer ceased to operate, or if the insured chose to cancel coverage, these unearned premiums would have to be refunded to the insureds.

The relationship between assets and liabilities can easily be demonstrated by examining the situation of a typical homeowner who has a house worth $300,000 and an unpaid mortgage balance of $200,000. The house is an asset valued at $300,000. The mortgage is a liability valued at $200,000. The

Unearned premium reserve
The insurance premiums prepaid by insureds for insurance coverage that the insurer will provide in the future.

difference between the house's value and the amount owed on the mortgage is the owner's equity in the house, in this case $100,000. As the mortgage is paid off, the owner's equity in the house increases while the liability decreases.

The owners' equity of an insurer is the policyholders' surplus. This term "policyholders' surplus" emphasizes the priority given to satisfying insured obligations. So, for an insurer, the accounting equation could be stated as follows:

$$\text{Assets} = \text{Liabilities} + \text{Policyholders' surplus.}$$

When the insurer's assets increase without a corresponding increase in liabilities, policyholders' surplus increases. As policyholders' surplus grows, the insurer gains an increasingly large cushion that can absorb losses. Therefore an increase in the policyholders' surplus increases an insurer's capacity to write new business. Conversely, the policyholders' surplus of an insurer decreases whenever its assets decrease without a corresponding decrease in liabilities. Such a decline will occur, for example, when the value of investments decreases.

The income statement is the financial statement that reports an organization's profit or loss for a specific period by comparing the revenue generated with the expenses incurred to produce that revenue. Exhibit 7-8 contains an example of an insurer's income statement. The difference between revenue and expenses, after income tax, is the organization's net income. Net income can therefore be expressed using the following basic formula:

$$\text{Net income} = \text{Revenue} - \text{Expenses} - \text{Income taxes.}$$

Net income is also called the organization's earnings. Some organizations, including insurers, may report net income as revenue minus expenses, and then refer to the after-tax figure as net income after taxes. Regardless of the layout of the income statement and the terminology used, if expenses exceed revenue for the period, then the organization has a net loss and is not operating profitably.

EXHIBIT 7-8

Insurer's Income Statement

Barnley Insurance Group, Income Statement as of December 31, 20X5

	GAAP		SAP	
Earned premiums	$138.5	100.0%	$138.6	100.0%
Losses & LAE incurred	95.1	68.7	95.1	68.6
Other underwriting expenses	74.9	54.1	72.3	52.2
Net underwriting gain (loss)	$(31.5)	−22.8%	$ (28.8)	−20.8%
Net investment income	77.4	55.9	72.8	52.5
Net realized capital gains	51.2	37.0	34.5	24.9
Net investment gain (loss)	$128.6	92.9%	$107.3	77.4%
Provision for income taxes	34.4	24.8	9.7	7.0
Net income	$ 62.7	45.3%	$ 68.8	49.6%

Most financial performance measures depend on measures of revenue and expenses reported on insurers' financial statements.

Revenue

Revenue is generated for individual insurers from the following two major sources:

1. Premiums—payments by insureds to purchase insurance
2. Investments—interest, dividends, capital gains, and other earnings on funds held by the insurer

Comparatively small amounts of revenue might also come from other sources, such as selling loss control or other real services or renting property to others.

Premiums

The first major source of revenue, premiums, is generated by the sale of insurance products and services to consumers. For most insurance policies, the insurer collects the premium at policy inception and provides coverage for a specific length of time, usually one year. An insurer's revenue from premiums is generally characterized in one of two ways: written premiums or earned premiums.

An insurer's written premiums are the total premiums on all policies written (put into effect) during a particular period. An insurer's written premiums are comprised of two components, earned premiums and unearned premiums. **Earned premiums** are the portion of written premiums that corresponds to coverage that has already been provided. An insurer does not recognize premiums as revenue until they can be classed as earned premiums. The portion of written premiums that corresponds to coverage that has not yet been provided is called the **unearned premiums**. Unearned premiums are set aside in the previously discussed unearned premium reserve and are a liability, not an asset.

Earned premiums
The portion of written premiums that corresponds to coverage that has already been provided.

Unearned premiums
The portion of written premiums that corresponds to coverage that has not yet been provided.

Written Premium Compared With Earned Premium

Assume that a company writes only one policy during the year—a one-year policy with an annual premium of $100 written on October 1. The written premium for the year would be $100, the entire premium for the policy. At the insurer's fiscal year end at midnight, December 31, the earned premium for the year would be $25, because only three months of protection would have been provided during the year. The remaining $75 of premium for the policy would be earned in the next year. The $75 not earned by December 31 would be shown on the liabilities side of the company's year-end balance sheet as part of the unearned premium reserve.

	Oct 1	Dec 31	Mar 31	Jun 30	Sep 30
Earned premium	$0	$25	$50	$75	$100
Unearned premium	$100	$75	$50	$25	$0

Investments

The second major source of revenue for an insurer is investments. Insurers typically invest any money available that is not immediately being used to pay claims and other expenses. The three most common areas of investment for insurers are bonds, stocks, and real estate. The insurers' resulting investment income can be quite substantial, especially during periods in which the bond or the stock market is performing well. Conversely, when stock or bond markets are performing poorly, an insurer can suffer significant investment losses.

Premiums provide the primary source of funds that can be invested to increase an insurer's earnings until such time as those funds are required to pay claims. The policyholders' surplus provides a second source of funds that is invested to produce investment income.

As stated previously, insurers' investment income indirectly serves to reduce insurance premiums. Because insurance is highly competitive, insurers base their premiums not only on expected losses and expenses, but also on the investment income they expect to earn.

Expenses

An insurer's expenses are generated from paying claims and from expenses incurred for handling those claims. An insurer also has expenses associated with selling, delivering, and servicing its insurance products, as well as expenses associated with investing available funds. Typically the six largest expenses for an insurer are losses, loss adjustment expenses, acquisition expenses, general expenses, taxes and fees, and investment expenses.

Although the amount of losses vary widely by insurer, losses can be up to 80 percent (or more) of all expenses. Because not all losses are paid when they occur, insurers establish loss reserves. For any given year, an insurer only knows with certainty the amount of its paid losses, not the amount of its incurred losses. **Paid losses** are losses that have been paid to, or on behalf of, insureds during a given period. **Incurred losses** are the losses that have occurred during a specific period, no matter when claims resulting from the losses are paid. Incurred losses for any given period are equal to paid losses plus or minus changes in loss reserves over that period.

In addition to the amounts that must be paid to insureds or third-party claimants in satisfying a claim, insurers incur additional expenses, called loss adjustment expenses. **Loss adjustment expenses (LAE)** are expenses that an insurer incurs to investigate, defend, and settle claims. LAE can include not only the expenses an insurer incurs in-house for claims adjustment and legal defenses, but also the fees paid to third-party providers of loss adjustment services.

Acquisition expenses are expenses that an insurer incurs when selling a policy to a new customer, including marketing, advertising, and underwriting

Paid losses
Losses that have been paid to, or on behalf of, insureds during a given period.

Incurred losses
The losses that have occurred during a specific period, no matter when claims resulting from the losses are paid.

Loss adjustment expenses (LAE)
Expenses that an insurer incurs to investigate, defend, and settle claims.

expenses. Because most of the expenses of selling an insurance policy are paid up front (for example, producers receive a commission when the policy is sold and delivered), the insurer is spending some of the money it expects to earn during the policy period at the outset of the policy.

Insurers have various general expenses that do not relate directly to claims, marketing, or underwriting. These general expenses include overhead (such as staffing) and expenses incurred by departments not directly involved with the provision of the insurance product, such human resources, accounting, legal, research, product development, customer service, and building maintenance.

Insurers pay income tax and a variety of additional government-imposed taxes and fees, such as premium taxes. In addition, insurers usually must pay for licenses in each state where they operate and participate in various state insurance programs, such as guaranty funds or residual markets. Guaranty funds are designed to provide for insureds having claims against insurers that have become insolvent.

Insurers incur expenses to pay for professional investment managers to oversee the insurers' investment programs. Even if an insurer imparts all its investment tasks on major mutual fund or investment firms, the insurer incurs expenses to find the right fund managers and to assess and oversee the performance of such managers periodically. Other investment expenses include brokerage, registration and transfer, and custodial fees.

All of the above expenses, in combination with the previously discussed revenue, are combined to determine the overall financial performance of an insurer. However, determining the profitability of an insurer is not as straightforward as revenue minus expenses.

Profitability

Like any business, an insurer generates income, or profits, when its revenue exceeds its expenses. However, insurers face a special challenge compared with other organizations because the largest portion of an insurer's expenses involves losses that will occur in the future and that are, by definition, more difficult to project than past or current expenses. Estimating these future expenses and setting aside the funds to pay for them is done through reserving. Because reserving is an estimate subject to errors, and is a substantial portion of an insurer's expenses, it makes it difficult to measure the profitability of an insurer's financial performance.

Over the long run, the profitability of an insurer will become apparent as the estimates of losses (loss reserves) are replaced with certain amounts (paid losses). However, an insurer's profitability in any given quarter or year is significantly influenced by the loss reserve estimates. Estimating insurer profitability is generally done by examining either underwriting performance (underwriting gain or loss) or overall operating performance (gain or loss from operations).

Net Underwriting Gain or Loss

Net underwriting gain or loss
An insurer's earned premiums minus its incurred losses and underwriting expenses for a specific period.

An insurer's **net underwriting gain or loss** is its earned premiums minus its incurred losses and underwriting expenses for a specific period. Incurred losses include loss adjustment expenses and underwriting expenses include acquisition expenses, general expenses, taxes, and fees. Because this figure ignores investment income (or investment losses) and investment expenses, it represents the extent of the insurer's profit or loss derived strictly from the sale of insurance products. The formula for calculating net underwriting gain or loss can be expressed as follows:

Net underwriting gain or loss = Earned premiums − (Incurred losses + Underwriting expenses).

Three specific ratios are used to measure an insurer's underwriting performance: the loss ratio, the expense ratio, and the trade basis combined ratio. Each of these ratios is shown in the following text box and discussed in greater detail in other CPCU courses.

Measuring an Insurer's Underwriting Performance

The loss ratio compares an insurer's incurred losses with its earned premiums for a specific period. The figure for incurred losses includes loss adjustment expenses. The loss ratio is calculated as follows:

Loss ratio = Incurred losses ÷ Earned premiums.

The expense ratio compares an insurer's underwriting expenses with its written premiums for a specific period. The expense ratio is calculated as follows:

Expense ratio = Incurred underwriting expenses ÷ Written premiums.

The trade basis combined ratio combines the loss ratio and the expense ratio to compare inflows and outflows from insurance underwriting. There are two widely accepted ways of calculating the combined ratio: the financial basis combined ratio and the trade basis combined ratio. The trade basis combined ratio is calculated as follows:

$$\text{Trade basis combined ratio} = \frac{\text{Incurred losses (including LAE)}}{\text{Earned premiums}} + \frac{\text{Incurred underwriting expenses}}{\text{Written premiums}}.$$

This can be simplified as follows:

Trade basis combined ratio = Loss ratio + Expense ratio.

Overall Gain or Loss From Operations

Overall gain or loss from operations
An insurer's net underwriting gain or loss plus its net investment gain or loss for a specific period.

An alternative way to measure an insurer's profits is through overall results from operations. An insurer's **overall gain or loss from operations** is its net underwriting gain or loss plus its net investment gain or loss for a specific period. This overall figure gives a more complete picture of an insurer's profitability because investment income generally helps to offset any underwriting losses. The formula for overall gain or loss from operations is as follows:

Overall gain or loss from operations = Net underwriting gain or loss + Investment gain or loss.

After an insurer pays losses, expenses, and taxes, and reserves money to pay additional incurred losses, the remainder is net operating income, which belongs to the company's owners. The owners (stockholders or policyholders) may receive a portion of this remainder as dividends. The amount that is left after dividends are paid is added to the policyholders' surplus. The increase in policyholders' surplus enables the insurer to expand its operations in the future and provides a cushion against catastrophic losses. To obtain an accurate picture of an insurer's profitability, it is important to analyze the overall gain or loss from operations for several years, because any company might have a single bad year that is offset by a pattern of profitability over a longer period.

Insurers may lose money on their underwriting activities (that is, the combined ratio is more than 100 percent) and yet still generate a profit on investments. Ideally, the investment profit is more than enough to offset the underwriting loss so that the insurer has an overall gain from operations, and the policyholders' surplus grows through time and generates a suitable return on equity for the insurer's owners.

The investment income ratio, overall operating ratio, and return on equity are more specific measures of an insurer's operational performance. Each of these ratios is shown in the following text box and discussed in greater detail in other CPCU courses.

Measuring an Insurer's Overall Performance

The investment income ratio compares the amount of net investment income (investment income minus investment expenses) with earned premiums over a specific period of time. The investment income ratio is calculated as follows:

$$\text{Investment income ratio} = \text{Net investment income} \div \text{Earned premiums.}$$

The overall operating ratio, the trade basis combined ratio minus the investment income ratio, can be used to provide an overall measure of the insurer's financial performance for a specific period. Of all the commonly used ratios, the overall operating ratio is the most complete measure of an insurer's financial performance. The formula for overall operating ratio is as follows:

$$\text{Overall operating ratio} = \text{Trade basis combined ratio} - \text{Investment income ratio.}$$

Return on equity, calculated by dividing the organization's net income by the average amount of owners' equity (policyholders' surplus) for a specific period, enables investors to compare the return that could have been obtained by investing in the insurer with the potential returns that could have been earned by investing their money elsewhere. In general, the owners' equity is invested in operations to generate income for the organization. For insurers, the policyholders' surplus is invested in underwriting activities. The formula for return on equity is as follows:

$$\text{Return on equity} = \text{Net income} \div \text{Owners' equity.}$$

The functional, economic, and financial views of an insurer show how an insurer operates within society. The social view of insurance looks at how the existence and operation of an insurer affects society and how it helps society to manage risk.

SOCIAL VIEW OF INSURANCE

The social view of insurance shows how insurance works as a pooling mechanism and how it adds to the social good by actually removing risk from society.

Pooling

One of the fundamental concepts used in risk management is pooling. Pooling is an arrangement that facilitates the grouping together of loss exposures and the resources to pay for any losses that may occur. In the context of risk financing, a pool is a financial arrangement that combines the loss exposures and financial resources of individuals or organizations within the group to share the losses experienced by members of the group.

Pooling arrangements function best (reduce the most risk to the group) when the loss exposures being pooled are independent of (uncorrelated with) one another. Losses are independent when a loss at one loss exposure has no effect on the probability of a loss at another loss exposure. For example, two warehouse properties, one in Hawaii and the other in Pennsylvania, would be independent loss exposures regarding the fire cause of loss. A fire at one warehouse would not affect the frequency or severity of a fire at the other. However, two warehouses in Miami would not be independent loss exposures with respect to the windstorm cause of loss, because one hurricane could cause damage to both locations.

Loss exposures do not necessarily have to be independent to benefit from pooling. Correlated loss exposures (exposures that are not independent) can still benefit from pooling arrangements provided the loss exposures are not perfectly positively correlated (that is, if a loss happens to one exposure, it definitely happens to the other). However, although pooling correlated loss exposures can reduce risk to the pool members, the risk is not as effectively reduced as when the exposures are independent.

Pooling Compared With the Law of Large Numbers

Although similar in concept, pooling is not the same as the law of large numbers. The law of large numbers indicates that as the number of independent exposures increases, the actual performance of the group of exposures more nearly approaches the true predicted performance. Pooling benefits from the law of large numbers in that as the pool size grows, the pool's results more closely resemble the predicted outcome. However, the pool includes not only the grouping of the loss exposures, but also the resources of the pool members to pay for the losses that do occur. Therefore, the pool members' grouped resources can help pay for any deviations from the expected outcome.

Pooling and Risk Reduction

Suppose that Rachel owns a $100,000 home that is exposed to the possibility of loss in the coming year. The loss distribution that Rachel faces is shown in Exhibit 7-9. There is an 85.5 percent chance that Rachel will not have a loss and a very small chance (0.5 percent) that the home will be completely destroyed. Based on the distribution shown and the formulas given in a previous chapter, without any pooling arrangements, Rachel's expected loss is $744, and the standard deviation of the loss is $7,131.

EXHIBIT 7-9

Rachel's Loss Distribution

Size of Loss (X)	Probability (p)	Expected Loss (p × X)	Standard Deviation Calculation $(X - EV)^2$	$p \times (X - EV)^2$
$ 0	0.855	$ 0	$ 553,536	$ 473,273
100	0.04	4	414,736	16,589
500	0.04	20	59,536	2,381
1,000	0.02	20	65,536	1,310
2,500	0.02	50	3,083,536	61,670
5,000	0.01	50	18,113,536	181,135
10,000	0.01	100	85,673,536	856,735
100,000	0.005	500	$9,851,753,536	$49,258,767
	Expected Loss	$744	Standard Deviation $	7,131

Further suppose that Rachel agrees to enter a pooling arrangement with Keith, who owns the same type of house and faces the same loss distribution as Rachel. Also assume that the two houses are independent of one another and that Rachel and Keith agree to evenly split any losses that the two might incur. That is, they are pooling both their loss exposures and their resources to pay for any losses to those exposures.

Exhibit 7-10 shows that when there are two pool members (in this case, Rachel and Keith), the expected losses of the pool are twice the expected losses of one member (2 × $744 = $1,488). However, although the standard deviation of the pool has increased ($10,085 compared with $7,131), it has not doubled. The standard deviation of the pool is calculated as follows:

$$\text{Standard deviation (pool)} = \sqrt{n} \times \text{variance (single member)},$$

where n is the number of members in the pool.

EXHIBIT 7-10

Loss Distribution for Pools

Number of Members in Pool (n)	Expected Loss		Standard Deviation	
	Pool	Per Member	Pool	Per Member
1	$744	$744	$7,131	$7,131
2	$ 1,488	$744	$ 10,084	$5,042
10	$ 7,440	$744	$ 22,550	$2,255
100	$ 74,400	$744	$ 71,310	$ 713
1,000	$744,000	$744	$225,502	$ 226

The standard deviation of the pool will increase as the number of members increases. However, the standard deviation increases at a decreasing rate, which means that the standard deviation of losses on a per member basis actually decreases. As shown in Exhibit 7-10, as the number of members in the pool increases, the expected losses and standard deviation of the pool increases, but on a per member basis the expected value remains unchanged and the standard deviation decreases. This occurs because the extreme outcomes become less likely at the pool level.

For example, because Rachel's losses are independent of Keith's losses, the probability that neither individual will have a loss is simply the probability that Rachel does not have a loss multiplied by the probability that Keith does not have a loss. Therefore, the probability of neither having a loss is .855 × .855 = .731, or 73.1 percent. Similarly, the probability of both of them having a total loss is .005 × .005 = 0.0025 percent. From Rachel's perspective, before the pooling arrangement, the chance of Rachel not having any loss (and not having to pay anything) was 85.5 percent. With the pooling arrangement, the chance of Rachel not having to pay anything has been reduced to 73.1 percent because Rachel has agreed to pay a part of Keith's losses as well as part of her own. As far as losses are concerned, without the pooling arrangement Rachel had a 0.5 percent chance of having to pay $100,000 in losses. With the pooling arrangement, Rachel will have to pay $100,000 in losses only if both she and Keith suffer total losses, which will happen only 0.0025 percent of the time.

As this example demonstrates, the pooling arrangement does not change the frequency or severity of the individual loss exposures. It does change the probability distribution of losses facing each person simply because the sources of the loss exposures and resources to pay for losses have been combined. The expected value remains the same, but the uncertainty around that expected value (as measured by standard deviation) has decreased. Therefore, both Rachel's and Keith's risks are reduced by pooling. Exhibit 7-10 also shows that as the number of members of the pool increases, the standard deviation per member continues to decrease. This is a social good of pooling because it helps to reduce risk in society. As more and more members of the pool are added, it becomes more and more likely that the pool members will have to pay closer to the expected loss rather than an amount at the extremes of the original loss distribution. In summary, the pooling arrangement does not change either person's expected cost, but it makes the actual cost more consistent and less variable, thereby reducing risk in society. Although pooling arrangements do not prevent losses or transfer risk, they reduce each individual's risk or uncertainty through sharing of losses and resources.

Pooling Arrangements With Correlated Losses

Pooling arrangements work best with loss exposures that are independent. However, most loss exposures are not independent. The occurrence of a loss is often the result of events that are common to many people or organizations. Catastrophes, such as hurricanes, tornadoes, wildfires, and earthquakes, cause property losses to many individuals at the same time. Consequently, property losses in certain geographic regions during a given period are positively correlated. Pooling arrangements still work when loss exposures are correlated, provided they are not perfectly positively correlated. With independent loss exposures, there is a high probability that one person's large losses will be offset by other participants' small losses. Therefore, the average loss becomes more predictable. When losses are positively correlated, similar losses are incurred by more participants; therefore, one person's large losses are less likely to be offset by other participants' small losses.

From Exhibit 7-10, if Rachel and Keith's houses were close together, their loss exposures would be positively correlated. Their proximity would determine how highly correlated. Therefore, although the expected loss would remain unchanged ($1,488 for the two of them), the standard deviation for the two of them would be higher. For example, the standard deviation for the two of them may be $15,000 rather than $12,899 if they were on the same street, or $17,000 if they were next-door neighbors. Therefore, although pooling would still reduce the risk to both Rachel and Keith if they were next-door neighbors, and the standard deviation would drop from $9,121 per member to $8,500 ($17,000 ÷ 2), it would not reduce as much risk as it would have had their loss exposures been uncorrelated.

Insurance Compared With Pooling

Both insurance and pooling often rely on the law of large numbers. That is, both pools and insurers can expect actual results to more closely resemble expected results as the number of members (or insureds) grows. Insurers benefit from pooling and, in fact, most insurers act as large, well-financed pools. However, although an insurer resembles a formal pooling mechanism, there are two key differences between pooling and insurance. First, pooling is a risk sharing mechanism whereas insurance is a risk transfer mechanism. With insurance, the insurance contract transfers the risk from the insured to the insurer in exchange for premiums. If the premiums are not adequate to cover the insureds' losses that year, the insurer cannot collect more from the insureds, as would happen in a pooling arrangement. Even with insurance products that are loss sensitive, such as retrospective rating plans, the risk sharing occurs between the insurer and the insured, not the insured and other insureds. In a retrospective rating plan, if the insured's losses were higher than expected, the insurer can adjust the premium amount. However, the insurer would not adjust all insureds' premiums because one insured's losses were higher. The insurer simply has to pay the additional losses from its policy-holders' surplus. With a pool, losses are shared among all pool members, not transferred to the pool. If the losses of the pool were greater than expected, each member of the pool would have to commit additional resources to pay for losses. Because there is no cost certainty, pools are risk sharing mechanisms rather than risk transfer mechanisms.

Second, the insurer introduces additional financial resources that enable it to provide a stronger guarantee that sufficient funds will be available in the event of a loss, further reducing risk. These additional financial resources are primarily derived from the following sources:

- Initial capital from investors—The initial capital is the money that investors provide to establish an insurer. The minimum amount of initial capitalization is established by law in the state where the insurer is chartered. This startup fund might be provided by stockholders, who expect a return on their investment, or by insureds, who want to establish an insurer that will provide a market for their particular insurance needs.

- Retained earnings—Retained earnings are derived from premiums in excess of amounts used to pay claims and expenses, and from earnings on invested money. Each premium should be sufficient to cover that insured's fair share of claims and expenses—and to provide a profit for the insurer. The premium might also include an amount to cover contingencies (known as a risk loading) to pay claims when aggregate loss experience is worse than expected without impairing the insurer's solvency.

Because the premiums charged are greater than the expected average loss costs and expenses, and because the insurer begins with an initial capitalization, the insurer can be comfortable agreeing to accept the transfer of risks from its insureds—provided the risks it accepts are within its capacity.

Exhibit 7-11 demonstrates the limitations on the financial resources of an insurer. The loss distribution is the same as that shown in Exhibit 7-9. In the Exhibit 7-11 example, assume the insurer has been funded by investors with $1 million in initial capital. If the insurer sells one policy to Rachel, the insurer assumes the risk that losses will be more than the premium it charged. Suppose that the insurer wants to ensure that it can pay losses that are two standard deviations above the expected loss. In this case, that means the insurer must have at least $18,986 to pay for losses to Rachel's policy. With $1 million in initial capital and only one policy sold, the insurer has more than enough capacity to pay any loss that Rachel may suffer. Therefore, the insurer does not need any significant additional resources from the premium on the policy, the second source of additional funds.

EXHIBIT 7-11

Pooling and Capital Requirements

Insurer's initial capital = $1,000,000.

Number in Pool	Expected Loss		Standard Deviation		Resources Needed to Pay Losses Two Standard Deviations From the Expected	Additional Resources per Policy
	Pool	Per Member	Pool	Per Member		
2	$ 1,488	$744	$ 12,899	$6,450	$ 27,286	$ 0
10	$ 7,440	$744	$ 28,843	$2,884	$ 65,126	$ 0
1,000	$744,000	$744	$288,431	$ 288	$1,320,862	$321

If the insurer sells ten identical policies to ten independent insureds, the resources needed to pay losses that are two standard deviations above the expected loss of $7,440 are $65,126. With ten policies, the initial capital still provides more than enough capacity. However, if the insurer sold 1,000 policies, it would need $1,320,862 to be able to pay losses two standard deviations above the expected losses of $744,000. In this case, the initial investment of $1,000,000 does not provide enough capacity. Therefore, the insurer would need to charge an extra $321 per policy to cover its desired contingencies. The additional $321 would be above expected losses, expenses, and profit margins and would be the retained portion of the premium necessary to meet the desired capacity.

Every insurer's capacity is limited by its financial resources, and its ability to fulfill its obligations is based on remaining solvent. Just as insurance buyers transfer risks that they are unwilling to retain to insurers, insurers can transfer risks that they are unwilling to retain to reinsurers. Through reinsurance, primary insurers pool or transfer risks, thereby staying within capacity constraints and helping to ensure their solvency. Reinsurance helps to reduce risk for insurers that accept risks transferred by insurance buyers. Therefore, reinsurance also contributes to the social function of insurance by assisting insurers in removing risk from society.

SUMMARY

When used as a risk financing technique within a risk management program, insurance helps an individual or organization achieve its risk financing goals and provides benefits to individuals, organizations, and society. These benefits include indemnifying the costs of covered losses and reducing financial uncertainty, promoting the insured's risk control measures, and providing a source of investment funds.

An insurer's core functions are marketing, underwriting, and claims. An insurer's marketing department gets business by developing relationships with, and providing information to, potential buyers of the insurer's products and services. Underwriting is the process of evaluating insurance risks, accepting or rejecting them, classifying accepted risks, and determining the appropriate insurance premium. The claim handling process is designed to achieve a fair settlement in accordance with the applicable insurance policy provisions. Other administrative functions include loss control, premium auditing, reinsurance, actuarial activities, investments, and information systems.

The dynamics of supply and demand are such that the seller (supplier) will not offer a product at a price lower than the minimum possible price. Similarly, the buyer will not pay more than the buyer's maximum possible price. If the seller's minimum possible price is lower than the buyer's maximum possible price, then a price exists between these two boundaries at which the transaction can occur such that both the seller and buyer are satisfied. For any product, demand is inversely proportional to its price: the higher the price, the smaller the quantity that consumers are willing to purchase, and vice versa. The opposite is true for supply: the higher the price of a product, the greater the quantity that sellers are willing to offer, and vice versa.

The supply of insurance is influenced by capacity to assume new business, investment opportunities, production costs, and the regulatory environment. The demand for insurance is influenced by insurance mandates and regulation, risk tolerance, financial status, real services rendered, and tax incentives. Insurers supply insurance at a price that is greater than the expected value of the losses they cover, and consumers purchase insurance when the premium is less than the cost to them of assuming the risk. Economic issues affecting insurance pricing include adverse selection, moral and morale hazard, actuarial compared with social equity, and timing.

An insurer will be financially successful if, over time, its revenues exceed its expenses by a satisfactory margin. Information with which to gauge an insurer's financial success can be found in the insurer's financial statements. The primary statements are the income statement (which shows revenues and expenses) and the balance sheet (which shows assets, liabilities, and policyholders' surplus).

Revenue is generated for individual insurers primarily from premiums and investments. An insurer's written premiums are the total premiums on all policies written (put into effect) for a particular period. Earned premiums are the portion of written premiums that corresponds to coverage that has already been provided. An insurer does not recognize premiums as revenue until they can be classed as earned premiums. The portion of written premiums that corresponds to coverage that has not yet been provided is called the unearned premiums. Insurers typically invest any money available that is not immediately being used to pay claims and other expenses. The three most common areas of investment for insurers are bonds, stocks, and real estate.

An insurer's expenses are generated from paying claims and from expenses incurred for handling those claims. Typically, the six largest expenses for an insurer are losses, loss adjustment expenses, acquisition expenses, general expenses, taxes and fees, and investment expenses. Insurers face a special challenge compared with other organizations because the largest portion of an insurer's expenses involves losses that will occur in the future and that are, by definition, more difficult to project than past or current expenses. Estimating these future expenses and setting aside the funds to pay for them is done through reserving. Because reserving is an estimate subject to errors and is a substantial portion of an insurer's expenses, it is difficult to measure the profitability of the insurer's financial performance. Estimating insurer profitability is generally done by examining either underwriting performance (underwriting gain or loss) or overall operating performance (gain or loss from operations).

The social view of insurance shows how insurance works as a pooling mechanism. Pooling is an arrangement that facilitates the grouping together of loss exposures and resources. It functions best when the loss exposures being pooled are independent of one another. However, correlated loss exposures can still benefit from pooling arrangements provided the loss exposures are not perfectly positively correlated (that is, if a loss happens to one exposure, it definitely happens to the other).

Although an insurer resembles a formal pooling mechanism, there are two key differences between them. First, an insurer transfers the risk from the insured to the insurer in exchange for premiums. If the premiums are not adequate to cover an insured's losses that year, the insurer cannot collect more from the insured, as would happen in a pooling arrangement. Second, the insurer introduces additional financial resources that enable the insurer to provide a stronger guarantee that sufficient funds will be available in the event of a loss, further reducing risk.

Direct Your Learning

Insurable Risks

After learning the content of this chapter and completing the corresponding course guide assignment, you should be able to:

- Explain why each of the six characteristics of an ideally insurable loss exposure is important to the insurance mechanism.

- Explain how the six characteristics of an ideally insurable loss exposure apply to commercial insurance loss exposures.

- Explain how the six characteristics of an ideally insurable loss exposure apply to personal insurance loss exposures.

- Explain how state and federal governments are involved in the insurance market and the rationale for, and level of, their involvement.

- Define or describe each of the Key Words and Phrases for this chapter.

Develop Your Perspective

What are the main topics covered in the chapter?

Organizations face a wide variety of loss exposures, not all of which are insurable. Insurers look for certain characteristics when evaluating the insurability of a loss exposure. In some instances, the government offers insurance programs to provide the coverage that private insurers are unwilling or unable to provide.

Analyze your organization's current insurance portfolio.

- For what types of loss exposure does your organization carry insurance?
- Does your organization participate in any property-casualty government insurance programs?

Why is it important to learn about these topics?

Knowing about insurability will help you understand why insurers choose to insure some loss exposures over others; why insurers cannot always assume risks they might otherwise choose to insure; and why government insurance complements, reinsures, or competes with private insurance.

Examine your organization's insurance coverages.

- How many different insurers provide the necessary coverages? Does any one insurer cover multiple loss exposures?
- Do any constraints prevent an insurer from covering multiple loss exposures?

How can you use what you will learn?

Evaluate your organization's insurance needs for which the government provides coverage.

- What are some reasons why the government would provide this coverage?
- Why might a private insurer be unable or unwilling to provide this coverage?

Chapter 8
Insurable Risks

Individuals and organizations face risk from a wide variety of sources. For example, organizations have loss exposures associated with hazard, operational, financial, and strategic risks. Although a wide range of insurance products are available in the insurance markets, relatively few of the loss exposures faced by individuals and organizations are insurable. In a previous chapter, the risk transfer mechanism of insurance was discussed as a viable option when a loss exposure has a low frequency and high severity of loss. However, in addition to frequency and severity considerations, other characteristics of a loss exposure influence its suitability for insurance. Six of these characteristics are commonly referred to as the characteristics of an ideally insurable loss exposure.

The loss exposures that insurers are willing to assume (and for which they provide coverage) generally possess most if not all of the six characteristics of an ideally insurable loss exposure. Nonetheless, some loss exposures that do not exhibit one or more of these characteristics (that is, the loss exposure is not ideal) are still insured. Insurability becomes an issue when a particular loss exposure deviates too far from the ideal. Determining what is "too far" is subjective and varies not only by insurer, but also with market conditions over time. Some loss exposures that are routinely insured today were once considered uninsurable, and vice versa.

When a loss exposure is considered uninsurable in the insurance market, other risk transfer techniques may be viable options. However, if suitable alternatives are not available in the private market, a circumstance often referred to as a market failure, then either state or federal governments may decide to provide insurance. The government-supplied insurance may be the only insurance coverage offered, may compete with insurance supplied by private insurers, or may be government-supplied reinsurance designed to facilitate private market insurance coverage.

Industry Language—What Does Private Mean?

Insurance organizations that are not owned or operated by federal or state governments are generally referred to as private insurers. The insurance products they sell are sold in the private insurance market. The term "private" may be confusing because some insurers are publicly traded stock organizations (owned by the public), not privately owned. Furthermore, the markets they compete in are open to all consumers, not restricted to certain parties. When federal or state governments compete with private insurers, they compete in the private insurance market. When federal or state governments are the only source of an insurance product, then no private market exists.

CHARACTERISTICS OF AN IDEALLY INSURABLE LOSS EXPOSURE

Private insurers insure some, but not all, loss exposures. Insurable loss exposures ideally have certain characteristics. Exhibit 8-1 lists the six characteristics of an ideally insurable loss exposure.

EXHIBIT 8-1

Six Characteristics of an Ideally Insurable Loss Exposure

1. Pure risk—involves pure risk, not speculative risk.

2. Fortuitous losses—subject to fortuitous loss from the insured's standpoint.

3. Definite and measurable—subject to losses that are definite in time, cause, and location and that are measurable.

4. Large number of similar exposure units—one of a large number of similar exposure units.

5. Independent and not catastrophic—not subject to a loss that would simultaneously affect many other similar loss exposures; not catastrophic.

6. Affordable—premiums are economically feasible.

Note that these are *ideal* characteristics, not requisite ones. In fact, most insured loss exposures do not completely meet all of these criteria. However, each of these characteristics is important to a loss exposure's insurability.

Industry Language: What Does Insurability Mean?

Although a particular loss exposure has the characteristics of a commercially insurable loss exposure, an insurer still may prefer not to sell an insurance policy for it. This may be the result of externally or internally imposed constraints placed on the insurer or simply because the insurer prefers not to cover those types of exposures. Internal constraints may be a lack of expertise or resources to offer insurance coverages in that particular line of business. External constraints include state regulation.

State laws regulate the types of insurance that can be written in each state and prescribe the minimum capital and surplus an admitted insurer must have to transact business. Some financial requirements are so high that an insurer might forgo writing a type of business it would otherwise prefer to include in its portfolio. In addition, state insurance departments regulate forms and rates for some types of coverage, which could involve substantial paperwork, making it relatively unattractive for an insurer to offer those coverages. Finally, regulatory approval is often a slow process that constrains insurers' ability to provide new products and services because various marketing practices are also regulated, and some activities are prohibited.

Pure Risk

The first ideal characteristic of an insurable loss exposure is that the loss exposure should be associated with pure risk, not speculative risk. Unlike many other risk financing measures, such as hedging, insurance is not designed to finance speculative risks. One purpose of insurance is to indemnify the insured for the loss, not to enable the insured to profit from the loss. Indemnification is the process of restoring an individual or organization to a pre-loss financial condition. If the loss exposure has the possibility of gain, the insurance premium the insurer would need to charge would offset the potential gain. For example, assume a gambling opportunity involves a roulette wheel that has only red and black numbers (50 percent red and 50 percent black; no green), a mandatory $5 bet, and an insurer that is willing to insure a red number outcome. Consider the following two scenarios:

1. *The insurer does not charge a premium.* If a roulette player can place a bet on black, knowing that if the result is black, he or she will win $5.00, and if the result is red, an insurer will refund the bet, the player can gain without any risk of loss. This is arbitrage (or risk-free) profits. The roulette player would win $5 with a black number and $0 with a red number (the $5 bet is refunded by the insurer). In the long run, the roulette player can expect to win $2.50 ([$5 × .50] + [$0 × .50] = $2.50) every spin of the roulette wheel, without ever losing.

2. *The insurer charges an appropriate premium.* The insurer can expect to lose $2.50 every spin of the roulette wheel. If the outcome is a black number (which happens 50 percent of the time), the insurer loses nothing and if the outcome is a red number, the insurer loses $5.00. This gives an expected value of a loss of $2.50 ([$5 × .50] + [$0 × .50] = $2.50). If the insurer has no expenses, makes no profit, and has no risk charges, then the premium it would charge would be $2.50 per spin (the expected loss). Therefore, the minimum premium an insurer would have to charge offsets any potential gain the insured could have earned from the speculative risk.

Although this example is not realistic, it demonstrates that to insure the downside in a speculative risk, an insurer would have to charge a premium that removed all the expected profits for the insured. In addition, to cover an insurer's expenses, risk charges, and profitability, the minimum premium an insurer would have to charge more than offsets any expected profits. This in turn removes the incentive for the insured to buy the insurance. Furthermore, limiting insurance coverage only to pure risks helps reduce the complexity of the loss exposures insured by the policy and therefore reduces the difficulty in analyzing the loss exposures during the underwriting process. Insuring speculative risks would require the underwriter to calculate all the possible bad outcomes that would involve the claims against the insurer in order to accurately price the insurance policy. The additional work required in the underwriting process would add to the cost of insurance for all policyholders.

Fortuitous

Fortuitous loss
A loss that is accidental and unexpected.

The second characteristic of an ideally insurable loss exposure is that the loss associated with the loss exposure should be fortuitous from the insured's standpoint. A **fortuitous loss** is a loss that is accidental and unexpected. Some causes of loss may be fortuitous only from one point of view. For example, vandalism and theft are intentional (and therefore not fortuitous) acts from the perspective of the individual or organization committing the acts. However, they are fortuitous from the victim's or insured's standpoint because they were not intended or expected by the victim or insured. Other causes of loss are fortuitous regardless of the perspective from which they are examined. For example, naturally occurring events such as windstorms, hail, or lightning are fortuitous events whether one is the insurer, the insured, or any third party associated with the loss exposure.

If the insured has some control over whether or when a loss will occur, the insurer is at a disadvantage because the insured might have an incentive to cause a loss (moral hazard). Also, if losses are not fortuitous, the insurer cannot calculate an appropriate premium because the chance of loss could increase as soon as the policy is issued. Ideally, private insurance is suitable for situations in which there is reasonable uncertainty about the probability or timing of a loss without the threat of moral or morale hazard. If policyholders were compensated for losses they cause, they may be encouraged to generate losses for property they no longer wish to own. This could undermine the pricing structure for insurance and increase insurance premiums for all policyholders.

Definite and Measurable

The third characteristic of an ideally insurable loss exposure is that the loss exposure is subject to losses that are definite in time, cause, and location and that are measurable. For a loss exposure to be definite in time, cause, and location, the insurer must be able to determine the event (or series of events) that led up to the loss, when that event or series of events occurred, and where it occurred. All insurance policies have a policy period that specifies the precise dates and times of coverage. A typical property-casualty policy has a policy period ranging from six months to one year. Although other periods may be specified, shorter or longer policy periods are not as common. As an example, the policy period for a homeowners policy is shown in Exhibit 8-2. In this policy, the policy period appears in the declarations.

The insurer usually needs to be able to determine that the event occurred during the policy period. For some events, this may be a difficult process; insurers are reluctant to insure such events. For example, suppose an insurer was considering insuring a gas station against environmental pollution. A definite loss would be a fire that ruptured an underground gas tank if the gasoline that was in the tank leaked into the surrounding soil and caused a large environmental pollution loss. A less measurable loss might be an inspector's discovery of a high concentration of gasoline in the soil of an

EXHIBIT 8-2

Homeowners Policy Declarations

Homeowners Policy Declarations

POLICYHOLDER: David M. and Joan G. Smith   **POLICY NUMBER:**   296 H 578661
(Named Insured) 216 Brookside Drive
Anytown, USA 40000

POLICY PERIOD: **Inception:** March 30, 2004   **Policy period begins 12:01 A.M. standard time**
Expiration: March 30, 2005   **at the residence premises.**

Includes copyrighted material of Insurance Services Office, Inc., with its permission. Copyright, ISO Properties, Inc., 1999.

adjacent property that has been caused by a leaking underground gas tank. It is impossible to pinpoint the exact date or the cause of the leak. The leak could have been occurring for months or even years. Therefore, it may be impossible to determine a precise cause of loss or whether the event occurred during the policy period. Because they are not definite, these types of loss exposures are not ideally insurable.

As well as being definite, the loss needs to be measurable in order to be ideally insurable. Insurers cannot determine an appropriate premium if they cannot measure the frequency or severity of the potential losses. As discussed, when evaluating a loss exposure, an insurance professional needs to be able to quantify both the frequency and severity of potential losses to determine what future losses may be. The fact that the future losses may be immeasurable creates a substantial amount of uncertainty for the insured and the insurer. Insurers are reluctant to insure losses that are highly uncertain without receiving substantial compensation (high premiums) from the insured.

In summary, if a loss cannot be defined in time or measured, it would be extremely difficult for an insurer to write a policy that specifies what claims to pay and how much to pay for them. If multiple insurance policies issued by different insurers were issued to cover the loss exposure at various renewals, it would be difficult to determine which policy applied and which insurer was responsible for the loss. At a minimum, the costs of adjusting losses would increase and the likelihood of litigation would be greatly increased.

Large Number of Similar Exposure Units

The fourth characteristic of an ideally insurable loss exposure is that the loss exposure is one of a large number of similar exposure units. Some common loss exposures that satisfy this requirement include homes, offices, and automobiles.

Industry Language—Loss Exposure, Exposure Units, Exposures

In a previous chapter, the term loss exposure was defined as any condition or situation that presents a possibility of loss, whether or not an actual loss occurs. An exposure unit is defined as a fundamental measure of the loss exposure assumed by an insurer. The terms "exposure" and "exposure unit" are often used interchangeably by insurance professionals. However, this practice can lead to confusion as to whether the individual is referring to loss exposures or exposure units.

A loss exposure may be made up of multiple exposure units. For example, Henry may own a $300,000 house (a property loss exposure). Similarly, Alison may own a $500,000 house (also a property loss exposure). From each of the insured's points of view, these are single loss exposures. To the insurer, they are not identical exposure units, because one house is more valuable than the other. The insurer may use $100,000 as a single exposure unit. Therefore, Henry's house is equivalent to three exposure units and Alison's house is equivalent to five exposure units. The three exposure units that comprise Henry's house are not independent exposure units, but those three exposure units are independent of the five exposure units that comprise Alison's house. The insurer can increase the number of independent exposure units ($100,000 units) it insures by increasing the number of independent loss exposures (houses) it insures.

There are two risk transfer functions that insurance can provide—cross-sectional and intertemporal risk transfer. The most common risk transfer function that insurance provides is the spreading of risk across a large number of similar exposure units within the same period. This is commonly referred to as cross-sectional risk transfer, and it requires a large number of similar loss exposures. Cross-sectional risk transfer is achieved through pooling, which takes advantage of the law of large numbers. As discussed, the law of large numbers has three criteria:

1. The events have occurred in the past under substantially identical conditions and have resulted from unchanging, basic causal forces.

2. The events can be expected to occur in the future under the same unchanging conditions.

3. The events have been, and will continue to be, independent and sufficiently numerous.

The third criterion ensures that the loss exposures are numerous enough for the insurer to pool a large number of exposure units. This large pool enables the insurer to more accurately project losses and determine appropriate premiums because loss statistics can be maintained over time and losses for similar exposure units can be projected with a higher degree of accuracy.

Another risk transfer function insurance can provide is the spreading of risk through time, known as intertemporal risk transfer. This function does not require a large number of similar exposure units; therefore insurers are willing to insure unique loss exposures where there is little or no pooling of similar exposure units.

Independent and Not Catastrophic

The fifth characteristic of an ideally insurable loss exposure is that the loss exposure is not subject to a loss that would simultaneously affect many other similar loss exposures (that is, the loss exposure would be independent) and that the loss exposure would not be catastrophic to the insurer. This characteristic is similar to the characteristic of a large number of similar exposure units in that they are both tied to the third criterion of the law of large numbers. The difference is that this characteristic focuses on the independence of the loss exposures, not their number and similarity.

For insurers to utilize pooling most effectively, the insured exposure units need to be independent. Although pooling will work to some degree if the exposure units are correlated (not independent), it will not be as effective. An example of correlated loss exposures would be two adjacent houses. Given the proximity of the houses to each other, certain causes of loss, such as a tornado, hurricane, or fire, could affect both houses at the same time. The fact that one of the houses is on fire does not mean the other house will catch fire, but the probability of the second house catching fire is much higher. Therefore, these two loss exposures are correlated.

Insurance operates economically because many insureds pay premiums that are small relative to the cost of the potential losses they could each incur. The cost can stay relatively small because insurers project that they will incur far fewer losses than they have loss exposures. However, if a large number of insureds who are covered for the same type of loss were to incur losses at the same time, the insurance mechanism would not operate economically and losses to the insurer could be catastrophic.

Following Hurricane Andrew in 1992 (and reinforced by Hurricane Katrina in 2005), property-casualty insurers are much more aware of the catastrophic risk that a correlated portfolio of insured loss exposures presents. Geographic diversification, line of business diversification, and reinsurance can help insurers both to improve the independence of their insured loss exposures and to minimize their catastrophic exposure.

In addition to correlated losses, single events or a series of events can also present catastrophic risk to an insurer. Consequently, an insurer should not insure any single loss exposure that would pose a serious financial hardship if a loss occurred. For example, a small insurer should not insure a multimillion dollar property, such as an oil refinery. Although the loss exposure may be independent of the other properties the insurer has chosen to insure, a loss at such a single location may cause insurer severe financial difficulty.

Economically Feasible Premium

The final characteristic of an ideally insurable loss exposure is that the insurer is able to charge an economically feasible premium—one that the insured can afford to pay. Of all the characteristics of an ideally insurable loss exposure, this is probably the most important. Supply and demand of insurance demonstrate that if an insurer cannot provide the insurance product at a reasonable premium, there will be no demand. The first five characteristics are designed to ensure that the insurer can provide insurance at a reasonable premium.

Loss exposures involving only small losses, as well as those involving a high probability of loss, are generally considered uninsurable. Providing insurance to cover small losses may not make economic sense when its expense exceeds the amount of potential losses. It also may not make economic sense to insure losses that are almost certain to occur. The expense of providing insurance increases with the frequency of claims because insurers incur some of their largest expenses settling insured claims. In such a situation, the premium would probably be as high as or higher than the potential loss.

To maintain the balance of supply and demand, it is important that the insurance mechanism establish a pricing structure that adequately supports the expenses for providing coverage at a price (premium) appropriate for the purchaser when compared with the potential loss.

The concept of ideally insurable loss exposures is best explained by reference to some of the typical commercial loss exposures faced by organizations and personal loss exposures faced by individuals.

COMMERCIAL LOSS EXPOSURES

Insurers sell insurance policies to cover a wide variety of loss exposures, many of which are not ideally insurable. This should not imply, however, that insurers do not strive to select ideally insurable loss exposures. For each type of loss exposure (property, liability, personnel, and net income), insurers will try to insure the loss exposures that exhibit as many of the ideally insurable characteristics as possible. Although a comprehensive discussion of all insurable loss exposures and all related insurance products is beyond the scope of this text, examining a sample of loss exposures against the six ideally insurable characteristics demonstrates why insurers may choose to insure some loss exposures and not others.

Property

All organizations have property loss exposures related to their business operations. Some organizations may rely more on real property and others may rely more on personal property, but all rely on property to some extent. This section focuses on a real property loss exposure—the building that houses an organization's main operations—and on three different causes of loss: fire, windstorm, and flood.

Property Loss Exposures: Brick-and-Mortar Compared With Dot-Coms

Technological innovations over the last two decades have spurred the development of the dot-com business model. The term "dot-com organization" refers to an organization that conducts a substantial portion of its business over the Internet. Well-known examples of dot-com businesses are eBay and Amazon. Although these organizations do not have a large number of physical locations as do traditional "brick-and-mortar" retailers such as Wal-Mart, they do have some physical locations and large distribution centers and therefore are exposed to property loss exposures. Whereas brick-and-mortar retailers tend to have significant real property loss exposures diversified geographically because of the number of retail outlets, dot-com organizations have a greater reliance on personal property, such as computer servers, to conduct their daily operations. Although these more concentrated types of business models may not face the same frequency of loss on their property loss exposures as the more localized brick-and-mortar model, they may face a greater severity of losses when they occur because of the higher chance that a cause of loss will interrupt their entire business operation.

A review of how and why the property loss exposure generally meets the ideally insurable criteria reveals that this widely insured loss exposure may not always meet these criteria. Exhibit 8-3 summarizes whether the building that houses an organization's main operations meets the six ideally insurable characteristics for fire, windstorm, and flood.

EXHIBIT 8-3

Ideally Insurable Characteristics: Commercial Property Loss Exposures

	Fire Cause of Loss	Windstorm Cause of Loss	Flood Cause of Loss
Pure risk	Yes (except arson-for-profit)	Yes	Yes
Fortuitous	Yes (except for arson-for-profit)	Yes	Yes
Definite and measurable	Yes	Yes	Yes
Large number of similar exposure units	Depends on property location, property type and use	Depends on property location, property type, and use	Depends on property location, property type, and use
Independent and not catastrophic	Yes	Can be catastrophic	Can be catastrophic
Premiums are economically feasible	Yes	Depends on location	Depends on location

Fire Cause of Loss

For most property loss exposures, the main underwriting criteria focus on the threat of the fire cause of loss. As shown in Exhibit 8-3, commercial property loss exposures associated with the fire cause of loss generally meet all six characteristics.

Fire loss to a building is a pure risk rather than a speculative risk because it generally involves only the possibility of loss and no possibility of gain. An exception would be arson-for-profit. For example, an organization might own an obsolete, run-down building in a prime location whose land is worth more without the building. In an arson-for-profit, the organization would deliberately burn down the building, both to claim on the insurance and to increase the value of the land. Insurance underwriters guard against knowingly providing insurance for such obviously potential moral hazards. Insurance policies can be modified to limit losses for these exceptions.

An accidental fire loss would be fortuitous from the perspective of both parties. However, not all fires are accidents. Again, arson committed by the insured (arson-for-profit) is the exception because it is intentional Similarly, other intentional fires may not be started by the insured, such as fires resulting from riots or civil commotion. As long as the intentional fire is not started by the insured, it is fortuitous from the perspective of both the insurer and insured. An insurer can project aggregate claims from fortuitous fire losses with reasonable confidence, based on past experience. However, it is not as easy to project the number and extent of claims that are not fortuitous. So although fires generally meet the fortuitous criteria, the fact that they can be deliberately set detracts from their being considered an ideally insurable loss exposure.

Property fires are typically definite and measurable. Occasionally, pinpointing the time of an unobserved property fire is difficult, such as when the fire that destroys an office building occurs over a weekend. Because fire insurance is usually written for a one-year policy period, loss timing becomes critical only if the loss occurs near the policy's expiration date and a question exists about whether the loss occurred during the policy period. In some cases, continuous coverage exists (such as a renewal policy), but the question remains as to which policy was in force at the time of the loss.

Knowing the value of a building or its contents is critical in measuring the amount of a fire loss. Such value can be measured in different ways (discussed subsequently). It is often necessary to specify—before a loss occurs—whether the insured loss will be the amount necessary to repair or replace the loss with like kind and quality, or whether the insured loss will be a depreciated actual cash value. Some insurance provides coverage for additional living expenses, fair rental value, or other financial losses resulting from a building that cannot be used. These losses are somewhat more difficult to measure because they depend on an estimate of what an insured's financial position would have been had the event not occurred.

Therefore, with respect to being definite and measurable, fire loss exposures are usually ideally insurable because a fire's occurrence typically is obvious. However, uncertainty about the timing of a fire's occurrence or the value of the property at the time of the loss may make insuring such a fire loss less than ideal.

Many properties present a large number of similar loss exposures for an insurer. For example, many retail organizations are located in malls, which tend to be rather homogenous. However, many organizations have unique locations, or perform a unique function at their locations, making pooling by the insurer very difficult. Whether a specific commercial property location meets this ideally insurable criterion depends on the location, type, and usage of the property.

The characteristic of being independent and not catastrophic applies to the insurer's perspective, based on its portfolio of insurance policies. The insurer needs to consider whether a loss exposure under consideration for insurance coverage could be subject to a loss that would simultaneously affect many other similar insured loss exposures. For example, a retail shop in an enclosed mall would not be an independent loss exposure if its insurer covered other retail shops in the same mall. A large fire at the mall could simultaneously affect all of the shops, which could be catastrophic if a single insurer had insured most or all of the shops. If an insurer is insuring only one retail shop in the mall, the loss exposure would be independent of the other loss exposures it has chosen to insure and a fire loss would not be catastrophic.

Fires at an organization's main location tend to be low-frequency, high-severity (from the insured's perspective) events that insureds could not usually recover from financially without insurance. Although the frequency of fire loss to any one specific building is usually too small for insurers to project with confidence, aggregate fire losses generate credible statistical information on which insurance rates can be based. Because fires tend to be low-frequency events, and because a fire loss exposure typically exhibits most or all of the first five ideally insurable characteristics, this cause of loss is usually economically feasible to insure.

Windstorm Cause of Loss

As shown in Exhibit 8-3, many of the ideally insurable characteristics that are met by the fire cause of loss are also met by the windstorm cause of loss. Windstorm damage to commercial property loss exposures is generally a pure risk subject to fortuitous losses that are definite and measurable. However, it may not meet the last three ideally insurable characteristics. This drastically changes how some insurers view the insurability of the windstorm cause of loss.

As with the fire cause of loss, the windstorm cause of loss can be insured on many similar buildings. However, identical buildings at different locations can face substantially different windstorm exposure. With the fire cause of loss, property type and use are significant factors in determining if there are a large number of similar exposure units. With the windstorm cause of loss, those factors are still important, but not as important as location. Hurricanes and tornadoes, the most common windstorms, are geographically concentrated, making pooling a large number of similar, yet independent loss exposures more difficult. Exhibit 8-4 shows the geographic regions of the United States that have the highest exposure to hurricane activity.

Different buildings in the same geographic area are not independently exposed to windstorm loss. Unlike fire, a single windstorm is likely to damage many buildings; for example, hurricanes generally affect a widespread geographic area. Although tornadoes are more concentrated, they can still cause catastrophic damage to all property in a limited area, sometimes wiping out an entire community. For small insurers in geographic locations that are exposed to hurricane or tornado activity, the windstorm cause of loss can therefore be catastrophic. Adverse selection (when high-risk individuals or organizations are more likely to demand insurance than low-risk individuals or organizations) is present because property owners in windstorm-prone areas are more likely to demand insurance.

The catastrophic nature of some windstorms—notably hurricanes—makes windstorm insurance difficult to underwrite, especially for insurers with a high volume of business in a limited geographic area. Appropriate rating is complicated by the fact that premium and loss calculations are performed in one-year periods, whereas weather cycles are much longer. Advances in catastrophe modeling have increased the accuracy of predicting storm damage. These models indicate that, in high-risk areas, higher premiums are typically necessary to offset the insurer's predicted losses. As catastrophe modeling improves, it may lead to economically infeasible premiums for some insureds.

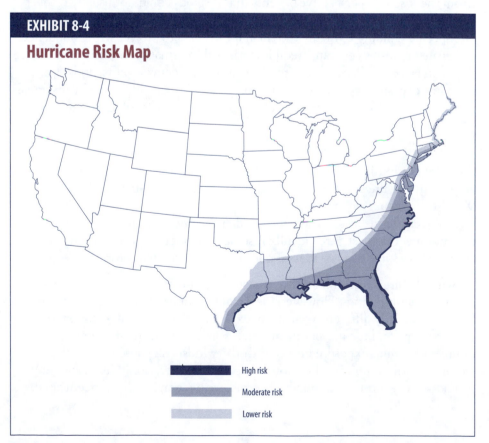

EXHIBIT 8-4

Hurricane Risk Map

High risk

Moderate risk

Lower risk

The windstorm cause of loss does not meet as many of the ideal characteristics of an insurable loss exposure as does the fire cause of loss. Although common commercial property insurance policies have previously tended to cover the windstorm cause of loss, this has been changing in states where the probability of hurricane activity is highest. For example, insurers in some coastal states such as Florida, Texas, and South Carolina are able to sell homeowners insurance policies in the highest-risk coastal regions that do not cover windstorm damage. Homeowners can obtain coverage for windstorm damage through state-run windstorm pools.

Flood Cause of Loss

Flood damage to property at fixed locations has traditionally been considered uninsurable by private insurers, even for property that was insured against fire and windstorm losses. In contrast, flood insurance is readily available for autos and other personal property that can easily be moved in order to avoid damage. Similar to the windstorm cause of loss, the flood cause of loss generally involves pure risk and losses that are fortuitous, definite, and measurable. Whether property is part of a large number of similar loss exposures suitable for pooling again depends on the location, property type, and use. The main issue is that the flood cause of loss is geographically concentrated, so loss exposures tend not to be independent, and losses could be catastrophic from the insurer's perspective. As a result of the potentially catastrophic losses resulting from floods, flood loss premiums are high and flood can be economically unfeasible to insure for some organizations.

Although some uncertainty exists about whether a flood will occur at a particular location in a particular year, in many areas the long-term probability of flood can be forecast. Property located within a 10-year, 20-year, or 100-year flood plain is almost certainly exposed to loss. Although that does not mean a flood occurs at specified intervals, (a 100-year flood could occur in two consecutive years), on average, a flood can be expected with certain regularity. Premiums in these flood zones would be too high for most insureds to pay without government assistance. Flood insurance is now available under the National Flood Insurance Program (NFIP). The federal government has also devoted engineering resources to evaluating flood zones, and these evaluations have facilitated underwriting flood insurance by private insurers.

Hurricane Damage: Windstorm or Flood?

For commercial properties with windstorm coverage, distinguishing between covered windstorm damage and not-covered flood damage can be difficult because a storm may produce both perils. For example, hurricanes produce a phenomenon known as storm surge, in which ocean waves are larger and ocean levels rise. Flooding caused by storm surge is not covered by property insurance policies that exclude flood coverage. Damage caused by flood must then be covered by separate policies sold by the National Flood Insurance Program. Ongoing litigation in those states severely affected by Hurricane Katrina in 2005 is challenging the validity of the flood exclusion in many property policies where it has been difficult to discern the cause of loss because of the extent of the damage. For example, consider the properties for which all that remained of a structure was a concrete slab. Was it wind or flood that caused the complete destruction of the building and contents?

Liability

The second category of loss exposures is liability loss exposures. The frequency and severity of liability losses associated with these exposures vary widely, depending on factors such as the organizations' operations and product lines, and on the legal environment in which the organizations operate.

Industry Language—Liability Loss Exposures

There are a variety of sources of liability loss exposures facing individuals and organizations. Insurance professionals often categorize liability loss exposures by cause of loss. These categories include premises and operations, products liability, automobile, workers' compensation, environmental, and professional liability. Insurance professionals use these categories as descriptors. For example, an insurance professional would not use the term "liability loss exposure" to describe losses associated with products. They would use the term "products liability." Similarly, insurance professionals rarely talk about the liability of employee injury; they discuss workers' compensation.

This section focuses on liability loss exposures stemming from two sources of risk faced by many organizations—premises and operations liability and products liability. Exhibit 8-5 summarizes how well these two categories of liability loss exposures meet the six characteristics of an ideally insurable loss exposure.

EXHIBIT 8-5

Ideally Insurable Characteristics: Commercial Liability Loss Exposures

	Premises and Operations Liability	Products Liability
Pure risk	Yes	Yes
Fortuitous	Yes	Yes
Definite and measurable	Yes	Depends on product
Large number of similar exposure units	Yes	Depends on product
Independent and not catastrophic	Yes	Can be catastrophic
Premiums are economically feasible	Yes	Depends on product

Premises and Operations Liability

The premises and operations liability loss exposure is the possibility that an organization will be held liable because of injury or damage caused by either of the following:

- An accident occurring on premises owned or rented by the organization
- An accident occurring away from such premises, but only if it arises out of the organization's ongoing operations

An organization owes a duty of care to visitors to their premises or to off-site locations where the organization's operations are taking place. The extent of that duty of care, which varies based on the visitor's reasons for being on the premises, is beyond the scope of this text. Examples of accidents that would be classified as premises or operations liability loss exposures include the following:

- A customer's bodily injury resulting from a slip-and-fall in ice, snow, or wet conditions
- A visitor's bodily injury or property damage resulting from an individual's or organization's failure to provide sufficient premises security

Premises and operations liability loss exposures exhibit all the characteristics of an ideally insurable loss exposure. The loss exposures involve pure risk and generate fortuitous losses that are definite in time, cause, and location and are measurable. Some organizations are more exposed to premises and operations liability loss exposures than others. For example, retail stores have a large volume of customers visiting their premises relative to other types of organizations, such as manufacturers. Therefore, retail stores are more likely to see a higher frequency of liability claims from customers. Given the large number of retail stores in the U.S., the premises and operations liability loss exposure is one of a large number of similar exposures. Each loss would be independent and not catastrophic, and premiums should be economically feasible because all the other five characteristics are met.

Products Liability

Products liability loss exposures arise out of injury or damage that results from defective or inherently dangerous products. Unlike the premises and operations liability loss exposures, not all products liability loss exposures exhibit all the characteristics of an ideally insurable loss exposure. Although they involve pure risk and fortuitous losses, the losses are not necessarily definite in cause. For example, the cause of a person's injury is not always definite. There could be several potential causes, only one of which is the insured's product. The loss may also not be measurable. For example, it may be difficult to measure the monetary value of an injury. If the product has been widely distributed, then the loss may simultaneously affect many individuals or organizations. Therefore, the loss could be catastrophic in terms of the number of claims. As a result, some products may not be economically feasible to insure.

Personnel

The third category of loss exposures are personnel loss exposures. A personnel loss exposure is a condition that presents the possibility of loss caused by a key person's death, disability, retirement, or resignation that deprives an organization of that person's special skill or knowledge that cannot be readily replaced. The frequency and severity of personnel losses vary widely by organization and industry. In general, personnel losses are fairly infrequent, but their severity will depend on the personnel involved. The more valuable the key person is to the organization, the more severe the loss. Unlike property, liability, and net income loss exposures, personnel loss exposures are generally not insured through property-casualty insurers. Personnel loss exposures resulting from the death of a key person can be insured by employer-owned life insurance policies, but the remaining causes of loss are often uninsurable.

This section focuses on two causes of personnel losses—death and retirement. Exhibit 8-6 summarizes how well personnel loss exposures associated with these two causes of loss meet the six characteristics of an ideally insurable loss exposure.

EXHIBIT 8-6

Ideally Insurable Characteristics: Commercial Personnel Loss Exposures

	Death	Retirement
Pure risk	Yes	Yes
Fortuitous	Yes	Depends on circumstances and personnel involved
Definite and measurable	Depends on personnel involved	Depends on personnel involved
Large number of similar exposure units	Depends on personnel involved	Depends on personnel involved
Independent and not catastrophic	Yes	Yes
Premiums are economically feasible	Yes	N/A

Death Cause of Loss

Unless a disaster occurs, an organization's losses from death are of low frequency, with the loss severity depending on the employee's value to the organization. Because of the low frequency of employee deaths in many organizations, it is difficult to predict their number over a given period with much accuracy.

Personnel loss exposures associated with the death cause of loss generally exhibit the six characteristics of an ideally insurable loss exposure. The loss exposure involves pure risk that is fortuitous, independent, and not catastrophic, and that is usually economically feasible to insure. The two characteristics the death cause of loss may not meet are that losses are definite and measurable and that they are among a large number of similar exposure units.

Although the death of a key employee is typically definite in time, cause and location, it may be difficult to measure the actual loss to the organization. Personnel losses are often difficult to quantify because a single employee's value to an organization may be incalculable.

Many organizations have hundreds or thousands of employees. This can make it difficult to quantify their number of key employees. In some industries, qualified employees are difficult to find and replace. For example, very few individuals in the world are experts in oil location and extraction. In these cases, there are not a large number of similar exposure units to create an ideally insurable loss exposure.

Retirement Cause of Loss

Although death often occurs suddenly, retirement is usually planned. Therefore, most personnel losses resulting from retirement can be handled with proper planning by the organization. However, sudden retirements can cause severe personnel losses. Similar to the death cause of loss, the personnel loss exposures associated with the retirement cause of loss involve pure risk; are definite in time, cause, and location (although they may be hard to measure); may not be one of a large number of similar loss exposures; and are generally independent and not catastrophic. The characteristics that retirement causes of loss do not meet are that the loss may not be fortuitous and it may not be economically feasible to insure.

Organizations can influence key employees' retirement decisions through a variety of methods. For example, benefits such as early retirement packages may induce key employees to retire. Alternatively, organizations may lose key employees to retirement because of poor work conditions or poor compensation packages. Therefore, a personnel loss resulting from a key employee's retirement may not be fortuitous from the organization's perspective.

Because it is not possible to purchase retirement insurance on key employees to compensate the organization if they retire, it is impossible to determine whether premiums are economically feasible. Given that a loss may not be fortuitous, premiums for such a product would have to account for the moral hazard and adverse selection that would exist in the market, making premiums less likely to be affordable.

Net Income

The fourth category of loss exposures is net income loss exposures. Net income is the difference between an organization's total revenues and its total expenses (including taxes). In a broad sense, a net income loss could involve any decrease in net income an organization incurs, for whatever reason. Net income can be higher or lower than expected as a result of either the business environment or fortuitous events (such as a property, liability, or personnel losses).

Net income losses caused by the business environment clearly do not meet the first characteristic of the loss exposure involving pure risk. The remainder of this section therefore focuses on net income loss exposures associated with two causes of loss that are pure risks—property losses and liability losses.

Exhibit 8-7 summarizes how well net income loss exposures associated with property and liability causes of loss exhibit the six characteristics of an ideally insurable loss exposure.

EXHIBIT 8-7

Ideally Insurable Characteristics: Commercial Net Income Loss Exposures

	Net income loss associated with property losses	Net income loss associated with liability losses
Pure risk	Yes	Yes
Fortuitous	Yes	Yes
Definite and measurable	Yes	May not be definite
Large number of similar exposure units	Yes	Yes
Independent and not catastrophic	May be catastrophic	Yes
Premiums are economically feasible	Yes	N/A

Net Income Loss Associated With Property Losses

Net income losses stemming from property losses result from physical damage to property (either property the organization owns or property of others on which the organization depends) that either prevents the organization from operating or that reduces its capacity to operate. Net income losses associated with property losses are insured by a variety of business income insurance coverages. Net income loss exposures associated with property losses exhibit almost all the characteristics of an ideally insurable loss exposure. The net income loss exposure associated with the property cause of loss involves pure risk, with losses that are fortuitous, definite and measurable, one of a large number of similar exposure units, and economically feasible to insure. Net income losses may not be independent and can be catastrophic if the property losses they are associated with were caused by catastrophic causes of loss such as a windstorm. A substantial portion of insured losses following hurricanes, such as Hurricane Katrina in 2005, are business income losses stemming from the property damage done to businesses in the affected areas.

Net Income Loss Associated With Liability Losses

Unlike the net income losses associated with property losses, there are no insurance products that provide coverage for net income losses stemming from liability losses. The major difference between net income losses stemming from property losses and those stemming from liability losses involves the determination of the time of the loss. For net income losses associated with property losses, insurance coverage is provided until the property has been restored or should have been restored (plus some additional time to return to normal operations). The restoration of the property provides a definite end to the payment of benefits by the insurance policy. There is no similar end point for net income losses that are associated with liability losses. For example, a restaurant could suffer a net income loss because customers stop frequenting it after it is found liable in a food poisoning case. There is no definite end point in such a case, because there is no definite time when customers will return.

PERSONAL LOSS EXPOSURES

This section focuses on the categories of loss exposures to which most individuals are exposed. As with the section on commercial loss exposures, this section does not present a comprehensive list of loss exposures or insurance coverages. It is designed to provide an understanding of how the six characteristics of an ideally insurable loss exposure may or may not be present in certain categories of loss exposures faced by most individuals. Examining loss exposures against these criteria will help insurance professionals understand why insurers may choose to insure some loss exposures and decline to insure others.

In general, many of the loss exposures faced by organizations are also faced by individuals. For individuals, these loss exposures can be divided into property, liability, and net income loss exposures. Although individuals do not typically have personnel loss exposures, they do have life, health, and retirement loss exposures that organizations do not face.

Property

An individual's key property loss exposure is typically a residence. Therefore, this section focuses on how the fire, windstorm, and flood causes of loss affect the insurability of that residence. Although all homes are different, they generally can be grouped into classes that face essentially the same loss potential. Individual homes are easier to group together than commercial property exposures, mainly because they all serve the same function. Insurers still must identify buildings with higher-than-normal hazards, guard against arson-for-profit, avoid excessive concentration of loss exposure, ensure adequate diversification of exposures, and carefully establish the insurable value of property subject to loss. Exhibit 8-8 summarizes whether an individual's residence meets the six ideally insurable characteristics for fire, windstorm and flood causes of loss.

The property loss exposures associated with the fire cause of loss are ideally suited to insurability because the loss exposure involves a pure risk, a large number of similar, yet independent exposure units, and losses that are fortuitous, definite, measurable, and not catastrophic. These characteristics make premiums economically feasible. However, the windstorm and flood causes of loss can be catastrophic in nature and, depending on the location of the residence, may not be economically feasible to insure.

EXHIBIT 8-8

Ideally Insurable Characteristics: Personal Property Loss Exposures

	Fire cause of loss	Windstorm cause of loss	Flood cause of loss
Pure risk	Yes (except for arson-for-profit)	Yes	Yes
Fortuitous	Yes (except for arson-for-profit)	Yes	Yes
Definite and measurable	Yes	Yes	Yes
Large number of similar exposure units	Yes	Yes	Yes
Independent and not catastrophic	Yes	Can be catastrophic	Can be catastrophic
Premiums are economically feasible	Yes	Depends on location	Depends on location

Liability

Individuals are exposed to personal liability loss exposures through the property they own, which may be real property, such as a home, or personal property, such as an automobile, lawnmower, or jewelry. Similar to organizations, individuals owe a duty of care to visitors to their property. An additional significant source of liability loss exposures for individuals is their behavior toward others. For example, if an individual fails to stop at a stop sign while driving and hits a pedestrian, he or she may be liable for any bodily injury or property damage that results. Similarly, individuals often face liability loss exposures from a pet. For example, many homeowners' insurers refuse to sell homeowners' insurance policies to applicants with certain breeds of dogs, such as pit bulls, because of the liability issues associated with them.

Exhibit 8-9 focuses on liability loss exposures stemming from two common sources of risk faced by many individuals: real property ownership (premises) liability loss exposures and automobile liability loss exposures. The exhibit summarizes how well these two categories of liability loss exposures meet the six characteristics of an ideally insurable loss exposure.

Exhibit 8-9 shows that both premises and automobile liability loss exposures display all six of the characteristics of an ideally insurable loss exposure. Premises liability loss exposures are generally covered by the variety of homeowners insurance policies available and the automobile liability loss exposures are covered by a personal auto policy.

EXHIBIT 8-9

Ideally Insurable Characteristics: Personal Liability Loss Exposures

	Premises liability	Automobile liability
Pure risk	Yes	Yes
Fortuitous	Yes	Yes
Definite and measurable	Yes	Yes
Large number of similar exposure units	Yes	Yes
Independent and not catastrophic	Yes	Yes
Premiums are economically feasible	Yes	Yes

Net Income

A net income loss could involve any decrease in net income, regardless of the reason. Revenues (such as salary) and expenses (such as housing) can be higher or lower than expected as a result of either the economic environment or fortuitous events such as a property or liability loss. Net income losses caused by the economic environment clearly do not meet the first characteristic of the loss exposure involving pure risk. For example, rising gas and oil prices would cause an individual's expenses to increase, resulting in a net income loss. However, falling gas and oil prices would result in a net income gain. Net income losses caused by fortuitous events such as a fire to an individual's residence, would involve pure risk because there is no potential for the individual to gain.

Exhibit 8-10 focuses on one net income loss exposure associated with an individual's loss of employment. Unemployment leads to a reduction in revenues and therefore a net income loss. The exhibit summarizes how well a net income loss exposure associated with the unemployment cause of loss exhibits the six characteristics of the ideally insurable loss exposure.

There are many reasons an individual may become unemployed. One reason could be that economic conditions result in a layoff. Another could be the individual was not a productive employee (was fired) or chose to leave the position (quit). Although the unemployment cause of loss for personal net income loss exposures does meet many of the characteristics of an ideally insurable loss exposure, the one it may not meet—fortuitous—is very important to its insurability. To an extent, individuals can influence whether they become unemployed. Their actions may be direct, such as quitting their job, or indirect, such as poor work performance. Unemployment insurance is widespread, but it does not cover individuals who become unemployed by quitting. This approach helps ease some of the moral hazard problems in unemployment insurance; for example, an individual will not be able to insure an event that is not fortuitous, such as resignation.

EXHIBIT 8-10

Ideally Insurable Characteristics: Personal Net Income Loss Exposures

	Unemployment cause of loss
Pure risk	Yes
Fortuitous	Depends on person involved
Definite and measurable	Yes
Large number of similar exposure units	Yes
Independent and not catastrophic	Yes
Premiums are economically feasible	Yes

Life, Health, and Retirement

In addition to the property, liability, and net income personal loss exposures, individuals and families can face financial difficulty resulting from life, health, and retirement loss exposures. These loss exposures are generally managed through the life and health insurance industry and also through government programs. A variety of causes of loss contribute to the life, health, and retirement personal loss exposures. Although some of these causes of loss are fortuitous, others are under the control of the person involved and therefore make life, health, and retirement causes of loss subject to moral and morale hazard problems.

Exhibit 8-11 shows how life, health, and retirement causes of loss meet the characteristics of an ideally insurable loss exposure.

EXHIBIT 8-11

Ideally Insurable Characteristics: Personal Life, Health, and Retirement Loss Exposures

	Life loss exposures	Health loss exposures	Retirement loss exposures
Pure risk	Yes	Yes	Yes
Fortuitous	Yes (except for suicide)	Depends on cause of loss	Not usually, but may be forced retirement
Definite and measurable	Yes	Depends on cause of loss	Yes
Large number of similar exposure units	Yes	Yes	Yes
Independent and not catastrophic	Yes	Yes	Yes
Premiums are economically feasible	Usually	Usually	N/A

Life Loss Exposures

Although life is not generally considered a loss exposure, the loss of life to premature death is. Premature death is a term used to refer to the death of a person with outstanding financial obligations. These financial obligations, such as children to support or mortgage payments, can result in financial difficulty for the family that depended on the deceased's earnings if they are unable to generate replacement income from other sources. There are individual circumstances, such as health conditions or hazardous occupations, that may prevent insurers from offering an economically feasible premium. However, for most individuals, life loss exposures satisfy all six of the ideally insurable characteristics.

Health Loss Exposures

Poor health is another personal loss exposure that can create serious financial problems for individuals and families. First, an individual might incur significant medical bills. Without health insurance or significant personal savings, these expenses can cause financial distress or bankruptcy. Second, if a person is unable to work because of poor health or disability, earnings can also be lost, again resulting in financial difficulties.

Similar to the life loss exposures, widely available health insurance appears to indicate that health loss exposures have the ideally insurable characteristics. However, health insurance is subject to adverse selection as well as moral and morale hazard. Unlike life loss exposures, for which most causes of loss are fortuitous, many causes of loss to health are under some control of the individual involved. Smoking and obesity are examples of health-related causes of loss over which an individual may have some control. These factors have contributed to some of the issues in the health insurance market. The two major issues are availability and affordability of health insurance. Whereas most Americans obtain health insurance through their employer, those who need to purchase coverage individually often have difficulty obtaining coverage, or obtaining coverage at an economically feasible premium. Furthermore, pre-existing health conditions exacerbate the problem for those shopping for coverage individually. The affordability issue exists for employers as well. Rising healthcare costs are a major concern for both small and large organizations.

Retirement Cause of Loss

The possibility of insufficient income during retirement is another important loss exposure faced by individuals. Although workers are not typically forced to retire, most retire by age sixty-five. If the replacement income generated by Social Security, private retirement plans, and personal savings is not sufficient to cover expenses, financial hardship may result. This situation is compounded by increasing life expectancy, which lengthens the retirement period. If the individual has underestimated the number of years that could be spent in retirement, his or her savings may not be adequate.

The retirement cause of loss does not usually exhibit the fortuitous characteristic of ideally insurable loss exposures because the individual has control over savings and choice of retirement dates. Consequently, individuals are not able to purchase retirement insurance.

When loss exposures significantly fail to meet the criteria of ideally insurable loss exposures, private insurers are often unwilling to provide insurance coverage. This leaves a gap in coverage that can be devastating to individuals, organizations, and communities. For example, when property insurance is unavailable for office buildings and residences, it can be difficult to sell the property because mortgage companies require property insurance on the mortgaged property. To prevent such difficulties, the government offers insurance programs to provide the coverage that private insurers are unwilling or unable to provide.

GOVERNMENT PROGRAMS

Government insurance programs vary based on their purpose or rationale, the level of government involvement, and whether the program is run at the state or federal level. Government insurance programs can be grouped into one of the following three broad categories: property-casualty insurance plans, social insurance plans, and financial security plans. Examples of social insurance and financial security plans include social security, unemployment insurance, the Federal Deposit Insurance Corporation (FDIC), and the Pension Benefit Guaranty Corporation (PBGC). Although the social insurance and financial security plans are vital to the success of the U. S. economy, an in-depth discussion of them is beyond the scope of this text. Therefore, this section focuses on the property-casualty insurance plans in order to provide an insurance professional with an understanding of why government insurance programs exist, how they are structured and why some are run at the state level while others are federal programs. It is not designed to provide a detailed analysis of all property-casualty government insurance programs.

One of the major differences between private market insurance products and public (government provided) insurance lies in the primary objective of each party. Private insurance seeks to provide actuarial equity; that is, to treat policyholders fairly by charging premiums directly proportional to the loss exposure borne or the benefits paid. Public insurance programs typically aim to provide social equity; that is to provide benefits to the public in response to a far-reaching cause of loss. For example, consider auto insurance—making auto insurance mandatory for all drivers benefits society because it ensures that funds are available to pay for accidents. Private auto insurers attempt to provide actuarial equity by requiring each driver to pay a premium related to his or her expected loss. However, the residual markets for auto insurance run by individual states ensure that auto insurance is available to all drivers at a reasonable cost, even if that means some low-risk drivers have to pay higher premiums in the private market to subsidize the premiums of high-risk drivers in the residual market.

Rationale for Government Involvement

The U.S., like most developed countries, has a very mature private property-casualty insurance market that provides a mechanism for consumers and insurers to interact in the demand and supply of insurance products. Although much of the market is heavily regulated, and behaves in a somewhat cyclical manner, in general it functions properly. That is, consumers are able to purchase insurance products they desire for a price determined by the market, and insurers can earn an appropriate rate of return on their capital. In a perfectly functioning market, there is no need for state or federal governments to supply insurance products. However, private insurance markets do not always function perfectly. Occasionally, insurers are unable or unwilling to supply an insurance product to consumers at a mutually acceptable price. In addition to market failures, other reasons for government involvement in insurance include the following:

- To fill insurance needs unmet by private insurers
- To compel people to buy a particular type of insurance
- To obtain greater efficiency and/or provide convenience to insurance buyers
- To achieve collateral social purposes

Fill Unmet Needs

When private insurers are unable or unwilling to satisfy certain insurance needs, government programs can provide insurance to meet legitimate public demands. By doing this, the government provides protection against loss that would otherwise not be provided. An example of a government insurance program formed to fulfill an unmet need in the private insurance market is the Terrorism Risk Insurance Program (TRIP), formed by the Terrorism Risk Insurance Act of 2002 (TRIA). The program was intended as a temporary provider of reinsurance for losses caused by terrorism and was designed to run until the end of 2005, when it was assumed that the private insurance market would have developed its own terrorism insurance products. In December 2005, the Terrorism Risk Extension Act of 2005 was passed, which reauthorized TRIP for two more years. Although the private market role was increased and the federal share of compensation for losses insured under TRIP was decreased, the private market for terrorism insurance and reinsurance has not made government involvement unnecessary.

Compel Insurance Purchase

Another reason federal and state governments are involved in insurance is to facilitate compulsory insurance purchases. For example, workers' compensation insurance has proven to efficiently manage workplace injuries. However, it is possible that some employers would not purchase workers' compensation insurance if they were not required to do so. As states require employers to purchase this insurance (or provide proof of self-insurance), they must have a mechanism to ensure that workers' compensation insurance is available at a reasonable cost. Another example is personal automobile liability insurance. As auto liability coverage is required in almost all states, each state has some type of mechanism in place to provide insurance for those drivers who cannot obtain coverage at a reasonable price in the private market.

In the workers' compensation and auto liability insurance markets, most consumers obtain coverage through private insurers. Government programs are necessary to fulfill the needs of those who cannot obtain the required coverage in the private market; they are not required to insure all consumers.

Obtain Efficiency and Provide Convenience

Two related rationales for government involvement in insurance are providing efficiency in the market and convenience to insureds. In economic terms, these two rationales are essentially the same. Providing convenience to insureds, by reducing either the time or the resources they need to expend to obtain the desired insurance coverage, adds to the efficiency of the market.

Legislators often find it is more straightforward to establish government insurance plans for particular purposes than to invite and analyze bids from private insurers and then supervise and regulate the resulting plans. When insurance provided by the government is compulsory, spending money on marketing or paying sales commissions (two large expenses for insurers) is unnecessary. Governments sometimes try to avoid sales costs by setting up their own distribution channels. Alternatively, as is the case with the National Flood Insurance Program (NFIP), they market through established insurance producers who also market other insurance.

Achieve Collateral Social Purpose

The government may participate in insurance to accomplish social goals because insurance is often seen as a social good. By making use of the pooling mechanism, insurance can reduce risk to society. This is beneficial both to society and to the overall economy. In economic terms these benefits are often referred to as positive externalities.

An issue arises when individuals do not have an incentive to purchase insurance, even though it would benefit society. Individuals and organizations make decisions that are in their best interest. If, for example, an organization conducted a cost-benefit analysis and determined that workers' compensation insurance was too expensive, it would not want to purchase the insurance. However, workers' compensation laws encourage injury prevention and injured workers' rehabilitation, a positive externality. Therefore, it falls to the government to provide incentives for the purchase of insurance. It does this through a combination of regulation and provision of insurance at a reasonable price. Organizations respond to these measures by purchasing insurance, which, as well as benefiting the organization, benefits society. Similarly, the NFIP provides strong incentives to amend and enforce building codes and otherwise reduce the loss exposure of new construction to floods. Without the involvement of the federal government in providing flood insurance, these incentives would be lacking.

Level of Government Involvement

The level of government involvement varies widely and depends on many factors, such as the rationale for government involvement, the availability and willingness of private insurers to partner with the government program, and the level of competition in the market. There are three levels at which the government can participate:

1. Exclusive insurer
2. Partner with private insurers
3. Competitor to private insurers

The government can be an exclusive insurer either because of law or because no private insurer offers a competing plan. A federal or state government can function as a primary insurer by collecting premiums, providing coverage, and paying all claims and expenses (with the backing of government funds if necessary). Examples include some state government-run workers' compensation programs. Alternatively, the government can function as a reinsurer, either by providing 100 percent reinsurance to private insurers writing a particular coverage (an exclusive reinsurer), or by reinsuring part of the risk in excess of the private insurer's retention. If the government is reinsuring only part of the risk, the program is essentially a partnership with private insurers.

Government partnerships with private insurers can develop when private insurers are no longer able to adequately provide coverages they had typically offered previously. Two examples of such partnerships are TRIP and NFIP. TRIP is an example of a partnership under which the government operates a reinsurance plan, providing reinsurance on specific loss exposures for which private insurers retain only part of the loss. The NFIP is an example of a partnership under which the federal government underwrites the insurance policy but private insurers and insurance producers deliver the policies to consumers. The private insurers take a percentage of the premium as a sales commission and pass the remainder of the premium on to the NFIP. Both terrorism and flood coverage had previously been offered by private insurers, but the nature of the loss exposures indicated that the insurance industry was not well suited to providing coverage alone. In addition to the TRIP and NFIP partnership structures, other partnerships use a wide variety of structures.

Government involvement may also take the form of operating an insurance plan in direct competition with private insurers. This type of involvement often evolves when the private insurance market has not failed, but is not operating as efficiently as regulators would like. In these instances, the government performs essentially the same marketing, underwriting, actuarial, and claim functions as a private insurer. Examples include the competitive workers' compensation funds offered in some states.

Federal Compared With State Programs

The final distinction among government property-casualty insurance programs is whether a state government or the federal government is involved with the program. Because federal government involvement in these types of issues is often a political decision, predicting what factors will influence federal government involvement is difficult. One motivating factor may be that if the rationale for government involvement extends beyond state boundaries or would affect interstate commerce, the federal government should be running the insurance program. This may explain why the federal government is involved with the NFIP and Federal Crop Insurance. However, it would not explain why windstorm and beach plans are state government-run insurance programs. Hurricanes often cause damage in multiple states. Although hurricane risk is regional, the same can be said for flood risk. In fact, when taking into account storm surge, hurricane risk and flood risk often go together.

Exhibit 8-12 contains examples of property-casualty insurance plans that involve the federal government and Exhibit 8-13 contains examples of property-casualty insurance plans that involve state governments.

EXHIBIT 8-12

Examples of Property-Liability Insurance Offered by the Federal Government

Plan	Characteristics of Government Plan	Relationship to Private Insurance
National Flood Insurance Program	• Meets previously unmet needs for flood insurance. • Serves the social purposes of amending and enforcing building codes and reducing new construction in flood zones.	• Federal government can act as primary insurer. • Federal government can partner with private insurers. Private insurers sell the insurance and pay claims; government reimburses insurers for losses not covered by premiums and investment income.
Terrorism Risk Insurance Program	• Designed to temporarily meet the unmet needs for a backstop to insured terrorism losses. • Serves the social purpose of preventing economic disruptions that market failures in terrorism coverage could have caused.	• Private insurers act as the primary insurer for terrorism coverages. • Federal government temporarily acts as reinsurer for terrorism coverage.
Federal Crop Insurance	• Provides crop insurance at affordable rates to reduce losses that result from unavoidable crop failures. • Covers most crops for perils such as drought, disease, insects, excess rain, and hail.	• Federal government subsidizes and reinsures private insurers; private insurers sell and service the federal crop insurance. • Private insurers also independently offer crop insurance for certain perils.

EXHIBIT 8-13

Examples of Property-Liability Insurance Offered by State Governments

Plan	Characteristics of Government Plan	Relationship to Private Insurance
Fair Access to Insurance Requirements (FAIR) Plans	• Make basic property insurance available to property owners who are otherwise unable to obtain insurance because of their property's location or any other reason.	• Organization varies by state. Typically it is an insurance pool through which private insurers collectively address an unmet need for property insurance on urban properties. • Does not replace normal channels of insurance; is only for consumers who could not obtain coverage in the private market.
Workers' Compensation Insurance	• Helps employers meet their obligations under state statutes to injured workers.	• Private insurers provide most workers' compensation insurance. • State government can operate as an exclusive insurer, as a competitor to private insurers, or as a residual market.
Beach and Windstorm Plans	• Make property insurance against the windstorm cause of loss available to property owners who are otherwise unable to obtain insurance because of their property's location.	• Organization varies by state: some states are insurance pools of private insurers; other states are ultimately guaranteed with taxpayer funds. • Does not replace normal channels of insurance; is only for consumers who could not obtain coverage in the private market.
Residual Auto Plans	• Make compulsory automobile liability coverage available to high-risk drivers who have difficulty purchasing coverage at a reasonable rate in the private market.	• Organization varies by state. Typically it is an insurance pool through which private insurers collectively address an unmet need for compulsory auto liability coverage. • Does not replace normal channels of insurance; is only for consumers who could not obtain coverage in the private market.

SUMMARY

The following are the six characteristics of an ideally insurable loss exposure:

1. Pure risk—involves pure risk, not speculative risk
2. Fortuitous losses—subject to fortuitous loss from the insured's standpoint
3. Definite and measurable—subject to losses that are definite in time, cause, and location, and that are measurable
4. Large number of similar exposure units—one of a large number of similar exposure units
5. Independent and not catastrophic—not subject to a loss that would simultaneously affect many other similar loss exposures; loss would not be catastrophic
6. Affordable—premiums are economically feasible

With respect to commercial loss exposures, many insurance products have been developed to handle the four broad types of loss exposures to which organizations are exposed: property, liability, personnel, and net income. For most property loss exposures, the main underwriting criteria focus on the threat of fire. Other key causes of loss are windstorm and flood. The fire cause of loss meets most, if not all, of the ideally insurable characteristics. As a result, fire insurance is typically available. In contrast, the windstorm and flood causes of loss do not meet all of the characteristics, and therefore private insurers have had difficulty providing windstorm and flood insurance.

The frequency and severity of liability losses vary widely depending on factors such as the organizations' operations, product lines, and the legal environment in which they operate. Two common sources of risk faced by many organizations are premises and operations liability loss exposures and products liability loss exposures. Premises and operations liability loss exposures exhibit all the characteristics of an ideally insurable loss exposure. The loss exposures involve pure risk and generate fortuitous losses that are definite in time, cause, and location and are measurable. Unlike the premises and operations liability loss exposures, not all products liability loss exposures exhibit all the characteristics of an ideally insurable loss exposure. Although they involve pure risk and fortuitous losses, the losses are not necessarily definite in cause and may not be measurable. Also, if the product has been widely distributed, then the loss may simultaneously affect many individuals or organizations and could therefore be catastrophic in terms of the number of claims. As a result, some products may not be economically feasible to insure.

The frequency and severity of personnel losses vary widely by organization and industry. In general, personnel losses are fairly infrequent, but their severity will depend on the personnel involved. The more valuable the employee is to the organization, the more severe the loss. Personnel loss exposures meet some, but not all, of the ideally insurable characteristics. Personnel losses may not be definite and measurable and there may not be a large number of similar exposure units. Unlike property and liability loss exposures, personnel loss exposures are generally not insured through property-casualty insurers.

In a broad sense, a net income loss could involve any decrease in net income an organization incurs, for whatever reason. Net income can be higher or lower than expected as a result of either the business environment or fortuitous events (such as property, liability, or personnel losses). Net income losses caused by the business environment clearly do not meet the first characteristic of the loss exposure involving pure risk. Net income losses stemming from property losses do meet many of the ideally insurable characteristics and may be insured through a variety of business income insurance coverages. Net income losses stemming from liability losses may not meet the definite and measurable characteristic and no such coverage exists.

In general, many of the loss exposures faced by organizations are also faced by individuals. For individuals, these loss exposures can be divided into property, liability, and net income loss exposures. Although individuals do not typically have personnel loss exposures, they do have life, health, and retirement loss exposures that organizations do not face. Most individual loss exposures meet all or a majority of the ideally insurable characteristics, and insurance coverage is widely available for most of those loss exposures.

Government insurance programs may provide insurance coverage when insurers are unwilling or unable to insure loss exposures that do not exhibit ideally insurable characteristics. These government programs vary based on their purpose or rationale, the level of government involvement, and whether the program is run at the state or federal level. The three broad categories of government insurance programs are property-casualty insurance plans, social insurance plans, and financial security plans. Examples of social insurance and financial security plans include social security, unemployment insurance, the Federal Deposit Insurance Corporation (FDIC), and the Pension Benefit Guaranty Corporation (PBGC).

The rationale for government involvement in insurance is as follows:

• To fill insurance needs unmet by private insurers
• To compel people to buy a particular type of insurance
• To obtain greater efficiency and/or provide convenience to insurance buyers
• To achieve collateral social purposes

The level of government involvement varies widely and depends on many factors, such as the rationale for government involvement, the availability and willingness of private insurers to partner with the government program, and the level of competition in the market. There are three levels at which the government can participate. The first is as an exclusive insurer, either because of law or because no private insurer offers a competing plan. The second is in partnership with private insurers—for example, operating as a reinsurer for private insurers. The third level of participation is as a competitor to private insurers.

Direct Your Learning

Legal Environment of Insurance

After learning the content of this chapter and completing the corresponding course guide assignment, you should be able to:

- Describe the common-law system.

- Contrast civil and criminal law.

- Explain how liability is determined and remedied under tort law.

- Explain the ways in which contract law influences the insurance industry.

- Given a case, determine whether the elements of a contract are present.

- Explain how void, voidable, and canceled contracts are unenforceable.

- Explain how fraud, concealment or misrepresentation, mistake, duress, or undue influence affect the genuineness of assent and insurance contract enforcement.

- Describe the common agency relationships in the insurance industry.

- Define or describe each of the Key Words and Phrases for this chapter.

Develop Your Perspective

What are the main topics covered in the chapter?

A foundational understanding of the legal environment is vital to analyzing insurance products and services. Because insurance policies are contracts, laws governing legal liability and contract law form their basis. Tort law governs the relationship between parties when no contract or statute is present. Further, the relationships between insurers and producers are agencies and are governed by agency law.

Identify the elements of negligence.

- How are legal duties of care created?
- How do the courts determine if a person is in breach of the duty of care?

Why is it important to learn about these topics?

Understanding the legal environment of insurance allows an insurance professional to respond to issues of tort law, contract law, agency law, and coverage disputes.

Consider what contractual elements might be missing in an insurance contract.

- What are the three requirements for an offer to be valid?
- When might an insurer be barred from denying a claim based on lack of consideration?

How can you use what you will learn?

Examine the factors that can affect genuine assent in an insurance contract that you purchase.

- What happens when genuine assent is not present?
- What types of mistakes can affect genuine assent?

Chapter 9
Legal Environment of Insurance

Insurance professionals must be familiar with the legal environment in which they operate. Although insurance professionals need not understand all facets of law related to insurance, they should understand the general principles so that they can identify and respond to potential liability issues and coverage disputes.

The legal systems that operate in the United States are the civil-law system and the common-law system. The U.S. civil-law and common-law systems can be further classified as criminal law or civil law. Three areas of civil law that are prevalent in the insurance industry are tort law, contract law, and agency law.

LEGAL FOUNDATIONS

There are two different legal systems in the U.S.—the civil-law system and the common-law system. The **civil-law system** is a basic legal system that relies on scholarly interpretations of codes and constitutions rather than court interpretations of prior court decisions, as in common-law systems. Therefore, civil-law systems include comprehensive codes of written laws (statutes) applicable to all legal questions. The civil-law system is the basis of law in some U.S. states, such as Louisiana and California. **Common-law systems** are legal systems in which the body of law is derived more from court decisions as opposed to statutes or constitutions.

Current U.S. law consists of a combination of the foundation that English common law provides, the written laws that Congress and state legislatures pass, and the decisions resulting from U.S. court cases.

Common Law

The U.S. common-law system relies on prior case rulings, or precedents. A court's decision in a case serves as the basis for resolving similar future cases. This method of case resolution is the **doctrine of *stare decisis*** in which courts follow earlier court decisions when the same issues arise again in lawsuits. For example, if an insured sues an insurer in state court over a disagreement about a policy provision's meaning, the court analyzes prior cases in which other courts have determined the meaning of the same or a similar provision.

Civil-law system
A basic legal system that relies on scholarly interpretations of codes and constitutions rather than court interpretations of prior court decisions, as in common-law systems.

Common-law system
A legal system in which the body of law derived more from court decisions as opposed to statutes or constitutions.

Doctrine of *stare decisis*
A method of case resolution in which courts follow earlier court decisions when the same issues arise again in lawsuits.

The court first seeks similar cases in its own state. If it finds none, it seeks similar cases in other states. If there are still no cases to use as reference, the court might analyze the rulings in reasonably similar cases. The court will also scrutinize the facts of the current case to determine distinctions and similarities between that case and prior cases. Courts often encounter situations for which they can find no prior case or previous law that directly applies. These situations for which no applicable precedent exists are called "threshold cases" because they present new legal questions. When courts encounter a threshold case, the judges consult all applicable law in an attempt to arrive at a fair decision.

This common-law doctrine adds certainty to the law on which citizens can rely in conducting their affairs. This approach helps give stability to society and business. Courts need not decide all similar cases exactly the same way, but they need to provide strong reasons to depart from the rulings in precedents.

Common law is not an absolute—it reflects the evolution of society's values and attitudes. What was acceptable law in the U.S. a century ago would, in many instances, be unacceptable today. Furthermore, a court can find that a prior decision was clearly wrong and therefore decide not to use it as precedent. Similarly, courts generally do not follow precedent when the earlier rule of law has lost its usefulness or when the original reasons for the rule no longer exist. However, the common-law system permits courts to overrule prior decisions only when they have sound supportive judicial reasons.

The U.S. civil-law and common-law systems can be further classified as either criminal law or civil law.

Criminal and Civil Law

Criminal law
A classification of law that applies to acts that society deems so harmful to the public welfare that government is responsible for prosecuting and punishing the perpetrators.

Civil law
A classification of law that applies to legal matters not governed by criminal law and that protects rights and provides remedies for breaches of duties owed to others.

Criminal law is a classification of law that applies to acts that society deems so harmful to the public welfare that government is responsible for prosecuting and punishing the perpetrators. This body of law defines offenses; regulates the investigating, charging, and trying of accused offenders; and establishes punishments for convicted offenders. **Civil law** is a classification of law that applies to legal matters not governed by criminal law and that protects rights and provides remedies for breaches of duties owed to others. Civil law applies to all legal matters that are not crimes and involve private rights. The term "civil law" is not, within this classification context, the same as the civil-law system discussed previously.

One distinguishing factor between civil and criminal law is the burden of proof, that is, the requirement to prove a charge or an allegation. The extent of the proof required varies depending on the type of case. The prosecution in a criminal case must establish guilt beyond a reasonable doubt. In civil actions, the injured party need establish a case only by a preponderance of the evidence; that is, the evidence supporting the jury's decision must be of greater weight than the evidence against it.

Burden of Proof and Insurance Coverage

Few, if any, insurance policies specifically address the question of burden of proof. Generally, the burden of proof is on the insured to show that coverage applies in a disputed case. With liability insurance, for example, if a third party makes a claim against the insured because of bodily injury or property damage resulting from the insured's products, the insured must show that it had purchased products liability insurance and that the alleged injuries meet the policy definition of bodily injury or property damage. The burden of proof then shifts to the insurer, which, to preclude coverage, must demonstrate that one or more exclusions apply.

With property insurance, the issue is often not whether covered property has been damaged but whether it was damaged by a covered peril. Although neither type of policy specifically says so, named-perils policies (basic or broad cause of loss forms) place the burden of proof on the insured, but special cause of loss forms (all-risks, open-perils) policies place it on the insurer. If a property insurance policy is issued with the basic or broad cause of loss form, the insured has to prove that the loss was caused by one of the perils listed in the cause of loss form for the policy to provide coverage. If the policy is issued with a special cause of loss form, the insurer has to prove that the loss was caused by an excluded peril to exclude coverage. From the insured's standpoint, "all-risks" special-form property policies have two important advantages. First, they cover more causes of loss than named-peril forms cover. Second, and perhaps more importantly, they implicitly shift the burden of proof to the insurer. The party with the burden of proof is more likely to lose the dispute.

Society uses criminal law to prescribe a standard of conduct to which all citizens must adhere. A crime can be major (such as murder) or minor (such as a traffic violation). A felony is a major crime involving long-term punishment. A minor crime, or misdemeanor, is punishable by a monetary fine or short-term imprisonment. Summary offenses are crimes that are not felonies or misdemeanors under state law and that usually result in monetary fines rather than imprisonment.

Written laws, such as statutes and ordinances (local laws), specify the nature of crimes and their punishments. Unlike in civil law, under which an individual victim can file charges, in criminal law the government decides whether it is in society's best interests to press charges and to prosecute on society's behalf.

Civil law protects rights and provides remedies for breaches of duty other than crimes. In a civil action, the injured party usually requests reimbursement, in the form of monetary damages, for harm.

Damage Compared With Damages

In legal terminology, a distinction is made between damage and damages. "Damage" is used to refer to harm such as physical loss, bodily injury, or deterioration of value. In contrast, "damages" refers to monetary compensation for the loss or injury.

One act can be both a criminal and a civil wrong. In such a case, both an injured party and the government can bring a legal action. The injured party can bring a civil suit requesting monetary damages and the government can prosecute a criminal case requesting fines or imprisonment. For example, suppose an insurance agent defrauds an insured, misleading the insured about insurance coverage. This action can be both a civil fraud and the crime of fraud and can result in separate civil and criminal trials. The insured sues in a civil trial, and a public prosecutor prosecutes the agent in a criminal trial.

Although the insurance industry is influenced by criminal law, the products and services it offers are more focused on civil law. The three areas of civil law that are most relevant to the insurance industry are tort law, contract law, and agency law. Each of these areas affects some aspect of the insurance industry. Tort law affects the determination of legal liability under liability insurance policies, contract law has a significant effect on the interpretation of insurance policies, and agency law determines the relationship between insurers and their producers.

TORT LAW

Tort

A wrongful act or omission, other than a crime or breach of contract, for which the remedy is usually monetary damages.

Tortfeasor

One who commits a tort.

A **tort** is a wrongful act or omission, other than a crime or breach of contract, for which the remedy is usually monetary damages. The person who commits the tort is referred to as the **tortfeasor**. The torts that result in legal liability can be classified into three broad types: (1) negligence, (2) intentional torts, and (3) strict liability torts. In practice, there can be some overlap between these three categories. However, they provide a useful framework for examining the nature of specific kinds of torts that can generate legal liability.

A basic understanding of tort law is vital to insurance professionals because tort law governs the relationship between parties when no contract or statute applies. Because many relationships are not governed by contract or statute, tort law is the prevalent determinant of legal liability. For individuals, tort law can determine legal liability in cases such as bodily injury or property damage stemming from auto accidents, use of defective products, or injuries to visitors of a residence. Similarly, for organizations, tort law can determine legal liability arising from cases such as bodily injury or property damage caused by defective products or from injuries to visitors of premises.

Torts can involve actions directed toward people or their property. Some torts are simultaneously private wrongs and crimes. Similarly, the same act can be both a tort and a breach of contract. For example, suppose that a person riding a train is injured through the train crew's negligence. The party may have an action in tort for negligence but may also have an action for breach of a contract for safe transportation between the injured person and the train company. In the typical medical malpractice situation, the injured person usually has a right to sue for the cost of medical services in tort or for breach of a contract.

Negligence

The most important tort classification for insurance professionals to understand is negligence, which is the basis of most property-casualty insurance claims. Many acts are legal wrongs even if they are not intentional. For example, a driver who is in a hurry may fail to see a stop sign and run through it, causing an accident. In this case, the driver did not intend to cause the accident; however, the driver failed in his or her duty to drive carefully and was therefore negligent.

Negligence is the failure to exercise the degree of care that a reasonable person in a similar situation would exercise to avoid harming others. If a person does something that a reasonably prudent person would not have done under similar circumstances, the person's conduct is referred to as a negligent act (or act of commission). If a person fails to do something that a reasonably prudent person would have done under similar circumstances, the person's conduct is referred to as a negligent omission (or act of omission).

Negligence
The failure to exercise the degree of care that a reasonable person in a similar situation would exercise to avoid harming others.

When a claimant (the "plaintiff") brings a lawsuit against an allegedly negligent person (the "defendant"), legal liability will be imposed on the defendant only if the following four essential elements of negligence are established to the satisfaction of the court hearing the suit:

1.   The defendant owed a legal duty of care to the plaintiff.
2.   The defendant breached the duty of care owed to the plaintiff.
3.   The defendant's breach of duty was the proximate cause of the plaintiff's injury or damage.
4.   The plaintiff suffered actual injury or damage.

The first element of negligence is a legal duty of care owed to the plaintiff. In the context of negligence law, the legal duty is the obligation to exercise reasonable care for the safety of others. For example, the driver of an auto has a legal duty to obey posted speed limits, stay in his or her lane of travel, and not cross over the center line into oncoming traffic. Such legal duties are created either by the common law or by statutes or ordinances.

The second element of negligence is the breach of the duty of care. A person who owes a legal duty to another must exercise reasonable care to observe that duty. Otherwise, he or she is in breach of that duty. For example, an auto mechanic who fails to bleed a car's brake lines of air, thereby enabling the brakes to fail, is in breach of the duty of care owed to the car's owner.

Courts have adopted the reasonably prudent person test to evaluate the conduct of a defendant. The issue is whether the fact-finder (usually a jury) believes that the defendant behaved in the way that a reasonable person of ordinary prudence would have behaved under similar circumstances. If the fact-finder believes that a reasonably prudent person would not have indulged in the act or omission committed by the defendant because of its foreseeable consequences to others, the fact-finder can conclude that the defendant failed to observe the standard of care that was required by the particular circumstances involved.

The third element of negligence is proximate cause. A court cannot hold a person liable for negligence merely for proof of a wrongful act and an injury. The wrongful act must also have been the proximate, or direct, cause of the injury. **Proximate cause** is the event that sets in motion an uninterrupted chain of events leading to a loss. An event that is a proximate cause cannot be interrupted by any new and independent cause.

Proximate cause
The event that sets in motion an uninterrupted chain of events leading to a loss.

For example, a law may require sprinklers be installed in a hotel. A fire destroys the defendant's hotel and severely injures the plaintiff. Establishing that the hotel did not have sprinklers and was therefore in violation of the law is not enough to create liability on the hotel owner's part. The plaintiff must prove that the absence of the sprinklers was the proximate cause of his or her injuries. If, for instance, the plaintiff could easily have escaped the fire but did not for some reason unrelated to the absence of sprinklers, the chain of events was broken and proximate cause not established.

The fourth element of negligence is actual injury or damage. The plaintiff must establish that he or she suffered actual harm as a result of the alleged negligent act or omission.

If the plaintiff has succeeded in establishing all four elements of negligence, the appropriate court remedy is usually monetary damages, although in some cases the plaintiff may be awarded an injunction (discussed subsequently).

Intentional Torts

Intentional tort
A tort committed with intent to cause harm or with intent to do the act that causes harm.

An **intentional tort** is a tort committed with intent to cause harm or with intent to do the act that causes harm. The most common forms of intentional torts are as follows:

- Intentional physical torts against persons—including battery, assault, false imprisonment, false arrest, and infliction of emotional distress
- Defamation—libel and slander
- Invasion of right of privacy—interference with a person's right to be free from unwarranted public intrusion
- Fraud—deliberate misrepresentation
- Bad faith—reckless act causing severe emotional distress that results in physical injury
- Interference with relationships between others—including unfair competition, interference with employment, and injurious falsehood
- Intentional torts against property—including trespass and conversion
- Nuisance—interfering with another's use or enjoyment of property

Although there are a variety of defenses for both unintentional and intentional torts, a discussion of them is beyond the scope of this text. Insurance policies generally exclude most intentional torts. However, insurance professionals should recognize and understand the intentional torts that can result in legal disputes involving both insureds and insurers.

> ### Physical and Nonphysical Intentional Torts
>
> Sometimes torts are classified by whether they involve physical acts on another's person or property, as distinguished from nonphysical acts that might also violate a legal right. Examples of physical torts are battery (illegal touching), false imprisonment, and false arrest. Nonphysical torts do not involve physical acts or contacts. Examples are defamation (libel and slander), which involves only written or spoken words; outrage; malicious prosecution; and fraud. Assault is a nonphysical tort a person commits when threatening another person with physical harm, but without physical touching. Battery is the physical act of harming a person by actual touching.

Strict Liability

In some situations, tort liability can be imposed even when the defendant is shown to have acted neither negligently nor with intent to cause harm. This type of legal liability is called **strict liability**, or **absolute liability**, which is liability that arises from inherently dangerous activities, resulting in harm to another, regardless of the degree of care taken. Strict liability can be imposed through torts or imposed by certain statutes, such as workers' compensation laws. Situations in which strict liability is imposed by tort law include the following:

- Ultrahazardous activities
- The sale of dangerously defective products

Ultrahazardous activities can include using dangerous substances, such as dynamite, gasoline, noxious chemicals, or explosives; or engaging in dangerous activities, such as blasting, oil well drilling, mining, manufacturing dangerous chemicals, or handling propane gas. It can also refer to keeping wild animals in captivity or keeping domesticated animals known to be abnormally dangerous. Any person engaged in hazardous activities can be held liable to someone who is injured by the activity, regardless of whether the person exercised due care.

Strict liability generally applies to the sale of products that are defective and unreasonably dangerous to the person or property of users or consumers. Mere proof of the defect and the resulting damages are sufficient to support a cause of action against the seller. Liability can be imposed even though the seller has exercised all possible care in the preparation of the product.

Strict liability, or **absolute liability**
Liability that arises from inherently dangerous activities, resulting in harm to another, regardless of the degree of care taken.

Remedies

The primary remedy in tort actions, damages, can either be compensatory or punitive. **Compensatory damages** are a payment awarded by a court to indemnify a victim for actual harm. These damages represent the total of monetary losses actually sustained by the victim plus any additional monetary losses that can be inferred from the facts and circumstances of the case. Compensatory damages are customarily divided into two categories: special damages and general damages.

Special damages are compensatory damages for actual losses that the plaintiff claims resulted from the defendant's wrongful act. Assuming that they are the direct result of the defendant's wrongful actions, special damages could include any of the following:

- Reasonable medical expenses incurred by the plaintiff.
- Damage to property owned by the plaintiff, as measured by the lesser of the cost to repair the damage or the cost to replace the damaged property with undamaged property of like kind and quality.
- Damages resulting from the loss of use of damaged property, such as loss of earnings.
- If the plaintiff dies or is physically disabled by the negligence of the defendant, (1) any loss of earnings from personal services up to the date of the trial and (2) the present value or lump-sum equivalent of potential future earnings from personal services, from the date of the trial to the date of the anticipated retirement or based on the life expectancy of the plaintiff. Personal services are services for which there is no acceptable substitute. For example, an actor who agrees to perform in a play cannot send someone else.

Once the plaintiff has established special damages, an additional amount may also be awarded for general damages. **General damages** are compensatory damages that do not have an economic value and that are presumed to follow from the type of wrong claimed by the plaintiff. Examples of general damages are damages for pain and suffering, mental anguish, bereavement from the death of a loved one, and the loss of the consortium of a deceased or disabled spouse. (Loss of consortium refers to loss of the benefits that one spouse is entitled to receive from the other, including companionship, affection, and sexual relations.) Any general damages awarded are intended to compensate the plaintiff with the monetary equivalent of the intangible loss suffered. The total amount of general damages is determined by the jury deciding the case or, if the claim is settled out of court, by negotiation between the two parties.

Punitive, or **exemplary damages** are a payment awarded by a court to punish a defendant for a reckless, malicious, or deceitful act or to deter similar conduct. These damages need not bear any relationship to a party's actual injury or harm. In certain cases, punitive damages are awarded to the plaintiff as an additional amount, over and above what is awarded as compensatory damages.

Compensatory damages
A payment awarded by a court to indemnify a victim for actual harm.

Special damages
Compensatory damages for actual losses that the plaintiff claims resulted from the defendant's wrongful act.

General damages
Compensatory damages that do not have an economic value and that are presumed to follow from the type of wrong claimed by the plaintiff.

Punitive, or exemplary damages
A payment awarded by a court to punish a defendant for a reckless, malicious, or deceitful act or to deter similar conduct; need not bear any relationship to a party's actual damages.

Historically, punitive damages were rarely awarded in ordinary negligence lawsuits—they were imposed on defendants only in gross negligence or intentional interference lawsuits when the conduct of the defendant was particularly malicious. Although that is still the general rule, the frequency and severity of punitive damage awards have increased noticeably.

Although there is ordinarily no upper dollar limit on the amount a court may award, some statutes impose limits on the amount of damages plaintiffs can collect in certain types of lawsuits. For example, a states tort reform statute may limit recovery for general damages in a medical malpractice suit to $500,000.

In some legal actions, plaintiffs seek to obtain an injunction instead of, or in addition to, monetary damages. An **injunction** is a court-ordered equitable remedy requiring a party to act or refrain from acting. The injunction may require a party to stop doing something (such as practicing unfair employment discrimination) or to do something (such as clean up a toxic landfill).

Injunction
A court-ordered equitable remedy requiring a party to act or refrain from acting.

CONTRACT LAW

Contract law governs the relationship between two or more parties that have entered into a contract. If a party to a contract breaches that contract, the other party, if injured by the breach, may seek a remedy through the courts. There are two ways in which contract law influences the insurance industry. First, violations of contract law can lead to legal liability that may lead to claims under liability insurance policies. For example, organizations can be exposed to liability from warranties that are made in conjunction with the products or services they provide to their customers. Second, because an insurance policy is a contract, contract law influences the way courts will interpret an insurance policy.

A **contract** is a legally enforceable promise. A promise is an expression of intent to do or not do something in the future, communicated in a way that assures another person of a firm commitment. The party to a contract making a promise is called the **promisor**. The party to a contract to whom a promise is made is the **promisee**. People regularly make promises or enter into agreements for many purposes, but not all of these promises are legally enforceable contracts. Examples of promises that constitute contracts include agreements to purchase food, clothing, or insurance; to rent housing; to pay debts; and to buy property. In contrast, a promise to have dinner with a friend is not legally enforceable. Understanding what circumstances give rise to legally enforceable promises or agreements is essential to understanding contract law. Contracts can create, transfer, or remove legal liability and courts can enforce all these agreements.

Contract
A legally enforceable promise.

Promisor
The party to a contract making a promise.

Promisee
The party to a contract to whom a promise is made.

Privity of contract
The connection or relationship between parties to a contract because they have mutual interests.

Breach of contract
The failure of a party to a contract, without legal excuse, to perform all or part of the contract.

When two or more parties enter into a contract, they are said to be in privity of contract. **Privity of contract** is the connection or relationship between parties to a contract because they have mutual interests. A **breach of contract** is the failure of a party to a contract, without legal excuse, to perform all or part of the contract. Ordinarily, a party cannot sue for breach of contract without being in privity of contract with the other party.

Elements of an Enforceable Contract

To understand how an insurance policy can be formed, an insurance professional needs to understand what is required to form an enforceable contract. A contract is enforceable only if it contains all of the following four elements:

1. Agreement
2. Capacity to contract
3. Consideration
4. Legal purpose

If any one of these elements is missing, then no contract exists. Therefore, during policy analysis, an insurance professional must ensure that all four elements are present. This does not mean that the insurer will pay for a loss if all the elements of a contract are present in the insurance policy. It means that the courts will find that the policy is an enforceable contract and will interpret the policy to determine coverage. If, for example, the insured fails to fulfill one of the policy's conditions, the courts may decide that the insurer is not obligated to pay for a particular loss, despite the fact that a valid contract exists.

Agreement

The first element of an enforceable contract is agreement. Agreement is reached when one party (the offeror) makes a specific offer and the other party (the offeree) gives specific and genuine acceptance of the exact terms of that offer. Determining what constitutes a specific offer and a specific and genuine acceptance can be difficult and is determined on a case-by-case basis. However, the following three requirements must be met by the offeror and the offeree for an offer to be valid:

1. Intent to contract—The offeror must express, by word or conduct, the intent to enter into a contract.
2. Definite terms—The terms of the proposed contract must be sufficiently definite.
3. Communication to offeree—The offer must be communicated to the offeree.

An offeree may exercise one of the following three alternatives:

1. Accept the offer
2. Reject the offer
3. Make a counteroffer

A counteroffer cancels the original offer and constitutes a new offer. Therefore, the offeree becomes the offeror, and the offeror becomes the offeree. The party who was originally the offeror may accept or reject the counteroffer—or make yet another counteroffer, thereby generating another new offer.

Acceptance occurs when a party to whom an offer has been made either agrees to what has been proposed or completes the action required by the offer. An acceptance must meet the following three requirements:

1. It must be made by the offeree.
2. It must be unconditional and unequivocal; that is, it must be consistent with the offer's exact terms and not be a counteroffer.
3. It must be communicated to the offeror by appropriate word or act.

With respect to an insurance policy, what constitutes an offer and what constitutes acceptance varies according to situation. For example, if an insurance applicant submits a completed application along with the appropriate premium to an insurer, the applicant is making an offer and is therefore the offeror. If, in response, the insurer (the offeree) issues a policy on the same terms as the application, the policy issuance constitutes acceptance, but only once it has actually been communicated to the offeror or to the offeror's authorized agent. When insurance transactions are handled by mail, the policy is considered communicated when the acceptance is mailed, not when it is received. If the policy introduces new terms not covered by the application, then the policy is a counteroffer.

As an alternative example, if an applicant submits an application to an insurer to find out if the insurer is prepared to offer insurance, then the application is not an offer, it is simply an invitation to the insurer to make an offer. If the insurer issues a quote in response, then the quote is the offer and the applicant's payment of the appropriate premium is the acceptance.

Capacity to Contract

The second element of an enforceable contract is that the parties to the contract must have the capacity to contract; that is, they must be considered legally capable of entering into an agreement. A contract may be voidable (that is, it can legally be rejected or avoided at the option of one or both of the parties to the contract) if any contracting party was not legally competent at the time of agreement.

Age and mental capacity are the two main criteria for determining competency. Each state has its own statute that sets the age of majority for contracts, the most common age being eighteen. In general, minors cannot enter into contracts without parental consent unless the contract is for a necessity. Examples of necessities include food, water, and clothing, as well as student loan contracts.

Impaired mental capacity does not only cover psychological state, it also covers intoxication from drugs or alcohol. Courts have not always agreed on whether a party who has voluntarily taken drugs or alcohol is considered competent. Some courts have found that simply being intoxicated, regardless of how, is grounds for finding the party incompetent; others have not. However, a majority of states will void a contract if one of the parties was voluntarily intoxicated (partially incapacitated) and the other party attempted to take advantage of the situation.

In insurance, questions of capacity to contract are not as common as questions about offer and acceptance—encountering incompetent parties in insurance policies is unusual. If questions of capacity to contract are raised, they tend to concern the principal-agent relationship between an insurer and its agents. Competency for an insurer involves its legal authority to do business in a state. Insurers are licensed by the various states to sell insurance, and their activities are regulated by state insurance departments. Authority to act as an insurance agent is also granted at the state level. States impose some basic competency standards through pre-license exams and continuing education requirements.

An insured can be deemed incompetent to form a contract because of age or mental incapacity. As a practical matter, insureds who want to avoid an insurance contract rarely raise the issue of competency because the same effect can be accomplished simply by exercising a cancellation right or not paying premiums.

Consideration

Consideration

Something of value or bargained for and exchanged by the parties to a contract.

The third element of an enforceable contract is consideration. **Consideration** is something of value or bargained for and exchanged by the parties to a contract. Both parties to the contract must offer some type of consideration. Without consideration from both parties, the contract is considered a gift and is therefore not a contract. The consideration might be paying money, giving a promise in return for money, performing an act, or relinquishing a right to do what one is legally entitled to do. Past consideration and pre-existing duties are not classed as consideration.

Consideration does not have to be adequate for it to be valid consideration. For example, two parties could agree to sell 100 acres of prime real estate for $500. The courts would determine only whether the parcel of real estate and the $500 constitute valid consideration (which they do), not whether $500 is adequate consideration for that real estate.

Questions of consideration in insurance are not particularly common. In an insurance policy, the insurer's consideration is its promise to make payment on the occurrence of an insured event. The insurer may also offer additional consideration, such as loss prevention services, in exchange for the premium. The insured's consideration is payment of the premium or the promise to pay the premium. With property or liability insurance policies, the insured does not necessarily have to pay the premium to the insurer immediately.

The courts will find a property or liability insurance policy to be valid without prepayment of the premium, provided they can find a readily implied promise to pay the premium. For example, suppose the insured does not pay the premium before the policy's inception date, but authorizes the insurer to deduct premium payments monthly from the insured's bank account. If a covered event happens a few days after the inception date, but before the initial premium is paid, the contract is valid because the insured implicitly promised to pay the premium. The courts will not support the insurer's denial of the claim based on a lack of consideration by the insured.

However, if the insured fails to make the initial premium payment when due, the insurer can cancel the policy for lack of consideration (nonpayment of premium). This is an example of flat cancellation. A **flat cancellation** is the cancellation of an insurance policy as of its effective date. With a flat cancellation, it is as if the policy never existed. However, there are circumstances in which the insurer cannot make a flat cancellation for nonpayment of premium. For example, it is generally not feasible to make a flat cancellation if an insured event has occurred. The insured must be given the option of providing the promised consideration for the contract. Assuming the amount of premium involved is less than the amount of the loss, the insured would almost always prefer to pay the overdue premium than to retain an uninsured loss. Alternatively, the insured may not have paid the premium because of a delay between policy issuance and billing. Permitting insurers to deny a claim arising before the insured has had a chance to pay the initial premium would be against public policy.

Flat cancellation
The cancellation of an insurance policy as of its effective date.

Legal Purpose

Legal purpose is the fourth element of an enforceable contract. Any contract must serve a legal purpose that is not contrary to the public interest. A contract is illegal when either its formation or its performance is a crime or wrongful act. For example, a contract to murder a person would be illegal. The courts will also consider contracts to be illegal if they are against public policy, such as a contract to bribe a public official in exchange for a government job.

Courts refuse to enforce any insurance policy that harms the public or is illegal. Policies that tend to increase crime or encourage violations of the law may also be deemed unenforceable for lack of legal purpose. The following examples illustrate how certain insurance coverages for some types of losses could be against public policy:

- Liability insurance coverage for punitive damages—In a liability claim, courts sometimes award not only compensatory damages but also punitive damages, which are intended to punish the defendant for greater culpability than simple negligence. Some states prohibit insurers from paying punitive damages on an insured's behalf on the grounds that liability coverage for these types of damages is against public policy because it would be the insurer, not the defendant, who is punished.

- Homeowners insurance coverage for child molestation and spousal abuse—In some cases, convicted child molesters have sought protection against civil suits under the liability portion of their homeowners policy. In response, many states have enacted laws (which insurers have reflected in policy exclusions) declaring that no such coverage exists because this coverage would shield molesters from the financial consequences of their illegal behavior.

- Property insurance coverage on illegal goods—Property insurance coverage on illegally owned or possessed goods (such as illegal drugs) is unenforceable and against public policy because the public suffers the consequences of the illegal activity, such as higher crime rates.

- Property insurance coverage in the absence of an insurable interest— Without an insurable interest requirement, people could obtain insurance on other people's property, essentially wagering on insured events. An insured party with no insurable interest in the property would have nothing to lose but the premium, but everything to gain if a loss occurred. This is against the public interest because it creates a moral hazard.

In general, insurance is a social good. Through the ability to pool insureds, insurance actually reduces risk to society. However, insurance is not a social good if it provides coverage for actions that are against public policy. Therefore, insurance policies are specifically worded to avoid the implication that coverage would be provided for criminal acts.

Oral and Temporary Contracts

In general, contracts do not need to be in writing to be valid. An oral contract can be as binding as a written contract. Therefore, in the absence of statutory or common-law prohibitions, insurance policies need not be in writing. The courts generally enforce oral contracts of insurance, provided that they are specific enough to show the parties' mutual assent on key matters, such as the identities of the parties, the loss exposures insured, and the policy limits.

When Does a Contract Need to Be in Writing?

One exception to the rule that contracts do not need to be in writing applies to agreements that are within the Statute of Frauds. The Statute of Frauds was an English statute that changed common law by requiring that certain contracts, such as those involving real estate, be in writing and signed by the party responsible for performing the contract. The aim of the statute is to reduce the possibility of fraud. All states have now enacted laws containing certain statute of frauds provisions for particular types of contracts. In addition, the Uniform Commercial Code (UCC) contains a statute of frauds provision that requires contracts for the sale of goods for a price of $500 or more to be in writing.

In insurance, a **binder** is a temporary contract outlining the coverage provided. Both written and oral binders are enforceable insurance contracts. However, the exact terms of an oral binder can easily be disputed. Insurers routinely issue written binders to confirm to the insured that the specified coverage is in effect despite the lack of a complete, written contract. Binders, such as the one shown in Exhibit 9-1, are typically simple documents that take up only one page. Although they may contain form names or numbers, binders do not contain all the provisions that ultimately appear in the final written policy.

If a loss occurs before the actual policy is issued, the insurer and the insured might dispute the extent of the coverage to which they agreed. No single rule applies to all such disputes, and each must be considered on its own merits, taking into account any state or local statutes that may apply.

Binder

In insurance, a temporary contract outlining the coverage provided.

Certificates of Insurance

A certificate of insurance is a document issued by an insurer or its authorized representative as evidence that a policy has been issued providing coverage in a certain amount. Certificates of insurance are used in many situations. Mortgagees require evidence that property subject to a mortgage is properly insured and that the mortgagee's interests are protected. Businesses that engage a contractor require the contractor to demonstrate that it has liability insurance. Like binders, certificates of insurance summarize coverage. If the certificate and the policy differ, courts usually enforce the policy.

Contract Enforcement

If an enforceable contract is breached by any party to the contract, the other party, if injured by the breach, may seek a remedy through the legal system. The two most common legal remedies for breach of contract are damages (both compensatory and, if appropriate, punitive) and specific performance. Specific performance is the term for a court order to a party to perform its duties as specified in the contract; therefore, specific performance is similar to an injunction.

Some contracts are not legally enforceable because they do not contain one or more of the elements of an enforceable contract. In these cases, the courts will neither require the parties to perform specific duties nor require the payment of damages. A contract can be unenforceable if it is void, voidable, or canceled. Alternatively, a contract may be unenforceable because there is a lack of genuine assent as a result of fraud, concealment, misrepresentation, mistake, duress, or undue influence.

EXHIBIT 9-1

ACORD Insurance Binder

ACORD®	INSURANCE BINDER		DATE (MM/DD/YYYY)

THIS BINDER IS A TEMPORARY INSURANCE CONTRACT, SUBJECT TO THE CONDITIONS SHOWN ON THE REVERSE SIDE OF THIS FORM.

AGENCY

COMPANY | BINDER #

	EFFECTIVE		EXPIRATION	
DATE	TIME	DATE	TIME
		AM		12:01 AM
		PM		NOON

PHONE (A/C, No, Ext):   FAX (A/C, No):

THIS BINDER IS ISSUED TO EXTEND COVERAGE IN THE ABOVE NAMED COMPANY PER EXPIRING POLICY #:

CODE: SUB CODE:

AGENCY CUSTOMER ID:

DESCRIPTION OF OPERATIONS/VEHICLES/PROPERTY (Including Location)

INSURED

COVERAGES

LIMITS

TYPE OF INSURANCE	COVERAGE/FORMS	DEDUCTIBLE	COINS %	AMOUNT
PROPERTY CAUSES OF LOSS BASIC ☐ BROAD ☐ SPEC ☐				
GENERAL LIABILITY		EACH OCCURRENCE	$	
COMMERCIAL GENERAL LIABILITY		DAMAGE TO RENTED PREMISES	$	
☐ CLAIMS MADE ☐ OCCUR		MED EXP (Any one person)	$	
		PERSONAL & ADV INJURY	$	
		GENERAL AGGREGATE	$	
RETRO DATE FOR CLAIMS MADE:		PRODUCTS - COMP/OP AGG	$	
AUTOMOBILE LIABILITY		COMBINED SINGLE LIMIT	$	
☐ ANY AUTO		BODILY INJURY (Per person)	$	
☐ ALL OWNED AUTOS		BODILY INJURY (Per accident)	$	
☐ SCHEDULED AUTOS		PROPERTY DAMAGE	$	
☐ HIRED AUTOS		MEDICAL PAYMENTS	$	
☐ NON-OWNED AUTOS		PERSONAL INJURY PROT	$	
		UNINSURED MOTORIST	$	
			$	
AUTO PHYSICAL DAMAGE DEDUCTIBLE ☐ ALL VEHICLES ☐ SCHEDULED VEHICLES		ACTUAL CASH VALUE		
COLLISION:		STATED AMOUNT	$	
OTHER THAN COL:		OTHER		
GARAGE LIABILITY		AUTO ONLY - EA ACCIDENT	$	
☐ ANY AUTO		OTHER THAN AUTO ONLY:		
		EACH ACCIDENT	$	
		AGGREGATE	$	
EXCESS LIABILITY		EACH OCCURRENCE	$	
☐ UMBRELLA FORM		AGGREGATE	$	
☐ OTHER THAN UMBRELLA FORM	RETRO DATE FOR CLAIMS MADE:	SELF-INSURED RETENTION	$	
		WC STATUTORY LIMITS		
WORKER'S COMPENSATION AND EMPLOYER'S LIABILITY		E.L. EACH ACCIDENT	$	
		E.L. DISEASE - EA EMPLOYEE	$	
		E.L. DISEASE - POLICY LIMIT	$	
SPECIAL CONDITIONS/ OTHER COVERAGES		FEES	$	
		TAXES	$	
		ESTIMATED TOTAL PREMIUM	$	

NAME & ADDRESS

☐ MORTGAGEE	☐ ADDITIONAL INSURED
☐ LOSS PAYEE	
LOAN #	

AUTHORIZED REPRESENTATIVE

ACORD 75 (2004/09)   NOTE: IMPORTANT STATE INFORMATION ON REVERSE SIDE   © ACORD CORPORATION 1993-2004

Void, Voidable, and Canceled Contracts

A **void contract** is an agreement that, despite the parties' intentions, never reaches contract status and is therefore not legally enforceable or binding. A void contract never had any legal existence—even though one or more parties might have considered it a contract—because it lacks one or more elements of an enforceable contract. For example, lack of consideration by one party makes the contract void. The parties to a void contract may choose to treat the contract as though it is a valid contract, provided all parties agree.

A **voidable contract** is a contract that one of the parties can reject (avoid) based on some circumstance surrounding its execution. A voidable contract legally exists, but its existence is tenuous because it can legally be rejected (made void, or avoided) at the option of one or both of the parties to the contract.

A **canceled contract** is a legally enforceable contract that is no longer in effect. Many contracts include provisions detailing how and when either party may cancel the contract. To cancel a contract, a party to the contract must first acknowledge that it is a legally valid contract and then terminate it according to its own contractual terms.

Void contract
An agreement that, despite the parties' intentions, never reaches contract status and is therefore not legally enforceable or binding.

Voidable contract
A contract that one of the parties can reject (avoid) based on some circumstance surrounding its execution.

Canceled contract
A legally enforceable contract that is no longer in effect.

Void, Voidable, and Canceled Contracts

Insurers have several possible methods for circumventing insurance contracts. The following example shows when an insurer may choose not to cover a policyholder and how the insurer can handle the coverage situation.

Scenario: Peggy owns a 100-year-old house. She submitted and signed a homeowners insurance application to XYZ Insurance Company and included a check for the first year's premium. In exchange, XYZ issued a homeowners insurance policy to Peggy.

XYZ later discovered that Peggy misrepresented the age of the house as only two years old. Because XYZ does not write insurance on homes over thirty years old, Peggy's misrepresentation of the house's age resulted in the insurer's assuming a risk (the old house) that the insurer would not otherwise choose to assume. XYZ wanted to circumvent this insurance contract and identified the following options for doing so:

Option 1—XYZ considered denying coverage because of a void contract; however, given the above scenario, the insurance policy between XYZ and Peggy is not void; the contract had legal existence.

Option 2—XYZ Insurance Company could have the policy avoided based on Peggy's misrepresentation in the insurance application. The policy is voidable by XYZ because the company's offer to Peggy was based on the information misrepresented by Peggy. In this case, the contract is not enforceable.

Option 3—XYZ Insurance Company could have the house inspected. Upon learning its actual age, XYZ could send a notice to Peggy advising that her policy is being canceled because the house's age does not agree with the house's age identified in the insurance application. In this case, the contract is not enforceable.

Genuine Assent

A significant portion of litigation regarding the enforceability of insurance contracts involves genuineness of assent. An insurance policy that appears valid might still be unenforceable if either party's assent was not genuinely given. Without genuine assent, the parties cannot achieve the legally required agreement. **Genuine assent** is contracting parties' actual assent to form a contract or their indication of intent to contract by their actions and words. An innocent party whose genuine assent was lacking may avoid the contract.

Genuine assent
Contracting parties' actual assent to form a contract or their indication of intent to contract by their actions and words.

Genuine assent can be found lacking under the following circumstances:

- Fraud
- Concealment or misrepresentation
- Mistake
- Duress
- Undue influence

Fraud
An intentional misrepresentation resulting in harm to a person or an organization.

Fraud is an intentional misrepresentation resulting in harm to a person or an organization. For example, fraud occurs when someone knowingly makes a false representation with the intent to deceive someone to enter into a contract. Courts consider six elements when evaluating allegations of fraud. The first five elements must be present to cancel a contract on the basis of fraud and the sixth must be present in order for the plaintiff to obtain damages. These elements are as follows:

1. A false representation
2. Of a material fact
3. Knowingly made
4. With intent to deceive
5. On which the other party has place justifiable reliance
6. To his or her detriment

If an insurance agent fraudulently misrepresents the nature of the document the applicant is signing or the protection that is being purchased, the fraud victim may cancel the agreement and recover any premium paid. An insurer also is permitted to avoid a contract based on the applicant's fraud in procuring the policy.

Material fact
In insurance, a fact that would affect the insurer's decision to provide or maintain insurance or to settle a claim.

Because both parties rely on full disclosure for the correct assessment of risk and a mutual understanding of contract terms, concealment or misrepresentation by either party affects genuine assent. The existence of concealment or misrepresentation is determined by looking at material facts. In insurance, a **material fact** is a fact that would affect the insurer's decision to provide or maintain insurance or to settle a claim. Any fact the insurer specifically asks about is material. Failure to disclose the answers to specific questions in the insurance application is strong evidence of concealment that may give the insurer adequate grounds for denying any obligation to make payment under the policy. Incorrect answers to questions in the application are strong evidence of misrepresentation.

What Constitutes Material Facts?

Consider the following scenarios:

Scenario 1: Ken and Val have just moved into a new home. When notifying their auto insurance agent of the relocation, Ken mistakenly transposes two of the numbers in their new address. Instead of telling the agent that they now live at 123 Apricot Lane, he reported that they live at 132 Apricot Lane.

Scenario 2: Ken and Val have just moved into a new home. When notifying their auto insurance agent of the relocation, Ken mistakenly transposes two of the numbers in their new zip code. Instead of telling the agent that they now live in the 19115 zip code, he reported that they live in the 19151 zip code.

Scenario 3: Ken and Val have just moved into a new home. One of the neighbors tells Val that their auto insurance premiums increased significantly when they relocated to the neighborhood, because the zip code in which they now live has an abnormally high rate of auto thefts. When notifying their auto insurance agent of the relocation, Ken intentionally provides a different address and zip code in the hope of getting a lower auto insurance premium.

Scenario 1 does not involve the misrepresentation of any material facts. Both scenarios 2 and 3 are misrepresentations of material facts. Although scenario 2 was not an intentional misrepresentation, it still involved material facts that could affect an insurer's decision to provide insurance at a stated price. Because many auto insurers use zip code data to determine premiums, the zip code is a material fact for auto insurance.

Most courts would find that facts unrelated to the policy's coverage are not material. For example, an applicant's misstatement of a lienholder's address in an auto insurance application would not likely be misrepresentation. Likewise, an applicant's accidental omission of his or her telephone number would not likely be concealment.

Another situation that can affect genuine assent involves a mistake. A mistake is a perception that does not agree with the actual facts. Mistakes can be made regarding the facts of the transaction or the law affecting the agreement. Alternatively, mistakes can involve errors in data entry, arithmetic errors, or misstatements about the property's value. Although some mistakes do not affect the rights of the parties to a contract, others make the agreement voidable or unenforceable. When a mistake occurs in an insurance transaction, the courts sometimes interpret the policy to determine how or whether coverage applies. Sometimes courts may act to reform or change a formal contract so that it conforms to both parties' true intention.

For example, an insured may want to add an endorsement to her homeowners policy to provide $500,000 coverage for an expensive diamond ring. On the application, the insured mistakenly applied for $50,000 in coverage, which the insurer willingly provided. When the insured realized the mistake, she tried to obtain her desired $500,000 coverage, but the insurer refused to provide a limit that high for jewelry. When the insured filed a lawsuit to force the insurer to provide coverage, the insurer argued that the mistake affected its genuine consent to the contract.

Duress
The use of restraint, violence, or threats of violence to compel a party to act contrary to his or her wishes or interests.

A party may seek to avoid or cancel a contract on the basis that the other party used duress to obtain assent to the agreement. **Duress** is the use of restraint, violence, or threats of violence to compel a party to act contrary to his or her wishes or interests. To establish sufficient duress to escape liability under a contract, the plaintiff must show that the threat of violence or other harm actually restrained the plaintiff's free choice. Economic pressure alone, even if significant, is usually not considered duress.

Tie-In Sales and Duress

Tie-in sales—those that require the purchase of one or more products or services in addition to the desired product or service—usually do not constitute duress. In the insurance industry, there was concern regarding tie-in sales of banking and insurance products by lenders (for example, whether a mortgage lender could require the borrower buy homeowners insurance from the lender's insurance subsidiary).

The Gramm-Leach-Bliley Act of 1999 includes certain "safe harbor" provisions to prevent this type of abuse from occurring. Section 104 of the act prohibits states from "preventing or significantly interfering with" the ability of a depository institute or an affiliate to engage in insurance sales, solicitation, and cross-marketing activities. However, the act adopts thirteen "safe harbor" provisions that permit states to adopt rules targeted specifically at bank-insurance sales activities, including insurance sales conducted by bank affiliates. These safe harbors include the following restrictions:

1. Prohibiting the rejection of an insurance policy by a depository institution or an affiliate solely because the policy has been issued or underwritten by an unaffiliated entity

2. Prohibiting a requirement that any debtor or unaffiliated insurer or agent pay a separate charge in connection with the handling of insurance required in connection with a loan, extension of credit, or other traditional bank product or service unless the same charge would be required of an affiliated insurer or agent

3. Requiring depository institutions to provide customers with "free-choice" disclosures when loans are pending—that is, notice that the customer's choice of insurance provider will not affect the loan decision process. The depository institution may, however, impose reasonable requirements concerning the insured's creditworthiness and the scope of the coverage chosen

4. Requiring that when a customer obtains insurance (other than credit or flood insurance) and credit from a depository institution or an affiliate, the credit and insurance transactions be completed through separate documents

---

Undue influence
The improper use of power or trust to deprive a person of free will and substitute another's objective, resulting in lack of genuine assent to a contract.

Finally, genuine assent is affected when one party unduly influences another to make certain decisions. Most legal cases involving undue influence concern gifts, wills, or the selection of insurance beneficiaries. **Undue influence** is the improper use of power or trust to deprive a person of free will and substitute another's objective, resulting in lack of genuine assent to a contract. Mere persuasion and argument are not undue influence. For undue influence to occur, the following situations must be present:

- A confidential relationship must exist between the parties.

- One party must exercise some control and influence over the other. For example, the relationships of parent and child, attorney and client, doctor and patient, guardian and ward, or agent and principal give one party a position of dominance over the other.

- An element of helplessness or dependence must be involved.

In contracts between such individuals, the law will assist a person who is a victim of undue influence. The dominating party must prove that he or she did not unduly influence a contract from which the dominated party obtains inadequate benefits.

AGENCY LAW

Agency law governs the relationship between a principal and its agent(s). **Agency** is a legal, consensual relationship that exists when one party, the agent, acts on behalf of another party, the principal. Agency law enforces the duties of the principal and agent toward one another. Agency relationships are extremely prevalent in the insurance industry. Not only do insurance contracts provide coverage for liability that may stem from agency relationships, but also the majority of insurance products and services involve principals and agents. Both insurers and insureds (the principals) may be represented by agents, such as independent agents, exclusive agents, or brokers in insurance contract negotiations. An understanding of agency law will allow insurance professionals not only to better understand the liability loss exposures of insureds in agency relationships but also to better understand the role that the principal-agency relationship plays in the insurance transaction.

An agent of a principal can be an employee of the principal or an independent contractor. For example, claim representatives are employees of the insurer and their representative agents. Similarly, independent insurance agents are both independent contractors and also agents of the insurer. Insurance brokers are also usually independent contractors who may be agents of the insurer or the insured, depending on the function they are serving at that time.

The authority that an agent has to act on the principal's behalf can be actual or apparent. Actual authority is the authority, both express and implied, that a principal intentionally gives to an agent. In the insurance industry, the insurance producer and the insurer typically enter into a principal-agent relationship through a formal written contract. This contract grants the producer express authority to act on the insurer's behalf. Actual authority can also be granted by less formal means than a written contract, in which case it is referred to as implied authority. An example of implied authority is when an insurer accepts insurance applications from a producer with whom it does not have a written agreement. Because the insurer has accepted applications in the absence of a written contract in the past, the producer has implied authority to submit insurance applications again in the future.

Agency
A legal, consensual relationship that exists when one party, the agent, acts on behalf of another party, the principal.

The principal-agent relationship may also be established through apparent authority. If, for example, customers who visit an insurance agent see that the agent has the insurer's application forms, signs, and stationary, it would be reasonable for the customer to assume that an agency relationship exists. Should the insurer subsequently try to deny that relationship to the detriment of the customer, that customer may have legal protection based on his or her reasonable belief that the agent had authority to deal with that insurer.

Legal liability can arise under agency law when either party fails to meet the obligations required by the agency relationship. Principals and agents owe different obligations to each other, as outlined in an insurance context in Exhibit 9-2.

EXHIBIT 9-2

Obligations in Agency Relationships

Agent's Fiduciary Duty to Principal/Producers' Duty to Insurers	Principal's Duty to Agent/Insurers' Duty to Producers
Loyalty and accounting—duty to receive and process premium checks and forward to insurer properly	Agreed-upon period of employment—duty to honor any employment contracts
Obedience—duty to follow insurer's general and specific instructions	Duty of compensation—duty to make prompt and accurate payment to producers of any salary, bonus, or commissions
Reasonable care—duty to disclose risks to insurer	Duty of reimbursement—duty to make prompt and accurate payment to producers for any covered expenses
Information—duty to transmit material information regarding insureds properly to insurer	Duty of indemnity—duty to provide for defense costs and indemnity of losses for losses stemming from agency relationship

In insurance contract cases regarding agency relationships, courts must answer questions about the existence of the agency contract, the extent of the agent's authority, and the fulfillment of agency obligations. In tort cases regarding agency relationships between an insurer and its employees, courts must answer questions about whether any employment relationship existed and whether the tort in question was within the scope of that employment. If an employee (other than an independent contractor) causes harm to another while acting in the scope of his or her employment, the employer will be liable for the harm.

SUMMARY

There are two different legal systems in the United States, the civil-law system and the common-law system. The civil-law system is a basic legal system that relies on scholarly interpretations of codes and constitutions rather than court interpretations of prior court decisions. In common-law systems, the body of law is derived more from court decisions as opposed to statutes or constitutions. Criminal law is a classification of law that applies to acts that society deems so harmful to the public welfare that government is responsible for prosecuting and punishing the perpetrators. Civil law is a classification of law that applies to legal matters not governed by criminal law and that protects rights and provides remedies for breaches of duties owed to others. One distinguishing factor between civil and criminal law is the burden of proof, that is, the requirement to prove a charge or allegation. Three areas of civil law that are prevalent in the insurance industry are tort law, contract law, and agency law.

Tort law governs the relationship between parties when no contract or statute is present. A tort is a wrongful act or omission, other than a crime or breach of contract, for which the remedy is usually monetary damages. Torts are either unintentional or intentional. "Negligence" is the broad term used for unintentional torts— all other torts are intentional. Most property-casualty insurance claims are based on negligence, which is the failure to exercise the degree of care that a reasonable person in a similar situation would exercise to avoid harming others. In addition to negligence or intentional torts, strict liability is a source of legal liability under tort law. The primary remedy in tort actions, damages, can either be compensatory or punitive.

Contract law governs the relationship between two or more parties that have entered into a contract. A contract is a legally enforceable promise. Any enforceable contract must contain the following four elements: (1) agreement, (2) capacity to contract, (3) consideration, and (4) legal purpose.

In general, contracts do not need to be in writing to be valid. An oral contract can be as binding as a written contract. The courts generally enforce oral contracts of insurance, provided that they are specific enough to show the parties' mutual assent on key matters such as the identities of the parties, the loss exposures insured, and the policy limits. In insurance, a binder is a temporary contract outlining the coverage provided. Both written and oral binders are enforceable insurance contracts.

A contract can be unenforceable if it is void, voidable, or canceled. A void contract is an agreement that, despite the parties' intentions, never reaches contract status and is therefore not legally enforceable or binding. A voidable contract is a contract that one of the parties can reject (avoid) based on some circumstance surrounding its execution. A canceled contract is a legally enforceable contract that is no longer in effect.

A contract may also be unenforceable because there is a lack of genuine assent between its parties. Genuine assent is contracting parties' actual assent to form a contract or their indication of intent to contract by their actions and words. An innocent party whose genuine assent was lacking may avoid the contract. Genuine assent can be found lacking under the following circumstances: fraud, concealment or misrepresentation, mistake, duress, and undue influence.

Agency law governs the relationship between a principal and its agent(s). Agency is a legal, consensual relationship that exists when one party, the agent, acts on behalf of another party, the principal. An agent of a principal can be an employee of the principal or an independent contractor. The authority that an agent has to act on the principal's behalf can be actual or apparent. Actual authority is the authority, both express and implied, that a principal intentionally gives to an agent. Apparent authority exists when it would be reasonable for customers to assume that there is an agency relationship, such as when they see an insurer's forms and signs in an agent's office.

Direct Your Learning

The Insurance Policy

After learning the content of this chapter and completing the corresponding course guide assignment, you should be able to:

■ Describe the following distinguishing characteristics of insurance policies:

- Indemnity
- Utmost good faith
- Fortuitous losses
- Contract of adhesion
- Exchange of unequal amounts
- Conditional
- Nontransferable

■ Explain why some insurance policies do not have the distinguishing characteristics common to most insurance contracts.

■ Explain the role of the courts in resolving coverage disputes:

- Compare questions of liability and questions of coverage.
- Compare questions of law and questions of fact.

■ Describe waiver and estoppel.

■ Describe an insurer's alternatives in coverage disputes regarding property claims and liability claims.

■ Describe the damages and other penalties that may be assessed against an insurer in a coverage dispute.

■ Define or describe each of the Key Words and Phrases for this chapter.

Develop Your Perspective

What are the main topics covered in the chapter?

Certain distinguishing characteristics apply to insurance policies, though not necessarily in all cases. When a policy's coverage is disputed, questions of liability, coverage, fact, and law must be determined. An insurer has various alternative courses of action it can take in response to property and liability claims, but may ultimately pay damages.

Identify the distinguishing characteristics of an insurance policy.

- In what way is the policy a conditional contract?
- When might a policy be transferable?

Why is it important to learn about these topics?

An insurance professional needs to identify and understand the distinguishing characteristics of a particular insurance policy in order to effectively analyze it. In addition, an insurance professional needs to be aware of the potential liability an insurer faces in order to take the appropriate action to deal with the claim and mitigate any potential damages awards.

Consider a property claim that a policyholder may file against an insurer.

- Why might an insurer want to issue a reservation of rights letter?
- In what circumstances might an insurer enter into a nonwaiver agreement?

How can you use what you will learn?

Examine a property insurance policy.

- What sections of the policy limit the claim payment to ensure that the policyholder is indemnified for the loss?
- Does the policy cover any losses that are not fortuitous from the insured's standpoint?

Chapter 10

The Insurance Policy

The legal basis of all insurance transactions is the insurance policy. An insurance policy is a formal written contract by which an insurer provides protection if an insured suffers specified losses. The terms "insurance contract" and "insurance policy" are used interchangeably by insurance professionals. For policy analysis, an insurance professional needs to be able to identify and understand the distinguishing characteristics of a particular insurance policy and understand the methods of resolving many of the coverage disputes that can arise between an insurer and insured. Several of the policy provisions discussed in subsequent chapters are based on these distinguishing characteristics or on avoiding or resolving coverage disputes.

Industry Terminology—Insurance Contract or Insurance Policy?

The terms "insurance contract" and "insurance policy" are used interchangeably in the insurance industry. Insurance Services Office (ISO), which has developed standardized insurance contracts used by many insurers, uses the term "policy" (for example, "the personal auto policy" or "the personal umbrella liability policy").

Furthermore, most insurance contracts use terms such as "policy period," "policy provisions," or "policy limits." These terms have the following specific meanings:

- A provision is any statement in an insurance policy.

- A condition is an insurance policy provision that qualifies an otherwise enforceable promise of the insurer or the insured.

- A clause is a particular article, stipulation, or provision in a formal document.

However, in practice, these terms are somewhat interchangeable and their usage often depends on custom.

In some circumstances, an insurance professional will analyze an insurance policy to avoid or resolve a coverage dispute that has arisen between the insurer and an insured. When insurance-related issues are not resolved by insurance policy language, courts may be called upon to resolve questions of liability, questions of coverage, questions of law, or fact. In some cases, insureds may claim that insurers have forfeited the right to refuse coverage because of either estoppel or a waiver of a defense. Furthermore, the actions an insurer takes when presented with a claim affect the likelihood of a coverage dispute arising and the methods of resolving that dispute. If an insurer is found to be in breach of contract, to be in breach of fair claims settlement practices, or to have acted in bad faith, then a court may order the insurer to pay damages. An insurance professional should be able to recognize not only the insurer's perspective on the insurance policies it sold, but also the insured's understanding of the insurance policies purchased. An understanding of the insured's position may help the insurance professional to avoid or resolve coverage disputes.

DISTINGUISHING CHARACTERISTICS OF AN INSURANCE POLICY

Insurance policies are unique legal contracts that display certain distinguishing characteristics not often found in other types of contracts. Some of the distinguishing characteristics that apply to insurance policies are also called insurance principles because they adhere to the economic theory behind the business of insurance discussed in a previous chapter. The distinguishing characteristics of insurance policies are as follows:

- Indemnity
- Utmost good faith
- Fortuitous losses
- Contract of adhesion
- Exchange of unequal amounts
- Conditional
- Nontransferable

Although these characteristics are unique to insurance policies, not all insurance policies exhibit every one of these characteristics. Indeed, some insurance policies exhibit only a few of the characteristics discussed in this section. Nonetheless, many of the clauses in insurance policies discussed in subsequent chapters are based on these characteristics. Therefore, an understanding of these characteristics will help an insurance professional accurately analyze insurance policies.

Indemnity

Principle of indemnity
The principle that insurance policies should compensate the insured only for the value of the loss.

Contract of indemnity
A contract in which the insurer agrees, in the event of a covered loss, to pay an amount directly related to the amount of the loss.

The goal of an insurance policy is to indemnify (make whole) the insured who has suffered a covered loss. An insurance policy adheres to the **principle of indemnity**, which is the principle that insurance policies should compensate the insured only for the value of the loss. That is, the policyholder should not profit from insurance. This adherence to the principal of indemnity means that an insurance policy is a contract of indemnity. A **contract of indemnity** is a contract in which the insurer agrees, in the event of a covered loss, to pay an amount directly related to the amount of the loss.

In practice, an insurance policy does not necessarily pay the full amount necessary to restore an insured who has suffered a covered loss. Most insurance policies contain a dollar limit, a deductible, or other provisions or limitations that result in the insured being paid less than the entire loss amount. Furthermore, insurance policies do not always indemnify the insured for the inconvenience, time, and other nonfinancial expenses involved in recovering from an insured loss. How the loss is valued is also a major factor in determining the level of indemnity the insured receives from the insurance policy. Subsequent chapters of this text focus on valuation methods and amounts payable under property and liability policies.

Some insurance policies violate the principle of indemnity. For example, certain insurance policies are valued policies, not contracts of indemnity. Under the terms of a valued policy, the insurer agrees to pay a preestablished dollar amount in the event of an insured total loss. That dollar amount may be more or less than the value of the insured loss. For example, rare pieces of art are often insured with a valued policy. If the artwork is destroyed, the policy pays the dollar value specified, regardless of the value of the artwork at the time of the loss. Therefore, valued policies are not contracts of indemnity, because they do not attempt to directly relate the insurer's obligations to the loss's value. Although insurers exercise care in issuing valued policies where the preestablished dollar value is greater than the value of the insured object, a valued policy does have the potential to pay the insured more than was lost.

Despite the fact that some policies do not adhere to the principle of indemnity; in order to reduce or avoid moral hazards, insurance policies should *not* do either of the following:

- Overindemnify the insured
- Indemnify insureds more than once per loss

Insurance Should Not Overindemnify

Insureds should be compensated, but not overcompensated (overindemnified) for a loss. Ideally, the insured should be restored to approximately the same financial position that he or she was in before the loss. The principle of indemnity implies that an insured should not profit from an insured loss. The potential for overindemnification can constitute a moral hazard. For example, a run-down building that is insured for more than its value might be a tempting arson target for an insured owner who could use the insurance money to build a better building on that site. Insurers can reduce moral hazard (and thereby reduce the potential for overindemnification) by clearly defining the extent of a covered loss in the policy provisions and by carefully setting policy limits.

Insureds Should Not Be Indemnified More Than Once per Loss

Ideally, a loss exposure should be the subject of only one insurance policy and only one portion of that insurance policy. Multiple sources of recovery (payment from many policies or more than one portion of the same policy) could result in the insured's overindemnification. To limit overindemnification, most property and liability insurance policies contain clauses called "other-insurance provisions" that limit multiple sources of recovery.

However, sometimes duplicate recovery is both available and justifiable. For example, people can be insureds under more than one policy when they carry multiple policies, such as auto and health insurance. If an insured that has overlapping coverage has been charged an actuarially fair premium for the duplicate portion of coverage, it may be unfair for an insurer to deny coverage simply because the insured has more than one policy. In some instances, prohibiting duplicate recovery for an insured could unfairly absolve the responsible parties from bearing the financial consequences of the loss. To illustrate, if a person (the plaintiff) sues another (the defendant) for injuries suffered as a result of the defendant's negligence and the court finds in favor of the plaintiff, it is not acceptable for the negligent party to avoid paying some or all of those damages, because the plaintiff can also recover money under his or her own insurance policies. This is known as the **collateral source rule**, which is a legal doctrine that provides that the damages owed to a victim should not be reduced because the victim is entitled to recover money from other sources, such as an insurance policy.

Collateral source rule
A legal doctrine that provides that the damages owed to a victim should not be reduced because the victim is entitled to recover money from other sources, such as an insurance policy.

Utmost Good Faith

An insurance policy is generally more vulnerable to abuses such as misrepresentation or opportunism than other contracts for two reasons: information asymmetry and costly verification. Information asymmetry exists when one party to a contract has information important to the contract that the other party does not. For example, a homeowner may know that an insured home is in a state of disrepair that makes a loss more likely. If the insurer does not know this, then information asymmetry exists. To reduce information asymmetry, the insurer attempts to gather as much relevant information as possible during the underwriting process. For example, the insurer could conduct an inspection to verify the condition of the property. If the property is in disrepair, the insurer may charge a higher premium or require a higher deductible than it would have charged had the house been in good condition. However, verification of information is often time consuming and expensive (costly verification). The harder or more costly it is to verify information provided by the insured, the less likely it is that the insurer will expend the resources to verify information, and the information asymmetry will remain.

Information asymmetry can lead to adverse selection; that is, the insurer may improperly price insurance policies by charging a higher-risk insured a lower than actuarially fair premium. Similarly, it may lead to the insurer's issuing a policy on a loss exposure that it may not want to insure at all. Such situations can be prevented if all parties exercise the utmost good faith in the insurance transaction. **Utmost good faith** is an obligation to act with complete honesty and to disclose all relevant facts. The characteristic of utmost good faith has

Utmost good faith
An obligation to act with complete honesty and to disclose all relevant facts.

its roots in early marine insurance transactions, when underwriters could not verify the condition of ships and their cargoes. Therefore, insurance policies became agreements founded in the utmost good faith that the statements made by both the insured and insurer could be relied upon as accurate fact. Although some of the principle of utmost good faith has been eroded by court decisions, the doctrines of misrepresentation, fraud, and concealment in insurance policies are based on utmost good faith.

Utmost good faith requires that a person applying for insurance make a full and fair disclosure of the risk presented by the loss exposures to be insured. An insurance buyer who intentionally conceals material facts from the insurer, or who misrepresents material facts in an insurance application or a claim, does not act in good faith (a material fact is one that, if known by the insurer, would alter the insurer's underwriting decision). If an insurer discovers concealment or misrepresentation of material facts, it may refuse to provide the insurance, or may provide the insurance under different terms, conditions, or premiums. If an insured conceals or misrepresents a material fact or commits fraud that is not discovered by the insurer or is discovered after the policy is effected, the insurance policy can be voided.

The good faith requirement also applies to the insurer—the insurer must fulfill its promises as outlined in the contract. This requirement extends to the claim settlement process, in which insurers are obligated to investigate and pay claims promptly. Failure to abide by various laws and regulations concerning claim settlement practices (discussed subsequently in this chapter) exposes insurers to legal liability. A variety of claim settlement practices may expose the insurer to legal liability, including failing to promptly settle claims, denying claims without performing the proper due diligence, misrepresenting material facts, or failing to promptly acknowledge or respond to correspondence from a claimant.

The most common violations of the concept of utmost good faith in insurance policies involve fraud and/or buildup in insurance claims filed by insureds. Fraud is the misrepresentation of key facts of a claim and buildup is the intentional inflation of an otherwise legitimate claim. For example, filing a claim for an auto accident that never occurred would be fraud. Overstating the extent of injuries suffered in a legitimate auto accident is buildup. The Insurance Research Council estimates that fraud and buildup added between $4.3 and $5.8 billion (11 to 15 percent) to auto injury settlements in 2002.[1]

Fortuitous Losses

As stated in a previous chapter, fortuitous losses are losses that happen accidentally or unexpectedly. For a loss to be fortuitous, reasonable uncertainty must exist about its probability or timing. For insurance purposes, the loss must be fortuitous from the insured's standpoint. For example, although robbery is an intentional act from the perpetrator's standpoint, it is a fortuitous loss from the victim's standpoint.

If an insured knows in advance that a loss will occur and the insurer does not, the insured has an information advantage over the insurer. This information asymmetry, if acted on by the insured (the insured purchases an insurance policy covering the known loss), promotes adverse selection, thereby changing the loss distribution in the pool the insurer insures. Therefore, the premium the insurer charges the pool is no longer actuarially fair, because the loss distribution on which the premium was based has changed. Underwriting is designed to minimize the effect that adverse selection can have on the insurer's loss distribution. One method of avoiding adverse selection is precluding coverage for losses that are not fortuitous.

Fortuitous losses are not necessarily covered by insurance. Many losses happen fortuitously but are not covered, such as losses caused by wear and tear or inherent vice (a characteristic of property that causes it to destroy itself, such as, for example, the perishable nature of fruit). Conversely, some losses are not fortuitous but are still covered by insurance policies. For example, an insurer writing a "claims-made" liability insurance policy might be willing to cover a claim that occurs outside the policy period, assuming that the loss occurred after a retroactive date (the date on or after which bodily injury or property damage must occur in order to be covered) specified in the policy. Many finite risk insurance contracts cover losses that have occurred but have not been settled. In such cases, some uncertainty remains about the final settlement values. For example, an auto manufacturer may have recalled a model because of a faulty part that was responsible for fifty accidents that involved bodily injury and property damage. Although all the accidents have been reported, none of the claims have been settled. Both the auto manufacturer and insurer would have an estimate of what the claims would ultimately settle for; however, there is still some uncertainty regarding both the timing and the amount of the settlements. The insurer may be willing to provide liability insurance coverage to the auto manufacturer for these fifty accidents after the fact for a very high premium because the insurer believes that it will be able to negotiate settlements that would make the transaction profitable.

Contract of Adhesion

The amount of negotiation required to formulate a contract varies widely. Some contracts are the result of extensive negotiation between parties, in which every clause is discussed before agreement is reached. Other contracts involve little or no negotiation. Between these two extremes are contracts that contain some standard clauses, leaving the remainder of the contract to be negotiated.

Insurance policies typically involve little or no negotiation (except for unique loss exposures that require special underwriting consideration, such as a highly valued property). An insurer generally chooses the exact wording in the policies it offers (or uses the wording developed by an advisory organization), and the insured generally has little choice but to accept it. A basic insurance policy might be altered by endorsements, but the insurer or advisory organization also typically develops these endorsements. Consequently, a party who wants to purchase an insurance policy usually has to accept and adhere to the standard policy forms the insurer or advisory organization drafts. The typical insurance policy is, therefore, a contract of adhesion. A **contract of adhesion** is a contract to which one party must adhere as written by the other party.

Courts have ruled that any ambiguities or uncertainties in contracts are to be construed against the party who drafted the agreement because that party had the opportunity to express its intent clearly and unequivocally in the agreement. Therefore, unless the insured drafted the policy (which is rare), ambiguities in an insurance policy are interpreted in the insured's favor. The insurer has a good-faith obligation to draft a policy that clearly expresses what it intends to cover. Any policy provision that can reasonably be interpreted more than one way can be considered ambiguous.

Standard insurance policies are sometimes constructed with acceptable ambiguities. If an insurance policy can be interpreted in two different ways and the insurer is satisfied with either interpretation, no expansion of the policy is necessary to make it more precise.

Contract of adhesion
A contract to which one party must adhere as written by the other party.

Acceptable Ambiguity

Insurance policies are often ambiguous when there is no need for them to be more precise because the interpretation most generous to the insured is acceptable to the insurer.

For example, the Insurance Services Office (ISO) Building and Personal Property Coverage Form's definition of building in the "building" insuring agreement includes some items of personal property:[2]

> Personal property owned by you that is used to maintain or service the building or structure or its premises, including:
>
> (a) Fire extinguishing equipment;
>
> (b) Outdoor furniture;
>
> (c) Floor coverings; and
>
> (d) Appliances used for refrigerating, ventilating, cooking, dishwashing or laundering....

If the owner-occupant of a building purchases both "building" coverage and coverage on "your business personal property," both coverages would apply to these items.

The writers of this policy could have added a provision to clarify how this situation would be handled, but the ambiguity is acceptable because it usually does not matter whether a loss to these personal property items is paid as a building loss or as a personal property loss. If limits or valuation provision differences between the building coverage and personal property coverage do matter, the ambiguity would be resolved in favor of the insured.

For example, suppose outdoor furniture was stolen and the building coverage was written on a special-form basis including theft, while the personal property coverage was written on a broad named perils (without theft) basis. Any insured who understood the policy would claim the theft as a building loss, and the insurer would pay it. In this case, because of the ambiguity, the insurer is obligated to pay the claim under the building coverage, even if the claim is submitted as a personal property loss.

An important consideration affecting the interpretation of a contract's ambiguity is the level of sophistication of the parties to the contract. With some contracts, such as investment contracts, both parties are likely to be well-informed, financially sophisticated parties who have a thorough knowledge of the contract's specifications and interpretations. This is typically the case in insurance contracts formulated chiefly through negotiation, but often is not the case in contracts of adhesion. Whether a contract is ambiguous is a question of fact often determined by the courts.

In cases concerning insurance policies, the level of sophistication of the insured has had the following effects on court decisions:

- *Unsophisticated insured.* Usually, the insurer has drafted a ready-made policy and the insured has little or no control over the policy's wording. This is true of most homeowners and personal auto insurance policies. Ambiguities in these cases are typically interpreted against the insurer. This is the case for most personal insurance consumers.

- *Sophisticated insured.* In a minority of cases, the insured (or its representatives) draft all or part of the insurance policy. Alternatively, the insurer and a sophisticated insured negotiate the policy wording. In these cases, the contract of adhesion doctrine may not apply. Courts do not necessarily interpret any ambiguity in the insured's favor if the insured had some understanding and ability to alter the policy wording before entering the agreement. Sophisticated insureds include many medium to large organizations with dedicated risk management functions.

The courts consider several factors when determining whether an insured can be considered sophisticated. These factors include the size of the insured organization, the size of the insured organization's risk management department, use of an insurance broker or legal counsel with expertise in insurance policies, and the relative bargaining power of the insured in relation to the insurer.

The most common examples of insurance policies that are not contracts of adhesion are manuscript policies or policies that contain manuscript forms (discussed in a subsequent chapter). When the insured contributes to the precise wording of the contract, courts generally do not apply the standards that are common under contracts of adhesion.

Reasonable expectations doctrine
A legal doctrine that provides for an ambiguous insurance policy clause to be interpreted in the way that an insured would reasonably expect.

An extension of the contract of adhesion doctrine is the **reasonable expectations doctrine**, which is a legal doctrine that provides for an ambiguous insurance policy clause to be interpreted in the way that an insured would reasonably expect. For example, the reasonable expectations doctrine is sometimes applied to the renewal of insurance policies that contain a change from the original policy. Unless an oral or a written notification and explanation accompanies the renewal policy, the insured can reasonably expect that the renewal policy is the same as the expiring policy.

The reasonable expectations doctrine is an important extension of the contract of adhesion doctrine because it accounts for the fact that most insureds are not practiced in policy interpretation. However, insureds should not rely on this doctrine because not all courts recognize the reasonable expectations doctrine.

Exchange of Unequal Amounts

For insurance policies, the consideration offered by the insured is the premium; the consideration offered by the insurer is the promise to indemnify the insured in the event of a covered loss. There is no requirement that the amounts exchanged be equal in value. In most insurance policies, the tangible amounts exchanged, the premium from the insured, and any payments made by the insurer, will be unequal.

For example, consider an insurer that charges a $1,500 premium to insure a property valued at $500,000. An infinite number of potential losses could occur. However, the potential losses fall into the following four categories:

1. The insured does not suffer a loss during the policy period. The insured paid the $1,500 premium, and the insurer pays nothing to the insured. In this case, the insured provides substantially more consideration than the insurer.

2. The insured suffers losses of less than $1,500 during the policy period. The insured pays the $1,500 premium and the insurer reimburses the insured for the loss amount (ignoring any deductible). In this scenario, the insured provides more (albeit not substantially more) consideration than the insurer.

3. The insured suffers losses exactly equal to $1,500 during the policy period. In this situation, both the insurer and insured provide the same consideration.

4. The insured suffers losses of more than $1,500 during the policy period. Here, the insurer provides more consideration than the insured.

It is impossible to predict which of the four possible situations will occur, but it is highly unlikely that the tangible amounts exchanged between the insurer and insured will be equal. The four situations consider only the exchange of tangible values—the premium paid by the insured and the recovery of losses paid by the insurer (if any)—not the intangible value of the insurance promise. It is difficult to explicitly value the reduction in volatility of losses and the reduction in the maximum amount at risk that insurance policies provide for an insured because they vary based on the insured's level of risk aversion. However, when both the tangible and intangible values are jointly considered, the values exchanged between the insurer and the insured are closer in value.

Although the tangible values exchanged between an insurer and insured may not be equal, in general they are equitable—that is, the premium the insurer charges the insured is directly proportional to the insured's expected losses on an actuarially sound basis. This is often called the equitable distribution of risk costs. That is, the insured's premium should be commensurate with the risk it presents to the insurer. By charging the appropriate premium, the insurer can ensure that the tangible consideration offered by the insured is equitable compared with the intangible consideration offered by the insurer.

Equitable Distribution of Risk

Insurance achieves an equitable distribution of risk costs in various ways, including the following:

- Rating plans—Actuaries typically develop complex rating systems that project expected loss costs and expenses for each insurance policy so that the insurers can charge premiums commensurate with the insured's loss exposures, as well as with the insurer's projected expenses.

- Coinsurance—The purpose of coinsurance (a policy with a limit that is some percentage of the property value being insured) is to provide an incentive for people to avoid a penalty by purchasing amounts of insurance that reflect their loss exposures.

- Subrogation—Through subrogation (recovery of insurance claim payments from negligent third party who caused the loss), loss costs are ultimately allocated to the party responsible for the loss.

However, other forces can affect actuarial equity. These include the following:

- Insurance regulation—Most insurance regulators must approve many of the rates charged by insurers. Such rate approval can sometimes affect the free-market economic forces intended to match insurance premiums with insured loss exposures.

- Social equity—Social equity is a system to redistribute wealth. Under the concept of social equity, good drivers subsidize the cost of insurance for bad drivers; owners of "safe" property subsidize the owners of "high-hazard" property.

- No-fault insurance—No-fault laws assign the costs of auto-related injuries to the insurer of the party who is injured, not the at-fault party. Although this results in an inequitable distribution of loss costs, it can also eliminate the substantial expenses otherwise involved in determining which party was at fault in any given accident. The no-fault concept violates the fundamental assumption that losses should be charged to the party who causes them. Nevertheless, the no-fault approach is supported in a number of states because it serves other goals, such as reducing the number of claims that are resolved through litigation.

Therefore, although insurers generally strive for the equitable distribution of risk costs in theory, certain forces work against it in practice.

Finite risk insurance policies involve an exchange of amounts closer in value than other types of policies, because their premiums are often close to the present value of the limit stated on the policy. Finite risk insurance involves little or no actual risk transfer and often functions as a loan.

Conditional

Insurance policies are conditional contracts. A **conditional contract** is a contract that one or more parties must perform only under certain conditions. Insurance policies are conditional contracts because the insurer is obligated to pay for losses incurred by the insured only if the insured has fulfilled all of the policy conditions. For example, under a property insurance policy, an insured must allow the insurer to inspect the damaged property after a covered cause of loss, such as a fire. The insurer is not obligated to fulfill the insurance policy (pay for any covered losses) unless the insured meets this condition. If the property is not available for inspection, the insurer has the right to deny the claim because the insurer was unable to verify that the loss actually occurred. Policy conditions are discussed in greater detail in subsequent chapters.

The most common exception to "the conditional nature of an insurance policy" is when the insurer is willing to waive some of the conditions of the insurance policy. This often occurs in practice. For example, an insurer may be willing to pay a claim without making an inspection, thereby waiving the condition that the insured make damaged property available for inspection.

Conditional contract
A contract that one or more parties must perform only under certain conditions.

Nontransferable

Insurance policies are sometimes referred to as "personal contracts" to indicate their nontransferable or nonassignable nature. An insurance policy is a contract between two parties; the insured cannot assign (transfer) the policy to a third party without the insurer's written consent.

For example, although property, such as a residence or a business, can be sold to a third party, the insurance policy that covers the property cannot be sold with it unless the insurer approves the transfer in writing. Exhibit 10-1 contains the policy wording under the common policy conditions of the commercial package policy that requires the insurer's written consent to transfer a policy. These policy conditions apply to all the optional coverage forms (including commercial property and commercial general liability) available under the commercial package policy. Similar wording appears in both the personal auto policy and homeowners insurance policies.

In most standard insurance policies, the assignment or nontransfer clause prevents the *insured* from transferring the insurance policy to a third party without the insured's written consent. However, no clause prevents the *insurer* from transferring or assigning the policy to a third party without the insured's written consent. Insurers frequently transfer policies to other insurers. Insureds are notified of the transfer or assignment, but their written approval is not required. For example, if an insurer wants to exit from a line of business or geographic area, the insurer can sell its entire portfolio for that business or area to another insurer. Alternatively, an insurer can transfer all of its business if it is acquired by another insurer, or a state regulator can assign insurance policies from an insolvent insurer to other insurers that are licensed in that state.

EXHIBIT 10-1

Insurance Policy Transfer Wording

Common Policy Conditions, Commercial Property

F. Transfer of Your Rights and Duties Under This Policy

Your rights and duties under this policy may not be transferred without our written consent except in the case of death of an individual named insured.

If you die, your rights and duties will be transferred to your legal representative but only while acting within the scope of duties as your legal representative. Until your legal representative is appointed, anyone having proper temporary custody of your property will have your rights and duties but only with respect to that property.

Includes copyrighted material of Insurance Services Office, Inc., with its permission. Copyright, ISO Properties, Inc., 1998.

If insureds are not receptive to the transfer or assignment by the insurer, they essentially have two choices. First, they may cancel their policies and purchase policies from other insurers. Second, they may pursue claims through the courts based on the notion that the consideration offered by the transferee (new insurer) is lower than the consideration offered by the transferor (original insurer). In essence, the insured would be claiming that the transferee's claim-paying ability is not equal to the transferor's. However, typically the consideration offered by the new insurer is equal to or greater than that of the original insured, improving the insured's position. When a policy is transferred from an insolvent insurer, insureds' coverage is more secure.

Maritime policies (insurance policies covering sea-going vessels) include exceptions to the nontransferable clause for when a change in ownership occurs while the ship is at sea. For example, assume a cargo ship is at sea when its owner sells the ship to another company. The insurance policy covering the ship would remain in force for the new owner without the written consent of the insurer. This exception to the nontransferable clause is designed to ensure that coverage remains in force, given that the change in ownership would have little or no effect on the risk of loss to the ship and cargo while at sea. Once the ship reaches port, the new owner must transfer the policy or apply for new insurance.

Some of these distinguishing characteristics of insurance policies can give rise to coverage disputes between the insurer and insured. If disputes do arise, mechanisms exist to help resolve them.

RESOLVING COVERAGE DISPUTES

Disputes between an insurer and insured can arise when it is unclear if coverage applies to a particular claim. Resolving coverage disputes can be expensive for both parties and lead to strained relationships between insurers and insureds. Although a variety of policy provisions are designed to reduce the frequency of coverage disputes, they do arise regularly. Coverage disputes can arise from disagreement over the facts of the case, the interpretation of the insurance policy, the actions or inactions of the insurer or insured, or applications of waiver and estoppel. If an insurer is found to be in breach of contract, to be in breach of fair claims settlement practices, or to have acted in bad faith, then a court may order the insurer to pay damages.

When coverage disputes arise, courts may be called upon to consider whether the dispute concerns questions of coverage or questions of liability. In addition, questions of law and questions of fact may need to be considered either by a judge alone, or by a judge and jury, depending on the nature of the dispute.

Generally, courts resolve questions about the following four types of insurance-related issues that are not necessarily addressed by insurance policy language:

1. Questions of liability
2. Questions of coverage
3. Questions of law
4. Questions of fact

Questions of Liability and Questions of Coverage

Questions of liability and questions of coverage can easily be confused. Courts often must resolve these questions as follows:

- *Questions of liability.* For liability claims, the courts can apply the law to determine if the *insured* is legally obligated to pay damages to a third party.
- *Questions of coverage.* For both property and liability claims, the courts can apply the law to interpret the insurance policy and to determine whether the *insurer* is obligated to pay the claim to, or on behalf of, the insured and, if so, to what extent.

The insurer's liability to pay damages to, or on behalf of, the insured can involve both questions of liability and questions of coverage. Not only does the insurer's liability to pay depend on the interpretation of the insurance policy, it also may depend on the insured's liability to pay damages to an injured third party. As an example, assume a commercial tenant, Sean, operated a restaurant in a rented building. A fire originated in the original wiring inside the building's walls, damaging the restaurant. Sean immediately notified his insurer under his commercial general liability policy, which included liability coverage for "damage by fire to property rented to you." A claim representative explained to Sean that he was not liable to anyone for the fire damage because he was not responsible for the wiring.

Suppose the landlord's property insurer sued Sean to recover the cost of repairing fire damage to the building, claiming that the fire occurred as a result of Sean's negligence. Sean's insurer would defend him and attempt to prove that he was not liable for the damage. If the court found Sean liable for damages, then Sean's insurer would pay the claim unless another basis existed for holding that the claim was not covered.

Questions of coverage arise frequently. A tool used by insurers and insureds to help resolve questions of coverage is a declaratory judgment action. A **declaratory judgment action** is a legal action in which the insurer (or insured) presents a coverage question to the court and asks the court to declare the rights of the parties under the applicable insurance policy. A declaratory judgment action resolves questions of coverage rather than questions of liability. The action could involve questions about whether there has been an "occurrence," whether a given exclusion applies, or whether the insurer has an obligation to defend the insured against a specific set of allegations.

Declaratory judgment action
A legal action in which the insurer (or insured) presents a coverage question to the court and asks the court to declare the rights of the parties under the applicable insurance policy.

Declaratory judgment actions are particularly useful when an insurer faces a substantial third-party claim involving a coverage question. If handled promptly, a declaratory judgment provides a decision on the coverage issue before the question of liability is litigated. If the court declares that coverage applies, the insurer can decide how best to fulfill its obligations. If the court declares the insurer has no duty under the policy, the insurer may close the claim. The defendant must then arrange his or her own defense.

Declaratory Judgment Action Regarding an Ambiguity

Excluded Watercraft in HO Policy Includes Jet Ski [3]

James McGinnis was killed when a jet ski operated by seventeen-year-old Jeremy Wittekind collided with a jet ski on which James was a passenger. Jeremy's parents, Roger and Jane Wittekind, had a homeowners policy issued by Nationwide; however, it excluded bodily injury arising out of a watercraft owned by or rented to an insured if the watercraft had inboard or inboard-outdrive motor power of more than 50 horsepower (HP). In this case, both jet skis had 60 HP power plants.

Nationwide filed an action for a declaratory judgment to determine its liability, if any, to the insureds arising out of James's death. The trial court granted Nationwide's motion that it was an excluded injury based on the policy exclusion.

The insureds appealed, contending that the term "watercraft" was ambiguous and should have been construed in their favor. The higher court stated that the accepted meaning of the word is a "vessel used on water." It said that the term was not ambiguous simply because it included all boats, ships, and other vessels that travel on water. In this case, the policy excluded liability arising out of the insured's use of a "watercraft" and, therefore, excluded the use of a personal watercraft.

The appeals court affirmed the summary judgment entered in the trial court in favor of Nationwide.

Questions of Law and Questions of Fact

Court decisions apply the law to the facts. In cases with no jury, the trial judge determines the law, finds facts, and applies the law to the facts. In jury trials, the jury hears the evidence and decides the facts, and the judge decides all questions of law. Judges do not make factual determinations in jury trial cases, and juries do not answer legal questions.

A question of law in a negligence case might be whether a defendant owed a plaintiff any duty. A question of fact in the same case might be whether the plaintiff suffered any harm. In a property insurance case with a valued policy, a question of law might involve the issue of whether any laws govern valued policies. A question of fact in the same case might involve the cash value of the damaged or destroyed property.

Waiver and Estoppel

The issues of waiver and estoppel are prominent in insurance policy coverage disputes. They usually arise when an insured sues for payment of damages under the policy and the insurer denies the claim based on a defense such as fraud, misrepresentation, concealment, mistake, or breach of a condition. In turn, the insured argues that the insurer has forfeited or is prevented from asserting the defense by one of the following:

- Waiver of the defense
- Estoppel from asserting the defense

Waiver is the intentional relinquishment of a known right. A waiver can be expressed or implied, depending on the circumstances. In insurance, waiver means that an insurer's conduct has the legal effect of surrendering its option to defend a lawsuit. For example, a homeowner makes a claim for water damage to the contents of his basement. The adjuster instructs the homeowner to make a list of the damaged items, then to dispose of them. Under these circumstances, the adjuster's instructions resulted in a knowing waiver of the insurer's right to inspect the contents. The insurer cannot later deny the claim on the basis that the insured failed to make the contents available for inspection.

Waiver
The intentional relinquishment of a known right.

Estoppel is a legal principle that prohibits a party from asserting a claim or right that is inconsistent with that party's past statement or conduct on which another party has detrimentally relied. In other words, estoppel bars a person from asserting a claim or right that contradicts what that person has said or done previously. Estoppel generally arises in insurance law from the following sequence of events:

Estoppel
A legal principle that prohibits a party from asserting a claim or right that is inconsistent with that party's past statement or conduct on which another party has detrimentally relied.

1. The insurer falsely represents a material fact.
2. The insured assumes a reasonable reliance on the representation.
3. The insured suffers resulting injury or detriment.

For example, an insurer issues a fire insurance policy on a building on leased land, a fact the insured disclosed on the application. The agent delivers the policy to the insured, saying, "Here is the policy, and it fully covers your building." However, the policy expressly provides that it is void if the building insured is located on leased land. The insured accepts the policy without reading it. When the building later burns, the insurer denies the claim.

All the elements leading to estoppel are present in this case. The insurer, through its agent, made a false representation by stating that the policy covered the building. The insured reasonably relied on the representation by accepting the policy and not purchasing other insurance. The insured's failure to read the policy does not mean reliance is unreasonable. Denying coverage would harm the insured, who would have no insurance coverage. The insurer is prevented, or estopped, from denying coverage. No waiver is effective because the insurer did not intend to give up any right under the policy.

Waiver and Estoppel Example

One of an insured's duties is to report a loss promptly. This notice should include how, when, and where the loss happened. The notice also should include any injured parties' and witnesses' names and addresses. The insured's failure to perform this obligation could result in a denial of coverage by the insurer.

Notification that the insured experienced a loss could come from anyone, not necessarily the insured, and is usually sufficient for the claim department to create a file and begin an investigation. Assuming the insurer accepts such notice without issuing a reservation of rights letter (discussed subsequently) to the insured, the insurer has waived its right to deny coverage at a later date on the basis that the insured has failed to fulfill the obligation to report the loss fully. As a result of this waiver, the insurer would be estopped from asserting a coverage denial based on the insured's failure to fulfill the notice obligation.

The insurer has accepted whatever notice was given and begins an investigation without a reservation of rights letter. The insured relies on the assumption that the insurer will fulfill its contractual obligation to indemnify and defend the insured. The insurer's refusal to indemnify and defend based on insufficient notice would put the insured in a detrimental position. The insured would not have a chance to investigate the loss or preserve evidence. Therefore, the insurer would be estopped from denying coverage based on the insured's failure to meet the specific requirements of proper notification.

Courts resolving coverage disputes involving waiver or estoppel may decide questions of coverage, law, or fact.

Insurer's Alternatives When a Property Claim Is Filed

When an insured files a claim with the insurer under a property insurance policy, the insurer may pursue one of the following three alternatives, any of which can lead to coverage disputes:

1. Deny the claim with appropriate justification—justified refusal
2. Investigate the claim under a reservation of rights letter, nonwaiver agreement, or both—preserving the insurer's rights
3. Investigate and/or pay the claim without any reservation

The insurer's denial of a claim is justified if the policy does not cover the claim. Court opinions generally agree that an insurer who justifiably denies a claim has not breached the policy. The insurer has no obligation under the policy concerning any claim arising out of a noncovered loss. Most justified refusals of property insurance claims involve causes of loss that are excluded. An insurer's justified refusal can lead to coverage disputes if the insured disagrees with the insurer's rationale for the denial. For example, an insurer may deny a homeowner's claim for damage caused by hurricane winds (a covered cause of loss) on the grounds that the damage resulted from storm surge (not a covered cause of loss). The insurer may believe that it acted appropriately in denying the claim; however, the insured disagrees. Resolving this type of coverage dispute could be a question of fact—the cause of the damage—left for the courts to decide.

When an insurer even implies that a loss is covered, it may be prohibited from disclaiming coverage later. Insurers use a reservation of rights letter to preserve their ability to disclaim coverage if the facts reveal that the policy does not cover the loss. A **reservation of rights letter** is a notice sent by an insurer advising the insured that the insurer is proceeding with a claim investigation but that the insurer retains the right to deny coverage later. A reservation of rights letter has the following two purposes:

1. To protect the insurer's right to subsequently deny coverage, if warranted, without facing the accusation that its previous actions waived that right
2. To inform the insured that a coverage problem might exist and give the insured an opportunity to protect its interests

To prevent bad-faith actions, discussed subsequently, the insurer should send a reservation of rights letter to the insured immediately upon identifying any potential problem that may cause the insurer to decide to deny the claim. The letter should be specific and concise, clearly stating the insurer's position and quoting pertinent policy language. Many claim representatives send reservation of rights letters by certified mail, return receipt requested, to verify the insured's receipt. A sample reservation of rights letter appears in Exhibit 10-2.

Reservation of rights letter
A notice sent by an insurer advising the insured that the insurer is proceeding with a claim investigation but that the insurer retains the right to deny coverage later.

EXHIBIT 10-2

Reservation of Rights Letter
Notice of Reservation of Rights

Date:

RE: Policyholder

Claimant

Date of Loss

Policy Number

We have received notice of an occurrence that took place at (location) on (date), for consideration under policy number _____, which was issued to (policyholder) by (insurance company). In order that the company may continue to handle this matter, we want you to know that we are proceeding under a reservation of rights. We are reserving our rights under the policy for the following reason(s):

(Specify reasons, identifying actual policy provisions.)

Our continued handling of this matter does not constitute an admission of any kind on our part. No act of any company representative while investigating, negotiating settlement of the claim, or defending a lawsuit shall be construed as waiving any company rights. The company reserves the right, under the policy, to deny coverage to you or anyone claiming coverage under the policy.

You may wish to discuss this matter with your own attorney. In any event, we would be pleased to answer any questions you have concerning our position as outlined in this letter.

Sincerely,   By

(INSURANCE COMPANY)   (FOR THE COMPANY)

A reservation of rights letter implies a conflict between the insured's interests and the insurer's interests that can lead to coverage disputes. Although the insurer must defend the insured as long as it is handling the case, the insurer may at any time deny coverage and cease handling the case. The insured who receives a reservation of rights letter often hires its own legal counsel to protect its interest.

Nonwaiver agreement
A written contract in which the insured and the insurer agree that neither will waive any of its rights under the policy as a result of the investigation or defense of a lawsuit against the insured.

If an insurer does uncover a problem when investigating a claim, then, before issuing a reservation of rights letter, it may approach the insured about entering into a nonwaiver agreement. A **nonwaiver agreement** is a written contract in which the insured and the insurer agree that neither will waive any of its rights under the policy as a result of the investigation or defense of a lawsuit against the insured. The contract is bilateral in that both parties make promises and requires the signatures of both parties. If the insured is unwilling to enter into a nonwaiver agreement, a reservation of rights letter may be sent. A reservation of rights letter differs from a nonwaiver in that the notice is unilateral, usually in the form of an insurer's letter to an insured.

Resolving coverage disputes that include reservation of rights letters or non-waiver agreements could involve court decisions regarding misrepresentation of material facts, fraud, or other potential problems that the insured discovered during the claims investigation.

Even an insurer's paying a claim without reservation can lead to coverage disputes if the insured and insurer cannot agree on the settlement value. For example, an insurer and insured may disagree on the value of a building or item of personal property. When these types of coverage disputes arise, policy provisions regarding appraisal or arbitration, discussed in subsequent chapters, can aid in resolving the dispute.

Insurer's Alternatives When a Liability Claim Is Filed

A liability insurance policy contains more than the insurer's agreement to pay damages on the insured's behalf; it also includes the insurer's duty to defend the insured. As part of the duty to defend, the insurer agrees to pay the costs of defending the insured and often contributes substantial experience and expertise to the defense process. Many insurance buyers consider the insurer's defense services to be one of the most important reasons to buy liability insurance.

With liability insurance policies, the insurer's alternatives when faced with a claim are similar to those available under property insurance contract: (1) justified refusal, (2) preserving the insurer's rights with a reservation of rights letter and/or nonwaiver agreement, or (3) investigate and/or defend the claim.

Similar to property insurance contracts, the insurer may be justified in refusing to defend the insured because the claim is not covered by the contract. If there is some question about whether the claim is covered, the insurer may preserve its rights by entering into a nonwaiver agreement with the insured or issuing a reservation of rights letter. If the insurer decides to investigate or defend the insured without reservation, the insurer is assuming its duty to defend as outlined in the liability insurance contract.

Courts have consistently held that the liability insurer's duty to defend is broader than its duty to pay damages. Even if a lawsuit appears to be groundless, false, or fraudulent, the insurer must defend an insured whenever the plaintiff alleges damages that could conceivably be covered by the policy. Even if only a single allegation among many would be covered, in most states the insurer is obligated to defend the insured.

Although the insurer's defense obligation is theoretically unlimited, practical constraints apply. Most policies give the insurer the exclusive right to control the defense. The insurer can select its own defense counsel, monitor the case, and attempt to negotiate a settlement if costs threaten to become disproportionately high.

The benefits of a sound legal defense stemming from the duty to defend include the following:

- Often a strong defense results in a judgment favoring the insured and consequently neither the insurer nor the insured are required to pay damages.
- A legal decision in the insured's favor may establish case law that discourages similar claims.
- A strong defense signals plaintiffs' attorneys and would-be claimants that the insurer will vigorously defend similar claims rather than pay them.
- The amount of damages payable can be substantially reduced because of evidence introduced through a sound, if costly, defense.

However, an insurer's duty to defend can also result in coverage disputes. For example, consider a doctor that is sued for malpractice by a former patient. The doctor may be concerned about her reputation and unwilling to settle with the plaintiff. She may want to let the courts decide whether malpractice has been committed. However, the defense counsel chosen by the insurer may want to settle the case because the defense costs of continuing the case would be greater than the amount the plaintiff is requesting. Policy provisions typically resolve this type of dispute. The liability insurer usually has control of the defense and has a right to settle the case without the insured's consent.

Damages or Other Penalties Assessed Against the Insurer

Any payment the insurer must make is directly associated with its obligations under an insurance contract, as determined or enforced by the courts, if necessary. If an insurer is found to have mishandled a claim, it may be subject to additional payments, such as compensatory damages for breach of contract, fines or penalties assessed by regulatory authorities for violations of Unfair Claims Settlement Practices Acts, or punitive damages for bad faith.

Compensatory Damages for Breach of Contract

An insurer that has breached its contract with the insured might be required to pay compensatory damages. A general rule of contract law permits the recovery of compensatory damages for breach of an implied covenant of good faith and fair dealing (that is, a covenant that is not expressly stated in the policy). Both the insurer and the insured are subject to this implied covenant. The insured, for example, owes a duty to the insurer to provide truthful underwriting and claim information, and the insurer has an obligation to be fair and reasonable in handling claims.

In many cases, an insured can show that the insurer's breach of the contract caused a definite financial loss. Suppose, for example, the insurer fails to pay a valid $500,000 property insurance claim when business property is destroyed, and the business fails as a result. The businessowner may convince the court that, as a direct result of the insurer's failure to fulfill its obligations, the insured lost not only the $500,000 value of the building, but also $2 million the business would have earned if insurance proceeds had permitted prompt reconstruction of the building. In such situations, courts sometimes award damages that far exceed the limits of the original policy. The goal of this type of lawsuit is not to enforce the coverage provided by the insurance contract itself, but rather to seek damages for the breach of the insurance contract created by the insurer's failure to pay the claim.

Penalties Under Unfair Claims Settlement Practices Acts

Each state has adopted some version of the National Association of Insurance Commissions (NAIC) Model Regulation on Unfair Claims Settlement Practices. These adaptations are usually referred to as "unfair claims settlement practices acts." The acts are designed to define a minimum set of standards by which insurers are to abide during claim settlements. Many aspects of claim handling are addressed, including insurers' responsibility for prompt communications with their insureds, adequate investigation, detailed explanations of coverage denials, and so on. Generally, these acts require that insurers handle claims promptly, which requires timely investigation and evaluation, and, where warranted, swift settlement.

Frequent violations of these minimum requirements may constitute a violation of the act. An insurer that violates an unfair claim settlement practices act might be fined or sanctioned by the state. Unfair claim settlement practices acts are not intended to change coverage, exclusions, or loss settlement provisions in insurance policies. However, a state insurance department can assess penalties and sanctions against an insurer that is found to have violated a provision of an unfair claim practices act with such frequency as to indicate a general business practice. If an insurer has been found in violation of the acts, the claimant can also bring a separate tort action against the insurer alleging bad faith. In some cases, the results of the unfair claim settlement practices proceeding can be used as evidence in the insured's bad-faith action. Possible penalties and sanctions include the following:

- Fines
- Interest on an overdue claim payment
- Payment of other fees and costs
- Injunctions or cease-and-desist orders
- Suspension of a claim representative's or an insurer's license
- Revocation of a claim representative's or an insurer's license

If insurers have been penalized or sanctioned, they usually take corrective action to prevent further violations. Insurers pay fines to the state department of insurance, not to the policyholder. Suspension and revocation of licenses are extreme measures, usually imposed only after other penalties have proven ineffective.

Punitive Damages for Bad Faith

In addition to the breach of contract compensatory damages just discussed, punitive damages can also be awarded against an insurer for acting in bad faith. Bad-faith claims are often generated by an insurer wrongfully denying a claim. However, delaying a claim investigation or payment, improper investigation of a claim, misrepresenting material facts, and many other improper behaviors by an insurer can provide a basis for an insured's bad-faith claim. The threat of punitive damages awards in bad-faith claims can serve to discourage insurers from any action that even appears to involve bad faith. In some states, only a policyholder can bring a bad-faith claim (a first-party claim) against an insurer. In other states, many parties including policyholders, claimants, and excess insurers can bring bad-faith claims (both first- and third-party claims) against insurers. Although these types of claims may seem to be extreme solutions to coverage disputes, they are influential in insurance markets. For example, the Government Accounting Office Report on Medical Malpractice Insurance reports that bad-faith claims are an issue that is affecting medical malpractice insurance premiums in three of the four states studied.[4]

SUMMARY

The distinguishing characteristics of insurance policies are as follows:

- Indemnity—Insurance policies should compensate the insured for the value of the loss but should not provide a benefit greater than the loss.

- Utmost good faith—Utmost good faith is an obligation to act with complete honesty and to disclose all relevant facts.

- Fortuitous losses—The covered loss should be fortuitous from the insured's standpoint.

- Contract of adhesion—Most policies are contracts of adhesion, that is, contracts to which one party must adhere as written by the other party. Any ambiguities or uncertainties are interpreted in the insured's favor.

- Exchange of unequal amounts—There is no requirement that the amounts being exchanged in an insurance transaction are equal in value.

- Conditional—Insurance policies are conditional contracts because the insurer is obligated to pay for losses incurred by the insured only if the insured has fulfilled all of the policy conditions.

- Nontransferable—An insurance policy is a contract between two parties; the insured cannot assign (transfer) the policy to a third party without the insurer's written consent.

Coverage disputes arise when the insurer and insured do not agree on some aspect of the coverage provided by the insurance policy. These coverage disputes can be resolved by policy provisions but also may involve the courts. Generally, courts resolve questions about four types of insurance-related issues that are not necessarily resolved by insurance policy language: (1) questions of liability, (2) questions of coverage, (3) questions of law, and (4) questions of fact. For questions of liability, the courts determine if the *insured* is legally obligated to pay damages to a third party. For questions of coverage, the courts determine whether the *insurer* is obligated to pay the claim to, or on behalf of, the insured and, if so, to what extent.

In cases with no jury, the trial judge determines questions of both law and fact. In jury trials, the jury decides the facts and the judge decides all questions of law. A question of law might be whether a defendant owed a plaintiff any duty or whether a particular statute applies. A question of fact might entail deciding whether the policyholder suffered any harm or determining the cash value of damaged or destroyed property.

Waiver and estoppel may also lead to coverage disputes. In insurance, waiver means that an insurer's conduct has the legal effect of giving up a defense to a lawsuit. Estoppel generally arises in insurance law from the following sequence of events: (1) false representation of a material fact, (2) reasonable reliance on the representation, and (3) resulting injury or detriment to the insured.

When an insured files a claim with the insurer under a property insurance policy, the insurer has the following three alternatives: (1) deny the claim with appropriate justification—justified refusal, (2) investigate the claim under a reservation of rights letter, nonwaiver agreement, or both—preserving the insurer's rights, or (3) investigate and/or pay the claim without any reservation, all of which can lead to coverage disputes. Insurers use reservation of rights letters and nonwaiver agreements to preserve their ability to disclaim coverage if the facts reveal that there should be no coverage under the policy. A nonwaiver agreement is a written contract in which the insured and the insurer agree that neither will waive any of its rights under the policy as a result of the investigation or defense of a lawsuit against the insured.

A liability insurance policy contains more than the insurer's agreement to pay damages on the insured's behalf; it also includes the insurer's duty to defend the insured, which can lead to coverage disputes. As part of the duty to defend, the insurer agrees to pay the costs of defending the insured, and the insurer often contributes substantial experience and expertise to the defense process. With liability insurance policies, the insurer's alternatives when faced with a claim are similar to those available under property insurance contract: (1) justified refusal, (2) preserving the insurer's rights with a reservation of rights letter and/or nonwaiver agreement, or (3) investigate and/or defend the claim. Courts have consistently held that the liability insurer's duty to defend is broader than its duty to pay damages.

If an insurer is found to have mishandled a claim, it may be subject to additional payments such as compensatory damages for breach of contract, fines or penalties assessed by regulatory authorities for violations of unfair claims settlement practices acts, or punitive damages for bad faith.

Additional possible penalties and sanctions include interest on an overdue claim payment, payment of other fees and costs, injunctions or cease-and-desist orders, suspension of a claim representative's or an insurer's license, or revocation of a claim representative's or an insurer's license.

CHAPTER NOTES

1. Insurance Research Council, *Fraud and Buildup in Auto Injury Insurance Claims* (Malvern, Pa., Insurance Research Council, 2004), p. 7.

2. Includes copyrighted material of Insurance Services Office, Inc., with its permission. Copyright, ISO Properties, Inc., 1999.

3. *Nationwide Mutual Fire Insurance Company v. Wittekind et al.*, Ohio Ct. App., 4th Dist. 730 NE. 2d. 1054 (1999). *Source*: "Court Decisions." From case reports published in the *North Eastern Reporter 2d*, St. Paul, Minn.: West Publishing Co., and *Rough Notes*, April 2001, p. 8.

4. Government Accounting Office Web site, www.gao.gov/new.items/d03702.pdf (accessed March 30, 2006).

Direct Your Learning

Insurance Policy Analysis

After learning the content of this chapter and completing the corresponding course guide assignment, you should be able to:

- Explain how the physical construction of an insurance policy influences policy analysis.

- Given an insurance coverage case, explain how common policy provisions affect the coverage provided and the actions taken by the insured or insurer.

  - Describe the contents and purpose of the six categories of policy provisions of a property-casualty insurance policy.

  - Explain the six reasons that policies contain exclusions.

- Differentiate between pre-loss and post-loss policy analysis.

- Define or describe each of the Key Words and Phrases for this chapter.

Develop Your Perspective

What are the main topics covered in the chapter?

All insurance policies contain a relatively standard physical structure—typically they are a collection of various preprinted forms. Common provisions within these policies include declarations, definitions, insuring agreements, conditions, exclusions, and other miscellaneous provisions. Understanding these provisions enables an insured or insurance professional to analyze a policy, either pre-loss or post-loss.

Identify policy provisions that differ between a self-contained policy and a modular policy.

- Why do the provisions differ?

- Why might an insurer choose one type of policy over the other?

Why is it important to learn about these topics?

Knowing how to read and interpret an insurance policy is a fundamental skill for insurance professionals. This skill can be applied to a wide range of insurance policies, and it enables the insurance professional to determine whether a particular loss would be covered under the policy's terms and, if covered, the amount that would be payable.

Consider how you would approach a policy that you had never seen before.

- Why would determining the physical construction of the insurance policy be your first step?

- Why would you identify the various sections of the policy?

- What information would you look for in each of the policy sections?

How can you use what you will learn?

Analyze an auto insurance policy to determine whether a loss is covered.

- What information about the loss must you determine to be able to analyze the policy?

- Which policy provisions are most relevant in determining whether the loss is covered?

Chapter 11
Insurance Policy Analysis

An insurance policy communicates the details of a binding agreement between the insurer and the insured. All insurance policies have a relatively standard physical structure and typically consist of a collection of various preprinted forms. Although insurers have tried to improve the readability of these policies, they remain complex legal documents that may vary widely. There are many different lines of insurance, such as property insurance, liability insurance, life insurance, health insurance, and disability insurance and many different policies within each line. Each policy is designed to provide a certain type of insurance and contains provisions that can be grouped into six categories: declarations, definitions, insuring agreements, conditions, exclusions, and miscellaneous provisions. Insurance professionals must be able to read and interpret these provisions, either pre-loss or post-loss, in order to understand how the policy provisions grant, clarify, qualify, or eliminate insurance coverage.

PHYSICAL CONSTRUCTION OF INSURANCE POLICIES

An insurance policy is made up of one or more forms. A form is simply a physical document within an insurance policy. In some cases, one form, combined with a declarations page (discussed subsequently), constitutes the entire insurance policy. In other cases, multiple forms are combined with a declarations page to form the policy. In addition to the forms physically present in the insurance policy, other components (related documents) that are attached to, or incorporated by reference in, the policy become part of the policy. For example, if a workers' compensation insurance policy makes reference to a state-mandated schedule of benefits, that schedule becomes part of the insurance policy.

An insurance policy can provide insurance coverage for one or more different lines of insurance. A **monoline policy** is an insurance policy that covers a single type of insurance. A **package policy**, also called a multiline policy, is an insurance policy that covers more than one type of insurance. For example, a commercial package policy may cover property, liability, and crime insurance. Commercial package policies often contain multiple coverage parts. A **coverage part** is one or more forms that together provide coverage for a line of insurance. The term "coverage part" should not be confused with the use of the term "part" to describe a section of a policy form that provides a particular coverage. For example, the

Monoline policy
An insurance policy that covers a single type of insurance.

Package policy
An insurance policy that covers more than one type of insurance.

Coverage part
One or more forms that together provide coverage for a line of insurance.

liability section of the Insurance Services Office (ISO) Personal Auto Policy is captioned "Part A – Liability Coverage." In this example, "Part" is used as a section heading, rather than as a reference to a coverage part.

Self-Contained and Modular Policies

Self-contained policy
A single document that contains all the agreements between the insured and the insurer and that forms a complete insurance policy.

A **self-contained policy** is a single document that contains all the agreements between the insured and the insurer and that forms a complete insurance policy. This document identifies the insurer and the insured and details the amounts, terms, and conditions of coverage. Endorsements can be added to a self-contained policy to provide additional, optional coverages or to exclude unnecessary coverages. An endorsement is a document that amends an insurance policy.

A self-contained policy is appropriate for insuring loss exposures that are similar among many insureds. For example, private passenger auto insurance is typically provided in a self-contained policy (such as the ISO Personal Auto Policy). Such a policy is used for each of an insurer's individual auto policyholders throughout a state—and potentially in several different states. Endorsements, such as the Towing and Labor Costs Coverage endorsement or the Customizing Equipment Coverage endorsement, can be added as needed.

Modular policy
An insurance policy that consists of several different documents, none of which by itself forms a complete policy.

A **modular policy** is an insurance policy that consists of several different documents, none of which by itself forms a complete policy. The policy is designed around one basic policy component (such as a "policy jacket") and is created by combining a set of individual components. The policy jacket of a modular policy often includes common policy conditions, definitions, or other provisions that apply to all other policy components used with it.

The modular approach is often used in commercial insurance because the insured's loss exposures are typically unique and require more customization of the insurance policy than other lines of insurance. Exhibit 11-1 illustrates the structure of an ISO commercial package policy. Every ISO commercial package policy contains common policy conditions and common declarations. If only one line of insurance is covered (that is, it is a monoline policy), the policy is completed by adding the necessary forms to constitute that coverage part. For example, if the policy provides commercial property insurance, the commercial property coverage part includes a commercial property declarations page, the necessary commercial property coverage forms, a causes of loss form, and a commercial property conditions form. These forms, in combination with the common policy conditions and common declarations, would complete the insurance policy.

An advantage of the modular approach is that a single policy can include several lines of insurance. The resulting combination is then a package policy, rather than a monoline policy. The commercial package policy referred to in Exhibit 11-1 is flexible enough to cover the majority of loss exposures faced by most organizations.

The various coverages shown in Exhibit 11-1 do not have to be combined in a single commercial package policy. Similar coverage could be provided with separate self-contained commercial property policies, commercial general liability policies, crime policies, and so on. The insured has the option of purchasing multiple, stand-alone policies or a single commercial package policy to cover the same loss exposures. However, relative to self-contained policies, the modular approach to policy construction has the following advantages:

- Carefully designed and coordinated provisions in the various forms minimize the possibility of gaps and overlaps that might exist when several monoline policies are used.
- Consistent terminology, definitions, and policy language make coverage interpretation easier for the insured.
- Fewer forms are required to meet a wide range of needs.
- Underwriting is simplified because much of the basic information that must be analyzed applies to all lines of insurance.
- Adverse selection problems can be reduced when the same insurer provides several lines of insurance for an individual insured.
- Insurers often give a package discount when several coverages are included in the same policy.

Minimal coverage gaps, consistent terminology, and fewer forms are important advantages to insurance professionals conducting policy analysis. Although analyzing a single self-contained policy may be straightforward, most organizations are protected by more than one self-contained policy. Analyzing multiple self-contained policies is more difficult than analyzing a modular policy. The self-contained policies will often include multiple copies of related forms and endorsements, use inconsistent terminology, and have gaps and overlaps in coverage, all of which make policy analysis more difficult. Well-coordinated modular policies offer insurance professionals a better framework for policy analysis than multiple self-contained policies.

EXHIBIT 11-1

Components of the ISO Commercial Package Policy (CPP)

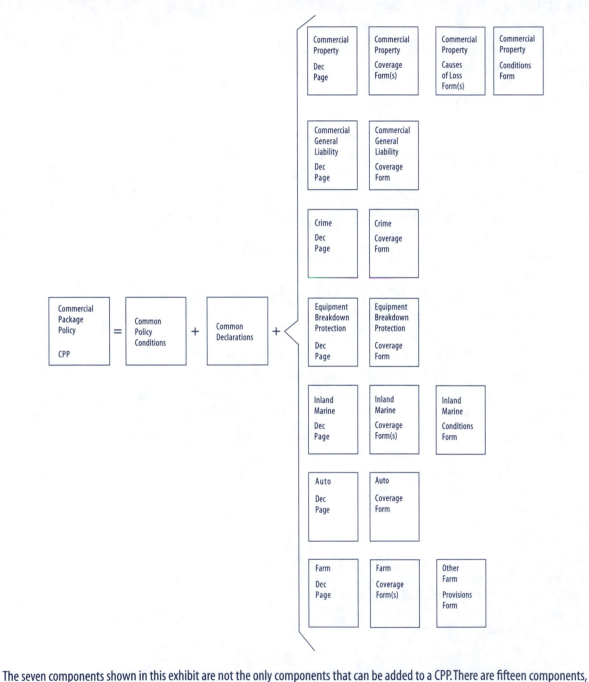

The seven components shown in this exhibit are not the only components that can be added to a CPP. There are fifteen components, including employment practices liability insurance, umbrella, capital assets, and management protection components, that can be included in the ISO CPP.

Preprinted Forms

Most insurance policies are assembled from one or more preprinted forms and endorsements. Preprinted forms are developed for use with many different insureds. Therefore, they refer to the insured in general terms (such as "the insured" or "you") so that the forms can be used in multiple insurance policies without customization. The declarations page then adds the specific information about the insured that customizes the insurance policy.

Using preprinted forms significantly reduces the paperwork necessary for an insurance policy. When the policy is issued, insurers send the insured the generic preprinted policy and the customized declarations page. The declarations page indicates the form number or numbers and edition dates of the insurer's form or forms that apply to the insurance policy. Exhibit 11-2 contains a sample homeowners insurance declarations page. The next-to-last line, "FORMS AND ENDORSEMENTS IN POLICY," specifies the particular preprinted policy forms and endorsements forms that make up the remainder of the policy. When insureds update (for example, change deductibles) or renew their policies, the insurer can simply send the insureds new declarations pages without having to resend entire new policies containing copies of the preprinted forms (provided the preprinted forms have not been changed).

Furthermore, if they are using preprinted forms, the insurer and its producer do not have to keep a complete duplicate of each insured's entire policy in their files. All that needs to be filed is the declarations page, either on paper or as an electronic file. Details of specific coverage can be obtained by examining copies of the preprinted forms referenced in the declarations page.

> ## Preprinted Forms as Electronic Forms
>
> Although they are still referred to as preprinted forms in the insurance industry, printing technology has reduced the need for producers and insurers to maintain a supply of actual preprinted forms. Producers and insurers can now quickly print the electronic copies of all the forms and endorsements as needed.

Standard Forms

An insurer may use the standard forms that are also used by other insurers, or it may develop its own nonstandard forms. A nonstandard form drafted or adapted by one insurer is sometimes called a company-specific or proprietary form.

Insurance service and advisory organizations, such as ISO and the American Association of Insurance Services (AAIS), have developed standard insurance forms for use by individual insurers. These standard forms are usually accompanied by a portfolio of coordinated endorsements that reflect necessary state variations or customize coverage. Because they are widely used, standard forms provide benchmarks against which nonstandard forms can be evaluated. Preprinted standard forms are typically the easiest forms for insurance professionals to evaluate during policy analysis. These forms are widely used and usually have been more consistently interpreted by the courts than other forms. Furthermore, most insurance professionals have more experience working with preprinted standard forms than most other forms, especially manuscript forms.

EXHIBIT 11-2

Example of Reference to Preprinted Policy Forms

Homeowners Policy Declarations

POLICYHOLDER:	David M. and Joan G. Smith	**POLICY NUMBER:**	296 H 578661
(Named Insured)	216 Brookside Drive		
	Anytown, USA 40000		

POLICY PERIOD: **Inception:** March 30, 2004   Policy period begins 12:01 A.M. standard time
                    Expiration: March 30, 2005   at the residence premises.

FIRST MORTGAGEE AND MAILING ADDRESS:

Federal National Mortgage Assn.
C/O Mortgagee, Inc.
P.O. Box 5000
Businesstown, USA 55000

We will provide the insurance described in this policy in return for the premium and compliance with all applicable policy provisions.

SECTION I COVERAGES	LIMIT	
A—Dwelling	$ 160,000	**SECTION I DEDUCTIBLE:** $ 250
B—Other Structures	$ 16,000	(In case of loss under Section I, we cover
C—Personal Property	$ 80,000	only that part of the loss over the
D—Loss of Use	$ 48,000	deductible amount shown above.)

SECTION II COVERAGES	LIMIT	
E—Personal Liability	$ 300,000	**Each Occurrence**
F—Medical Payments to Others	$ 1,000	**Each Person**

CONSTRUCTION: Masonry Veneer   **NO. FAMILIES:** One   **TYPE ROOF:** Approved

YEAR BUILT: 1990   **PROTECTION CLASS:** 7   **FIRE DISTRICT:** Cook Township

NOT MORE THAN 1000 FEET FROM HYDRANT

NOT MORE THAN 5 MILES FROM FIRE DEPT.

FORMS AND ENDORSEMENTS IN POLICY: HO 00 03, HO 04 61

POLICY PREMIUM: $ 480.00   **COUNTERSIGNATURE DATE:** March 30, 2004   **AGENT:** A.M. Abel

> ## ISO Form Numbers
>
> Exhibit 11-2, the Homeowners Policy Declarations, references two forms and endorsements in the policy: HO 00 03 and HO 04 61. The first form number refers to ISO's Homeowners 3—Special Form (ISO HO-3). The full ISO form number for this form is HO 00 03 05 01. This number includes the following elements:
>
> - HO is the line of insurance.
>
> - 00 is the form or category number.
>
> - 03 is the category identifier.
>
> - 05 01 extension refers to the effective month and year of the form.

Nonstandard Forms

Many insurers have developed their own company-specific preprinted forms, especially for high-volume lines of insurance (such as auto or homeowners) or for coverages in which the insurer specializes (such as recreational vehicle insurance). Nonstandard forms include provisions that vary from standard-form provisions and often contain coverage enhancements not found in standard forms.

Similar to the preprinted standard forms, preprinted nonstandard forms are easier for insurance professionals to evaluate during policy analysis than forms that are not preprinted. Although these preprinted forms are referred to as nonstandard, many of them are widely used by some of the largest insurers in the United States.

Both standard and nonstandard preprinted forms typically form contracts of adhesion. The wording of preprinted forms and endorsements is carefully chosen by the insurer (or developed by an advisory organization and then adopted by the insurer). Courts tend to interpret any ambiguities in policy language in favor of the insured, because the insured did not have an opportunity to choose the policy wording.

Manuscript Forms

In contrast to preprinted forms, manuscript forms are custom forms developed for one specific insured—or for a small group of insureds—with unique coverage needs. A **manuscript form** is an insurance form that is drafted according to terms negotiated between a specific insured (or group of insureds) and an insurer. If an insurance policy includes a manuscript form, it is often referred to as a manuscript policy. A manuscript form can be specifically drafted or selected for a particular need, such as products liability coverage for a manufacturer of a new type of explosives or property coverage on a unique building. Manuscript endorsements can also be used to customize insurance coverage.

Manuscript form
An insurance form that is drafted according to terms negotiated between a specific insured (or group of insureds) and an insurer.

Because the insurer and the insured develop policy language together, manuscript policies are not generally considered to be contracts of adhesion. Therefore, there is no preference in favor of the insured if the courts are called upon to interpret policy ambiguity.

Manuscript forms are the most difficult forms for insurance professionals to interpret during policy analysis. These forms, because they often contain unique wording, can vary widely in their interpretation. Manuscript forms will not have the same history of court interpretations for insurance professionals to rely on during policy analysis. This can lead to differences between how an insurance professional interprets a manuscript form and how the insured or courts will interpret the same form. Consequently, there can be substantial delays in claim adjusting or strained relations between the insurer and insured. To reduce the likelihood of such problems occurring, most manuscript forms are not individually composed but are adapted from wording previously developed and used in standard forms or other insurance policies.

Related Documents

Several other documents can become part of an insurance policy, either by being physically attached or by being referenced within the policy. Examples include the completed insurance application, endorsements, the insurer's bylaws, and the terms of relevant statutes.

An insurance application is the documented request for coverage, whether given orally, in writing, or electronically (for example, over the Internet). The application contains information about the insured and the loss exposures presented to the insurer. Underwriters use the information provided on the application to price the policy. Although the declarations page often contains much of the same information as the application, the insurer usually keeps the completed application to preserve the representations made by the insured. The application can be used, if necessary, to provide evidence of misleading or false material information supplied by the insured. In some jurisdictions, statutes explicitly require that any written application be made part of the policy for certain lines of insurance.

Endorsements, if added to the policy, form part of the policy. Terms that might be used instead of "endorsement" include "policy change," "addition," "amendment," and "codicil." Alternatively, an endorsement might have a descriptive title, such as "Loss Payable Clause." An endorsement may be a preprinted, computer-printed, typewritten, or handwritten line, sentence, paragraph, or set of paragraphs on a separate sheet of paper attached to other documents forming the policy. Although rare, an endorsement may also take the form of a handwritten note in the margin of a basic policy, form, or coverage part, and be dated and initialed by an insured and the insurer's authorized representative.

Because endorsements are usually intended to modify a basic policy form, the endorsement provisions often differ from basic policy provisions. This difference can lead to questions of policy interpretation. The following two general rules of policy interpretation apply to endorsements:

1. An endorsement takes precedence over any conflicting terms in the policy to which it is attached.

2. A handwritten endorsement supersedes a computer-printed or typewritten one. Handwritten alterations tend to reflect true intent more accurately than do preprinted policy terms.

In several lines of business, policies are issued with what many practitioners call "standard" endorsements included in the policy. These are endorsements that are included with most of the policies written in that line. Because they are so common, they essentially become part of the basic policy form. In addition, certain states require state-specific endorsements to be included with every policy sold in that state. This results in most policies having some type of an endorsement attached.

In certain circumstances, the insurer's bylaws or the provisions of pertinent statutes are incorporated into an insurance policy. For example, the policyholders of mutual and reciprocal insurers typically have some rights and duties associated with managing the insurer's operations, and these rights and duties are specified in the policy.

Policies providing workers' compensation insurance or auto no-fault insurance are among those that provide benefits specified by state statute. The relevant statutes are usually not printed in the insurance policy—they are incorporated by reference. For example, Exhibit 11-3 contains a portion of the standard National Council on Compensation Insurance (NCCI) workers' compensation and employers' liability insurance policy that references the state's workers' compensation laws. In this exhibit, the term "Information Page" is used to refer to the declarations page.

EXHIBIT 11-3

Example of Reference to Statute Within a Policy

PART ONE

WORKERS' COMPENSATION INSURANCE

B. **We Will Pay**

We will pay promptly when due the benefits required of you by the workers' compensation law.

GENERAL SECTION

C. **Workers' Compensation Law**

Workers' Compensation Law means the workers or workmen's compensation law and occupational disease law of each state or territory named in Item 3. A. of the Information Page. It includes any amendments to that law which are in effect during the policy period. It does not include any federal workers or workmen's compensation law, any federal occupational disease law or the provisions of any law that provide nonoccupational disability benefits.

Source: Workers' Compensation and Employers' Liability Policy WC 00 00 00 A, © 1991 National Council on Compensation Insurance, Inc. All rights reserved. Reprinted with permission.

Insurance policies sometimes incorporate the insurer's rating manual (or the insurer's rules and rates, whether found in the manual or elsewhere) by referring to it in the policy language. Although the rules and rates themselves do not appear in the policy, reference to them makes them part of the policy. The applicable rules and rates often have been approved by an insurance regulator.

Subject to statutory or regulatory constraints, insurance policies may incorporate virtually any documents. Some frequently incorporated documents include premium notes (promissory notes that are accepted by the insurer in lieu of a cash premium payment), inspection reports, and specification sheets or operating manuals relating to safety equipment or procedures. If, for example, an insurer and an applicant agree that the coverage provided by a particular property or liability insurance policy is conditional on the use of certain procedures or safety equipment, then a set of operating instructions or a manual of specifications can be incorporated into the policy by reference and then used to define the agreed-upon procedures or equipment.

States are increasingly requiring insurers to provide a "notice to policyholders," informing them of significant changes when an insurance policy is revised. Insurers are also sometimes required to furnish policyholders with documents summarizing the coverage options available to them and choices that must be made. However, these informational documents are not typically part of the insurance policy.

Any of these related documents can alter the basic forms that are included in a policy. Therefore, related documents make policy analysis more difficult for insurance professionals because they add to the volume and complexity of forms that must be evaluated. As the number of related documents grows, so does the likelihood that one or more of the documents may contradict, exclude, or expand provisions in the basic forms.

COMMON POLICY PROVISIONS

Every insurance policy is composed of numerous policy provisions. A policy provision is a contractual term included in an insurance policy that specifies requirements or clarifies intended meaning. Some policy provisions are common to most insurance policies, whereas others are unique to specific policies. Despite the wide variation in property-casualty insurance policy provisions, each provision can typically be placed into one of six categories, depending on the purpose it serves. Exhibit 11-4 lists the six categories, briefly describes each category, and summarizes the effect that policy provisions in each category may have on coverage. Subsequent chapters provide in-depth analysis of the policy provisions found in insurance policies. Each of the policy provisions must be examined during policy analysis to determine its exact effect on coverage.

EXHIBIT 11-4

Property-Casualty Insurance Policy Provisions

Policy Provision	Description	Effect on Coverage
Declarations	Unique information on the insured; list of forms included in policy	Outline who or what is covered, and where and when coverage applies
Definitions	Words with special meanings in policy	May limit or expand coverage based on definitions of terms
Insuring Agreements	Promise to make payment	Outline circumstances under which the insurer agrees to pay
Conditions	Qualifications on promise to make payment	Outline steps insured needs to take to enforce policy
Exclusions	Limitations on promise to make payment	Limit insurer's payments based on excluded persons, places, things, or actions
Miscellaneous Provisions	Wide variety of provisions that may alter policy	Deal with the relationship between the insured and the insurer or establish procedures for implementing the policy

Insurance policies usually contain several sections, or "coverages," and often use headings and subheadings that do not necessarily coincide with these six categories of policy provisions. For example, a policy may contain a definitions section, but may not contain a miscellaneous provisions section. However, the categories present a useful way to group policy provisions in terms of the purpose they serve.

Declarations

Insurance policy declarations typically contain not only the standard information that has been "declared" by both the insured and the insurer but also information unique to the particular policy. The declarations (commonly referred to as the information page or declarations page) typically appear as the first page (or one of the first pages) in an insurance policy and contain the following information:

- Policy or policy number
- Policy inception and expiration dates (policy period)
- Name of the insurer
- Name of the insurance agent
- Name of the insured(s)
- Names of persons or organizations whose additional interests are covered (for example, a mortgagee, a loss payee, or an additional insured)
- Mailing address of the insured
- Physical address and description of the covered property or operations

- Numbers and edition dates of all attached forms and endorsements
- Dollar amounts of applicable policy limits
- Dollar amounts of applicable deductibles
- Premium

Sometimes other policy forms or endorsements also contain information that qualifies as part of the declarations. This information is often referred to as a "schedule." For example, an endorsement to a homeowners policy may list descriptions and limits of coverage of valuable pieces of personal property that need special insurance treatment. In contrast to the homeowners declarations page shown in Exhibit 11-2, Exhibit 11-5 shows an example of a commercial property declarations page.

Definitions

Many insurance policies or forms contain a section titled "Definitions" that defines the terms used throughout the entire policy or form. Although the definitions section can appear anywhere in the policy or form, it is usually near the beginning of the policy for personal lines policies (such as homeowners or personal auto policies) and in the back of the policy for commercial lines policies. Boldface type or quotation marks are typically used to distinguish words and phrases that are defined elsewhere in the policy. The following excerpt from the Definitions section of the ISO Personal Auto Policy shows the use of quotation marks:[1]

> **Personal Auto Policy Definitions**
>
> I. "Trailer" means a vehicle designed to be pulled by a:
>
>   1. Private passenger auto; or
>   2. Pickup or van.
>
> It also means a farm wagon or farm implement while towed by a vehicle listed in 1. or 2. above.

Many insurance policies refer to the insurer as "we" and the named insured as "you." These and other related pronouns, such as "us," "our," and "your," are often defined in an untitled preamble to the policy rather than in a definitions section.

Words and phrases defined within an insurance policy have special, defined meanings when they are used within that particular policy. Undefined words and phrases are interpreted according to the following rules of policy interpretation:

- Everyday words are given their ordinary meanings.
- Technical words are given their technical meanings.
- Words with an established legal meaning are given their legal meanings.
- Consideration is also given to the local, cultural, and trade-usage meanings of words, if applicable.

Many of the definitions that appear in insurance policies are there because of real or perceived ambiguity that has arisen regarding the use of those terms in previous policies.

EXHIBIT 11-5

Commercial Property Declarations

COMMERCIAL PROPERTY
CP DS 00 10 00

COMMERCIAL PROPERTY COVERAGE PART DECLARATIONS PAGE

POLICY NO. SP 0001   **EFFECTIVE DATE** 10 / 1 / 2005   ☒ **"X" If Supplemental Declarations Is Attached**

NAMED INSURED

AMR Corporation

DESCRIPTION OF PREMISES

Prem. No.	Bldg. No.	Location, Construction And Occupancy
001	001	2000 Industrial Highway, Workingtown, PA 19000 Joisted Masonry Storm Door Manufacturing

COVERAGES PROVIDED   Insurance At The Described Premises Applies Only For Coverages For Which A Limit Of Insurance Is Shown

Prem. No.	Bldg. No.	Coverage	Limit Of Insurance	Covered Causes Of Loss	Coinsurance*	Rates
001	001	Building	2,000,000	Special	80%	(See Sched.)
		Your Business Personal Prop.	1,120,000	Broad	80%	
		Personal Prop. of Others	50,000	Broad	80%	
		Business Income & Extra Expense	680,000	Special	80%	

*If Extra Expense Coverage, Limits On Loss Payment

OPTIONAL COVERAGES   Applicable Only When Entries Are Made In The Schedule Below

Prem. No.	Bldg. No.	Agreed Value			Replacement Cost (X)		
		Expiration Date	Cov.	Amount	Building	Pers. Prop.	Including "Stock"
001	001	10/1/2004	Building	$2,000,000	X		

	Inflation Guard (%)		*Monthly Limit Of Indemnity (Fraction)	Maximum Period Of Indemnity (X)	*Extended Period Of Indemnity (Days)
	Bldg.	Pers. Prop.			
	3%	3%			

*Applies to Business Income Only

MORTGAGEHOLDERS

Prem. No.	Bldg. No.	Mortgageholder Name And Mailing Address
001	001	Workingtown Savings and Loan Assn. 400 Main Street Workingtown, PA 19001

DEDUCTIBLE

$1,000.   **Exceptions:**

FORMS APPLICABLE

To All Coverages: CP 00 10, CP 00 30, CP 00 90, CP 10 30

CP DS 00 10 00   Copyright, Insurance Services Office, Inc., 1999   Page 1 of 1   ☐

Insuring Agreements

Insuring agreement
A statement in an insurance policy that the insurer will, under certain circumstances, make a payment or provide a service.

An **insuring agreement** is a statement in an insurance policy that the insurer will, under certain circumstances, make a payment or provide a service. Following the declarations, and possibly preceded by a section containing definitions, the body of most insurance policies begins with an insuring agreement.

Policies typically contain an insuring agreement for each coverage they provide. Consequently, package policies contain multiple insuring agreements. For example, the ISO Personal Auto Policy typically provides "liability," "medical payments," "uninsured motorists," and "damage to your auto" coverages. Therefore, the ISO Personal Auto Policy contains four insuring agreements, as shown in Exhibits 11-6 through 11-9. Similarly, the ISO Homeowners 3—Special Form (ISO HO-3) contains six insuring agreements: "dwelling," "other structures," "personal property," "loss of use," "personal liability," and "medical payments to others."

EXHIBIT 11-6

Personal Auto Policy Liability Insuring Agreement

PART A – LIABILITY COVERAGE

INSURING AGREEMENT

A. We will pay damages for "bodily injury" or "property damage" for which any "insured" becomes legally responsible because of an auto accident. Damages include prejudgment interest awarded against the "insured". We will settle or defend, as we consider appropriate, any claim or suit asking for these damages. In addition to our limit of liability, we will pay all defense costs we incur. Our duty to settle or defend ends when our limit of liability for this coverage has been exhausted by payment of judgments or settlements. We have no duty to defend any suit or settle any claim for "bodily injury" or "property damage" not covered under this policy.

B. "Insured" as used in this Part means:

1. You or any "family member" for the ownership, maintenance or use of any auto or "trailer".

2. Any person using "your covered auto".

3. For "your covered auto", any person or organization but only with respect to legal responsibility for acts or omissions of a person for whom coverage is afforded under this Part.

4. For any auto or "trailer", other than "your covered auto", any other person or organization but only with respect to legal responsibility for acts or omissions of you or any "family member" for whom coverage is afforded under this Part. This Provision (B.4.) applies only if the person or organization does not own or hire the auto or "trailer".

Includes copyrighted material of Insurance Services Office, Inc., with its permission. Copyright, ISO Properties, Inc., 1997.

EXHIBIT 11-7

Personal Auto Policy Medical Payments Insuring Agreement

PART B – MEDICAL PAYMENTS COVERAGE

INSURING AGREEMENT

A. We will pay reasonable expenses incurred for necessary medical and funeral services because of "bodily injury":

1. Caused by accident; and

2. Sustained by an "insured".

We will pay only those expenses incurred for services rendered within 3 years from the date of the accident.

B. "Insured" as used in this Part means:

1. You or any "family member":

a. While "occupying"; or

b. As a pedestrian when struck by;
a motor vehicle designed for use mainly on public roads or a trailer of any type.

2. Any other person while "occupying" "your covered auto".

Includes copyrighted material of Insurance Services Office, Inc., with its permission. Copyright, ISO Properties, Inc., 1997.

EXHIBIT 11-8

Personal Auto Policy Uninsured Motorist Insuring Agreement

PART C – UNINSURED MOTORISTS COVERAGE

INSURING AGREEMENT

A. We will pay compensatory damages which an "insured" is legally entitled to recover from the owner or operator of an "uninsured motor vehicle" because of "bodily injury":

1. Sustained by an "insured"; and

2. Caused by an accident.

The owner's or operator's liability for these damages must arise out of the ownership, maintenance or use of the "uninsured motor vehicle".

Any judgment for damages arising out of a suit brought without our written consent is not binding on us.

B. "Insured" as used in this Part means:

1. You or any "family member".

2. Any other person "occupying" "your covered auto".

3. Any person for damages that person is entitled to recover because of "bodily injury" to which this coverage applies sustained by a person described in 1. or 2. above.

Continued on next page.

C. "Uninsured motor vehicle" means a land motor vehicle or trailer of any type:

1. To which no bodily injury liability bond or policy applies at the time of the accident.

2. To which a bodily injury liability bond or policy applies at the time of the accident. In this case its limit for bodily injury liability must be less than the minimum limit for bodily injury liability specified by the financial responsibility law of the state in which "your covered auto" is principally garaged.

3. Which is a hit-and-run vehicle whose operator or owner cannot be identified and which hits:

    a. You or any "family member";

    b. A vehicle which you or any "family member" are "occupying"; or

    c. "Your covered auto".

4. To which a bodily injury liability bond or policy applies at the time of the accident but the bonding or insuring company:

    a. Denies coverage; or

    b. Is or becomes insolvent.

However, "uninsured motor vehicle" does not include any vehicle or equipment:

1. Owned by or furnished or available for the regular use of you or any "family member".

2. Owned or operated by a self-insurer under any applicable motor vehicle law, except a self-insurer which is or becomes insolvent.

3. Owned by any governmental unit or agency.

4. Operated on rails or crawler treads.

5. Designed mainly for use off public roads while not on public roads.

6. While located for use as a residence or premises.

Includes copyrighted material of Insurance Services Office, Inc., with its permission. Copyright, ISO Properties, Inc., 1997.

EXHIBIT 11-9

Personal Auto Policy Damage to Your Auto Insuring Agreement

PART D – COVERAGE FOR DAMAGE TO YOUR AUTO

INSURING AGREEMENT

A. We will pay for direct and accidental loss to "your covered auto" or any "non-owned auto", including their equipment, minus any applicable deductible shown in the Declarations. If loss to more than one "your covered auto" or "non-owned auto" results from the same "collision", only the highest applicable deductible will apply. We will pay for loss to "your covered auto" caused by:

1. Other than "collision" only if the Declarations indicate that Other Than Collision Coverage is provided for that auto.

2. "Collision" only if the Declarations indicate that Collision Coverage is provided for that auto.

If there is a loss to a "non-owned auto", we will provide the broadest coverage applicable to any "your covered auto" shown in the Declarations.

B. "Collision" means the upset of "your covered auto" or a "non-owned auto" or their impact with another vehicle or object.

Loss caused by the following is considered other than "collision":

1. Missiles or falling objects;

2. Fire;

3. Theft or larceny;

4. Explosion or earthquake;

5. Windstorm;

6. Hail, water or flood;

7. Malicious mischief or vandalism;

8. Riot or civil commotion;

9. Contact with bird or animal; or

10. Breakage of glass.

If breakage of glass is caused by a "collision", you may elect to have it considered a loss caused by "collision".

C. "Non-owned auto" means:

1. Any private passenger auto, pickup, van or "trailer" not owned by or furnished or available for the regular use of you or any "family member" while in the custody of or being operated by you or any "family member"; or

2. Any auto or "trailer" you do not own while used as a temporary substitute for "your covered auto" which is out of normal use because of its:

    a. Breakdown;

    b. Repair;

    c. Servicing;

    d. Loss; or

    e. Destruction.

Includes copyrighted material of Insurance Services Office, Inc., with its permission. Copyright, ISO Properties, Inc., 1997.

The term "insuring agreement" is usually applied to statements that introduce a policy's coverage section. However, "insuring agreement" can also be used to describe statements introducing coverage extensions, additional coverages, supplementary payments, and so on. Even unlabeled statements within declarations, definitions, exclusions, or conditions can serve as insuring agreements.

Scope of Insuring Agreements

Insuring agreements can be divided into the following two broad categories:

1. *Comprehensive, all-purpose insuring agreements.* This category provides extremely broad, unrestricted coverage that applies to virtually all causes of loss or to virtually all situations. This broad coverage is both clarified and narrowed by exclusions, definitions, and other policy provisions.

2. *Limited or single-purpose insuring agreements.* Insuring agreements in this category restrict coverage to certain causes of loss or to certain situations. Exclusions, definitions, and other policy provisions serve to clarify and narrow coverage, but may also broaden the coverage.

Whether comprehensive or limited, insuring agreements state the insurer's obligations in relatively broad terms. The full scope of coverage cannot be determined without examining the rest of the policy because the insurer's obligations are clarified or modified by other policy provisions.

In commercial property insurance, a comprehensive insuring agreement is called special-form coverage (or all-risks coverage) and a limited insuring agreement is called either basic-form or broad-form coverage (or named perils coverage). The declarations page of the commercial property policy lists which of these causes of loss forms (basic, broad, or special) applies to the policy.

The special-form coverage provides protection against causes of loss that it does not specifically exclude. This comprehensive approach covers all the named causes of loss included in the basic- or broad-form coverage, as well as additional causes of loss that are not otherwise excluded. The following clause from the insuring agreement in the ISO Causes of Loss Special Form illustrates how special-form coverage can be provided:[2]

> **A. Covered Causes of Loss**
>
> When Special is shown in the Declarations, Covered Causes of Loss means Risks of Direct Physical Loss unless the loss is:
>
> **1.** Excluded in Section **B.**, Exclusions; or
>
> **2.** Limited in Section **C.**, Limitations;
>
> that follow.

The limited insuring agreements in commercial property insurance are the named-perils, specified-perils, or specified-causes of loss coverage, referred to as the basic-form or broad-form coverages. The basic-form coverage protects against a list of named causes of loss and the broad-form coverage provides protection against the named causes of loss in the basic form plus some additional named causes of loss. The following clause from the insuring agreement in the ISO Causes of Loss Broad Form illustrates how broad-form coverage can be provided:[3]

> **A. Covered Causes of Loss**
>
> When Broad is showing in the Declarations, Covered Causes of Loss means the following:

1. Fire

2. Lightning

3. Explosion…

14. **Water Damage**

In liability insurance, a limited or single-purpose insurance agreement (which uses specific policy language to define the policy terms) applies to a limited number of incidents. On the other hand, comprehensive liability insurance agreements are much broader and do not limit coverage to a particular location, operation, or activity. Additional policy provisions, such as exclusions, limit the coverage on these policies.

Insuring Agreements for Secondary or Supplemental Coverages

Many insurance policies include secondary or supplemental coverages in addition to the main coverage in the insuring agreement. These coverages are described by terms such as "coverage extensions," "additional coverages," or "supplementary payments." Generally, a "coverage extension" extends a portion of the basic policy coverage to apply to a type of property or loss that would not otherwise be covered. An "additional coverage" adds a type of coverage not otherwise provided. "Supplementary payments" clarify the extent of coverage for certain expenses in liability insurance. All of these coverages are considered insuring agreements. However, the labels for such coverages vary by policy.

An example of an additional coverage from the ISO HO-3 policy is shown in Exhibit 11-10. The debris removal additional coverage insures a loss consequence that might not otherwise be covered by the policy: the cost of removing the debris of covered property that has been damaged by a covered cause of loss. Payment is limited to an additional 5 percent of the limit applicable to the damaged property.

EXHIBIT 11-10

Insuring Agreement Under Additional Coverages

E.   Additional Coverages

   1.   Debris Removal

      a.   We will pay your reasonable expense for the removal of:

         (1)   Debris of covered property if a Peril Insured Against that applies to the damaged property causes the loss; or

         (2)   Ash, dust or particles from a volcanic eruption that has caused direct loss to a building or property contained in a building.

     This expense is included in the limit of liability that applies to the damaged property. If the amount to be paid for the actual damage to the property plus the debris removal expense is more than the limit of liability for the damaged property, an additional 5% of that limit of liability is available for such expense.

Other Provisions Functioning as Insuring Agreements

Other policy provisions may also serve as insuring agreements by granting or restoring coverage otherwise excluded. These other policy provisions could be anywhere in the policy. Exhibit 11-11 contains an example of an insuring agreement that appears in the definitions section.

The Bodily Injury and Property Damage Liability insuring agreement in the ISO Commercial General Liability Coverage Form is broad enough to include claims involving liability for motor vehicle accidents. An exclusion in the form removes coverage for liability arising out of autos in most instances, but the form's definition of "auto" states that mobile equipment, as defined in the form, is not an auto. Therefore, the effect of the definition is to grant coverage (restore coverage otherwise excluded) for liability arising out of mobile equipment (subject to other policy provisions). An insurance professional might refer to the "mobile equipment coverage" of the CGL, even though the grant of coverage appears only within a definition. Consequently, the final sentence of the definition of "auto" in Exhibit 11-11 technically qualifies as an insuring agreement, despite not being specifically labeled in that way.

Similarly, Exhibit 11-12 contains an example of an insuring agreement appearing as an exception to the CGL Liquor Liability exclusion. Because of the exception in the final sentence of that exclusion, coverage applies to liquor liability resulting from office parties or other functions held by insureds that are not in the alcoholic beverage business. This exception to the Liquor Liability exclusion is commonly called "host liquor liability coverage," and it is, in effect, an insuring agreement.

EXHIBIT 11-11

Insuring Agreement in the Definitions Section

The insuring agreement of the ISO Commercial General Liability (CGL) policy (CG 00 01 12 04) provides broad liability coverage, but this broad coverage is restricted by an auto exclusion, which reads in part as follows:

> This insurance does not apply to:...."Bodily injury" or "property damage" arising out of the ownership, maintenance, use or entrustment to others of any..."auto"...owned or operated by or rented or loaned to any insured. Use includes operation and "loading or unloading".

The definition of "auto" reads as follows:

2. "Auto" means:

   a. A land motor vehicle, trailer or semitrailer designed for travel on public roads, including any attached machinery or equipment;...

   However, "auto" does not include "mobile equipment".

Includes copyrighted material of Insurance Services Office, Inc., with its permission. Copyright, ISO Properties, Inc., 2003.

EXHIBIT 11-12

Insuring Agreement Appearing in the Exclusions Section

The CGL also grants liquor liability coverage for most businesses through an exception to the liquor liability exclusion. The entire exclusion, which concludes with the exception, reads as follows:

2. Exclusions

This insurance does not apply to:...

   c.   Liquor Liability

   "Bodily injury" or "property damage" for which any insured may be held liable by reason of:

   (1) Causing or contributing to the intoxication of any person;

   (2) The furnishing of alcoholic beverages to a person under the legal drinking age or under the influence of alcohol; or

   (3) Any statute, ordinance or regulation relating to the sale, gift, distribution or use of alcoholic beverages.

   This exclusion applies only if you are in the business of manufacturing, distributing, selling, serving or furnishing alcoholic beverages.

Includes copyrighted material of Insurance Services Office, Inc., with its permission. Copyright, ISO Properties, Inc., 2003.

Conditions

A **policy condition** is any provision in an insurance policy that qualifies an otherwise enforceable promise of the insurer. Some policy conditions are found in a section of the policy titled "Conditions," whereas others are found in the forms, endorsements, or other documents that constitute the policy. For example, the homeowners insurance policy has three major sections in which conditions are listed: Section I Conditions, Section II Conditions, and Sections I and II Conditions.

In a policy's insuring agreement, the insurer promises to pay to the insured, to pay on behalf of the insured, to defend the insured, and/or to provide various additional services. However, such promises are not unconditional. The insurer's promises are enforceable only if an insured event occurs and only if the insured has fulfilled its contractual duties as specified in the policy conditions.

Examples of common policy conditions include the insured's obligation to pay premiums, report losses promptly, provide appropriate documentation for losses, cooperate with the insurer in any legal proceedings, and refrain from jeopardizing an insurer's rights to recover from responsible third parties (under subrogation actions). If the insured does not do these things, then the insurer may be released from any obligation to perform some or all of its otherwise enforceable promises.

Policy condition
Any provision in an insurance policy that qualifies an otherwise enforceable promise of the insurer.

Exclusions

Exclusions state what the insurer does not intend to cover. The word "intend" here is important; the primary function of exclusions is not only to limit coverage but also to clarify the coverages granted by the insurer. Specifying what the insurer does not intend to cover is a way of clarifying what aspects the insurer does intend to cover. The six purposes of exclusions in a property-casualty insurance policy are described in Exhibit 11-13.

EXHIBIT 11-13

Six Purposes of Exclusions

1. Eliminate coverage for uninsurable loss exposures

   Some loss exposures (such as war) possess few if any of the ideal characteristics of an insurable loss exposure. Exclusions allow insurers to preclude coverage for these loss exposures.

2. Assist in managing moral and morale hazards

   Some insureds' behavior is altered when they purchase insurance. Exclusions enable insurers to limit the moral and morale hazard incentive by limiting coverages for causes of loss over which the insured had some control.

3. Reduce likelihood of coverage duplications

   In some cases, two insurance policies provide coverage for the same loss. Exclusions ensure that two policies work together to provide complementary, not duplicate, coverage and that insureds are not paying duplicate premiums.

4. Eliminate coverages not needed by the typical insured

   Exclusions allow insurers to exclude coverage for loss exposures not faced by the typical insured. This means that all insureds would not have to share the costs of covering the loss exposures that relatively few insureds have.

5. Eliminate coverages requiring special treatment

   Exclusions eliminate the coverages that require rating, underwriting, loss control, or reinsurance treatment substantially different from what is normally required by the insurance policy.

6. Assist in keeping premiums reasonable

   Exclusions allow insurers to preclude risks that would otherwise increase costs. By keeping costs down, insurers can offer premiums that a sufficiently large number of insurance buyers consider reasonable.

Any exclusion can serve more than one of these six purposes. For example, all exclusions fulfill the last purpose of keeping premiums reasonable. A higher premium would be required to pay for the additional losses that might be covered whenever a policy is broadened by eliminating an exclusion.

Eliminate Coverage for Uninsurable Loss Exposures

Some loss exposures possess few, if any, of the ideal characteristics of an insurable loss exposure. The first purpose of exclusions is to eliminate coverage for those loss exposures that are considered uninsurable by private insurers. For example, most property and liability insurance policies exclude loss exposures relating to war. (The main exception is the "war risks coverage" often available in ocean marine insurance policies covering vessels or cargoes, even those that might pass through war zones. Insurers charge appropriately higher rates for such coverage.) Exhibit 11-14 contains the War exclusion that applies to the ISO CGL policy.

EXHIBIT 11-14

Exclusions

2. Exclusions

    i. War

        "Bodily injury" or "property damage", however caused, arising, directly or indirectly, out of:

        (1) War, including undeclared or civil war;

        (2) Warlike action by a military force, including action in hindering or defending against an actual or expected attack, by any government, sovereign or other authority using military personnel or other agents; or

        (3) Insurrection, rebellion, revolution, usurped power, or action taken by governmental authority in hindering or defending against any of these.

Includes copyrighted material of Insurance Services Office, Inc., with its permission. Copyright, ISO Properties, Inc., 2003.

In addition to war, examples of loss exposures that most private insurers consider to be uninsurable, and therefore widely exclude, are injury or damage intended by the insured, criminal acts committed by the insured, and normal wear and tear of property. Each of these excluded loss exposures is lacking one or more of the characteristics of an ideally insurable loss exposure. For example, war involves an incalculable catastrophe potential, and the other examples involve losses that are not fortuitous from the insured's standpoint.

Assist in Managing Moral and Morale Hazards

The second purpose of exclusions is to assist in managing moral and morale hazards. Both moral and morale hazards can cause individuals and organizations to behave differently when they are insured because they do not have to assume the entire cost of a loss. Exclusions help insurers minimize these hazards because they ensure that the individual or organization remains responsible for certain types of loss. For example, the liability section of the ISO HO-3 uses the following exclusion to manage moral hazards:[4]

E. **Coverage E – Personal Liability and Coverage F – Medical Payments to Others**

> Coverages **E** and **F** do not apply to… "Bodily injury" or "property damage" which is expected or intended by an "insured"….

This exclusion reduces moral hazard incentives by eliminating coverage for intentional harmful results. Other conditions and miscellaneous provisions manage moral hazard by making it difficult to exaggerate losses.

Some exclusions, such as the provisions from the ISO HO-3 shown in Exhibit 11-15, assist in managing morale hazards by making insureds themselves bear the losses that result from their own carelessness. This exclusion appears not under the heading "Exclusions," but within the description of the "freezing" peril in Section I — Perils Insured Against.

EXHIBIT 11-15

Policy Wording to Manage Morale Hazards

SECTION I — PERILS INSURED AGAINST

A.   **Coverage A — Dwelling and Coverage B — Other Structures**

    2.   We do not insure, however, for loss…

        c.   Caused by:

            (1) Freezing of a plumbing, heating, air conditioning or automatic fire protective sprinkler system or of a household appliance…This provision does not apply if you have used reasonable care to:

            (a) Maintain heat in the building; or

            (b) Shut off the water supply and drain all systems and appliances of water.

            However, if the building is protected by an automatic fire protective sprinkler system, you must use reasonable care to continue the water supply and maintain heat in the building for coverage to apply.

Reduce Likelihood of Coverage Duplications

The third purpose of exclusions is to reduce the likelihood of coverage duplications. Having two insurance policies covering the same loss is usually unnecessary and inefficient. It is unnecessary because coverage under one policy is all that is needed to indemnify the insured (unless policy restrictions or limits of insurance preclude full recovery). It is inefficient because, at least in theory, each policy providing coverage for certain types of losses includes a related premium charge. Therefore, an insured with duplicated coverage is paying higher premiums than is necessary. Exclusions ensure that multiple policies can work together to provide complementary, not duplicate, coverage and that insureds are not paying duplicate premiums.

For example, assume Karim has both a personal auto policy and a homeowners policy. If Karim leaves his laptop computer in his car and the car is stolen, he can submit a claim for the laptop under his homeowners insurance. Therefore, the loss of the laptop does not need to be covered under his personal auto policy. If it were covered under his auto policy, Karim would likely be paying more than is necessary for his auto insurance. Excluding the laptop under the auto insurance avoids duplication of coverage. Exhibit 11-16 shows the ISO Personal Auto Policy exclusion that avoids this type of duplication.

EXHIBIT 11-16

Exclusions That Reduce Coverage Duplications

Exclusions

We will not pay for:

5.   Loss to any electronic equipment that receives or transmits audio, visual or data signals and any accessories used with such equipment. This includes but is not limited to:

    a.   Citizens band radios;

    b.   Telephones;

    c.   Two-way mobile radios;

    d.   Scanning monitor receivers;

    e.   Television monitor receivers;

    f.   Video cassette recorders;

    g.   Audio cassette recorders; or

    h.   Personal computers.

Includes copyrighted material of Insurance Services Office, Inc., with its permission. Copyright, ISO Properties, Inc., 1997.

Eliminate Coverages Not Needed by the Typical Insured

The fourth purpose of exclusions is to eliminate coverages that are not needed by the typical purchaser of that line of insurance. Elimination of such coverages avoids the situation of all insureds having to share the costs of covering loss exposures that relatively few insureds have. For example, the typical individual does not own or operate private aircraft or rent portions of the family home for storage of others' business property. Therefore, homeowners policies typically exclude coverage for such loss exposures. People who do have these loss exposures may be able to obtain coverage separately through endorsements to their policies (for an additional premium) or by purchasing separate insurance policies.

Insurers are not always permitted to exclude coverage for loss exposures not faced by the typical insurance purchaser. For example, insurers may want to exclude auto liability coverage for drivers who have accidents while driving under the influence of alcohol. However, state insurance regulators are unlikely to approve such an exclusion because it tends to eliminate a source of recovery for the victims of drunken drivers. The effect is that auto policyholders who never drink and drive are required to share the costs of accidents caused by those who do.

Eliminate Coverages Requiring Special Treatment

The fifth purpose of exclusions is to eliminate coverages requiring special treatment. Such special treatment may entail underwriting, loss control, or reinsurance that is substantially different from what is normally required for the policy containing the exclusion. For example, commercial general liability policies issued to professionals are usually endorsed to exclude their professional liability loss exposures. One example is the exclusion for engineers, architects, or surveyors shown in Exhibit 11-17. These and other types of professionals can purchase separate professional liability insurance to cover claims alleging that they made errors or omissions in providing their professional services. Insurers exclude professional liability loss exposures from CGL policies not because such exposures are rare (there are thousands of individuals involved in these professions) but because of the special underwriting, loss control, or reinsurance treatment necessary to adequately insure professional liability loss exposures.

EXHIBIT 11-17

Exclusion—Engineers, Architects or Surveyors Professional Liability

This endorsement modifies insurance provided under the following:

COMMERCIAL GENERAL LIABILITY COVERAGE PART

The following exclusion is added to Paragraph **2., Exclusions of Section I – Coverage A – Bodily Injury And Property Damage Liability** and Paragraph **2., Exclusions of Section I – Coverage B – Personal And Advertising Injury Liability**:

This insurance does not apply to "bodily injury," "property damage" or "personal and advertising injury" arising out of the rendering of or failure to render any professional services by you or any engineer, architect or surveyor who is either employed by you or performing work on your behalf in such capacity.

Professional services include:

1. The preparing, approving, or failing to prepare or approve, maps, shop drawings, opinions, reports, surveys, field orders, change orders or drawings and specifications; and

2. Supervisory, inspection, architectural or engineering activities.

Includes copyrighted material of Insurance Services Office, Inc., with its permission. Copyright, ISO Properties, Inc., 1997.

As another example, many standard policies covering valuable personal property exclude coverage for loss exposures involving property exhibited at a convention or trade fair. Paintings, stamps, coins, and other collectors' items that are displayed in public exhibits are vulnerable to loss by theft and other perils. As with professional liability coverage, an underwriter may agree to provide coverage for property in exhibitions for an additional premium.

Assist in Keeping Premiums Reasonable

The sixth purpose of exclusions is to assist in keeping premiums at a level that a sufficiently large number of insurance buyers will consider reasonable. All exclusions serve this purpose to some extent. However, for some exclusions it is the primary or sole purpose, whereas for others it is simply one of the effects.

Excluded losses are not necessarily uninsurable. In many cases, few people are willing to pay the premiums necessary to include coverage for losses that ordinarily are excluded. For example, the ISO Personal Auto Policy excludes coverage for mechanical breakdown and road damage to tires. These loss exposures are not uninsurable. In fact, many auto dealers, tire shops, and various other organizations offer insurance-like service warranties covering such loss exposures. An insurance policy could probably be priced to reflect the expected costs of mechanical breakdowns or tire losses, but the insured would be paying the projected costs of maintenance plus the insurer's expenses in administering insurance to cover the maintenance costs. The additional premium might exceed the typical costs associated with these losses.

Miscellaneous Provisions

In addition to declarations, definitions, insuring agreements, conditions, and exclusions, insurance policies often contain miscellaneous provisions that deal with the relationship between the insured and the insurer or help to establish working procedures for implementing the policy. However, such provisions do not have the force of conditions. Consequently, even if the insured does not follow the procedures specified in the miscellaneous provisions, the insurer may still be required to fulfill its contractual promises.

Miscellaneous provisions often are unique to particular types of insurers, as in the following examples:

- A policy issued by a mutual insurer is likely to describe each insured's right to vote in the election of the board of directors.
- A policy issued by a reciprocal insurer is likely to specify the attorney-in-fact's authority to implement its powers on the insured's behalf.

Once an insurance professional understands how the six categories of policy provisions grant, clarify, qualify, or eliminate insurance coverage, he or she can analyze any type of policy.

POLICY ANALYSIS

Ideally, all insureds should read their policies as soon as they receive them so that they have a basic understanding of their agreement with their insurers and what potential losses are covered by the policy. However, many insureds do not read their insurance policies. Many review the declarations page to ensure that the limits of coverage and premiums are correct, but do not read the policy in detail until after a loss has occurred. This may result in a strained relationship between the insurer and insured when a loss occurs that is excluded by the policy but that the insured believes should be covered. To ensure that an insured receives consistent information regarding policy interpretation, it is important that all the insurers' representatives (producers, customer service representatives, underwriters, and claim adjusters) who interact with the insureds have a thorough and correct understanding of the policy.

Since most insurers' underwriters, claim representatives, and insurance producers already have a basic understanding of the policy, aside from reviewing the declarations page for the accuracy of the unique information for the particular insured, they have little need to thoroughly review each policy issued. However, each pre-loss question posed or post-loss claim filed by an insured is a unique situation that may require a review of policy provisions to determine coverage for a loss reported by the insured.

As discussed previously, policy analysis starts with determining whether an enforceable contract exists. The remainder of this section is based on the assumption that all four elements of an enforceable contract have been met, that is, that the insurer and insured have entered into a legally enforceable insurance policy. Therefore, the policy analysis shifts focus to determining the extent of coverage provided by the policy. This analysis can take place either before a loss (pre-loss) or after a loss (post-loss).

Pre-Loss Policy Analysis

Both insurance professionals and insureds conduct pre-loss policy analysis. Insurance professionals should conduct pre-loss analysis to be better able to answer insureds' coverage questions that arise before any claims are filed. Furthermore, insurance professionals should conduct pre-loss policy analysis to ensure that the insurance policies being sold are appropriate for the insured's loss exposures. Failure to understand the insurance policy can lead to errors or omissions liability claims against insurance producers and their employers.

Insureds should conduct pre-loss policy analysis to ensure that the insurance policy being purchased is appropriate for their loss exposures. Determining whether and how much coverage applies before a loss has occurred can be extremely difficult. Pre-loss policy analysis requires a wide range of skills, including the following:

- Understanding the alternative ways in which insurance policies customarily describe coverage in addressing loss exposures
- Identifying and evaluating insurance policy provisions that depart from the customary approach
- Understanding the loss exposure or loss exposures to which the policy applies

Pre-loss policy analysis almost exclusively relies on scenario analysis to determine the extent of coverage (if any) the policy provides for the losses generated by a given scenario. For insureds, the primary source of information for generating such scenarios is the insured's past loss experience. Frequently, insureds have developed a thorough understanding of a particular loss exposure(s) to which the policy applies through losses that have been associated with that exposure. They can examine the past losses that have occurred and analyze the current insurance policy to ensure that it will provide coverage if any of those past losses were to occur again in the future. For example, assume that five years ago an infant car seat manufacturer had to recall a particular model of car seats because of a design defect. The manufacturer's risk management professional may want to determine whether the manufacturer's current ISO CGL policy would provide coverage if a recall were necessary this year. A review of the policy would reveal that unless it was endorsed, the policy would not cover recalls.

Friends, neighbors, co-workers, and family members can also be sources of information for scenario analysis for individuals who purchase personal insurance policies, particularly if those individuals have never suffered a loss that triggered insurance coverage. By gathering information from others about their experiences with losses and the claim process, insureds can formulate scenarios they can use to conduct pre-loss policy analysis.

Another source of information for an insured to develop scenarios for pre-loss policy analysis is the insurance producer or customer service representative consulted in the insurance transaction. Because insureds may rely on these insurance professionals as sources of information, they need to be able to accurately interpret coverage questions raised. Frequently, the producer has specialized knowledge of the loss exposures to which the policy applies. Furthermore, producers understand the alternative ways in which insurance policies may describe coverage and know the policy provisions that depart from the customary wordings. For example, homeowners who have read news articles about toxic mold may consult their insurance producers to determine whether their homeowners insurance policy covers mold, fungus, or wet rot.

One of the limitations of scenario analysis is that because the number of possible scenarios is infinite, events will always occur that are not envisioned. For example, the terrorist attacks of September 11, 2001, would not have been envisioned by most insurance professionals or insureds. Alternatively, the insured or insurance professional may recognize the possibility of an event but underestimate the extent of potential loss. For example, the amount of damage that Hurricane Andrew caused in 1992 was unprecedented, as was the extent of flooding that New Orleans experienced following Hurricane Katrina in 2005. These events prompted insurers to fundamentally change the methods used to evaluate these types of risks. Because no pre-loss analysis can evaluate every possible scenario, post-loss policy analysis is also necessary to determine the extent of coverage for losses that have occurred.

Post-Loss Policy Analysis

The most efficient method of performing post-loss policy analysis is to have a systematic approach for determining whether the loss triggers coverage from the insurer and, if so, the extent of that coverage. It is typically more efficient to determine if the loss triggers coverage prior to determining the amount that may be payable by the policy. However, it may be unnecessary to conduct the first step in some cases. For example, if it is clear that the amount payable is zero even if the loss is covered (perhaps because the policy's deductible is larger than the loss amount), then determining whether coverage applies is unnecessary.

There are several methods used to perform post-loss policy analysis, and each method has its strengths and weaknesses. One common method is the question-and-answer method discussed in the following textbox. The method of post-loss policy analysis this text follows is the DICE method.

Question and Answer Policy Analysis

After a loss occurs, an individual can analyze a policy to determine if the loss is covered by answering the following six questions:

1. Does an enforceable insurance policy exist?

2. Did the loss occur to an insured party who has an insurable interest?

3. Has the insured met all policy conditions?

4. Has an insured event occurred?

5. What dollar amount, if any, is payable?

6. Do any external factors affect the claim?

If the answer to any of questions 1 through 4 is no, then the insurance policy does not provide coverage. Questions 5 and 6 determine how much is payable under an insurance policy that does provide coverage.

DICE Review

The DICE acronym represents four of the six categories of property-casualty policy provisions: declarations, insuring agreements, conditions, and exclusions. The DICE method creates a decision tree to determine whether the policy provides coverage. Once the DICE method has been used to determine coverage, the insurance professional determines the amount payable under the insurance policy. This systematic approach can be used by producers, claim representatives, and insureds alike. It serves all parties to the insurance policy well by ensuring that the coverage intended to be provided by the insurance policy is actually delivered as promised.

Although the DICE acronym represents only four of the six categories of policy provisions, every policy provision must be examined to determine whether it affects coverage. Accordingly, the definitions section should be analyzed in conjunction with whichever provisions (declarations, insuring agreements, conditions, or exclusions) contain the terms to which the definitions apply. Miscellaneous provisions seldom affect policy coverage but can be considered with the exclusions.

Exhibit 11-18 contains the DICE decision tree.

The DICE method begins with the individual examining the declarations page of the insurance policy. An insurance professional can examine the information provided by the insured to determine if any of that information precludes coverage. For example, an insured may report to the property insurer that a fire occurred at the insured premises on May 5. The declarations page contains both the policy inception and expiration dates (the policy period). If the policy period ended on April 30, then the policy does not provide coverage for this loss. If, however, no information in the declarations precludes covering the claim, the insurance professional proceeds to reviewing the insuring agreement(s).

The insuring agreement or agreements often contain policy provisions regarding the covered property or events, covered causes of loss, and coverage territories. If the insuring agreement or agreements contain specially defined terms, those definitions should be analyzed in this step of the analysis. If a policy provision in an insuring agreement precludes coverage, the claim will be denied. If not, the insurance professional proceeds to analyze the conditions.

Policy conditions specify the duties of the insurer and the insured. Violating a condition can change the coverage on an otherwise-covered claim. Examining the policy conditions can help the insurance professional clarify important points, such as the following:

- Whether fulfillment of certain conditions, such as premium payment conditions, is required for there to be an enforceable policy
- Whether coverage will be denied if an insured party breaches a policy condition
- Whether coverage triggers and coverage territory restrictions affect the loss
- Whether conditions concerning the rights and duties of both parties to maintain the insurance policy apply (for example, the insurer's right to inspect covered premises and audit the insured's books, the rights of either or both parties to cancel the policy, the insurer's right to make coverage modifications, and so on)

- Whether the post-loss duties of the insured and the insurer affect coverage
- Whether conditions have been or need to be followed regarding claim disputes
- Whether subrogation and salvage rights and conditions have to be considered

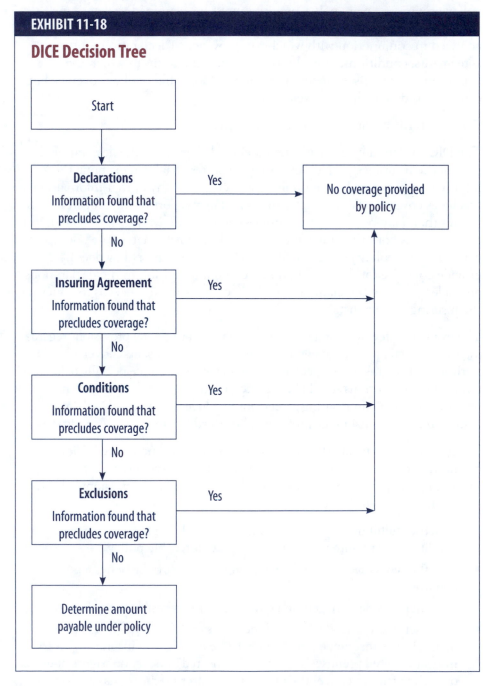

EXHIBIT 11-18

DICE Decision Tree

If the insurance professional finds a condition that precludes coverage, the claim is denied. If not, the insurance professional analyzes the exclusions to determine whether any exclusions would preclude coverage.

Exclusions can appear anywhere in the policy, from the definitions or insuring agreements to endorsements. It is during this step of the DICE method that any remaining provisions that were not evaluated in the first three steps need to be considered. Therefore, this step involves evaluating exclusions, endorsements, miscellaneous provisions and any other related documents that are included in the policy. If no preclusions to coverage apply after completing all four steps of the DICE method, the claim is covered and the insurance professional can then move on to determining the amount that is payable under the policy.

Determining Amounts Payable

After using the DICE method to determine whether the claim is covered, the next step is to determine how much is payable under that insurance policy. The amount payable under a given insurance policy can be affected not only by the value of the loss but also by policy limits and deductibles or self-insured retentions. For property insurance, the amount payable is affected by several issues. First, the valuation provision in the policy indicates whether property is valued on the basis of its replacement cost, its depreciated actual cash value, or some other basis. The amount payable is also affected by applicable policy limits and can be limited by a coinsurance provision or other insurance-to-value provisions. A deductible might also be subtracted from the amount otherwise payable.

For liability insurance, the valuation of a covered loss is set by the courts or, more commonly, by a negotiated settlement. The amounts payable for both property and liability insurance losses can also be affected by other insurance.

The remaining chapters in the text provide a more detailed analysis of insurance policies using the DICE method as well as methods of determining the amounts payable for both property and liability insurance policies.

SUMMARY

An insurance policy is made up of one or more forms. In some cases, one form, combined with a declarations page, constitutes the entire insurance policy. In other cases, multiple forms are combined with a declarations page to form the policy. A monoline policy is an insurance policy that covers a single line of insurance. A package policy, also called a multiline policy, is an insurance policy that covers more than one line of insurance.

A self-contained policy is a single document that contains all the agreements between the insured and the insurer and that forms a complete insurance policy. Endorsements can be added to a self-contained policy to provide additional, optional coverages or to exclude unnecessary coverages. A modular policy consists of several different documents, none of which by itself forms a complete policy. The policy is designed around one basic policy component (such as a "policy jacket") and is created by combining a set of individual components.

As compared with self-contained policies, the modular approach to policy construction has certain advantages, including fewer coverage gaps and over-laps, consistent terminology, fewer forms, simpler underwriting, reduced adverse selection problems, and package discounts from insurers. These advantages can be important to insurance professionals conducting policy analysis.

Most insurance policies consist of one or more preprinted forms and endorsements. Preprinted forms are developed for use with many different insureds. An insurer may use the standard forms that are also used by other insurers, or it may develop its own company-specific preprinted forms, especially for high-volume lines of insurance or for coverages in which the insurer specializes. Pre-printed standard forms are typically the easiest forms for insurance professionals to work with during policy analysis.

In contrast to preprinted forms, manuscript forms are custom forms developed for one specific insured—or for a small group of insureds—with unique coverage needs. Manuscript forms are the most difficult forms for insurance professionals to interpret during policy analysis because they often contain unique wording and can therefore vary widely in their interpretation.

Several other documents can become part of an insurance policy, either by being physically attached or by being referenced within the policy, such as the completed insurance application, endorsements, the insurer's bylaws, and the terms of relevant statutes. Any of these related documents can alter the basic forms that are included in a policy. Therefore, related documents make policy analysis more complicated because they add to the volume and complexity of forms that must be evaluated.

Every insurance policy is composed of numerous policy provisions. Each provision can be placed into one of the following six categories, depending on the purpose it serves:

1. *Declarations.* Declarations typically contain not only the standard information that has been "declared" by the insured but also information unique to the particular policy.

2. *Definitions.* Many insurance policies or forms contain a section titled "Definitions" that defines the terms used throughout the entire policy or form.

3. *Insuring agreements.* An insuring agreement is a statement that the insurer will, under certain circumstances, make a payment or provide a service. Policies typically contain an insuring agreement for each coverage they provide.

4. *Conditions*. A condition qualifies an otherwise enforceable promise of the insurer. Examples of common policy conditions include the insured's obligation to pay premiums, report losses promptly, provide appropriate documentation for losses, cooperate with the insurer in any legal proceedings, and refrain from jeopardizing an insurer's rights to recover from responsible third parties.

5. *Exclusions*. Exclusions state what the insurer does not intend to cover. The six reasons for having exclusions are to eliminate coverage for uninsurable loss exposures, to assist in managing moral and morale hazards, to reduce the likelihood of coverage duplications, to eliminate coverages not needed by the typical insured, to eliminate coverages requiring special treatment, and to assist in keeping premiums reasonable.

6. *Miscellaneous provisions*. Insurance policies often contain miscellaneous provisions that deal with the relationship between the insured and the insurer or help to establish working procedures for implementing the policy. However, such provisions do not have the force of conditions.

Policy analysis starts with determining whether an enforceable contract exists and then shifts focus to determining the extent of coverage provided by the policy. This analysis can either take place before a loss (pre-loss) or after a loss (post-loss). Pre-loss policy analysis almost exclusively relies on scenario analysis to determine the extent of coverage. The primary source of information for generating such scenarios is the insured's past loss experience. A limitation of scenario analysis is that because the number of possible scenarios is infinite, events will always occur that are not envisioned.

The method of post-loss policy analysis that this text follows is the DICE method. The DICE acronym represents four of the six categories of property-casualty insurance provisions: declarations, insuring agreements, conditions, and exclusions. The DICE method creates a decision tree to determine if the insurance policy provides coverage. Once the DICE method has been used to determine coverage, the insurance professional determines the amount payable under the insurance policy.

CHAPTER NOTES

1. Includes copyrighted material of Insurance Services Office, Inc., with its permission. Copyright, ISO Properties, Inc., 1997.

2. Includes copyrighted material of Insurance Services Office, Inc., with its permission. Copyright, ISO Properties, Inc., 2001.

3. Includes copyrighted material of Insurance Services Office, Inc., with its permission. Copyright, ISO Properties, Inc., 2001.

4. Includes copyrighted material of Insurance Services Office, Inc., with its permission. Copyright, ISO Properties, Inc., 1999.

Direct Your Learning

Policy Analysis: Declarations and Insuring Agreement

After learning the content of this chapter and completing the corresponding course guide assignment, you should be able to:

■ Given a case involving a property or liability insurance policy, analyze each of the following to determine whether coverage exists:

- Insured parties, including insured parties identified by name, insured parties identified by relationship, additional insured parties, multiple insured parties, and parties not insured

- Insurable interest

- Premiums

- Policy period and coverage territory provisions

- Insured events and cause of loss

■ Define or describe each of the Key Words and Phrases for this chapter.

Develop Your Perspective

What are the main topics covered in the chapter?

This chapter identifies which provisions are commonly found in property-casualty insurance policies, where in the policy the provisions are typically located, and how these provisions affect coverage.

Consider how the policy provisions define the terms and scope of the agreement between the insurer and the insured.

- How do the provisions regarding the covered time period clarify the promises between the insurer and the policyholder?

Why is it important to learn about these topics?

Understanding how policy provisions affect coverage helps an insurance professional analyze an insurance policy. Consulting the provisions is just one aspect of determining whether a given loss is covered by the policy.

Imagine that you have presented a claim to your insurer and that a dispute exists about the amount to be paid or the applicability of coverage.

- What process would you apply to review all the policy provisions to determine whether the claim is covered and the amount of coverage that may be applicable?

How can you use what you will learn?

Examine your auto insurance policy.

- Who is an insured under the policy, and who is a named insured?

- How might distinctions between the insured and named insured affect coverage?

- How might the coverage territory affect your decisions to drive an auto outside the United States and Canada?

Chapter 12

Policy Analysis: Declarations and Insuring Agreement

After a loss has occurred and a claim has been filed, an insurance professional begins the process of examining the applicable insurance policy to determine if coverage exists, and, if so, to what extent. As discussed in the previous chapter, this text follows the DICE method of post-loss policy analysis. The DICE acronym represents four of the six sections of a property-casualty insurance policy: declarations page (declarations), insuring agreement, conditions, and exclusions. This chapter examines those provisions related to the declarations and insuring agreement sections of the policy. A subsequent chapter examines the provisions related to the conditions and exclusions sections.

Not all the policy provisions that are related to a specific section of a policy appear in the section they address. For example, policy provisions that relate to the declarations may appear in the conditions, exclusions, or endorsements section or in any other section of the policy. Furthermore, each property or liability insurance policy has a different structure, making it impossible to definitively state where various provisions can be found. Therefore, when examining a particular section, this text discusses both the provisions related to the section that appear in that section and other related provisions that may appear outside the section. For example, when discussing the inclusion of the named insured in the declarations, the section also refers to other insured parties covered by the insurance policy, even though some of the provisions related to insured parties appear outside the declarations.

This chapter also examines some of the variations among the policy provisions related to the declarations and insurance agreements sections. These variations illustrate why it is not advisable to make broad generalizations across property-casualty insurance policies. Assuming that all provisions of a specific type are identical can result in faulty policy analysis. Furthermore, insurance professionals should not assume that any particular policy contains all the provisions discussed in this text. The absence of a policy provision that is commonly found in other policies can have a significant effect on policy analysis.

Finally, although following the DICE method can be useful, a provision that affects coverage might not be explicitly covered by this method. Consequently, the importance of reading the entire policy when performing post-loss policy analysis cannot be overemphasized.

DECLARATIONS

The first section of the policy to be analyzed in the DICE method is the declarations. The declarations contain the unique information provided by and about the insured. For many insurance policies, the only customized portion of the policy is the declarations. Declarations typically contain information important to policy analysis about the following:

- Numbers and edition dates of all attached coverage forms and endorsements
- Name of the insured(s) and names of persons or organizations whose additional interests are covered
- Premium
- Policy inception and expiration dates (policy period)
- Coverage territory
- Physical address and description of the covered property or operations
- Dollar amounts of applicable policy limits
- Dollar amounts of applicable deductibles

All this information is important in determining coverage as part of post-loss policy analysis. Post-loss policy analysis begins by ensuring that the complete insurance policy is available for analysis. An insurance professional should determine that all applicable endorsements listed in the declarations are with the policy. For example, the homeowners policy declarations, shown in Exhibit 12-1, reference the coverage and endorsement forms (in addition to the declarations) that constitute the complete policy for Anthony and Ria Jones. Without both of these (HO 00 03 and HO 04 61), an insurance professional would be unable to accurately analyze the Jones's homeowners policy if a loss were to occur.

Having obtained the complete policy, post-loss policy analysis continues by analyzing the following common policy provisions related to the declarations:

- Insured parties
- Insurable interest
- Premiums
- Policy period
- Coverage territory

EXHIBIT 12-1

Homeowners Policy Declarations

Homeowners Policy Declarations

POLICYHOLDER: **(Named Insured)**	Anthony M. and Ria C. Jones 192 Alderton Street Anytown, USA 40000	**POLICY NUMBER:**	872 H 235771

POLICY PERIOD: **Inception:** April 30, 2005 Policy period begins 12:01 A.M. standard time
Expiration: April 30, 2006 at the residence premises.

FIRST MORTGAGEE AND MAILING ADDRESS:

State Local Mortgage Assn.
C/O Mortgagee, Inc.
P.O. Box 2000
Businesstown, USA 55000

We will provide the insurance described in this policy in return for the premium and compliance with all applicable policy provisions.

SECTION I COVERAGES	LIMIT	
A—Dwelling	$ 192,000	**SECTION I DEDUCTIBLE:** $ 300
B—Other Structures	$ 19,200	(In case of loss under Section I, we cover
C—Personal Property	$ 96,000	only that part of the loss over the
D—Loss of Use	$ 57,600	deductible amount shown above.)

SECTION II COVERAGES	LIMIT	
E—Personal Liability	$ 360,000	Each Occurrence
F—Medical Payments to Others	$ 1,200	Each Person

CONSTRUCTION: Masonry Veneer   **NO. FAMILIES:** One   **TYPE ROOF:** Approved

YEAR BUILT: 1990   **PROTECTION CLASS:** 7   **FIRE DISTRICT:** Cook Township

NOT MORE THAN 1000 FEET FROM HYDRANT

NOT MORE THAN 5 MILES FROM FIRE DEPT.

FORMS AND ENDORSEMENTS IN POLICY: HO 00 03, HO 04 61

POLICY PREMIUM: $ 576.00   **COUNTERSIGNATURE DATE:** April 30, 2005   **AGENT:** W.R. Vincent

Insured Parties

The policy provisions related to insured parties include the named insured and other persons or organizations that qualify as insured parties and have an insurable interest. These provisions are important because, although the declarations provide the name(s) and address(es) of the named insured(s), they do not include the names of the other insured parties.

Insured party

A person, corporation, or other entity contractually entitled to a loss payment or other benefits according to an insurance policy's terms.

An **insured party** is a person, corporation, partnership, or other entity contractually entitled to a loss payment or other benefits according to an insurance policy's terms. Insured parties—especially those who qualify as named insureds—have a wide variety of contractual rights under the terms of a typical policy. A **named insured** is a person, corporation, partnership, or other entity identified as an insured party in an insurance policy's declarations page.

Named insured

A person, corporation, partnership, or other entity identified as an insured party in an insurance policy's declarations page.

Insurable interest is an interest in the subject of an insurance policy that is not unduly remote and that would cause the interested party to suffer financial loss if an insured event occurred. An insurable interest can arise as a result of a relationship with a person or a right over property. Whether a person legally has an insurable interest depends on the relationship between the claiming party and the property, person, or event in question. Insurable interests are discussed in greater detail subsequently in this chapter.

Insurable interest

An interest in the subject of an insurance policy that is not unduly remote and that would cause the interested party to suffer financial loss if an insured event occurred.

Differences Between "You" and "An Insured"

When analyzing a typical insurance policy, it is important to understand the distinction between (1) "you" (the named insured) and (2) "an insured" (which includes, but is not limited to, the named insured) because the distinction can determine whether a particular loss is covered.

- "You" means the named insured shown in the declarations and any other person or organization qualifying as a named insured or meeting the policy's definition of "you." Personal insurance policies typically include the named insured's spouse within the definition of "you," effectively making the spouse a named insured even if that person's name does not appear in the declarations.

- "An insured," "the insured," or "any insured" includes not only the named insured but also any other person or organization that qualifies as an "insured" under the policy. For example, under the Commercial General Liability (CGL) Coverage Form, the named insured's employees are insureds even though their names do not appear in the declarations.

The distinction between the two definitions can be crucial. For example, a liability insurance policy exclusion of damage to property in the custody of "the insured" applies to property in the custody of any party qualifying as "the insured" and against whom a claim is made. In contrast, an exclusion of damage to property in "your" custody applies only to property in the named insured's custody (or in the custody of anyone else who meets the policy's definition of "you").

All insured parties have some rights in an insurance policy, but the extent of these rights can vary. The types of insured parties that typically appear in an insurance policy are as follows:

- Insured parties identified by name
- Insured parties identified by relationship
- Additional insureds
- Multiple insured parties

Policies also typically specify which parties are not insured.

Insured Parties Identified by Name

Some policy provisions apply to all insureds, whereas others apply only to named insureds. An insurance policy's declarations may specifically name both the named insured(s) and any loss payees or mortgagees (who are typically secured creditors). Throughout the policy, "you" refers to the named insured or anyone else meeting the policy's definition of "you."

Although all named insureds are eligible for coverage under the policy, the order in which named insureds are listed in the declarations can be important. The first named insured (the first name that appears in the declarations) is usually responsible for premium payment and is the only insured who can cancel the policy, receive notice of cancellation, make policy changes with the insurer's consent, receive claim and occurrence data from the insurer, and receive returned premiums.

A **loss payee** is a secured creditor, identified by name as a loss payee, to whom the debtor (named insured) has pledged specific personal property as collateral for a loan. Although loss payees may be entitled to some payment under the policy, they are neither insureds nor named insureds—even if their name appears in the declarations. Loss payees' interests in personal property are typically protected by a **loss payable clause**, which is a policy provision that protects the creditor's interest in personal property pledged as collateral for a loan. The typical loss payable clause amends the definition of the insured to include the loss payee (creditor) with respect to the personal property in which the loss payee has an interest. This amendment does not give the creditor any greater rights than the debtor/insured has under the policy, and it does not create a separate policy with the loss payee.

Some loss payable clauses extend additional rights to the loss payee. For example, the loss payee might be entitled to receive the same advance notice of policy cancellation as the named insured, or the loss payee's rights might be protected even when the loss results from the named insured's fraudulent acts or omissions. The following is the loss payable clause from the ISO HO-3 policy:[1]

Loss payee
A secured creditor to whom the debtor has pledged specific personal property as collateral for a loan.

Loss payable clause
A policy provision that protects the creditor's interest in personal property pledged as collateral for a loan.

R. Loss Payable Clause

If the Declarations show a loss payee for certain listed insured personal property, the definition of "insured" is changed to include that loss payee with respect to that property.

If we decide to cancel or not renew this policy, that loss payee will be notified in writing.

Mortgagee
A lender in a mortgage arrangement, such as a bank or another financing institution.

Mortgage clause
A policy provision that protects the creditor's (mortgagee's) insurable interest in real property pledged as collateral for a mortgage loan.

A **mortgagee** is a lender in a mortgage arrangement, such as a bank or another financing institution. A mortgagee's rights are typically protected by a **mortgage clause**, which is a policy provision that protects the creditor's (mortgagee's) insurable interest in real property pledged as collateral for a mortgage loan. The rights of a mortgagee (who has an insurable interest in real property) are somewhat stronger than those of a typical loss payee (who has an insurable interest in personal property). Unlike a typical loss payable clause, the standard mortgage clause is viewed as a separate policy between the insurer and the mortgagee. Exhibit 12-2 contains the mortgage clause from the ISO HO-3 policy.

EXHIBIT 12-2

K. Mortgage Clause From the ISO HO-3 Policy

Mortgage Clause

1. If a mortgagee is named in this policy, any loss payable under Coverage **A** or **B** will be paid to the mortgagee and you, as interests appear. If more than one mortgagee is named, the order of payment will be the same as the order of precedence of the mortgages.

2. If we deny your claim, that denial will not apply to a valid claim of the mortgagee, if the mortgagee:

   a. Notifies us of any change of ownership, occupancy or substantial change in risk of which the mortgagee is aware;

   b. Pays any premium due under this policy on demand if you have neglected to pay the premium; and

   c. Submits a signed, sworn statement of loss within 60 days after receiving notice from us of your failure to do so. Paragraphs **E.** Appraisal, **G.** Suit Against Us and **I.** Loss Payment under Section I – Conditions also apply to the mortgagee.

3. If we decide to cancel or not to renew this policy, the mortgagee will be notified at least 10 days before the date cancellation or nonrenewal takes effect.

4. If we pay the mortgagee for any loss and deny payment to you:

   a. We are subrogated to all the rights of the mortgagee granted under the mortgage on the property; or

   b. At our option, we may pay to the mortgagee the whole principal on the mortgage plus any accrued interest. In this event, we will receive a full assignment and transfer of the mortgage and all securities held as collateral to the mortgage debt.

5. Subrogation will not impair the right of the mortgagee to recover the full amount of the mortgagee's claim.

The mortgagee's rights under the policy cannot be impaired by an act or omission of the insured. For example, the mortgage clause shown in Exhibit 12-2 clarifies that the mortgagee can still protect its interests—that is, the mortgagee can still be covered by the insurance policy—even if the insured violates policy conditions by any of the following:

- Failing to report material changes to the insurer
- Failing to pay premiums when due
- Failing to submit a proof of loss as required by the policy

The mortgagee is also entitled to receive advance notice of cancellation or nonrenewal.

Insured Parties Identified by Relationship

Most property and liability policies cover as an insured one or more parties identified only by their relationship to the named insured or to another insured party. Some insured parties are members of a class (a spouse of the named insured, for example), whereas others receive protection as legal substitutes for the named insured.

In a homeowners or personal auto policy, the definition of "you" encompasses both the named insured and the named insured's spouse if the spouse resides in the same household as the named insured. The spouse is covered even if, as is typical, he or she is not named in the policy. The definition of "you" often appears in the definitions section of the policy. Unless the spouses are legally separated, the pronouns "you" and "your" throughout these policies refer collectively to the named insured and the named insured's spouse. Therefore, the spouse possesses the same rights and privileges as the named insured. For example, Becca marries her fiancé, Greg, who has no insurance, and he moves into her house. Following the marriage, Greg automatically becomes a named insured under both Becca's auto policy and her homeowners policy, even though he is not specifically named in either.

In addition to spouses, various parties may qualify for status as an insured because they belong to the following classes:

- Family members
- Household residents
- Employees
- Officers and directors
- Other classes stated in the policy based on personal or business relationships with the named insured

Exhibit 12-3 contains an excerpt from ISO's Personal Auto Policy that illustrates how coverage applies to several classes of insureds, as well as how the extent of coverage varies within a single policy.

EXHIBIT 12-3

Liability Coverage Clause From ISO Personal Auto Policy

PART A—LIABILITY COVERAGE

Insuring Agreement

B.   "Insured" as used in this Part means:

1.   You or any "family member" for the ownership, maintenance or use of any auto or "trailer".

2.   Any person using "your covered auto".

3.   For "your covered auto", any person or organization but only with respect to legal responsibility for acts or omissions of a person for whom coverage is afforded under this Part.

4.   For any auto or "trailer", other than "your covered auto", any other person or organization but only with respect to legal responsibility for acts or omissions of you or any "family member" for whom coverage is afforded under this Part. This Provision (**B.4.**) applies only if the person or organization does not own or hire the auto or "trailer".

Includes copyrighted material of Insurance Services Office, Inc., with its permission. Copyright, ISO Properties, Inc., 1997.

The provision in Exhibit 12-3 (which is sometimes called the "omnibus" clause) potentially includes broad classes of individuals or organizations as insureds. For example, assume Javier uses his personal automobile for work as well as personal business. Javier's employer is an insured if any claim or suit is brought against the employer because Javier has an accident while using his own or any other car on business.

In addition to members of a class, a legal substitute for the named insured can also become an insured under the named insured's policy. For example, some property and liability insurance policies define an insured to include one or more of the following parties:

- Legal representatives—such as an executor or administrator of a deceased insured's estate, or a receiver in a bankruptcy proceeding

- Personal representatives—such as a son who has been granted power of attorney to conduct his aging mother's business affairs

- Heirs and assignees—parties who will inherit the named insured's property either by a will or by applicable state law

These individuals do not expressly qualify as separate insureds—they are acceptable legal substitutes for the named insured and are legally empowered to act on behalf of the named insured or the named insured's estate. Because legal substitutes have only the legal rights possessed by the named insured, they can collect only for the named insured's covered losses, not for their own.

Additional Insureds

In addition to being a named insured, being a member of some class of insureds, or being the named insured's legal representative, a party may acquire insured status as an additional insured to the named insured's policy.

An additional insured endorsement can be used to add coverage for one or more additional insureds. Many standard and nonstandard additional insured endorsements are available that address a variety of individuals. Such endorsements include the following:

- *Additional Insured—Club Members*. Members of a golf club or some other club are added as insureds to the club's general liability policy for liability arising out of club activities or activities performed on the club's behalf.

- *Additional Insured—Engineers, Architects, or Surveyors*. Architects, engineers, or surveyors engaged by the named insured are added as insureds for liability arising out of the named insured's premises or operations. Professional liability is specifically excluded.

- *Additional Insured—Owners, Lessees or Contractors—Scheduled Person or Organization*. Owners or lessees are added as insureds on policies covering contractors, and contractors are added as insureds on policies covering subcontractors. The party named in the endorsement is included as an insured under the named insured's policy to which it is attached, but coverage applies only to liability for operations performed for the named insured.

Multiple Insured Parties and Separation of Interests

Many insurance policies insure more than one party. Therefore, policies must address how the actions of one insured might affect coverage for other insureds. When several parties are insured under the same policy, questions such as the following may arise:

- Does the intentional damage exclusion in a property insurance policy preclude coverage for one insured or for all insureds if one insured intentionally causes property damage that results in a financial loss for all insureds?

- How do the policy limits apply if each insured has separate coverage?

- Do the other insureds have coverage if one insured breaches a policy condition in a property or liability insurance policy?

- Can one insured sue another insured for a loss that may be covered by their liability policy?

- Does one insured's concealment, misinterpretation, or fraud void the policy for all insureds, or only for the one who committed the act?

Many insurance policies contain a separation of interests provision to addresses these issues like these. A **separation of interests provision** is a policy provision that clarifies the extent to which coverage may apply separately to more than one insured party.

For example, the liability conditions of an ISO HO-3 policy include the following policy provision:[2]

> **B. Severability of Insurance**
>
> This insurance applies separately to each "insured". This condition will not increase our limit of liability for any one "occurrence".

Separation of interests provision
A policy provision that clarifies the extent to which coverage may apply separately to more than one insured party.

This provision means that the liability coverage of the homeowners policy (Section II Liability Coverages) applies as follows:

- Coverage applies to one insured even if another insured causes an intentional loss or breaches a policy condition. However, violations of the concealment or fraud provision may still preclude coverage. To determine how separation of interests applies in cases of concealment, misrepresentation, or fraud, applicable provisions must also be analyzed.

- Coverage applies to each insured separately when a claim is brought against two or more insureds. However, the insurer's total liability under the policy is not increased.

- Coverage applies when one insured makes a liability claim against another insured. However, separate exclusions in this policy—for property damage to an insured's property or bodily injury to an insured—exclude coverage for some liability claims.

Although many policies contain conditions relating to concealment, misrepresentation, or fraud, their treatment is not necessarily consistent between policies. In the ISO HO-3 policy, the concealment or fraud provision (which also addresses misrepresentation) indicates that coverage is not provided to an insured who commits the concealment, fraud, or misrepresentation but that such action does not void coverage for other insureds.

Parties Not Insured

In addition to extending coverage to many different named and unnamed parties, a typical insurance policy also contains policy provisions addressing parties that may not be insured. The most common example of policy provisions related to parties not insured are the no benefit to bailee provisions that are found in many property policies. Another related policy provision is the assignment provision.

Bailee
A party having possession of another's personal property and a duty either to return it to the owner or to deliver or dispose of it as agreed.

No benefit to bailee provision
A property insurance policy provision that states that it is the insured, and not the bailee, who is protected when covered property is in a bailee's custody.

Insurance deals with many types of property that can, at times, be in the care, custody, or control of someone other than the property owner. A **bailee** is a party having possession of another's personal property and a duty either to return it to the owner or to deliver or dispose of it as agreed. When compensation is involved, the bailee is a bailee for hire. When no compensation is involved, the bailment is a gratuitous bailment. A **no benefit to bailee provision** is a property insurance policy provision that states that it is the insured, and not the bailee, who is protected when covered property is in a bailee's custody. The following is the no benefit to bailee provision from the ISO Personal Auto Policy:[3]

NO BENEFIT TO BAILEE

This insurance shall not directly or indirectly benefit any carrier or other bailee for hire.

This provision relates specifically to bailees for hire, such as an auto mechanic. It does not preclude coverage for a gratuitous bailee, such as another driver to whom an insured lends his or her auto.

Policy language varies, reflecting different types of property loss exposures. However, the effect of any no benefit to bailee provision is typically as follows:

- The bailee (and the bailee's own insurer, if any) cannot benefit from the property owner's coverage. Such coverage does not relieve the bailee of the legal responsibility to safeguard the property. Consequently, the insurer's subrogation rights are preserved.

- An insured does have protection for loss to property in the custody of a bailee for hire, subject to other policy terms.

A bailee for hire is not legally responsible for all damage to property in its care, custody, or control but only for damage caused by its own negligence. For example, suppose Angela's car is in the custody of an auto repair shop when a tornado blows the car from the shop's raised hoist. Because the shop owner did not cause the tornado, he or she cannot be charged for the destruction of Angela's car. However, if, instead, her car slips off the hoist because a mechanic is careless, the mechanic could be liable for the damage. Angela's auto insurer could pay her claim, provided Angela has auto physical damage coverage, then attempt to recover its payment from the bailee (the repair shop) through subrogation. Angela, the property owner, is protected by her insurance, but her insurance is not intended to provide protection for the bailee. The auto repair shop's garagekeepers coverage is designed to protect the mechanic and would also cover the damage to Angela's vehicle.

As well as excluding bailees from coverage, many policies exclude coverage for parties to whom the policyholder has transferred the covered property. Contract law permits anyone who possesses a contract to transfer that contract to another party. The transfer of property from one party (the assignor) to another party (the assignee) is called **assignment**. However, it is usually not possible to transfer (assign) insurance coverage from the named insured to another party (the assignee) without the insurer's written approval.

Assignment
The transfer of property from one party (the assignor) to another party (the assignee).

To guard against moral hazard, adverse selection, and other issues, insurers want to be able to decide whom to insure. Therefore, most property and liability insurance policies contain an assignment provision. An **assignment provision** is a policy provision that prohibits an insured from transferring ownership of an insurance policy to another party without the insurer's written consent. Many property and liability insurance policies call the assignment provision the "Transfer of Your Rights and Duties Under This Policy" provision.

Assignment provision
A policy provision that prohibits an insured from transferring ownership of an insurance policy to another party without the insurer's written consent.

The following assignment provision from the ISO HO-3 policy is typical of assignment provisions in many property-casualty policies:[4]

E. Assignment

Assignment of this policy will not be valid unless we give our written consent.

For example, if Ricardo sells his single family home to Alison, he cannot include his homeowners insurance policy as part of the sale unless the insurer agrees in writing. In practice, insurance policies rarely are assigned. It would be more likely that Ricardo would cancel his homeowners policy and Alison would purchase a new policy.

If Ricardo and Alison attempted to assign Ricardo's homeowners policy without the insurer's written consent, neither party would receive coverage. Ricardo would no longer have an insurable interest in the home he has sold, and Alison would not be an insured on the home she now owns.

Although most insurance policies prohibit assignment, there are some exceptions. For example, insurance on oceangoing cargo is usually assignable. The ownership of the cargo can change several times while it is in transit from one port to another, and the policy can be assigned to new owners as they gain ownership. Insurers are willing to agree to such assignment for two reasons: the risks associated with the cargo do not change with ownership, and the owners' underwriting characteristics are not an issue because the cargo is normally outside any owner's control. Other types of property insurance policies may also allow assignment because they are written to cover multiple insurable interests by using phrases such as "for whom it may concern" or "the named insured or its assignees." Both of these phrases are broad enough to include an assignee as an insured.

In summary, due diligence during post-loss policy analysis requires that the insurance professional properly determine the claiming party's insured status. The party may be the named insured, related to the named insured, one of multiple insured parties, or an additional insured. If the claiming party does not fall into one of these categories, then the insurance policy will probably not provide coverage for that party. Although determining the claiming party's insured status is based on the information provided in the declarations, the insurance professional must be aware that other policy provisions (such as bailee or assignment provisions) may affect the insured status of the claimant.

Insurable Interest

Having determined who qualifies as an insured party, the insurance professional must ensure that the claiming party actually faces a potential loss; that is, an insured party must have an insurable interest in the subject of the policy in order to have a legitimate claim.

Insurable interest is different in property-casualty insurance policies than in life insurance policies. In life insurance policies, insurable interest must be present at the time the policy is purchased; that is, the beneficiary must have insurable interest in the life of the insured individual when the policy is purchased, not at the time of the insured individual's death. While the life insurance policy is in force, circumstances may change that cause the beneficiary to no longer have insurable interest. For example, a wife may be the beneficiary on the life insurance policy of her husband. If the couple were to divorce, the wife may no longer have an insurable interest in her ex-husband's life, but would not be prevented from collecting the proceeds of the life insurance policy in the event of his death.

In contrast, insurable interest in property-casualty insurance policies must be present at the time of the loss. For example, if a homeowner sold his or her home but did not cancel the homeowners policy, then the homeowner cannot present a valid claim if the property subsequently suffers a loss because the homeowner did not have an insurable interest when the loss occurred.

The policy provision of insurable interest is designed to ensure that the insured is actually exposed to potential loss. The following is the insurable interest policy provision from the ISO HO-3 policy:[5]

> **SECTION I – CONDITIONS**
>
> **A. Insurable Interest And Limit Of Liability**
>
> Even if more than one person has an insurable interest in the property covered, we will not be liable in any one loss:
>
> 1. To an "insured" for more than the amount of such "insured's" interest at the time of loss; or
> 2. For more than the applicable limit of liability.

Reasons for Insurable Interest Requirement

Insurance policies have an insurable interest requirement for the following three reasons:

1. It supports the principle of indemnity.
2. It prevents the use of insurance as a wagering mechanism.
3. It reduces the moral hazard incentive that insurance may create for the insured.

Insurable interest supports the principle of indemnity by indemnifying only those parties whose relationships to insured events would cause them to suffer financial losses, and then only to the extent of those losses. Requiring an insurable interest prevents individuals or organizations from wagering (gambling) on an event from which they would not suffer a loss by paying the premium on an insurance policy and profiting when an insurable event occurs. Further, because the insurable interest requirement limits insureds' ability to profit from insurance, the incentive to intentionally cause losses (moral hazard incentive) is reduced.

Basis of Insurable Interest

Insurable interest can arise from a legal relationship between the party filing the claim and the subject of insurance. The legal bases for insurable interest include the following:

- Ownership interest in property
- Contractual obligations

- Exposure to legal liability
- Factual expectancy
- Representation of another party

Having ownership interest in property creates insurable interest in that property. The rights a party possesses regarding owned property are legally protected. For example, property owners have a legal right to sell, give away, and use their property. The extent of legal ownership determines the extent of insurable interest in the property. Although the term "property" is commonly applied to tangible objects, property also includes intangible property, such as copyrights, patents, trademarks, intellectual property, and stock certificates. These intangible property rights have economic value and are guaranteed and protected by law.

Insurable interest can also arise through contractual obligations. Generally, contractual rights and related insurable interests fall into the following two major categories:

1. *Contractual rights regarding persons.* A contract may give a party the right to bring a claim against a second party without entitling the first party to make a claim against any specific property belonging to the second party. For example, if Anthony does not pay his credit card debt, the credit card company can bring a claim against Anthony for the outstanding amount but does not have the right to repossess any of Anthony's property as payment for the debt. In this situation, the credit card company is an unsecured creditor. Unsecured creditors do not have insurable interest in debtors' property.

2. *Contractual rights regarding property.* Some contracts allow one party to bring a claim against specific property held by the second party. For instance, if Anthony purchases an auto subject to a secured loan, the lender may repossess the car if Anthony fails to make payments. This type of contract generally creates an insurable interest in the secured property equal to the debt's remaining balance.

Sometimes property is not owned by a party but that party still has legal responsibility for, or a financial interest in, the property. Examples of legal responsibility for or financial interests in property include the following:

- A hotelkeeper has an insurable interest in guests' property.
- A tenant has an insurable interest in the portion of the premises the tenant occupies.
- A contractor typically has an insurable interest in a building under construction.

In these cases, the responsible party has an insurable interest based on potential legal liability. The extent of that insurable interest is the property's full value, including the owner's use value.

A majority of states have accepted factual expectancy as a valid basis for an insurable interest. **Factual expectancy** is a situation in which a party experiences an economic advantage if an insured event does not occur or, conversely, economic harm if the event does occur. In states that recognize factual expectancy, the insured does not have to establish a specific property right, contractual right, or potential legal liability to prove insurable interest. The person has to show only potential financial harm resulting from the event to be insured. The focus is on the insured's financial position rather than on a legal interest.

Factual expectancy
A situation in which a party experiences an economic advantage if an insured event does not occur or, conversely, economic harm if the event does occur.

As an example of factual expectancy without a legal property right, assume that one of Richard's friends gave him an MP3 player for his birthday. The MP3 player was then taken along with several other items when his home was burglarized. Richard subsequently discovered that the MP3 player was one of a batch that had been stolen from a warehouse. Because a person cannot legally obtain title to property owned by another, Richard was never the legal owner. Therefore, he has no insurable interest in the MP3 player based on ownership rights. Nonetheless, courts would probably find that Richard would be entitled to recover for the player under his homeowners policy based on his factual expectancy of loss.

Finally, insurable interest can be based on one party's acting as a representative of another. Examples of how a person who represents someone else may have an insurable interest by virtue of the representative status include the following:

- *Agents*. An agent may insure property in the agent's name for the principal's benefit. Although the insurance proceeds are ultimately payable to the principal, the agent has an insurable interest.

- *Trustees*. A trustee may insure property in the trustee's name for the trust's benefit. The trustee has an insurable interest but must give the insurance proceeds to the trust.

- *Bailees*. A bailee may insure property in the bailee's name for the bailor's benefit. The bailee has an insurable interest and then pays the insurance proceeds to the bailor.

In these situations, the party obtaining the insurance is not required to have an independent insurable interest in the property. The party derives its interest from its relationship with the party it represents.

Multiple Parties With Insurable Interests

Under some circumstances, multiple parties each have an insurable interest in a property and, as a result, the sum of all insurable interests exceeds the property's value. For example, a mortgage lender and property owner typically both have an insurable interest in the same insured property. The mortgage lender's interest is the extent of the unpaid loan, and the owner's interest is the property's full value. Combined (and if actually paid), the amount of these two interests could greatly exceed the property's value. To illustrate, assume Nina has purchased a $500,000 home using $100,000 of her savings and a $400,000 mortgage. The mortgage lender's interest is $400,000 and Nina's interest is the full amount, $500,000, because she has full use of the property. Therefore, their combined interest is $900,000, well above the total value of the property. However, if the home was completely destroyed, neither Nina nor the mortgage lender could claim more than their actual loss under the homeowners policy. The insurer would pay $100,000 to Nina and $400,000 to the mortgage lender.

When more than one person owns the same property, the nature of the ownership affects the extent of each party's insurable interest. Property may be jointly owned under one of the following interests:

- Joint tenancy

- Tenancy by the entirety

- Tenancy in common

- Tenancy in partnership

Joint tenancy

A concurrently owned and undivided interest in an estate that transfers to a surviving joint tenant upon the death of the other.

Joint tenancy is a concurrently owned and undivided interest in an estate that transfers to a surviving joint tenant upon the death of the other. In joint tenancy, each tenant has a right of survivorship, that is, an automatic right to the share of the joint tenant when the joint tenant dies. For example, if Manuel and Gerard are joint tenants of a restaurant building, each owns the entire building. If Manuel died, Gerard would automatically become the sole owner of the building and vice versa. Because any one joint tenant could become the property's sole owner, each tenant has an insurable interest to the extent of the property's full value. If the restaurant was insured for $1 million, both Manuel and Gerard would have a $1 million interest. Therefore, their combined interest would be $2 million, or twice the value of the property. Nonetheless, if the restaurant was destroyed by fire, their insurance policy would pay out only $1 million. That payment would probably be made to the first named insured in the declarations.

Tenancy by the entirety

A joint tenancy between husband and wife.

Tenancy by entirety is a joint tenancy between husband and wife. As with a joint tenancy, if spouses jointly own a property, each of them owns the entire property and if one of them dies, the other becomes the sole owner. Therefore, in a tenancy by the entirety, each spouse has an insurable interest to the full extent of the property value. As a result, the combined interests of the spouses would be twice the property value. However, as with a joint tenancy, an insurance policy would pay out only up to the property value.

Tenancy in common

A concurrent ownership of property, in equal or unequal shares, by two or more joint tenants who lack survivorship rights.

Tenancy in common is a concurrent ownership of property, in equal or unequal shares, by two or more joint tenants who lack survivorship rights. Unlike joint tenants or tenants in the entirety, tenants in common do not have survivorship rights. For example, if Andrew, Colin, and Rita were tenants in common of a factory, each holding a one-third interest, then if Andrew died, Colin and Rita would still own one-third of the factory, not half each. Andrew's third would pass to his heirs. With tenants in common, each party's insurable interest is therefore limited to that owner's share of the property. Therefore, in this example, each has an interest worth one-third of the value of the property, so their combined interests are equal to the property value. Any insurance payouts would probably be made to the first named insured, who would then be responsible for distributing the appropriate share of the money to the other tenants in common.

Tenancy in partnership is a concurrent ownership by a partnership and its individual partners of personal property used by the partnership. This type of tenancy is similar to a joint tenancy in that the partnership and all partners have rights of survivorship. Therefore, with a tenancy in partnership, both the partnership entity and the individual partners have an insurable interest in property used by the partnership. Depending on the size of the partnership, the combined interests could be many times the actual property value because each partner, and the partnership, would have an interest worth the entire insurable amount. If a loss occurred, the insurer payments would be made to the first named insured, which could be the partnership entity or one of the partners.

Tenancy in partnership
A concurrent ownership by a partnership and its individual partners of personal property used by the partnership.

Premiums

A contract requires both parties to provide consideration. In an insurance policy, the insured's consideration is the payment of premium—or the promise to pay the premium. The premium amount to be paid by the insured is typically stated in the declarations. In addition to the premium amount shown in the declarations, many policies and endorsements also include a payment of premium provision, which states that coverage is granted in consideration of the premium. The insured's use of the premium as consideration is reinforced by payment of premium provisions. The following is one of the payment of premium provisions from a standard workers' compensation and employers' liability insurance policy:[6]

> **PART FIVE - PREMIUM**
>
> D.   Premium Payments
>
> You will pay all premium when due. You will pay the premium even if part or all of a workers compensation law is not valid.

Some policies include additional provisions relating to premium calculation. For example, they include provisions about how premiums are determined and whether they may be changed while the policy is in force. Some provisions might indicate who is responsible for handling premiums and renewal options. During the analysis of the declarations, the insurance professional needs to ensure that the insured did not violate any premium payment policy provisions.

Policy Period

Once it has been determined that the party filing the claim is an insured party, has an insurable interest, and has paid the premium, an insurance professional should analyze whether the loss occurred during the policy period. The **policy period** is the timeframe, beginning with the inception

Policy period
The timeframe, beginning with the inception date, during which insurance coverage applies.

date, during which insurance coverage applies. The policy period dates, or at least the inception date, are usually shown in the declarations. Although six-month and one-year policies are typical with property-casualty insurance, other timeframes are also common.

Some property insurance policies may depart from the general rule that coverage applies for a specified period and terminate coverage when the loss exposure ceases to exist. For example, a builders risk policy (covering a building under construction) expires before the stated expiration date if construction is completed prior to that date. Similarly, coverage under a crop-hail insurance policy ends when the crop is actually harvested, provided the harvest precedes the policy expiration date.

Many package policies provide both property and liability coverage, and it is desirable that the entire policy begin at the same time. Many property, liability, and other policies begin and expire at 12:01 AM, that is, one minute after midnight. The additional minute eliminates any ambiguity about whether 12:00 means noon or midnight, or whether "midnight" means the instant at which the specified date begins or the one at which it expires.

In addition to the period specified in the declarations, policy period provisions appearing elsewhere in the policy address when something must happen to trigger coverage. The following is an excerpt from the ISO Commercial Property Conditions in which the policy period is referenced as a condition of coverage:[7]

H. POLICY PERIOD, COVERAGE TERRITORY

Under this Coverage Part:

1. We cover loss or damage commencing:
    a. During the policy period shown in the Declarations; and
    b. Within the coverage territory.

Property insurance typically applies to losses that actually start during the policy period. For example, assume Policy A covers a loss that commences during the policy period. Policy A expires at 12:01 AM on Monday, at which time Policy B becomes effective. If a building covered by these policies experiences a fire that begins at 11 PM on Sunday and continues to burn until 1 AM on Monday, the entire loss is covered by Policy A because the fire commenced during Policy A's policy period.

This provision is especially significant for claims, such as business income claims, concerning losses that extend for a long time after they commence. An insurer could be required to pay business income losses for many months after a business income policy expires, provided the loss-producing event began during the policy period.

Liability insurance triggers can vary. Many liability policies refer to bodily injury or property damage that occurs during the policy period, but others trigger coverage when a claim is first made, regardless of the time the event occurred that gave rise to the claim. In some cases, coverage has been found under a series of policies for events that were considered to occur throughout the terms of several consecutive policies.

Coverage Territory Provisions

As well as specifying when an event must occur to be covered, an insurance policy must specify where the event must happen. Whereas the policy period is frequently contained in the declarations, the coverage territory may appear in the declarations, definitions, or other policy sections.

Although other policy provisions may be much more restrictive, the coverage territory provisions help identify broad geographical borders beyond which coverage does not apply. For example, real property may be covered only at the address specified in the policy declarations, and long-haul trucking loss exposures may be covered only within a described radius of operations.

Exhibit 12-4 contains the definition of coverage territory from the ISO Commercial General Liability policy as it appears in the definitions section.

After analyzing the declarations for insured parties, insurable interests, premiums, policy period, and territory, the second section of the policy to be analyzed in the DICE method is the insuring agreement.

EXHIBIT 12-4

Coverage Territory Provisions From ISO CGL Policy

SECTION V DEFINITIONS

4. "Coverage territory" means:

   a. The United States of America (including its territories and possessions), Puerto Rico and Canada;

   b. International waters or airspace, but only if the injury or damage occurs in the course of travel or transportation between any places included in **a.** above; or

   c. All other parts of the world if the injury or damage arises out of:

      (1) Goods or products made or sold by you in the territory described in **a.** above;

      (2) The activities of a person whose home is in the territory described in **a.** above, but is away for a short time on your business; or

      (3) "Personal or advertising injury" offenses that take place through the Internet or similar electronic means of communication provided the insured's responsibility to pay damages is determined in a "suit" on the merits, in the territory described in **a.** above or in a settlement we agree to.

INSURING AGREEMENT

A policy's insuring agreement section contains the promise from the insurer to pay for covered losses when an insured event occurs. An insurer may be contractually obligated to make a payment to an insured if all of the policy provisions related to the declarations have been met; that is, the claiming party qualifies as an insured, the claiming party has an insurable interest, and the insured event occurs during the policy period and in the coverage territory.

The insurer's obligations are not triggered by an insuring agreement unless an insured event occurs. Insured events and insured property or activities are often mentioned explicitly in the insuring agreement and then clarified subsequently in the conditions, endorsements, exclusions, or other miscellaneous provisions. An event is insured only if it meets all five elements of an insured event. These five elements differ somewhat between property and liability insurance policies, as shown in Exhibit 12-5.

EXHIBIT 12-5

Elements of an Insured Event

Property Insurance	Liability Insurance
1. Covered property	1. Covered activity
2. Covered cause of loss	2. Alleged legal responsibility to pay covered damages
3. Covered consequences	3. Covered consequences
4. Covered location	4. Covered location
5. Covered period	5. Covered period

As the elements of an insured event differ between property insurance policies and liability insurance policies, each type of policy should be considered individually.

Insured Events in Property Insurance Policies

Property insurance (either in a stand-alone property policy or as part of a package policy) provides coverage for real or personal property lost or damaged by a covered cause of loss. The policy may also provide coverage for consequential financial losses resulting from property damage. Furthermore, property coverage may be limited to a single cause of loss, such as in a flood insurance policy, or include multiple causes of loss, such as in the ISO HO-3 policy.

Covered Property

The first element of an insured event in property insurance policies is covered property. An insurance policy may cover either real property or personal property. Real property refers to rights in land, including rights to water, minerals, structures permanently attached to the land (such as buildings), and whatever is growing on the land (such as trees). It also includes rights closely related to land, such as the right to have access to or use of the land belonging to another. Personal property refers to property that is not real property and includes both tangible and intangible property.

The declarations of property insurance policies often either specify the address or give a description of the real property being covered. Additional real property, such as newly acquired locations, may also be covered, despite not being specifically identified in the declarations. The personal property covered by a property insurance policy may be specified in the declarations, but may be covered as part of a broad category of coverage being offered by the insuring agreement. For example, a personal auto policy lists the automobiles being covered in the declarations, but the insured may also have coverage for automobiles that are rented. This coverage is not specifically listed in the declarations.

Most property insurance policies, including commercial building, personal property, and homeowners forms, share a similar format, as follows:

- An insuring agreement describing broad classes of covered property. Some limited or single-purpose insurance policies cover only items specifically described in a list, or policy schedule. A **policy schedule** (also just called a schedule) is a list that identifies specific items, usually with values attached, that are covered by a property insurance policy.

- An exclusionary section describing narrower subclasses of property that are not covered.

- Other provisions within the policy form or in endorsements that may add or exclude specific types of property or exclude damage for certain causes of loss.

Policy schedule
A list that identifies specific items, usually with values attached, that are covered by a property insurance policy.

Examining Other Provisions to Determine Covered Property

The insuring agreement often broadens covered property beyond the real or personal property listed in the declarations. Furthermore, determining covered property involves more than analyzing the insuring agreement. The declarations, insuring agreement, conditions, endorsements, exclusions, definitions, and miscellaneous provisions all affect the determination of covered property. Because so many provisions are involved, it is difficult to say whether determining covered property is part of the insuring agreement analysis, or part of the analysis of any other section of policy provisions. Discussing determination of covered property as part of analyzing the insuring agreement is just one of several possible approaches.

Most policies begin with a broad description of the types of property that are covered. Exclusions then further define the coverage by removing coverage that would not be provided under specific circumstances or for specific reasons. What remains of the original covered property is what is then covered under the policy.

For example, in ISO's Building and Personal Property Coverage form, property is divided into three categories: (1) "Building," (2) "Your Business Personal Property," and (3) "Personal Property Of Others." Generally, the "Building" definition provides coverage for real property. The "Your Business Personal Property" definition complements the "Building" coverage with a description of covered personal property of the insured, sometimes called "contents coverage." The "Personal Property Of Others" definition covers insureds whose contents include some personal property owned by others but that the insured might choose to insure. Newly acquired property, or property at new locations, can also be insured.

Covered Cause of Loss

The second element of an insured event in property insurance policies is covered cause of loss. Coverage for a loss is provided under a property insurance policy only if a covered cause of loss is the proximate cause of a covered consequence. A proximate cause is the event that sets in motion an uninterrupted chain of events leading to a loss. Coverage may not be provided under a property insurance policy if the chain of events is broken by an intervening force that is not covered by the policy.

Insurers typically use the following three common approaches to describe covered causes of loss in commercial property policy forms:

1. Basic-form
2. Broad-form
3. Special-form

Additional specified perils can be added through endorsements, such as flood or earthquake coverage, to any of those forms.

The basic and broad forms use the specified-perils or named-perils approach, meaning that they specifically name covered perils. To enforce coverage, the insured has the burden of proof to show that a covered peril was the proximate cause of covered loss consequences. The special-form coverage, however, provides very broad coverage and names the excluded hazards and causes of loss. To successfully deny coverage, the insurer, not the insured, must be able to prove that the loss resulted from a peril or hazard that the policy excludes. The difference in who has the burden of proof is a major difference between the basic and the broad cause of loss forms compared with the special cause of loss form.

In addition to the covered causes of loss, most property policies provide some coverage for ensuing losses. An **ensuing loss** is the loss attributable to a subsequent peril that results from loss by an initial peril. For example, the water (flood) exclusion of the ISO Causes of Loss—Special Form ends with the following words:

Ensuing loss
The loss attributable to a subsequent peril that results from loss by an initial peril.

But if Water, as described…results in fire, explosion or sprinkler leakage, we will pay for the loss or damage caused by that fire, explosion or sprinkler leakage.[8]

The ensuing losses that are covered, and the causes of loss that are covered, vary among policies and even within a single policy.

Covered Consequences

The third element of an insured event in a property insurance policy is covered consequences. When a cause of loss damages or destroys property, only some of the damage is covered by property insurance policies. The phrase "covered consequences" refers to the damage or adverse effects the policy covers.

Covered consequences fall into four major categories. The first two categories reflect direct property losses. The second two reflect indirect loss, that is, a loss that is a consequence of a direct property loss. The categories are as follows:

1. *Reduction in value.* Reduction in property value because of damage by a covered cause of loss is sometimes called a direct loss. A policy usually contains provisions that determine how the reduction in value can be determined.

2. *Increased cost to replace or repair.* Replacing damaged or destroyed property often costs more than the property was worth before the damage. Consequently, replacement cost coverage, which provides sufficient coverage to replace property if it is damaged, is often available for real property and many types of personal property.

3. *Loss of revenue.* Damage to property can cause a business slowdown or shutdown, cutting off the stream of income that normally pays operating expenses and ultimately reducing profits. The loss of income resulting from property damage is a covered consequence under many property insurance policies.

4. *Extra expense.* A business or family can incur extra expense during a period when it cannot use damaged or destroyed property that has not yet been repaired or replaced. Both business and family extra expenses are covered consequences under some insurance policies.

Indirect property losses are covered consequences that may be more difficult to estimate than direct property losses. For example, consider the catastrophic damage to Alabama, Louisiana, and Mississippi caused by Hurricane Katrina in 2005. Although billions of dollars in direct property losses occurred, a majority of the insured losses stemming from Hurricane Katrina are indirect, business income losses. For example, the casino hotels in Biloxi, Mississippi, and other areas along the Gulf coast lost millions of dollars a day in revenue.

Covered Location

The fourth element of an insured event in property insurance policies is covered location. A covered location is both of the following:

- Within the "coverage territory," as defined in the policy
- A place where coverage applies within the coverage territory

Location is not usually an issue in real property insurance claims because the property has a fixed location. By definition, "contents" also have a permanent location—the building that contains them. However, many personal property items periodically or regularly change locations. For example, when a manufacturer's finished stock is moved from one warehouse to another, the stock is no longer the contents of the first warehouse.

Different policies have different covered locations for personal property. A homeowners policy's coverage extends worldwide. Specialized inland marine coverages can also provide worldwide coverage for business personal property. However, most commercial property forms cover business personal property only in or within 100 feet of the premises described in the declarations. Likewise, most crime coverages are restricted to property inside the premises described in the declarations—or even inside a safe or vault on the premises.

A growing number of organizations have loss exposures outside the United States. Whenever property loss exposures exist, even if they are temporary, property insurance policies should be scrutinized to ensure that otherwise insured events also involve a covered location. The covered location should be investigated and confirmed when claims for damage to personal property off-premises or out of the country are involved.

Covered Period

The fifth element of an insured event in a property insurance policy is the covered period, which is the period during which the insured has a contract with the insurer. This may not always be the same as the policy period written in the declarations, as in the following examples:

- The policy period might begin before a written policy is issued. Sometimes an insurance agent binds coverage, orally or in writing, as soon as the insured agrees to buy the policy, but several weeks pass before a written policy is issued. Once issued, the written policy would normally have the same effective date as the binder (the temporary agreement to provide insurance coverage until a formal written policy is issued). This type of situation arose after the terrorist attacks on the World Trade Center in 2001. The property insurance program that was being designed to insure the World Trade Center had been agreed to, but not all of the contracts had been formalized at the time of the attacks. The result was that the insurers who had agreed to provide coverage had a legal obligation to pay for the damage to the World Trade Center.

- After a policy is issued, coverage may be terminated by cancellation before the end of the policy period, when it would otherwise expire.

- A policy could be renewed for many successive years, as shown in an endorsement that does not replace the original declarations.

Generally, only the onset or beginning of the loss-producing event must fall within the covered period. It is not necessary for the entire covered consequences to fall entirely within the policy period. For example, if a fire starts to damage covered property ten minutes before policy inception, the loss is not an insured event, even if the fire continues to burn well into the policy period. Conversely, if a fire starts to damage covered property ten minutes before the policy expires, then the loss is an insured event, even if most of the damage occurs after policy expiration.

Insured Events in Liability Insurance Policies

Although insured events under both property insurance and liability insurance share three elements—covered consequences, covered location, and covered period—there are major differences in how those elements are defined. In addition, the first two elements of an insured liability event—covered activity and an alleged legal responsibility to pay covered damages—differ from the first two elements of a property insurance insured event.

Covered Activity

The first element of an insured event under a liability insurance policy is covered activity. The broadest personal and commercial liability policies have a comprehensive insuring agreement offering protection for a wide range of activities. These liability policies do not specify what types of activities are covered, but they apply to all activities not excluded. Therefore, they could be loosely compared to special-form property coverage that applies to causes of loss and hazards that are not specifically excluded. Other liability policies—auto policies, for example—have single-purpose or limited insuring agreements that provide coverage for only one activity or a few types of activities.

The name of a policy or coverage often indicates what activities it covers. For example, a Commercial General Liability Coverage Form and the personal liability coverage of homeowners policies provide broad, comprehensive protection against a range of common business or personal activities, whereas the coverage of a business auto policy or a personal auto policy is limited to auto-related activities. However, although the policy name provides some indication of coverage, the full range of activities covered under a particular liability policy can be understood clearly only by analyzing the entire policy, including all endorsements.

Alleged Legal Responsibility to Pay Covered Damages

The second element of an insured event in a liability insurance policy is alleged legal responsibility to pay covered damages. A liability loss is caused whenever something happens for which an insured allegedly becomes legally responsible to pay damages to a third-party claimant because of bodily injury or property damage that the policy covers.

Most liability insurance policies agree to pay for damages that the insured is legally obligated to pay or the insurer agrees to during a settlement. The legal obligation to which various liability policies refer can stem from the following bases of legal liability:

- Negligence or other tort liability—failure to fulfill a duty imposed by tort law
- Contractual liability—failure to meet an obligation assumed under contract
- Statutory liability—failure to meet a duty imposed by statute

A variety of claims can be made under these legal bases, including premises and operations, products, completed operations, automobile, workers' compensation, environmental, or professional liability claims.

Covered Consequences

The third element of an insured event in a liability insurance policy is covered consequences. The covered consequences of a liability insurance policy (which are not the same as the covered consequences of a property insurance policy) typically cover consequences in the following two broad categories:

1. Damages for which the insured is legally liable to a third party
2. Defense costs incurred to defend the insured against a third-party claim for covered bodily injury or property damage, including miscellaneous expenses

Whether the allegation involves bodily injury, property damage, or some other offense, an insured event does not occur unless the covered consequences involve a claim for damages that are covered under the policy. A typical liability insuring agreement refers to "sums that the insured becomes legally obligated to pay as damages." Insurers usually do not define "damages," and the common meaning of the term would obligate the insurer to pay any compensatory damages as well as punitive damages that the insured is legally liable to pay. However, some states prohibit insurers from paying punitive damages awards because relieving an insured from paying damages designed to punish wrongdoing is considered to be against public policy.

In addition to paying damages that the insured is legally liable to pay, liability insurers are required to defend the insured even when a claim seems to be false or fraudulent or most of the claim's allegations are outside of the coverage provided by the insurance policy. As long as at least one of the claim's allegations is potentially within the coverage the policy provides, most liability insurance policies require the insurer to provide a defense, using a counsel of the insurer's choice and to pay all costs of the defense provided. For example, the insurer would be required to defend a homeowners liability claim alleging damages for both bodily injury (which is covered) and slander (which is not covered by most unendorsed homeowners policies). The insurer agrees to pay the costs of defending the insured, and the insurer often contributes substantial experience and expertise to the defense process. Many insurance buyers consider the insurer's defense services to be one of the most important reasons to buy liability insurance.

Knowing whether defense costs are paid within or in addition to policy limits is important because the amount of insurance available to pay damages can be significantly reduced when defense costs are paid as part of the policy limits, as shown in Exhibit 12-6.

EXHIBIT 12-6

Limits on Defense Costs Example

Suppose an insurer has issued a professional liability insurance policy with a $100,000 policy limit covering a dentist. The insurer incurs $40,000 in costs to defend a professional liability claim, and the trial court holds the insured liable for $90,000 in damages.

- If defense costs are within limits, the insurer pays $40,000 in defense costs and $60,000 in damages, consuming the entire $100,000 limit. The insured will be responsible for the remaining $30,000.

- If defense costs are payable in addition to policy limits, the insurer pays the $40,000 in defense costs plus the full $90,000 in damages. Additionally, if the claimant appeals the case to a higher court, the insurer pays the costs of defending the appeal, and its defense obligation does not end until the insurer pays $100,000 in damages.

Under the majority of liability insurance policies, defense costs are payable in addition to the maximum amount payable for damages. No dollar limit is placed on the amount the insurer might be required to pay in defending the insured against a claim for covered damages. A typical liability insurance policy stipulates that the insurer's obligation to defend against any given claim for damages terminates when the amount it pays for damages equals the policy limits. For example, the following provision from the ISO Commercial General Liability Policy describes when the duty to defend ends:[9]

1. **Insuring Agreement**

a. ...

  (2) Our right and duty to defend end when we have used up the applicable limit of insurance in the payments of judgments or settlements under Coverages **A** or **B** or medical expenses under Coverage **C**.

In cases in which the damages clearly exceed the policy limits, the insurer cannot just pay the limits and withdraw from the case. If the claimant is not willing to settle for policy limits, the insurer is obligated to continue defending the insured until a final court judgment has been rendered or a settlement has been reached.

Although the insurer's defense obligation is theoretically unlimited, practical constraints apply. Most policies give the insurer the exclusive right to control the defense. The insurer can select its own defense counsel, monitor the case, and attempt to negotiate a settlement if costs threaten to become disproportionately high. In practice, limitations usually exist on how much an insurer will spend defending a claim before agreeing to a settlement.

The benefits of a sound legal defense stemming from the duty to defend include the following:

- Often a strong defense results in a judgment favoring the insured. Therefore neither the insurer nor the insured are required to pay damages.
- A legal decision in the insured's favor may establish case law that discourages similar claims.
- A strong defense signals to plaintiffs' attorneys and would-be claimants that the insurer will vigorously defend similar claims rather than pay them.
- The amount of damages payable can be substantially reduced because of evidence introduced through a sound, if costly, defense.

The outcome of litigation can never be predicted with complete confidence. Insurers do not always prevail when they choose to defend cases, and defense costs sometimes are incurred on claims that could have been reasonably settled out of court by paying the claimant's original settlement demand. Rather than incur defense costs, insurers sometimes pay small, questionable claims (known as nuisance claims), even those they could probably win, in order to avoid defense costs or the possibility of a large adverse judgment.

Supplementary payments

Payments for a range of additional claim-related expenses as specified in a liability policy.

Primary liability insurance policies invariably cover defense costs, as well as a range of additional expenses (generally called supplementary payments). In the context of insurance, **supplementary payments** are payments for a range of additional claim-related expenses as specified in a liability policy. An example of the supplementary payments that may be made by the liability section of the ISO personal auto policy is shown in Exhibit 12-7.

EXHIBIT 12-7

ISO Personal Auto Policy Supplementary Payments

1. Up to $250 for the cost of bail bonds required because of an accident, including related traffic law violations. The accident must result in "bodily injury" or "property damage" covered under this policy.

2. Premiums on appeal bonds and bonds to release attachments in any suit we defend.

3. Interest accruing after a judgment is entered in any suit we defend. Our duty to pay interest ends when we offer to pay that part of the judgment which does not exceed our limit of liability for this coverage.

4. Up to $200 a day for loss of earnings, but not other income, because of attendance at hearings or trials at our request.

5. Other reasonable expenses incurred at our request.

Includes copyrighted material of Insurance Services Office, Inc., with its permission. Copyright, ISO Properties, Inc., 1997.

Covered Location

The fourth element of an insured event in liability insurance policies is covered location. With liability insurance, two distinct locations can be relevant: (1) the location of the incident and (2) the location of a lawsuit brought by a claimant against an insured.

Most liability insurance policies provide protection at any location within a broadly defined policy territory. In auto insurance, for example, the policy territory is usually defined as the United States (including its territories or possessions), Puerto Rico, or Canada. Accidents involving a covered auto while being transported between these locations are also covered by these policies. The broadest definitions of covered locations can be found in liability policies that apply "anywhere in the world." Others apply "anywhere" or do not specify their territorial scope.

An insurance policy providing defense coverage sometimes places a territorial restriction on lawsuits. For example, the ISO Commercial General Liability Coverage Form provides coverage for personal and advertising injury offenses that occur through the Internet, provided that the insured's responsibility to pay damages is determined in a lawsuit in the U.S. (including its territories and possessions), Puerto Rico, or Canada.

Covered Period

The fifth element of an insured event in a liability insurance policy is a covered period. It is essential to know whether coverage is triggered when an adverse event occurs, when the insured becomes aware that it happened, when a claim is made for damages arising out of that event, or at some other point in time. Like property insurance policies, liability policies usually have a one-year term, but three- or six-month personal auto policies are common, and multi-year policies also exist.

Many discussions of periods covered by liability insurance policies include the term "tail," a term that does not actually appear in liability insurance policies. Most claims—and nearly all property claims—involve a relatively short period, or tail, between the insured event, the discovery, the claim, and the settlement. Other claims, called long-tail claims, may involve years from the date of the bodily injury or property damage, the date it is discovered, the date a claim is made, the date a claim is settled, and the date of final claim payment.

Claims involving long-tail loss exposures raise challenging questions about the point at which a covered event occurs. Most liability insurance is written on an occurrence-basis. Some liability coverages, however, are written on a claims-made basis. The difference between the two approaches lies in their coverage triggers. **Occurrence-basis coverage** is triggered by the actual happening of bodily injury or property damage during the policy period. **Claims-made coverage** is triggered by a claim alleging bodily injury or property damage that is made during the policy period, even if the claim arises from an event that happened before policy inception.

Many claims-made liability policies are subject to a **retroactive date**, which is the date on or after which injury, damage, or another insured event must occur in order to be covered under a claims-made policy. Ideally, a retroactive date is designated on the insured's first claims-made policy to avoid any gaps in coverage, and that date remains fixed even when the initial policy is renewed or replaced. A replacement claims-made policy with a different retroactive date would create a potential time gap. An insured who replaces a claims-made policy with an occurrence policy might also face a time coverage gap.

Exhibit 12-8 contains the insuring agreement in the claims-made version of the ISO Commercial General Liability Coverage Form.

Occurrence-basis coverage
Coverage that is triggered by the actual happening of bodily injury or property damage during the policy period.

Claims-made coverage
Coverage that is triggered by a claim alleging bodily injury or property damage that is made during the policy period, even if the claim arises from an event that happened before policy inception.

Retroactive date
The date on or after which injury, damage, or another insured event must occur in order to be covered under a claims-made policy.

EXHIBIT 12-8

Claims-Made Insuring Agreement From ISO CGL Coverage Form

This insurance applies to "bodily injury" and "property damage" only if...

(2) The "bodily injury" or "property damage" did not occur before the Retroactive Date, if any, shown in the Declarations or after the end of the policy period; and

(3) A claim for damages because of the "bodily injury" or "property damage" is first made against any insured, in accordance with paragraph c. below, during the policy period or any Extended Reporting Period we provide under Section V — Extended Reporting Periods.

Includes copyrighted material of Insurance Services Office, Inc., with its permission. Copyright, ISO Properties, Inc., 2003.

An insurance professional should be careful in analyzing liability policies to determine whether an event occurred in the covered period. Overlaps and gaps in coverage may arise if the insured has switched from a claims-made liability policy to an occurrence liability policy or vice-versa. A coverage gap could also arise from an unforeseen claim that results from an event that happened before the policy's retroactive date. Insurers writing claims-made coverage are sometimes willing to provide retroactive coverage for a period long enough to cover any claims that were previously incurred but unknown and unreported. Alternatively, insureds that are aware of these types of time gaps in coverage can purchase additional policies to bridge the gaps. A detailed discussion of these bridge policies is beyond the scope of this text.

SUMMARY

Post-loss policy analysis begins with the analysis of an insurance policy's declarations and insuring agreements. Analyzing the declarations involves analyzing the policy provisions relating to insured parties, insurable interest, premiums, policy period, and coverage territory. Insured parties include the named insured and other persons or organizations that qualify as insured parties and have an insurable interest. Insured parties—especially those who qualify as named insureds—have a variety of valuable contractual rights under the terms of a typical policy. Although policies grant rights to all insured parties, the extent of these rights can vary. Policy provisions that typically appear in a policy refer to insured parties identified by name, insured parties identified by relationship, additional insureds, and multiple insured parties. Policies also typically specify which parties are not insured.

An insurable interest can arise as a result of a relationship with a person or a right over property. Whether a person legally has an insurable interest depends on the relationship between the claiming party and the property, person, or event in question. Insurable interest is different in property-casualty insurance policies than in life insurance policies. In life insurance policies, insurable interest must be present at the time the policy is purchased, not at the time of the insured individual's death. In contrast, insurable interest in property-casualty insurance policies must be present at the time of the loss. The legal bases for insurable interest include ownership interest in property, contractual obligations, exposure to legal liability, factual expectations, and representation of another party. Under some circumstances, multiple parties each have an insurable interest and, as a result, the sum of all interests may exceed the property's value.

In an insurance policy, the insured's consideration is the payment (or promise of payment) of premiums. The premium amount that is to be paid by the insured is typically stated in the declarations. The policy period is the time-frame, beginning with the inception date, during which insurance coverage applies. The policy period dates, or at least the inception date, are usually shown in the declarations. In addition to the period specified in the declarations, policy period provisions appearing elsewhere in the policy address when something must happen to trigger coverage. Property insurance typically applies to losses that actually start during the policy period. Liability insurance triggers can vary. Many liability policies refer to bodily injury or property damage that occurs during the policy period, but others trigger coverage when a claim is first made, regardless of the time the event occurred that gave rise to the claim.

Whereas the policy period is frequently contained in the declarations, the coverage territory may appear in the declarations, definitions, or other policy sections. Although other policy provisions may be much more restrictive, the coverage territory provisions help identify broad geographical borders beyond which coverage does not apply.

The insuring agreement section contains the promise from the insurer to pay for covered losses when an insured event occurs. The insurer's obligations are not triggered by an insuring agreement unless an insured event occurs. Insured events and insured property or activities are often mentioned explicitly in the insuring agreement and then clarified subsequently in the conditions, endorsements, exclusions, or other miscellaneous provisions. An event is insured only if it meets all five elements of an insured event. These five elements differ somewhat between property and liability insurance policies. In property insurance policies, the five elements of an insured event are covered property, covered cause of loss, covered consequences, covered location, and covered period. For liability insurance policies, the five elements of an insured event are covered activity, alleged legal responsibility to pay covered damages, covered consequences, covered location, and covered period.

Having determined that nothing in the policy provisions related to the declarations, definitions, and insuring agreement precludes coverage for a claim, the insurance professional must examine the conditions, exclusions and endorsements, and miscellaneous provisions of a policy before determining the amounts payable under the policy.

CHAPTER NOTES

1. Includes copyrighted material of Insurance Services Office, Inc., with its permission. Copyright, ISO Properties, Inc., 1999.

2. Includes copyrighted material of Insurance Services Office, Inc., with its permission. Copyright, ISO Properties, Inc., 1999.

3. Includes copyrighted material of Insurance Services Office, Inc., with its permission. Copyright, ISO Properties, Inc., 1997.

4. Includes copyrighted material of Insurance Services Office, Inc., with its permission. Copyright, ISO Properties, Inc., 1999.

5. Includes copyrighted material of Insurance Services Office, Inc., with its permission. Copyright, ISO Properties, Inc., 1999.

6. Includes copyrighted material of National Council on Compensation Insurance with its permission. Form WC 00 00 00 A 1991.

7. Includes copyrighted material of Insurance Services Office, Inc., with its permission. Copyright, ISO Properties, Inc., 1987.

8. Includes copyrighted material of Insurance Services Office, Inc., with its permission. Copyright, ISO Properties, Inc., 2001.

9. Includes copyrighted material of Insurance Services Office, Inc., with its permission. Copyright, ISO Properties, Inc., 2003.

Direct Your Learning

Policy Analysis: Conditions and Exclusions

After learning the content of this chapter and completing the corresponding course guide assignment, you should be able to:

■ Given a case, analyze each of the following to determine whether coverage exists:

- Concealment, misrepresentation, or fraud provisions

- Coverage maintenance provisions

- Insured's duties in event of loss provisions

- Insurer's duties in event of loss provisions

- Property insurance exclusions

- Liability insurance exclusions

■ Define or describe each of the Key Words and Phrases for this chapter.

Develop Your Perspective

What are the main topics covered in the chapter?

This chapter analyzes the conditions and exclusions section of an insurance policy. This is a continuation of the post-loss policy analysis applying the DICE method.

Consider how the policy provisions define the terms and scope of the coverage between the insurer and the insured.

- How do policy conditions grant or restrict coverage between the insurer and the insured?

- How do policy exclusions refine the insurer's intentions in providing coverage?

Why is it important to learn about these topics?

Understanding how conditions and exclusions operate helps an insurance professional to determine whether coverage exists under a particular policy.

Imagine that you have presented a claim to your insurer and that there is a dispute about the amount to be paid or the applicability of coverage.

- What policy provisions might you review to resolve this dispute?

How can you use what you will learn?

Examine one of your insurance policies.

- What are your duties in the event of a loss?

- What exclusions eliminate coverage for your significant loss exposures?

Chapter 13
Policy Analysis: Conditions and Exclusions

As discussed in the previous chapters, this text uses the DICE method of post-loss policy analysis. The DICE acronym represents four of the six sections of a property-casualty insurance policy: declarations, insuring agreement, conditions, and exclusions. This chapter examines the policy provisions related to the conditions and exclusions sections of the policy. Subsequent chapters discuss the amounts payable under an insurance policy once it has been determined what coverage exists and to what extent.

It is important to understand that not all of the policy provisions that are related to a specific section of a policy appear in that section. Each property-casualty insurance policy has a different structure, which complicates locating various provisions. Insurance professionals should be familiar with common policy provisions to better analyze frequently used policies. The importance of reading the entire policy when performing post-loss policy analysis cannot be overemphasized.

CONDITIONS

The conditions section contains the insurance policy provisions that qualify an otherwise enforceable promise of the insurer. The policy conditions that affect all coverages offered in the policy are typically found in a section of the policy titled "Conditions," whereas conditions that are specific to a particular coverage in the policy are often found in the section that contains that particular coverage. Examples of widely used policy conditions include concealment, misrepresentation, or fraud provisions; coverage maintenance provisions; suspension or reduction in coverage provisions; insurer and insured's duties in the event of a loss provisions; and dispute resolution, subrogation, and salvage provisions.

The extensive variety of conditions that appear in property and liability insurance policies prohibit an in-depth discussion of every condition. However, certain policy conditions are found in many insurance policies, and certain conditions have a direct effect on coverage. This chapter covers some, but not all of these conditions. Notable exceptions are provisions concerning transfer of rights and duties, appraisal, legal action, loss payment, other insurance, and separation of insureds. All these conditions can be found in either property or liability insurance policies (which are discussed in detail in other CPCU courses, but are beyond the scope of this discussion). An insurance professional must read each insurance policy completely to determine all of the applicable policy conditions.

The concealment, misrepresentation, and fraud provisions and the coverage maintenance provisions are designed to elicit accurate information from the insured both before and after losses occur. The duties of the insured and insurer are provisions that apply only after a loss occurs. The concealment, misrepresentation, or fraud provision and the insured's duties in the event of a loss provision are the provisions that are most likely to be violated by an insured seeking coverage from an insurer.

Concealment, Misrepresentation, or Fraud Provisions

The concealment, misrepresentation, or fraud provision, also commonly referred to as "representations," serves to affirm that the information the insured has provided is complete and accurate and that the insurer has used it to issue the policy. The insured's concealment, misrepresentation, or fraud can provide sufficient grounds for the insurer to void the insurance policy if it relates to a material fact or circumstance relating to the insurance policy. Many insurance policies contain a concealment, misrepresentation, or fraud provision that explicitly states this condition. Such a provision provides reinforcement of the principle of utmost good faith and helps insurers deal with moral hazard concerns regarding insurance policies. The following is the concealment, misrepresentation, or fraud provision contained in the ISO Homeowners 3—Special Form policy (ISO HO-3 policy):[1]

> Q. Concealment Or Fraud
>
> We provide coverage to no "insureds" under this policy if, whether before or after a loss, an "insured" has:
>
> 1. Intentionally concealed or misrepresented any material fact or circumstance;
>
> 2. Engaged in fraudulent conduct; or
>
> 3. Made false statements;
>
> relating to this insurance.

Insurance professionals often look for certain indicators in insurance claims that may signal an increased likelihood of concealment, misrepresentation, or fraud by the insured. For example, they may look for patterns in bodily injury claims from auto accidents. An examination of claims may reveal that the same groups of doctors, chiropractors, or lawyers are involved in a disproportionate percentage of auto bodily injury claims in a particular area. This pattern may indicate that some of the claimants are misrepresenting their injuries and may lead insurance professionals to more closely examine the claims made by these parties.

Actions of Parties Beyond the Insured's Control

Coverage may be voided if a named insured's actions breach policy conditions, such as those in the concealment, misrepresentation, or fraud provision. However, if the actions of another party not acting under the named insured's direction, lead to a breach of policy conditions, then, typically, the insured is not held responsible (contract is not voided).

For example, assume Alisa operates a retail photo shop protected by a burglar alarm. Alisa's special-form property insurance policy includes a protective safeguards endorsement in which she agrees to maintain the alarm system. After a burglary, Alisa discovers that workers hired by her landlord and not controlled by Alisa had disconnected the alarm without her knowledge or approval. This act of the landlord's workers does not affect Alisa's rights to collect from her insurer.

Other policy provisions address similar issues. For example, the control of property provision in the ISO Commercial Property Conditions Form clarifies the extent to which a breach of conditions at one location affects coverage at other locations. In general, a breach of policy conditions at one location does not have a detrimental effect on coverage at other locations covered by the same policy.

A separation of interests provision, a policy provision that clarifies the extent to which coverage might apply separately to more than one insured party, may specify that coverage applies to one insured even if another insured breaches a policy condition. However, the various property and liability insurance policies are not consistent in their treatment of this if the policy condition breached is concealment, misrepresentation, or fraud by one insured. If that is the case, the specific insurance policy providing coverage needs to be evaluated to determine if coverage still exists for the other insureds.

Coverage Maintenance Provisions

A variety of provisions are relevant to maintaining coverage under an insurance policy. These provisions include the following:

- Cancellation provisions
- Policy modification provisions
- Examination of books and records provisions (audit) provisions
- Inspections and surveys provisions
- Increase in hazards provisions

These provisions are intended to help the insurer avoid both moral hazard and adverse selection. They help minimize the insured's moral hazard incentive by granting the insurer access to information to verify data provided by the insured (or applicant) and provide any other relevant information that the underwriter needs to properly assess the exposure. This information can be gathered by inspecting property or examining books and records. The provisions also reduce adverse selection by giving the insurer access to information before a loss—for example, by way of an inspection or survey.

Cancellation Provisions

Cancellation is an action taken by either the insurer or the insured to terminate coverage that otherwise would continue until policy expiration. A policy's cancellation provision states who may cancel the policy and under what circumstances. It is typically the first provision found in the common policy provisions section of a policy. The cancellation provision also addresses who has the right to initiate the cancellation, how much advance notice is required, what procedures must be followed, and how any necessary premium charges or refunds will be determined.

In addition to cancellation, the contractual relationship between the insurer and the insured may end through policy expiration or nonrenewal. Policy expiration is the ending of the contractual relationship between the insured and insurer when the policy reaches the end of its term without action to renew the policy. Renewal (extending coverage for another term) requires action by both the insurer and the insured. For renewal to occur, the insurer must offer a renewal policy, and the insured must accept the offer, similar to the original policy issuance. Expiration can occur if either of the parties to the policy takes no action.

Nonrenewal is the ending of the contractual relationship between the insured and insurer by an action of the insurer to terminate coverage on the policy's expiration date. Typically the insurer provides the insured with a written statement (notice of cancellation or nonrenewal) informing the insured that the insurer has chosen not to renew the policy. Although not as commonly used, the term "nonrenewal" is also used to refer to an insured's decision not to continue coverage with the insurer for an additional policy period.

Whatever the reason, the ending of the contractual relationship between the insured and insurer by cancellation, expiration, or nonrenewal is called **policy termination**. A policy typically expires, is renewed, or is nonrenewed on its **anniversary date**, which is the specific day and month that the policy initially became effective. The anniversary date does not include a year (for example, July 30), whereas inception and expiration dates do include a year (for example, July 30, 2006) and change with each renewal.

It is customary to keep a property-casualty insurance policy in force until expiration and, when changing insurers, to change only on an expiration date, commonly called an "x-date." An insured can usually discontinue future coverage by not paying a renewal premium. Generally, an insurer can avoid future coverage by choosing not to renew the policy. Advance written nonrenewal notice to the insured may be required by law or by contract.

Although people usually change insurers or drop policies or coverages at a policy's anniversary, it is possible to cancel a policy midterm. Therefore, insurance policies must include provisions indicating whether, when, or under what circumstances the policy may be canceled, who has the right to initiate the cancellation, how much advance notice is required, what procedures must

Cancellation
An action taken by either the insurer or the insured to terminate coverage that otherwise would continue until policy expiration.

Nonrenewal
The ending of the contractual relationship between the insured and insurer by an action of the insurer to terminate coverage on the policy's expiration date.

Policy termination
The ending of the contractual relationship between the insured and insurer by cancellation, expiration, or nonrenewal.

Anniversary date
The specific day and month that a policy initially became effective.

be followed, and how any premium charges or refunds are determined. These matters are generally addressed in the cancellation provision. In most states, the only requirement to effect cancellation is mailing the notice, not demonstrating receipt of the notice.

Exhibit 13-1 contains both the nonrenewal and cancellation policy provisions that appear in the ISO HO-3 policy.

EXHIBIT 13-1

Cancellation and Nonrenewal Policy Provisions in the ISO HO-3 Policy

C. Cancellation

1. You may cancel this policy at any time by returning it to us or by letting us know in writing of the date cancellation is to take effect.

2. We may cancel this policy only for the reasons stated below by letting you know in writing of the date cancellation takes effect. This cancellation notice may be delivered to you, or mailed to you at your mailing address shown in the Declarations. Proof of mailing will be sufficient proof of notice.

    a. When you have not paid the premium, we may cancel at any time by letting you know at least 10 days before the date cancellation takes effect.

    b. When this policy has been in effect for less than 60 days and is not a renewal with us, we may cancel for any reason by letting you know at least 10 days before the date cancellation takes effect.

    c. When this policy has been in effect for 60 days or more, or at any time if it is a renewal with us, we may cancel:

        (1) If there has been a material misrepresentation of fact which if known to us would have caused us not to issue the policy; or

        (2) If the risk has changed substantially since the policy was issued.

        This can be done by letting you know at least 30 days before the date cancellation takes effect.

    d. When this policy is written for a period of more than one year, we may cancel for any reason at anniversary by letting you know at least 30 days before the date cancellation takes effect.

3. When this policy is canceled, the premium for the period from the date of cancellation to the expiration date will be refunded pro rata.

4. If the return premium is not refunded with the notice of cancellation or when this policy is returned to us, we will refund it within a reasonable time after the date cancellation takes effect.

D. Nonrenewal

We may elect not to renew this policy. We may do so by delivering to you, or mailing to you at your mailing address shown in the Declarations, written notice at least 30 days before the expiration date of this policy. Proof of mailing will be sufficient proof of notice.

How an insurance policy is terminated has important implications for insureds. For example, an insured that has had an insurance policy cancelled by an insurer often has difficulty purchasing a policy from another insurer. Insurance applications usually ask whether the applicant has had an insurance policy cancelled.

Although some states subject to high catastrophe hazards have tried to limit insurer nonrenewals on homeowners insurance, insurers almost always have the right not to renew a policy. The insurer does not have to provide a justification for nonrenewal. Common reasons that insurers choose not to renew are high claim activity, geographic or product line diversification, or lack of profitability.

In most cases, the insurer must provide justification for cancellation if the policy has been in force for more than sixty days. During the first sixty days of a policy's coverage, an insurer can cancel for any reason. After that period has passed, the insurer can use only a limited number of reasons to cancel a policy. For example, under the policy shown in Exhibit 13-1, the insurer could cancel for material misrepresentation of fact. Had the insurer originally known the facts, it would not have issued the policy or would have issued the policy under different conditions.

When cancelling an insurance policy, the insurer also notifies any mortgagee, loss payee, or additional insured listed in the policy. Depending on the financial arrangement between the insured and the mortgagee, loss payee, or additional insured, cancellation of the insurance policy could alter the agreement. For example, the insured's mortgage may contain a clause that states that the full mortgage becomes immediately due if the insured's insurance is canceled and the insured is unable to obtain coverage elsewhere.

When determining whether to pay a claim, an insurance professional must ensure that the policy had not terminated at the time of the claim.

Policy Modification Provisions

The term "policy modification provision" is not one that an insurance professional will find in an insurance policy. It is a term used in this text to jointly refer to two policy provisions—a changes provision and a liberalization clause—that address the rights of either the insured or the insurer to modify an insurance policy once it is in force.

Changes provision
A policy provision that states the procedure that must be followed to alter the policy and who has the authority to request an alteration.

A **changes provision** states the procedure that must be followed to alter the policy and who has the authority to request an alteration. Most changes provisions state that the changes must be in writing and be agreed to by the insurer. This provision's most significant feature is not that it authorizes policy changes, but that policy changes are limited to what the insurer is willing to agree to. Also, the provision states that all agreements concerning the coverage are contained in the written policy. Therefore, any oral agreements that the insured may have reached with the producer are superseded by the written insurance policy.

The following is the changes provision for the ISO Common Policy Conditions Form for the commercial package policy (CPP):[2]

B. Changes

This policy contains all the agreements between you and us concerning the insurance afforded. The first Named Insured shown in the Declarations is authorized to make changes in the terms of this policy with our consent. This policy's terms can be amended or waived only by endorsement issued by us and made a part of this policy.

Under this changes provision, the first named insured may request a policy change, and the change will be made provided the insurer agrees. However, no change is effective unless it is indicated in a policy endorsement. In other words, oral agreements to modify coverage are not permitted.

A **liberalization clause** is a policy provision that explains the expansion of coverage that occurs when an insurer introduces a revised or updated version of the policy that is broader than the insured's current policy. Some policies include a liberalization clause within the changes provision. Others contain a separate liberalization clause, such as the following clause from the ISO Commercial Property Conditions:[3]

E. LIBERALIZATION

If we adopt any revision that would broaden the coverage under this Coverage Part without additional premium within 45 days prior to or during the policy period, the broadened coverage will immediately apply to this Coverage Part.

The liberalization clause gives existing insureds the same broadened coverage the insurer offers to new insureds provided the revision occurs during the period specified in the clause. Automatically providing the new coverage to existing insureds is practical and eliminates administrative inconvenience. If insurance policies did not automatically provide broadened coverage, insurers would be inundated with requests that outstanding policies be endorsed or replaced whenever existing insureds discover that an insurer has improved its coverage. This clause helps an insurer reduce expenses associated with policy reissuance or endorsement and therefore to operate more efficiently. However, liberalization clauses may present ethical challenges to insurance professionals.

Some liberalization clauses distinguish between policy revisions and revised policy editions and do not apply to new editions. Typically, a new policy edition includes some provisions that broaden coverage and others that narrow coverage. Restrictions of coverage could not be enforced unless restrictive language is added to the insured's policy. Insurers consider it inequitable to give insureds the choice of the broader provisions of either the existing policy or the replacement policy, but only the restrictions of the original policy.

Liberalization clause
A policy provision that explains the expansion of coverage that occurs when an insurer introduces a revised or updated version of the policy that is broader than the insured's current policy.

Ethics and the Liberalization Clause

The liberalization clause challenges insurance professionals, particularly claim professionals, to remain aware of policy changes that sometimes mean the insured has the right to benefit from coverage that is not written in the insured's policy.

For example, the first edition of ISO's Building and Personal Property Coverage Form inadvertently eliminated coverage that would otherwise have applied to insureds' forklift trucks used to move stock in a warehouse. A revision to the form restored the coverage. As soon as any insurer adopted the revised form, insureds with a prior version of the form also had forklift coverage because of the liberalization clause, even though their written contracts precluded coverage.

An insurance producer faced with a claim from a client for forklift damage under the first edition of the policy faces the combined challenge of (1) knowing coverage has changed in a way that activates the liberalization clause and (2) informing clients that previously precluded coverage, because of the liberalization clause, is now applicable. This may present an ethical issue if the producer's compensation is based on the performance of his or her books of business. Informing clients that forklift losses are not covered by the policy may lead to higher producer compensation, but to the client's detriment.

Examination of Books and Records Provision

Examination of books and records provision
A policy provision that indicates the insured's duty to permit a premium auditor representing the insurer to conduct the audits necessary to determine the final premium when the premium is based on an auditable exposure or to confirm the amount payable on a claim.

An **examination of books and records provision** indicates the insured's duty to permit a premium auditor representing the insurer to conduct the audits necessary to determine the final premium when the premium is based on an auditable exposure or to confirm the amount payable on a claim. An auditable exposure is any loss exposure with a value that fluctuates and is recorded by the insured. For example, an organization's workers' compensation loss exposure varies with the type of employees and the wages paid. A workers' compensation insurer can audit the insured's records to determine the types of employees hired and the wages paid to ensure that premiums are correct.

Premium audit
An examination of an insured's operations, records, and accounts to determine exposure for the insurance coverages provided.

An insurance **premium audit** is an examination of an insured's operations, records, and accounts to determine exposure for the insurance coverages provided. Once the audit is complete, the auditors produce a report of the findings. Audit provisions in an insurance policy ensure that the insurer and auditors have access to the appropriate information.

Insurers employ premium auditors to determine the appropriate premium to charge for certain commercial insurance policies. For these policies, the initial premium is based on the insured's projected annual payroll, annual sales, or inventory at hand at policy inception. The premium audit then determines the final premium based on the insured's actual annual payroll, annual sales, or inventory on hand during the policy term.

The insurer must also be able to audit the insured's financial records for other reasons. For example, the insurer may want to audit income statements for business income insurance because business income insurance premiums and losses are related to income levels. The examination of books and records provisions explicitly gives the insurer a right to perform these activities. The following is the examination of books and records provision as it appears in the ISO Common Policy Conditions:[4]

> **C. Examination Of Your Books And Records**
>
> We may examine and audit your books and records as they relate to this policy at any time during the policy period and up to three years afterward.

The examination of books and records provision ensures the insurer has access to information necessary to calculate a premium. Although many policies have other provisions that deal with records that should be made available at the time of a loss, the examination of books and records provision relates only to policies for which the premium is based on an auditable exposure. Personal auto policies and homeowners policies, for example, do not contain an audit provision.

When dealing with policies that do contain the records examination provision, the insurance professional should verify with the insurer's premium auditors that the insured has not prevented the insurer from conducting an examination of the books and records. Violation of this provision provides the insurer with a basis to deny claims on the grounds that the insured failed to fulfill the policy conditions.

Inspections and Surveys Provision

An **inspections and surveys provision** states the insured's duty to permit an insurer representative to enter the insured's premises and make loss control inspections and surveys. This provision does not require the insurer to inspect the premises; its purpose is to give the insurer the option to inspect. Whereas insurers have the right, but not the obligation, to inspect the premises, the insured is required to allow the inspections.

Inspections and surveys provisions are most relevant to property insurance policies. To properly manage these policies, the insurer needs to be able to inspect the insured's premises and operations. The inspections may be completed for a variety of reasons. For example, the insured's premium on a commercial property policy may vary based on the type of security equipment that has been installed. By conducting inspections and surveys, the insurer may become aware of an increased probability of loss resulting from previously unknown hazards. The inspections and surveys provision may also apply to liability insurance policies. For example, the insurer may want to verify that the insured is following the loss control requirements necessary for a workers' compensation policy.

Many insurers employ loss control representatives who may inspect the premises and operations of businesses that apply for insurance. Once a policy is in force, loss control representatives may also inspect the premises and operations, provide reports to the insured and the insurer, and make safety

Inspection and surveys provision
A policy provision that states the insured's duty to permit an insurer representative to enter the insured's premises and make loss control inspections and surveys.

recommendations. However, an inspections and surveys provision states that it is not a safety inspection, that the insurer does not assume the responsibility of protecting workers or the public from injury, and that the insurer does not warrant that the business inspected is safe or compliant with applicable laws. This disclaimer is used to protect insurers from liability for losses related to the insured's using the insurer's inspections as a certification of safety.

Exhibit 13-2 contains the inspections and surveys provision in the ISO Common Policy Conditions Form, which would apply to any coverages sold as part of the commercial package policy. This provision extends inspection rights not only to the insurer but also to various rating and advisory organizations, such as ISO, as well as to other organizations that provide loss control services to insurers for a fee.

EXHIBIT 13-2

ISO Common Policy Conditions Inspections and Surveys Provision

D. **Inspections And Surveys**

1. We have the right to:

    a. Make inspections and surveys at any time;

    b. Give you reports on the conditions we find; and

    c. Recommend changes.

2. We are not obligated to make any inspections, surveys, reports or recommendations and any such actions we do undertake relate only to insurability and the premiums to be charged. We do not make safety inspections. We do not undertake to perform the duty of any person or organization to provide for the health or safety of workers or the public. And we do not warrant that conditions:

    a. Are safe or healthful; or

    b. Comply with laws, regulations, codes or standards.

3. Paragraphs **1.** and **2.** of this condition apply not only to us, but also to any rating, advisory, rate service or similar organization which makes insurance inspections, surveys, reports or recommendations.

4. Paragraph **2.** of this condition does not apply to any inspections, surveys, reports or recommendations we may make relative to certification, under state or municipal statutes, ordinances, or regulations, of boilers, pressure vessels or elevators.

Includes copyrighted material of Insurance Services Office, Inc., with its permission. Copyright, ISO Properties, Inc., 1998.

Inspection and survey provisions are common in commercial insurance policies and may appear in homeowners policies. Although the provision allows inspections and surveys of any building, they are generally only conducted on high-value properties. An insurance professional needs to ensure that the insured has not prevented the insurer from conducting inspections or surveys.

Violation of this provision provides the insurer with a basis to deny claims on the grounds that the insured failed to fulfill the policy conditions.

Increase in Hazard Provisions

An **increase in hazard provision** limits or suspends coverage during the period in which a specified hazard has increased. A finding of an increase in hazard usually requires a physical change in property. Conditions within an insured's control may change during the policy period and may increase loss frequency or severity. To provide the insured with an incentive not to increase hazards or allow hazards to build up, many property insurance policies contain provisions that will limit or suspend coverage if hazard levels increase. If coverage is suspended during a particular increase in hazard, all or part of the policy is temporarily inactive but it is not canceled. When the increase in hazard no longer exists, coverage may be restored.

> **Increase in hazard provision**
> A policy provision that limits or suspends coverage during the period in which a specified hazard has increased.

The increase in hazard provision is specifically designed for hazards within the insured's control. Therefore, the provision limits or suspends coverage only in specific hazards, not all hazards. For example, a fire at warehouse A increases the hazard related to fire at warehouse B next door. The increase in hazard provision in warehouse B's commercial property insurance policy would not suspend coverage during a fire at warehouse A, but it may limit coverage from certain specified causes of loss, such as vandalism, if warehouse B were to be vacant for more than sixty days.

Although insurance policies typically do not exclude coverage for most situations involving an increase in specific hazards, policies containing an increase in hazard provision may do the following:

- Automatically suspend coverage against losses related to the hazard
- Automatically suspend all coverage
- Permit the insurer to suspend coverage immediately
- Automatically limit or reduce coverage

Some policy provisions automatically suspend coverage for related losses while a specific hazard is present. One such provision, shown in Exhibit 13-3, is contained within the freezing cause of loss of the ISO HO-3 policy. Under this policy provision, loss by freezing is not covered during any period in which the insured has not taken reasonable measures to prevent freezing. However, coverage against loss by another cause of loss (fire, for example) is not affected.

To illustrate, a loss by freezing would not be covered if the insured went on vacation and turned off all heat in the house when freezing weather was forecast. However, coverage for freezing damage would not be excluded if the damage instead resulted from an unexpected breakdown in the home heating system that had been left on while the insured was on vacation.

EXHIBIT 13-3

Increase in Hazard Provision in the ISO HO-3 Policy

B.   Coverage C—Personal Property

We insure for direct physical loss to the property described in Coverage C caused by any of the following perils unless the loss is excluded in Section I – Exclusions.

14. Freezing

a. This peril means freezing of a plumbing, heating, air conditioning or automatic fire protective sprinkler system or of a household appliance but only if you have used reasonable care to:

(1) Maintain heat in the building; or

(2) Shut off the water supply and drain all systems and appliances of water.

However, if the building is protected by an automatic fire protective sprinkler system, you must use reasonable care to continue the water supply and maintain heat in the building for coverage to apply.

Includes copyrighted material of Insurance Services Office, Inc., with its permission. Copyright, ISO Properties, Inc., 1999.

Some policy conditions grant the insurer the right to suspend coverage, but do not require the insurer to do so. An example, shown in Exhibit 13-4, is found in the ISO Equipment Breakdown Coverage Form.

EXHIBIT 13-4

Increase in Hazard Provision in the ISO Equipment Breakdown Coverage Form

13. Suspension

Whenever "covered equipment" is found to be in, or exposed to, a dangerous condition, any of our representatives may immediately suspend the insurance against loss from an "accident" to that "covered equipment." This can be done by delivering or mailing a written notice of suspension to:

a. Your last known address; or

b. The address where the "covered equipment" is located.

Once suspended in this way, your insurance can be reinstated only by an endorsement for that "covered equipment."

If we suspend your insurance, you will get a pro rata refund of premium for that "covered equipment" for the period of suspension. But the suspension will be effective even if we have not yet made or offered a refund.

Includes copyrighted material of Insurance Services Office, Inc., with its permission. Copyright, ISO Properties, Inc., 2001.

The success of equipment breakdown insurance depends greatly on the insurer's ability to prevent losses through periodic equipment inspections. In rare cases in which an inspector discovers a serious hazard, the inspector will request that the equipment be shut down until the hazard is eliminated. If the insured is not willing to shut down hazardous equipment, the insurer's representative has the right to immediately suspend insurance coverage. The threat of suspension is often sufficient to persuade the insured to take immediate action. However, if action is not taken, the inspector has a contractual right to suspend coverage immediately, provided the action is documented in writing. By mentioning a pro rata premium refund, the provision in Exhibit 13-4 suggests that suspensions are normally final. The suspension can be lifted, but doing so requires a written endorsement. Insurers are likely to be unwilling to reinstate coverage for an insured that was not willing to address a serious hazard.

Some policy provisions do not suspend coverage altogether but reduce it by reducing the amount payable under certain conditions involving an increase in hazard. An example appears in the vacancy condition of the ISO Building and Personal Property Coverage Form, shown in Exhibit 13-5, which suspends coverage for certain causes of loss and reduces coverage for others.

EXHIBIT 13-5

Increase in Hazard Provisions in the ISO Building and Personal Property Coverage Form

6. **Vacancy**

    b. **Vacancy Provisions**

    If the building where loss or damage occurs has been vacant for more than 60 consecutive days before that loss or damage occurs:

    (1) We will not pay for any loss or damage caused by any of the following even if they are Covered Causes of Loss:

    (a) Vandalism;

    (b) Sprinkler leakage, unless you have protected the system against freezing;

    (c) Building glass breakage;

    (d) Water damage;

    (e) Theft; or

    (f) Attempted theft.

    (2) With respect to Covered Causes of Loss other than those listed in b.(1)(a) through b.(1)(f) above, we will reduce the amount we would otherwise pay for the loss or damage by 15%.

Includes copyrighted material of Insurance Services Office, Inc., with its permission. Copyright, ISO Properties, Inc., 2001.

Paragraph (1) of the provision in Exhibit 13-5 describes a suspension in coverage, whereas paragraph (2) describes a reduction in coverage. Even though no business operations occur in a vacant building, the vacancy itself is an increase in hazard. Vacant buildings are easier targets for vandals and thieves, are susceptible to undetected water damage or water damage relating to deterioration, and are susceptible to damage by any cause of loss that may not be detected and addressed if no one is in the building to see it.

Protective safeguards provision
A policy provision that suspends coverage when a protective device is not functioning.

A provision related to an increase in hazard provision is the protective safeguards provision. A **protective safeguards provision** suspends coverage when a protective device is not functioning. This provision provides an incentive to insureds to verify that the safeguards they have in place are functioning properly. A protective safeguards provision is often included within the standard language of policies covering loss exposures that frequently involve safeguards, such as restaurants or buildings with sprinkler systems. Alternatively, it can be added as a protective safeguards endorsement.

The American Association of Insurance Services (AAIS) Camera and Musical Instrument Dealers Coverage Form contains a protective safeguards provision (labeled "Premises Protection"), as shown in Exhibit 13-6.

EXHIBIT 13-6

Protective Safeguards Provision in the AAIS Camera and Musical Instrument Dealers Coverage Form

Premises Protection—"You" must maintain in proper working order the protective devices that were in operation at the premises described on the "schedule of coverages" on the effective date of this policy.

If "you" fail to keep the protective devices:

a.   in working condition at the premises described on the "schedule of coverages"; or

b.   in operation when "you" are closed to business,

coverage for property at such locations is automatically suspended. This suspension will stay in effect until equipment or services are back in operation.

Form IM 1050 01 05, Contains copyrighted material of the American Association of Insurance Services, 2005.

Whenever common protective safeguards are in place (such as automatic sprinkler systems, burglar alarms, and fire alarms), an insurance professional should determine whether the insurance contract has a protective safeguards provision and evaluate its effect. Such provisions should be analyzed to determine what protective devices are affected, whether coverage is suspended at one or all locations when a safeguard is inoperative, whether the suspension applies to loss by any peril, and whether coverage is automatically reinstated when the safeguard is restored. Some protective safeguards provisions allow for a protective system's temporary outages or maintenance. Most protective safeguards provisions suspend coverage only if the insured was aware of the discontinuance of the safeguard and failed to notify the insurer.

Although an insurance professional may not find many violations of the policy provisions related to maintaining coverage, a thorough analysis of any of these provisions appearing in the insurance policy must be completed to determine whether coverage exists. The most likely provision to be violated is the increase in hazard provision. Technological advances in reporting and maintaining records helps ensure that the insurer is aware of any violations of the other provisions related to maintaining coverage before any claim being filed.

Insured's Duties in the Event of Loss

A property insurance policy requires an insured to perform certain duties in the event of a loss. A liability policy requires an insured to perform certain duties in the event of occurrence, offense, claim, or suit. Although the wording is different in the two types of policies, the provisions related to the insured's duties serve the same purpose. These duties are a condition of the policy and are designed to help mitigate the severity of loss, if possible. Many insurance policies expressly state that the insurer is not obligated to pay benefits unless the insured has complied with these duties. Most policies also state that the insured cannot sue the insurer unless the insured has fully complied with the duties stated in the policy.

A technical error in performing these duties does not necessarily preclude coverage. Nonetheless, to avoid disputes over procedural matters, insureds should attempt to fulfill all of their post-loss duties. Both property and liability insurance policies impose the following duties on the insured:

- Report losses promptly to the insurer
- Cooperate with the insurer in evaluating and settling the claim

Report Losses Promptly to the Insurer

Liability insurance policies contain policy provisions that require a prompt report of an occurrence or offense that might result in a claim (notice of a potential claim), as well as a report of an actual claim or suit. For example, if a customer were to slip and fall on a wet floor in a supermarket, then the supermarket may be required to notify its liability insurer (put the liability insurer on notice) that the slip and fall occurred and that there is a potential liability claim against the supermarket. In addition, the supermarket is also required to notify the insurer of any actual liability claims filed against it. For example, the supermarket may receive a notice from a lawyer that a client wants the supermarket to pay for property damage to the client's car caused by a loose supermarket cart in the parking lot.

The notice requirement under a liability policy enables an insurer to conduct a prompt investigation, which aids the insurer in defending the insured against a third-party lawsuit. Over time, obtaining evidence and witnesses becomes increasingly difficult, and minor injuries may become magnified. Prompt notice of one loss can also help prevent and minimize future losses because the insurer has an opportunity to evaluate the circumstances that led to the loss and because the insured has an opportunity to correct any dangerous conditions before another loss occurs. This result is in the interest of the insured, the insurer, and the public. Timely notice also enables the insurer to control claims, promotes favorable settlements, and reduces litigation expenses.

Similar to liability insurance policies, property insurance policies require prompt notification of a loss, enabling the insurer to investigate the claim and estimate its liabilities. For example, it can become increasingly difficult over time to determine the cause of a loss and, therefore, to determine whether a covered peril caused the loss.

The following is the prompt reporting provision from the ISO Building and Personal Property Coverage Form:[5]

> **3. Duties In The Event Of Loss Or Damage**
>> a. You must see that the following are done…
>>> (2) Give us prompt notice of the loss or damage. Include a description of the property involved.
>>>
>>> (3) As soon as possible, give us a description of how, when and where the loss or damage occurred.

The policy provisions related to prompt reporting use vague language such as "as soon as possible" to allow both the insured and insurer some flexibility on a case-by-case basis to determine what constitutes "prompt." In some cases, the insured may not notice a loss for days, weeks, or even months. In more extreme cases, such as the flooding that followed Hurricane Katrina in 2005, it may be impossible for the insured to return to the property to assess the damage for weeks. Although helpful in some circumstances, this vague language can also be the basis for legal challenges by both the insured and insurer.

Cooperate With the Insurer

The insured's duty to cooperate with the insurer after a loss in evaluating and settling the claim differs between property insurance policies and liability insurance policies. For property insurance, once the loss has occurred and the insurer has been notified, the insured has a duty to work with the insurer to assess the nature and extent of the loss. Exhibit 13-7 contains the duties in the event of loss or damage from the property section of the ISO Businessowners Coverage Form related to cooperating with the insurer.

The mitigation of loss provision in a typical property insurance policy (such as, **3.a.(4)** in Exhibit 13-7) reinforces the insured's obligation to protect damaged property against further damage. Any further loss can be excluded from coverage if the loss is caused by a peril that is not covered or if the insured did not take all reasonable means to protect property.

Provision **3.b.** in Exhibit 13-7 states that the insurer has the right to obtain an insured's sworn testimony. This right can be important to insurers in cases of suspected arson or fraud, or when the adjuster has otherwise been unable to obtain information. Examination under oath also provides a way to support or refute information in the written records provided by the person being examined. This provision treats examination under oath as a right, not a request. However, some policies may limit this right to examining the named insured. An insurer can always request an insured to submit to examination under oath, but if it is not a contractual requirement, the insured also has a right to deny the request.

EXHIBIT 13-7

Insured's Duties in the Event of a Loss in the ISO Businessowners Coverage Form

E. **Property Loss Conditions**

1. **Abandonment**

    There can be no abandonment of any property to us.

. . .

3. **Duties In The Event Of Loss Or Damage**

    a. You must see that the following are done in the event of loss or damage to Covered Property:

    (1) Notify the police if a law may have been broken.

    (2) Give us prompt notice of the loss or damage. Include a description of the property involved.

    (3) As soon as possible, give us a description of how, when and where the loss or damage occurred.

    (4) Take all reasonable steps to protect the Covered Property from further damage, and keep a record of your expenses necessary to protect the Covered Property, for consideration in the settlement of the claim. This will not increase the Limits of Insurance of Section I - Property. However, we will not pay for any subsequent loss or damage resulting from a cause of loss that is not a Covered Cause of Loss. Also, if feasible, set the damaged property aside and in the best possible order for examination.

    (5) At our request, give us complete inventories of the damaged and undamaged property. Include quantities, costs, values and amount of loss claimed.

    (6) As often as may be reasonably required, permit us to inspect the property proving the loss or damage and examine your books and records.

    Also permit us to take samples of damaged and undamaged property for inspection, testing and analysis, and permit us to make copies from your books and records.

    (7) Send us a signed, sworn proof of loss containing the information we request to investigate the claim. You must do this within 60 days after our request. We will supply you with the necessary forms.

    (8) Cooperate with us in the investigation or settlement of the claim.

    (9) Resume all or part of your "operations" as quickly as possible.

    b. We may examine any insured under oath, while not in the presence of any other insured and at such times as may be reasonably required, about any matter relating to this insurance or the claim, including an insured's books and records. In the event of an examination, an insured's answers must be signed.

Abandonment provision
A policy provision that specifies the insurer's post-loss position on the rejection of damaged property abandoned by the insured.

Exhibit 13-7 also contains an abandonment provision (provision **1.**). An **abandonment provision** specifies the insurer's post-loss position on the rejection of damaged property abandoned by the insured. Many insurance policies state that the insurer has the option of paying for damaged property and taking over its ownership. In some situations, abandonment would be an attractive alternative for the insured. For example, an insured may want an insurer to take over ownership of a seriously damaged car in exchange for cash payment of the pre-loss value. However, an abandonment provision typically states that the insured has no right to elect this option. Insurers may be reluctant to take on property repair and resale. Also, ownership of damaged property can present a considerable liability in some situations, especially if the property is toxic, radioactive, or otherwise contaminated.

Similar to property insurance policies, liability insurance policies require the insured to cooperate with the insurer. It is the duty and obligation of the insured to notify the insurer of potential liability claims, cooperate with the insurer, and protect the rights of the insurer in defending and settling claims. However, what constitutes cooperation is different in liability policies compared with property policies. Exhibit 13-8 contains the insured's duties in the event of occurrence, offense, claim, or suit from the ISO Businessowners' Coverage Form.

In addition to the provisions requiring prompt notice (provisions **2.a.** and **b.**) in Exhibit 13-8, other provisions require insureds to cooperate with the insured. The insured is required to send copies of any demands or legal papers received as well as share any records or documents related to the claim or suit. Furthermore, the insured is required to assist the insurer in the enforcement of rights against liable parties.

Another requirement of liability insurance policies is that the insured is not to admit responsibility or otherwise prejudice the insurer's opportunity to defend a claim (provision **2.d.** in Exhibit 13-8). By agreeing to assume responsibility, an insured might appear to admit liability for the loss, seriously weakening the insurer's ability to defend against the claim. An exception within this provision specifically authorizes insureds to incur first-aid expenses without jeopardizing their insurance coverage. For example, when someone is seriously injured, an insured may call an ambulance or hire a taxicab to take the injured person to a hospital.

An insurance professional may encounter claims in which an insured has failed to fulfill one or more duties after a loss. Failure to fulfill these duties, whether accidental or intentional, provides the insurance professional with a basis to deny the insured's claim. If the failure to fulfill duties is the result of an oversight or some other accidental cause, the insurer will often still pay the claim. However, if the failure to fulfill the duties is intentional, the insurer must decide, usually on a case-by-case basis, if this failure warrants denying the claim.

EXHIBIT 13-8

Insured's Duties in the Event of Occurrence, Offense, Claim or Suit in the ISO Businessowners Coverage Form

2. **Duties In The Event Of Occurrence, Offense, Claim Or Suit**

    a. You must see to it that we are notified as soon as practicable of an "occurrence" or an offense which may result in a claim. To the extent possible, notice should include:

        (1) How, when and where the "occurrence" or offense took place;

        (2) The names and addresses of any injured persons and witnesses; and

        (3) The nature and location of any injury or damage arising out of the "occurrence" or offense.

    b. If a claim is made or "suit" is brought against any insured, you must:

        (1) Immediately record the specifics of the claim or "suit" and the date received; and

        (2) Notify us as soon as practicable.

        You must see to it that we receive written notice of the claim or "suit" as soon as practicable.

    c. You and any other involved insured must:

        (1) Immediately send us copies of any demands, notices, summonses or legal papers received in connection with the claim or "suit";

        (2) Authorize us to obtain records and other information;

        (3) Cooperate with us in the investigation, or settlement of the claim or defense against the "suit"; and

        (4) Assist us, upon our request, in the enforcement of any right against any person or organization that may be liable to the insured because of injury or damage to which this insurance may also apply.

    d. No insured will, except at that insured's own cost, voluntarily make a payment, assume any obligation, or incur any expense, other than for first aid, without our consent.

Insurer's Duties in the Event of Loss

In addition to the insured's duties, both property and liability insurance policies have provisions in the conditions section that address the insurer's duties in the event of a loss. The insurer's primary duty is payment, which is expressed in the insuring agreement. The insurer's duties in the event of loss are mostly procedural and must be fulfilled after report of a claim or a loss. These duties do not have as significant an influence on the determination of coverage as the insured's duties in the event of a loss. As with the insured's duties, the insurer's duties differ between property and liability insurance policies.

Property Insurance Policies

The insurer provisions found in most property insurance policies offer several options in settling a property insurance claim, and they do not all include paying money. The property insurer has the option to pay the value of the lost or damaged property or the amount spent to repair or replace it, whichever is less (Exhibit 13-9, provision **6.a.**). The insurer also has other options. Exhibit 13-9 contains the Loss Payment provision from the Property Loss Conditions section of the ISO Businessowners Coverage Form.

EXHIBIT 13-9

Insurer's Duties Following a Loss in the ISO Businessowners Coverage Form

6. **Loss Payment**

    In the event of loss or damage covered by this policy:

    a. At our option, we will either:

        (1) Pay the value of lost or damaged property;

        (2) Pay the cost of repairing or replacing the lost or damaged property;

        (3) Take all or any part of the property at an agreed or appraised value; or

        (4) Repair, rebuild or replace the property with other property of like kind and quality...

    b. We will give notice of our intentions within 30 days after we receive the sworn proof of loss.

    c. We will not pay you more than your financial interest in the Covered Property.

    ...

    e. Our payment for loss of or damage to personal property of others will only be for the account of the owners of the property. We may adjust losses with the owners of lost or damaged property if other than you. If we pay the owners, such payments will satisfy your claims against us for the owners' property. We will not pay the owners more than their financial interest in the Covered Property.

    f. We may elect to defend you against suits arising from claims of owners of property. We will do this at our expense.

    g. We will pay for covered loss or damage within 30 days after we receive the sworn proof of loss, provided you have complied with all of the terms of this policy, and

        (1) We have reached agreement with you on the amount of loss; or

        (2) An appraisal award has been made.

Includes copyrighted material of Insurance Services Office, Inc., with its permission. Copyright, ISO Properties, Inc., 2001.

(Provision **6.d.** in the policy shown in Exhibit 13-9 covers how property is valued and is discussed in a subsequent chapter.) Provisions **6.b.** and **g.** in Exhibit 13-9 show that the insurer has thirty days after receiving the sworn statement of loss to announce whether it intends to pay the value of destroyed property, pay the cost of repairs, pay the full value of damaged property and take title to the property, or perform the repair or replacement service. The insurer makes payment within thirty days provided both parties agree to the value and the insured has fulfilled all the policy conditions. Other policies may specify different time periods. The thirty-day period is triggered only after an agreement is reached on the amount of the loss or upon an appraisal award. An investigation may be necessary to determine the actual cause of loss or some other factor critical to determining whether a claim is covered. An insurer that delays a claim payment, waiting for proof that a claim was not covered, may rightfully be accused of breaching the contract. By including these provisions, insurers let insureds know that claims will be handled promptly, but with adequate information.

Another clause in the loss payment provision in Exhibit 13-9 (**6.c.**) limits payment to the extent of the insured's insurable interests in the property. This provision does not say the insurer will not pay an amount greater than the named insured's insurable interest, only that the insurer will not pay more than the insurable interest to *the named insured*. An additional amount may be payable to a mortgagee based on its insurable interest in the property.

Many property insurance policies also include some coverage for personal property of customers, employees, guests, or others on the insured's premises or in the insured's care, custody, or control. Because the contract is between the insurer and the insured, others have no contractual rights against the insurer. However, provisions such as provision **6.e.** in Exhibit 13-9 allow the insurer the right to settle claims directly with bailors, whose personal property is in the custody of an insured bailee, or with other property owners. If the property owner is not satisfied with the settlement and sues the insured, the insurer may choose to defend the insured at the insurer's own expense because the insurer was responsible for the initial settlement.

Liability Insurance Policies

Unlike property insurance, relatively few liability insurance policy conditions relate specifically to the insurer's procedural post-loss duties. The two main duties of the insurer in a liability insurance policy are the duty to pay claims and the duty to defend, both of which are covered in the insuring agreement. The one condition that relates to an insurer's duties in the event of occurrence, offense, claim, or suit is the bankruptcy provision. A **bankruptcy provision** states that the insurer is obligated to pay claims on behalf of an insured who is bankrupt. The following is the bankruptcy provision from the ISO Businessowners Coverage Form:[6]

Bankruptcy provision
A policy provision stating that the insurer is obligated to pay claims on behalf of an insured who is bankrupt.

1. **Bankruptcy**

   Bankruptcy or insolvency of the insured or of the insured's estate will not relieve us of our obligations under this policy.

Bankruptcy provisions are generally not necessary with property insurance because claims are paid to the insured, not on behalf of the insured. The bankruptcy clause is designed to protect third-party claimants so that their status is not adversely impaired by bankruptcy laws that might alter the insured's obligation to pay their debts.

Insurance professionals need to ensure that they are fulfilling all the insurer's duties after a loss. These provisions act as guidelines of behavior for the insurer and its representatives to protect the insurer from future liability claims, such as a bad faith claim.

EXCLUSIONS

Exclusions clarify the coverages granted by the insurer, as well as excluding or restricting coverage. By clarifying the coverage granted by the insurer, exclusions help to keep premiums reasonable by eliminating coverage for uninsurable loss exposures and for coverages not needed by the typical insured, assisting in managing moral and morale hazards, reducing the likelihood of coverage duplications, and eliminating coverages requiring special treatment.

Insurance professionals must examine the exclusions section of an insurance policy in addition to the main policy when determining if coverage applies. In property insurance, even if covered property is damaged or destroyed by a covered cause of loss, the loss is not covered if it falls under a policy exclusion. The same applies for liability insurance, in which a covered activity resulting in a covered consequence is not covered if an exclusion applies. For example, the ISO Commercial General Liability (CGL) policy provides liability coverage for amounts that the insured becomes legally obligated to pay for bodily injury or property damage that occurs during the policy period. An insured may be legally obligated to pay for bodily injury that was intentionally inflicted, but the CGL specifically excludes bodily injury or property damage that is intended or expected.

Analyzing the exclusions section of a liability insurance policy can be particularly difficult because many liability policies restore coverages through exceptions to the exclusions. For example, the CGL policy excludes intentional injury, unless that injury was inflicted when the insured was using reasonable force to protect persons or property.

As with conditions, a variety of exclusions are commonly added to both property and liability insurance policies, not all of which are discussed in this section. A few of the "standard" exclusions are presented to demonstrate the types of exclusions that an insurance professional can expect to see in common property or liability insurance policies. Common property exclusions include ordinance or law, earth movement, government action, nuclear hazard, utility, war, water, fungus, and bacteria. Common liability exclusions include expected or intended injury, pollution, certified acts of terrorism, and contractual liability.

Why Exclude Intentional Acts?

In most cases, exclusions are logical; for example, insureds should not be able to intentionally destroy their own property and collect insurance proceeds. Otherwise, many people would have an incentive to dispose of obsolete or unsaleable property by "selling" it to the insurance company. Arson-for-profit on buildings, prearranged thefts of cars, and other fraudulent claims do occur, and when they are detected, coverage is denied. Detecting and proving fraud can be a challenge, which is the primary reason that underwriters generally prefer to avoid coverage presenting a moral hazard.

Most insurance policies contain carefully worded provisions that exclude coverage for intentional losses. But even without an intentional loss exclusion, the courts permit an insurer to deny coverage that allows a party to profit by intentionally causing an insured loss.

Although many intentional acts are excluded, the separation of insureds provision does provide coverage for some of the damage done by intentional acts. For example, the intentional acts of an employee are covered when paid on behalf of the employer.

Property Insurance Exclusions

The extent of the exclusions section in a property insurance policy varies depending on whether the property insurance policy is a named perils policy or special coverage form (commonly called an "all-risks" policy). A named perils policy lists the causes of loss the policy covers. Its exclusions section is typically not as extensive as that for a special coverage form, in which all losses are covered unless they are specifically excluded. Nonetheless, a named perils coverage form may still have an extensive list of exclusions. The following is the introduction statement to the Section I exclusions in the ISO HO-3 policy and is typical of most property insurance policies in how it states the extent of the exclusions to follow:[7]

> SECTION I—EXCLUSIONS
>
> A. We do not insure for loss caused directly or indirectly by any of the
>   following. Such loss is excluded regardless of any other cause or event
>   contributing concurrently or in any sequence to the loss. These
>   exclusions apply whether or not the loss event results in widespread
>   damage or affects a substantial area.

Following this introductory statement, the policy lists nine excluded causes of loss. These nine exclusions (ordinance or law, earth movement, water damage, power failure, neglect, war, nuclear hazard, intentional loss, and governmental action) are commonly found in both commercial property insurance policies and personal property insurance policies. All these exclusions (and any other exclusions that are listed in a specific policy) must be evaluated by an insurance professional to determine applicability.

Ordinance or Law Exclusion

Exhibit 13-10 contains the ordinance or law exclusion from the ISO HO-3 policy. This policy, like many insurance policies, provides some coverage for increased cost of construction resulting from an ordinance or law. The ordinance or law provision adds up to an additional 10 percent to the policy limit in order to help offset the increased cost of construction to make an older building meet newer building codes or other regulations. The provision even includes bringing undamaged portions of the building up to code after a covered loss. For example, some municipalities require that for any buildings damaged beyond a certain percentage of their value, even the undamaged portions must be brought up to current building codes during their repair. For older buildings with outdated plumbing, electrical systems, and heating systems, the costs of bringing the building up to current code can be significant.

The ordinance or law exclusion in Exhibit 13-10 states that the policy does not cover the reduction in value to a property or costs incurred to deal with pollution that may be incurred by changes in laws or regulations.

EXHIBIT 13-10

Ordinance or Law Exclusion in the ISO HO-3 Policy

SECTION I—EXCLUSIONS

A.   We do not insure for loss caused directly or indirectly by any of the following . . .

　　1.   Ordinance Or Law

　　　Ordinance Or Law means any ordinance or law:

　　　a.   Requiring or regulating the construction, demolition, remodeling, renovation or repair of property, including removal of any resulting debris. This Exclusion **A.1.a.** does not apply to the amount of coverage that may be provided for in **E.11.** Ordinance Or Law under Section I—Property Coverages;

　　　b.   The requirements of which result in a loss in value to property; or

　　　c.   Requiring any "insured" or others to test for, monitor, clean up, remove, contain, treat, detoxify or neutralize, or in any way respond to, or assess the effects of, pollutants.

　　　　Pollutants means any solid, liquid, gaseous or thermal irritant or contaminant, including smoke, vapor, soot, fumes, acids, alkalis, chemicals and waste. Waste includes materials to be recycled, reconditioned or reclaimed.

　　This Exclusion **A.1.** applies whether or not the property has been physically damaged.

Includes copyrighted material of Insurance Services Office, Inc., with its permission. Copyright, ISO Properties, Inc., 1999.

Earth Movement

Exhibit 13-11 contains the earth movement exclusion from the ISO HO-3 policy. This exclusion appears in many property policies. However, most insureds can add an earthquake endorsement or purchase a separate earthquake insurance policy to cover losses stemming from earth movement. Evaluating a property's exposure to earth movement requires special underwriting attention. In an effort to keep premiums reasonable, the cost of the special underwriting for this exposure is borne only by those insureds interested in obtaining coverage.

EXHIBIT 13-11

Earth Movement Exclusion in the ISO HO-3 Policy

SECTION I—EXCLUSIONS

A. We do not insure for loss caused directly or indirectly by any of the following...

   2. **Earth Movement**

   Earth Movement means:

   a. Earthquake, including land shock waves or tremors before, during or after a volcanic eruption;

   b. Landslide, mudslide or mudflow;

   c. Subsidence or sinkhole; or

   d. Any other earth movement including earth sinking, rising or shifting;

   caused by or resulting from human or animal forces or any act of nature unless direct loss by fire or explosion ensues and then we will pay only for the ensuing loss.

   This Exclusion **A.2.** does not apply to loss by theft.

Includes copyrighted material of Insurance Services Office, Inc., with its permission. Copyright, ISO Properties, Inc., 1999.

Although the exclusion in Exhibit 13-11 excludes earth movement, the policy does cover certain ensuing losses (fire or explosion). Distinguishing between losses caused by earth movement and losses caused by the ensuing fire or explosion is often difficult and a source of coverage disagreements.

War

The war exclusion is an example of the type of exclusion that keeps premiums reasonable by not providing coverage for causes of loss that may be catastrophic. This exclusion also excludes property losses caused by the accidental discharge of a nuclear weapon, which is different than general exposure to nuclear hazards. Nuclear hazards have their own set of exclusions. The following is the war exclusion from the ISO HO-3 policy:[8]

6. War

   War includes the following and any consequence of any of the following:

   a. Undeclared war, civil war, insurrection, rebellion or revolution;

   b. Warlike act by a military force or military personnel; or

   c. Destruction, seizure or use for a military purpose.

   Discharge of a nuclear weapon will be deemed a warlike act even if accidental.

Courts have generally adhered to a very strict doctrine regarding what constitutes war, and typically require warlike acts between sovereign nations. The war exclusion was the subject of media coverage following the terrorist attacks on September 11, 2001. At that time, President Bush announced that the United States considered the attacks to be an act of war. Although this caused media speculation that insurers would invoke the war exclusion to avoid paying for the damage that was inflicted, none attempted to do so.

Governmental Action

The following is the governmental action exclusion from the ISO HO-3 policy:[9]

> **9. Governmental Action**
>
> Governmental Action means the destruction, confiscation or seizure of property described in Coverage **A**, **B** or **C** by order of any governmental or public authority.
>
> This exclusion does not apply to such acts ordered by any governmental or public authority that are taken at the time of a fire to prevent its spread, if the loss caused by fire would be covered under this policy.

Although the wording of the governmental action exclusion is broad enough to cover destruction, confiscation, or seizure of property by any governmental or public authority for any reason, insurers often use this exclusion to avoid paying criminals for property taken because of its use in criminal activity. For example, assume Jason's home was confiscated by the government because he was growing marijuana on the property. Without the governmental action exclusion, Jason's homeowners policy would have to compensate Jason for the loss of his property, because government confiscation is not specifically excluded elsewhere.

An insurance professional needs to ensure that none of the exclusions included in the policy affect the insured's claim. The type of property, its location, and its use are all factors in determining which exclusions are included in the policy.

Liability Insurance Exclusions

The extent of the exclusions section in a liability insurance policy varies depending on whether the liability insurance policy is a general liability insurance policy or a more specialized liability insurance policy. A general liability insurance policy, such as the CGL policy, businessowners coverage form, or the homeowners insurance policy, covers a broad range of liability loss exposures but also has an extensive list of exclusions. Common exclusions in these types of liability policies include auto or watercraft liability, employment practices liability, workers' compensation and employers' liability, and professional liability. Many of these exclusions are necessary because the loss exposures are not present for the majority of insureds or may require special underwriting attention. Although these liability loss exposures are excluded by general liability insurance policies, coverage is available through specialized liability policies. An insurance professional must ensure that the liability loss exposure is not excluded by the insured's specific liability policy.

Expected or Intended Injury

Insurance is designed to protect against fortuitous losses; liability insurance policies are not designed to provide insurance protection for losses a reasonable person could foresee or for intentional losses. For example, a reasonable person should foresee the likelihood of bodily injury to children from a toy designed with sharp edges. Similarly, an individual who intentionally injures a neighbor should not be protected by the liability portion of his or her homeowners insurance policy if the neighbor sought restitution. The following is the expected or intended loss exclusion from the liability section of the ISO Businessowners Coverage Form:[10]

> B. Exclusions
>
> 1. **Applicable To Business Liability Coverage**
>
>   This insurance does not apply to:
>
>   a. **Expected Or Intended Injury**
>
>   "Bodily injury" or "property damage" expected or intended from the standpoint of the insured. This exclusion does not apply to "bodily injury" resulting from the use of reasonable force to protect persons or property.

The expected or intended injury (loss) exclusion reduces the moral hazard incentive an insured may have to behave recklessly or endanger others. An exception to the exclusion is granted for expected or intentional loss if the insured used reasonable force to protect persons or property.

This exclusion, like many other exclusions, provides a broad exclusion to coverage but then restores limited coverage through an exception to the exclusion. Exceptions often make analyzing general liability insurance policies' exclusions more difficult than analyzing property insurance exclusions.

Pollution

Another common exclusion in general liability insurance policies is the pollution exclusion. Exhibit 13-12 contains the pollution exclusion from the ISO Businessowners Coverage Form. Pollution loss exposures can be very difficult to analyze because they often do not exhibit the definite and measurable characteristics of an ideally insurable loss exposure. Determining exactly when pollution began is often difficult. Therefore, the loss exposure may not be definite in time. Furthermore, pollution detection and remediation costs are high and difficult to estimate, complicating the analysis of the potential severity of losses.

EXHIBIT 13-12

Pollution Exclusion in the ISO Businessowners Coverage Form

B. **Exclusions**

   1. Applicable To Business Liability Coverage

      This insurance does not apply to:...

      f. Pollution

         (1) "Bodily injury" or "property damage" arising out of the actual, alleged or threatened discharge, dispersal, seepage, migration, release or escape of "pollutants":

            (a) At or from any premises, site or location which is or was at any time owned or occupied by, or rented or loaned to, any insured. However, this subparagraph does not apply to:

               (i) "Bodily injury" if sustained within a building and caused by smoke, fumes, vapor or soot from equipment used to heat that building;

               (ii) "Bodily injury" or "property damage" for which you may be held liable, if you are a contractor and the owner or lessee of such premises, site or location has been added to your policy as an additional insured with respect to your ongoing operations performed for that additional insured at that premises, site or location and such premises, site or location is not and never was owned or occupied by, or rented or loaned to, any insured, other than that additional insured; or

               (iii) "Bodily injury" or "property damage" arising out of heat, smoke or fumes from a "hostile fire";

            (b) At or from any premises, site or location which is or was at any time used by or for any insured or others for the handling, storage, disposal, processing or treatment of waste;

            (c) Which are or were at any time transported, handled, stored, treated, disposed of, or processed as waste by or for:

               (i) Any insured; or

               (ii) Any person or organization for whom you may be legally responsible; or

            (d) At or from any premises, site or location on which any insured or any contractors or subcontractors working directly or indirectly on any insured's behalf are performing operations if the "pollutants" are brought on or to the premises, site or location in connection with such operations by such insured, contractor or subcontractor. However, this subparagraph does not apply to:

(i) "Bodily injury" or "property damage" arising out of the escape of fuels, lubricants or other operating fluids which are needed to perform the normal electrical, hydraulic or mechanical functions necessary for the operation of "mobile equipment" or its parts, if such fuels, lubricants or other operating fluids escape from a vehicle part designed to hold, store or receive them. This exception does not apply if the "bodily injury" or "property damage" arises out of the intentional discharge, dispersal or release of the fuels, lubricants or other operating fluids, or if such fuels, lubricants or other operating fluids are brought on or to the premises, site or location with the intent that they be discharged, dispersed or released as part of the operations being performed by such insured, contractor or subcontractor;

(ii) "Bodily injury" or "property damage" sustained within a building and caused by the release of gases, fumes or vapors from materials brought into that building in connection with operations being performed by you or on your behalf by a contractor or subcontractor; or

(iii) "Bodily injury" or "property damage" arising out of heat, smoke or fumes from a "hostile fire".

(e) At or from any premises, site or location on which any insured or any contractors or subcontractors working directly or indirectly on any insured's behalf are performing operations if the operations are to test for, monitor, clean up, remove, contain, treat, detoxify or neutralize, or in any way respond to, or assess the effects of, "pollutants".

(2) Any loss, cost or expense arising out of any:

(a) Request, demand, order or statutory or regulatory requirement that any insured or others test for, monitor, clean up, remove, contain, treat, detoxify or neutralize, or in any way respond to, or assess the effects of, "pollutants"; or

(b) Claim or "suit" by or on behalf of a governmental authority for damages because of testing for, monitoring, cleaning up, removing, containing, treating, detoxifying or neutralizing, or in any way responding to, or assessing the effects of, "pollutants".

However, this paragraph does not apply to liability for damages because of "property damage" that the insured would have in the absence of such request, demand, order or statutory or regulatory requirement or such claim or "suit" by or on behalf of a governmental authority.

The pollution exclusion, similar to the expected or intended injury (loss) exclusion, is a broad exclusion with more limited coverage restored as an exception to the exclusion. Section **f.(1)** states that injury or damage arising out of the actual, alleged or threatened discharge, dispersal, seepage, migration, release or escape of "pollutants" is excluded. However, section **f.(1)(iii)** restores coverage for injury or damage arising out of heat, smoke or fumes from a "hostile fire," which is any fire that is uncontrollable or spreads beyond where it was intended to be.

Exclusion of Certified Acts of Terrorism

In December 2005, Congress passed an extension of the original Terrorism Risk Insurance Act (TRIA), which had been set to expire at the end of 2005. The Terrorism Risk Insurance Extension Act (TRIEA) extended the original act for two years. Concerned that TRIA would not be renewed, most states allowed exclusions for terrorism coverage to be added to policies. For example, if an insured purchasing a CGL policy declines terrorism insurance coverage that is supported by TRIEA, the war or terrorism exclusion (CG 69 01 02) shown in Exhibit 13-13 is added to the policy. There are a variety of other terrorism exclusions that exclude specific types of terrorism. These exclusions can be added to the policies such as the CGL, liquor liability, pollution liability, underground storage tank, and a variety of others. Unlike the previous exclusions discussed in this section, a war or terrorism exclusion does not have exceptions to the exclusion to restore limited coverage.

EXHIBIT 13-13

War or Terrorism Exclusion in the ISO Commercial General Liability Coverage Part

THIS ENDORSEMENT CHANGES THE POLICY. PLEASE READ IT CAREFULLY.

WAR OR TERRORISM EXCLUSION

This endorsement modifies insurance provided under the following:

COMMERCIAL GENERAL LIABILITY COVERAGE PART

A.   Exclusion i. under Paragraph **2., Exclusions** of **Section I—Coverage A—Bodily Injury And Property Damage Liability** is replaced by the following:

   2.   **Exclusions**

   This insurance does not apply to:

   i.   **War Or Terrorism**

   "Bodily injury" or "property damage" arising, directly or indirectly, out of:

   (1)   War, including undeclared or civil war; or

   (2)   Warlike action by a military force, including action in hindering or defending against an actual or expected attack, by any government, sovereign or other authority using military personnel or other agents; or

(3) Insurrection, rebellion, revolution, usurped power, or action taken by governmental authority in hindering or defending against any of these; or

(4) "Terrorism", including any action taken in hindering or defending against an actual or expected incident of "terrorism"

regardless of any other cause or event that contributes concurrently or in any sequence to the injury or damage.

However, with respect to "terrorism", this exclusion only applies if one or more of the following are attributable to an incident of "terrorism":

(1) The total of insured damage to all types of property exceeds $25,000,000. In determining whether the $25,000,000 threshold is exceeded, we will include all insured damage sustained by property of all persons and entities affected by the "terrorism" and business interruption losses sustained by owners or occupants of the damaged property. For the purpose of this provision, insured damage means damage that is covered by any insurance plus damage that would be covered by any insurance but for the application of any terrorism exclusions; or

(2) Fifty or more persons sustain death or serious physical injury. For the purposes of this provision, serious physical injury means:

   (a) Physical injury that involves a substantial risk of death; or

   (b) Protracted and obvious physical disfigurement; or

   (c) Protracted loss of or impairment of the function of a bodily member or organ; or

(3) The "terrorism" involves the use, release or escape of nuclear materials, or directly or indirectly results in nuclear reaction or radiation or radioactive contamination; or

(4) The "terrorism" is carried out by means of the dispersal or application of pathogenic or poisonous biological or chemical materials; or

(5) Pathogenic or poisonous biological or chemical materials are released, and it appears that one purpose of the "terrorism" was to release such materials.

Paragraphs **(1)** and **(2)**, immediately preceding, describe the thresholds used to measure the magnitude of an incident of "terrorism" and the circumstances in which the threshold will apply for the purpose of determining whether the Terrorism Exclusion will apply to that incident. When the Terrorism Exclusion applies to an incident of "terrorism", there is no coverage under this Coverage Part.

In the event of any incident of "terrorism" that is not subject to the Terrorism Exclusion, coverage does not apply to any loss or damage that is otherwise excluded under this Coverage Part.

Multiple incidents of "terrorism" which occur within a seventy-two hour period and appear to be carried out in concert or to have a related purpose or common leadership shall be considered to be one incident.

Continued on next page.

B. The following exclusion is added to Paragraph **2., Exclusions** of **Section I—Coverage B—Personal And Advertising Injury Liability**:

2. **Exclusions**

This insurance does not apply to:

War Or Terrorism

"Personal and advertising injury" arising, directly or indirectly, out of:

(1) War, including undeclared or civil war; or

(2) Warlike action by a military force, including action in hindering or defending against an actual or expected attack, by any government, sovereign or other authority using military personnel or other agents; or

(3) Insurrection, rebellion, revolution, usurped power, or action taken by governmental authority in hindering or defending against any of these; or

(4) "Terrorism", including any action taken in hindering or defending against an actual or expected incident of "terrorism"

regardless of any other cause or event that contributes concurrently or in any sequence to the injury.

However, with respect to "terrorism", this exclusion only applies if one or more of the following are attributable to an incident of "terrorism":

(1) The total of insured damage to all types of property exceeds $25,000,000. In determining whether the $25,000,000 threshold is exceeded, we will include all insured damage sustained by property of all persons and entities affected by the "terrorism" and business interruption losses sustained by owners or occupants of the damaged property. For the purpose of this provision, insured damage means damage that is covered by any insurance plus damage that would be covered by any insurance but for the application of any terrorism exclusions ; or

(2) Fifty or more persons sustain death or serious physical injury. For the purposes of this provision, serious physical injury means:

(a) Physical injury that involves a substantial risk of death; or

(b) Protracted and obvious physical disfigurement; or

(c) Protracted loss of or impairment of the function of a bodily member or organ; or

(3) The "terrorism" involves the use, release or escape of nuclear materials, or directly or indirectly results in nuclear reaction or radiation or radioactive contamination; or

(4) The "terrorism" is carried out by means of the dispersal or application of pathogenic or poisonous biological or chemical materials; or

(5) Pathogenic or poisonous biological or chemical materials are released, and it appears that one purpose of the "terrorism" was to release such materials.

Paragraphs (1) and (2), immediately preceding, describe the thresholds used to measure the magnitude of an incident of "terrorism" and the circumstances in which the threshold will apply for the purpose of determining whether the Terrorism Exclusion will apply to that incident. When the Terrorism Exclusion applies to an incident of "terrorism", there is no coverage under this Coverage Part.

In the event of any incident of "terrorism" that is not subject to the Terrorism Exclusion, coverage does not apply to any loss or damage that is otherwise excluded under this Coverage Part.

Multiple incidents of "terrorism" which occur within a seventy-two hour period and appear to be carried out in concert or to have a related purpose or common leadership shall be considered to be one incident.

C.   Exclusion h. under Paragraph 2., **Exclusions** of **Section I—Coverage C—Medical Payments** does not apply.

D.   The following definition is added to the **Definitions** Section:

"Terrorism" means activities against persons, organizations or property of any nature:

1.   That involve the following or preparation for the following:

a.   Use or threat of force or violence; or

b.   Commission or threat of a dangerous act; or

c.   Commission or threat of an act that interferes with or disrupts an electronic, communication, information, or mechanical system; and

2.   When one or both of the following applies:

a.   The effect is to intimidate or coerce a government or the civilian population or any segment thereof, or to disrupt any segment of the economy; or

b.   It appears that the intent is to intimidate or coerce a government, or to further political, ideological, religious, social or economic objectives or to express (or express opposition to) a philosophy or ideology.

Exclusions are necessary to ensure that premiums remain reasonable. However, they often complicate the readability of an insurance policy and may lead to confusion on the insured's part. An insurance professional should have an in-depth understanding of the common exclusions in insurance policies to conduct a thorough analysis of the loss exposures that are and are not covered by the insurance policies. As with other policy sections, what does not appear in the exclusions section may be just as important as what does appear. An insurance policy may grant coverage for something that is typically excluded in a standard insurance policy but not specifically excluded in the policy being analyzed.

SUMMARY

The second two letters of the DICE acronym stand for conditions and exclusions. The conditions section of a policy contains provisions that qualify an otherwise enforceable promise of the insurer. Examples of widely used policy conditions include the concealment, misrepresentation, or fraud provisions and the coverage maintenance provisions.

The concealment, misrepresentation, or fraud provision serves to affirm that the information provided is complete and accurate and that the insurer has used this information to issue the policy. The insured's concealment, misrepresentation, or fraud can provide sufficient grounds for the insurer to void the insurance policy if it relates to a material fact or circumstance relating to the insurance policy. A variety of provisions are relevant to maintaining coverage under an insurance policy. These provisions include those concerning cancellation, policy modification, examination of books and records, inspections and surveys, and increases in hazards.

Both property and liability insurance policies impose a duty on the insured to report losses promptly to the insurer and to cooperate with the insurer in evaluating and settling claims. Liability insurance policies contain policy provisions that require a prompt report of an occurrence or offense that might result in a claim (notice of a potential claim), as well as a report of an actual claim or suit. Property insurance policies require prompt notification of a loss.

The insured's duty to cooperate with the insurer after a loss in evaluating and settling the claim also differs between property insurance policies and liability insurance policies. For property insurance, once the loss has occurred and the insurer has been notified, the insured has a duty to work with the insurer to assess the nature and extent of the loss. Under liability insurance policies, it is the duty and obligation of the insured to notify the insurer of potential liability claims, cooperate with the insurer, and protect the rights of the insurer in defending and settling claims. Another requirement of liability insurance policies is that the insured is not to admit responsibility or otherwise prejudice the insurer's opportunity to defend a claim. Failure to fulfill these duties, whether accidental or intentional, provides the insurance professional with grounds to deny the insured's claim. However, if the failure to fulfill duties is the result of an oversight or some other accidental cause, the insurer will often pay the claim.

The insurer's primary duty in the event of loss is to make any appropriate payments. As with the insured's duties, the insurer's duties differ between property and liability insurance policies. A property insurer has the option to pay the value of the lost or damaged property or the amount spent to repair or replace it, whichever is less. Many property insurance policies also include some coverage for personal property of customers, employees, guests, or others on the insured's premises or in the insured's care, custody, or control. The two main duties of the insurer in a liability insurance policy are the duty to pay claims and the duty to defend.

Exclusions clarify the coverages granted by the insurer, as well as excluding or restricting coverage. Exclusions help to keep premiums reasonable by eliminating coverage for uninsurable loss exposures and for coverages not needed by the typical insured, assisting in managing moral and morale hazards, reducing the likelihood of coverage duplications, and eliminating coverages requiring special treatment. Many liability policies add excluded coverages back through what are called exceptions to the exclusions.

Exclusions vary widely between property insurance policies and liability insurance policies. As with conditions, there are a wide variety of exclusions that are commonly added to both property and liability insurance policies. Some of these exclusions are so common that many practitioners consider them to be part of the standard insurance policy. Common property exclusions include ordinance or law, earth movement, government action, nuclear, utility, war, water, fungus, and bacteria. Common liability exclusions include expected or intended injury, pollution, certified acts of terrorism, and contractual liability.

CHAPTER NOTES

1. Includes copyrighted material of Insurance Services Office, Inc., with its permission. Copyright, ISO Properties, Inc., 1999.

2. Includes copyrighted material of Insurance Services Office, Inc., with its permission. Copyright, ISO Properties, Inc., 1998.

3. Includes copyrighted material of Insurance Services Office, Inc., with its permission. Copyright, ISO Properties, Inc., 1983, 1987.

4. Includes copyrighted material of Insurance Services Office, Inc., with its permission. Copyright, ISO Properties, Inc., 1998.

5. Includes copyrighted material of Insurance Services Office, Inc., with its permission. Copyright, ISO Properties, Inc., 2001.

6. Includes copyrighted material of Insurance Services Office, Inc., with its permission. Copyright, ISO Properties, Inc., 2001.

7. Includes copyrighted material of Insurance Services Office, Inc., with its permission. Copyright, ISO Properties, Inc., 1999.

8. Includes copyrighted material of Insurance Services Office, Inc., with its permission. Copyright, ISO Properties, Inc., 1999.

9. Includes copyrighted material of Insurance Services Office, Inc., with its permission. Copyright, ISO Properties, Inc., 1999.

10. Includes copyrighted material of Insurance Services Office, Inc., with its permission. Copyright, ISO Properties, Inc., 2001.

Chapter 14

Direct Your Learning

Amounts Payable: Property Insurance

After learning the content of this chapter and completing the corresponding course guide assignment, you should be able to:

- Explain why insurance to value is important to the insured and to the insurer in property insurance, what problems are associated with maintaining insurance to value, and what can be done to minimize these problems.

- Given a case, apply valuation methods, policy limits, deductibles, and coinsurance or insurance-to-value provisions separately or in combination, to determine the amount payable. In support of this objective:

  - Describe the valuation approaches used in property insurance policies.

  - Explain the reasons for policy limits.

  - Analyze the following types of policy limits used in property insurance: individual property limits, specific limits, blanket limits, sublimits, variable limits, and nondollar limits.

  - Explain why deductibles are applied, how various types of deductibles are applied, and why some policies contain no deductibles.

  - Analyze the purpose and function of coinsurance, insurance-to-value policy provisions, and alternatives to coinsurance.

  - Apply the coinsurance formula.

- Explain how appraisal provisions aid in resolving disputed claims.

- Explain how subrogation and salvage provisions can help keep premiums reasonable.

- Define or describe each of the Key Words and Phrases for this chapter.

Develop Your Perspective

What are the main topics covered in the chapter?

The amount payable when a claim is made depends on the policy's valuation provisions, limits, deductibles, and coinsurance and other insurance-to-value provisions. Disputes over claim settlements may be addressed by the policy's appraisal provision. After a claim, an insurer may try to recover all its loss payments through subrogation or salvage.

Review a property insurance policy.

- What policy limits are included for coverage?
- What property loss exposures are covered by each of these limits?

Why is it important to learn about these topics?

Knowing this information will help you understand how to analyze a policy to determine the available coverage and the process for evaluating losses and amounts payable.

Explain how coinsurance and other insurance-to-value provisions encourage insureds to insure to value.

- Why is coinsurance alternately called a penalty and a reward?

How can you use what you will learn?

Consider a property loss exposure your organization might face. Investigate the coverage that applies to the loss.

- Do the policy limits provide adequate coverage for the possible loss exposures?
- How might you determine the amount that would be paid for the loss?

Chapter 14

Amounts Payable: Property Insurance

Once an insurance professional determines that a policy covers a claim, he or she must then determine the amounts that are payable under that policy. Provisions regarding amounts payable differ between property insurance policies and liability insurance policies. This chapter focuses on property insurance. The following chapter focuses on liability insurance policies and explains the implications of the other-insurance provisions of a policy.

Every insurance policy must indicate how an insurer determines the amount payable for a covered loss. Under a property insurance policy, the amount payable depends on the policy's valuation methods, policy limits, deductibles, and the coinsurance or other insurance-to-value provisions. Each of these features must be evaluated to accurately determine the amount of payment an insured should receive from the insurer for a claim. In addition, because disputes may arise in relation to the amount payable, insurance professionals need to understand which property insurance policy provisions address disputed claims. To help keep premiums at a reasonable level, and to ensure the accountability of those responsible for a loss, a property insurance policy also contains provisions pertaining to subrogation and salvage.

Before evaluating any of these provisions, an insurance professional must understand why property insurance policies require that the property exposure be fully insured—referred to as requiring insurance to value—and how the failure to do so has detrimental effects on both insurers and insureds.

INSURANCE TO VALUE

Insurance to value is the choice of a limit in property insurance that approximates the maximum potential loss. Therefore, a building with an insurable value of $100,000 that is covered by $100,000 of insurance is insured to value. Insurance buyers and sellers usually attempt to closely align the insurable value of property with the amount of insurance that covers it. Insurance to value is best understood by first examining loss frequency and loss severity.

During the risk management process, loss exposures are assessed to determine potential loss frequency and loss severity. For property loss exposures, the severity loss distribution is often skewed. That is, most of the losses that occur to property loss exposures, especially real property, are small losses (low severity), with a total loss being a rare occurrence. Exhibit 14-1 contains a hypothetical severity distribution of a typical property valued at $150,000.

Insurance to value
The choice of a limit in property insurance that approximates the maximum potential loss.

EXHIBIT 14-1

Probability Distribution of Loss Severity of Residential Property Losses

Size Category of Losses (bins)	Probability of Loss	Cumulative Probability of Loss	Average Bin Value	Expected Value of Loss	Expected Value Truncated	
$0–$1,000	.700	.700	$ 500	$ 350	$ 350	Probability of Loss × Average Bin Value
$1001–$5,000	.200	.900	3,000	600	600	
$5,001–$10,000	.050	.950	7,500	375	375	
$10,001–$15,000	.020	.970	12,500	250	250	
$15,001–$25,000	.015	.985	20,000	300	300	
$25,001–$50,000	.0075	.993	37,500	281		Expected Value of Insured Losses: $25,000 Policy Limit
$50,001–$100,000	.005	.998	75,000	375		
$100,001–$150,000	.0025	1.000	125,000	313		
Total	1.000			$2,844	$1,875	Expected Value of Insured Losses: Insured to Value

The severity distribution shown in Exhibit 14-1 shows that if a loss occurs, 90 percent of the time that loss is less than $5,000 (because the cumulative probability is 90 percent). Because the cumulative probability of a loss less than $25,000 is 98.5 percent, then only 1.5 percent of the time is the loss greater than $25,000. The maximum possible loss for the property is $150,000, which would occur only if the property were totally destroyed.

To calculate the insurance rate and premium to insure the property, an insurer would combine the severity distribution shown in Exhibit 14-1 with a frequency distribution. For example, the severity distribution in Exhibit 14-1 has an expected value of approximately $2,844. If an insurer were to assume a simple frequency distribution that has only two possibilities—80 percent of the time no loss would occur and 20 percent of the time one loss would occur—then the insurer would be able to calculate an expected loss of approximately $569 [(0.8 × $0) + (0.2 × $2,844) = $569]. If the insurer had a 40 percent expense ratio, the premium it would charge would be $948 [$569 ÷ (1 − .40) = $948].

The importance to the insurer of insurance to value can be illustrated by showing how the lack of insurance to value affects premium adequacy. For example, suppose that an insurer provides a property insurance policy with a policy limit of $150,000 and that the premium is based on an insurance rate per $100 of coverage. Dividing $150,000 by $100 yields 1,500 units of coverage that the insurer is providing. The insurer, charging a premium of $948 for a policy with a limit of $150,000 (the value of the property), is using an insurance rate of approximately $0.63 per unit of coverage ($948 ÷ 1,500 = $0.63). Further, suppose that the insured evaluated the severity distribution and chose to retain the 1.5 percent probability that losses would be above $25,000 by buying a policy with a limit of only $25,000. The insurer would lose money on the

$25,000-limit policy (250 units of coverage) if it charged the same rate ($0.63 per unit of coverage) as for the policy with the $150,000 limit, because it would result in a premium of only $158 (250 units × $0.63 = $158). This lower premium would not be enough to cover the expected losses under the policy.

If the severity distribution that the insurer faces stops at $25,000, the expected value of that distribution is now $1,875. With the same frequency distribution as previously, the expected loss is now $375 [(0.8 × $0) + (0.2 × $1,875) = $375], and assuming the same expense loading, the premium would be $625 [$375 ÷ (1 − 0.4) = $625]. For a policy limit of $25,000, the insurer is offering 250 units of coverage with a rate of $2.50 per unit of coverage, which is substantially higher than the $0.63 per unit rate that was calculated when the property insurance limit was equal to the property's total value. The insurer is then faced with a decision to either charge a higher rate for property insurance when the policy limit is less than the property's value or require insureds to choose policy limits that are close to the full value of the property. The second choice is what is referred to as insurance to value.

The insurable value of property is partly determined by the valuation provision in the applicable insurance policy. The insurance amount depends on the applicable policy limits. Insuring to value is typically beneficial for both the insurer and the insured. The insurer benefits in two ways. First, the premium is adequate to cover potential losses. Second, it simplifies the underwriting process by reducing the need to determine exact values during underwriting. The determination of underinsurance (not insuring to value) is made at the time of loss; therefore, the underwriter does not need to determine whether the property is being underinsured. The insured benefits because sufficient funds are available in the event of a total loss and the uncertainty associated with large retained losses is reduced.

Industry Language—Insurance to Value, Coinsurance, and Insurance-to-Value

The property policy limit chosen should be close to the value of the insured property. Many insurance professionals call this fully insuring the property, but it is also called insurance to value. The term insurance to value is often confused with provisions in homeowners and businessowners insurance policies called insurance-to-value provisions. The distinction is important. Insurance to value (without the hyphens) refers to the relationship between the policy limit and the insured property's value. Insurance-to-value (with hyphens) refers to the provisions in specific property insurance policies that determine the amounts payable by the policy based on the relationship between the policy limit and the insured property's value. Insurance-to-value provisions are similar to coinsurance provisions in commercial property insurance policies. They both are based on the relationship between policy limits and the insured property's value. However, they determine the amounts payable using different formulas, described subsequently in this chapter.

This text refers to the relationship between policy limits and the insured property's value as insurance to value.

Maintaining insurance to value is important to avoid coinsurance penalties (discussed subsequently) and other insurance-to-value provision penalties that might reduce the amount payable in the event of a loss. Underinsurance penalties are not a concern for those who maintain property insurance limits that meet or exceed coinsurance requirements or the insurance-to-value requirement. However, maintaining such limits is difficult, for at least the following reasons:

- The amount of insurance necessary to meet coinsurance requirements is based on the insured property's value at the time of the loss, but the policy limit is selected when the policy is purchased.
- When selecting insurance limits, an insurance buyer typically estimates property values based on an informed guess.
- The insurable value at the time of the loss often cannot be precisely measured until the property is actually rebuilt or replaced.
- Values change over time.

Insurance professionals can help property insurance buyers minimize problems associated with valuation by recommending that they do the following:

- Hire a qualified appraiser to establish the property's current replacement cost value. The property owner should adjust the appraisal using indexes and/or a record of additions and deletions each year and should reappraise the property every few years.
- Purchase an inflation guard coverage option. Inflation guard coverage is designed to ensure that policy limits rise as the property values increase as a result of inflation.
- Purchase a peak season endorsement if a business's personal property values fluctuate in a cyclical pattern. A peak season endorsement automatically increases the policy limits during the specified peak season of the organization.
- Review and revise limits periodically to ensure that the policy limits are adequate to cover potential losses.

In order to ascertain whether a property is being insured at or near its value, and to determine the amount payable under a policy, an insurance professional needs to understand the various valuation methods available and the differences that can result from taking alternate valuation approaches.

VALUATION METHODS

When covered property is lost or damaged, the amount payable under a property insurance policy depends on the property's value. Every property policy states how the insurer and the insured determine that value. The policy's valuation method is contained in its valuation provision. For some policies, actual cash value (ACV) is the standard valuation method, with replacement cost available as an option. For other policies, replacement cost is the standard valuation method, with ACV available as an option. Although ACV and replacement cost are the most common valuation methods, property insurance policies may also use other methods, such as actual loss sustained.

Actual Cash Value

Actual cash value is one of the most prevalent methods property insurance policies use to determine the amount payable for a property loss because it supports the principle of indemnity. **Actual cash value (ACV)** is a valuation method typically calculated as the replacement cost at the time of loss minus depreciation. **Replacement cost** is the cost to repair or replace property using new materials of like kind and quality with no deduction for depreciation.

The term actual cash value is rarely defined in insurance policies, and the definition adopted by courts often varies by jurisdiction and the type of property insured. Although the traditional definition of ACV has been limited to replacement cost minus depreciation, other methods of determining ACV have evolved, including the use of market value and the broad evidence rule (discussed subsequently).

When a property insurance policy specifies that property will be valued on an ACV basis, the insured must choose a policy limit to fully insure the property on that basis. The following is the actual cash value policy provision from the Insurance Services Office (ISO) Building and Personal Property (BPP) Coverage Form (subsections **b.–e.** change the valuation methods for special items such as glass, outdoor equipment, and tenant's improvements and betterments):[1]

> 7. **Valuation**
>
> We will determine the value of Covered Property in the event of loss or damage as follows:
>
> **a.** At actual cash value as of the time of loss or damage, except as provided in **b., c., d.** and **e.** below.

Replacement Cost Minus Depreciation

Most property has its highest value when new and depreciates at a fairly steady rate as a result of age and use. **Depreciation** is the reduction in value caused by the physical wear and tear or technological or economic obsolescence of property. Depreciation reflects the value of the use the insured has already received from the property. Although it can be based on physical wear and tear, which usually increases with age, it can be based on age alone. Depreciation can also be based on obsolescence caused by fashion, technological changes, or other factors that occur rapidly and suddenly. Disagreements regularly develop about how to determine the appropriate amount of depreciation to deduct.

Actual cash value (ACV)
A valuation method typically calculated as the replacement cost at the time of loss minus depreciation.

Replacement cost
The cost to repair or replace property using new materials of like kind and quality with no deduction for depreciation.

Depreciation
The reduction in value caused by the physical wear and tear or technological or economic obsolescence of property.

The important distinction about depreciation in calculating ACV is that the ACV calculation is based on economic depreciation, not accounting depreciation.

Accounting Depreciation and Economic Depreciation

In accounting, if property is expected to have a useful life greater than one year, organizations can depreciate the property over its useful life rather than expensing it in the year of the purchase. This accounting depreciation expense is the allocation of the property's value, as reflected in an organization's accounting and tax records, over the property's useful life (usually a schedule set by tax codes). The most common method of accounting depreciation is the straight-line depreciation method, in which the property's original value is divided by the number of years of useful life. The result is the annual accounting depreciation of that property.

Accounting depreciation is distinct from the economic depreciation of property. Economic depreciation is the difference between the replacement cost of the property and its current market value. Economic depreciation is typically the result of physical or functional depreciation. Physical depreciation is the wear and tear on the property and is usually reflected in a reduction in the property's ability to perform its intended function, regardless of use. For example, a building continues to depreciate (the roof wears, the paint ages, and so on) even if business operations are shut down. In contrast, the depreciation of some equipment is clearly related to use. For example, motors that must be rebuilt after a stated number of hours of use may depreciate little when not in use.

Functional depreciation is usually the result of technological advances because the function performed by the capital expenditure is no longer needed or can be performed better by other methods. For example, personal computers that an organization purchased three years ago would have a greatly reduced current value even if they had never been taken out of their original cartons.

Generally, ACV valuation restores the insured to its pre-loss condition and therefore supports the concept of indemnity. Some policies explicitly state that the insured should not be made better off by the policy, as does the following provision from the ISO Personal Auto Policy:[2]

LIMIT OF LIABILITY

C. If a repair or replacement results in better than like kind or quality, we will not pay for the amount of the betterment.

Market Value

Market value
The price at which a particular piece of property could be sold on the open market by an unrelated buyer and seller.

Many courts have ruled that ACV means market value (also referred to as fair market value). **Market value** is the price at which a particular piece of property could be sold on the open market by an unrelated buyer and seller. Market value is easily established for autos, personal computers, and other property that has many buyers and sellers and for which information is available about recent sales. However, it can be difficult to establish market value if there have been few recent transactions involving comparable property. For example, it may be difficult to determine a market value using recent sales of unique manufacturing machinery and equipment.

Market valuation is also useful when property of like kind and quality is unavailable for purchase, such as with antiques, works of art, and other collectibles. These types of property may be irreplaceable, making replacement cost calculations impossible. Although these types of property may not fit the standard of having many comparable sales, examining the sales history of a piece of art and recent transactions involving other pieces of similar quality may be the only method of determining its value. Market valuation can also be the most accurate way to determine the value of some older or historic buildings built with obsolete construction methods and materials.

The market value of real property reflects the value of the land and its location, as well as the value of any buildings or structures on the land. Because most insurance policies cover buildings and structures but not land, the land's value must be eliminated in establishing insurable values of property.

Conversely, the value of land usually excludes the value of any building or structure on it, so any damage to the building does not affect the land's value. However, there are exceptions. For example, some zoning restrictions prohibit reconstruction of a building at its current location, and, consequently, the land loses value if the building is destroyed. Alternatively, a deteriorating structure on a prime piece of real estate can detract from the land's value, because any developer would have to tear down the building before a new one could be constructed. In this situation, the building's destruction, by any cause, is likely to increase the land's value.

Broad Evidence Rule

The **broad evidence rule** is a method for determining actual cash value based on court decisions that require all relevant factors to be considered. The broad evidence rule arose when courts stipulated that insurers had to consider more than just depreciation or market value when determining ACV. Exhibit 14-2 contains a sample of some of the elements that various courts have used in applying the broad evidence rule to determine a building's ACV.

Broad evidence rule
A method for determining actual cash value based on court decisions that require all relevant factors to be considered.

EXHIBIT 14-2

Factors Considered in Determining a Building's ACV

- Obsolescence
- Building's present use and profitability
- Alternate building uses
- Present neighborhood characteristics
- Long-term community plans for the area where the building is located, including urban renewal prospects and new roadway plans
- Inflationary or deflationary trends
- Any other relevant factors

Court decisions about personal property valuation can be summarized as follows:

- *Residential personal property.* Residential personal property is valued at its replacement cost new at the time of loss, minus depreciation. Its value in the secondhand market (used furniture and clothing stores) is not the test of its value.

- *Business personal property in use.* Business personal property (such as furniture, fixtures, and machinery) is generally valued at its replacement cost new at the time of loss, minus depreciation. This class of property has a used market. For secondhand property, the market value of similar property in the same condition is its ACV.

- *Stocks of merchandise.* Stocks of merchandise, a special class of personal property, are valued at the cost of replacing the property rather than at the property owner's selling price. Freight and other transportation charges are added. However, active (on the sales floor) merchandise that cannot be replaced within a reasonable time is worth its selling price. Depreciation (which includes obsolescence) is generally deducted.

- *Personal property held by the manufacturer.* Personal property held by the manufacturer is typically valued at the cost of materials, plus transportation costs to get those materials to the manufacturer, plus the cost of labor and other expenses, unless this valuation standard is inconsistent with policy provisions.

Returning an Insured to Pre-Loss Condition

Direct damage property insurance usually pays repair costs but does not pay the insured for any diminution in value that might result if repaired property has a lower market value than property that has not been damaged. For example, an auto that has been involved in an accident and repaired may be functionally the same but have a lower market value than a similar auto that has not been involved in an accident. Some motorists have requested additional payment under their collision coverage for diminution in value. Their argument was that the insurer was not returning them to "pre-loss condition" as was promised in their insurance policies, because the vehicle after repair was worth less in terms of market value. To clarify insurers' intentions, many auto policies now include an endorsement noting that coverage for diminution in value is specifically excluded.

Replacement Cost

The second valuation method in property insurance policies is replacement cost. Replacement cost is commonly used in insurance policies covering buildings and in many policies covering personal property. Exhibit 14-3 contains the replacement cost valuation provision from the ISO HO-3 policy.

EXHIBIT 14-3

Replacement Cost Valuation Provision in the ISO HO-3 Policy

C.   Loss Settlement

2.   Buildings covered under Coverage **A** or **B** at replacement cost without deduction for depreciation, subject to the following:

   a.   If, at the time of loss, the amount of insurance in this policy on the damaged building is 80% or more of the full replacement cost of the building immediately before the loss, we will pay the cost to repair or replace, after application of any deductible and without deduction for depreciation, but not more than the least of the following amounts:

   (1) The limit of liability under this policy that applies to the building;

   (2) The replacement cost of that part of the building damaged with material of like kind and quality and for like use; or

   (3) The necessary amount actually spent to repair or replace the damaged building.

   If the building is rebuilt at a new premises, the cost described in **(2)** above is limited to the cost which would have been incurred if the building had been built at the original premises.

   b.   If, at the time of loss, the amount of insurance in this policy on the damaged building is less than 80% of the full replacement cost of the building immediately before the loss, we will pay the greater of the following amounts, but not more than the limit of liability under this policy that applies to the building:

   (1) The actual cash value of that part of the building damaged; or

   (2) That proportion of the cost to repair or replace, after application of any deductible and without deduction for depreciation, that part of the building damaged, which the total amount of insurance in this policy on the damaged building bears to 80% of the replacement cost of the building.

   d.   We will pay no more than the actual cash value of the damage until actual repair or replacement is complete. Once actual repair or replacement is complete, we will settle the loss as noted in **2.a.** and **b.** above.

   However, if the cost to repair or replace the damage is both:

   (1) Less than 5% of the amount of insurance in this policy on the building; and

   (2) Less than $2,500;

   we will settle the loss as noted in **2.a.** and **b.** above whether or not actual repair or replacement is complete.

   e.   You may disregard the replacement cost loss settlement provisions and make claim under this policy for loss to buildings on an actual cash value basis. You may then make claim for any additional liability according to the provisions of this Condition **C.** Loss Settlement, provided you notify us of your intent to do so within 180 days after the date of loss.

According to the terms set out in Exhibit 14-3, if property covered on a replacement cost basis is damaged or destroyed, the insured is entitled to the current cost of repairing damaged property or of buying or building new property of like kind and quality, even if the destroyed property is several years old, and even if its replacement cost exceeds the original purchase price. If the cost of new property has decreased, as often happens with computers or other electronic equipment, replacement cost coverage pays the current lower cost.

Often, a particular model or style of electronic equipment is no longer made. Although the equipment is technically irreplaceable, the replacement cost for property of comparable material and quality can still be determined. For example, a manufacturer might have discontinued a particular television model. However, a comparable television can be purchased, often from the same manufacturer. The insured is usually willing to settle a claim based on the existing model's cost, provided the replacement item is not inferior.

Even when the replacement cost method of valuation is specified by the property insurance policy, certain types of property are not valued using that method. For example, replacement cost coverage often does not apply to property such as antiques or artwork, primarily because there is no adequate replacement for such property. These types of property are typically valued at their ACV determined by market value.

Technically, replacement cost coverage violates the principle of indemnity. An insured who sustains a loss to old, used property and receives insurance payment for new property has profited from the loss. To reduce the moral hazard, most replacement cost policies pay out only after the insured has actually replaced the damaged or destroyed property or, in some cases, only if the loss is a relatively low value. Some building policies also require the insured to rebuild the building with identical construction, in the same location, or for the same purpose. Otherwise, depreciation is deducted. In many policies with replacement cost provisions, the insured has the option of settling the claim based on ACV and then has 180 days to refile the claim on the replacement cost basis. This gives the insured the opportunity to obtain funds from the insurer at the time of loss, use those funds to help pay for the rebuilding, and then collect the full replacement cost value on completion.

If the policy specifies that property is covered on a replacement cost basis, the insured must select a policy limit to fully insure the replacement cost property value. For buildings, the replacement cost value is usually higher than the property's depreciated ACV. Property insurance rates per $100 of insurance are usually the same whether the property is insured for replacement cost or ACV. However, replacement cost insurance is more costly because higher limits are required to insure to value because replacement cost is generally higher than ACV.

Do Insurers Always Settle Claims With Cash?

No. Many property insurance policies permit the insurer to repair or replace damaged property, rather than make a cash settlement. Although most claims are paid in cash, insurers sometimes exercise the option to repair or replace when it minimizes the claim's cost to the insurer or when it eliminates an insured's ability to profit from the claim.

Actual Loss Sustained

Another valuation method in property insurance, less common than ACV or replacement cost, is actual loss sustained. **Actual loss sustained** is a valuation method in business income policies designed to make the insured whole by demonstrating the actual amount of loss that occurs during the period of restoration. The period of restoration is the time during which business income losses are covered by a business income policy. The following is the actual loss sustained policy provision from the ISO Business Income (And Extra Expense) Coverage Form:[3]

> A. Coverage
>
> 1. **Business Income**
>
> We will pay for the actual loss of Business Income you sustain due to the necessary "suspension" of your "operations" during the "period of restoration".

The policy also defines how the actual sustained losses are to be calculated. The effect of actual loss sustained in business income coverages is comparable to ACV for direct property losses. The intent is to support the principle of indemnity by making the insured whole but not create an opportunity for enrichment.

> **Actual loss sustained**
>
> A valuation method in business income policies designed to make the insured whole by demonstrating the actual amount of loss that occurs during the period of restoration.

Other Valuation Methods

Although insurers usually settle losses by paying the replacement cost or ACV of lost or damaged property, many other valuation provisions are used for special classes of property, sometimes within policies that value most property on a replacement cost or ACV basis. Some of the more common other valuation methods are as follows:

- Agreed value method
- Functional valuation method
- Cost of reproduction valuation method
- Pair or set clauses valuation method
- Money and securities valuation method

Agreed Value Method

Agreed value method
A valuation method in which the insurer and the insured agree on the value of the insured object and state it in a policy schedule.

Some property insurance policies are valued policies, not contracts of indemnity. These policies typically cover antiques, paintings, and other objects whose value can be difficult to determine. The valuation provision in such policies uses the **agreed value method**, in which the insurer and the insured agree on the value of the insured object and state it in a policy schedule. If a total loss occurs, the insurer will pay the amount specified in the policy. Partial losses are paid based on actual cash value, repair cost, replacement cost, or whatever other valuation method the policy specifies. Although the agreed value method is not a specific formula as are some of the other valuation methods, it is nonetheless useful when it would otherwise be difficult to calculate a precise value. The agreed value method does not stipulate what the agreed value has to be relative to the true value of the property. The only stipulation is that both parties have to agree to the value in the policy. The agreed value method should not be confused with agreed value coverage, which is an arrangement for suspending the coinsurance clause (discussed subsequently in this chapter) in commercial property insurance coverages such as the Building and Personal Property Coverage Form or the Business Income Coverage Form.

Functional Valuation Method

Functional valuation method
A valuation method that determines the value of property by comparing it to the cost of property that can perform the same function even if it is not identical.

The functional valuation method is sometimes used when replacing buildings or personal property with property of like kind and quality is not practical and when the ACV method does not match insurance needs. The **functional valuation method** determines the value of property by comparing it to the cost of property that can perform the same function even if it is not identical. For example, suppose an organization that has been using a former schoolhouse as an office suffered a fire that destroyed the building. The functional valuation method would value the building at the cost to rebuild an office, not a schoolhouse. In the functional valuation method, the insurer is required to pay no more than the cost to repair or to replace the damaged or destroyed property with property that is its functional equivalent. This method is available by an endorsement to a commercial property policy. It is also used for residential buildings covered by the ISO Homeowners Modified Coverage Form, sometimes called Form HO-8.

When applied to personal property, the functional valuation method requires the insurer to pay no more than the cost to replace with equivalent but less expensive property. This method is commonly used with electronics and computers, where new computers may be more functional but less expensive than the models that have to be replaced. The insurer might also pay the actual repair cost or the applicable policy limit, if either is less than the cost of functionally equivalent property.

When applied to real property, the functional valuation method permits the insurer to use common construction methods and materials. For example, a three-coat plaster wall might be replaced with wallboard, restoring its function but not using the same material.

Cost of Reproduction Valuation Method

The cost of researching, reproducing, or transcribing is a commonly used valuation method for valuable papers and records. The value of these items lies in the value of the information they contain and the cost of reproduction is essentially the cost of restoring the information.

Cost of reproduction is not a suitable valuation method for papers and records that could never be restored. An example would be a dentist's file recording a patient's dental history. Unless duplicate records exist, recreating historical records showing the patient's dental X-rays, treatment, or other data is not possible. It may be more appropriate to insure irreplaceable items like these using an agreed value method. This would provide some compensation for the loss of goodwill and/or the expense of repeating the processes that generated the original records—to the extent feasible.

Pair or Set Clauses Valuation Method

Replacement cost, actual cash value, and the other valuation methods do not specify how to deal with the loss of part of a matched pair or set, such as a pair of earrings or a set of silverware. With matched pairs or sets, the loss of one item affects the value of the remaining item(s).

Many commercial and personal insurance policies address this valuation issue through a pair or set clause. A **pair or set clause** is a policy provision that indicates how values will be determined when part of a pair or set is lost, damaged, or destroyed. The following is the pair or set clause from the ISO HO-3 policy:[4]

Pair or set clause
A policy provision that indicates how values will be determined when part of a pair or set is lost, damaged, or destroyed.

> **D. Loss To A Pair Or Set**
>
> In case of loss to a pair or set we may elect to:
>
> 1. Repair or replace any part to restore the pair or set to its value before the loss; or
> 2. Pay the difference between actual cash value of the property before and after the loss.

The differential actual cash value (value before the loss minus value after the loss) of the entire pair or set is used for valuation. The pair or set clause explicitly acknowledges the insurer's right to repair or replace any part of a pair or set to restore its pre-loss value. Indirectly, the clause also tells the insured that loss of half the pair does not constitute a total loss—unless the remaining part or parts have become completely and absolutely worthless.

Money and Securities Valuation Method

Because crime insurance policies cover money and securities, they must address the valuation issue of such property. When a loss involves money, the insurer pays no more than its face value. Losses to money issued by countries other than the United States are paid at either (a) the face value in the currency issued by the applicable country or (b) the U.S. dollar equivalent, determined by the exchange rate on the day the loss was discovered. The insurer chooses which option to exercise. When a loss involves securities, the insurer pays no more than the value of the securities at the close of business on the day the loss was discovered. The insurer has the option of paying the value of the securities or replacing them in kind.

Regardless of how property is valued, the amount an insurer ultimately pays in respect to loss of that property loss is restricted by the limits set out in the policy.

POLICY LIMITS

Policy limits, which state the maximum amount payable for most claims covered by the policy, are usually stated in the declarations. These limits may apply to the policy as a whole or to a specific policy coverage, such as the property coverage or liability coverage in a homeowners policy. Most policy limits are expressed as dollar amounts. For example, a homeowners policy may have a $200,000 property limit and a $1 million liability limit. Some policies use nonmonetary limits, such as time (number of hours or days), and a few policies or coverages contain no explicit policy limit.

Industry Language—Limits of Liability

Insurance professionals often refer to policy limits as limits of liability. Although this is an accurate term, it can create confusion because the liability it refers to is to the insurer's responsibility to pay damages. Some may misinterpret the term "limits of liability" to mean that the policy limit applies only to liability insurance. To avoid confusion, many policies use the term "limits of insurance." This text uses the term "policy limits."

Most property insurance policy limits apply to each loss event (occurrence). If coverage is on an occurrence basis, covered property that is lost or damaged in each occurrence is covered up to the stated limit. The original policy limit remains in effect for each new occurrence. For example, if a homeowners policy provides $75,000 coverage on unscheduled personal property (all personal property not listed on a policy schedule) and a covered cause of loss destroys property worth $10,000, then the insurer pays a claim for $10,000. The insured still has $75,000 of coverage against losses resulting from future occurrences.

Reasons for Policy Limits

Policies contain limits for the following four major reasons:

1. *Limit the insurer's obligations.* Without policy limits, occasional losses under some policies could be extremely large, making it difficult for insurers to project losses and charge appropriate premiums. Limits also put a ceiling on the insurer's obligations to pay for a "priceless" art item or a catastrophe loss that is impossible to accurately measure. Few insurers are willing to risk bankruptcy on a single loss exposure.

2. *Accommodate consumer preferences.* Consumers are able to select policy limits that balance their coverage needs with their ability to pay premiums. This flexibility enables consumers to select policy limits appropriate to their specific loss exposures rather than having to pay for coverage they do not need. For example, consumers would be unwilling to pay the premium associated with a $1 million property insurance policy when their property is valued at only $200,000.

3. *Reflect insurer financial capacity.* Every insurer has a limited financial capacity to accommodate losses. Regulators often measure an insurer's ability to absorb losses based on their policyholders' surplus. Policy limits enable an insurer to remain within its financial capacity and to diversify its exposure by selling different types of insurance to a range of consumers.

4. *Substitute for exclusions.* Insurers sometimes use policy limits as a substitute for an exclusion. Instead of excluding problematic loss exposures, insurers may find it more effective to provide explicit coverage subject to a modest limit. For example, although pollution losses are not ideally insurable, courts have been reluctant to allow insurers to completely exclude coverage for these losses. Therefore, rather than excluding pollution losses, insurers provide explicit coverage that is subject to an aggregate limit.

Many types of policy limits can be used in relation to property insurance. Some types of policy limits, such as fixed dollar amounts, are common and are found in most property insurance policies. Others, such as no specified limit, are rare and are used only in particular types of policies. Limits can apply to all property or just to individual pieces of personal property and can be specified as fixed dollar values, variable amounts, or nondollar limits. Furthermore, multiple policy limits can be applied to a single event or claim, with one overall limit and various sublimits applying. Finally, policy limits may be specified on a per occurrence or an aggregate basis. With all of these possibilities, the potential number of combinations of policy limits is extensive. Some of the more commonly occurring types of policy limits are discussed in this section; however, this is not a comprehensive discussion of all possible limits that may apply. Therefore, each property insurance policy must be analyzed to determine what limits apply and when.

Individual Property Limits

In general, two types of policy limits apply to individual pieces of personal property: scheduled property limits and unscheduled property limits. Property is said to be "scheduled" when the policy covers a list (schedule) of particular property items. Each scheduled item is listed and precisely identified with descriptions, serial numbers, or other identifying marks or characteristics. Each item of scheduled property typically is subject to a limit that reflects the amount of insurance applying only to that property. For example, a scheduled personal property endorsement to a homeowners policy might describe a specific diamond engagement ring and state the ring's limit of insurance.

> ### What Happens If a Scheduled Item Is Destroyed?
>
> If a scheduled item is destroyed, nothing remains to insure, and no further insurance limit is needed, unless the item is replaced with another scheduled item. At least the following two approaches are possible if a scheduled item is destroyed:
>
> 1. Some policies explicitly state that limits are restored after a loss or that payment of a loss shall not reduce the policy limits.
>
> 2. Other policies state that limits are not reduced by a partial loss. However, after paying a total loss, the insurer usually refunds the unearned premium for that item's coverage.
>
> Some policies providing per item coverage contain a restoration of limits provision that clarifies the situation.

Most property insurance policies do not individually list, or schedule, personal property items, and the policy limits apply to all unscheduled items of covered property as a group. For example, the personal property coverage of a home-owners policy applies a single limit to all of the insured's personal property without listing individual items.

Some policies cover both scheduled and unscheduled items. For example, a stamp collector might purchase an insurance policy that covers specific prized stamps on a scheduled basis, with a separate amount of insurance listed for each specifically described stamp. The same policy might also provide a limit of unscheduled coverage (sometimes called blanket coverage) on several books of less valuable stamps. Similarly, a construction contractor might purchase scheduled insurance on a bulldozer and on other specific pieces of earthmoving equipment, and purchase a separate limit of unscheduled (blanket) insurance on other tools and equipment.

Specific Limits

Specific limit
The maximum dollar amount the insurer will pay, per item or per occurrence, for each loss of a particular item or class of property.

A **specific limit** is the maximum dollar amount the insurer will pay, per item or per occurrence, for each loss of a particular item or class of property. Specific limits can apply to either a single item of property (such as a build-ing) or a class of property (such as business personal property).

A property insurance policy may have several specific limits. These limits are for the maximum dollar amounts the insurer will pay for several items or classes of property. For example, an insured may own buildings and personal property as described in Exhibit 14-4. The insured can purchase a Building and Personal Property Coverage Form with the specific limits specified in the exhibit.

EXHIBIT 14-4

Examples of Specific and Blanket Limits

Property	Value	Specific Limits	Blanket Limit
Building at 114 Main Street	$240,000	$240,000	
Business Personal Property at 114 Main Street	$160,000	$160,000	
Building at 312 South Street	$280,000	$280,000	$720,000
Business Personal Property at 312 South Street	$120,000	$120,000	

Blanket Limits

A **blanket limit** is the maximum dollar amount the insurer will pay for two or more items or classes of property at one or more locations.

Using the example in Exhibit 14-4, the owner could purchase specific insurance with separate limits on each of these four items. Alternatively, with blanket insurance, the owner could purchase $800,000 (the total dollar amount of all property values) coverage applying to loss to any or all of them. With blanket insurance, insureds can often purchase slightly lower limits on the blanket policy than the sum of all the specific limits that would have been needed and still meet all the contractual requirements. For example, instead of purchasing $800,000 for the four previous items, the owner might purchase blanket coverage of $720,000 because a total loss at both locations simultaneously is highly unlikely.

A blanket limit is especially helpful when the total value of a firm's movable property is fairly constant, but the values may shift between covered locations. In the previous example, specific insurance in the amounts shown would not be adequate if at the time of the loss the insured had, for example, $180,000 of business personal property at 312 South Street and $80,000 at 114 Main Street. One location would be overinsured (a waste of premium dollars), whereas the other would be underinsured. Blanket insurance would provide sound protection at either location. However, blanket insurance can make underwriting, rating, and claim settlement more complicated because of the fluctuating values among locations.

Blanket insurance is less important for buildings than for personal property because building values usually do not change rapidly. However, blanket insurance is often used for buildings as a hedge against inaccurate valuation. By purchasing an insurance policy with blanket limits for all buildings rather

Blanket limit
The maximum dollar amount the insurer will pay for two or more items or classes of property at one or more locations.

than a specific limit for each building, the insured reduces the likelihood of a penalty after a loss at one location for underestimating that building's value and underinsuring it.

Sublimits

Sublimit
A policy provision that imposes smaller limits for certain kinds of property or lines of insurance.

The policy limits previously examined are usually shown in the policy declarations and represent upper limits on the amounts of recovery. Within these upper limits, many property insurance policies contain one or more sublimits. A **sublimit** is a policy provision that imposes smaller limits for certain kinds of property or lines of insurance.

For example, the ISO HO-3 policy contains a sublimit for personal property usually located at an insured's secondary residence, as shown in Exhibit 14-5.

EXHIBIT 14-5

Sublimits in the ISO HO-3 Policy

C.   **Coverage C – Personal Property**

2.   **Limit For Property At Other Residences**

Our limit of liability for personal property usually located at an "insured's" residence, other than the "residence premises", is 10% of the limit of liability for Coverage **C**, or $1,000, whichever is greater. However, this limitation does not apply to personal property:

a.   Moved from the "residence premises" because it is being repaired, renovated or rebuilt and is not fit to live in or store property in; or

b.   In a newly acquired principal residence for 30 days from the time you begin to move the property there.

Includes copyrighted material of Insurance Services Office, Inc., with its permission. Copyright, ISO Properties, Inc., 1999.

In the example in Exhibit 14-5, the sublimit is followed by two exceptions, similar to the exceptions to the exclusions discussed previously.

Variable Limits

Other limits that affect amounts payable are variable limits. Changing property values raise questions about the adequacy of property insurance limits expressed in fixed dollar amounts. Barely adequate amounts of insurance can easily become inadequate before the end of a policy period. The alternative, buying insurance that exceeds current values, involves paying more premium than necessary for the insurance that is needed.

During periods of economic inflation, some insurers automatically increase property insurance limits and premiums at each renewal unless the insured rejects the increase. The increase is usually based on a relevant price level index. For example, a construction cost index might be applied to building replacement cost values. However, there are drawbacks associated with this approach. First, a policyholder who is underinsured at policy inception is probably still underinsured at renewal because this approach adjusts only established policy limits. Second, coverage that was adequate at the beginning of a policy period may become inadequate sometime during the policy period because limits are increased only on renewal dates.

Automatically changing policy limits as they change during the policy period (rather than only at policy renewal) may be the best approach. Limits can be automatically changed by using an inflation guard endorsement, a peak season endorsement, or value reporting form.

Inflation Guard Protection

Inflation guard protection is a method of protecting against inflation by increasing the applicable limit for covered property by a specified percentage over the policy period. Inflation guard protection can be written into the policy or added to a policy through an endorsement. Many insurers selling homeowners insurance offer inflation guard protection as an option on their standard homeowners insurance policies but include it automatically on their preferred policies. Exhibit 14-6 shows an example of the effect of an inflation guard endorsement.

Inflation guard protection
A method of protecting against inflation by increasing the applicable limit for covered property by a specified percentage over the policy period.

EXHIBIT 14-6

Inflation Guard Endorsement Example

Assume a building is covered by a property insurance policy with a $365,000 limit and an endorsement with a 10 percent inflation guard. Coverage will be increased by $36,500 (10 percent of $365,000) during a one-year policy period. One hundred dollars of that increase ($1/365$ of $36,500) applies each day. If a loss occurs after the policy has been in force for 100 days, the applicable policy limit is not the policy limit in the declarations—$365,000, but $375,000, that is, the $365,000 limit plus $100 per day for 100 days ($10,000).

Although inflation guard protection automatically increases coverage on a daily basis, it has its disadvantages. First, if the property is not adequately insured at the outset, inflation guard protection does not correct the basic coverage inadequacy. Second, the selected inflation percentage might bear little or no relationship to actual inflation rates. To address the second disadvantages, linking the increase to some index rather than using an arbitrary percentage may be more appropriate.

Indexed Limits

Some insurers offer policy limits linked to a price level index, such as the U.S. Department of Commerce Construction Cost Index. Indexes can be more accurate than an inflation guard percentage, but the indexed limit approach also has one major shortcoming: Government price indexes (typically used because they are readily available) measure aggregate price level changes, not increases in local labor or material costs at the time and location of a loss. Despite this shortcoming, indexing can help maintain limits that reflect current values.

Peak Season Endorsement

For some businesses, keeping policy limits in line with inflation is difficult because of seasonal fluctuations. For example, the inventory in a toy shop greatly increases before the holiday season and declines through the end of December. Other businesses have their own seasonal patterns, such as ski resorts and summer camps.

Peak season endorsement
A commercial property endorsement that covers the fluctuating values of business personal property by providing differing amounts of insurance for certain periods during the overall policy period.

A **peak season endorsement** is a commercial property endorsement that covers the fluctuating values of business personal property by providing differing amounts of insurance for certain periods during the overall policy period. The peak season endorsement adjusts policy limits according to a specified schedule, regardless of policy inception and expiration dates. For example, a toy store owner might use a peak season endorsement to establish one policy limit for January through July and a higher limit for August through December. Other businesses might structure their coverage based on different seasonal patterns, possibly reflecting two or more peak seasons during the year.

A peak season endorsement is a relatively simple variable limits method that does not require either the insured or the insurer to do anything during the policy term. Its major disadvantages are that it depends on an advance estimate of the pattern of variable values during a future policy period and it does not respond to any unprojected changes. For example, the peak season endorsement for a toy store would not adjust limits or premiums if the store were to experience delayed or canceled shipments of merchandise that reduced its overall personal property loss exposures. Some policies, like the ISO Businessowners Policy, contain a peak season endorsement automatically.

Value Reporting Forms

Another way to accommodate fluctuations in property values is to use a value reporting form. The value reporting form is a commercial property form that bases the insured's premium on the business personal property values that the insured reports to the insurer periodically during the policy period.

Value reporting form policies are different from inflation guard and peak season endorsements in that the limits do not actually vary. In a value reporting form, policy limits remain constant but the premium adjusts to reflect changes in the covered property's value. A value reporting form is typically used to cover a merchant's or a manufacturer's stock.

Nondollar Limits

Property insurance policies do not always contain dollar limits. However, policies without dollar limits generally work on the assumption that some other factor restricts the insurer's financial obligations so that the insurer's liability in the event of a loss is still limited. For example, liability may be limited by the maximum possible loss to the property or on a time limit on coverage. The following two coverages illustrate nondollar limits:

- *Auto physical damage coverage.* No dollar value is stated in a typical personal auto policy. The policy limit for auto physical damage coverage usually is the actual cash value of the stolen or damaged property or the amount to repair or replace the property, whichever is less.

- *Business income coverage in businessowners policies.* Many businessowners policies include coverage for loss of business income that is incurred within twelve consecutive months after the date of direct physical loss or damage. Although twelve months is a time limit, this additional coverage is not subject to any dollar limits.

Policy limits reflect the upper end of an insurer's financial obligations. The amount an insurer pays out in the event of a loss is also affected by the deductible applicable to the policy.

DEDUCTIBLES

Most property insurance policies contain one or more deductibles that can affect the amounts payable under that policy. A **deductible** is a portion of a covered loss that is not paid by the insurer. In a property insurance policy, the deductible is subtracted from the amount of loss or the amount the insurer would otherwise be obligated to pay to the insured. In most cases, the deductible is stated as a dollar amount.

Deductible
A portion of a covered loss that is not paid by the insurer.

Reasons for Deductibles

Deductibles are a risk financing technique that requires the insured to retain a portion of the loss that is being transferred to an insurer. By requiring the insured to retain some of the loss, deductibles reduce the premium cost to the insured because they achieve the following:

- Reduce moral and morale hazard incentives and encourage risk control by the insured

- Eliminate the need for the insurer to process small losses, thereby reducing the insurer's loss costs and loss adjustment expenses

Reduce Moral and Morale Hazards and Encourage Loss Control

Having some of the insured's own funds at stake theoretically gives the insured the risk control incentive to prevent or reduce losses. A deductible serves this purpose most effectively when it is large enough to have a noticeable financial effect on the insured. Deductibles that are too small do not offer enough financial incentive, and deductibles that are too large defeat the purpose of transferring the loss exposure to the insurer.

Deductibles are not particularly effective when used with large property exposures, especially those that are not likely to incur a partial loss. For example, consider the costs involved in launching a satellite. With hundreds of millions of dollars at stake, even a $100,000 deductible on satellite launch insurance would neither encourage risk control nor substantially reduce the insurer's costs.

Reduce Insurer's Costs

A typical property deductible eliminates the insurer's involvement in low value losses. It is not cost-efficient for an insurer to deal with low value losses because the insurer's loss adjustment expenses often exceed the amount of indemnity payable to the insured.

The expensive and inefficient process of insuring small claims is sometimes called dollar trading (or trading dollars). **Dollar trading** is an insurance premium and loss exchange in which the insured pays the insurer premiums for low value losses, and the insurer pays the same dollars back to the insured, after subtracting expenses. Risk transfer mechanisms in general—and insurance in particular—are not designed to cope with these types of low-severity losses.

Dollar trading

An insurance premium and loss exchange in which the insured pays the insurer premiums for low value losses, and the insurer pays the same dollars back to the insured, after subtracting expenses.

Sizable property insurance deductibles help to eliminate dollar trading. The insured retains small losses as normal, out-of-pocket expenses and uses insurance to protect against major, unpredictable losses. Deductibles are most effective in reducing insurers' expenses for coverages such as auto collision, in which small, partial losses are common.

Deductibles reduce the premiums insurers must charge and ultimately benefit the insured because they (1) reduce insurers' overall loss costs and loss adjustment expenses, (2) provide insureds with loss control incentives, and (3) reduce the morale and moral hazard incentives. For most property insurance policies, insureds can choose from a variety of deductible levels. In making this choice, the insured must balance the benefits of the premium reduction with the need for insurance protection for large losses.

For most property insurance policies, the premium reduction is not directly proportional to the size of the deductible. Because small losses are more frequent than large losses, the premium reduction is on a sliding scale, that is, the premium credit increases much more slowly than the size of the deductible, as illustrated in Exhibit 14-7.

As shown in the exhibit, shifting from a $1,000 deductible to a $2,500 deductible reduces premiums by $300 while increasing retained loss exposures by $1,500. The premium reduction for shifting from a $50,000 deductible to a $75,000 deductible is also $300, but retained losses are increased by $25,000. Given these figures, shifting from a $1,000 deductible to a $2,500 deductible would be attractive in many cases. However, shifting from a $50,000 deductible to a $75,000 deductible is not as attractive. Even if the pricing is actuarially sound, and a risk management professional's organization could absorb the extra $25,000 loss, few risk management professionals would choose to retain an extra $25,000 in property losses to save $300 in premium unless other factors were involved, such as the insurer offering much broader coverage when the high deductible applies.

EXHIBIT 14-7

Premium Credits for Various Deductibles

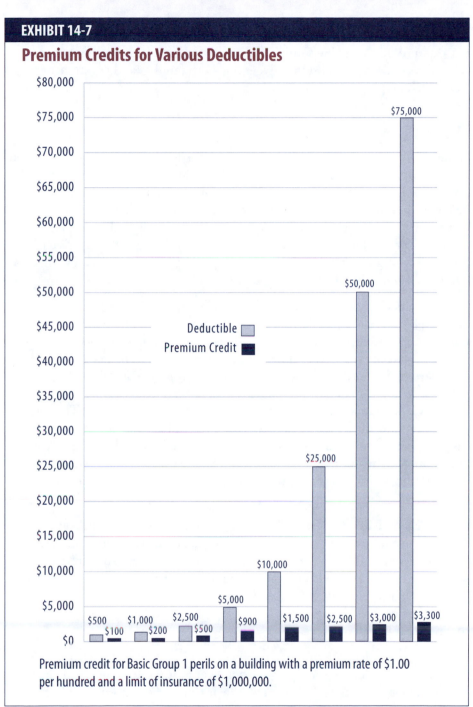

Premium credit for Basic Group 1 perils on a building with a premium rate of $1.00 per hundred and a limit of insurance of $1,000,000.

Source: *Commercial Lines Manual*, Copyright, Insurance Services Office, Inc., 2000, 4th ed. p. CF-99.

When premium costs are considered, premium credits tend to encourage the use of medium-sized deductibles that eliminate dollar trading for small losses but that provide a reliable source of recovery for large losses. What constitutes "medium-sized" varies substantially among both families and organizations that purchase property insurance.

Types of Deductibles

A variety of types of deductibles are used. Some deductibles can be applied on a per event or aggregate basis. Others may be a specified dollar figure (straight deductible), be a percentage of the loss amount (percentage deductible), or be based on time (time deductible). The type of deductible used in a property insurance policy varies based on the type of property covered by the policy, the frequency and severity of expected losses, and the type of incentive the insurer is trying to offer the insured. Some policies are offered even without a deductible, with the insurer paying losses from the first dollar.

Per event deductible
A deductible that applies to each item, each location, each claim, or each occurrence.

Generally, deductibles can be placed into two broad categories: per event deductibles and aggregate deductibles. A **per event deductible** applies to each item, each location, each claim, or each occurrence. Per event deductibles can be variously expressed as dollar amounts, percentages of some value, or time periods. These deductibles are the most common deductibles found in property insurance policies but can leave the insured exposed to substantial retained losses if many covered losses occur within a short period. The larger the per event deductible, the quicker the retained losses accumulate for the insured. Therefore, when per event deductibles are included in property insurance policies, the insured must be concerned about the cumulative effect of all deductibles during a year as well as about the deductible's effect on any one occurrence.

Aggregate deductible
A deductible that applies collectively to all losses occurring during a specific period, typically a policy year.

An **aggregate deductible** applies collectively to all losses occurring during a specific period, typically a policy year. Aggregate deductibles are usually stated as a dollar figure (called a straight deductible). An aggregate deductible minimizes retained losses resulting from a high frequency of small losses because all losses that occur during the specified period are accumulated. After the insured has retained losses in the amount of the aggregate, the insurer begins to pay any subsequent losses.

An aggregate deductible can be combined with a per event deductible, with the per event deductible applying to each event after the aggregate deductible has been met. Exhibit 14-8 shows the effects that per occurrence and aggregate deductibles can have on an insured's retained losses.

EXHIBIT 14-8

Deductibles and a Fleet of Cars

With seven losses, a $1,000 per event deductible results in different retained losses than a $10,000 aggregate deductible. With less frequent losses, aggregate deductibles typically will result in a higher proportion of the losses being retained. As the frequency of loss increases, per event deductibles can significantly increase retained losses.

Policy 1: $1,000 per event deductible

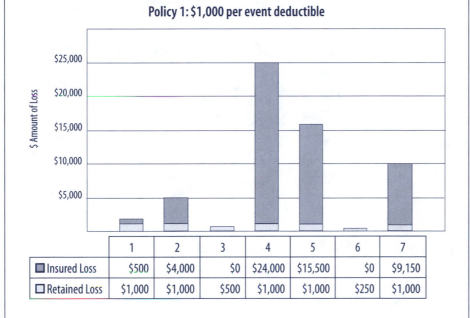

	1	2	3	4	5	6	7
■ Insured Loss	$500	$4,000	$0	$24,000	$15,500	$0	$9,150
☐ Retained Loss	$1,000	$1,000	$500	$1,000	$1,000	$250	$1,000

Policy 2: $10,000 aggregate deductible

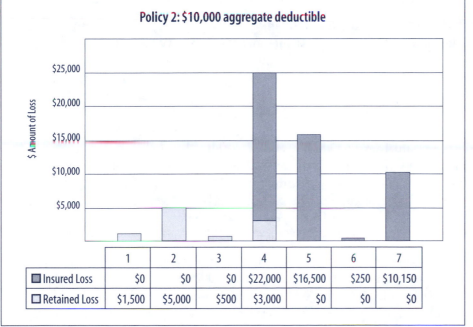

	1	2	3	4	5	6	7
■ Insured Loss	$0	$0	$0	$22,000	$16,500	$250	$10,150
☐ Retained Loss	$1,500	$5,000	$500	$3,000	$0	$0	$0

Continued on next page.

Accident	Physical Damage to Auto	Aggregate Losses	Auto Policy 1 $1,000 Per event deductible		Auto Policy 2 $10,000 Aggregate deductible	
			Retained Loss	Insured Loss	Retained Loss	Insured Loss
1	$1,500	$1,500	$1,000	$500	$1,500	$0
2	$5,000	$6,500	$1,000	$4,000	$5,000	$0
3	$500	$7,000	$500	$0	$500	$0
4	$25,000	$32,000	$1,000	$24,000	$3,000	$22,000
5	$16,500	$48,500	$1,000	$15,500	$0	$16,500
6	$250	$48,750	$250	$0	$0	$250
7	$10,150	$58,900	$1,000	$9,150	$0	$10,150
Total Retained Losses:			$5,750		$10,000	
Total Insured Losses:				$53,150		$48,900

Straight Deductibles

Straight deductible

A dollar amount the insured must pay toward a covered loss.

A **straight deductible** is a dollar amount the insured must pay toward a covered loss. In personal insurance, straight deductibles are relatively small, typically $1,000 or less. In commercial insurance, straight deductibles can range from $1,000 to several million dollars. The deductible provisions in the insurance policy specify how the straight deductible will be applied.

The most common method of applying a straight deductible is to subtract the deductible from the loss amount. The property insurer pays nothing unless the covered loss exceeds the deductible amount. For losses greater than the deductible amount, the insurer pays the loss after subtracting the deductible. To illustrate, if the insured has a $100,000 policy limit, a $10,000 covered loss, and a $1,000 deductible, the insurer will pay $9,000 ($10,000 – $1,000 = $9,000). This method becomes more complex if the loss amount is greater than the policy limit. Most property insurance policies specify that the insured can collect the full policy limit by subtracting the deductible from the loss amount and then applying the policy limit, such as the deductible provision from the BPP Coverage Form shown in Exhibit 14-9. Some other property insurance policies do not specify whether the deductible is subtracted from policy limits for losses exceeding limits.

The insured can collect the full policy limit if the loss is large enough. For example, assume an insured suffers a $110,000 loss under a policy with a $100,000 policy limit and a $5,000 straight deductible. Also assume the insured has fully insured the property so that no coinsurance penalty applies.

EXHIBIT 14-9

Deductible Policy Provision, ISO Building and Personal Property Coverage Form

D. Deductible

In any one occurrence of loss or damage (hereinafter referred to as loss), we will first reduce the amount of loss if required by the Coinsurance Condition or the Agreed Value Optional Coverage. If the adjusted amount of loss is less than or equal to the Deductible, we will not pay for that loss. If the adjusted amount of loss exceeds the Deductible, we will then subtract the Deductible from the adjusted amount of loss, and will pay the resulting amount or the Limit of Insurance, whichever is less.

Includes copyrighted material of Insurance Services Office, Inc., with its permission. Copyright, ISO Properties, Inc., 2001.

The insurer pays the policy limit of $100,000. This is an example of absorbing a deductible. To absorb a deductible means to apply the deductible to the loss amount before applying any coverage limits. If a property loss exceeds the coverage limit by at least the amount of the deductible, then the insured can collect the full coverage limit without further application of a deductible. The $5,000 deductible in this example is subtracted from the amount of the loss ($110,000 – $5,000 = $105,000). Because this result is greater than the policy limit, the deductible has been absorbed and the insurer pays the full policy limit ($100,000).

Order of Operations Is Important

When losses are at or above the policy limit and a deductible applies, the order in which the deductible and limit apply is important. For most policies, the correct order is to subtract the deductible from the loss amount and then compare the result to the limit. The policy pays the lesser of the loss minus the deductible or the policy limit. This is often termed "losses minus deductible, subject to the policy limit" and is the order of operations that was specified by the BPP Coverage Form in Exhibit 14-9.

The alternative order of operations is to compare the loss amount with the policy limit, choose the lesser of the two, and then subtract the deductible. However, in this case the full policy limit would never be paid. The policy would pay the lesser of the loss and the policy limit, minus the deductible. This alternative method is not as common.

Further complicating the deductible calculations is the fact that the deductible in a property insurance policy may be applied separately to each item or location, or it may apply to each loss or occurrence. Depending on which of these approaches is used, the same dollar deductible can produce dramatically different results. Exhibit 14-10 contains an example of how different applications of deductibles affect the insured's retained losses.

EXHIBIT 14-10

Comparison of per Item, per Location, and per Occurrence/ Per Loss Deductibles

Suppose a commercial bakery owns twenty trucks that are parked on two lots several blocks apart when a severe hailstorm causes at least $500 in damage to each truck. The trucks have physical damage coverage for the hail cause of loss. With a $500 deductible, the bakery's retained loss could be either $10,000, $1,000, or $500:

- If the $500 deductible applies per vehicle, the bakery retains $500 for each of the twenty vehicles, for a total of a $10,000 deductible.

- If the $500 deductible applies per location, the bakery retains $500 for each of the two locations, for a total of a $1,000 deductible.

- If the $500 deductible applies per occurrence/per loss, the bakery retains a $500 deductible.

Split deductible
A deductible provision that applies one deductible for most causes of loss but a different, higher deductible for other specified causes of loss.

Insurance policies occasionally use a split deductible. A **split deductible** is a deductible provision that applies one deductible for most causes of loss but a different, higher deductible for other specified causes of loss. For example, a higher theft deductible could be used to give the insured a greater risk control incentive to guard against theft. Alternatively, a higher windstorm deductible might be used to reflect the high probability of windstorm damage to property at some locations.

Split deductibles are common in auto insurance, which often contains one deductible for the peril of collision and another, often smaller, deductible for "other-than-collision" losses.

Percentage Deductibles

Percentage deductible
A deductible expressed as a percentage of some other amount, such as the amount of insurance, the covered property's value, or the amount of the loss.

Not all deductibles are expressed in dollar amounts. A **percentage deductible** is a deductible expressed as a percentage of some other amount, such as the amount of insurance, the covered property's value, or the amount of the loss. Consequently, the dollar amount of these percentage deductibles increases as the insurance amount, the property's insurable value, or the loss amount increases.

When property is insured to 100 percent of its insurable value, the dollar amount of a percentage deductible based on the amount of insurance is the same as the dollar amount of a percentage deductible based on insurable value. The difference in these approaches is relevant only when policy limits and insurable values differ. For example, percentage deductibles would result in different dollar amounts if property is insured to only 80 percent of its value, either to meet coinsurance requirements or because a total loss is not considered likely.

To illustrate, assume XYZ Company purchases $100,000 of earthquake coverage on a building valued at $500,000. The earthquake coverage is subject to a 10 percent deductible. XYZ retains the following losses:

- $10,000 of each insured loss if the percentage deductible applies to the amount of insurance.
- $50,000 of each insured loss if the percentage deductible applies to the property's insurable value.

Percentage deductibles are normally based on the amount of insurance. However, this approach tends to discourage insurance to value, because insureds who purchase less insurance are rewarded with a lower dollar deductible. Consider what would happen to XYZ if it had purchased $500,000 with a percentage deductible applying to the amount of insurance rather than the $100,000. The deductible would have been $50,000 rather than $10,000. Consequently, insurers sometimes base a percentage deductible on a property's insurable value.

A percentage deductible can also apply to the loss amount. This approach is common with health insurance and is called a coinsurance clause. It is also used in some professional liability insurance policies. In property insurance, stating the percentage deductible as a percentage of the loss amount might be used with windstorm or hail coverage when blanket limits apply and coverage is written on a reporting form basis.

Time Deductibles

A **time deductible** is a deductible expressed in terms of the time delay between when a loss occurs and when coverage begins. Although it has the same effect as other deductibles, a time deductible, or waiting period, usually is not captioned as a deductible in the policy.

One example of a time deductible appears in the ISO Personal Auto Policy, which provides coverage up to a specified dollar sublimit per day with a dollar maximum for transportation expenses (such as renting a substitute auto) if a covered auto has been stolen. However, the payment does not begin until forty-eight hours after the theft, and many stolen cars are recovered within this timeframe. Therefore, even though it is not called a "deductible," this forty-eight-hour period constitutes a two-day time deductible.

In addition to determining values, setting policy limits, and establishing deductibles, the amounts payable under a policy are affected by provisions called either coinsurance or insurance-to-value provisions that are designed to encourage insurance to value.

Time deductible
A deductible expressed in terms of the time delay between when a loss occurs and when coverage begins.

COINSURANCE AND OTHER INSURANCE-TO-VALUE PROVISIONS

The amount payable under a property policy can be reduced—but not increased—through the effect of a coinsurance clause or insurance-to-value provision designed to provide an incentive for insuring to value.

Coinsurance

Coinsurance clauses serve a dual purpose, both rewarding those who have insured to value and penalizing those who have not. Coinsurance is a requirement in most property insurance policies that makes the insured responsible for part of a loss if the property is underinsured below some specified percentage of the property's insurable value. The concept of coinsurance may be described as a penalty the insurer imposes on the insured for not buying enough insurance. However, coinsurance is also effectively a reward for insuring property to full value. If the insured insures property to full value, then the insurer agrees to waive the insured's participation in the loss, except to the extent of the deductible.

Coinsurance in Property Insurance and in Health Insurance

Coinsurance means something different in the context of property insurance than it does in the context of health insurance.

- A coinsurance clause in a property insurance policy provides that the insurer pays losses in full (subject to other policy provisions) for any insured who carries an amount of insurance that equals or exceeds some stated percentage of the covered property's insurable value. For example, in a property policy with an 80 percent coinsurance clause, an insured who carries $80,000 or more of property insurance on a building with an insurable value of $100,000 recovers in full for a covered loss (subject to any applicable deductible and the policy limit). Only a policyholder who does not insure to value shares the loss with the insurer, thereby becoming a coinsurer.

- A coinsurance clause in a health insurance policy is, in effect, a percentage deductible in which the insured and the insurer each agree to pay a stated percentage of covered losses. For example, in a health insurance policy with an 80 percent coinsurance clause, the insurer pays 80 percent of every covered claim, and the insured pays 20 percent. In a claim for $1,000 of covered medical expenses, the insurer pays $800, and the insured pays $200 (subject to other applicable policy provisions). Every policyholder shares the loss with the insurer and is therefore a coinsurer.

Coinsurance Clause

A coinsurance clause in a property insurance policy requires the insured to carry an amount of insurance equal to or greater than the stated coinsurance percentage of the covered property's insurable value in order to pay a lower rate per unit of coverage and avoid a partial recovery for a covered loss. The most common coinsurance percentages for buildings and personal property are 80, 90, and 100 percent. The insurable value is the ACV, the replacement cost value, or whatever other value is determined according to the policy's valuation clause.

The more insurance a consumer agrees to buy—in other words, the more closely the amount of insurance purchased reflects the covered property's full insurable value—the lower the rate for insurance that consumer will pay. Insurers charge a lower rate per $100 of coverage to those who agree to meet the 80 percent coinsurance requirement. This rate is reduced by another 5 percent for those who purchase a policy with a 90 percent coinsurance percentage, and a further 5 percent for those who opt for 100 percent coinsurance. Insureds buy more insurance (higher limits), but each unit of insurance costs less. Insurance professionals usually call this the "coinsurance requirement" although it is not literally required. Failure to meet a coinsurance requirement does not void coverage. If the requirement is not met, the policy remains in effect, but the insured will receive only a partial recovery when a covered loss occurs.

Given the coinsurance requirement, it might seem to be most cost-effective for property insurance buyers to choose a 100 percent coinsurance clause and insure to full value. This approach essentially provides full coverage at the lowest rate per $100 of insurance. However, 80 percent coinsurance is the most common, for several reasons, including the following:

- It is traditional practice. For many years, 80 percent coinsurance has been viewed as the standard approach.

- Few property losses are total losses. Insurance to 80 percent of the full insurable value provides adequate insurance limits to cover the majority of losses.

- Eighty percent coinsurance allows some margin for error in predicting the full insurable value of property at the time of the loss.

- The total premium for insurance to 80 percent of value with an 80 percent coinsurance clause is less than the total premium for insurance to 100 percent of value with a 100 percent coinsurance clause. However, when property insurance rates are low, this is not a significant factor.

Some property insurance buyers use a conservative approach, insuring to approximately 100 percent of the estimated full insurable value, subject to an 80 percent coinsurance clause. If the estimated value is accurate, this approach provides insurance limits adequate to provide indemnity for a total loss. It also provides a margin of error that usually prevents a coinsurance penalty if the property is underinsured at the time of the loss. Coinsurance penalties can also be avoided by using the agreed value coverage.

Exhibit 14-11 contains the coinsurance clause from the ISO BPP Coverage Form.

EXHIBIT 14-11

Coinsurance Clause in the ISO BPP Coverage Form

F.   Additional Conditions

1. Coinsurance

If a Coinsurance percentage is shown in the Declarations, the following condition applies.

a.   We will not pay the full amount of any loss if the value of Covered Property at the time of loss times the Coinsurance percentage shown for it in the Declarations is greater than the Limit of Insurance for the property.

Instead, we will determine the most we will pay using the following steps:

(1)   Multiply the value of Covered Property at the time of loss by the Coinsurance percentage;

(2)   Divide the Limit of Insurance of the property by the figure determined in Step **(1)**;

(3)   Multiply the total amount of loss, before the application of any deductible, by the figure determined in Step **(2)**; and

(4)   Subtract the deductible from the figure determined in Step **(3)**.

We will pay the amount determined in Step **(4)** or the limit of insurance, whichever is less. For the remainder, you will either have to rely on other insurance or absorb the loss yourself.

Includes copyrighted material of Insurance Services Office, Inc., with its permission. Copyright, ISO Properties, Inc., 2001.

Coinsurance Formula

The coinsurance formula explains how the amount payable is determined if the coinsurance requirement has not been met, and can be expressed as follows:

$$\text{Amount payable} = \frac{\text{Limit of insurance}}{\text{Value of covered property} \times \text{Coinsurance}} \times \text{Total amount of covered loss.}$$
$$\phantom{\text{Amount payable} = \frac{\text{Limit}}{\text{Value (at time of loss)}\quad\text{percentage}}}$$

Insurance students often remember this formula as "did over should times loss," which can be written as follows:

$$\text{Amount payable} = \frac{\text{Did}}{\text{Should}} \times \text{Loss,}$$

where

"Did" = The amount of insurance carried (the policy limit), and

"Should" = The minimum amount that should have been carried to meet the coinsurance requirement based on the insurable value at the time of the loss.

The following three points are crucial in applying the coinsurance formula:

1. Applying the coinsurance formula is necessary only when the coinsurance requirement is not met, because the policy limits are less than the insurable value multiplied by the coinsurance percentage. In other words, the coinsurance penalty applies only when the "did" is less than the "should." If the coinsurance requirement is met ("did" is greater than or equal to "should"), the amount payable is the full loss amount, subject to the deductible, applicable policy limits, and other relevant policy provisions.

2. The insurer never pays more than the loss amount. If the amount of insurance carried is greater than the minimum policy limit required ("did" is greater than or equal to "should"), the coinsurance formula itself would indicate that the insurer should pay more than the loss amount.

3. The insurer never pays more than the applicable policy limits. If the loss amount is greater than the minimum policy limits required by the coinsurance clause ("loss" is greater than "should"), the formula might indicate that the insurer would pay more than the policy limits. However, the insurer's obligation would not exceed the applicable policy limits.

Exhibit 14-12 illustrates how to use the coinsurance formula.

Coinsurance can be critical in the event of a major partial loss and substantial underinsurance. To impose a coinsurance penalty, an insurer must accurately appraise the full insurable value of all covered property at the time of the loss subject to the applicable policy limits. This process alone can be time-consuming and costly and can lead to disputes over the appraisal estimate's accuracy. If the appraised value of the property results in a value high enough to invoke the coinsurance penalty, it can even lead to litigation. For these and other practical reasons, many property claims are settled without any attempt to determine precisely whether a coinsurance requirement has been met. Coinsurance calculations usually are invoked only when both clear evidence of substantial underinsurance and a sizable loss exist.

Coinsurance clauses apply in policies covering direct damage to buildings and personal property. The coinsurance requirement in these policies is based on the building's full insurable value, normally the ACV or replacement cost. Coinsurance clauses are also used in business income policies for indirect losses. In those policies, the coinsurance formula requires an amount of insurance based on net income and operating expenses that, if no loss had occurred, would have been earned or incurred during the current policy period.

EXHIBIT 14-12

Coinsurance Example

Barbara and Carlos own a building with a replacement cost value of $300,000. They insure the building for $200,000 with a property insurance policy providing replacement cost coverage subject to a 100 percent coinsurance clause. A covered peril causes $60,000 of damage to the building. How much will the property insurer pay Barbara and Carlos for the damage to the building?

Insured value = $300,000

Coinsurance percentage = 100%

Loss amount = $60,000

Policy limit = $200,000

Alternatively:

Did = Policy limit = $200,000

Should = Insured value × Coinsurance percentage = $300,000 × 100% = $300,000.

Is "did" greater than or equal to "should"?

    If yes, the policy pays the loss amount subject to policy limits and deductible.

    If no, the policy pays [(Did ÷ Should) × Loss amount].

In this case the answer was no. Therefore, Barbara and Carlos did not meet the coinsurance requirement, and the policy pays the following:

$$\text{Policy payout} = \frac{\text{Did}}{\text{Should}} \times \text{Loss amount}$$

$$= \frac{\$200,000}{\$300,000} \times \$60,000$$

$$= \$40,000.$$

Because Barbara and Carlos did not meet the coinsurance clause, even though the loss was well below the policy limits, the amount payable under the property insurance policy was reduced.

Insurance-to-Value Provisions in Homeowners and Businessowners Policies

Despite similarities, the insurance-to-value provisions in homeowners and businessowners policies are different from coinsurance. With insurance-to-value provisions, the amount payable by the insurer will not be less than the ACV (subject to policy limits). These provisions are found within a loss payment or loss settlement condition that resembles the coinsurance provision. Exhibit 14-13 contains a portion of the loss settlement condition from the ISO HO-3 policy.

Under the insurance-to-value provisions of the policy in Exhibit 14-13, the amount payable by the insurer will be one of the following:

- The replacement cost value of the property—effectively a reward for those insured to at least 80 percent of the replacement cost value of the property

- The actual cash value of the property—effectively a penalty for those not insured to at least 80 percent of replacement cost value of the property

- An amount between the replacement cost value and the ACV of the property, determined by the same "did over should times loss" formula used in the coinsurance penalty, where the loss amount is on a replacement cost basis

The advantage of the insurance-to-value requirement compared with the coinsurance requirement is that the penalty for underinsurance is limited. The worst penalty for underinsurance is for a loss amount based on a depreciated ACV basis, rather than on an replacement cost basis, as the insurance-to-value provision states that the policy will pay the greater of ACV or the "did over should times loss" penalty.

Even if the property is substantially underinsured, the insurer will not pay less than the property's ACV, provided that amount is within policy limits. Another difference between the insurance-to-value requirement and coinsurance requirements is that policies containing insurance-to-value provisions do not give the insured a choice of percentages. Unlike the coinsurance provisions, under which the insured can choose from a variety of percentages, the insurance-to-value provision has a stated 80 percent requirement.

EXHIBIT 14-13

Insurance-to-Value Provision in the ISO HO-3 Policy

Section I – Conditions

C. Loss Settlement

...Covered property losses are settled as follows:...

2. Buildings covered under Coverage **A** or **B** at replacement cost without deduction for depreciation, subject to the following:

a...

b. If, at the time of loss, the amount of insurance in this policy on the damaged building is less than 80% of the full replacement cost of the building immediately before the loss, we will pay the greater of the following amounts, but not more than the limit of liability under this policy that applies to the building:

(1) The actual cash value of that part of the building damaged; or

(2) That proportion of the cost to repair or replace, after application of any deductible and without deduction for depreciation, that part of the building damaged, which the total amount of insurance in this policy on the damaged building bears to 80% of the replacement cost of the building.

Alternatives to Coinsurance

Maintaining insurance to value is only one way of avoiding coinsurance penalties or other insurance-to-value penalties. Several techniques and forms are available that avoid insurance-to-value penalties, including the following:

- Flat policies
- Agreed value
- Monthly limit of indemnity
- Maximum period of indemnity

Flat Policies

Flat policy

A property insurance policy without a coinsurance clause.

A **flat policy** is a property insurance policy without a coinsurance clause. Some insurers will remove the coinsurance clause for a substantial additional charge—such as a 300 percent increase in the rate per $100 of insurance. Usually this option is prohibitively expensive, and it is therefore more attractive to spend premium dollars on higher policy limits.

Some coverages are usually written on a flat (no coinsurance) basis, such as the unscheduled personal property coverage on a tenant's policy. Determining the ACV of a typical residential tenant's personal property prior to a loss is usually difficult, and values constantly change as specific items are acquired, worn or used, or discarded. Because of fluctuating values of personal property, it may be difficult to ensure that coinsurance requirements are being met without overinsuring. To avoid these types of problems, some portions of insurance policies may be written on a flat basis.

Agreed Value

The term "agreed value" applies to the following two concepts:

1. The agreed value method of valuation, discussed previously, applies to property whose value is difficult to determine after a loss. The insurer and the insured agree on the insured property's value and specify that value in a policy schedule. For a total loss to the insured property, the insurer pays the amount specified in the policy.

2. The agreed value coverage that avoids coinsurance penalties also requires that the insurer and the insured agree on an amount. In this case, however, what is agreed on is not necessarily the property's value but is an amount of insurance that meets the requirement of the coinsurance formula. If the insured carries an amount of insurance at least equal to that of the agreed value, the insurer will not impose a coinsurance penalty at the time of loss. The amount payable is the ACV, replacement cost, or other amount specified in the policy's valuation clause.

Agreed value coverage addresses one major challenge of insurance-to-value provisions—the difficulty of establishing values before a loss. This approach is so popular that it is preprinted as an option in the ISO BPP Coverage Form. It operates as follows:

- The insurer and the insured agree to what amount of insurance is sufficient to meet the "should" requirement of the coinsurance clause.

- If the insured carries an amount of insurance at least equal to that agreed value, the insurer will not impose a coinsurance penalty at the time of the loss.

- A rate increase, typically 5 percent (compared with the rate charged on a policy with 80 percent coinsurance), is applied when premiums are calculated.

The agreed value is based on a statement of values. The statement of values, which must be submitted by the insured and acceptable to the insurer, specifies the full ACV or replacement cost of the covered property. Many insurers require an appraisal to support the statement of values submitted by the insured. The policy's coinsurance percentage is applied to the full ACV or replacement cost to produce the agreed value. The coinsurance clause is suspended if the amount of insurance equals or exceeds the agreed value.

Agreed value coverage eliminates only one risk of a coinsurance penalty. If the amount of insurance equals the agreed value but the agreed value is only 80 percent of the full property value, the coinsurance penalty is suspended, but the insured still retains 20 percent of a total loss. Similarly, agreed value coverage does not convert the policy to a valued policy. The policy's loss valuation provision continues to apply, and the insurer is still obligated to pay only the insurable value of the loss or the policy limits, whichever is less.

Monthly Limit of Indemnity

Another alternative to coinsurance is the stipulation of a monthly limit of indemnity. The **monthly limit of indemnity** is a limit in business income policies on the amount of insurance that can be collected during any thirty-day period, subject to the limit of insurance. The monthly limit of indemnity provides a popular alternative to coinsurance for business income policies. The indemnity is preprinted as an option in the standard ISO business income forms and activated by an entry on the policy's declarations page. This alternative to coinsurance focuses less on the total dollar amount exposed to loss and more on the period during which a loss of business income may occur. Rather than require an amount of insurance that equals a specified percentage of the insurable value (as coinsurance does), this approach limits the total amount of insurance that can be collected. No limit is set on the overall length of an interruption during which loss payments may be made.

Exhibit 14-14 contains the monthly limit of indemnity option from the ISO Business Income and Extra Expense (BIC) Coverage Form.

Monthly limit of indemnity
A limit in business income policies on the amount of insurance that can be collected during any thirty-day period, subject to the limit of insurance.

> **EXHIBIT 14-14**
>
> ## Monthly Limit of Indemnity Option in the ISO BIC Coverage Form
>
> **E.   Optional Coverages**
>
> If shown as applicable in the Declarations, the following Optional Coverages apply separately to each item.
>
> **2.   Monthly Limit of Indemnity**
>
> **a.** The Additional Condition, Coinsurance, does not apply to this Coverage Form at the described premises to which this Optional Coverage applies.
>
> **b.** The most we will pay for loss of Business Income in each period of 30 consecutive days after the beginning of the "period of restoration" is:
>
> **(1)** The Limit of Insurance, multiplied by
>
> **(2)** The fraction shown in the Declarations for this Optional Coverage.

Includes copyrighted material of Insurance Services Office, Inc., with its permission. Copyright, ISO Properties, Inc., 2001.

As an example, assume Mike's Phone Store has business income coverage on a monthly limit of indemnity basis with a policy limit of $40,000 and a fraction of one-fourth shown in the policy declarations. During any thirty-day period after a covered business income loss, Mike could recover either the amount of business income loss actually sustained or $10,000 (that is, one-fourth of the $40,000 limit), whichever is less. If the interruption continues for more than four months, Mike could continue to recover up to $10,000 per month until the $40,000 limit had been consumed.

Business income coverage on a coinsurance basis requires an accurate estimate of future insurable values. Sound estimates can be difficult for some businesses, especially small start-up operations. The monthly limit of indemnity alternative presents a simple alternative because the business needs to estimate only what it must recover in any thirty-day period for a worst-case period of interruption.

Maximum Period of Indemnity

Maximum period of indemnity
An option in business income policies in which the insurer agrees to pay the amount of covered losses and expenses sustained during a 120-day period, up to the limit of insurance.

The **maximum period of indemnity** is an option in business income policies in which the insurer agrees to pay the amount of covered losses and expenses sustained during a 120-day period, up to the limit of insurance. As with the monthly limit of indemnity, it is preprinted as an option in the standard ISO business income forms. When this option is activated by an entry in the declarations, the coinsurance requirement does not apply, and the insurer agrees to pay the amount of covered loss and expenses sustained during a 120-day period, up to the policy limits. No per-month limitation applies. For example, suppose Mike's Phone Store has business income coverage on a maximum period of indemnity basis with a policy limit of $40,000. During the period of restoration after a covered business income loss, Mike could recover either the amount of business income loss actually sustained or $40,000, whichever is less. However, if the interruption continued for more than 120 days, Mike would recover no more than the amount of covered loss and expense sustained during the first 120 days.

EXAMPLES COMBINING VALUATION, LIMITS, DEDUCTIBLES, AND COINSURANCE

For a given loss, the amount payable under a property insurance policy depends on the interaction between its loss valuation provisions, policy limits, deductibles, and coinsurance or other insurance-to-value provisions. Except as noted, these examples are based on the ISO BPP Coverage Form. The coinsurance provision in that form was previously quoted in Exhibit 14-11, but is repeated here in Exhibit 14-15 and is referred to in the examples.

EXHIBIT 14-15

Coinsurance and Deductible Clauses in the ISO BPP Coverage Form

F. Additional Conditions

1. Coinsurance

If a Coinsurance percentage is shown in the Declarations, the following condition applies.

  a. We will not pay the full amount of any loss if the value of Covered Property at the time of loss times the Coinsurance percentage shown for it in the Declarations is greater than the Limit of Insurance for the property.

  Instead, we will determine the most we will pay using the following steps:

  (1) Multiply the value of Covered Property at the time of loss by the Coinsurance percentage;

  (2) Divide the Limit of Insurance of the property by the figure determined in Step **(1)**;

  (3) Multiply the total amount of loss, before the application of any deductible, by the figure determined in Step **(2)**; and

  (4) Subtract the deductible from the figure determined in Step **(3)**.

  We will pay the amount determined in Step **(4)** or the limit of insurance, whichever is less. For the remainder, you will either have to rely on other insurance or absorb the loss yourself.

The deductible provision is also relevant in determining amounts payable:

D. Deductible

In any one occurrence of loss or damage (hereinafter referred to as loss), we will first reduce the amount of loss if required by the Coinsurance Condition or the Agreed Value Optional Coverage. If the adjusted amount of loss is less than or equal to the Deductible, we will not pay for that loss. If the adjusted amount of loss exceeds the Deductible, we will then subtract the Deductible from the adjusted amount of loss, and will pay the resulting amount or the Limit of Insurance, whichever is less.

When the occurrence involves loss to more than one item of Covered Property and separate Limits of Insurance apply, the losses will not be combined in determining application of the Deductible, but the Deductible will be applied only once per occurrence.

Includes copyrighted material of Insurance Services Office, Inc., with its permission. Copyright, ISO Properties, Inc., 2001.

ACV Valuation/Adequate Insurance Example

Alpha Company's building is covered on an ACV basis under an ISO BPP Coverage Form. Exhibit 14-16 sets out the assumptions that can be made about this case at the time of the loss.

EXHIBIT 14-16	
Specific Insurance Example Assumptions	
Alpha Company	
ACV of Alpha's building	$275,000
Replacement cost (RC) of Alpha's building	$375,000
Coinsurance percentage	80%
Policy limits	$250,000
Deductible	$500
Loss amount (ACV)	$40,000
Loss amount (RC)	$50,000

The steps in determining the amount payable are as follows:

Step 1: Determine whether a coinsurance penalty applies. In this case, the minimum amount of insurance to meet coinsurance requirements (the "should" in the coinsurance formula) on an ACV basis is $220,000 (80% × $275,000 = $220,000). The $250,000 policy limit (the "did" in the coinsurance formula) meets or exceeds the $220,000 minimum requirement. Because the coinsurance requirement has been met, the coinsurance penalty does not apply.

Step 2: Determine the amount of the coinsurance penalty. In this case, no coinsurance penalty applies. However, the deductible and limit provisions apply according to the following formula:

Amount payable = (Loss amount − Deductible) subject to policy limits.

Therefore, the following two additional steps are taken:

Step 3: Subtract the deductible from the loss amount to ascertain the amount payable, subject to policy limits. The amount payable is $39,500 ($40,000 − $500 = $39,500).

Step 4: Pay the resulting amount or the policy limits, whichever is less. As $39,500 (the resulting loss amount) is less than the $250,000 policy limits, the insurer pays $39,500.

Note that the insurer does not pay $40,000 and absorb the deductible. As previously mentioned, a deductible can be absorbed only when a property loss exceeds the coverage limit by at least the deductible amount. In this case, the $40,000 property loss does not exceed the policy limits.

Replacement Cost Valuation/Underinsurance Example

If Alpha's building had been insured on a replacement cost basis, the coinsurance requirement would not be met, and the calculations would produce a different amount payable, based again on the assumptions in Exhibit 14-16. The steps in determining the amount payable are as follows:

Step 1:   Determine whether a coinsurance penalty applies. In this case, the minimum amount of insurance to meet coinsurance requirements (the "should" in the coinsurance formula) on an RC basis is $300,000 (80% × $375,000 = $300,000). The $250,000 policy limit (the "did" in the coinsurance formula) does not meet or exceed the $300,000 requirement. Because the minimum amount of insurance to meet coinsurance requirements on an RC basis was not met; a coinsurance penalty applies. In this case, the formula to use to determine the amount payable (subject to policy limits) when a coinsurance penalty applies is as follows:

$$\text{Amount payable} = \left[\left(\frac{\text{Did}}{\text{Should}} \times \text{Loss amount}\right) - \text{Deductible}\right] \text{subject to policy limits.}$$

Step 2:   Calculate Did ÷ Should.

$$\frac{\text{Did}}{\text{Should}} = \frac{\$250,000}{\$300,000}$$
$$= 0.83 \text{ (rounded).}$$

Step 3:   Multiply (Did ÷ Should) by the loss amount. In this case the loss is $50,000, which is the replacement cost value of the loss.

$$\frac{\text{Did}}{\text{Should}} \times \text{Loss amount} = 0.83 \times \$50,000$$
$$= \$41,500.$$

Step 4:   Subtract the deductible from the amount calculated in Step 3.

$$\left(\frac{\text{Did}}{\text{Should}} \times \text{Loss amount}\right) - \text{Deductible} = \$41,500 - \$500$$
$$= \$41,000.$$

Step 5:   The insurer pays the amount determined in Step 4 or the policy limits, whichever is less, so the amount payable by the insurer is $41,000.

Blanket Insurance/Underinsurance Example

To illustrate blanket insurance and underinsurance, Exhibit 14-17 sets out the assumptions for Beta Company.

EXHIBIT 14-17	
Blanket Insurance Example	
Beta Company	
ACV of Beta's building at Location 1	$75,000
ACV of Beta's building at Location 2	$100,000
ACV of Beta's personal property at Location 1	$10,000
ACV of Beta's personal property at Location 2	$65,000
Coinsurance percentage	90%
Blanket policy limit for buildings and personal property at Locations 1 and 2	$135,000
Deductible	$1,000
Amount of loss to building at Location 1 (ACV)	$30,000
Amount of loss to personal property at Location 1 (ACV)	$20,000

The steps in determining the amount payable to Beta Company are as follows:

Step 1: Determine whether a coinsurance penalty applies. In this case, the minimum amount of insurance to meet coinsurance requirements (the "should" in the coinsurance formula) on an ACV basis is as follows:

$$\text{Minimum amount of insurance} = \text{Sum of ACV values} \times \text{Coinsurance percentage}$$
$$= (\$75{,}000 + \$100{,}000 + \$10{,}000 + \$65{,}000) \times 90\%$$
$$= \$225{,}000.$$

The $135,000 policy limit (the "did" in the coinsurance formula) does not meet or exceed the $225,000 requirement. Because the minimum amount of insurance to meet coinsurance requirements on an ACV basis was not met, a coinsurance penalty applies. The formula to use to determine the amount payable (subject to policy limits) when a coinsurance penalty applies is as follows:

$$\text{Amount payable} = \left[\left(\frac{\text{Did}}{\text{Should}} \times \text{Loss}\right) - \text{Deductible}\right] \text{ subject to policy limits.}$$

Step 2: Calculate Did ÷ Should.

$$\frac{\text{Did}}{\text{Should}} = \frac{\$135{,}000}{\$225{,}000}$$
$$= 0.60.$$

Step 3: Multiply (Did ÷ Should) by the loss amount. In this case the loss is $50,000 (30,300 + $20,000 = $50,000).

$$\frac{Did}{Should} \times Loss\ amount = 0.6 \times \$50,000$$
$$= \$30,000.$$

Step 4: Subtract the deductible from the amount calculated in Step 3 (the deductible is applied once per occurrence).

$$\left(\frac{Did}{Should} \times Loss\ amount \right) - Deductible = \$30,000 - \$1,000$$
$$= \$29,000.$$

Step 5: The insurer does not pay more than the amount determined in Step 4 or the policy limits, whichever is less. The insurer pays $29,000, and the remaining loss of $21,000 is not covered.

Deductible Application Example

Property insurance policies can differ in how they combine coinsurance and deductibles, and these differences affect the amount an insured recovers for a loss. Using the same set of assumptions presented in Exhibit 14-16, the next example uses the AAIS counterpart to the ISO policy to illustrate a policy form that applies the deductible before coinsurance calculations. Exhibit 14-18 shows the coinsurance provision in the AAIS Building and Personal Property Coverage Part.

EXHIBIT 14-18

Coinsurance Provision in the AAIS Building and Personal Property Coverage Part

4. **Coinsurance** —When a coinsurance percentage is shown on the "declarations", "we" only pay a part of the loss if the "limit" is less than the value of the covered property at the time of the loss multiplied by the coinsurance percentage shown for it on the "declarations". "Our" part of the loss is determined using the following steps:

   a. Multiply the value of the covered property at the time of the loss by the coinsurance percentage;

   b. Divide the "limit" for covered property by the figure determined in 4.a. above; and

   c. Multiply the total amount of loss, after the application of any deductible, by the figure determined in 4.b. above.

   The most "we" pay is the amount determined in 4.c. above or the "limit", whichever is less. "We" do not pay any remaining part of the loss.

Source: Form CP 0012 12 99. Contains copyrighted material of the American Association for Insurance Services, 1999.

Applying this formula to the Alpha Company assumptions in Exhibit 14-16 produces the following results, assuming coverage applies on a replacement-cost basis:

Step 1:   Determine whether a coinsurance penalty applies. In this case, the minimum amount of insurance to meet coinsurance requirements (the "should" in the coinsurance formula) on an RC basis is $300,000 (80% × $375,000 = $300,000). The $250,000 amount of insurance (the "did" in the coinsurance formula) does not meet or exceed the $300,000 requirement. Because the minimum amount of insurance to meet coinsurance requirements on an RC basis was not met, a coinsurance penalty applies. In this example, the formula to use to determine the amount payable (subject to policy limits) when a coinsurance penalty applies is as follows:

$$\text{Amount payable} = \frac{\text{Did}}{\text{Should}} \times (\text{Loss} - \text{Deductible})$$

Step 2:   Calculate Did ÷ Should.

$$\frac{\text{Did}}{\text{Should}} = \frac{\$250{,}000}{\$300{,}000}$$

$$= 0.83 \text{ (rounded)}.$$

Step 3:   Subtract the deductible from the loss amount

$$\text{Loss Amount} - \text{Deductible} = \$50{,}000 - \$500$$

$$= \$49{,}500.$$

Step 4:   Multiply the figure calculated in Step 3 by (Did ÷ Should) to determine the amount payable.

$$\text{Amount payable} = \frac{\text{Did}}{\text{Should}} \times (\text{Loss} - \text{Deductible})$$

$$= 0.83 \times \$49{,}500$$

$$= \$41{,}085.$$

Step 5:   The insurer pays the amount determined in step 4 or the policy limit, whichever is less. Therefore the amount payable by the insurer is $41,085.

The difference between the ISO and the AAIS commercial property forms is that the deductible in the AAIS form is subtracted from the loss before the coinsurance calculation, whereas in the ISO form the deductible is subtracted after the coinsurance calculation. When the deductible is applied as specified in the AAIS policy, the insured recovers $85 more than under the ISO policy.

In the insurance-to-value provisions of the ISO HO-3 policy, the calculations are done in a similar order to the AAIS example. The deductible is subtracted from the loss before any adjustment is made for underinsurance.

Some insurance policies do not specify where in the calculation the deductible should be subtracted. When the issue is not addressed, the adjustment usually depends on the practices of the insurer or on the claim representative handling the case.

DISPUTED CLAIM RESOLUTION: APPRAISAL PROVISIONS

After a loss, the insurer and insured may dispute the amounts payable under a property insurance policy. For example, the insured may believe that a damaged piece of machinery was undervalued by the insurer. The appraisal clause included in most property insurance policies addresses these types of disputes. The **appraisal clause** is a policy provision that prescribes a method for resolving a disputed claim about the value of property or the amount of a property loss.

The appraisal clause is useful when the insurer and the insured agree that a given property loss is covered but cannot agree on the property's value or the loss amount, or when the insured thinks the claim is worth more than the insurer is willing to pay.

Such disputes usually do not involve bad faith by either party. Many factors affect property's value or repair cost, and reasonable parties can differ dramatically in their determinations of value. Negotiation usually resolves the dispute, but the appraisal clause clarifies how an impasse can be resolved. Indirectly, the appraisal clause also encourages the parties to negotiate between themselves to avoid hiring appraisers to do the same thing. The appraisal provisions in some policies also specify when the appraisal process must occur.

Exhibit 14-19 contains the appraisal clause from the ISO BPP Coverage Form.

Appraisal clause

A policy provision that prescribes a method for resolving a disputed claim about the value of property or the amount of a property loss.

EXHIBIT 14-19

Appraisal Clause; BPP Coverage Form

2. **Appraisal**

   If we and you disagree on the value of the property or the amount of loss, either may make written demand for an appraisal of the loss. In this event, each party will select a competent and impartial appraiser. The two appraisers will select an umpire. If they cannot agree, either may request that selection be made by a judge of a court having jurisdiction. The appraisers will state separately the value of the property and amount of loss. If they fail to agree, they will submit their differences to the umpire. A decision agreed to by any two will be binding. Each party will:

   a. Pay its chosen appraiser; and

   b. Bear the other expenses of the appraisal and umpire equally.

   If there is an appraisal, we will still retain our right to deny the claim.

Includes copyrighted material of Insurance Services Office, Inc., with its permission. Copyright, ISO Properties, Inc., 2001.

Some insurance claims are ultimately taken to court, especially when large amounts are at stake and the insurer and the insured interpret the policy differently. The court is the ultimate authority on the insurance policy's meaning and enforceability. However, an insured's right to sue the insurer and ask the court to enforce the policy is limited by a common provision, traditionally called a lawsuit or suit provision. This provision specifies that the insured must comply with other policy provisions before bringing a lawsuit against the insurer. A lawsuit should not be used as a shortcut to circumvent the policy or to address issues that the policy adequately handles. Many policies also state a time limit within which any lawsuit must be brought. A lawsuit on the claim cannot be started after this specified time has elapsed. The following clause is the suit provision in the ISO Commercial Property Conditions:[5]

D. LEGAL ACTION AGAINST US

No one may bring a legal action against us under this Coverage Part unless:

1. There has been full compliance with all of the terms of this Coverage Part; and
2. The action is brought within 2 years after the date on which the direct physical loss or damage occurred.

To help keep premiums reasonable, and to ensure that any parties that caused a loss are held accountable, property insurance policies also contain subrogation and salvage provisions.

SUBROGATION AND SALVAGE

After an insurer has paid a property loss to an insured or has paid a liability loss on an insured's behalf, the insurer may decide to try to recover all or part of its loss payment through the processes of subrogation and salvage. **Subrogation** is the process by which an insurer recovers payment from a liable third party who has caused a property or liability loss that the insurer has paid to, or on behalf of, an insured. **Salvage** is the process by which an insurer takes possession of damaged property for which it has paid a total loss and recovers a portion of the loss payment by selling the damaged property. Policy provisions outline how these provisions operate.

Subrogation and salvage activities within the claim department enable insurers to recover a portion of the money paid out to satisfy claims. By reducing the insurer's overall loss ratio, subrogation and salvage activities reduce the premiums the insurer needs to charge.

Subrogation applies whenever an insured's property is damaged through another person's fault. The insured has a legal right to recover from the responsible party and also has a right to recover from his or her property insurer. However, the insured should not receive a double recovery. Under subrogation provisions, the insured makes a claim for the loss under his or her property insurance policies and the property insurer then assumes any rights of recovery against the responsible third party. The property insurer then has

Subrogation

The process by which an insurer recovers payment from a liable third party who has caused a property or liability loss that the insurer has paid to, or on behalf of, an insured.

Salvage

The process by which an insurer takes possession of damaged property for which it has paid a total loss and recovers a portion of the loss payment by selling the damaged property.

the right to make a claim against the responsible party, seeking to recover whatever money it has paid to the insured. For example, suppose a thief broke into an electronics store and stole several televisions. The thief was ultimately apprehended by the police. The electronics store files a claim and collects payment from its property insurer. The property insurer then brings a legal action against the thief to collect the payment made to the electronics store under its insurance policy.

Liability losses are handled similarly. After paying a third-party claim, the insurer assumes any rights of recovery the insured previously possessed and may seek to recover loss amounts from another responsible party. Responsible parties might turn their claims over to their own liability insurers, which will ultimately pay the claims.

Property and liability insurance policies contain a variety of subrogation provisions reflecting the policies' own varied nature. Sometimes a subrogation provision is included in policy section called something other than "subrogation," such as "Transfer of Your Rights of Recovery." The ISO HO-3 Policy includes the "subrogation" label in its policy condition that applies to both the policy's property and liability coverages, as shown in Exhibit 14-20.

EXHIBIT 14-20

Subrogation Provision in the ISO HO-3 Policy

F.   Subrogation

An "insured" may waive in writing before a loss all rights of recovery against any person. If not waived, we may require an assignment of rights of recovery for a loss to the extent that payment is made by us.

If an assignment is sought, an "insured" must sign and deliver all related papers and cooperate with us.

Subrogation does not apply to Coverage **F** or Paragraph **C.** Damage to Property Of Others under Section **II** – Additional Coverages.

Includes copyrighted material of Insurance Services Office, Inc., with its permission. Copyright, ISO Properties, Inc., 1999.

The subrogation provision in Exhibit 14-20 permits the insured, before a loss occurs, to waive its rights of recovery against a third party that might be responsible for the loss. These types of pre-loss waivers are common. Typical subrogation provisions prohibit the insured from waiving any of its rights of recovery after a loss because it is in the insurer's interests to preserve these rights of recovery. After a loss, the insured would, in effect, be waiving not its own rights, but the insurer's. Before the loss, the situation might be different. The purpose of a pre-loss waiver, sometimes referred to as a waiver of subrogation, is to prevent an insurer from exercising its right of subrogation against someone who has been released from liability by the insured.

For example, a landlord (lessor) may give her tenant (lessee) a waiver only to the extent that the lessor's property policy provides coverage. In other words, both parties agree that the tenant is not responsible for any damage to property covered by the landlord's insurance.

Although the subrogation provisions in most property insurance policies permit waivers of subrogation before loss, not all policies do. In some cases, the existence of a pre-loss waiver could void the entire policy.

Salvage involves the insurer's taking possession of damaged property for which it has paid a total loss and then selling that property. The proceeds from the sale of the damaged property are used to offset the claim settlement cost. Salvage can help keep premiums reasonable. Closely related to the salvage provision is the **recovered property provision**, which clarifies the insured's options when a claim based on the loss of property has been settled but the property is later recovered.

Recovered property provision
A policy provision that clarifies the insured's options when a claim based on the loss of property has been settled but the property is later recovered.

For example, suppose a camera is covered for theft under a special-form property insurance policy. The camera is stolen and the insurer pays the claim after subtracting a deductible. The camera is subsequently recovered by the insurer or by the insured. The recovered property policy provision outlines the steps to be taken by the insurer and insured in such situations. The following is the recovered property policy provision in the ISO HO-3 policy:[6]

N. Recovered Property

> If you or we recover any property for which we have made payment under this policy, you or we will notify the other of the recovery. At your option, the property will be returned to or retained by you or it will become our property. If the recovered property is returned to or retained by you, the loss payment will be adjusted based on the amount you received for the recovered property.

The insured determines whether to take back recovered property, but the insured does not keep both the property and the loss amount the insurer paid. Because of this provision, the insured can consider the case closed once a property claim has been paid, and the insured can proceed to purchase replacement property without worrying that the case will be reopened because property has been recovered. At the same time, the insured is given the opportunity to take back any recovered property and sell it for salvage.

SUMMARY

Insurance to value is the choice of a limit in property insurance to approximate the maximum potential loss. The insurable value of property is partly determined by the policy's valuation provision and the insurance amount depends on the policy limits. The insurer benefits from insuring to value because the premium is adequate to cover potential losses. The insured benefits because sufficient funds are available in the event of a total loss and the uncertainty of large retained losses is reduced. Maintaining insurance to value is important in order to avoid coinsurance penalties and other insurance-to-value provision penalties. However, maintaining such limits is difficult, because of factors such as difficulty in measuring values and the change in values over time. Insurance professionals can help property insurance buyers to address the valuation challenge by recommending that they hirer appraisers, purchase inflation guard coverage, purchase a peak season endorsement (if necessary) and periodically review and revise limits.

Every property policy states how the insurer and the insured determine the value of property that is lost or damaged. The valuation method that is being applied by the policy is contained in the policy's valuation provision. The most common methods used are actual cash value (ACV) and replacement cost, although other methods may be used. Actual cash value (ACV) is a valuation method calculated as the replacement cost at the time of loss minus depreciation. Replacement cost is the cost to repair or replace property using new materials of like kind and quality with no deduction for depreciation. Other valuation methods include actual loss sustained, agreed value method, functional valuation method, cost of reproduction valuation method, pair or set clauses valuation method, and money and securities valuation method.

Policies contain limits on the insurer's obligations and limits to accommodate consumer preferences to reflect insurer financial capacity, and as a substitute for exclusions. Many types of policy limits affect amounts payable in property insurance. Limits can apply to all property or just to individual pieces of personal property. Furthermore, multiple policy limits can be applied to a single event or claim, with one overall limit and various sublimits applying. Finally, policy limits may be specified on a per occurrence or an aggregate basis. With all of these possibilities, the potential number of combinations of policy limits is extensive. Types of limits used include individual property limits, specific limits, blanket limits, sublimits, variable limits, and nondollar limits.

The amount an insurer pays out in the event of a loss is also affected by the deductible applicable to the policy. A deductible is a portion of a covered loss that is not paid by the insurer. In a property insurance policy, the deductible is subtracted from the amount of loss or the amount the insurer would otherwise be obligated to pay to the insured. In most cases, the deductible is stated as a dollar amount. Deductibles reduce the premium cost to the insured because they reduce moral and morale hazard incentives, encourage risk control by the insured, and eliminate the need for the insurer to process small losses, thereby reducing the insurer's loss costs and loss adjustment expenses. Some deductibles can be applied on a per event or aggregate basis. Others may be a specified dollar figure (straight deductible), be a percentage of the loss amount (percentage deductible), or be based on time (time deductible).

The amount payable under a property policy might be reduced—but not increased—through the effect of a coinsurance clause or insurance-to-value provision designed to provide an incentive for insuring to value. Coinsurance clauses serve a dual purpose, both rewarding those who have insured to value and penalizing those who have not. The coinsurance formula explains how the amount payable is determined if the coinsurance requirement has not been met, and can be expressed as follows:

$$\text{Amount payable} = \frac{\text{Limit of insurance}}{\substack{\text{Value of covered property} \\ \text{(at time of loss)}} \times \substack{\text{Coinsurance} \\ \text{percentage}}} \times \text{Total amount of covered loss.}$$

Insurance students often remember this formula as "did over should times loss," which can be written as follows:

$$\text{Amount payable} = \frac{\text{Did}}{\text{Should}} \times \text{Loss,}$$

where

"Did" = amount of insurance carried, and

"Should" = the minimum amount that should have been carried to meet the coinsurance requirement based on the insurable value at the time of the loss.

Despite similarities, the insurance-to-value provisions in homeowners and businessowners policies are different from coinsurance. With insurance-to-value provisions, the amount payable by the insurer will not be less than the ACV (subject to policy limits). The policy will pay the greater of ACV or the "did over should times loss" penalty if insurance-to-value requirement is not met.

Maintaining insurance to value is only one way of avoiding coinsurance penalties or other insurance-to-value penalties. Several techniques and forms are available that avoid insurance-to-value penalties, including flat policies, agreed value, monthly limit of indemnity, and maximum period of indemnity. After a loss, the insurer and insured may dispute the amounts payable under a property insurance policy. The appraisal clause is a policy provision that prescribes a method for resolving a disputed claim about the property's value or the loss amount. The appraisal clause is useful when the insurer and the insured agree that a given property loss is covered but cannot agree on the property's value or the loss amount.

After an insurer has paid a property loss to an insured or has paid a liability loss on an insured's behalf, the insurer may decide to try to recover all or part of its loss payment through the processes of subrogation and salvage. Subrogation is the process by which an insurer recovers payment from a liable third party who has caused a property or liability loss that the insurer has paid to, or on behalf of, an insured. Salvage is the process through which an insurer takes possession of damaged property for which it has paid a total loss and recovers a portion of the loss payment by selling the damaged property.

CHAPTER NOTES

1. Includes copyrighted material of Insurance Services Office, Inc., with its permission. Copyright, ISO Properties, Inc., 2001.

2. Includes copyrighted material of Insurance Services Office, Inc., with its permission. Copyright, ISO Properties, Inc., 1997.

3. Includes copyrighted material of Insurance Services Office, Inc., with its permission. Copyright, ISO Properties, Inc., 2001.

4. Includes copyrighted material of Insurance Services Office, Inc., with its permission. Copyright, ISO Properties, Inc., 1999.

5. Includes copyrighted material of Insurance Services Office, Inc., with its permission. Copyright, ISO Properties, Inc., 1983, 1987.

6. Includes copyrighted material of Insurance Services Office, Inc., with its permission. Copyright, ISO Properties, 1999.

Chapter 15

Direct Your Learning

Amounts Payable: Liability Insurance and Other Sources of Recovery

After learning the content of this chapter and completing the corresponding course guide assignment, you should be able to:

- Explain why determining adequate liability policy limits is difficult.

- Given a liability insurance claim, apply policy limits and valuation provisions to determine the amounts payable.

  - Explain how liability losses are valued and how that affects amounts payable after a loss.

  - Describe the following types of liability policy limits and their effects on the amounts payable after a loss: single limits, split limits, aggregate limits, limits for defense costs, limits for nonfault-based coverages, and limits on workers' compensation.

- Explain when and why deductibles and self-insured retentions are applied to liability insurance policies.

- Explain how arbitration is used to settle disputed liability claims.

- Describe the following five other sources of recovery that affect amounts payable:

  - Noninsurance agreements

  - Negligent third parties

  - Other insurance in the same policy

  - Other insurance in a similar policy

  - Other insurance in dissimilar policies

- Describe the three types of other-insurance provisions.

- Explain how conflicts are resolved for other-insurance provisions.

- Define or describe each of the Key Words and Phrases for this chapter.

Develop Your Perspective

What are the main topics covered in the chapter?

The amounts that should be paid for losses under liability insurance policies depend on the function, type, and amount of policy limits; the loss valuation methods; and deductibles and self-insured retentions. There may also be other sources of recovery that affect the amounts payable. Various types of other-insurance policy provisions determine how to resolve other-insurance conflicts in the face of other sources of recovery.

Consider a liability insurance policy.

- What types of policy limits may be included?
- What types of other-insurance provisions may be included?

Why is it important to learn about these topics?

Knowing this information helps an insurance professional understand how amounts payable differ under liability insurance and also how to interpret a policy to determine the available coverage and the process for evaluating losses.

Consider the different methods for valuing losses under liability insurance and property insurance.

- Why might the methods for valuing losses differ under each policy?
- How is coverage affected if another possible source of recovery is available?

How can you use what you will learn?

Consider a liability loss exposure your organization might face. Evaluate the coverage that applies to the loss.

- Do the policy limits provide adequate coverage for the possible loss exposures?
- How might you determine amounts payable for the loss?

Chapter 15

Amounts Payable: Liability Insurance and Other Sources of Recovery

If, by following the DICE method for analyzing insurance policies, an insurance professional determines that a policy covers a claim, he or she must then determine the amounts that are payable under the insurance policy. The amounts payable under a liability insurance policy depend on factors such as valuation methods, policy limits, deductibles, and self-insured retentions for liability insurance policies.

Payment issues may arise when an insured has other sources of recovery, such as noninsurance agreements, third-party liability, or other insurance policies. Most insurance claims are covered by a single insurance policy, and the policy's wording (which is usually drafted by the insurer) governs the insurer's obligations. If there are multiple insurance policies covering the same loss exposure, the relationship between the insurance policies is governed by the "other-insurance" provisions in either a property or liability insurance policy. Because an insurer cannot control the wording of policies written by other insurers, conflicts about payment obligations sometimes occur. Various types of other-insurance provisions provide methods to resolve these conflicts.

AMOUNTS PAYABLE: LIABILITY INSURANCE

As with property insurance, several types of liability insurance policies are available to individuals and organizations. Coverages such as commercial general liability, professional liability, environmental liability, directors and officers' liability (D&O), employment practices liability (EPL), auto liability, workers' compensation (WC), homeowners, and umbrella liability offer a wide array of protection, as shown in the text box. The amounts payable under each policy vary, and this discussion uses examples of specific policy provisions from different liability policies to illustrate these variations. Several factors can affect the amount payable, such as policy limits, the valuation of losses, and the amount of deductibles or self-insured retentions. Policies may also include provisions on how to deal with disputes, should they arise.

Covered Injury or Damage in a Liability Policy

An insurer is obligated to pay damages under a liability insurance policy only when the nature of the injury, damage, offense, wrongful act, and so forth is covered by that policy. Liability policies commonly cover bodily injury, personal injury, advertising injury, property damage, professional liability, and wrongful acts.

Bodily injury—liability stemming from injury, sickness or disease sustained by a person, including death resulting from any of these at any time, some courts have held that emotional distress is bodily injury even when it does not involve physical harm.

Personal injury—liability stemming from libel, slander, defamation, wrongful entry or eviction, false arrest, wrongful detention, and malicious prosecution. These offenses fall into the broad legal category of intentional torts, but only the intentional torts (offenses) listed in the policy are covered.

Advertising injury—liability stemming from libel or slander; publishing material that constitutes an invasion of privacy; misappropriation of advertising ideas; and infringement of copyright, title, or slogan.

Property damage—liability stemming from physical damage to tangible property. It also includes the resulting loss of use, as well as loss of use of tangible property that has not been physically injured. This definition does not encompass loss of use of intangible property (such as goodwill, copyrights).

Professional liability—liability stemming injury or losses that result from the improper rendering of professional services, errors in judgment, or omissions.

Wrongful acts—liability stemming from a harmful act or omission, allegedly committed or attempted by an insured.

Adequate Policy Limits

Adequate policy limits are important in both property and liability insurance to cover losses as fully as possible. For property insurance, this is accomplished by insuring to value. Determining the value of most liability loss exposures can be more challenging because it can be difficult to evaluate an individual or organization's maximum potential liability loss and, in theory, the loss can be limitless. Liability often stems from two sources: bodily injury to others or property damage to others' property. However, liability may also stem from other sources, such as emotional distress or failure to adhere to statutes or regulations. The complexity of determining the potential value of liability loss exposures can make it difficult to assess whether the limits on liability insurance policies are adequate.

Some liability loss exposures can be insured to value because the maximum potential loss for liability exposures involving possible damage or destruction to specific property items (property of others) can be determined. An example is a tenant's liability exposure to a landlord for fire damage, which can be insured with fire legal liability coverage. The maximum possible loss for a tenant is the value of the leased building plus its use value. Similarly, statutory limits on the maximum loss, such as those imposed by statute in workers' compensation insurance, limit the maximum possible loss.

Unlike liability claims for property damage, liability claims arising from bodily injury, wrongful death, emotional distress, and so on are much more difficult to value. Common liability insurance limits vary based on the individual's or organization's activities, income, and asset level. Producers and risk management professionals can be consulted regarding common practices in setting liability insurance policy limits.

Because individuals and organizations recognize the need for high limits of liability coverage, and because the necessary limits may not be available from a single insurer, liability insurance is often purchased in layers of coverage. A primary insurance policy provides a working layer of coverage. Most losses are likely to fall within the policy limits of this working layer. For an individual or a family, the working layer might involve $100,000 of personal liability coverage limits under a homeowners policy. For a business, it might involve coverage limits of $500,000, $1,000,000, or more. In addition to primary policy coverage, exceptionally large liability loss exposures usually require one or more layers of excess or umbrella insurance coverage.

Large Liability Loss Exposures: Who Is at Risk?

Large organizations and those engaging in hazardous activities are most likely to have large liability loss exposures. However, almost any person or organization could be exposed to the possibility of paying large liability losses. In 2002, the average dog bite liability claim cost homeowners insurers $16,600.[1] In 2003, the average products liability jury award was $6.4 million.[2] Individuals and organizations must determine the frequency and severity of potential losses and then determine risk financing measures, including which limits of liability insurance to purchase.

With liability insurance, many costs (such as defense costs) may not be subject to policy limits. Therefore, insureds need not be concerned with whether policy limits are high enough to cover those costs. For policies in which defense costs are in addition to policy limits, if policy limits are exhausted during the policy period, the insurer is no longer obligated to pay for the insured's defense costs. Also, insureds must be careful to stay adequately insured because policy limits are not usually adjusted unless the insured actually selects a new policy limit. Unlike workers' compensation policy limits, which are not explicitly stated on the policy (they are set by state mandates) but are changed when workers' compensation benefits are changed by statute, liability insurance policy limits do not automatically change. Therefore, a $100,000 liability insurance policy with policy limits set ten years ago may not adequately cover current liability exposures.

Valuation of Liability Losses

Policy provisions addressing the valuation of liability losses differ greatly from those that address the valuation of property losses. Property valuation is based on actual cash value, replacement cost, or other valuation provisions appearing in the policy. With liability insurance, although policy provisions provide information on the maximum amount payable, the determination of the amount payable is affected by many factors, including relevant policy provisions and extent of bodily injury and/or property damage to others.

Relevant Policy Provisions

Liability insurance policies do not generally specify how the amount of a loss is determined. Under most circumstances, the maximum amount the insurer pays is the lesser of the following:

1. The applicable policy limit
2. The compensable amount of the loss

Most liability claims do not go to a formal trial,[3] and the compensable amount of the loss is determined by negotiations between the liability insurer (or its attorney) and the claimant (or the claimant's attorney). During these negotiations, the parties try to anticipate what a court or jury would do if presented with the same facts. Both parties have an incentive to reach an out-of-court settlement because of the uncertainty, time, and expense involved in a formal trial.

Most liability insurance policies give the insured/defendant no right to prohibit the insurer and the claimant from reaching a settlement within policy limits. Often, an insured wants its insurer to mount a vigorous defense and vindicate the insured. However, the insurer's goal is usually to minimize its total costs for defense or damages. Sometimes the insurer pays a claim that might successfully have been defended because defending the claim would cost more than paying damages. In other cases, the insurer does not want to risk losing a lawsuit that would set a dangerous precedent for other, similar claims.

If a settlement cannot be reached by the parties involved, the liability claim will go to trial and the extent of the insured's liability to the claimant is then based on legal principles. When a jury trial is involved, the compensable amount of the loss is the amount the jurors decide to award to the plaintiff as damages. Subject to policy conditions and limits, the insurer pays that amount on the insured's behalf. In some situations, the judge exercises the power to reduce or set aside an award or reduce or overturn an award on appeal. This may be done if the judge believes the jury award was excessive or not based on legal principles. Although policy limits restrict the insurer's liability, neither the jury nor the judge is bound to confine an award to policy limits. If the court awards a judgment that exceeds policy limits, the insured/defendant is responsible for paying the excess award.

For claims exceeding policy limits, the insured has a right to legal counsel, usually at the insured's expense, to protect the insured's interests. Otherwise, the liability insurer usually has control over defense costs and the amount it wants to offer as a settlement.

Extent of Damages

When the insured is liable for damages, the key issue affecting the valuation of a liability claim is the amount of monetary compensation that will reasonably indemnify the party who incurred the loss. Although a judge or jury may ultimately determine this amount, the insurer, the insured, and the claimant try to estimate this amount during any settlement negotiations.

The United States common-law system requires the amount of damages awarded to compensate the claimant for loss incurred as of the trial date. This presents a problem if not all damage has been repaired by the trial date or settlement date. In some cases, such as those involving permanent disability, damages must be partly based on an estimate of future expenses.

The claimant usually has the burden of proof regarding bodily injury and property damage. The claimant must establish what losses were proximately caused by the insured. However, even though the insured caused the loss, the claimant has a duty to mitigate loss. Consequently, the claimant may not recover for damages that result from the claimant's lack of care after the accident. The collateral source rule may apply, and the insured's liability to pay damages may not be reduced by any recovery the claimant might receive from health insurance or other sources.

When property is damaged, the owner may recover the reasonable cost to repair the property or to replace the property if it cannot economically be repaired. When property must be replaced, the owner is entitled to the property's reasonable market value before damage or destruction. Generally, the owner may also recover damages to compensate for the loss of use of the property for a reasonable period. For example, a claimant could recover the cost of renting a substitute car while a damaged car is being repaired.

Under certain circumstances, a claimant may also recover for profits lost from the inability to use the damaged or destroyed property. For example, the owner of a damaged truck or tractor-trailer might lose revenue while the vehicle is being repaired, especially if the owner cannot rent a substitute vehicle. Similarly, the owner of a damaged building might lose rent from tenants or sales from customers while a building is out of use. A few jurisdictions also permit third-party damages for the reduction in value of property that has been damaged and repaired.

Unlike property damage claims, evaluation of bodily injury claims considers a much broader range of damage elements for the claimant, such as the following:

- Reasonable and necessary medical expenses incurred and those expected to be incurred in the future
- Type of bodily injury

- Wage loss or loss of earning capacity because of the bodily injury
- Other out-of-pocket expenses, such as household assistance
- Current and future pain and suffering resulting from the bodily injury
- Extent and permanency of disability and impairment
- Disfigurement resulting from the bodily injury
- Preexisting conditions that could have contributed to the bodily injury

When bodily injury results in a claimant's death, the claim is generally categorized as either a survival action (how much would have been recovered if the claimant had lived) or a wrongful death action (monetary loss to the survivors). The category into which the claim falls affects its valuation.

Policy Limits

As discussed in a previous chapter, insurance policies have policy limits to restrict the insurer's obligations, accommodate consumer preferences, reflect insurer capacity, and substitute for exclusions. Unlike property insurance policies, it is rare for a liability insurance policy to use a policy limit as a substitute for an exclusion. Furthermore, policy limits in liability policies can be more confusing than those in property policies because interaction between per occurrence limits, aggregate limits, and sublimits is more common in liability policies than in property policies. An insurance professional needs to analyze how the various policy limits interact to ultimately determine the amounts payable under the liability policy.

In liability insurance, policy limits are generally expressed in one of the following three ways:

1. Single limit
2. Split limits
3. Aggregate limits

Single Limit

Liability insurance policies typically contain a single dollar limit that applies for (1) each occurrence (accident), (2) each person (or organization), or (3) each claim. **Single limit** (sometimes called a combined single limit) is a limit that applies to all bodily injury and property damage for a single occurrence, a single person incurring a loss, or a single claim.

Occurrences include events that happen suddenly and result in immediate bodily injury or property damage, such as an auto accident. Occurrences also include adverse conditions that continue over a long period and eventually result in bodily injury or property damage, such as exposure to

Single limit
A limit that applies to all bodily injury and property damage for a single occurrence, a single person incurring a loss, or a single claim.

asbestos. The following is an excerpt from the ISO Commercial General Liability (CGL) Coverage Form that has several limits and sublimits, including an each occurrence limit:[4]

SECTION III – LIMITS OF INSURANCE

5. ...the Each Occurrence Limit is the most we will pay...because of all "bodily injury" and "property damage" arising out of any one "occurrence".

The same policy defines "occurrence" as follows:[5]

13. "Occurrence" means an accident, including continuous or repeated exposure to substantially the same general harmful conditions.

Sometimes determining whether a given set of circumstances involves a single occurrence or a series of occurrences is difficult. To illustrate this difficulty, suppose the tailgate of a gravel truck traveling down the highway is not completely closed, and gravel falling from the truck damages the windshields of many cars. The release of gravel damaging multiple vehicles could be seen as a single occurrence, or each broken windshield could be seen as a separate occurrence. Ultimately, the issue is a question of fact for a court to decide.

The ISO CGL policy is an example of a liability insurance policy that contains a policy limit that applies per person or organization. Some liability insurance policies, including the CGL, cover intentional torts (such as libel and slander) that do not technically qualify as occurrences (accidents) because of their intentional nature. In the CGL policy, these torts are subject to a separate personal and advertising injury limit that applies for each person or organization, as follows:[6]

SECTION III – LIMITS OF INSURANCE

4. ... the Personal and Advertising Injury Limit is the most we will pay under Coverage **B** for the sum of all damages because of all "personal and advertising injury" sustained by any one person or organization.

The CGL policy limit applies to each person or organization for all damages resulting from personal or advertising injury. Several claimants can incur loss in a single occurrence. For example, the publication of a single magazine article can offend several people, each of whom presents a separate libel claim.

Finally, a single occurrence causing a loss to one person can generate multiple claims. Some policies, notably professional liability policies, provide limits on an each claim basis. Exhibit 15-1 contains an example from the Shand Morahan & Company, Inc. Physicians, Surgeons, and Dentists Professional Liability Policy.

EXHIBIT 15-1

Per Claim Limits: Professional Liability Policy

LIMITS OF LIABILITY

1. **COMPANY'S LIMITS OF LIABILITY:**

    As stated in Item 6. of the Declarations, Coverage and Limits of Liability:

    (a) COVERAGE A:

        (i) <u>Limit of Liability/Each Claim</u>

            The liability of the Company for loss payments and claim expenses against each COVERAGE A Insured for each claim shall not exceed the amount stated in Item 6.(a) of the Declarations.

Reprinted with permission from Shand Morahan & Company, Inc.

Split Limits

Split limits
Separate limits for bodily injury claims and for property damage liability claims.

Split limits are separate limits for bodily injury claims and for property damage liability claims. For example, a policy might provide a $500,000 bodily injury liability limit and a $100,000 property damage liability limit. Such a limit would customarily be written as "500/100 limits" or orally expressed as "five hundred, one hundred limits."

Policies containing split limits, such as personal auto policies, usually contain the following three types of limits:

1. Bodily injury limit (called a sublimit) applicable to each injured person
2. Bodily injury limit applicable to two or more injured persons (this limit is usually greater than the each-person limit)
3. Property damage limit

As an example of split limits, assume that Audrey is an insured under an auto policy with 25/50/10 ("twenty-five, fifty, ten") limits. The following three examples illustrate how these limits apply:

1. Audrey negligently causes a covered accident resulting in no injuries but in $15,000 damage to another driver's car. The insurer would pay no more than $10,000—the property damage liability limit—for this damage. Audrey could not apply any of the separate bodily injury liability limits to cover the property damage liability claim.
2. In a separate accident, Audrey negligently causes $27,000 in bodily injury to Mrs. Smith and $4,000 to Mr. Smith. Audrey's insurer would pay no more than $25,000 to Mrs. Smith (the per person sublimit) and $4,000 to Mr. Smith.

3. In another accident, Audrey is responsible for $134,000 in bodily injury to all five members of the Jones family, as well as for $15,000 in property damage to the Joneses' car. The insurer would pay the claimants no more than $60,000; that is, $50,000 for bodily injury to two or more persons and $10,000 for property damage. $60,000 is the maximum amount payable for any one accident under a policy with 25/50/10 limits.

Aggregate Limits

An **aggregate limit** is a specific limit on the maximum amount an insurer will pay for total damages from all covered occurrences during the covered period. An aggregate limit typically is two or three times the each occurrence limit and usually is expressed as an annual limit for each policy year.

Aggregate limits are common in commercial liability policies. Personal insurance policies, such as personal auto and homeowners policies, usually do not contain aggregate limits—an individual or a family rarely incurs two or more separate, substantial liability losses during a covered period (typically a year or less). As an example of aggregate limits, suppose liability Policy A has a single limit of $1,000,000 per occurrence and an annual aggregate limit of $3,000,000. The covered losses occur in the following amounts during the one-year covered period of the policy term, which begins on February 1:

Aggregate limit
A specific limit on the maximum amount an insurer will pay for total damages from all covered occurrences during the covered period.

Date	Loss Amount	Amount Paid	Aggregate Limit (before loss)	Remaining Aggregate Limit (after loss)
February 15	$500,000	$500,000	$3,000,000	$2,500,000
April 11	$1,200,000	$1,000,000 (per occurrence limit)	$2,500,000	$1,500,000
June 5	$2,000,000	$1,000,000 (per occurrence limit)	$1,500,000	$500,000
August 31	$1,000,000	$500,000 (aggregate limit)	$500,000	$0

The insurer would pay the full amount of $500,000 for the first loss because it is less than the each occurrence limit. Subsequently, the insurer would pay the each occurrence limit of $1,000,000 for each of the second and third losses, for a cumulative total of $2,500,000 during the first six months. At this point, the insured has accumulated $2,500,000 in insured losses and has only $500,000 of coverage available for the remaining six months of the covered period because the policy has an aggregate limit of $3,000,000 per year. The August 31 loss of $1,000,000 exhausts the remaining $500,000 in the aggregate limits. The insurer would pay $500,000 for the August loss, and the insured would be responsible for the remaining $500,000. The insured would no longer have liability coverage for the remainder of the covered period.

Some liability insurance policies have more than one aggregate limit. For example, the ISO CGL policy has two separate aggregate limits. One applies to all bodily injury and property damage arising out of products liability and completed operations and the other applies to all other bodily injury and property damage claims.

Other Policy Limits

In addition to the three general methods of expressing policy limits, liability insurance policies may specifically mention other policy limits. Examples of the other types of policy limits that may appear in liability insurance policies include limits on defense costs and limits on some nonfault-based coverages—such as medical payments or state-mandated benefits in workers' compensation. The limits presented in this section are a selection of the limits that insurance professionals may need to evaluate when determining amounts payable for a liability insurance policy. This selection is meant to be illustrative, not comprehensive.

Limits for Defense Costs

Most liability insurance policies contain more than the insurer's agreement to pay damages on the insured's behalf; they also include the insurer's duty to defend the insured. As part of the duty to defend, the insurer also agrees to pay the costs of defending the insured, and the insurer often contributes substantial experience and expertise to the defense process. Many insurance buyers consider the insurer's defense services to be one of the most important reasons to buy liability insurance.

Knowing whether defense costs are paid either within or in addition to (outside) policy limits is important because the amount of insurance available to pay damages can be significantly reduced when defense costs are paid as part of the policy limits. For example, suppose an insurer has issued a professional liability insurance policy covering a dentist with a $100,000 policy limit. The insurer incurs $40,000 in costs to defend a professional liability claim, and the trial court holds the insured liable for $90,000 in damages. If defense costs are within limits, the insurer pays $40,000 in defense costs and $60,000 in damages, consuming the entire $100,000 limit. The insured will be responsible for the remaining $30,000. Alternatively, if defense costs are payable in addition to policy limits, the insurer pays the $40,000 in defense costs plus the full $90,000 in damages. In addition, if the claimant appeals the case to a higher court, the insurer pays the costs of defending the appeal, and its defense obligation does not end until the insurer pays $100,000 in damages.

Under the majority of liability insurance policies, defense costs are payable in addition to (outside) the maximum amount payable for damages. Although no dollar limit is placed on the amount the insurer might be required to pay in defending the insured against a claim for covered damages, the insurer's obligations are not entirely limitless. A typical liability insurance policy stipulates that the insurer's obligation to defend against any given claim for damages terminates when the amount it pays for damages equals the policy limits. For example, the following is the pertinent provision from the ISO CGL Policy:[7]

> Our right and duty to defend end when we have used up the applicable limit of insurance in the payments of judgments or settlements under Coverages **A** or **B** or medical expenses under Coverage **C**.

In cases in which the damages clearly exceed the policy limits, the insurer cannot just pay or "tender" the limits and remove itself from the case. In policies with the wording similar to that in the ISO CGL policy, the insurer's duties do not end until it has paid the full policy limits in fulfilling a judgment or settlement. If the claimant is not willing to settle for an amount within the policy limits, the insurer is obligated to continue defending the insured until a final court judgment has been rendered or a settlement has been reached.

In some cases, insurers will pay small, questionable ("nuisance") claims—even those they could probably win—in order to avoid defense costs or the possibility of a large adverse judgment.

Limits for Nonfault-Based Coverages

Another type of coverage in a liability policy that affects amounts payable is the nonfault-based coverage. Many insurance policies that cover liability arising out of bodily injury include coverage for medical bills incurred by the claimant—without requiring proof of the insured's liability (fault). Because these medical payments coverages are provided regardless of fault, they are called nonfault-based coverages. Nominal limits of medical payments coverage enable an insurer to pay small claims in a way that eliminates the need for litigation and preserves the insured's goodwill, while preserving the insurer's defenses in the event of a larger liability claim.

Preserving Goodwill

Doris injured her knee and incurred medical expenses of $500 when she fell in her friend Jim's driveway. Doris asked Jim to pay her medical expenses because she believed they were caused by a hazard in his driveway. Jim notified his homeowners insurer, and it readily paid Doris's claim under that policy's "medical payments to others" coverage. If Jim did not have medical payments coverage and the insurer attempted to defend Jim, at some expense, by showing that Doris's fall was caused by her own carelessness and not by Jim's negligence, then Jim's insistence that he was not negligent might have cost him Doris' friendship. Alternatively, rather than lose Doris' friendship, Jim might have agreed with her version of the story to help her recover her expenses from his insurer. If the insurer was reluctant to pay the claim because they did not believe Doris's story, ill-will could arise between Jim and his insurer.

The standard homeowners policy limit for medical payments to others is usually $1,000 per person as the result of one accident. Under the following policy provisions from the ISO Homeowners 3 Policy—Special Form (HO-3), coverage does not apply to bodily injuries of the named insured or to regular household residents:[8]

> **Medical Payments to Others**
>
> **B. Coverage F – Medical Payments to Others**
>
> > We will pay the necessary medical expenses that are incurred or medically ascertained within three years from the date of an accident "bodily injury".

As with the limit for medical payments to others coverage, a $1,000 limit is printed in the body of standard ISO homeowners policies for coverage for damage to the property of others. This additional coverage, coupled with a nominal limit, allows the insurer to pay small claims without determining liability or implying that the insured was liable for the property damage. The insured need not be legally responsible for the property damage for the insurer to pay a claim.

Similar to the homeowners' policy, the limit for medical payments coverage, usually $5,000, is automatically built into the ISO CGL policy. The limit is the most the insurer will pay for all medical expenses because of bodily injury sustained by any one person resulting from an accident on the insured's premises or because of the insured's operations. Covered medical expenses must be incurred and reported within one year from the date of the accident. Coverage does not apply to an insured or its employees, among others.

Limits also apply for auto medical payments coverage and are typically offered in modest amounts, such as $5,000. However, auto medical payments coverage differs significantly from homeowners or commercial general liability medical payments coverage in that auto medical payments cover the named insured's bodily injuries and those of family members, in addition to covering passengers' injuries. Coverage for the insured and family members provides a first-party benefit. Coverage for others' bodily injuries is comparable to the medical payments coverage of homeowners policies—a third-party benefit.

In some states, auto liability insurance policies are endorsed to include auto no-fault personal injury protection (PIP) coverages. Although PIP coverages vary by state, almost all PIP endorsements provide specified policy limits, restricted solely to losses resulting from auto accidents, regardless of who is at fault. The typical endorsement contains modest limits for medical expenses, funeral expenses, survivor benefits, loss of income, and replacement of essential services.

Limits for Workers' Compensation

Unlike most liability insurance policies, some liability insurance policies do not state a dollar limit. For example, there are no dollar limits in the Workers' Compensation Coverage (Part One) of a Workers' Compensation and Employers' Liability Policy. Although the employers' liability portion of the policy (Part Two) does specify a limit, the workers' compensation insuring agreement simply states that the insurer will promptly pay the due benefits required by workers' compensation law. The applicable states or territories are listed in the policy's declarations, which are referred to in the policy as the "information page." The workers' compensation portion of the policy itself is not required to include dollar limits, because state workers' compensation statutes indicate the applicable limits. These legally specified limits become the amounts payable.

Deductibles and Self-Insured Retentions

Most property insurance policies include a deductible and, if so, specify the deductible amount. As previously discussed, by requiring the insured to share in the loss, deductibles do the following:

- Reduce moral and morale hazards and encourage risk control
- Eliminate the insurer's need to process small losses, thereby reducing the insurer's loss costs and loss adjustment expenses
- Reduce the premium cost to the insured

Although deductibles serve these purposes well with most types of property insurance policies, deductibles are much less effective with liability insurance. If a liability insurance policy had deductibles, insureds may not report seemingly minor incidents until the situation had escalated. However, because insurers want to control liability claims from the outset, they want to be involved in even small liability claims. Liability claim investigation involves determining not only the nature and extent of damages, but also who is legally responsible for paying those damages.

In addition, for most liability insurance policies, deductibles would not noticeably reduce premiums. One reason for this is that relatively few liability claims involve small amounts. Although most property losses are small enough for the insurer to avoid them by using a moderate deductible, liability losses tend to be larger. More important, as mentioned, the liability insurer wants to be involved in all claims, including small ones. Even with a deductible, the liability insurer usually pays "first dollar" expenses (the insurer pays all costs without contribution from the insured) for investigation and defense coverage, just as it does for policies without deductibles. Usually the deductible applies only to the amount paid to the claimant in settling the claim, not to defense costs.

With property insurance, the insurer simply subtracts the deductible from the covered loss amount to determine the amount payable to the insured. However, in liability insurance, the insurer must recover the deductible from the insured. The insurer usually must pay the third-party liability insurance claimant the agreed-upon settlement in full, without reduction for any deductible. The insurer then has the right to recover the amount of the deductible from the insured. Sometimes, the insured may be financially unable or unwilling to pay the deductible. So, in addition to incurring what could be significant expense costs, the insurer may also have to incur the deductible cost.

Consequently, insurers are selective in choosing the insureds for which they will even consider a liability deductible because the deductible, although it provides a premium discount to the insured, can present problems for the insurer.

Deductibles are not usually included in commercial general liability, personal liability, or auto liability policies. However, large deductibles are common with some specialty liability policies, such as those involving professional liability or directors and officers liability. By involving the insured in each loss, these large deductibles are used primarily to encourage risk control. Deductibles are also common in bailee legal liability policies, such as those for warehouses and garagekeepers. These policies provide property damage liability coverage against loss to a specified category of property, and the deductibles function similarly to those used with property insurance.

Some liability insurance policies include a self-insured retention (SIR). The differences between a deductible and self-insured retention are as follows:

- With a liability insurance deductible, the insurer defends on a first-dollar basis, pays all covered losses, and then bills the insured for the amount of losses up to the deductible.

- With an SIR, the insurer pays only losses that exceed the SIR amount. The insurer does not defend claims below the SIR amount. Consequently, the organization is responsible for adjusting and paying its own losses up to the SIR amount.

To compensate for the insurer's lack of control over self-insured claims, a policy with a self-insured retention usually requires strict reporting to the insurer of any claims that have the potential of exceeding the self-insured retention amount.

SIRs are common in professional liability insurance policies and some other specialty policies. SIRs are also commonly found in the "drop-down" coverage of umbrella policies. The drop-down coverage of an umbrella policy provides primary coverage, subject to the SIR, on claims that are not covered by an underlying primary insurance policy and not excluded by the umbrella policy.

Disputed Claims Resolution: Arbitration Provisions

Similar to the appraisal provisions in property insurance policies, liability insurance policies contain provisions designed to help resolve disputed claims. In liability policies, this provision is referred to as the arbitration provision. Unlike the appraisal process, which deals only with the loss amount, the arbitration process outlines a specific procedure for resolving the following two types of disagreements:

1. Disagreements about whether the insured is legally entitled to recover damages

2. Disagreements about the amount of damages

Whether coverage applies may not be settled through arbitration, in which case a court decides. Otherwise, the arbitration process closely resembles the appraisal process outlined in property insurance policies. Exhibit 15-2 contains the arbitration clause from the uninsured motorists coverage part of the ISO Personal Auto Policy.

EXHIBIT 15-2

Arbitration Clause in the ISO Personal Auto Policy

ARBITRATION

A. If we and an "insured" do not agree:

1. Whether that "insured" is legally entitled to recover damages; or

2. As to the amount of damages which are recoverable by that "insured";

from the owner or operator of an "uninsured motor vehicle", then the matter may be arbitrated. However, disputes concerning coverage under this Part may not be arbitrated.

Both parties must agree to arbitration. If so agreed, each party will select an arbitrator. The two arbitrators will select a third. If they cannot agree within 30 days, either may request that selection be made by a judge of a court having jurisdiction.

B. Each party will:

1. Pay the expenses it incurs; and

2. Bear the expenses of the third arbitrator equally.

C. Unless both parties agree otherwise, arbitration will take place in the county in which the "insured" lives. Local rules of law as to procedure and evidence will apply. A decision agreed to by two of the arbitrators will be binding as to:

1. Whether the "insured" is legally entitled to recover damages; and

2. The amount of damages...

Includes copyrighted material of Insurance Services Office, Inc., with its permission. Copyright, ISO Properties, Inc., 1997.

Insurance coverage analysis generally begins with the premise that one insurance policy or coverage, standing alone, covers a given loss. However, in some cases, the insured might also have access to additional sources of compensation covering all or part of the same loss.

OTHER SOURCES OF RECOVERY

Additional sources of compensation may violate the principle of indemnity—in that the insured could be indemnified more than once for the amount of loss. Insurance policy provisions have been developed to manage situations in which multiple recoveries may be possible. A multiple-recovery rule applies only to other sources against which the insured has a legally enforceable right, including the following five sources:

1. Noninsurance agreements (such as hold-harmless agreements or service agreements)

2. Negligent third parties (legal rights of recovery under tort law)

3. Other insurance in the same policy (multiple coverages in a package policy)

4. Other insurance in a similar policy (such as two homeowners policies or two commercial property policies)

5. Other insurance in a dissimilar policy (such as one homeowners policy and one auto policy)

Although some additional sources of recovery involve noninsurance agreements and negligent third parties, most multiple sources of recovery generally involve a situation in which more than one insurance source provides recovery for the same loss.

Noninsurance Agreements

Individuals and organizations often have a contractually enforceable source of recovery that does not involve insurance. Examples of noninsurance agreements that may overlap with insurance coverage of the loss include the following:

- A lease contract or bailment agreement might make a tenant, equipment lessee, or bailee responsible for damage to leased or bailed property that is also covered by insurance.

- A credit card protection plan might protect the cardholder against claims for damage to a rented car, partially duplicating auto physical damage coverage in the renter's personal auto policy.

- A credit card protection plan might protect property purchased with the card against theft or accidental damage. The same property is probably covered under a homeowners policy.

- An extended auto warranty, home warranty, appliance service agreement, or other plan can provide a contractually enforceable source of recovery that may overlap with an auto or homeowners policy, depending on the cause of loss.

Although credit card benefits are often underwritten by an insurer, the benefit itself is provided through a contract between the credit card company and the cardholder. The cardholder is contractually entitled to the benefits promised by the credit card company, which often duplicate insurance benefits. Even if the property is also insured, a cardholder might find it desirable to claim benefits from the credit card company. Unlike property insurance, the credit card benefit generally is on a first-dollar basis with no deductible.

To respond to the overlap in coverage provided by noninsurance agreements, the 2000 revision of the property section of the ISO HO-3 policy includes the following provision addressing noninsurance (service) agreements:[9]

F. Other Insurance and Service Agreement

If a loss covered by this policy is also covered by:...

2. A service agreement, this insurance is excess over any amounts payable under such agreement. Service agreement means a service plan, property restoration plan, home warranty or other similar service warranty agreement, even if it is characterized as insurance.

This provision indicates that the coverage provided by the homeowners policy is excess over any recovery that the insured may be able to get from the service agreement provider. The last line of this provision reflects the fact that service agreements are sometimes described as "insurance" when they are marketed, even if they do not meet a legal definition of insurance.

Third-Party Liability

As a matter of law, a party who is injured or whose property is damaged by a negligent third party generally has a right to recover damages from the third party—regardless of whether the third party has liability insurance. The recovery from a third party (or the third party's liability insurance) could overlap with any first-party property insurance coverage (the insured's own property insurance policy). Most first-party insurance policies have policy provisions that address these situations. Although two types of policies might be involved (the third party's liability insurer and the insured's property insurer), the relevant policy language is captioned "subrogation" rather than "other insurance." For example, Tara and David are both drivers in a state that does not have no-fault insurance (the example may not apply in no-fault states). Tara's car is struck and damaged by David, a negligent driver. David has liability insurance; that is, an insurer has agreed to pay liability claims on his behalf. Tara has a right under tort law to seek recovery from David, who will file a claim with his insurer. Tara also has a contractual right to recover under her own insurer's collision coverage. Tara's first-party right of recovery from her insurer does not reduce or eliminate David's obligation to pay damages to Tara. Nor can Tara's insurer deny her claim because David has liability insurance.

Regardless of whether a careless driver like David has liability insurance, his legal obligation to pay damages does not affect the contractual obligations of the insurer providing first-party property coverage—unless the insurance contract specifies otherwise. David is legally obligated, and Tara's insurer is contractually obligated, to pay for the damage to her car. However, that does not mean Tara will recover double the amount of loss she incurred. According to the subrogation provision in Tara's personal auto policy, if she recovers from her own insurer, that insurer can attempt to recover from David or his insurer. If David's insurer pays Tara directly, she is required to reimburse her insurer.

Other Insurance in the Same Policy

The third other source of recovery that affects amounts payable in liability insurance is other insurance in the same policy. Property and/or liability insurance policies may provide two or more coverages under the same policy. When these package policies are used, a given loss may be covered by more than one of the coverages offered. Therefore, an insurance professional needs to analyze the policy to determine if a policy provision exists that limits the number of coverages that apply. The following are examples of losses having insurance provided by more than one coverage:

1. A scheduled personal property endorsement (personal articles floater) attached to a homeowners policy provides coverage for scheduled items, many of which are also covered under the unscheduled personal property coverage of the homeowners policy.

2. A crime insurance form, as well as a building and personal property special-form on a building, can both be parts of a commercial package policy, and both might provide coverage against building damage by burglars.

3. Personal property used to maintain or service a building—such as fire extinguishing equipment, outdoor furniture, or refrigerators—is specifically covered under the building coverage of many commercial property insurance forms. The same items may also qualify for coverage as personal property under another insuring agreement of the same form.

4. A passenger injured while riding in a car may have medical payments coverage for medical expenses regardless of who was at fault; the passenger may also bring a bodily injury liability claim against the driver of the car (if the driver was partly at fault for the accident) and may also have a right of action against any other drivers involved. Coverage might apply under the liability, medical payments, and uninsured motorists coverages of the car owner's personal auto policy, depending on the facts of the case.

Because the insured's loss is covered, it might not seem important to know which coverage applies. However, although each of these examples may appear to involve a distinction that does not have a material effect on the claim, the distinction may be material to the amounts payable. Consequently, it is important to be aware of the applicability of more than one coverage in an insurance policy and to know which coverage applies in a given situation.

If the multiple coverages involved have different valuation provisions or deductibles, the insured may be able to recover more by filing under one coverage than another. The third example shows that under certain commercial property insurance policies, personal property used to maintain the building may be considered part of the building as well as personal property. For example, if the insured suffers a fire that destroys a storage shed and all the landscaping equipment that was stored in it, the insured may claim the equipment as a personal property loss or a building loss. If the building is insured on a replacement cost basis and personal property is insured on an ACV basis, the insured may be better off claiming the loss as a building loss.

Alternatively, the insured may have the option of combining (stacking) the limits of coverage of all the coverages that apply. That is, the insured can combine the various limits to cover losses that are larger than any one individual limit. To illustrate, suppose Rick and Ann have two cars insured under their personal auto policy and each vehicle has $50,000 in uninsured motorists coverage. Rick suffers a $75,000 loss resulting from bodily injury caused by an auto accident with an uninsured motorist. Based on the statutory regulations of the state in which they live, if the uninsured motorist limits are stackable, Rick and Ann have a total of $100,000 in uninsured motorist coverage that will pay for the entire $75,000 in bodily injury losses.

Other Insurance in a Similar Policy

The fourth other source of recovery that affects amounts payable in liability insurance is other insurance in a similar policy. In some cases, coverage overlaps because the same party is protected by two or more policies usually issued by different insurers. For example, suppose ABC Realty's property loss exposures exceed the capacity of any single insurer, so several insurers issue policies that, together, provide adequate policy limits. Alternatively, suppose Fred moves to a new home and buys a homeowners policy to cover the new home, but does not cancel the homeowners policy on his old home, which is still for sale. Both policies simultaneously cover some of Fred's loss exposures, such as personal property at other locations. Other-insurance situations like these usually involve more than one insurer as well as more than one policy. The question is therefore not simply which coverage applies, but which insurer will pay and how much. These situations are often resolved with each insurer sharing some portion of the loss.

Other Insurance in Dissimilar Policies

A fifth other source of recovery that affects amounts payable in liability insurance is other insurance in dissimilar policies. A loss is sometimes covered by more than one type of insurance, often from two or more insurers. Some examples of losses that may be covered by dissimilar policies include the following:

- An individual owns a utility trailer. Under some circumstances, liability claims involving the trailer might be covered by both the individual's homeowners policy and his or her personal auto policy.

- A restaurant offers valet parking on its premises. The valet parking activity might be covered under both the restaurant's general liability policy and its commercial auto liability policy.

- A pizza delivery company offers a delivery service for which employees use their own cars. The company's liability for an employee's acts or omissions might be covered under both the employee's own personal auto policy and the company's commercial auto policy.

- An employee is injured in an auto accident while performing work-related activities. The employee may be able to recover under his or her auto insurance (depending on the state), the employer's auto insurance, individual or group medical expense or disability insurance purchased by the employee, or the employer's workers' compensation insurance.

Dissimilar insurance policies do not necessarily include provisions that clearly coordinate coverage with other types of policies. Because of the typical lack of provisions governing coordination of coverage for dissimilar policies, these types of overlaps in coverage are often the most difficult to resolve. In some cases, the relationship between policies when more than one policy is in place is governed by the policies' "other-insurance" provisions.

OTHER-INSURANCE PROVISIONS

In general, other-insurance provisions include all policy provisions, regardless of their title, that attempt to specify in advance of a loss how an insurer's obligations (amounts payable) will be affected by other insurance applying to the same loss. Significant characteristics of other-insurance provisions include the following:

- Other-insurance provisions are not necessarily labeled "other insurance" within the policy document. An excess clause or a subrogation provision, among others, may address other insurance situations.

- Other-insurance provisions, regardless of their title, are usually found in the Conditions section of an insurance policy.

- Policies with more than one distinct coverage section often contain more than one other-insurance provision.

- A single other-insurance clause often includes more than one other-insurance provision. For example, the clause may address several possible types of other insurance situations.

- Two other-insurance provisions of the same general type are not necessarily consistent with one another.

- Group medical insurance policies include a coordination of benefits provision that addresses other-insurance situations.

Using these characteristics, a subrogation provision often qualifies as an other-insurance provision. So do provisions labeled "other insurance."

Types of Other-Insurance Provisions

Most other-insurance provisions that appear in property and liability insurance policies are one of three broad types, based on how the provision allows for the sharing of the claim payments. The three types are as follows:

1. Primary/excess provisions
2. Proportional provisions
3. Escape clauses

Overall, these provisions resolve insurers' responsibilities when more than one policy may provide coverage for the same loss. This relieves each insurer from having to prove its responsibility when there is conflicting language in multiple policies.

Primary/Excess Provisions

The first type of other-insurance provision is the primary/excess provision. A policy's other-insurance provisions may specifically indicate that the policy provides either primary coverage or excess coverage. A **primary coverage provision** is an other-insurance provision that specifies that the policy pays the loss amount before other applicable policies until its own limits have been exhausted. An **excess coverage provision** is an other-insurance provision that specifies that the policy pays any remaining loss amount, up to its policy limits, after the primary policy's coverage limits have been exhausted.

To illustrate, assume Sue owns property insured under the following two policies:

- Policy A with a $6,000 limit states that it is primary coverage.
- Policy B with a $10,000 limit states that it is excess coverage.

Further assume that Sue has an $8,000 loss covered by both policies. The insurer with Policy A pays its $6,000 limit of coverage. The insurer with Policy B then pays an additional $2,000.

An excess other-insurance provision should not be confused with an excess insurance policy. An excess insurance policy covers losses over either underlying primary insurance or a large self-insured retention amount. An excess other-insurance provision is usually found in a primary insurance policy that provides payment only after the coverage of other primary policies is exhausted.

Proportional Provisions

The second type of other-insurance provision is the proportional provision. **Proportional other-insurance provisions** are policy provisions that limit the insurer's obligations to a portion of the overall loss. Insurers typically share the loss amount proportionally when two policies both state that they are primary, when both state that they are excess, or when no statement of primary/excess coverage is indicated.

Proportional provisions may be perceived as prescribing an equitable way for two or more insurers to share in a loss. Equitable loss-sharing is the result only when every applicable policy has the same type of other-insurance provision. The purpose of any proportional provision is to limit the obligations of the insurer issuing that policy.

The following two points are crucial to understanding proportional other-insurance provisions:

1. *An other-insurance provision affects only the policy in which it appears.* One insurer's policy cannot specify the coverage that will be provided by another insurer.

2. *A proportional provision limits an insurer's amount payable, but it does not reduce coverage.* If losses exceed the total policy limits available, each insurer pays its full policy limit, barring indications to the contrary elsewhere in the policy.

Primary coverage provision
An other-insurance provision that specifies that the policy pays the loss amount before other applicable policies until its own limits have been exhausted.

Excess coverage provision
An other-insurance provision that specifies that the policy pays any remaining loss amount, up to its policy limits, after the primary policy's coverage limits have been exhausted.

Proportional other-insurance provision
A policy provision that limits the insurer's obligations to a portion of the overall loss.

Contribution by equal shares
A method of paying losses in which both policies pay the loss equally until the limits under one policy have been exhausted; thereafter the other policy alone pays.

Losses are typically proportioned between insurers either by equal shares or by pro rata sharing based on policy limits. **Contribution by equal shares** is a method of paying losses in which both policies pay the loss equally until the limits under one policy have been exhausted; thereafter, the other policy alone pays. To illustrate, assume that two policies, Policy A and Policy B, specify contribution by equal shares. Policy A's limit is $90,000 and Policy B's limit is $10,000. In the event of a $40,000 loss, Policies A and B would pay equal shares until Policy B has paid its $10,000 limit. At that point, each policy has paid $10,000, so $20,000 of the loss would remain. Policy A would pay the remaining $20,000. Therefore, Policy A would pay a total of $30,000 ($10,000 + $20,000), and Policy B would pay $10,000.

Contribution by equal shares is often used in liability insurance policies in which each insurer's premium is not directly proportional to policy limits. In other words, the first $100,000 layer of liability insurance generally costs much more than the next $100,000 layer of insurance, and so forth. Under these circumstances, contribution by equal shares tends to distribute losses among insurers in proportion to the premium they collected for the risk.

Pro rata sharing based on policy limits restricts the insurer's maximum amount payable to the proportion of the loss that the insurer's policy limit bears to the sum of all applicable policy limits. The following example of pro rata sharing based on policy limits specified in an other insurance policy provision is from the American Association of Insurance Services (AAIS) Building and Personal Property Coverage Part:

> 6. **Insurance Under More than One Policy – You** may have another policy subject to the same plan, **terms**, conditions, and provisions as this policy. If **you** do, **we** pay **our** share of the covered loss. **Our** share is the proportion that the applicable **limit** under this policy bears to the limit of all policies covering on the same basis.[10]

Pro rata sharing can be expressed by the following formula:

$$\text{Policy A's maximum amount payable} = \frac{\text{Policy A's limit}}{(\text{Policy A's limit} + \text{Policy B's limit} + \ldots + \text{Policy N's Limit})} \times \text{Loss}.$$

For example, suppose two insurers have insured the same property and that both insurance policies (Policy A and Policy B) specify that any loss will be shared on a pro rata basis based on policy limits. Policy A's limit is $90,000, Policy B's limit is $10,000, and a $40,000 loss occurs. The maximum amount payable under Policy A can be calculated as follows:

$$\text{Policy A's maximum amount payable} = \frac{\text{Policy A's limit}}{(\text{Policy A's limit} + \text{Policy B's limit})} \times \text{Loss}$$

$$= \frac{\$90,000}{(\$90,000 + \$10,000)} \times \$40,000$$

$$= 0.90 \times \$40,000$$

$$= \$36,000.$$

If B's policy has a similar proration by policy limits provision, Policy B's maximum amount payable can be calculated as follows:

$$\text{Policy B's maximum amount payable} = \frac{\text{Policy B's limit}}{(\text{Policy B's limit} + \text{Policy A's limit})} \times \text{Loss}$$

$$= \frac{\$10,000}{(\$10,000 + \$90,000)} \times \$40,000$$

$$= 0.10 \times \$40,000$$

$$= \$4,000.$$

Even if Policy B did not contain a pro rata other-insurance provision, the amount payable under Policy A is still limited to $36,000 because the insured also had coverage under Policy B. Policy A cannot dictate the amount payable by Policy B.

If a loss of $100,000 or more occurred, then Policy A would pay $90,000. If Policy B had a similar pro rata policy limits provision, then Policy B would pay $10,000. These amounts would not change if the loss were greater than $100,000 because an insurer is not obligated to pay more than its policies' limits.

Pro rata sharing based on policy limits is commonly used in property insurance policies. It provides an equitable way of allocating losses in situations in which each insurer's premium is directly proportional to policy limits. Pro rata sharing is not as prevalent in liability insurance policies; it is much more common to see contribution by equal shares.

Escape Clauses

The third type of other-insurance provision in insurance policies is the escape clause. An **escape clause** is an other-insurance provision that relieves the insurer of any obligation to pay a claim for which other insurance applies. Escape clauses generally function in one of the following four ways:

1. Prohibitions—forbidding other insurance
2. Exclusions—excluding property or activities covered by other insurance
3. Disclaimers—denying responsibility if other insurance applies
4. Offsets—reducing the coverage limit by the amount of other insurance

Prohibition escape clauses forbid the purchase of other insurance. An insurer may deny coverage to any insured who fails to comply with a policy provision that prohibits other insurance. For example, the ISO Personal Auto Policy contains an escape clause based on a prohibition. The automatic termination provision begins by stating that the policy ceases to provide further coverage at the end of the policy period if the insured does not accept the insurer's renewal offer. This statement is followed by the following escape clause:[11]

C. **Automatic Termination**

...If you obtain other insurance on "your covered auto", any similar insurance provided by this policy will terminate as to that auto on the effective date of the other insurance.

Escape clause
An other-insurance provision that relieves the insurer of any obligation to pay a claim for which other insurance applies.

People usually do not buy extra auto insurance deliberately. In most cases, this provision reflects the intent of the insured who decided to replace one policy with another. The provision also addresses the rare insurance fraud situation in which duplicate claims are filed with two or more insurers. However, the provision is effective only when the insurer knows a duplicate claim has been filed with another insurer.

Exclusion escape clauses negate coverage only if other insurance applies. These function as other-insurance provisions even if they appear in a policy's exclusions section. For example, the personal property coverage of an ISO HO-3 policy specifically excludes items insured elsewhere, as follows:[12]

> **4. Property Not Covered**
>
> We do not cover:
>
> a. Articles separately described and specifically insured, *regardless of the limit for which they are insured*, in this or other insurance; [emphasis added]

The italicized phrase was added in the 2000 policy edition to make it clear that this is an exclusion, not an offset. Coverage is completely excluded for items covered elsewhere in the homeowners policy, an endorsement to the homeowners policy, or a separate policy such as a personal articles floater. For example, suppose a firearms collection worth $10,000 is destroyed in a house fire and the collection has $5,000 of scheduled coverage under a Scheduled Personal Property Endorsement. Without the endorsement, the homeowners policy would provide $10,000 coverage on the collection (assuming its value could be proven). However, the endorsement provides only $5,000 of coverage. The homeowners policy does not pay the difference. This exclusion and others like it shift all responsibility for the loss to the policy that has generated a premium coverage on that valuable item, and it also encourages insurance to value on scheduled items. Exclusions in some policies reinstate coverage to the extent that other insurance is inadequate. These exclusions are properly categorized as excess provisions.

Because of the differences in the way they determine amounts payable, insurance professionals should be able to differentiate between an exclusion and an exclusion escape clause. Exclusions are not escape clauses because they apply even when the other insurance does not exist. For example, the liability coverage of homeowners policies excludes coverage for most auto-related losses. The exclusion applies even if a particular homeowner does not have an auto policy. In contrast, exclusion escape clauses apply only if the other insurance coverage is in effect.

Disclaimer escape clauses provide coverage only if no other insurance applies. Disclaimers usually apply only to fringe or supplemental coverages rather than the whole policy. For example, a state's no-fault law might prohibit stacking of coverages and prescribe the order in which insurance applies. To illustrate, insurance "on the car" might be the first to pay for injuries to any occupant, but if there is no insurance "on the car," a guest passenger's own personal injury protection would apply.

Offset escape clauses apply when available policy limits are reduced by policy limits of other insurance that applies to the same loss. If Policy A contains an offset, the following two scenarios are possible:

1. If the other insurance's policy limits equal or exceed the limit of Policy A, which has an offset escape provision, then the insurer pays nothing under Policy A. The offset essentially becomes an exclusion.

2. If Policy A's limits are higher than the other insurance's policy limits, the insurer with Policy A pays no more than the difference in policy limits.

The following example, part of the other-insurance provision under the uninsured motorists coverage of the ISO Personal Auto Policy, functions as an offset escape clause:[13]

> **OTHER INSURANCE**
>
> If there is other applicable insurance available under one or more policies or provisions of coverage that is similar to the insurance provided under this Part of the policy:
>
> 1. Any recovery for damages under all such policies or provisions of coverage may equal but not exceed the highest applicable limit for any one vehicle under any insurance providing coverage on either a primary or excess basis.

Conflict Resolution for Other-Insurance Provisions

Sometimes insurers disagree about each insurer's amounts payable when overlapping coverage exists, especially when neither policy's other-insurance provision clearly addresses the situation. The most common resolution is an agreement or a compromise between the two insurers. In cases of severe disagreement, arbitration might be used. Other procedures that can be used to resolve such differences include application of the Guiding Principles or resolution in court.

Guiding Principles

The Guiding Principles were developed by industry-wide associations in the 1960s to resolve conflicts between multiple insurers covering the same loss and are reproduced in the *Fire, Casualty, and Surety Bulletins* published by the National Underwriter Company. The Guiding Principles apply when other-insurance provisions are contradictory or when other-insurance clauses do not exist. These principles operate only when more than one policy covers a loss and none of the other policies' other-insurance provisions resolve how the respective coverages should apply.

The Guiding Principles indicate when policies are primary to or excess over one another, and they provide a method of proration for policies that are neither primary nor excess to one another. In establishing priority, the Guiding Principles make policies that cover more specifically described property at more specifically described locations primary over more general policies.

The Guiding Principles are complex, and adherence to them is voluntary. Arbitration can resolve disputes if insurers disagree with the outcome resulting from applying the Guiding Principles.

Court Resolution

When large amounts of money are involved, insurers sometimes find it necessary to take the case to court. Predicting the outcome in such cases is difficult because the courts have inconsistently ruled on overlapping coverage issues. The outcomes of court decisions vary by venue and over time. Because of the inability to predict court decisions, insurers are often reluctant to allow amounts payable decisions to be determined by the courts. Furthermore, insurers are also concerned that court decisions regarding amounts payable in one case may be applied broadly to other situations, and this may not be in the insurers' best interests.

SUMMARY

Several factors can affect the amount payable under liability insurance policies, such as policy limits, the valuation of losses, and the amount of deductibles or self-insured retentions. Adequate policy limits are important in both property and liability insurance to cover losses as fully as possible. Determining the value of most liability loss exposures can be challenging because it can be difficult to evaluate an individual or organization's maximum potential liability loss and, in theory, the loss can be limitless.

With liability insurance, although policy provisions provide information on the maximum amount payable, determination of the amount payable is affected by many factors, including relevant policy provisions and extent of bodily injury and/or property damage to others. Under most circumstances, the maximum amount the insurer pays is the lesser of the applicable policy limit and the compensable amount of the loss. When the insured is liable for damages, the key issue affecting the valuation of a liability claim is the amount of monetary compensation that will reasonably indemnify the party who incurred the loss. Although a court may ultimately determine this amount, the insurer, the insured, and the claimant try to estimate this amount during any settlement negotiations.

In liability insurance, policy limits are generally expressed as either single limits, split limits, or aggregate limits. Single dollar limits apply for each occurrence (accident), each person/organization, or each claim. This limit applies to all bodily injury and property damage for a single occurrence, a single person incurring a loss, or a single claim. Split limits are separate limits for bodily injury claims and for property damage liability claims. Policies containing split limits usually contain three types of limits: a bodily injury limit applicable to each injured person, a bodily injury limit applicable to two or more injured persons, and a property damage limit. An aggregate limit is a specific limit on the maximum amount an insurer will pay for total damages from all covered occurrences during the covered period. Liability insurance policies may also specifically mention other policy limits, such as limits on defense costs and limits on some nonfault-based coverages—such as medical payments or state-mandated benefits in workers' compensation.

Deductibles are much less effective with liability insurance than with property insurance. For most liability insurance policies, deductibles would not noticeably reduce premiums. One reason is that relatively few liability claims involve small amounts. Even with a deductible, the liability insurer usually pays "first dollar" expenses for investigation and defense coverage, just as it does for policies without deductibles. Usually the deductible applies only to the amount paid to the claimant in settling the claim, not to defense costs. In liability insurance, the insurer must recover the deductible from the insured.

Some liability insurance policies include a self-insured retention (SIR). With an SIR, the insurer pays only losses that exceed the SIR amount. The insurer does not defend claims below the SIR amount. Consequently, the organization is responsible for adjusting and paying its own losses up to the SIR amount.

Liability insurance policies contain provisions designed to help resolve disputed claims, referred to as the arbitration provisions. Arbitration is a process for resolving the disagreements about both whether the insured is legally entitled to recover damages and what the amount of damages are. Whether coverage applies is a question for the courts and may not be settled through arbitration.

Insurance policy provisions have been developed to manage situations in which multiple recoveries may be possible. Five other sources of recovery that affect amounts payable are noninsurance agreements, negligent third parties, other insurance in the same policy, other insurance in a similar policy, and other insurance in dissimilar policies.

Examples of noninsurance agreements that may overlap with insurance coverage of the loss include lease contracts, bailment agreements, credit card protection agreements, extended auto warranties, home warranties, and appliance service agreements.

As a matter of law, a party who is injured or whose property is damaged by a negligent third party generally has a right to recover damages from the third party—whether or not the third party has liability insurance. The recovery from a third party (or the third party's liability insurance) could overlap with any first-party property insurance coverage.

Property and/or liability insurance policies may provide two or more coverages under the same policy. When these package policies are used, a given loss may be covered by more than one of the coverages offered. If the multiple coverages have different valuation provisions or deductibles, the insured may be able to recover more by filing under one coverage than another. Alternatively, the insured may have the option to combine (stack) the various limits to cover losses that are larger than any one individual limit.

In some cases there is overlapping coverage because the same party is protected by two or more similar policies usually issued by different insurers. These situations are often resolved with each insurer sharing some portion of the loss. Alternatively, a loss may covered by more than one type of insurance, often from two or more insurers. Dissimilar insurance policies do not necessarily include provisions that clearly coordinate coverage with other types of policies. Therefore, these types of overlaps in coverage are often the most difficult to resolve.

Most other-insurance provisions that appear in property and liability insurance policies are of three broad types: primary/excess provisions, proportional provisions, and escape clauses. A primary coverage provision is an other-insurance provision that specifies that the policy pays the loss amount before other applicable policies until its own limits have been exhausted. An excess coverage provision is an other-insurance provision that specifies that the policy pays any remaining loss amount, up to its policy limits, after the primary policy's coverage limits have been exhausted.

Proportional other-insurance provisions limit the insurer's obligations to a portion of the overall loss. Insurers typically share the loss amount proportionally when two policies both state that they are primary, when both state that they are excess, or when no statement of primary/excess coverage is indicated. Losses are typically proportioned between insurers either by equal shares or by prorated sharing based on policy limits.

An escape clause is an other-insurance provision that relieves the insurer of any obligation to pay a claim for which other insurance applies. Escape clauses generally function as either prohibitions (forbidding other insurance), exclusions (excluding property or activities covered by other insurance), disclaimers (denying responsibility if other insurance applies), or offsets (reducing the coverage limit by the amount of other insurance).

The most common resolution for conflicts regarding other insurance is an agreement or a compromise between the two insurers. In cases of severe disagreement, arbitration might be used. Other procedures that can be used to resolve such differences include application of the Guiding Principles or resolution in court.

CHAPTER NOTES

1. www.iii.org/media/hottopics/insurance/dogbite (accessed December 6, 2005).

2. www.iii.org/media/facts/statsbyissue/litigiouness (accessed December 6, 2005).

3. Approximately 3 percent of tort cases ended in jury trials. G. Thomas Woodard, *The Economics of US Tort Liability: A Primer*, Chapter 2 (U.S. Congressional Budget Office, October 2003), www.cbo.gov/showdoc.cfm?index=4641&sequence=3 (accessed May 9, 2006).

4. Includes copyrighted material of Insurance Services Office, Inc., with its permission. Copyright, ISO Properties, Inc., 2003.

5. Includes copyrighted material of Insurance Services Office, Inc., with its permission. Copyright, ISO Properties, Inc., 2003.

6. Includes copyrighted material of Insurance Services Office, Inc., with its permission. Copyright, ISO Properties, Inc., 2003.

7. Includes copyrighted material of Insurance Services Office, Inc., with its permission. Copyright, ISO Properties, Inc., 2003.

8. Includes copyrighted material of Insurance Services Office, Inc., with its permission. Copyright, ISO Properties, Inc., 1999.

9. Includes copyrighted material of Insurance Services Office, Inc., with its permission. Copyright, ISO Properties, Inc., 1999.

10. Form CP-12, Ed 1.0, Copyright, American Association of Insurance Services, 1994.

11. Includes copyrighted material of Insurance Services Office, Inc., with its permission. Copyright, ISO Properties, Inc., 1997.

12. Includes copyrighted material of Insurance Services Office, Inc., with its permission. Copyright, ISO Properties, Inc., 1999.

13. Includes copyrighted material of Insurance Services Office, Inc., with its permission. Copyright, ISO Properties, Inc., 1997.

Index